FOUNDATIONS OF ORGANIZATIONAL COMMUNICATION: A READER

Steven R. Corman
ARIZONA STATE UNIVERSITY

Stephen P. Banks
UNIVERSITY OF IDAHO

Charles R. Bantz
ARIZONA STATE UNIVERSITY

and

Michael E. Mayer
ARIZONA STATE UNIVERSITY

Longman
New York & London

Foundations of Organizational Communication:
A Reader

Longman, 95 Church Street, White Plains, N.Y. 10601

Associated companies:
Longman Group Ltd., London
Longman Cheshire Pty., Melbourne
Longman Paul Pty., Auckland
Copp Clark Pitman, Toronto

Executive editor: Gordon T. R. Anderson
Production editor: Ann P. Kearns
Text design: Renée Edelman
Cover design: Thomas Slomka
Production supervisor: Kathleen M. Ryan

Library of Congress Cataloging-in-Publication Data

Foundations of organizational communication : a reader / edited by
  Steven R. Corman . . . [et al.].

     p. cm.
  Includes bibliographical references.
  ISBN 0-8013-0470-9
  1. Communication in organizations. I. Corman, Steven R.
HD30.3.F68 1990
658.4'5—dc20

89-36299
CIP

ABCDEFGHIJ-ML-99 98 97 96 95 94 93 92 91 90

CONTENTS

I.   COMMUNICATION AND ORGANIZATIONS   1

II.   PERSPECTIVES   63

III.   ORGANIZATIONAL COMMUNICATION CONCEPTS AND ISSUES   165

INTRODUCTION

A foundation is something that serves as a stable base for a structure. In houses, foundations are usually made of concrete. Walls are attached to the foundation, and they in turn support a roof. This keeps out rain and provides warmth and—well, you get the idea. It is very tempting to go for the corny analogy and compare this reader to a house: Part I would be like the concrete, Part II would be the walls and roof, and Part III would be the trim and so on.

But let us try a less corny and more useful tack: Think of the parts of this book as three layers of an apple. When you have studied the topics in all layers of this apple, you will have developed a foundation of knowledge about organizational communication. To this you can add your own layers later on.

As for the layers themselves, Part III, the skin, deals with issues closest to the "surface" of everyday life in organizations. It deals with topics like leadership, conflict, message-exchange, and networks—all things people in organizations commonly experience. Part II, the flesh, deals with explanations that we might say "lie below the surface." Theories in part II try to explain how communication and organization operate at a more general level to provide a context for everyday life. Part I, the core, focuses on broad issues of theory, organization, and communication. Articles in this part are meant to get you thinking about the philosophical aspects of what it is you are doing by studying organizational communication.

An apple is a good analogy for organizational communication because with an apple, any point you pick has other layers either above or below it that either support or protect it. Organizational communication, in a way, is also layered. Recall some "communication breakdown" you have observed in an organization and try to think of an explanation for it. Unless it was caused by a simple individual error, you will probably be looking for explanations in the organization's *structure*. But to even think about the organization as a structure assumes a particular philosophical core. Thus any explanation you make of organizational communication on the "surface" involves the other layers as well.

We selected readings to give you some exposure to good ideas other people have had about issues in each of these three layers. Some selections are classics, written by authors whose work most scholars respect. Other selections are application pieces, where the authors have taken a particular point of view and produced intriguing explanations with it. Still other articles review literature or survey ideas in a particular area to expand on material found in most basic texts. We hope that reading these different kinds of selections in each of the three layers will give you a solid survey of the different approaches to studying organizational communication. We count on you to take those different views and use them to develop your own perspective.

Unfortunately, we cannot layer the pages of this reader as an apple. We present our readings in a more linear fashion and ask you to keep the apple analogy in mind. The reader is organized in three parts plus an epilogue. Part I (the core) contains four readings, which look at the activity of studying and practicing organizational communication from a philosophical point of view—what the subject involves and what techniques are used to study it. Understanding this is crucial to understanding what organizational communication is "about." We tried to select readings that would show how people use theories from communication and other disciplines to understand and influence communication phenomena in organizations.

Part II has 13 readings, all focusing on a major theory or theoretical perspective that is important in the study of organizational communication: classical theory, human relations/human resources, systems theory, Weick's model, and organizational culture. These theories make different assumptions and look at events in organizations in different ways. But as a set they represent most of the major ways people think about organizations and communication on an organizational scale.

Part III contains notable attempts to explain the role and effects of communication in everyday organizational life. These are areas that generate much theory and research, and they build on ideas from the two layers underneath to help you understand specific communication phenomena. We include readings here covering interpersonal communication at work, leadership, gender and ethnicity, ethics, power, decision making, and communication networks.

The epilogue invites thinking about the future study of organizational communication. Existing organizational communication theory has developed with a strong orientation toward the concerns of the industrial age. The concluding reading recognizes evolution toward a new information age and notes many likely changes in the social forces that shape organizations. We hope this epilogue will provide food for thought about changes in the role of communication in organizations and new directions in theory and research to study that role.

No project involving as much coordination as editing a reader is done without help from many people. This book is no exception to that rule. At Arizona State University we have been fortunate to receive the advice of our colleagues Bill Arnold and Norm Perrill, the valuable skills of Linda Coddington, Earla Marshall, Jason Sato, and Marion Yakerson, the professional support of Marion Buckley and the staff of the Auxiliary Resources Center, and the resources of the Department of Communication. The expert editorial support from Tren Anderson, Ann Kearns, and David Fox of Longman has been essential to this project coming to fruition. Finally, we thank the anonymous reviewers, whose suggestions improved our selections. Our thanks to all of you.

1 COMMUNICATION AND ORGANIZATIONS

What, exactly, does it mean to study "organizational communication?" This is really a very good question and one that is not always easy to answer. Some people think it deals with report writing or with things like telephone systems and television. Others think it deals with running meetings and giving speeches. Some think it can tell you how to build a successful or effective structure for a business.

The fact is that *studying organizational communication involves all of these things* to varying degrees, but any one of these definitions is much too narrow. The subject you are studying is really better described as a *way of thinking about things* than as a means of doing something. In the broadest sense, it involves the study of how organization in social collectives is produced and affected by communication. This definition highlights three important aspects of organizational communication, and we have selected articles that we think expand on them in ways that will give you a clearer idea of what the subject is all about.

First, organizational communication involves *study*. Students of organizational communication mainly learn about different *theories* that have been developed to explain how organization is produced and affected by communication. Unfortunately, people often balk at the idea of learning about theories, feeling that they are impractical, complicated, and unrelated to real-world practice. The first essay, by Corman, attempts to dispel that misconception by arguing that understanding theory is the key to truly effective practice.

Second, it involves *organization*. Partly because of misconceptions about the functions of theory, organizations and organizing have bad reputations in the minds of some. They are thought of as things that complicate our lives and prevent things from getting done. Bureaucracies, the subject of more detailed attention in

Part II, are especially infamous in this regard. They are thought of as antiquated organizational forms that do little but generate "red tape." But Charles Perrow offers a compelling argument that this view is wrong: The real problem is that bureaucracies are spoiled when they implement policies through poor administrative practices and abuses of power. The idea of a bureaucracy and thus all the various ideas of organization in general are inevitable solutions to the human problems of coordinating activities in large social collectives.

Third, the definition deals with *communication*. Communication is increasingly seen as critical to the development of organization, and the selection by Hawes reflects that fact. He notes the trend toward viewing organizations as ongoing processes rather than static things. This idea makes communication one, if not *the*, critical phenomenon for explaining how organizations "happen." Hawes argues that organizations *are* communication and that the critical move in explaining how organizations organize is to study organizational talk.

These first three selections, then, are intended to help you explore organizational communication as a way of thinking about things. However, people have already been thinking about organizational communication for quite some time—some writers claim for thousands of years. Such a long tradition has accumulated a great deal of wisdom about what the subject does and does not entail, and the last piece in this unit, by Putnam and Cheney, is included to give you access to it. They provide a detailed account of the history of this area of study and suggest future directions in which it is likely to go. Their review provides an economical way for readers to get a grasp of how the study of organizational communication is pursued among a field of scientists and what they have discovered to date.

When reading the articles in this chapter, try to keep the general definition in mind, with an eye toward getting a deeper understanding of the terms it contains. What does it mean to *study* a subject like organizational communication? What are *organization* and *organizing*? What does *communication* have to do with them? What have people studied about these things in the past and what are they likely to study in the future? If you can answer these questions you will have developed a basic understanding of what you will be "doing" when you read the remaining selections in Parts II and III.

1 THAT WORKS FINE IN THEORY, BUT . . .
STEVEN R. CORMAN

What are theories good for? There is an all too common belief that theories are academic abstractions that have little or no use in the "real world." This is a critical issue for anyone studying organizational communication, because such study revolves around understanding the different theories that have been proposed to account for communication in organizations. If theories are really not practical, then the study of organizational communication is not practical either.

The following essay by Corman assumes that readers hold that attitude and tries to convince them that it is untrue. He argues that most intentional communication behavior in organizations is based on theories held by the organization members. Under this view, organizational communication theories are just extensively documented and well-tested instances of the same kinds of thinking used by everyday practitioners. Corman concludes by arguing that understanding theories that others have developed is the key to truly effective practice.

"That works fine in theory, but . . ." I asked an incidental sample of people on my campus to complete that sentence. The answers were all very similar:

"In practice it doesn't happen that way."

"In reality it just ain't gonna catch the train."

"Not in real life."

"Reality is a different story."

"In reality, things are a lot more complicated."

"In its application, it bites the big one."

These statements are typical of the opinions many people have about theories: Theories are high-minded, unrealistic abstractions. They are developed by strange people who sit in ivory towers and smoke funny cigarettes. They bear little or no relationship to reality. In the "real world" we must get things *done*; we can't spend all of our time thinking. *Doing* is the important thing, and theories usually make so many stupid assumptions that they no longer correspond to reality anyway.

You have surely heard people say things like this, and you may even think them yourself. They are very important criticisms because if they are true, then a class in something like organizational communication theory would be useless except to the most obscure theorists. We would be justified in asking why professors don't teach something useful rather than all of this theoretical mumbo-jumbo. Why study communication theory when you could learn something that can be applied in the "real world," where "real people" live?

In this essay, I hope to convince you, as a student of organizational communication, that theory is an important subject to study. My main argument is that although theory and practice are indeed different things, they are really inextricably linked. In the next section I offer definitions of theory and practice, then compare and contrast them to show that they are the logical complements of each other. I then review seven statements reflecting the more common variations of the argument that theory is useless. I refute each one as an oversimplification based on misunderstandings of the real nature of theory and practice before concluding that there are few things as practical as theories.

3

THEORY

A *theory* is any systematically related set of ideas used to describe and/or explain phenomena. To ensure clarity, I will unpack this definition by defining its important terms. Probably the most important term is the last: a *phenomenon* is anything an observer (e.g., you) finds extraordinary and in need of explanation. If this page detached spontaneously from the binding, flew around the room and burst into flames, that would be a phenomenon.

Of course, most phenomena are not so dramatic. A car that will not start is a phenomenon to most people. Organizational communication researchers study communication-related phenomena: a worker is constantly getting the wrong information about how to do the job; messages are distorted as they are passed through the organization; there is a "negative tone" to the communication in one organization; one work group makes a bad decision while a similar group makes a good one. All of these are things that someone finds extraordinary and in need of explanation.

Think of phenomena as the "seeds" of theory. When someone sees a phenomenon and is sufficiently interested, he or she tries to describe and/or explain it. To *describe* a phenomenon is to identify its relevant characteristics or components. To *explain* a phenomenon is to account for it or give reasons for it. People build descriptions and explanations of phenomena by putting together ideas they have about them in some logical way, which is why the definition talks about a *systematically related set of ideas*.

A quick example of theory might be useful. Patti the production manager ordered a machine part two weeks ago. It still has not arrived and the broken machine has slowed production below her quota. The vice president calls and wants to know what is going on, and Patti—horrified that the boss is angry—says she'll find out. The Parts Department was supposed to supply the part, so she calls there. It claims it never got the order. She talks to her secretary, who assures her that the order was mailed two weeks ago.

The Mail Department: It is known for moving mail about five feet per day. The order was probably lost in the mail, so Patti checks with the Mail Department. Sure enough, it sent her order to the Art Department (where she found an artist busily painting a picture of her part). She explained to the V.P. that the mail people had screwed up her order and claimed this was why she was below quota. The V.P. was in a good mood, so he forgave her. She lived happily ever after. The end.

We can identify the characteristics of theory in this simple story. The *phenomenon* was that two weeks had passed with no part being delivered. In applying *ideas* like "parts," "order," "quota," "supervisor," "parts department," "secretary," "mail department," "delivery," and "art department," Patti was *describing* the characteristics of the organization that were relevant to the phenomenon. She strung these ideas together in a *systematic* way that allowed her to give an *explanation* of the phenomenon. She then relayed this explanation to her boss, who lives in the . . .

REAL WORLD

Having a good explanation, Patti did not just compliment herself on her cleverness. She used the explanation to get herself out of trouble with the boss. If she is smart she will also use it to prevent her problem from happening again. For example, next time she orders a part, she might hand-deliver the order to avoid any trouble with the Mail Department.

This idea of hand-delivering her order may seem like an ordinary act, but it was born of a rather complex theory. Patti would be using her "mail-department interference theory" to predict that the Mail Department would probably send her order to the wrong place again. Having made this prediction, she would use her theory to control the way her order is communicated (i.e., she would not let the Mail Department touch it). In other words, she would be using her theory to guide her practice.

We can formally define *practice* as using descriptions and explanations of phenomena to predict and control them.[1] To *predict* is to estimate the state of a phenomenon in advance. This is related to *control*, which is to determine the state of a phenomenon in advance. This is how theory guides practice in the real world: Any time a person has seen something extraordinary and combined ideas to explain it, that person has developed a theory. When someone uses an explanation of a phenomenon to predict or control it, that person is engaging in real-world practice.

THE RELATIONSHIP BETWEEN THEORY AND PRACTICE

As you can tell from the definitions of theory and practice, there is an essential relationship between them. It is virtually impossible to engage in purposeful practice without a theory and be successful. To act purposefully is to have some desired future state of affairs and the means to predict and control events to bring that future state of affairs about. These "means" are usually explanations of why the events occur; in other words, theories are what make purposeful action possible. Without her explanation of the parts-ordering process at her company, Patti the production manager might have found some other way to get her parts. She might have resorted to witchcraft and cast a spell, or she might have sent up flares and smoke signals. But nobody is going to argue that acting on the basis of a good theoretical explanation is the most reliable way to get her part delivered quickly.

It is also virtually impossible to have theory without practice. It is possible that someone might explain a phenomenon just for fun, but constructing theories is not most people's idea of something you do for fun. People usually construct theories in order to *do* something useful with them, because they are needed to facilitate some kind of practice, even if "practice" is defined very generally. Not only that, but if theorists never came in contact with the real world they would never see phenomena, and I argued above that phenomena are what cause us to develop theory. This all sounds reasonable enough. But where does it leave our main idea that things frequently work fine in theory but not in the real world?

DIFFERENCES BETWEEN THEORY AND PRACTICE (REAL AND IMAGINED)

At the beginning of this chapter I reported the results of a survey. The people I surveyed were basically expressing their theories about theory and practice. In this section, I examine the main idea behind these opinions in order to show that for the most part, they do not work out very well in practice. Specifically, I outline six different statements that represent the most common reasons people think theories are of little use. I then refute each in turn based on the concepts of theory and practice just described.

"Theory and Practice Are Different."

Absolutely true. Theories are used to describe and explain phenomena. Practice uses descriptions and explanations of phenomena to predict and control them. Theory and practice are therefore completely different entities. But this is not an argument that practice is good and theory is bad; on the contrary, each requires the other.

"Theory Is Not Useful in the 'Real World.' "

This statement is incorrect but is probably based on a recognition of some true differences between theory and real-world practice. Theories are logical combinations of ideas that exist in the thoughts of observers. Nobody can see what thoughts an observer has, and the thoughts of others tend to be hard to understand. Therefore, theories (at least when they are originally made up) tend to be subjective and abstract.

Practice, on the other hand, consists of "real" events. We typically think of an event as real if two or more people see it happen and agree that they saw it happen. Practice is therefore more objective and concrete. Practice also "happens" in real time, whereas theory often explains general trends in events across time or across different time frames.

These differences show us that theory and practice are not the same. They say that theories exist in the idea world whereas practice exists in the real world. But this really amounts to hair-splitting. These two worlds are coextensive—they exist at the same time and in the same place and mutually influence one another. Saying that theory is not useful in the real world is like saying that understanding arithmetic is not useful when balancing a bank account. Arithmetic does not *equal* a balanced account. And as we all know, arithmetic by itself is not even sufficient to produce a balanced account. But it would be ridiculous to conclude from this that the theory of arithmetic is not useful to the practice of balancing.

It is equally ridiculous to say that theory is not useful in the real world. If people need theory in order to practice, and if we agree that practice is what people do in the real world, then theory is useful in the real world *by definition*. There are important conceptual differences between theory and practice, but in reality the two go hand-in-hand.

"Practice Is More Important Than Theory."

This statement is also incorrect but is also based on a true reading of some real differences between theory and practice. This difference is related to the specificity of theory and practice. I mentioned above that theories tend to be more abstract than practice, both logically and in terms of the way they treat time. Because they operate at this higher level of abstraction, theories often give more general explanations and descriptions of phenomena. They may try to explain and tie together several different phenomena or try to give explanations for classes of phenomena.

An example of this abstractness as it applies to communication is classical organizational theory. This theory tries to explain organizational communication as it occurs in the *general* case. A classical theorist would say that organization is accomplished primarily through downward communication from supervisors to subordinates, because such communication facilitates management control of an organization's resources.

Practice, on the other hand, is very concrete and specific. Practice involves doing specific things to accomplish specific tasks in the real world. A typi-

cal example of something we would want to explain with classical theory is a top manager telling division heads to gear up to produce a new product. Classical theory does not seem to give a very complete explanation for this phenomenon because it does not tell us why the top manager decided to produce this product or why he decided to communicate the decision to these division heads at this time in this way. It looks like classical theory gives us only a very general explanation: Top managers have authority over division heads by virtue of their position in the organization's hierarchy, so we should expect them to give orders to direct the division heads' actions. Because of this it is easy to conclude that theories deal only in vague generalities that tell us little about what people actually do in the real world. If this were true, then I would be forced to agree that theory is not very important when compared with practice.

But theories are used to *produce* explanations; they are not explanations themselves. They help us discover why people do things in the real world. For example, classical theory emphasizes the importance of formal upward and downward communication. It tells us, among other things, that the decision to produce the new product was very likely based on information that had come up the hierarchy from people "lower" in the organization. And it tells us that if we looked closely, say, at memos that had been sent in the past few months, we might be able to see just such a thing happening. A sales manager might have relayed information about customers' wants and needs for the new product up to the top manager. A marketing executive might have noted general trends in the markets favoring this kind of product and passed that information along. Manufacturing personnel might have noticed that their processes could be easily and cheaply modified to produce products of this type, and informed management of that fact. Of course, none of these events in itself is sufficient to cause the decision to make the new product. A top manager must also be in a position to receive all this information and have the authority to synthesize it all into a decision to produce a new product. This is another prediction of classical theory.

So while classical theory is not itself an explanation of this phenomenon, it tells us a lot about how we might go about developing an explanation of the phenomenon, and we know from the earlier discussion that you cannot have practice without explanations based on theory. Practice is therefore not more important, precise, or realistic than theory. Both are equally important, but are simply used for different purposes.

"Theories Make Unrealistic Assumptions."

Theories are often criticized for making unrealistic assumptions. For example, geologists who calculate the volume of the earth frequently assume that it is a prefect sphere. Of course, we know it is not a prefect sphere because it has mountains and oceans.

Assumptions are also made in organizational communication theory. Scientific management assumes that workers are motivated primarily by monetary rewards. While this may be true for some people, we like to think that most people are not only motivated by material goods, but also can be rewarded in more "human" ways, such as getting a sense of accomplishment from their jobs. This is one of the assumptions behind the human resources perspective, which is valid only for workers who have an interest in bettering themselves. But alas, this assumption is not always valid either: We all know people who tend to be lazy and unmotivated and are *not* interested in bettering themselves. The question is: Can theory be of any value when it is based on these kinds of admittedly incorrect assumptions?

Let us first acknowledge that it would be pretty hard to formulate *any* theory without making *some* assumptions. For example, most theories of social phenomena like organizational communication assume that the world will not change suddenly and radically from the way it is now. An evil dictator will not suddenly take over the world, there will not be nuclear war in the morning, and people who own organizations will not suddenly surrender all of their assets to their employees. Of course, any of these things could happen. Hitler could be reincarnated, a Russian general could wake up with a really mean vodka hangover and decide to push the button, and Donald Trump could have a religious vision and start throwing all of his money out the window. But it is probably safe to say that these things are ex-

tremely unlikely, and for the most part it would be absurd to make allowances for them in our theories. Therefore, devising any theory at least requires assumptions that these kinds of events will not happen.

If we cannot do without assumptions, the important question is: How do we decide whether any assumption we make is reasonable? Let us use an example to answer that question. Say that the management at SlobCo just took a course in organizational communication in which they learned about human resources theory. This theory holds that, assuming workers are interested in bettering themselves, the best way to increase productivity is to enrich jobs to make them more challenging and rewarding. Returning to their company, management tries this approach, but it fails to motivate the employees or produce any increase in productivity. It turns out that SlobCo employees do not want to improve themselves. They just want their paychecks so they can buy a fresh two-week supply of beer.

The management blames the failure on unreasonable assumptions by human resources theorists. In a sense, the assumptions are all there is to blame. Human resources theory gives an explanation of motivation that most people find quite logical. If the explanation did not work, then it almost must be because of faulty assumptions on the part of the theorists.

But this conclusion is drawn with the benefit of hindsight, which we all know to be 20/20. In fact, we can look at this situation in an entirely different way. The assumption that people want to better themselves is not "unreasonable." After all, human relations theorists could not be expected to anticipate every motivational state of every possible group of workers in every possible organization. Besides that, a lot of people *do* want to better themselves. The SlobCo program did not work because management tried to develop human resources in a situation where *the assumptions did not apply*; that is, where the employees were a bunch of lazy slobs motivated only by beer. They would have had better luck installing a tap in the break room or giving employees six-packs for doing good work. We might say that this was a failure by practitioners who applied a theory inappropriately, not a failure by theorists to anticipate the conditions at SlobCo.

Assumptions are not bad things that make theories unrealistic, and they are not unreasonable *or* reasonable. They are simply devices that theorists use like warning labels to ensure that theories are used properly. They say to the consumer of the theory: This theory is valid only under these circumstances: you should be attentive to the fact that these circumstances might not obtain in every organization and that the theory will probably not provide good explanations when they don't. To avoid problems like those at SlobCo, it is essential that practitioners have a clear understanding of the assumptions behind organizational communication theories and use that knowledge to make decisions about when and when not to apply them.

"Theories Often Contradict One Another."

It is true that different theories can yield differing explanations of one phenomenon. Let us say, for example, that Jane, the manager, and Dick, her subordinate, have a huge argument. Jane promised Dick a change in the way work gets distributed in their department (he was getting more than his share), but Jane never delivered. Dick was not pleased about this.

If the fight is the phenomenon we want to explain, there are almost as many explanations for it as there are theories to build them with. Conflict theory might tell us that Dick and Jane are fighting because they have not taken steps to defuse hostility and solve their problem in a productive manner. Interpersonal communication theory might attribute the argument to the violation of an implicit contract between Dick and Jane. Classical organizational theory might say that the problem is with Dick, who has no business second-guessing the decisions or actions of his boss; she has the formal authority to make such decisions. On the other hand, human relations theory might suggest that the problem is with Jane, who did not take seriously enough Dick's needs for a more fair distribution of work.

There are a virtual multitude of such explanations, and some of them, like the last two from the classical and human relations perspectives, even seem to contradict one another. But is this really a bad thing? Dick and Jane are not dealing with their conflict in a constructive manner if all they are doing is engaging in a protracted emotional fight. The fight has probably gotten emotional because an implicit contract between the two has been violated: Dick probably feels threatened and hurt by this, as if he can no longer trust Jane, while Jane probably thinks Dick is "turning on her." It is true that Jane has the authority to make these decisions, and her decision may have actually been the best one from the point of view of the company, in which case she could hardly have acted otherwise. At the same time, she should have recognized how unhappy her decision would make Dick and tried to find some other way to meet the need that caused his original request.

This simple example shows that different theories give different vantage points from which to analyze the problem; they provide us with *perspective*. Because each theory explains things in slightly different ways, each draws our attention to different important aspects of the problem, which gives us a deeper understanding of what is really going on. Among other results this keeps us from developing simplistic explanations and solutions. Our perspective on the Dick and Jane problem, for example, would tell us that we could not just give them bargaining training and expect the problem to go away. We would still be faced with the damage to their personal relationship and the fact that they are less able to trust one another.

I could go on about the perspective added by classical and human resources theories, but I think the point is fairly clear. The fact that different theories give competing explanations of phenomena is not a problem. On the contrary, it is one of the greatest and most useful things about theory because it give us a deeper understanding of phenomena.

"Theories Are Only for Scientists."

Not true. Everyone uses theories at one time or another. Social anthropologist William Kempton (1987) published an interesting article entitled *Two theories of home heat control*, in which he reported research describing people's theories about how their thermostats worked. He discovered two main theories: the *valve theory* says that a thermostat is like the valve on a faucet (the higher you turn up the thermostat the faster the heat comes out of the furnace), whereas the *switch theory* says the thermostat is just a switch that turns the furnace on and off (it produces a constant amount of heat whenever the switch turns on above a set temperature). Note that Kempton did not interview scientists about these theories; they came from everyday people.

As another example, ordinary people who have never even heard of organizational communication have many theories about communication at work. People in organizations frequently talk about "the grapevine" as an explanation for how supposedly confidential or private information is spread through an organization. Problems that happen at work are frequently explained as "communication breakdowns." Attempts by organizations to present themselves in a positive light are explained as "public relations."

There is also mounting agreement that humans *think* theoretically. Cognitive psychologists argue that our cognitive structures are in a way analogous to theories. Cognitive structures contain thoughts about phenomena we have experienced, previous descriptions and explanations of those phenomena, and judgments about the accuracy of predictions we have made. We act (i.e., practice) by continuously developing and refining our theories of the world. Wegner and Vallacher (1977) conclude that

> In a sense, then, every person is a naive psychologist who goes about his [or her] activities—collecting guesses about how people behave and think, testing his [or her] guesses about how people behave and think, building theories to explain the data and to predict and control future events—and yet is seldom aware that he [or she] is doing these things.

It is no wonder then that scientists construct theories: Theory building is a natural thing that everyone does.

There is, however, one important difference between the kinds of theories just described and theories you are likely to study in an organizational communication class. The former are known as *folk theories*. They are informal theories developed by nonscientists that are neither developed in detail nor rigorously tested. We might say that folk theories are valid as long as they are consistent with the experience of the folk theorist and help him or her practice effectively. The valve theory of heat control is technically incorrect, but Kempton presents evidence that people who hold it are better at managing the heat of their houses than people who subscribe to the switch theory.

Scientists working in their areas of expertise, on the other hand, produce *scientific theories*. These usually must conform to formal logical standards of internal validity, and are specified in great detail. This detail allows researchers to test the validity of the explanations the theory produces. Research conducted over time produces a body of evidence for or against the theory. Scientific theories are also subject to scrutiny and criticism by other scientists in a *field* or *discipline*. These are different names for organizations of scientists who (usually) work together to ensure that the most valid theories are supported and the least valid theories are discarded.

While there are important differences between folk theory and scientific theory, this does not mean that "folks" cannot make good use of scientific theories. On the contrary, scientific theories have usually undergone a lot of scrutiny and have been shown to produce generally valid explanations. As long as a "folk" understands the assumptions behind a theory and recognizes the particular point of view it provides, there is every reason to use it. It can only make his or her practice more effective.

CONCLUSION

There's nothing so practical as a good theory.
K. Lewin

So where do we stand on this theory/practice debate? Let me summarize my argument. Theory consists of descriptions and explanations of phenomena. Practice consists of using theories to predict and control the phenomena. The main point, then, is that theory and practice are different, but they are just different sides of the same coin. This means that theory is useful in the real world, if for no other reason than people require it for practice. And to say that practice is more important than theory leads quickly to a chicken-and-egg problem.

Theories are not perfect, and they cannot be: Some phenomena are just too complicated to explain all at once. So theorists are forced to limit the scope of their explanations by making assumptions. Fortunately, this does not prevent effective theory building because applying different theories of overlapping scope gives us perspective on phenomena. This helps ensure good explanations. Scientific theories are especially good at helping us explain phenomena because they usually have been formally described and tested, providing additional evidence of their validity.

So: That works fine in theory but . . . if something doesn't work in practice then it must not have *really* worked in theory after all. It is an oversimplification to think that theory and practice are separable things, that one is better or more important than another, or that one group of people does theory and another group does practice. Theories are thinking tools that thoughtful people learn about to get perspective and develop deeper understandings of phenomena like organizational communication.

And these kinds of deep understandings are the primary component of truly effective practice.

NOTE

1. Readers should note that there are other, more involved, notions of practice than the one employed here. For example, Banks (this volume) regards some practice as unconscious and routine. For this discussion, however, we will stick with the notion that practice makes use of theory, at least in cases in which practice is intentional.

REFERENCES

Kempton, W. (1987). Two theories of home heat control. In D. Holland & N. Quinn (eds.), *Cultural models in language and thought*, pp. 222–241. New York: Cambridge University Press.

Wegner, D. M., & Vallacher, R. R. (1977). *Implicit psychology: An introduction to social cognition.* New York: Oxford University Press.

2 WHY BUREAUCRACY?
CHARLES PERROW

Critics of bureaucracy are not hard to find. They often fault bureaucracy for being excessively rigid and for stifling employees' creativity and initiative. Charles Perrow challenges these common assumptions about the problems of bureaucracy, and he points out through concrete examples that in contemporary society bureaucracies are inescapable as a way of organizing because they are the most effective tools available for legitimizing power and authority in institutions. The problems, he says, are due not to the concept of bureaucracy but to the ways it is implemented in real organizations. Perrow claims that poor administrative practice and abuses of power are the *real* roots of problems people usually blame on "the bureaucracy."

Adapted from Charles Perrow, "Why Bureaucracy?" *Complex Organizations: A Critical Essay*, 3rd ed. New York: Random House, 1986. Reprinted with permission.

Thus, he advocates retaining many of the classical principles of organization, presented later in Part II.

This article is included to help you start thinking critically about organizations rather than just reacting to popular interpretation. Perrow is claiming that it is almost impossible to have a nonbureaucratic organization. After reading his article, think about the formal characteristics of bureaucracies and whether they are indeed true of most organizations. If you conclude that they are, you should also ask whether there is any evidence that bureaucracy *invites* abuses simply through its structure and/or function. Thinking about these issues will show you that a concept like bureaucracy can be extremely useful even if "bureaucracies" don't get good press.

Several miles from a medium-sized city near one of the Great Lakes, there was a plant that mined gypsum rock, crushed it, mixed it with bonding and foaming agents, spread it out on a wide sheet of paper, covered it with another sheet, let it set a bit, sliced it into large but inedible sandwiches, and then dried them. The resulting material was sold as wallboard, used for insulation and for dividing up rooms in buildings. Plants such as this were scattered about the country, some of them owned, as was this one, by General Gypsum Corporation (a pseudonym). A book by Alvin Gouldner, *Patterns of Industrial Bureaucracy*, described the plant and the surrounding communities as they existed in 1950.[1]

The towns around the plant were small and had been settled about a century before. The people in the area generally knew one another well and regarded strangers with considerable misgiving. They led a peaceful, semirural life, with an emphasis upon farming, hunting, and fishing. They were conservative in their outlook, strait-laced in their behavior, and, according to one member, "thrifty, religious, God-fearing, and anti-Semitic."[2]

The gypsum plant fitted comfortably into the style of life in the area. Most of the men working at the plant, some 225 including the miners, had worked there for many years. They knew one another well on the job and visited outside the plant in the surrounding hamlets. Indeed, perhaps as many as one-half of the workers were related to others employed in the plant. The personnel man who hired and fired people argued that it was good to learn something about a prospective employee by asking others in the plant or community about him and his

family. He did not want hostile employees or troublemakers. He also preferred farm boys over city boys. The former worked harder, he thought, and took greater pride in their work. The personnel man had few other rules for hiring, firing, or other matters with which he had to deal, however. He disliked paperwork and, as one employee said, "He regarded everything that happened as an exception to the rule." He had only an eighth-grade education, but since he relied so heavily on the community norms and his own rule-of-thumb methods, not much education seemed to be required. Apparently, hardly anyone was ever fired from the plant. Even those who left during the war years to work in defense plants paying much higher wages were welcomed back when those plants closed. A city boy, however, or a stranger laid off by a defense plant in the city had a hard time getting a job from this man.

In the plant itself, the workers had considerable leeway. The men were able to try different jobs until they found one that they liked, as long as they did so within the general limits of their union regulations. Moreover, they stretched out their lunch hours, were allowed to arrive late as long as they had some excuse, and were not required to keep busy. As long as their work was done, their time was their own. Production records were kept informally. The trouble was that the company management felt that not enough work was being done.

Further, the rhythm of the plant was, to some degree, determined by the men. During hunting season fewer showed up; the same thing sometimes occurred during planting season, since many employees farmed in their spare time. In cold weather more of them complained of sprains or other ailments so they could be transferred to the "sample room," where the work was light and the room was warm, until they were feeling better. This was preferable to staying at home and using up sick leave or to living off unemployment compensation. Mining operations fell off considerably on Mondays because of hangovers among the heavy-drinking miners. As a mill foreman explained, "You can't ride the men very hard when they are your neighbors. Lots of these men grew up together."[3]

Many employees used the plant materials and services freely. Men took dynamite home with them to explode in ponds (an easy way to fish) and for construction. They appropriated quantities of wallboard, even truckloads, for their personal use. They brought in broken items such as furniture to be fixed by the carpenters. And both employees and farmers in the area brought in broken parts for free welding.

For the workers, the plant was a pleasant and comfortable operation. One could hardly "get ahead," but few desired to go wherever "ahead" was. Those who showed a desire to advance in the company got transfers to company plants in different areas. Others left for the big city.

But for other interested parties, the plant was not all that satisfying. A job seeker found it difficult to get work if he was not well known, did not have relatives in the plant, or did not measure up to the vague standards of the personnel man—which had little to do with the ability to do the job. Customers found deliveries erratic. They might have suspected that if all gypsum plants were run this way, they would be paying a surcharge to cover the purloined materials, free repair work, and general slack. Top managers in the company headquarters, faced with postwar competition from other companies and competing products, were apparently climbing the walls.

When the plant manager died ("Old Doug," he was affectionately called), headquarters sent in an aggressive new manager with orders to tighten things up—increase productivity and cut costs. According to Gouldner's account, this man was not blessed with bountiful tact and insight, even though he was otherwise efficient. He cracked down rather hard and accumulated much ill will. He activated dormant rules, instituted new ones, demoted the

personnel man, and brought in one who applied a "universalistic" standard—the only thing that counted was a person's ability to do the job. The new manager successfully "bureaucratized" the surface plant. (He was unable to bureaucratize the more dangerous mine, for there was too much uncertainty and unpredictability in the work, and teamwork was extremely important.) However, some time later he was faced with a wildcat strike.

What had been a "traditional" form of organization, or in the terms of Max Weber,[4] a "traditional bureaucracy," became a "rational-legal bureaucracy." A rational-legal bureaucracy is based on rational principles (rational in terms of management's interests, not necessarily the worker's), is backed by legal sanctions, and exists in a legal framework. A miner fired for taking a case of dynamite, for example, was unsuccessful in his appeal that "everyone did it" and that the foreman "told him he could." Tradition or precedent was not binding; the material belonged to the company, not to the miner or the foreman.

Most of the key elements of the rational-legal bureaucracy are represented in this brief case history. They include:

1. Equal treatment for all employees.
2. Reliance on expertise, skills, and experience relevant to the position.
3. No extraorganizational prerogatives of the position (such as taking dynamite, wallboard, etc.); that is, the position is seen as belonging to the organization, not the person. The employee cannot use it for personal ends.
4. Specific standards of work and output.
5. Extensive record keeping dealing with the work and output.
6. Establishment and enforcement of rules and regulations that serve the interests of the organization.
7. Recognition that rules and regulations bind managers as well as employees; thus employees can hold management to the terms of the employment contract.

The rational-legal form of bureaucracy developed over many centuries of Western civilization. It grew slowly and erratically, beginning in the Middle

Ages, and reached its full form on a widespread basis only in the twentieth century.[5] Nearly all large, complex organizations in the United States, for example, are best classified as bureaucracies, though the degree and forms of bureaucratization vary.

Its "ideal" form, however, is never realized for at least three reasons. First, it tries to do what must be (hopefully) forever impossible—to eliminate all unwanted extraorganizational influences on the behavior of members. Ideally, members should act only in the organization's interests. The problem is that even if the interest of the organization is unambiguous, people do not exist just for organizations. They track all kinds of mud from the rest of their lives into the organization, and they have all kinds of interests that are independent of the organization.

Second, the ideal form also falls short of realization when rapid changes in some of the organizational tasks are required. *Bureaucracies are set up to deal with stable, routine tasks; that is the basis of organizational efficiency.* Without stable tasks there cannot be a stable division of labor, a prescribed acquisition of skills and experience, formal planning and coordination, and so on. But when changes come along, organizations must alter their programs; when such changes are frequent and rapid, the form of organization becomes so temporary that the efficiencies of bureaucracy cannot be realized. (The price of the product it delivers then goes up.) The gypsum mine could not be bureaucratized to the degree that the surface plant was because the unpredictability of the seams and the dangers and variability of the raw material made continual change and improvisation necessary.

Third, bureaucracy in its ideal form falls short of its expectations because people are only indifferently intelligent, prescient, all-knowing, and energetic. All organizations must be designed for the "average" person one is likely to find in each position, not the superhuman.

While bureaucracy always falls short of the ideal model that Weber outlined, neither Weber in his time nor many people today would be comfortable with the ideal. In fact, much can be said for the placid, community-oriented gypsum-plant organization before the owners decided it was not making enough money for them. There was job rotation and variability, consideration for special problems such as minor illnesses, and trust among the workers and between workers and management. Furthermore, to a small extent, workers could consider the resources of the organization (wallboard, the carpentry shop) to be theirs. Perhaps above all, they could farm and hunt and thus avoid complete dependence on wages paid by the gypsum plant. If all gypsum companies were like this, some of the "social costs" of bureaucracy—dependence on a wage, dull work, and inflexible demands—would be spread over all consumers of the product. But all companies are not like this, so this one could not compete and survive. In this sense, where all organizations strive toward efficiency as defined by the owners, the rational-legal form of bureaucracy is the most efficient form of administration known in industrial societies.

In the rest of this chapter, I am going to illustrate the essentials of bureaucracy by showing what happens when they are violated (as they constantly are). The chapter will give us all an appreciation for bureaucracy as a remarkable product of gradual, halting, and often unwitting social engineering. As we shall see, many of the "sins" of bureaucracy really reveal the failure to bureaucratize sufficiently. But while I will defend bureaucracy from many of the attacks we all are prone to make, I will attack it much more severely on quite different grounds, grounds that social scientists have been reluctant to explore. Let me explain my puzzling position briefly.

Critics usually attack bureaucracy for two reasons—it is unadaptive, and it stifles the humanity of employees. Both are legitimate criticisms to a degree. But what the first avoids noticing is that another description of unadaptiveness might be stability, steadfastness, and predictability. If we want a particular change and fail to get it, we blame the unadaptive bureaucracy. If it changes in ways we do not like though, we call for stability. The second criticism—that bureaucracies stifle spontaneity, freedom, and self-realization—is certainly true for many employees, but unfortunately, since they do not own what they produce and must work for someone else, expressions of spontaneity and self-realization are not likely to result in better goods and services for consumers. We have constructed a society where the satisfaction of our wants as consumers largely depends on restricting the employees who do the producing. Bureaucracy cannot be faulted for society's demands; if blame is to be placed it should fall on those elites who constructed bureaucracy over many generations and offered us no alternatives, a subject we will return to at the end of the book.

Most social scientists (almost all of them until the mid-1970s) have offered these two criticisms of bureaucracy—rigidity and employee discipline—if they have offered any. I would offer a third: bureaucracy has become a means, both in capitalist and noncapitalist countries, of centralizing power in society and legitimating or disguising that centralization. A full defense of this thesis is impossible here. But this book will sketch, through a critical review of historical and recent thought on organizational analysis, how social scientists have, until recently, avoided the "big" question of unregulated and unperceived power through bureaucratic organizations, even though the research that has been done points in this direction.

Bureaucracy is a tool, a social tool that legitimizes control of the many by the few, despite the formal apparatus of democracy, and this control has generated unregulated and unperceived social power. This power includes much more than just control of employees. As bureaucracies satisfy, delight, pollute, and satiate us with their output of goods and services, they also shape our ideas, our very way of conceiving of ourselves, control our life chances, and even define our humanity. As employees, whether we see ourselves as exploited or as pursuing "careers," we may dimly perceive this fact; as citizens in a society of organizations, where large organizations have absorbed all that used to be small, independent, personal, communitarian, religious, or ethnic, it is rarely perceived. We grow up in organizations; to stand outside them is to see their effect on what we believe, what we value, and, more important, how we think and reason.

At present, without huge, disruptive, and perilous changes, we cannot survive without large organizations. Organizations mobilize social resources for ends that are often essential and even desirable. But organizations also concentrate those resources in the hands of a few who are prone to use them for ends we do not approve of, for ends we may not even be aware of, and, more frightening still, for

ends we are led to accept because we are not in a position to conceive alternative ones. The investigation of these fearful possibilities has too long been left to writers, journalists, and radical political leaders. It is time that organizational theorists began to use their expertise to uncover the true nature of bureaucracy. This will require a better understanding both of the virtues of bureaucracy and its largely unexplored dangers.

PURGING PARTICULARISM

One of the many dilemmas of organizations is that they attempt to be efficient in producing their output of steel, court convictions, reformed delinquents, legislation, or whatever, and yet they seek to be quite particular about who shall enjoy the pay and the honor of doing the work. *Particularism* means that criteria irrelevant for efficient production (e.g., only relatives of the boss have a chance at top positions), in contrast to universalistic criteria (e.g., competence is all that counts), are used to choose employees. The criteria of efficiency and particularism are likely to clash, since the most efficient workers may lack the particular social characteristics desired. For example, few Jews ever rise very high in such industries as steel;[6] few blacks have thus far been able to break into many skilled trades in the construction industry. In a study of one manufacturing firm, Melville Dalton found that membership in the Masons was a prerequisite to advancement in management. Even though it is hard to imagine what there is about Masonic membership that would increase managerial efficiency,[7] ambitious managers were smart enough to join the fraternal order. Some levels in organizations, some work groups, and even whole plants are uni-ethnic—that is, all Irish or all Polish. One of the distinctive characteristics of voluntary associations such as patriotic societies or clubs is that they often specify membership criteria openly, while economic or governmental organizations can only do so informally. The Daughters of the American Revolution was founded at a time when many native-born Anglo-Saxons had parents who had lived during the days of the Revolution; the unqualified, then, were conveniently all immigrants.

The development of bureaucracy has been in part an attempt to purge organizations of particularism. This has been difficult, because organizations are profoundly "social," in the sense that all kinds of social characteristics affect their operation *by intent*. Take the relatively trivial matters of nepotism (giving preferred treatment to relatives) and personal favoritism. Both are very common—and very annoying, unless you are a favored relative or friend of the boss. But both reflect social solutions to the organizational problems of members. One of the things that you can do with the power that a decent position in an organization gives you is to reward people whom you like or are related to you or who will help you in return. Families, for example, are a major resource in society; relatives who work for you can be expected to hide your mistakes and incompetence, warn you about threats to your position, and support you in conflicts with others. Similarly, subordinates are well advised to defer to their superior because they will be protected and rewarded for covering for their boss, warning her, and lightening her workload. Two or three levels above the boss, the higher-ups will try to measure objective competence, but it is both hard to determine competence and easy to disguise incompetence. Since the subordinate's career and even comfort are always at risk in organizations, we can hardly expect them always to put the abstract "interests of the organization" ahead of their own interests and those of the bosses who control their fate.

The social character of organizations goes deeper. In a society where organizations provide the livelihood of eight out of ten of the "economically active" and where organizations are necessary for most other interests, merely being allowed to be a member of an organization is critical for well-being, if not survival. Assiduous efforts are made to restrict access to this resource; organizations discriminate on social, rather than objective, grounds in letting people in.

We view these particularistic criteria with suspicion partly because of our democratic ideas of equality. But we also view them with suspicion because we dimly recognize that organizations draw on resources provided by society in general and thus are beholden to all of society. In spite of this fact, though, there is, for example, a flourishing and byzantine structure of courts, laws, and law-enforcement facilities that is available to organizations to protect their interests. We support this structure through taxes. On campus, fraternities and sororities have special access to university facilities, receive special protection—and are tax-exempt. And private clubs that discriminate get quiet subsidies in one form or another. For example, in 1984 a county judge in Maryland ruled that an elite golf club, the Burning Tree Club, would lose its $186,000 real estate tax exemption because it would not admit women as members; indeed, even the kitchen staff had to be male. How could a club that charged an initiation fee of $12,000 and annual dues of $1,700 justify a yearly tax break of $186,000? Because the huge grounds preserved open spaces (in a suburb where the least expensive homes cost $400,000). The Burning Tree officials said they would appeal, cited the constitutional guarantee of freedom of association, and charged that the necessary increase in dues—about $292 per member—would turn the club into "a rich man's club."[8]

The factory is fairly free to pollute the air and water, to enforce its law through its own police force and its access to the courts, to hire and fire (and thus provide or deny livelihood), to utilize the services of the local chamber of commerce (which is tax-exempt and may even receive local tax support), and to draw upon tax-supported services of many state and federal agencies. These things cost all of us money. No matter that the factory pays taxes in return, or that the sorority provides housing and surveillance that the university might otherwise have to build and provide. Common resources are drawn from society, whatever the specific products returned. Thus, we feel the services should be common to all who desire them. Particularism or discrimination is frowned upon.

But these are political rather than bureaucratic reasons for distrusting particularism. The bureaucratic reason for frowning on particularism is that efficiency is forgone if recruitment or access is decided upon grounds that are not related to the members' performance in the organization. For most organizational goals or roles, social origins (race, ethnicity, and class) are not likely to be a measure of competence. The steel company or bank that bars Jews from middle management is possibly depriving itself of talent at the higher levels. The appointment of a large political campaign donor to the position of Ambassador to the Court of St. James suggests that the criteria are not knowledge of foreign affairs and skill in foreign diplomacy, but party loyalty and personal wealth. The son of the president of a corporation may well start out on the shop floor or as a sales trainee, but it is not his competence that moves him quickly to a vice-presidency. Moreover, the frequent practice of a professional person hiring staff members from the same university he or she attended suggests something other than universalistic criteria. One finds this in university departments ("only Eastern schools have a chance there," or "that's where Michigan sends its run-of-the-mill Ph.D.'s"), research and development labs ("someone from MIT doesn't stand a chance in that company"), social agencies ("they only give supervisory positions to Chicago graduates" [University of Chicago School of Social Work]), and hospital medical staffs ("that's a Johns Hopkins shop").

The problem with these practices is not only that there is little relationship between the social criteria for hiring or promoting people and the characteristics that affect performance in the organization. More serious, the particularistic criteria are likely to be *negatively* related to performance—the more these particularistic criteria are used, the poorer the performance. By hiring only Chicago graduates, one may have to take some who were among the poorer students, missing out on the good Michigan graduates. More serious still, one may end up with only one way of seeing the world and only one way of approaching a problem. By using broad or universalistic hiring criteria, the chances of getting different perspectives, and thus more ideas, are increased.

That particularistic criteria are often equivalent to favoritism also means that corruption is a likely accompaniment. The agency head who hires or favors primarily people from her own region, state, or university may get subtle returns in the bargain. She may be favored as a consultant to her former university or the state government and receive handsome fees; she may place herself at the head of the line for bigger and better appointments. Competence is hard to judge, so we rely on familiarity. The corruption may be less discreet, as in the political spoils system, whereby the elected official hires only people who are willing to contribute to his election campaign or to provide him with kickbacks.

Tenure and the Career Concept

Political patronage reached such a corrupting extreme in the late nineteenth century that the merit system and civil service examinations were instituted in the federal and most state governments. We now pay a price for that sweeping change, since merit systems may have little to do with merit. Once a civil service appointee receives "tenure," it is very hard to remove that employee for lack of competence. Over the years, as the organization changes and the demand for new skills increases, the person who may have once been a very competent employee may turn out to be quite incompetent. But the organization is stuck with him or her. One need look no further, for example, than university departments where skills change quickly, promise does not materialize into productivity, or people simply pass their prime. If research-oriented universities changed to the extent that teaching ability became a prime criterion for competence, rather than a secondary one, many tenured people might be found incompetent.

It is a tenet of the bureaucratic model of organizations that an employee is expected to pursue a "career" in the organization. Thus, if the person burns out too quickly or, more likely, if the skills demanded of the position change without the occupant changing (e.g., more emphasis on teaching and less on research), the organization is expected to retain him or her. The employee has tenure. Despite the frequency with which this annoyance is met in organizations, the career principle is a sound one. People would not be likely to master sets of skills through long technical training or experience in an organization if they knew they could not perpetually draw on the capital of their investment. There must be some guarantee that if the demands of the job change radically in the future, a person will still be credited with having met them in the present. Otherwise, personnel might be less willing to make large investments in skills.

In short, the benefits of universalistic standards clearly appear to exceed the costs; tenure may be a necessary inducement for mastering obscure skills and a necessary protection against arbitrary rulers. There are costs, but the alternatives are worse.

Universalism and Organizational Goals

Universalistic criteria, then, would appear to be a proper goal in organizations, and few would fault the bureaucratic model in this respect. But the situation is not that simple. To establish the standards, one has to know the real goals of the organization. Suppose a manufacturing firm favors members of a certain fraternal organization when it hires and promotes its managers. On the face of it, this sounds particularistic. Closer examination, though, might well reveal that the manufacturing organization receives a variety of tax benefits from the local government, and the local government is heavily loaded with Masons, Lions, Legionnaires, or whatever. If the firm gives preference to Masons, should they be the dominant group in the city government, it may avoid paying its fair share of the sewage system; it may get special arrangements for power supplies; zoning ordinances may be drafted so that it does not have to pay a heavy school tax; it may be able to get certain city streets closed to permit convenient expansion; and a good share of its security protection may come from the city's police department, rather than from plant guards. Furthermore, the local authorities may see that other plants are discouraged from coming in, through zoning ordinances or restrictions on transportation or available power supplies. Competing industry, particularly, would up the demand for skilled labor in one field and drive up wages. Moreover, the city planning commission may ensure that a new superhighway comes close to the front gate of the plant, even at the expense of cutting a residential district in two.

Showing favoritism within the manufacturing company to this fraternal organization is hardly, then, a particularistic criterion from the *company's* point of view. Any loss in managerial competence that may result from using selective criteria is more than offset by the gain of having sympathetic friends in the city administration. For similar reasons, defense industries have a disproportionate number of former military officers in their top echelons, even though it is questionable whether former procurement or inspection officers are particularly good

managers of large aerospace firms or conglomerates. For defense industries, political ties to the Pentagon are a universalistic criterion. Similarly, experience in the major corporations and investment houses is often crucial for top civilian positions in the State Department, the Defense Department, the CIA, and the Atomic Energy Commission; Richard Barnet found that seventy of the ninety-one top men in those agencies from 1940 to 1967 had such backgrounds.[9] The Polish foreman who favors Polish workers under him is acting no differently.

This reasoning also applies to voluntary associations such as fraternities and sororities. If the "real" goals of the Greek-letter societies were auxiliary support for the university, good fellowship, recreation, character building, and efficient housing, then discrimination against Jews and blacks would be unwarranted. However, if the goal of the fraternity or sorority also includes promoting social class and ethnic solidarity, ties that will lead to business or marital advantages, and reinforcement of religious, ethnic, and class sentiments, then the discrimination is certainly efficient. The Jew or the black is deemed an inappropriate resource for the organization; he or she does nothing for the group.

We may deplore the particularism of the Greek-letter society or the manufacturing firm and call for the universalism that is explicit in the bureaucratic model. There, at least, bureaucracy is virtuous in its impersonality. But to deplore particularism is only to advance an ideal and to neglect the reality of organizational affairs. The real cause for concern is not just the failure to apply universalism; rather it involves the uses the leaders make of the organization; these determine just what are universalistic or particularistic criteria. We are being naive when we deplore patronage, collusion, and snobbery in our political, economic, and voluntary organizations, as if those traits stemmed from a failure to apply sound organizational principles or even general moral principles. A more realistic view would question the uses to which owners and managers put these organizations, for these uses define what is efficient for those in control. Organizations are tools. The bureaucratic ideal assumes the uses are legitimate—that is, in society's interests. In doing so, it disguises some of the purposes to which people put organizations. Still, bureaucracy—with its ideals of clearly stated goals and rational instrumentation of legitimate purposes—is a clear advance over ancient satrapies, feudal domains, family dynasties, warlords and their retinues, and the autocracies of the past. At the least, since official goals are proclaimed, unofficial, unpublicized, and unlegitimated uses can be held up to scrutiny when they are found, and action can be taken. The hidden uses of organizations, always present, can be exposed and addressed.

The Contest for Control

Organizations generate power; control and use of that power are vital organizational issues. Particularism is a strategy to control and use that power, and it is not easily purged. It is a central theme of this book that organizations must be seen as tools, as having bundles of all sorts of resources that people inside and outside can make use of and try to control. Organizations are multipurpose tools because they can do many things for many people.

For example, regardless of their goals, organizations offer employment opportunities for friends and relatives, as well as for oneself. They also provide prestige and status for their members, as well as chances to make contacts and to strengthen social class ties. Obviously, there are opportunities for graft and corruption through organizations. But most important of all, *organizations are tools for shaping the world as one wishes it to be shaped.* They provide the means for imposing one's own definition of the proper affairs of humankind on others. The person who controls an organization has power that goes far beyond that of those lacking such control. The power of the rich lies not in their ability to buy goods and services, but in their capacity to control the ends toward which the vast resources of large organizations are directed.

Such power is naturally contested. People attempt to achieve control of organizations or even parts of an organization in order to gain that power. "If I were in charge I would do it this way." "We really should be doing such and such." "Top management should never let the union [or suppliers, or customers, or medical staff, or the prison guards, or the government, or middle management, or whatever] get away with this." "The trouble with top management is that it is only interested in immediate profits and not in long-term growth; I want to see this organization strong over the long run." "This agency should be serving lower-class people, not the middle class." "Top management is too tied to the industry way of doing things; it is preoccupied with traditions that are no longer relevant, and it does not want to rock the boat." "We should be revolutionizing things in this industry." "We don't want people of *that sort* in our company." "Business has a responsibility to protect the American way of life. We should make it clear to these groups that they can't get away with this." These are statements about power and the uses to which it can be put.

Retaining or gaining power is difficult because it is almost always contested, and the contest is not decided by measuring the "efficiency" or "productivity" of the contenders. The criterion is not narrow and testable, but general and vague. The principles of bureaucracy have little to do with the contest. One decidedly unbureaucratic principle is crucial—personal loyalty or loyalty to a superior rather than to the organization and its goals. One of the best ways to seize or retain control is to surround oneself with loyal people. If a person has a certain charisma or force of personality, the loyalty may be freely given by strangers and acquaintances. If one lacks this rare quality, there are other means of ensuring loyalty. The most powerful is dependence. The subordinate who is a relative of a superior or a friend of the family is more dependent than one who is not; his or her superior has privileged access to "significant others" in the subordinate's social world. The marginally competent manager who is promoted over others is vulnerable and thus had better be loyal.

Of course, one purchases some inefficiency along with this loyalty. Inefficiency means that the costs of doing business are increased. But the difference between a small increase in the operating cost and a threat to losing control of all or some of the resources of the organization is enormous. In most cases, the exchange of loyalty for competence is in the executive's interest.

Even less-than-exemplary subordinates can perform very well for their superiors. A man may lack good judgment in setting policies, be inefficient in organizing his work and his staff, and even spend an excessive amount of time on the golf course or traveling at company expense. However, if he manages to sniff out potential sources of opposition within the organization, nominate loyal subordinates and identify those who cannot be trusted, and generally keep track of the activities of ''internal enemies,'' he is worth a great deal to his boss. Such functions are commonplace in organizations of all types. As we have said, organizations are tools; they mobilize resources that can be used for a variety of ends. These resources and the goals of the organization are up for grabs, and people grab for them continually. Internecine warfare, often involving lawsuits, is a very prominent news item in the business press; it generally concerns the uses to which organizational power is to be put.

Viewing organizations as tools should reduce our tendency to cry incompetence when they do not do what we think they should. Incompetence certainly exists; organizations must contend with the distribution of incompetence in the general population, as well as the distribution of tendencies toward venality, stupidity, sycophancy, and so on, since they must draw upon the general population for employees. But a tool view alerts us to the possibility that what we see as incompetent performance or policy really reflects what some leaders wanted all along. A president will not announce that he or she intends to discipline labor and reduce inflation by creating a recession; it will be announced instead that the economy is not competitive enough. If an acquired firm goes downhill in performance, the new leaders need not be charged with incompetence in running the acquisition; they may have decided to appropriate its available cash and other liquid assets, its unused tax credits, and its best personnel and use them where they will provide greater returns. The acquired firm may then be sold, or even scrapped, possibly with significant tax breaks. Before assuming that an outcome was unintended, it is best to see if someone in top management might not have had reason to have intended the outcome. Bureaucracy is not the breeder of incompetence, as we often would like to believe. Instead, bureaucratic organization allows leaders to achieve goals, some of which are unannounced and costly for the rest of us and are only *attributed* to incompetence.

In conclusion, we have explored particularism in organizations, indicating the desirability of the bureaucratic ideal of universalism—hiring and promoting on the basis of performance ability (skills, competence, diligence, etc.) rather than on agreement to support the goals of the organization. We deplore particularism for several reasons. It goes against the values of a liberal society—that is, it yields racial or religious discrimination; it involves using public resources for the advantage of specific groups; it promotes inefficiency in organizations. But we also have been suggesting that much of the particularism we frown on is particularistic only if we think the goals of an organization should be other than what they are; from the point of view of those who control the organization, the criteria may really be universalistic and promote the efficiency of the organization. Better personnel practices, or standards, or screening criteria are irrelevant when only changes in the uses to which the organization is put would meet the criticisms. This is because organizations are tools designed to perform work for their masters, and particularism or universalism is relative to the goals of the masters. Because organizations generate power to get a variety of things done, people contend for that power, and favoritism and nepotism help to ensure loyalty to the contenders.

We also briefly touched on one other characteristic of bureaucracy—tenure, or the career principle; we argued that the costs of this principle, as seen in the frustration of dealing with incompetent personnel who have civil service protection or incompetent tenured professors, are more than made up for by its advantages. These include freedom from arbitrary authority, protection from changes in skill demands and declining ability, and assurance that one's investment in skills and experience will be secure. The bureaucratic model emphasizes efficiency in the long run, not the short run.

It is a tribute to the bureaucratic model as it developed since the Middle Ages that it has at least partially answered the problem of particularism and pursued it with vigor. Loyalty to the king or lord or chief was once everything; incompetence counted for little. With the rise of the university-educated scribes, jurists, and mathematicians, a class of presumably professional, neutral, and loyal personnel arose, the business administration students of yore.[10] The kings and chiefs could use these and get both competence and loyalty (through dependence) in their administration. The eunuch in the harem is the prototype of the modern professional; he can be trusted with everything except that which really counts—the uses to which the masters put the organization. We have come so far from the particularism of medieval days that nepotism and favoritism today are frowned on as both subversive and inefficient. A substantial residue of these practices remains in organizations simply because organizations, then as now, are tools in the hands of their masters; thus, control over them is a prize that many people seek. Particularism is one weapon in that struggle, but its use must be masked.

FEATHERING THE NEST

Organizations generate a great deal of power and leverage in the social world, power and leverage far beyond their ostensible goals. But one problem of organizations is that they are very leaky vessels. It is quite easy for a member of one to use some of his or her power and leverage for personal ends rather than for the ends of the organization. (The ends of the organization, we may say for the present, are those of a small group at the top of the organization or, in many cases, a small group outside the organization that controls those at the top). In the ideal world of the ideal bureaucracy, it should be possible to calculate neatly, and thus control, the relationship between a person's contribution to an organization and the rewards he or she receives. Theoretically, too, the rewards the organization has to pay should not exceed the contribution of the person. In practice, this is very difficult because it is hard to control people so closely and because organizations have permeable boundaries. People tend to act as if they own their positions; they use them to generate income, status, and other things that rightfully belong to the organization. Bureaucracy has made great strides in reducing the discrepancy between people's contributions, on the one hand, and the inducements necessary to keep them in the organization and make them work, on the other.[11] During the period when bureaucracies were just beginning to form, this problem was most acute.

During the late Middle Ages, the king who wanted revenues from the land and from the people he controlled would sell a tax franchise to someone, generally a nobleman. This official would agree to pay the king a set fee; he was then free to collect as much money as he could from the people and keep anything beyond the set fee. The king benefited because he did not have to organize and maintain a large bureaucracy to collect taxes. However, the collector might extract such a heavy toll that the subjects would revolt. Or the basis of the economy might be ruined so that fewer and fewer taxes could be collected. Or the collector might become so rich that he could challenge the power of the king. Eventually, the king or the state took control of taxation, centralized it, hired personnel on a salaried basis to run the system, and used the army to back up the collectors. In this way, the imbalance between the effort and reward of the tax collector was markedly reduced. The tax collectors were paid what they were worth on the labor market at that time.

Today, we do not find tax collectors paying a franchise fee to the state to collect as much as they can, but problems still remain because government units are empowered to force people to pay taxes. This power is a source of leverage for the officeholder. For example, local assessors (who determine the value of property for taxation purposes) have been known to make deals with business firms or other interests such that certain property is assessed at a lower value than it would normally be. Then the assessors receive a percentage of the reduction from the organization that is being assessed. Internal revenue agents have been known to make deals with taxpayers whereby the latter's taxes are reduced and the agents get a portion of the savings. The Internal Revenue Service spends a good deal of money on various forms of surveillance to minimize this practice and to keep the agent from using the power of that organization for his or her private purposes.

The medieval system of selling franchises is still legally practiced in some of the less-organized areas of our economy. For example, small businesspeople, particularly doctors and dentists, "sell" delinquent accounts to a tax-collecting firm; the tax-collecting firm gives the businessperson, say, 40 percent of the value of the account and then keeps anything above that amount, if it is able to collect. Most businesses are wary of using all the powers legally or illegally at hand to collect debts because they do not want to alienate people who might be future customers or clients. For the tax-collecting firm, however, this is not a constraint, so their methods of extracting money from debtors are more severe.[12] Of course, the agencies also do not care whether the debtors feel that the debt is unjust or not. It is irrelevant to the agency if the debtors failed to pay their full bill because they were overcharged or because they did not receive the goods or services. Furthermore, agencies stand to gain a great deal by collecting all or 70 percent of the debt rather than 40 percent, so they pursue their task with vigor. Agencies also find it easier to extract money from the poorer and less well-educated strata of society since those with few resources are more easily intimidated.

Another example of ancient practices in the less well-organized and rationalized sectors of our economy is the selling of professional services. Normally, one thinks that a client goes to a doctor, dentist, or lawyer on a voluntary basis. However, for a number of reasons, clients do not have effective choice in these matters. In varying degrees, professionals have captive clients. There is not much competition among doctors, for example, because clients have few ways to judge doctors and have to consider geographical accessibility; also, doctors have restricted entry to their profession to keep the numbers low. If the patient has been going to a particular doctor for any period of time at all, she has a "sunk cost" in this relationship—the doctor knows her and has X rays and other records. What happens, then, when a doctor or lawyer or dentist retires or moves away? If it is a sizable practice at all, it will be "sold" to another professional. Indeed, if the professional dies, his or her beneficiaries can sell the practice. Patients are not literally sold to the new buyer, of course, but in fact the new buyer has quite privileged access to them. Practices are put up for competitive bidding and go to the highest bidder. Of course, there is no guarantee of any relationship between ability and reward, since an incompetent doctor, for example, may be able to pay more for a practice than a good one. Given the highly entrepreneurial, even medieval, character of our independent professions, little was done until recently to rationalize or bureaucratize them in order to control the relationship between effort and reward.

However, rationalization of medical and legal services is beginning to appear as the demand for service has increased. Walk-in storefront medical clinics and law offices are opening; psychological counselors have formal ties with medical and legal professionals. Shopping-center emporiums with doctors, dentists, opticians, lawyers, accountants, tax experts, counselors, chaplains, chiropractors, and fitness experts will probably soon provide one-stop service for every conceivable personal need. We seem to have survived the loss of a personal relationship with our grocer or barber; we will probably accept, though not welcome, taking a number and standing in line for the next available professional. This is an efficient use of work power for the organizers of such groups, as for-profit hospital chains and franchises have learned. (The Kentucky Fried Chicken organization, for instance, has branched off into hospital franchises.)

The rationalization of professional services also reduces the occasions for the individual professional to feather his or her nest, though very likely at the expense of individualized service. The relationship between the effort the professional puts in and the reward he or she receives, open to abuse before such rationalization, is greatly controlled. But note that the consumer's definitions of effort and reward are no longer as potent; it is the entrepreneur who runs the service or the emporium who now sets the definition. Bureaucracy requires standardized inputs and outputs; after taking your number and waiting your turn for whichever professional is free, the professional will take note of your need and sort it into the nearest appropriate box for standard treatment, no exceptions please, in the interest of low fees and quick turnover. The relationship between effort and reward for the employee may be very rational, but for the consumer, an individualized, personal definition is lost. Why bureaucracy in the area of personalized services? Because most of us cannot afford the personalized attention, and our key needs would remain untended. We should not blame bureaucracy for not providing the personal services available only to the wealthy.

Once professionals have been bureaucratized, they will, like everyone else, seek to feather their nests from the copious amounts of down floating around in most organizations. Generally, such uses are simply taken for granted, as if they were fringe benefits written into the employment contract. No professor in his right mind (and they all have right minds in this regard) would think of buying his own paper, pencils, carbon paper, and so on to write a book from which he hopes to gain substantial income in the form of royalty. It does not occur to many professors that they should pay for the privilege of using a huge library that caters to their exotic tastes and allows them to keep books out for months or years without paying fines. Nor do many universities question a professor's use of secretarial time that is officially budgeted as an educational expense. When pressed, professors may insist that while they draw royalties on their books (which range from a few dollars a year to over $100,000), they are really contributing to the educational resources of society and that this is an inexpensive way to produce knowledge and teaching materials. This is true enough, but it is still remarkable that very few universities have attempted to require professors to pay back to the school some percentage of any outside income that comes from exploiting resources that are tax exempt or derived from students and, in public universities, from the taxpayers. A few have tried, and fewer actually do it; it meets with considerable resistance. In addition to royalties from books, there are the matters of lecture engagements and consulting jobs. A professor at a prestigious university is able to demand very high fees for consulting and lecturing and will get many opportunities to do these things. Since few prepare for these tasks only on Saturdays and Sundays, spending the other five days of the week busily teaching, these activities undoubtedly divert one from teaching duties.

Virtually all organizations offer opportunities to feather one's nest. Recall the dynamite that was readily taken from the gypsum mine described at the opening of this chapter. A more dramatic example is the scandals in the Chicago police department and other police departments in the early 1960s that were referred to as the "cops and/or robbers" syndrome. These scandals involved police officers who, by knowing when people were going to be away and when on-duty officers were not likely to be around, were able to burglarize stores and homes.

We may not expect a great deal of rectitude in police departments, but we might in voluntary hospitals supported by government funds, private, donations, community chest funds, and, of course, patient fees. Nevertheless, I was not surprised to

find that in some voluntary hospitals it was the custom for top-level administrators, physicians, and surgeons to receive expensive filets and other food from the hospital kitchens for use at home. Also, the maintenance staff occasionally remodeled or maintained the private houses of key executives, doctors, or board members. These illustrations may be trivial, but the principle is not. Organizations generate surpluses and leverage in our world, and those who have any power in them can use these for their own ends. The device of bureaucracy was designed to prevent *any but the masters* of the organization from doing this.

We might think that the more bureaucratized and rationalized the organization is, the less nest feathering will occur. This may be so, at least at the lower levels, but we have no research on the subject. However, to the extent that business and industrial organizations are among the most bureaucratized and rationalized, the generalization probably would not stand. Highly placed executives of business and industrial firms sometimes profit handsomely from giving lucrative contracts to suppliers in which they have invested their personal funds. These arrangements rarely become public because it is very difficult to gain such information. One did become public in 1960, when an aggressive stockholder pursued the matter with the Chrysler Corporation. Eventually, the president of Chrysler resigned, and, after being sued by the corporation, returned $450,000 to the company. He allegedly favored suppliers in whose firm he had a personal financial interest. (It is not often, however, that a stockholder with only a pittance of stock can bring down the administrative head of a large corporation.) Perhaps the reason that such an "unbureaucratic" practice could occur in a highly bureaucratized firm is that, as Max Weber noted long ago, the top of an organization is never bureaucratized. It always belongs to somebody. In this case, though, the board of directors and stockholders insisted that the organization was also theirs; it did not belong just to the president.

The practice of feathering one's nest in large part reflects the problem of separating the interests of the person from the interests of the organization. In our organizational society, this becomes increasingly difficult. For example, to whom does the experience of an employee belong? Does it belong to him or her or to the organization in which that experience was acquired? The growth of bureaucracy was equivalent to putting a label of "company property" on the skills, experience, and creativity of the employee. It is a measure of our socialization into a society of bureaucratic organizations that we no longer question this extraction at all in the case of blue-collar workers and most white-collar ones. But consider industry at the turn of the century. Most of the work in the large, mass-producing factories and mills (except textiles, which had been "rationalized" long before) was done by work crews that were recruited, organized, and paid by independent contractors.[13] They used the company's facilities, supplies, and tools but worked under yearly contracts to produce so many rifle barrels or parts of sewing machines or whatever. The contractors sometimes made very large profits and paid their workers presumably what the market would bear, or more likely, what the local custom dictated. The system was apparently quite efficient—technological changes were rapidly introduced and were in the interests of the contractors. It flourished in factories producing highly engineered products on a mass basis. Owners supplied the capital and organized the final assembly and marketing.

The genius of F. W. Taylor and others in the scientific management movement was to convince the owners that they should employ engineers to go around and find out how the men and women drilled the rifle barrels or made the gears for machine tools or cast the locomotive parts, centralize this information and study it, then break the tasks down into small parts so as to remove as much of the skill and accumulated experience as possible, hire a foreman who would supervise the crew for a wage, and assign the highly specialized "deskilled" tasks to the workers and pay them at a much lower wage rate. The owners "expropriated" the craft skills and craft system and designated as company property the ingenuity, experience, and creativity of the workers. Only now are we beginning to painfully rediscover and recommend giving back to the workers a small part of what had been their own property, in the form of such schemes as job enlargement, workers' participation, workers' autonomy, and group incentives.

What was settled for workers and most managers long ago (sometimes through bloody strikes)[14] still appears for top executives and scientists in new fields today. What happens when a team of researchers, or an executive and three or four subordinates who have been working together for a long time, leave the organization? At least two issues are involved. One is the charge that the leader raided the company by taking the subordinates along, since they had been trained by the organization; the other is the knowledge of the technology, business operations, market strategies, and so forth developed within the organization and now taken elsewhere. In both cases, the organization loses heavily. Such incidents have become frequent enough to produce a number of court rulings. The principles are still obscure, but in general the court has been ruling in favor of the former firm in requiring, for example, that the departing manager or scientist not work in the same product area for a period of five years. If he or she goes to work for firm B, after having worked in firm A, and firm B comes out with a product that is similar to the one he or she was working on in firm A, firm A can sue firm B on the grounds that the person left A with specific knowledge and gave it to B.

The executive and the subordinates need not go to another established firm, taking with them the fruit of years of experimentation, trial, gestation, and stimulation. They may start their own company. In one case, an engineer for IBM took thirty-six people with him and started a competing company that made integrated circuits for memory cores for large computers. IBM sued. Even if a large firm had little hope of winning such a suit, it could help persuade other employees that it is not wise to leave with so many company-provided resources in their hands. It is a measure of our organizational society that the courts are able to rule in favor of the organization rather than the creative individual.[15]

The case of the scientist who decides that what she has in her head belongs to her and not to the organization, even though organizational resources were used to develop it, is a borderline case in the basic question of who owns the office. As such it is illuminating. For there is no intrinsic difference between such a case and one in which an executive makes sure that the supplier in which he has a financial interest gets contracts from his company, even though that supplier's products may be inferior. In both cases, the organization provides a resource, which is then exploited by the individual for his or her own benefit and to the disadvantage of the organization. It does not matter whether the organization is considered a socially valuable one or whether the individual is moral or immoral. We are stuck with the organizational logic of our time; the official does not own his or her office—as Weber put it, and as the gypsum-plant employees and countless other workers discovered. The organization takes precedence over the individual.

Stated thusly, we are likely to deplore this concept. But as consumers of the goods and services of many organizations, we are likely to applaud it. Why bureaucracy if it takes precedence over the individual? Because our society has developed no alternative method of flooding us with goods and services just as cheaply.

"THERE OUGHT TO BE A RULE"

We have looked at several criticisms of bureaucracy and argued that some of its supposed sins have more to do with the uses to which organizations are put than any inherent evil and others are only abuses from the point of view of special interests, not the organization as a whole. But the weaknesses of bureaucracy considered so far are rather minor. Rules and red tape, hierarchy, and conservatism are more frequently identified as sins and considered more serious. First let us take the criticism that bureaucracies have too many rules.

A multitude of rules and regulations appears to be the very essence of a bureaucracy. The term "red tape" adequately conveys the problem. Rules govern everything; one cannot make a move unless one does it by the book or, to use military slang, by the numbers. Every office in every department has seen to it that its autonomy is protected by rules. An attempt to change one rule immediately runs into the problem that half a dozen other rules are connected to it; to change these, a geometric proportion of additional rules will be affected, and so on.

While it is obvious that some rules are needed in organizations, it is generally felt that most organiza-

tions have far too many rules. How might these be eliminated?

Reducing Rules

There are a number of ways to reduce the number of rules. One way is to mechanize as much as possible. A typewriter eliminates the need for rules about the size and clarity of script and the way letters will be formed. Rules on these matters were common before the appearance of typewriters. Any machine is a complex bundle of rules that are built into the machine itself. Machines ensure standardized products, thus eliminating rules regarding dimensional characteristics. They ensure even output time; they also indicate precisely what kind of material can be fed into them. The larger the machine, the more people it presumably replaces, and this eliminates rules about how workers are to interact, cooperate, and coordinate their activities. The thoroughly automated factory, of which we have none as yet, would be one with few or no written rules or regulations.

Another way to cut down on the number of rules is to insist on near uniformity of personnel in an organization. If we could hire people with the same physical characteristics, intelligence, amount of self-discipline, personality traits, and so on, we would need far fewer rules to govern the range of differences that we usually observe among personnel. If none of them had families, ever got sick, or needed vacations, and if all were thoroughly trained before they arrived at the office, plant, or agency, matters would also be simplified greatly. But, for the lack of a robot, we have people and thus rules.

If we could seal the organization off from its environment so that nothing ever affected it, we would need very few rules regarding relationships with the environment. We would also need few or no rules regarding changes in procedures—because nothing would change. Once things were started in the proper manner, they could run that way forever. Finally, if we could produce only simple products in our organizations, rather than complex ones in various sizes, shapes, and colors and with a lot of custom-made attributes, this would eliminate the need for a lot of rules.

As these comments suggest, we might not care for organizations that eliminate the need for rules—

they would be rather dull, mechanized, and inflexible. Rules are needed in organizations when complexity increases due to variability in personnel, customers, environment, techniques of producing the goods and services, and so on. When these matters are complex, it is not possible to allow personnel to "do their own thing," no matter how much we might prefer that. And every time variability in handling personnel is introduced by these complexities, rules are required to limit the discretion of those with power to handle people under them. There will be rules about favoritism and nepotism and discrimination on irrelevant grounds, rules about transferring people, rules about expectations regarding pay, promotion, accrued leave, and so on.

Professionalization and Rules. Buying and installing machines, as indicated above, is one way to reduce the number of rules in an organization. The rules are built into the machine itself, and the organization pays for those rules when it buys the machine. A quite similar means to reduce the number of written rules is to "buy" personnel who have complex rules built into them. We generally call these people professionals. Professionals, such as engineers and scientists, psychiatrists, doctors, social workers, teachers, and professors, are trained on the outside, usually at great public expense, and a large number of rules are inculcated into them. They bring these to the organization and are expected to act on them without further reference to their skills. While accounting practices differ more widely than some might expect, accountants in general are expected to be familiar with the rules and techniques of accounting. Doctors know when they should give certain drugs or what kinds of drugs should not be given to certain kinds of people; medicine is a complex body of rather imperfect rules. Professors, through long, arduous, and heroic training, learn rules about plagiarism in their writing, truth in their teaching, and deference to their more senior colleagues.

Professionals, like machines, cost a lot of money. There is a high initial investment in training that someone must pay, and the care and feeding of machines and professionals is expensive. Therefore, we tend to use them only when the economies are apparent or when there is no real choice. We charge more for services produced by complex machines or professionals than simple ones—other things, such as volume of production, being equal. It costs more to go to Harvard or to an outstanding hospital than it does to attend a city college or go to a substandard hospital. Were we able to thoroughly routinize the tasks performed by professionals and get around the restrictions that professionals are able to place on their positions, we would substitute machines for them. We are trying, for better or worse, with computerized teaching.

Expressive Groups. One other example of a way to avoid rules in an organization is rare but interesting. This involves organizations where all members agree on the goals of the organization (or, to put it more accurately, where the goals of the individual members are identical) and the techniques for achieving these goals are within the ability of all members. In such cases, few or no rules are required. Each will do his or her own thing, but this will fit with the thing of all other members. Such organizations are generally quite small and usually oriented around expressive needs. Few organizations have members solely on this basis. Most of the so-called voluntary associations rely on services to the members for which members pay in one form or another through dues, allowing their name to be used, or doing some work.[16] Since most voluntary associations provide services to members, they, like other organizations, also have a proliferation of rules and regulations.

Interdepartmental Regulations

So far, we have been talking about rules with respect to the whole organization. A quite different dimension of rules appears when we examine the relationships among units in an organization. Here many rules are clearly the basis of self-protection, predictability, and autonomy. Take the matter of distribution requirements in a university. The rule that students shall take a certain number of credits in various departments exists because students are not homogeneous when they enter the university; all cannot be expected to "know their own best interests." Only some would be motivated enough, the argument goes, to sample the sciences if they are majoring in the humanities or to sample the humanities if they are in the sciences, so a rule is promulgated. However, the matter does not end there. Departments, knowing there will be a big influx of students into their courses, want to control which courses the students come into. So they set rules regarding which courses are to be utilized for distribution requirements. This protects departmental autonomy and provides scheduling benefits and staffing economies. To change these rules when the characteristics of students or advances of knowledge have changed may prove to be quite difficult because a host of other practices have grown up in the department that depend on the designation of certain courses appropriate for distribution requirements. For example, perhaps only instructors and assistant professors assigned to teach these courses. Also, majors may be steered into more high-level courses where enrollment is kept down. A dean who attempts to force the department to make what seems to be eminently sensible changes from her point of view, or the point of view of the students or other departments, may run into serious opposition from the department. The change would threaten the department's whole fragile structure of work assignments and course requirements. The department might turn around in retaliation and change some of its rules on its own. For example, it might limit the enrollment in certain courses. Soon, if not immediately, a first-class *political* situation has evolved that has little to do with the original problem and can be solved only by bargaining. But bargaining threatens the status quo, involves other departments, and ramifies the changes. Because rules protect interests, and groups are interdependent, changing the rules is difficult.

Rules are like an invisible skein that bundles together all the technological and social aspects of organizations. As such, rules stem from past adjustments and seek to stabilize the present and future. When things are different in the future, an attempt to change these tough, invisible threads means that all kinds of practices, bargains, agreements, and payoffs will tumble out of the web and must be stuffed back in again. As a result of these kinds of interdependencies, changes in organizational rules (which go on continuously, if only informally)[17] are generally incremental—a little bit here and there. The

hope is that somehow the whole structure of the organization will gradually, painlessly, and, most of all, *covertly* change over time. It generally does.

In sum, rules protect those who are subject to them. Rules are means of preserving group autonomy and freedom; to reduce the number of rules in an organization generally means to make it more impersonal, more inflexible, more standardized. But even given this, rules are still a bore. We would all prefer to be free of them, or so it would seem. Actually, only *some* rules are bores. The good, effective rules are rarely noticed; the bad ones stand out. Bad rules are inevitable. Some merely reflect the fact that people make rules, and people are not generally geniuses. The problem is not rules in general, but particular ones that need changing.

Rules as Scapegoats

Rules are the scapegoats for a variety of organizational problems. Complaints about excessive rules or bad rules generally are symptomatic of more deep-seated problems that cannot be solved by changing rules. During the unhappy days of the breakdown in telephone service in New York in 1969–1970, a number of "stupid" rules surfaced and were held to have caused the difficulties. Actually, the difficulties appeared to be that the system was designed so that it would operate with a good deal of inefficiency and slack. Such an operation is easy when an organization has a monopoly and, despite the lack of risk, a guaranteed high rate of return. Savings from technical advances need not result in significant rate decreases, but simply in more inefficient ways of doing business—which is, after all, the easiest route. No one in the company gets upset, and since the public is uninformed and the rate-setting agencies are weak and generally captives of the utilities, the lack of rate reduction is not noticed. (The same appears to be true for the gas and electric utilities, which also are very profitable, inefficiently regulated monopolies.) When greater demands were made on the company than it could fulfill, it became apparent that, for example, the business-office side of the company in the New York area was not talking to the plant or operations side; both hid under a complex set of rules and regulations that governed their interrelationship and the operations within each of the divisions. As long as there was sufficient "fat," or surplus, in the system, it did not matter; when more efficiency was needed to meet demand for services, these inefficiencies surfaced, and rules got the blame. The rules were not bad in themselves. For example, they probably reduced contact and thus antagonisms between the operations and customer-service branches. A more efficient operation would require more contact, however, and under these situations the rules were inappropriate. But the whole premise on which the system operated would have to be changed; rules would be only one aspect that would be changed.

In a similar fashion, hidebound government bureaucracies are not unresponsive to their clients because of their rules but because of the premises they operate on and the system designed around those premises. The New York public school system[18] and the Bureau of Indian Affairs are two outstanding examples. In both cases, professionals have captured the organization and made it too difficult or expensive for policy makers—board members, staff of the Secretary of the Interior, politicians, and the like—to wrest control and change practices. The incredible rules of these agencies are only byproducts and symptoms of a commonplace fact of organization life: those who can will seize control of an organization and use it for their own ends—in these cases security, power, and expansion.

As we noted above, good rules are often those that are rarely noticed. They may be written down or just a matter of custom, but they are rarely challenged. They simply make sense. Some other good rules are those that cut the Gordian knots that inevitably bind organized endeavors of any complexity. Frequently, there is no clear ground for doing A instead of B; both will have unpleasant outcomes. Rather than agonize over a decision, a rule cuts the knot. Another function of good rules is to justify unpleasant decisions or actions: "Sorry, old boy, but I will have to discipline you for that." "I know it's not fair, from your point of view, but it's the rule." "It took a lot of extra work, and I made some enemies in the agency, but the rule is that these kinds of clients are entitled to more service." Without the rules, these necessary but unpleasant actions might not be taken.

The greatest problem with rules is that organiza-

tions and their environments change faster than the rules. Most bad rules were once good, designed for a situation that no longer exists. Nepotism was apparently a problem in university departments of the past, when they were dominated by one man who made all the decisions as to what the courses would be, what texts would be used, who was to be hired and who promoted. It was easy to extend this power by putting one's wife on the staff. Today, departmental chairpersons have much less power, and there are more finely graded criteria for performance. Yet, as more women once again come into the academic job market and have husbands who are also teachers, the nepotism rule becomes more burdensome and discriminatory. It is often stoutly defended, though, by those who resent women professors anyway, since they are a threat to male hegemony.

In sum, "there ought to be a rule" is as valid as saying "there are too damn many rules around here." Rules do a lot of things in organizations: they protect as well as restrict; coordinate as well as block; channel effort as well as limit it; permit universalism as well as provide sanctuary for the inept; maintain stability as well as retard change; permit diversity as well as restrict it. They constitute the organizational memory and the means for change. As such, rules in themselves are neither good nor bad, nor even that important. It is only because they are easy scapegoats for other problems that are more difficult to divine and analyze that we have to spend this much time on them. Social scientists, no less than the person in the street, love to denounce them and to propose ruleless organizations. But ruleless organizations are likely to be either completely automated, if they are efficient and have much output, or completely professionalized, turning out expensive and exotic services. Only a tiny fraction of organizations fit either case.

"WHO'S IN CHARGE AROUND HERE?"

For many social scientists, rules are a nuisance, but the existence of a hierarchical ordering of offices and authority is a barely tolerable evil. The principle of hierarchical ordering of offices and authority says that for every person there shall be one person above to whom he or she primarily reports and from whom he or she primarily receives direction. The organization is structured in the form of a pyramid, with the top controlling everything. Power is centralized. Though all aspects of bureaucracy—rules, universalism, impersonality, tenure, and stability—are criticized, hierarchy, the most characteristic aspect of bureaucracy, is judged its worst. It is the negation of individual autonomy, freedom, spontaneity, creativity, dignity, and independence.

The Collegial University

When we think of organizations with elaborate hierarchies, we often have the government and its bureaus in mind, or perhaps the large corporation. Professional organizations, according to theory, are not so arranged—colleagues are at more or less the same level.[19] I would probably be considered a professional, being a full professor of sociology in a university, so let us see what I might have had to go through at the University of Wisconsin in 1970 in order to make a suggestion, take up an issue, make a complaint, or whatever, if I wished to touch all bases. Theoretically, I would first go to the assistant chairman of my department, who would send the matter on to the chairman. The chairman might wish to consult with the departmental executive committee to be on "solid ground" before proceeding. The departmental chairman would then take it up with one of the appropriate assistant deans (there were eight to choose from) in the College of Letters and Science, who would refer it to one of the associate deans (there were four of them), who would take it up with the dean of the College of Letters and Science (there are Colleges of Agriculture, Engineering, etc., each of which has its dean and associate and assistant deans). If the matter involved the graduate program at all, it would next go to one of the two assistant deans, and then to one of the five associate deans of the Graduate School; then it would be taken up with the dean of the Graduate School (who would, of course, confer with the dean of the pertinent college). The Graduate School dean might consult with a student-faculty committee in

the process. After that, it would be taken up by one of the two assistants to the chancellor, who would refer it to one of the two vice-chancellors, who would take it up with the chancellor of the Madison campus (there are other campuses—Milwaukee, Green Bay, and Parkside among them). The chancellor of the Madison campus would send it along to one of the vice-presidents of the university (he had seven to choose from), who would take it up with the president of the university. If the matter were still unresolved and had not lost its power of ascent, the president would take it up with the university's regents. They, in turn, might have to refer to the State Coordinating Council for Higher Education (which has several staff layers of its own). It, though, receives its power from the legislature, whose actions can be vetoed by the governor. Were the matter important enough to go as far as the Coordinating Council, it would have gone through five major levels of authority, each with about three internal levels of authority, for a total of at least fifteen steps in the staircase.

Of course, it is not that simple. We have assumed that the matter did not involve any of the numerous other fiefdoms in the university, which is highly unlikely. There are numerous councils, committees, divisional organizations (e.g., a chairman of social studies), administrative units (such as the admissions office with its director, associate director, and four assistant directors), the libraries (an Egyptian-sized pyramid in itself), a jumble of business offices, the computing center, counseling services, and offices concerned with public relations, parking, physical plant, protection and security, purchasing, registration, student affairs, and so on—each of which could be involved. A professor has occasion to deal with all of these at times. In addition, much power is exercised by the campus university committee, the senate, the all-university faculty assembly, the university faculty council, the course committee, the divisional executive committee, the social studies committee of the graduate school, the research committee, the honors committee, various student-faculty committees (at the time an area of exponential growth in form, though with little substance), and various all-university committees. These committees plug the interstitial areas of the fifteen levels above me very effectively and relieve all the assistant deans or whatever of their back-breaking loads.

Of course, even with fifteen levels of authority and a tropical jungle of committee growth to go through to get to the top, I would not be at the bottom of the heap. Below me are strung out the associate professors, assistant professors, instructors, lecturers, teaching assistants, graduate students, and, somewhere down there, undergraduates. This is not a chain of command; undergraduates have been known to talk directly to full professors without going through a teaching assistant, for example. But these levels come into operation in numerous ways. For example, if two full professors desire the same office, the one who has been "in rank" longer will generally get it. We cannot really add six more levels below a full professor in terms of authority, though we can in terms of status.

In addition, I might have a secretary, research assistant, undergraduate work-study assistants, and graduate student trainees in a training program—that is, another little empire. (I have left out the enormous informal power of the head secretary of the department, other directors of training programs or of the graduate program, renowned colleagues, and those who somehow just manage to amass power.) Just to grasp this social structure intellectually, let alone maneuver in it, is a demanding task.[20]

So much for the myth that the university is a collegial body having a minimum of hierarchy and status difference. Nor should one assume that other professional bodies, such as the medical staff of a hospital or the U.S. Senate, also enjoy the advantages of lack of hierarchy. The medical personnel in hospitals are generally highly organized in a structure that parallels that of the administrative staff of the hospital. The medical staff has its own nursing committee, outpatient department committee, pharmacy committee, and so forth, and in between the major ranks of junior and senior attending staff are several clear distinctions in grade, with appropriate powers and entrance criteria.[21] The U.S. Senate is also more highly structured than one would expect on the basis of the contrast between bureaucratic and professional organizations, and it takes a new senator a long time to learn all the aspects of this struc-

ture. Even law firms are highly structured.[22] Indeed, any group with a division of labor, professional or not, will be hierarchically structured.

The Sins of Hierarchy

What is the consequence of this ubiquitous structuring of even "professional" organizations? For the critics of bureaucracy, the consequence is that the bulk of people in the lower and middle levels are prevented from really giving their all for goal achievement; they turn, instead, into infantile, fearful robots. The argument runs like this:

The hierarchy promotes rigidity and timidity. Subordinates are afraid of passing bad news up the ladder[23] or of suggesting changes.[24] (Such an action would imply that their superiors should have thought of the changes and did not.) They also are more afraid of new situations than of familiar ones, since with the new situations, those above them might introduce new evils, while the old ones are sufficient. The hierarchy promotes delays and sluggishness; everything must be kicked upstairs for a decision either because the boss insists or because the subordinate does not want to risk making a poor decision. All this indecision exists at the same time that superiors are being authoritarian, dictatorial, and rigid, making snap judgments that they refuse to reconsider, implementing on-the-spot decisions without consulting their subordinates, and generally stifling any independence or creativity at the subordinate levels. Subordinates are under constant surveillance from superiors; thus they often give up trying to exercise initiative or imagination and instead suppress or distort information. Finally, since everything must go through channels, and these are vertical, two people at the same level in two different departments cannot work things out themselves but must involve long lines of superiors.

At this point one may wonder how organizations can function at all, but it becomes even more alarming when we consider a contrasting series of complaints frequently made by members of a hierarchy. These are complaints about people in one department making decisions that affect other units without checking first with their respective superiors, and about the *lack* of clear lines of authority, the *failure* to exercise authority or to be decisive, and the *lack* of accountability. Some typical complaints:

1. Who's in charge here? Who am I supposed to take this matter to?
2. That bureau gets away with murder; no one will exercise authority over it, and it is not clear what their authority is supposed to be.
3. Some technician in engineering went ahead and made these design changes in conjunction with a department head in production, but they never bothered to check with the sales manager or the account supervisor in finance.
4. We make changes, and before we can see how well they are working out, we are making more changes.
5. What this place lacks is decisive leadership.
6. No one told me.

In such cases we hear of too much flexibility, too little attention to the hierarchy, too little forceful decision making. According to one survey,[25] managers in industrial firms are decidedly in favor of more, rather than less, clarity in lines of authority, rules, duties, specification of procedures, and so on. Only when the structure is clear can authority be delegated, they indicate, as did Wilfred Brown.[26]

If both the presence and the absence of hierarchy can be faulted, and if authority can be both excessive and absent, change too rapid and too infrequent, employees both fearful and aggressive, gutless and crafty, and flexible and rigid, the problem may not lie in hierarchy per se. Some degree of hierarchy is needed in any organized endeavor, but how much and in what kinds of endeavors? We are only beginning to phrase the problem in this fashion, and to get a glimpse of how hierarchies actually work.

Research on Span of Control

Take the matter of "span of control"—the number of subordinates whom a superior directly controls. This is the building block of hierarchy. If each superior controls few people—has a narrow span of control—there will be many levels in the organization; if he or she controls many, there will be few.

For twenty to thirty years, social scientists and management theorists debated regarding the optimum span of control—was it four, six, eight, or what? If only we knew, we could design our organizations properly. Embedded in this discussion was the assumption that if a manger had many people under her, she could not supervise them closely, and thus they would have more autonomy.[27] This assumption was furthered in an influential piece of reporting by a personnel officer with Sears Roebuck who described how morale and efficiency improved when the number of levels in the organization was reduced.[28]

Of course, as is true of most "principles" of organization, there was an alternative view—rarely stated as a principle, but acted on by management consulting firms. This principle said that if a manager had a lot of people reporting to him, he was centralizing power and would not want to give it up. Such a manager should establish an intermediate level in order to give his subordinates some leeway. A wide span of control meant reluctance to delegate, rather than delegation.

Few theorists took the rule-of-thumb wisdom of the management consultants seriously, however. One of the best theorists, for example, is Peter Blau. He and his associates conducted a study of 156 public personnel agencies, starting with "a few plausible considerations" that led to inferences "which appeared straightforward and perhaps even self-evident." They reasoned that if a person was well trained, he or she would need little supervision. The span of control would be wide. If personnel were not well trained, they would need more supervision, and the span of control would be narrow and the hierarchy higher. (In the language of journal articles, it reads like this: The inferences suggested, "as an initial hypothesis, that expert requirements decrease the ratio of managerial to nonsupervisory personnel in organizations, which widens the average span of control."[29])

To the admitted surprise of Blau and associates, the hypothesis was found to be incorrect. The more qualified the people, the *less* the span of control. They then suggested that the explanation might be that a narrow span of control—only two or three subordinates per superior—allows easy consultation on difficult problems and permits common problem solving. Though they did not state it directly, this would suggest that wide spans of control could mean close supervision but little consultation.

Actually, as is so true in much of organizational research, the resolution of the dilemma lies in distinguishing different types of organizations or situations. In some cases, a span of control of ten can mean close supervision through highly routinized controls over people performing routine tasks; in others, it can mean very little supervision, with the ten subordinates working out things with each other and only occasionally seeking the advice or direction of the boss.[30] The span of control, then, can be independent of the closeness of supervision. Supervision can be direct or indirect with either a wide or a narrow span of control.

The span of control, in turn, affects the degree of hierarchy, or the number of levels of supervision in an organization. Where spans of control are wide, the organization tends to be "squat"—there are not many levels of authority. Where spans of control are narrow, the organization tends to have a narrow, "tall" hierarchy, with many levels of authority. But we have argued that a squat organization does not necessarily mean either close or distant supervision. There are a number of factors that might affect the closeness of supervision (beyond, of course, the personality and leadership style of a manager), and they are worth listing to indicate the complexity of the matter:

1. The degree to which tasks are routine or nonroutine.
2. The difference between the expertise of the manager and that of his or her subordinates; the amount of interdependence among tasks under one manager; and the interdependence of these tasks with those performed under different managers.
3. The interdependence of the department as a whole with other departments in the organization, and the varying kinds of routine and nonroutine mixes of the departments.
4. The degree to which written rules and regulations or machines can reduce the need for personal supervision.

5. The extent to which flexibility and rapid response is necessary to the organization.

Given these relevant sources of variation, it remains to be seen whether, as Blau maintains, the relationship they suggested between span of control and supervision is likely to hold in all organizations.

Using the same data, Marshall Meyer concludes that there are two strategies available to organizations—control through direct supervision, utilizing a wide span of control, which promotes flexibility of response since the manager can change things quickly; and control through rules, regulations, and professional expertise, utilizing a greater number of hierarchical levels with a narrow span of control, which promotes more "rational" administration and more stable operations.[31] Blau also concludes that there are two types of organizations, but he labels the first the "old-fashioned bureaucracy." It has a "squat hierarchy with authority centralized at the top," little automation, and personnel rules that emphasize managerial discretion, seniority, and personal judgment. The second he calls the "modern organization" with a "tall, slim hierarchy with decentralized authority," relying upon experts, automation, and universalistic personnel procedures (objective merit standards).[32]

Meyer's data show only weak support for Blau's conclusions; the differences between the two types of strategies are in the predicted direction but are quite small. The important thing, however, is that they are *not* in the *opposite* direction; that is, the usual view of hierarchy would indicate that the higher the degree of hierarchy the greater the centralized control.[33] But that does not hold here. If anything, the greater hierarchy is associated with decentralization. Blau handles his data somewhat differently and finds somewhat stronger relationships, but more important, he finds the relationships consistent over three types of organizations: personnel departments, finance departments, and state employment agencies. Thus, even though the differences may not be large in any one sample, the consistency over the three is impressive.

Furthermore, a quite independent and large study in England, generally referred to as the Aston study because the team, headed by Derek Pugh, was then at the University of Aston in Birmingham, came to very similar conclusions.[34] In the Blau and the Aston studies, the gap between the indicators used and the concepts these indicators were supposed to represent is often very large. For example, the items that are used to measure the degree of delegation of authority, or decentralization, refer only to decisions that are visible, binary (either-or), and capable of clear statement in official rules, such as the level at which a certain amount of money can be spent without prior authorization. More subtle, basic, and certainly more powerful decisions are not measured; these may be quite centralized. We refer to this as the problem of ''operationalization,'' or making the measurement of concepts operational. The operationalization of the concept of hierarchy in the Aston study was particularly controversial. Nevertheless, one can have some confidence in the findings of the Blau and Aston studies for three important reasons: (1) they are independently arrived at, using different measures; (2) they were unexpected by both research teams; and (3) they are counterintuitive.

In short, we cannot assume that the more hierarchical the organization, the more centralized it is. If the limited data show anything, they indicate an inverse relationship. More important, the very characteristics that both Blau and Meyer ascribe to their tall, hierarchical, and decentralized organizations are those that Weber stressed in his bureaucratic model: expertise, written rules and regulations, clear ordering of positions, and hierarchy. The characteristics of the squat centralized organization are personal rule, personal evaluations, and low expertise. These are closer to the traditional model, which the development of bureaucracy attempted to supplant.

Hierarchy and Timidity

Another attribute often associated with tall hierarchies is timidity and caution on the part of subordinates who fear criticism from superiors and thus hesitate to pass unpleasant information up the line. That such an attitude exists in bureaucracies is clear, but that it is an inevitable concomitant of hierarchy, and thus its product, is far from evident. Timidity and caution appear to vary greatly among bureaucracies, on the basis of casual impressions. Peter Blau, in his study of two government agencies, commented that he found little evidence of this behavior.[35] It certainly does not show up among the more successful managers in Dalton's study,[36] nor among all managers in Gouldner's study.[37] Why, then, the variation?

It would seem that tendencies toward conservatism and self-protective behavior are natural outcomes of all organized activity that is not spontaneously coordinated and based on wholehearted cooperation. But it also would appear that organizations have mechanisms to minimize the danger and even reverse these tendencies. For example, people can be rewarded for passing critical items of information up the hierarchy; the reward may have to be high if it reflects on one's superior, but if it is that important to the organization it can be done. Actually, the opposite is sometimes a problem—a person gets ahead by showing up the superior. Between these two stances—timidity and cunning—there is the far more usual situation in which constructive criticisms are encouraged and rewarded because the boss can take the credit. Accounting departments are generally rewarded for critical information, which is why, in the organization Dalton studied, it was so essential for aggressive managers to neutralize or bribe the accountants. Innovative and risk-taking behavior may be harder to reward than conservative behavior, but it is possible to do it.

Timidity and caution appear to be functions of the technology and market of organizations, rather than of their degree of hierarchy. In some market situations—for example, Social Security administration, aid to dependent children, railroads, public utilities, mining (especially in such oligopolistic situations as sulfur mining)—there is little perceived need for risk taking. In other large and equally bureaucratic organizations—the Agency for International Development in its golden days of the late 1950s and early 1960s, the federal rehabilitation agencies during the 1950s and early 1960s, which used the money dumped on them by an uncomprehending Congress to upgrade physically healthy but untrained blacks, and the electronics and chemical industries—risk taking is much more in evidence. There is no evidence that these organizations had fewer levels of authority than more conservative organizations.

Still, problems remain. Some officials do insist that a great many minor matters be brought to their attention before action is taken. The explanation may be that they are poor or insecure administrators or have incompetent subordinates. This happens all the time, but it can hardly be attributed to hierarchy alone. Sometimes it is impossible to get an answer out of a higher officer; the explanation may simply be that he does not know and unfortunately will not admit it, or that he is still searching, or that he is perhaps hoping that the lower officer will go ahead and make the decision (and take the blame if it is wrong). But someone has to decide, and the principle of hierarchy at least specifies *who* should decide if ambiguity exists. Wilfred Brown observes that the principal function of a hierarchy is to resolve disputes or uncertainties; things go on well enough without slavishly going through channels if there is no dispute and no uncertainty.[38]

The Official and the Unofficial Hierarchical Order

One of the true delights of the organizational expert is to indicate to the uninitiated the wide discrepancy between the official hierarchy (or rules, for that matter) and the unofficial one. It is a remarkable phenomenon in many cases and well known to most people who spend their working lives as managers in organizations. Departmental secretaries in many universities have power far beyond their status. David Mechanic's well-known essay, "Sources of Power of Lower Participants in Complex Organization," touches on this and other examples.[39] Melville Dalton, in his excruciatingly unsettling study of a manufacturing plant, reveals top people with no power and those three or four levels below with extensive power.[40] Sociologists have been particularly fond of the contrast between the official and the unofficial because it indicates that organizations are natural systems rather than artificial or mechanistic ones—living things that the people within them create out of their own needs, rather than rational tools in the hands of a master. They are right, of course: between the conception and the reality, as the poet tells us, falls the shadow. The first thing the new employee should learn is who is really in charge, who has the goods on whom, what

are the major debts and dependencies—all things that are not reflected by the neat boxes in the organization chart. With this knowledge he or she can navigate with more skill and ease.

For the organizational theorists, however, a different kind of question is required: What are the systematic bases for the deviations? We should not expect the official map to be completely accurate because:

1. It is never up-to-date—it does not reflect the growing power of a subordinate who will be promoted over his or her boss in a year or two, or the waning power of a boss who has been passed by because of changes in technology or markets.
2. It does not pretend to make the finely graded distinctions that operating personnel have to live by—for example, three departments may be on the same official level, but one of them is three times the size of the other two and may carry commensurately more power.
3. It does not reflect all transactions in the organization, but primarily those disputes that can be settled formally.
4. Most important, the hierarchy functions primarily for routine situations; when new ones come along, someone two levels down may have more say for this or that situation, but unless the new situation itself becomes the persistent or frequent one, his or her authority will only be temporary. If it persists, that person may well move up fast.
5. Finally, hierarchical principles are sometimes violated intentionally. When, for example, the head office cannot get enough information about a division's operation, it sends in a spy. Dalton describes such a case. The man involved had a relatively unimportant job of manager of industrial relations, but his power over many other aspects of the organization was substantial because everyone knew that he was there to find out what was going on.

Few organizations keep an official chart of offices ranked by authority for very long or, if they do, such charts are rarely referred to. (Some organizations even refuse to draw them up.) Positions and units move up and down in authority over time, and the lag with the official chart is always there. Thus, we should not be surprised at the discrepancy, nor should we assume that the unofficial is necessarily a more accurate rendition than the official. The two are just different and only briefly join hands in their mutual evolution. While the "natural" or "living" system is important, it may only be a wistful and touching part of a rather mechanical and imperative whole. The fact that the dean and I (or the chancellor and I, or the president and I) are both professors in a collegial body of equals is as much a romance of the actual situation as the view that only the yeasty, vital, living, informal system counts in an organization. The official hierarchy is there, and no one who has both eyes open forgets it. One must know the hierarchy to survive it.

PROFESSIONALISM AND DISCIPLINE

The final criticism of bureaucracy that we shall consider is one of the most widespread. It concerns the discrepancy between the expertise of the subordinate and that of the superior. That is to say, it involves the manager or official who knows less about things than the people that work for him or her yet who exercises authority over them. Virtually every discussion of bureaucracy mentions this point. It is an attractive criticism because we all resent, more or less, those who have authority over us when we suspect that we know more about life on the firing line than they do. The outstanding example of this concerns professionals in organizations. The manager of professionals often simply cannot be as well informed as highly trained subordinates. Social scientists have always been preoccupied with the plight of professionals and have defended their interests extensively.

This whole line of thought started with a footnote in Talcott Parsons' introduction to his translation of parts of Weber's *Economy and Society*. Weber, Parsons said, confused two types of authority in his discussion—the authority that is based on "technical competence," and the authority based on "incumbency of a legally defined office."[41] Could there not be a discrepancy between the two? Could there not be officials who were not experts but who directed the work of those who were? Indeed, there

were examples, asserted Parsons. Unfortunately, his main example had little to do with organizations, and his second example was something less than relevant. But since this is possibly the most important footnote in the history of organizational theory, it is worth digging into at some length.

Parsons's main example was the physician whose "authority rests fundamentally on the belief on the part of the patient that the physician has and will employ for his benefit a technical competence adequate to help him in his illness." The trouble with the example is that in this role the physician does not function in an organization. Parsons recognizes this, but adds that where the physician does function in an organization, "instead of a rigid hierarchy of status and authority [hierarchies are always rigid, one gathers] there tends to be what is roughly, in formal status, a 'company of equals,' an equalization of status which ignores the inevitable gradation of distinction and achievement to be found in any considerable group of technically competent persons."[42] However, the evidence from studies of hospitals indicates that medical staffs are quite bureaucratic in their organizational functioning, with hierarchies that are apparent; moreover, they are quite sensitive to "inevitable gradations of distinction and achievement."[43]

His other example concerns "powers of coercion in case of recalcitrance." It is not logically essential, he says, that the person with this power "should have either superior knowledge or superior skill as compared to those subject to his orders. Thus, the treasurer of a corporation is empowered to sign checks disbursing large funds. There is no implication in this 'power' that he is a more competent signer of checks than the bank clerks or tellers who cash or deposit them for the recipient."[44] The example is irrelevant because the power of the treasurer rests in his knowledge that certain checks should be made out and sent, not in his ability to sign his name.

Nevertheless, despite these two quite weak illustrations, the idea took immediate root. (Many earlier writers had noted the possible discrepancy between authority and expertise, of course, but Parsons made it famous.) Everyone, it appears, could think of superiors who were less competent than their subordinates, and the bureaucratic dilemma of expertise and discipline was firmly established. Alvin Gouldner used it as the organizing basis for his previously mentioned study of a gypsum plant, *Patterns of Industrial Bureaucracy*.[45] In his hands, it became the explanation for two contrasting bureaucratic patterns—representative bureaucracy, which relied on expertise "based on rules established by agreement, rules which are technically justified and administered by specially qualified personnel, and to which consent is given voluntarily," and punishment-centered bureaucracy, "based on the imposition of rules, and on obedience for its own sake."[46] He, too, thought that Weber saw things two ways; in one, administration was based on expertise, and in the other "Weber held that bureaucracy was a mode of administration in which obedience was an end in itself."[47] (That Weber held nothing of the sort regarding obedience is not important here; it is the distinction that is. Gouldner's representative pattern, incidentally, is based on the slim reed of a safety rule.)

Stanley Udy, studying records of organizations in primitive societies, and Arthur Stinchcombe, in his discussion of the organization of the construction industry, come to much the same conclusion—that there are two fundamentally different forms of organizations, rational or professional organizations and bureaucratic ones.[48] But data on primitive organizations, and the statistics from the construction industry, have dubious relevance for modern large-scale organizations, though both of these studies are excellent for other purposes. The next use of the distinction is by Peter Blau in the article cited above, where it sets the stage for his analysis.[49] But it is apparent that the professionalized (and more hierarchical) organizations are the closest to the Weberian ideal, as we have seen. Blau's data thus support the opposite conclusion—professionalism is consistent with bureaucracy. While Weber asserted the importance of strict discipline, he was much more emphatic about the critical importance of expertise.[50]

But the most extensive use of this distinction has been in the voluminous literature on professionals in organizations; it was the hottest single topic in the field of organizational analysis during the early 1960s and continues to be discussed. With the increasing importance of university-trained scientists and engineers in organizations, the expense of these people, and the need to keep their morale high in a highly competitive employment market, a number of social scientists began to study their adjustment to industrial organizations. Some of these studies were concerned mostly with research laboratories, where the work was complex, innovative, unstructured, and unpredictable. These were truly new organizations that were difficult to cut to the bureaucratic pattern. Some sense of the enormous importance of charismatic leadership, individual autonomy, and serendipity can be gleaned from the fascinating account of the way J. Robert Oppenheimer directed the large Los Alamos laboratory, where the first atomic bombs were built, during World War II.[51] The efforts of General Groves (under whom Oppenheimer worked) to bureaucratize the enterprise—to treat it as if it were turning out Sherman tanks—had disastrous effects on morale and productivity. This example is more pertinent for understanding professionals than, say, studies of such research labs as Bell Laboratories or the DuPont experimental station, since in the Los Alamos case a single product was turned out—a bomb. In the labs, the administrative organization is an umbrella over scores of individual or small-group projects that produce diverse outputs unrelated to one another. To generalize from this highly decentralized type of operation to the usual case of large groups of professionals working on various aspects of one problem or product is misleading.

Many of the studies of scientists in industry, however, did deal with actual industrial organizations with a common problem focus rather than with universitylike basic research labs. They revealed, in keeping with antibureaucratic views, that scientists did indeed resent the constraints placed on them by the organization in general, and by their superiors in particular, and preferred the luxuries of academic life such as flexible schedules, few deadlines, uninhibited bull sessions, conference going, freedom to publish, and so on. This is not surprising. If you present yourself as a sociologist or a psychologist from a university and ask if these things are not valued more than profits, production deadlines, and restrictions on publications and inability to study whatever problem one is interested in, the answer is very likely to be yes. The hypothesis is confirmed:

there is a conflict between professional values and bureaucratic ones.

However, if one asked a question such as the following, the answer might be quite different: "Would you sooner spend most of your time working on a basic problem that might result in an academic journal publication, but be of little value to the company, or on a problem the company is interested in which might bring you a handsome bonus and a promotion?" Such a question has not been asked, but it poses the dilemma in realistic terms. I suspect that the majority of scientists and engineers in industry would choose the profitable project. The reasons are close at hand. The education these people receive in a university is from departments that are vocationally oriented.[52] Engineering departments and such science departments as chemistry and geology are designed to meet industrial needs, at least at the undergraduate level, and in many places at the graduate levels. Professors in these departments judge the quality of their teaching by the status of the companies in which their students obtain jobs. The professors also consult with industrial firms. The curriculum is designed to be relevant to industrial employment. The large majority of the students go into industry. Once there, they find that the route to power, prestige, and money is through serving the company and, in particular, through getting out of technical work and into management. Dalton has observed that the action and the rewards are in line positions rather than in staff (professional) positions.[53] A study by Fred Goldner and R. R. Ritti of recent engineering graduates, conceived without a bias in favor of a conflict between scientists and managers, found that "from the start of their business careers many engineers have personal goals that coincide with the business goals of the corporations."[54] Business-oriented goals, dealing with power and participation in the affairs of the company, were ranked far above professional goals.

Furthermore, although it is rarely noted, managers also are usually college-trained—for example in law, business administration, and economics. Are they not professionals, too? Presumably they would prefer to work in a universitylike atmosphere if they could have the power and the income provided by industry at the same time. They, too, resent supervi-

sion and discipline and if asked the proper questions would probably question the profit goal of business even as do scientists. In fact, the student with a master's degree in business administration will hear more about the "social responsibilities" of business than the scientist.

Finally, the distinction made by Parsons and invoked by so many since then fails to recognize the *technical* character of administration. That is, though the scientist promoted to a supervisory position will soon lose some of her *scientific* technical competence (she cannot keep up with the field; the new graduates know the latest things in some cases; she loses touch with the practical, daily problems), she is probably promoted on, and expected to exercise and increase, her *administrative* technical competence. The job of the scientific manager is to manage, not to do research. It is a very common observation in industry that the best scientists do not make the best managers; the skills required are quite different, even though the manager of scientists must know a good bit about the technical work of these specialists. The same is true of the manager in marketing, finance, personnel, and even production. By assuming that official incumbency of a supervisory role has no relationship to expertise (expertise in management, in this case), it is possible for critics of the bureaucratic model to suggest a hiatus between expertise and occupancy of an official position. It was Weber's simple but enduring insight to see how crucial expertise was as a requirement for holding office throughout the hierarchy. The critics of bureaucracy have failed to utilize that simple insight when they propose that the official is not an expert in anything but survival. Far more damning would be the criticism that bureaucracy, by enfeebling so many workers, has made management a specialized skill demanding expertise.

SUMMARY

When we attribute the ills of organizations and those of our society to the bureaucratization of large-scale organizations, as we are so wont to do, we may be only fooling ourselves. We may be talking about specific instances of maladministration, of which there will naturally be many since people are more or less imperfect, or we are talking about the uses to which the power generated by organizations is put. The presence of hierarchy, rules, division of labor, tenure provisions, and so on can hardly be blamed for maladministration or abuses of social power. Indeed, the bureaucratic model provides a greater check on these problems than do nonbureaucratic or traditional alternatives once you have managerial capitalism. Critics, then, of our organizational society, whether they are the radicals of the Left emphasizing spontaneity and freedom, the New Right demanding their own form of radical decentralization, or the liberals in between speaking of the inability of organizations to be responsive to community values, had best turn to the key issue of who controls the varied forms of power generated by organizations, rather than flail away at the windmills of bureaucracy. If we want our material civilization to continue as it is and are not ready to change the economic system drastically, we will have to have large-scale bureaucratic enterprises in the economic, social, and governmental areas. The development of industrialization has made this the most efficient way to get the routine work of a society done. If we were prepared to engineer a modest change in our economy, we could even reap more of the advantages of bureaucracy. Our present system of huge, inflexible firms dominating markets in highly concentrated industries costs us dearly. Large size distorts bureaucracy, encouraging the problems of outdated rules, improperly invoked hierarchies, particularism, and favoritism. If all but the few industries where capital investment must be enormous were limited to modest-sized firms of, say, less than 1,000 employees, they could be efficient, flexible, and limited in their market power.

In this chapter, we have, in effect, ranged over the model of bureaucracy drawn up by Weber, extending it in many places but rarely if ever modifying it greatly. I will summarize the basic Weberian model here.

Weber's model of bureaucracy contains three groups of characteristics: those that relate to the structure and function of organization, those that deal with means of rewarding effort, and those that deal with protections for the individuals.

Regarding the structure and functioning of the organization, Weber specified that the business of the organization be conducted on a continuous basis; that there be a hierarchy of offices, with each office under the control of a higher one; that this hierarchy entail a systematic division of labor based on specialized training and expertise; and that the division of labor specify the area of action for which the official is competent, the responsibilities he or she has in this regard, and the amount of his or her power or authority. The performance of duties is to be governed by written rules, imposed or enacted, and by written records (files) of acts and decisions already taken. This cluster of characteristics did two things for Weber's model: (a) it provided mechanisms for control over performance of individuals, and (b) it provided means for specialization and expertise and means for coordinating roles and preventing them from interfering with each other.

The second group of characteristics, dealing with rewards, specified that officials received fixed salaries, graded by rank; and that officials did not own the means of production or administration, could not appropriate their offices, had to separate their private affairs and property from the organization's affairs and property, had to render an accounting of the use of organizational property, and had to consider their offices as their sole or primary occupation. The provision of salary rather than other forms of reward and the clear role separation contrasted sharply with charismatic and traditional forms of administration, but charismatic and traditional forms of rewards still linger in bureaucracies.

Finally, in contrast to other forms of administration, the rights of individuals are protected in the Weberian bureaucratic model. This is necessary not only to ensure a source of personnel but also to prevent the arbitrary use of power in the service of nonorganizational or antiorganizational goals. Officials serve voluntarily and are appointed; service constitutes a career with promotions according to seniority or achievement; obedience is owed to the officeholder, not to the person; officials are subject to authority only with respect to their official obligations; compulsion can be exercised only under definite conditions; and there is the right of appeal of decisions and statements of grievances.

NOTES

1. Alvin Gouldner, *Patterns of Industrial Bureaucracy* (New York: Free Press, 1954).

2. Ibid., p. 35.

3. Ibid., p. 65.

4. The famous German sociologist, writing in the early decades of this century, laid out the model of bureaucracy and described and explained its origins. Weber's writings on bureaucracy appear in two different parts of an uncompleted draft of his opus, *Economy and Society*. The first part is presented in Max Weber, *The Theory of Social and Economic Organization*, trans. A. M. Henderson and Talcott Parsons (New York: Oxford University Press, 1947), pp. 324–340. The second part, which was actually written first and is a more discursive section, appears in Max Weber, *From Max Weber, Essays in Sociology*, trans. and ed. by Hans Gerth and C. Wright Mills (New York: Oxford University Press, 1946), pp. 196–244. The corresponding pages in the 1968 translation of Weber's work, *Economy and Society*, ed. Guenther Roth and Claus Wittich (New York: Irvington Publications, 1968) are vol. 1, pp. 212–225 and vol. 3, pp. 956–1001.

5. See Reinhard Bendix, ''Bureaucracy,'' in *International Encyclopedia of the Social Sciences* (New York: Free Press, 1977).

6. And not just steel, of course. In Detroit, only two-thirds of 1 percent of the white-collar jobs at the three major auto companies are filled by Jews. A 1960 study of 1,500 U.S. corporations showed that although Jews made up 8 percent of all college graduates and, even more important, 15 percent of the graduates of professional and business schools, they account for only 0.5 percent of management. See ''Has Bias Locked Up the Room at the Top?'' *Business Week*, January 24, 1970.

7. Melville Dalton, *Men Who Manage* (New York: Wiley, 1959).

8. *New York Times*, September 14, 1984, p. 1.

9. Richard Barnet, *Economy of Death* (New York: Atheneum House, 1969).

10. As Lewis Coser notes in *Greedy Institutions* (New York: Free Press, 1974), slaves, Jews, and others excluded from society could also be used because they owed to their lord their promotion from nonpersons to quasipersons.

11. The contributions-inducements theory of organizations was first formulated by Chester Barnard in the late 1930s and subsequently greatly refined by James G. March and Herbert A. Simon in their book, *Organizations* (New York: Wiley, 1958). Their contributions are cited as landmarks in organizational theory, despite the simplicity of the idea or perhaps because of it. We shall take them up later.

12. One of the most frequent consumer fraud devices is for a collection agency to send a fake social survey questionnaire out. Along with the usual attitude questions (''How do you feel about law and order?''), unsuspecting debtors are asked about their place of employment, the value of their car and other property, and whether their spouse works or not. The agencies also send letters on official-looking stationery saying that a heavily insured package is being held for them by the post office, and they should fill out the identification papers and mail them in to receive the package. Debtors thus disclose the information that the collection agency can use as leverage. Both practices are forbidden by law but are very hard to police.

13. Dan Clawson, *Bureaucracy and the Labor Process: The Transformation of U.S. Industry: 1860–1920* (New York: Monthly Review Press, 1980). See also the more general discussion of this issue in Harry Braverman, *Labor and Monopoly Capital* (New York: Monthly Review Press, 1975).

14. Katherine Stone, ''The Origins of Job Structures in the Steel Industry,'' *Radical America* 7, no. 6 (November/December 1973): 19–64, describes the process and conflicts for the steel industry. See also the seminal piece by Steven Marglin, ''What Do Bosses Do?'' *Review of Radical Political Economics* 6, no. 2 (Summer 1974): 33–60, and the book by Richard Edwards, *Contested Terrain: The Transformation of the Workplace in the Twentieth Century* (New York: Basic Books, 1979).

15. But on the other hand, it is striking that few creative individuals appear to start on their own, forming their own companies. Generally, they work first for a large firm. Only then can they attract the necessary capital from those arbitrators of the business scene, the banks.

16. Charles Perrow, ''Members as a Resource in Voluntary Organization,'' in *Organizations and Clients*, ed. W. Rosengren and M. Lefton (Columbus, Ohio: Charles E. Merrill, 1970), pp. 93–116.

17. Peter M. Blau, *The Dynamics of Bureaucracy*, 2nd rev. ed. (Chicago: University of Chicago Press, 1973).

18. David Rogers, *110 Livingstone Street* (New York: Random House, 1968).

19. Talcott Parsons, "Introduction," in Max Weber, *The Theory of Social and Economic Organization*, pp. 58–60. Amitai Etzioni, *A Comparative Analysis of Complex Organizations* (New York: Free Press, 1961), pp. 218–261.

20. I wish to thank Robert Taylor, former vice-president of the University of Wisconsin, for constructive comments on this material. As he points out, the chain of command works in a variety of ways, depending on who or what is involved. "Very little (maybe no) 'traffic' moves up or down this chain in this fashion. The fact is that most of it moves as your letter [to me] did—from professor to vice-president and back with all the other levels left in blessed ignorance. And, of course, no modern student would countenance such a chain for a moment—he'd pick up the phone and call the president or the president of the board of regents, if he thought either of these officials capable of acting on his request." (Private correspondence.) This is true, but in a crunch, the chain is there for those higher up to use it. As we shall see, much short-circuiting of the chain occurs in organizations that are not made up of "professionals."

21. Charles Perrow, "Goals and Power Structures: A Historical Case Study," and Mary E. W. Goss, "Patterns of Bureaucracy Among Hospital Staff Physicians," in *The Hospital in Modern Society*, ed. Eliot Freidson (New York: Free Press, 1963).

22. Erwin O. Smigel, *Wall Street Lawyer*, rev. ed. (Bloomington, Ind.: Indiana University Press, 1970).

23. Harold L. Wilensky, *Organizational Intelligence: Knowledge and Policy in Government and Industry* (New York: Basic Books, 1969), pp. 42–48.

24. Victor A. Thompson, *Modern Organization*, 2nd ed. (University, Ala.: Univ. of Alabama Press, 1977), Chapter 8.

25. Charles Perrow, "Working Paper on Technology and Structure," mimeographed, February 1970.

26. Wilfred Brown, *Exploration in Management* (New York: Wiley, 1960), pp. 97–98.

27. William F. Whyte, "Human Relations—A Progress Report," in *Complex Organizations, A Sociological Reader*, ed. Amitai Etzioni (New York: Holt, Rinehart & Winston, 1962), pp. 100–112.

28. James C. Worthy, "Organizational Structure and Employee Morale," *American Sociological Review* 15 (1950): 169–179.

29. Peter Blau, "The Hierarchy of Authority in Organizations," *American Journal of Sociology* 73 (January 1968): 453–457.

30. See, for example, the various discussions by Joan Woodward, *Industrial Organization: Theory and Practice* (London: Oxford University Press, 1965). In discussing span of control, Jay Lorsch generally finds a broad span is associated with nonroutine tasks, contrary to Blau. But on the other hand, in the routine production department of one of his companies, Lorsch also finds a broad span of control. See Jay W. Lorsch, *Product Innovation and Organization* (New York: Macmillan, 1965), p. 53. For a good discussion and additional evidence supporting Blau's view see Gerald Bell, "Determinants of Span of Control," *American Journal of Sociology* 73, no. 1 (July 1967): 90–101.

31. Marshall Meyer, "Two Authority Structures of Bureaucratic Organizations," *Administrative Science Quarterly* 13 (September 1968): 211–228.

32. Blau, "Hierarchy." There are complex problems here of different degrees of "tallness" in different units of an organization that are not relevant for these agencies, but would be for most organizations.

33. See, for example, Worthy, "Employee Morale." It is noteworthy that in a study of school teachers that used, by and large, unloaded questions to tap bureaucracy, it was found that, quite contrary to the authors' expectations, "Teachers in highly bureaucratic systems had a significantly higher, not lower, sense of power than those in less bureaucratic systems." See Gerald H. Moeller and W. W. Charters, "Relation of Bureaucratization to Sense of Power Among Teachers," *Administrative Science Quarterly* 10, no. 4 (March 1966): 457. These authors were as surprised as Blau and his associates but fell back upon the influence of other factors that might have clouded or reversed a relationship predicted by most schools of thought.

34. The best summary and introduction to these studies is that of John Child, "Predicting and Understanding Organization Structure," *Administrative Science Quarterly* 18, no. 2 (June 1973): 168–185. For a sample of the criticisms of this important survey see Howard Aldrich, "Technology and Organizational Structure: A Reexamination of the Findings of the

Aston Group.'' *Administrative Science Quarterly* 17, no. 1 (March 1972): 26–43; Sergio E. Mindlin and Howard Aldrich, ''Interorganizational Dependence: A Review of the Concepts and Reexamination of the Findings of the Aston Group,'' *Administrative Science Quarterly* 20, no. 3 (September 1975): 382–392; and especially William Starbuck, ''A Trip to View the Elephants and Rattlesnakes in the Garden of Aston,'' in *Perspectives on Organization Design and Behavior*, ed. Andrew H. Van de Ven and William F. Joyce (New York: Wiley, 1981), pp. 167–199.

35. Blau, *Dynamics*.
36. Dalton, *Men Who Manage*.
37. Gouldner, *Industrial Bureaucracy*.
38. Wilfred Brown, *Exploration in Management*.
39. David Mechanic, ''Sources of Power of Lower Participants in Complex Organization,'' *Administrative Science Quarterly* 7, no. 4 (December 1962): 349–364.
40. Dalton, *Men Who Manage*, Chapter 2.
41. Parsons, ''Introduction,'' in Weber, *The Theory of Social and Economic Organizations*, p. 59.
42. Ibid., p. 60.
43. Perrow and Goss in *The Hospital in Modern Society*.
44. Parsons, ''Introduction,'' in Weber, *The Theory of Social and Economic Organizations*, p. 60.
45. Gouldner, *Industrial Bureaucracy*.
46. Ibid., p. 24.
47. Ibid., p. 22.
48. Stanley H. Udy, Jr., '' 'Bureaucracy' and 'Rationality' in Weber's Organization Theory,'' *American Sociological Review* 24 (1959): 591–595; Arthur L. Stinchcombe, ''Bureaucratic and Craft Administration of Production,'' *Administrative Science Quarterly* 4 (1959): 168–187.
49. Blau, ''Hierarchy.''
50. See Weber, *The Theory of Social and Economic Organizations*, pp. 337–339, for the following: ''The primary source of bureaucratic administration lies in the role of technical knowledge. . . . Bureaucratic administration means fundamentally the exercise of control on the basis of knowledge. This is the feature of it which makes it specifically rational. . . . Bureaucracy is superior in knowledge, including both technical knowledge and knowledge of the concrete fact.''
51. Nuel Pharr Davis, *Lawrence and Oppenheimer* (New York: Simon & Schuster, 1968), Chapters 6 and 7.

General Groves is reported to have said, ''Here at great expense the government has assembled the world's largest collection of crackpots'' (pp. 173–174). He proceeded to run it like an asylum as well as a factory. Group leaders were required to turn in reports on the daily hours worked by Nobel laureates and other top scientists. The purpose, which they did not know, was to keep down absenteeism. ''The payroll office did not know what to do with work reports ranging up to a preposterous and unreimbursable eighteen hours a day.'' The military police closed up the labs at five o'clock every afternoon. Said a physicist, ''Apparently they didn't have orders to throw us out, but they did have orders to lock up the supplies. We sawed around the locks on the stockroom doors and just stayed and worked. We kept a refrigerator full of sandwich stuff because everybody was pretty hungry by four in the morning, our usual quitting time. After a while, whoever was directing the M.P.'s caught the spirit of the thing and stopped replacing the locks'' (p. 181). Another scientist contrasted the University of California lab at Berkeley, run by Ernest Lawrence, with the Los Alamos complex. They were similar only in the long hours put in. ''The difference was the atmosphere. There you did whatever task they assigned you and learned not to ask why. Here (Los Alamos) you asked what you liked and at least thought you did what you liked. There the pressure came from outside. Here there didn't seem to be any pressure'' (pp. 181–182).
52. See Harold L. Wilensky, ''The Professionalization of Everyone?'' *American Journal of Sociology* 70 (September 1964): 137–158, for a discussion of the role of the training institution in the process of professionalization.
53. Dalton, *Men Who Manage*; see also ''Conflicts Between Staff and Line Managerial Officers,'' *American Sociological Review* 15 (1950): 342–351.
54. Fred Goldner and R. R. Ritti, ''Professionalization as Career Immobility,'' *American Journal of Sociology* 73 (March 1967): 491. This article contains a good discussion of the issues raised here, as well as citations and review of the literature that views the goals of professionals and managers (or the company) as in conflict. See also the critical review of the literature in Norman Kaplan, ''Professional Scientists in Industry,'' *Social Problems* 13 (Summer 1965): 88–97.

3 SOCIAL COLLECTIVITIES AS COMMUNICATION
LEONARD C. HAWES

There is a bias (at least in Western culture) toward thinking of organizations as *things*—as if organizations were some kind of "magic containers" that hold resources, people, materials, products, and so on. A foundational change in thinking about organizational communication abandoned this view to conceive of organizations as *ongoing activities* that are accomplished mainly through communication. Karl Weick, whom you'll also read about in Parts II and III, championed this view by arguing that we should think about "organization" as a verb rather than a noun.

In the early 1970s organizational communication scholars began·exploring this idea that organizations are processes, not things, and that communication creates organizations. Leonard Hawes built on the teaching and writing of Weick to conceive of organizations *as* communication. He focused on the human activity of organizing, stimulated study of the everyday life of organizational members, and spurred the analysis of ordinary, routine organizational *talk*. This was not an easy transition to make. As you read Hawes's book review, think about how difficult it is to avoid referring to an organization as a thing or container and instead to consistently refer to organizing as an activity.

Contemporary social critics and pundits are fond of observing that our most pressing problems arise from our inability to cope with organized complexity. From a social-science viewpoint, that claim requires empirical verification and qualification. An assertion that the "Watergate affair," for example, resulted from certain people's inability to cope with organized complexity makes little sense to the social scientist. To transform that assertion into a testable proposition, he would have to specify the behaviors to which "Watergate affair" refers and the condition to which "organized complexity" refers. If that could be done satisfactorily, the proposition then could be examined from several social-science points of view.

An appropriate vantage point from which to investigate the forms and functions of "organized complexity" is the study of organizational behavior. In a defensible sense, the "Watergate affair" is an excellent example of certain of its dimensions. But it is apparent, from only a casual glance at the literature of organizational behavior, that one can adopt a variety of viewpoints within this social-science perspective. Political scientists, economists, sociologists, social psychologists, management scientists, business administrators, and anthropologists all conceive of organizational behavior differently. And even within disciplines, different perspectives appear frequently.

Books derived from each vantage point abound. However, few are written from a predominantly communication point of view; those, in turn, talk

Adapted from L. C. Hawes,"Social Collectivities as Communication."Reprinted with permission from *Quarterly Journal of Speech, 60*, 1974, 497–502. Copyright 1974 by the Speech Communication Association.

most often about communication practices that occur *within* business and/or industrial organizations. The existence of an "already organized organization" is assumed. Furthermore, it is assumed that organizations are containers *within which* people send messages, conduct meetings, write memoranda, make telephone calls, chat informally, etc.

As an alternative perspective for studying organized complexity, consider the following:

No a priori distinctions would be made among dyads, small groups, organizations, and societies. These distinctions frequently are made by using the convenient and arbitrary criterion of number of people involved. The behavioral phenomena to which these terms currently refer would all be treated as *social collectivities*. It seems safe to assume that differences among social collectivities will be found. But those differences ought to be determined by the questions being asked and the empirical data obtained rather than being assumed a priori on the basis of size.

In *The Social Psychology of Organizing*, Weick contends, "If you're going to learn about organizations, it is not necessary that you assume immediately that they are complex ('the currently popular term *complex organizations* conveys more information about organization theorists than about organization'; Weick, 1965, p. 205), or that they differ from groups of smaller size. Instead, assume that they are processes which create, maintain, and dissolve social collectivities, that these processes constitute the work of organizing, and that the ways in which these processes are continuously executed are the organization" (p. 1).

Most existing viewpoints on organizations are static. Macro-level constructs are placed in relation to one another and used to represent organizations and their characteristic behaviors. They resemble a still photograph in that they capture, at one instant in time, all the salient features of the organization that are readily apparent to the observer. An alternative perspective would be dynamic and would resemble a movie, representing the social collectivity behaving over time. But why is communication in a position to provide such a perspective and how could that perspective be accomplished empirically?

From a social collectivity, operationally defined as a corpus of observed and recorded communica-

tive behaviors, social rules or norms can be inferred. These rules or norms function both as a summary of all the observed behaviors and as a way of simulating or re-creating similar social collectivities in the future.

Given our concern in speech-communication with the notion of process, it is to be expected that we would strive to construct process models of social collectivities. Process has a space-and-time dimension; there is a spatial change over a given time frame. But to simulate and model these spatiotemporal changes, we must know the behavioral rules to which such changes conform.

Rather than assuming already organized organizations, the alternative perspective considers it necessary to determine *how* organizations come into existence in the first place, *how* such patterned behavior evolves, *how* the collectivities maintain themselves, and *how* they disengage. If we are to understand how social collectivities are created, maintained, and dissolved, we must infer from data the rules by which those social collectivities operate. Communicative behavior is easily accessible, is easily recordable and definable, and can function as the primary data from which operational rules of social collectivities can be inferred. In short, a social collectivity *is* patterned communicative behavior; communicative behavior does not occur *within* a network of relationships but *is* that network.

If we further assume, along with ethnomethodologists and social interactionists, that social collectivities are not *reflected in* communicative behavior but rather *are* communicative behavior, then we have no alternative but to treat observable communicative behavior as our primary data. To paraphrase Garfinkel's . . . argument . . . , communicative behavior is the operator that transforms the state of a system at Time One into the state as it exists in Time Two. Without communicative behavior, no transformational work can be accomplished and processes, by definition, cannot exist.

For the sake of arguing the feasibility of this alternative, compare the social collectivity of a medium-sized family with that of a large corporation. According to [many] . . . the large corporation would be considered an organization and the family as a type of small group on the grounds that the former is more permanent, complex, and interdependent than the latter. Let's begin with permanency.

It is argued that in a corporation, individual members are replaceable; consequently, the corporation retains its identity even though many of its original members are gone and have been replaced by new members. Calibrating our scale to the level of a family, the same conclusion can be reached. Any one of the members can die, or the husband or wife may get a divorce and may or may not remarry; but the family as a collectivity still exists in the eyes of the family members and the community. Granted, the particular configuration of the family has changed, but the configuration of the corporation also changes with member replacement. The difference between a large corporation and a medium- or small-sized family is one of degree, not of kind. The scale differs, but the principle of membership replaceability remains the same.

In relation to complexity, the differences between a family and a corporation are also of degree and not kind. In a large corporation there is a formal and informal structure. The same is true in a family collectivity. Legally and formally, family members have certain rights and obligations. Informally, the rights and obligations may be, and frequently are, quite different from the legal-formal structure. While corporations can be characterized in terms of power and influence structures, so can families. Both in families and corporations, the power and influence structures differ according to issue.

Another dimension of the supposed complexity of large corporations is that certain practices are formalized. For example, corporations have job descriptions, by-laws, official policy and procedure manuals, budgets, etc. In families the same functions are operative but are retained usually in the oral rather than written tradition. Again, the difference appears to be one of degree rather than kind.

One could argue that a large corporation consists of many interdependent parts that must operate in a complementary fashion in order for goals to be achieved. For most business and industrial organizations, goals are to survive and make a profit or provide services. But members of a family are also interdependent and must continue to take in as much or more money than they spend, and they must provide certain services. There are examples both of large corporations and of families that operate on the basis of deficit spending and that exist for long periods of time on "welfare." While large corporations have elaborate and complex accounting systems to record debits and credits, for most families the wife or the husband functions as the accountant. Keeping the checking account(s) balanced, keeping track of the savings account(s), if any, and projecting ahead for unusually heavy-spending months are necessary functions to be performed in both families and corporations.

Someone arguing against the concept of *social collectivity* might contend that these differences of degree, even if they are not differences of kind, make a substantive difference. Where those differences make an empirical difference depends upon the particular comparisons being made and the specific questions being posed. In some instances, one would not want to use the family collectivity as an analogue for a corporation collectivity. In other instances, a family or other small group might be a most efficient way of analoguing a corporation, which is one of the arguments Sarason (1972) makes.

The following questions, then, stimulate the development of an alternative communication perspective on social collectivities. In regard to their creation, maintenance, and dissolution, *how* are collectivities such as negotiations, interviews, families, communes, social movements, volunteer organizations, business/industrial organizations, and White House administrations similar and dissimilar? Rather than assuming the existence of organizational boundaries, we might ask *how* social collectivities set themselves apart from what is defined as not being part of the collectivity. In Weick's terms, the question is *how* are environments enacted (pp. 27–29)? *How* are resources such as information, men, and material defined and subsequently used? *How* are decisions accomplished, goals formulated, and policies defined? *How* are values established and *how* do they change? The communication perspective outlined assumes that these questions are answerable by observing the communicative behaviors that actually constitute social collectivities. Similarities in process, once identified, will be a valuable contribution to the overall social-science objective of understanding human behavior.

BOOKS REVIEWED

COMPLEX ORGANIZATIONS: A SOCIOLOGICAL PERSPECTIVE. By J. Eugene Haas and Thomas E. Drabek. New York: The Macmillan Company, 1973: pp. v + 416. $10.95.

ORGANIZATIONS, STRUCTURE AND PROCESS. By Richard H. Hall. Englewood Cliffs, N.J.: Prentice-Hall, Inc., 1972; pp. xi + 354. $9.95.

THE CREATION OF SETTINGS AND THE FUTURE SOCIETIES. By Seymour B. Sarason. San Francisco: Jossey-Bass Inc., 1972; pp. ix + 295. $10.50.

THE LIMITS OF ORGANIZATIONAL CHANGE. By Herbert Kaufman. University: The University of Alabama Press, 1971; pp. 124. $5.75.

MODERN ORGANIZATIONAL THEORY. By Anant R. Negandhi. Edited Kent, Ohio: The Kent State University Press, 1973; pp. 404. $10.00.

ORGANIZATIONAL SYSTEMS: A TEXT READER IN THE SOCIOLOGY OF ORGANIZATIONS. By Koya Azumi and Jerald Hage. Lexington, Mass.: D. C. Heath and Company, 1972; pp. v + 582. $10.95.

ORGANIZATIONAL COMMUNICATION. By Gerald M. Goldhaber. Dubuque, Iowa: Wm. C. Brown Company, Publishers, 1974; pp. v + 391. $6.95.

THE SOCIAL PSYCHOLOGY OF ORGANIZING. By K. A. Weick. Reading, Mass.: Addison-Wesley, 1969.

4   ORGANIZATIONAL COMMUNICATION: HISTORICAL DEVELOPMENT AND FUTURE DIRECTIONS
Linda L. Putnam and George Cheney

Putnam and Cheney provide an exhaustive history of organizational communication. They trace the history of organizational communication from the beginnings of business and professional speaking in the 1920s through major themes of research on less speaker-oriented approaches. They then indicate the major research perspectives that developed in the 1970s. Note that these more recent research perspectives include many more variables than the research perspectives that were pursued in the infancy of organizational communication research. They conclude by describing the relationship between research and practice, which, as Corman indicated, go hand in hand.

Adapted from Linda L. Putnam and George Cheney, "Organizational Communication: Historical Development and Future Directions." Adapted with permission from T. W. Benson (ed.), *Speech Communication in the 20th Century,* Carbondale: Southern Illinois University Press. Copyright 1985 by the Board of Trustees, Southern Illinois University.

Organizational communication as a specialized area of speech communication has experienced rapid growth in the past decade. Most colleges and universities with speech communication programs offer at least one course in this area. A master's degree in organizational communication can be obtained at approximately 75 institutions and 35 of these schools offer the Ph.D. Despite its growing popularity, however, organizational communication is a relative newcomer to the discipline. Its departmental roots date back to the early 1950s with the work of P.E. Lull at Purdue University; its origins can be traced to speech training for corporate executives in the 1920s. Its emergence in the field of speech communication parallels the entrance of speech communication into the mainstream of social science research.

The growth of organizational communication is concomitant with the development of industrial psychology, social psychology, organizational behavior, and administrative science; hence, experts in these fields have shaped the dominant theories, concepts, and issues that organizational communication scholars typically raise. Redding (1979b) acknowledges and laments this "wholesale transporting (borrowing? stealing?) of concepts and variables from our academic cousins" (p. 321). Recent breakthroughs, however, reflect the influence of a wider array of disciplines; namely, sociology, rhetoric, anthropology, philosophy, political science, and linguistics.

Organizational communication grew out of three main speech communication traditions: public address; persuasion; and social science research on interpersonal, small group, and mass communication. Definitions of both communication and organization were as diverse as the traditions that shaped research topics. Moreover, because definitions reflected various theoretical assumptions and concepts (Cusella, in press; Putnam, 1982a), it was unlikely that any one definition would gain wide acceptance (Porter & Roberts, 1976). In the early writings, definitions of communication had a distinctly "media-oriented" focus, shaping research on the accuracy and clarity of message composition (McMurray, 1965). Communication, in this sense, was the "process of sending and receiving messages" (Sanborn, 1964, p. 3). The publication of Lee Thayer's (1961) *Administrative Communication* and W. C. Redding's (1972) *Communication Within the Organization* shifted the focus of organizational communication from sender to receiver models. Communication referred to "those behaviors of human beings . . . which result in messages being received by one or more persons" (Redding, 1972, p. 25). This definition dismissed the notion that messages were literally transmitted from one person to another. Instead, it stressed that the message received was the one that mattered.

Recent studies have moved away from these conceptions to one of interaction, or the social creation of message and meaning (Hawes, 1974). *Process* assumes a central role in the interactive orientation, and organizational communication is broadly defined as "the processing and interpreting of messages, information, meaning, and symbolic activity within and between organizations" (Putnam, 1983a, p. 1). Definitions of *organization* have also shifted from a preoccupation with bureaucratic models to a focus on aggregates of persons arranged in patterned relationships (Barnard, 1938; Redding, 1972). Organizations are seen as involving dynamic activities rather than static collections of people; these activities are integrated through role coordination, interdependence, and interlocked behaviors (Redding, 1972; Weick, 1979).

This chapter traces the evolution of organizational communication—its major topics and research developments. In particular, it reviews the key research domains, breakpoints in new lines of work, and the interface between research and application from 1920 to 1980. Spatial limitations preclude a thorough synthesis of research findings in organizational communication. The reader is urged to consult Guetzkow (1965), Redding (1972), and Porter and Roberts (1976) for detailed state-of-the-art reviews. Other articles provide a definitive historical treatment of organizational communication (Hay, 1974; Porterfield, 1974; Redding, 1966; Richetto, 1977; Tompkins, 1967; Van Voorhis, 1974). Our chapter draws from these summaries to highlight historical developments.

Spatial limitations also preclude a review of major theorists and methodological developments in the study of organizational communication. Interested readers are directed to Tompkins (1984) and Pietri (1974) for a review of the contributions of such major theorists as Barnard, Fayol, Follett, Simon, Taylor, and Weber. Other review chapters focus on premises and metatheoretical assumptions that underlie research traditions (Putnam, 1982a; Redding, 1979b); ways of transforming traditional research into alternative approaches (Putnam, 1983b; Putnam & Cheney, 1983); research methodologies used to study organizational communication (Dennis, Goldhaber & Yates, 1978); and new models for research on systems theory and communication structure (Farace & MacDonald, 1974; Monge, 1982; Roberts, O'Reilly, Bretton & Porter, 1974; Thayer, 1967); hence, these topics will not be reviewed.

Instead, this essay reviews five areas of "traditional" organizational communication research—communication media, communication channels, networks, organizational climate, and superior-subordinate communication—and four emerging approaches: information-processing, rhetorical, cultural, and political orientations. It concludes with an overview of the practical side of organizational communication, its history, and its impact on training and consulting.

EARLY ORGANIZATIONAL COMMUNICATION RESEARCH: THE STUDY OF COMMUNICATION MEDIA

Topics covered in an introductory course on organizational communication typically begin with the research of the 1950s (Jablin, 1978b). But in actuality, one offshoot of industrial communication, business and professional speaking, dates back to the late 1920s. This section reviews publications on industrial public speaking, communication media, and the semantics of organizational messages. The first visible sign of courtship between the American business community and the speech-communication field occurred in the late 1920s. Encouraged by the popularity of Dale Carnegie's writings and courses, business began to link managerial effectiveness with communication skills (Sanborn, 1964). Even though academicians regarded Carnegie's courses as "gimmickry," they followed his lead in providing prescriptive texts for managerial success. Two textbooks that gained a widespread appeal were Hoffman's (1923) *Speaking for Business Men* and Sanford and Yeager's (1929) *Business and Professional Speaking*. These books adapted public speaking to the business scene by introducing briefs, reports, and presentational speeches as forms of public address. Most of the business speaking texts published before 1950 "provide no evidence to support their huge numbers of prescriptions" and treat communication as "speaker-centered, and success-oriented, manipulative, and simplistic" (Redding, 1966, p. 52).

Although Collins (1924) conducted a survey of public speaking courses in business administration and YMCA schools, systematic research on business speakers did not surface until the surveys of industrial training programs at Pennsylvania State University in the 1950s (Knapp, 1968; Zelko, 1951) and the studies of business rhetoric at the University of Missouri in the 1960s (Fisher, 1965). Fisher (1965) analyzed the persuasive strategies of 500 speeches delivered by top management officials. The speeches relied on a common enemy and used stylized platitudes and recurrent symbols as persuasive techniques. Shifting from content to speech preparation, Knapp (1970) reported that middle managers had very little preparation time before delivery, feared being misquoted, and relied heavily on prepared manuscripts for their delivery. A few academicians extended this work by studying audience responses to business rhetoric (Derry, 1969; Irwin & Brockhaus, 1963; Williams & Sundene, 1965). This early work on public speaking in industry laid the foundation for a plethora of courses and texts on business and professional speaking (see, for example, Bradley & Baird, 1980; Downs, Berg & Linkugel, 1977; Howell & Bormann, 1971; Zelko & Dance, 1965).

Public speaking was only one medium of communication that gained popularity in the early days of organizational research. Academicians also focused on written communication, particularly employee handbooks, company newsletters, memoranda, and information racks (Mahoney, 1954; Zelko,

1953). To understand what "information should be transmitted to whom in what media" (Van Voorhis, 1974, p. 14), studies centered on the accuracy (Beach, 1950), the readability (Paterson & Jenkins, 1948), and the functions (Dover, 1959) of written information. The few employee newsletters that existed before World War II contained mostly chitchat and notices of social events, but the number of company newsletters tripled in the 1940s, with their content shifting to information about company plans, operations, and policies (Dover, 1959). In the 1950s company publications became an arm of management, complete with persuasive appeals for action and with managerial interpretations of company events. Axley's (1983) recent study of employee publications echoed Dover's (1959) earlier observation that managerial philosophy influenced the amount of space devoted to information-giving news, status-conferring activities, and the language that depicted these events.

Typically, research in this vein compared the effectiveness of and preferences for particular types of media. Although management preferred written communiques, employees opted for supervisor conferences and group meetings as their preferred forms of communication (Peters, 1950). This finding in conjunction with Dahle's (1954) experimental comparison of five modes of communication led to the conclusion that a combination of written and oral media constituted the most effective means of communication (Sanborn, 1961), especially when message content and media use were adapted to particular audiences (Thayer, 1961). But when the sender and the receiver differed in vocabularies and problem orientations, written was more effective than oral communication. If the message required feedback or clarification, oral communication surpassed written media (O'Reilly & Pondy, 1979).

Research on communication media in organizations adopted a very narrow and often mechanical view of communication. With a zeal to improve routine practices, organizational researchers treated communications as a one-way, downwardly directed conduit for transmitting messages. Even studies that developed taxonomies of messages (Eilon, 1968) took a distinctly "media" focus; messages and media were treated as synonymous. Organizational communication consisted of "speech" media, often cast in simplistic, prescriptive principles that were devoid of any basic understanding of the complexities of communication (Redding, 1966).

A major breakpoint in this preoccupation with media came through the application of communication theory to organizational behavior. The focus of organizational communication shifted to message distortion, as characterized by two distinct lines of work—perceptual or semantic distortion and blockage in information flow. Both research strains questioned how misunderstanding occurred in organizations; one focused on the meanings of messages, and the other centered on transmission problems in message flow. Inspired by the general semanticists and under the leadership of Irving Lee at Northwestern University, perceptual distortion studies examined the effect of words and language on interpretations of organizational events. Haney (1973) discussed problems that resulted from equating inferences with observed behavior. Weaver (1958) tested the impact of labor-management semantic profiles on message flow. Triandis (1959a, 1959b) uncovered "cognitive disparity" between supervisory and work groups in making judgments about organizational events. Schwartz, Stark, and Schiffman (1970) found that concepts such as "strike," "solidarity," and "management" triggered different interpretations among union officers. Tompkins (1962) assessed what he termed "semantic information distance" between and among different levels of a nationwide trade union. Studies on semantic distance, while few in number, served as the forerunners for later work on organizational symbols. The second strain of research, message distortion, emerged in studies of upward communication, a subdivision of one of the four "traditional" domains of organizational communication.

TRADITIONAL DOMAINS OF ORGANIZATIONAL COMMUNICATION RESEARCH

From an early interest in the downward flow of information, four research "traditions" developed at roughly the same time. The four traditions—

communication channels, communication climate, network analysis, and superior-subordinate communication—"represent our discipline's struggle to establish the boundaries of organizational communication" (Putnam & Cheney, 1983, p. 213). These approaches date back to the human relations movement in the 1940s, when social scientists began systematic observations of information flow in collectivities.

Communication Channels

Channel research addresses the flow of information as it relates to organizational structure; that is, upward, downward, and horizontal. Although the majority of practitioners' books in the 1940s stressed one-way, downward communication, Given (1949), Heron (1942), and Pigors (1949) emphasized the two-way nature of information flow between lower and upper levels. At the same time, Lazarsfeld, Berelson, and Gaudet (1948) initiated research on "gatekeeping" and the "two-step flow" of information.

In the 1950s and 1960s channel research attracted great interest. A number of studies revealed that lower-level employees tended to distort messages they sent upward (Planty & Machaver, 1952; Read, 1962). This research interest has continued to be pursued. Athanassiades (1973) found that a sense of security reduced upward distortion, and high achievement drive increased the tendency to distort. Through extensive research on upward distortion, Roberts and O'Reilly concluded that trust, job satisfaction, and job performance reduced upward distortion (O'Reilly, 1978; O'Reilly & Roberts, 1974; Roberts & O'Reilly, 1974a). Moreover, positive feedback from one's superior also decreased the amount of upward distortion (Jablin, 1979). Following the work of Festinger (1950) and Cohen (1959), Bradley (1978) noted that the content of upwardly-directed messages was determined by the perceived power rather than the status of receivers. In a related vein, the term "Pelz Effect" emerged from studies showing that subordinates would initiate more upward messages if they believed their superiors had upward influence (Pelz, 1952). Examination of the "Pelz Effect" continued, but it became concerned

exclusively with the dyadic relationship of superior-subordinate (Jablin, 1980b).

Davis (1953), following Jacobson and Seashore (1951), developed a research technique, ECCO: Episodic Communication Channels in Organizations, to examine the spread of rumors through informal channels or the "grapevine." This body of research grew, but Davis (1978), the major analyst of informal channels, contended it was rather small. Informal communication was frequently linked with formal channels. Specifically, in effective organizations, informal and formal communication showed a positive relationship (Katz & Kahn, 1978). Tompkins's (1977, 1978) study of NASA's Marshall Space Flight Center reinforced this finding in his observation that the practices of managing and communicating fused through an emphasis on both formal and informal communication channels.

Message overload and information adequacy were also linked to frequency of message flow across different channels. Miller (1960) and O'Reilly (1980) observed the effects of "information overload" on organizational members. Miller (1960) described seven possible responses to overload conditions, including omission, error, delaying, filtering, and escaping. O'Reilly (1980) reported that perceived information overload was associated with higher satisfaction, but with lower decision-making performance. This overload, however, resulted from excess vertical rather than horizontal communication. Specifically, managers spent about two-thirds of their communication time on vertical messages to their superiors and subordinates and only one-third of their time on horizontal messages (Porter & Roberts, 1976). Perhaps as Goldhaber, Yates, Porter & Lesniak (1978) reported, horizontal coordinating functions in organizations typically occurred "on a rather informal, impromptu basis" (p. 86), rather than through formal communication channels. Several researchers extended work on communication channels by suggesting a link between perceived information adequacy and such organizational outcomes as communication satisfaction, job performance, and organizational effectiveness (Spiker & Daniels, 1981; Daly, McCroskey & Falcione, 1976; Downs & Hazen, 1977). In particular, O'Reilly and Pondy (1979) showed that relevant and accurate information contributed to individual job performance and to organizational effectiveness.

Guided by the metaphor of information flow, channel studies have treated messages and structures with misplaced concreteness; they have emphasized the "channel" through which messages are transmitted, rather than the nature or content of messages. In this perspective, communication becomes the accuracy of transmitting a message, a way of "getting information across" rather than a way of interpreting and giving feedback on the meaning of a message. Katz and Kahn (1978), while offering their own explanations for the types of messages that "move" in particular directions, bemoan the lack of empirical attention to message interpretation.

Communication Climate

In the 1960s channel research was applied to the study of communication "climate," communication that contributes to "the spirit or philosophy" responsible for organizational relationships (Koehler, Anatol, & Applbaum, 1981, p. 123). Thus, climate research incorporated communication channels into a framework of organizational relationships. The first studies of psychological or social climate were inspired by field theory (Lewin, 1951). Barnard (1938) and Roethlisberger and Dickson (1939) treated climates as implicit features of organizations; but as Jablin (1980a) noted, the first explicit linkage of psychological climate to organizational behavior appeared in McGregor's (1960) book. McGregor contended that "many subtle behavioral manifestations of managerial attitude create what is often referred to as the 'psychological climate' of the relationship" (p. 134).

"Organizational climate" differed from communication climate in its focus on organizational structure (e.g., rules, constraints), individual responsibility, rewards, job challenge, warmth, and tolerance (Litwin & Stringer, 1968). "Communication climate" became associated with such concepts as trust and openness (see Ireland, Van Auken & Lewis, 1978). Even though researchers characterized climate as a product of shared meanings among organizational members, they persisted in treating climate as having an existence of its own,

one that could be approximated through summary measures of individual perceptions.

Specifically, researchers employed questionnaires that measured individual perceptions; then they inappropriately applied summary statistics to indicate how organizational members felt on the average about climate factors (see the review by Falcione & Werner, 1978). Climate factors, then, became atmospheric or meteorological elements located in the organizational environment. For example, Roberts and O'Reilly (1974b) developed a climate-type measure of 16 "atmospheric conditions" of organizational communication, including trust, influence, accuracy, overload, percent of time spent communicating in different directions, and time spent on different communication media. Muchinsky (1977), in an assessment of the Roberts and O'Reilly questionnaire, concluded that it discriminated well among organizations on the basis of individual perceptions, but it was conceptually similar to job satisfaction.

Shifting the focus of climate to leadership functions, Redding (1972) offered a holistic prescriptive model for managers known as the "Ideal Managerial Climate" (IMC). The five components of the IMC consisted of supportiveness, participative decision making, trust, openness, and emphasis on high performance goals. The IMC represented an important attempt to bridge theory and practice in organizational communication, although it was limited by its managerial view of organizational effectiveness. During the 1970s, many organizational researchers adopted an applied interest in communication climate, linking it to job satisfaction. In a detailed review, Falcione and Werner (1978) discussed empirical support for this connection. Even though Redding (1972) acknowledged the "slippery" nature of this construct, he contended that climate was more important than were communication skills "in creating an effective organization" (p. 111).

In 1983 communication climate research took a dramatic shift from previous approaches. Poole and McPhee (1983) treated climate on the *intersubjective* level, based on members' beliefs, attitudes, values, and interpretations. This conceptualization introduced an intermediate level of analysis—one between objective and subjective variables. Further,

Poole and McPhee employed a ''structurational'' model (Giddens, 1979) to examine ''the production and reproduction'' of organizational climates through the use of generative rules and interaction resources. This conceptualization moved communication climate out of the confines of its meteorological metaphor by examining the way climate is produced through values and beliefs, rather than through ''atmospheric'' elements external to individuals.

Network Analysis

Climate research represented one attempt to characterize, understand, and explain communication patterns in the organization; another was network analysis. Jablin (1980a, p. 341) noted parallels between the two ''schools,'' but argued that a major reason they developed distinct traditions was that climate focused on communication consequences while network research concentrated on communication antecedents and determinants. In addition, the two approaches became associated with different speech-communication programs—climate work with Purdue University and network analysis with Michigan State and Stanford universities.

The origins of network analysis can be traced to (1) early sociometric studies (Moreno, 1953); (2) small-group studies (Bavelas, 1950; Leavitt, 1951; Shaw, 1964); (3) information diffusion (Rogers, 1962); and (4) the mass communication work of Lazarsfeld, Berelson, and Gaudet (1948). Simply put, ''a network consists of interconnected individuals who are linked by patterned communication flows'' (Rogers & Agarwala-Rogers, 1976, p. 110). Network analysis, which became popular both inside and outside the speech communication field, used data about communication flow to analyze interpersonal linkages and to identify the communication structure of a larger system (Rogers & Agarwala-Rogers, 1976). The earliest network studies were the 1950s' small-group laboratory experiments that contrasted different network structures, such as circle, wheel, and chain. They found that (1) centralization, as in the wheel network, contributed to rapid performance, especially of simple tasks; (2) decentralization, as in the circle network, was asso-

ciated with high satisfaction among members; (3) network structures affected leader emergence; and (4) persons in key network positions often experienced information overload (Rogers & Agarwala-Rogers, 1976).

In the 1970s organizational network research employed a systems model by treating linkages among all organizational members as ''nodes'' in a larger set of dyadic relationships (Farace, Monge & Russell, 1977; Monge, Edwards & Kiriste, 1978). Richards (1974b) suggested four key characteristics of linkages: (1) symmetry, (2) strength, (3) specificity, or the uniqueness of linkage function, and (4) transitivity, or consistency of linkages. Properties of network systems included centrality, connectedness, reachability, density, and range (Farace, Monge & Russell, 1977; Tichy, Tushman & Fombrun, 1979).

Research revealed that organizations were composed of a number of interrelated and often overlapping networks (Rogers & Agarwala-Rogers, 1976). In a study of three military organizations, Roberts and O'Reilly (1978) found that members rarely followed formal authority networks; rather they communicated in task-focused clusters. Moreover, the task network was larger and better developed than was the social one, but the two were closely related. Treating the group as the unit of analysis, Danowski (1980) found that production and innovation networks had stronger connectivity and greater uniformity in attitudes between groups than did maintenance networks. Researchers also investigated roles that individuals assumed in organizational networks. MacDonald (1976) observed that liaisons (persons who linked groups but were not necessarily members of them) were more satisfied with managerial messages and perceived themselves as more influential than did nonliaisons. Albrecht (1979) discovered that ''key'' communicators in a network identified more with management and with their jobs than did members who were not in key positions.

One type of communication role that attracted interest during the 1970s was boundary spanning. Boundary spanners are members who excel within their own work units and who also span the boundaries of work groups, departments, or organizations, or all three (Tushman & Scanlan, 1981a, 1981b). Boundary spanners, like liaisons and linking pins (members of two or more overlapping groups) perform essential integrative functions. Early studies by Blau (1954) and Erbe (1962) linked activity across organizational boundaries with professional relationships inside the company. Similarly, Tushman and his colleagues at Columbia University noted that professional employees typically assumed boundary-spanning roles and that roughly 40% of them were also "stars" within their own work groups (Tushman & Scanlan, 1981b). Thus, boundary spanning became fertile terrain for examining multiple roles in communication networks.

In the 1980s, as organizations became reliant on advanced technology, researchers began to examine the impact of computers on communication networks (Danowski, 1983; Fowler & Wackerbarth, 1980; Hintz & Couch, 1978; Plain, 1980; Rice, 1982a). In a dissertation completed at Stanford University, Rice (1982b), who gathered two years of computer-monitored conferencing data among 800 researchers, reported that group members typically exhibited reciprocal relationships and that nontask groups occupied more information-rich roles than did task groups. Computer-based network analysis might become even more prevalent as computers perform essential information processing functions for all employees.

Most network studies gathered data with self-report instruments and analyzed it with sociograms, matrix methods, and multidimensional scaling. In speech communication, the most popular data analysis technique was Richards' (1974a, 1974b) NEGOPY, developed at Stanford University. NEGOPY, designed to analyze an entire set of system relationships, accounted for indirect and direct communication links (Rogers & Agarwala-Rogers, 1976). Techniques such as NEGOPY, although useful for characterizing communication structures at particular points in time, over-emphasized the frequency of communication and gave little or no attention to the content and meanings of interaction (Putnam, 1982b). Albrecht and Ropp (1982) at the University of Washington suggested using nondirective interviews and ethnography to examine content and interpretations of network context and quantitative techniques to assess the frequency and configuration of communication systems.

Superior-Subordinate Communication

Similar to channel and climate research, the "tradition" known as superior-subordinate communication centered on information flow between subordinates and their supervisors. Jablin (1979) defined superior-subordinate communication as "exchanges of information and influence between organizational members, at least one of whom has formal . . . authority to direct and evaluate the activities of other organizational members" (p. 1202). Two key figures in research on superior-subordinate communication were W. C. Redding (1972) at Purdue University and Fredric Jablin (1979) at the University of Texas. Their reviews clustered this "tradition" into seven areas: (1) perceptions of the amount, frequency, and mode of interaction; (2) upward distortion; (3) upward influence; (4) openness; (5) feedback; (6) communicator style; and (7) effectiveness of superior-subordinate relationships. Because researchers found it natural in the 1960s and 1970s to apply concepts from channel and climate to the superior-subordinate dyad, most of the above research foci were borrowed from other "traditions." Three of the areas, however, accounted for specific task-oriented aspects of dyadic relationships: feedback, perceptual congruence, and communicator style. Studies on feedback noted that it was a multidimensional concept and that the quantity of feedback was less important than its relevance and accuracy (O'Reilly & Anderson, 1980). Cusella (1982) observed that a subordinate's intrinsic motivation increased with positive task-related feedback given by expert sources. But he posited that the timing, specificity, and rules for communicating the feedback would mitigate this effect (Cusella, 1980).

"Perceptual congruence," a concept similar to semantic information distance, referred to agreements between superiors and subordinates about aspects of their work life. Research concluded that superiors and subordinates generally disagreed about the requirements of their jobs (Boyd & Jensen, 1972), the amount of communication between them (Webber, 1970), and the personality traits of each other (Infante & Gorden, 1979). Effective supervisors were able to bridge these gaps through a relaxed, attentive communicator style

(Bradley & Baird, 1977) and through asking, persuading, and passing along information (Redding, 1972). Also, supervisors who exhibited an employee-centered communication style, tolerance for disagreement, and innovativeness achieved higher employee satisfaction scores than did other supervisors (Richmond & McCroskey, 1979; Richmond, McCroskey & Davis, 1982).

Because most studies highlighted task-related messages, a significant break occurred with research that emphasized the relational dimensions of superior-subordinate interaction. Jablin (1978a) demonstrated that subordinates who perceived an "open" relationship with their superior viewed certain types of superior-subordinate interaction as more appropriate than did subordinates who perceived a "closed" relationship, thus extending climate research on trust and openness. Openness, in this sense, referred to "candid disclosure of feelings" and "a willingness to listen to discomforting information" (Redding, 1972, p. 330). Jablin (1978a) also suggested that over time different norms and communication patterns developed for "open" as opposed to "closed" superior-subordinate dyads. In two recent studies Watson (1982a, 1982b) applied RELCOM, a coding scheme for relational control (Ellis, 1979), to an analysis of superior-subordinate interaction. She reported that superiors showed resistance to and subordinates showed compliance with each other's attempts to control the relationship.

Most superior-subordinate studies employ questionnaires, rarely matched for dyadic analysis. Smircich and Chesser (1981) address this failure to assess reciprocal influences directly. Other researchers are beginning to expand and enrich the literature by emphasizing how superior-subordinate relationships create and share symbolic realities (Pfeffer, 1981; Trujillo, 1983). In their comprehensive reviews of this literature, Jablin (1979) and Kelly (1982) lament the relative lack of attention to systemic variables that affect a dyadic relationship and urge researchers to consider situational and developmental approaches to superior-subordinate communication. In a pioneering effort to place superior-subordinate openness within an organizational system, Jablin (1982) reports that organizational size reduces openness while a supervisory position, especially at lower levels, tends to increase it.

NEW DIRECTIONS IN ORGANIZATIONAL COMMUNICATION RESEARCH

The emergence of any discipline or subdiscipline must be understood within a sociopolitical context. So it is with organizational communication. The research priorities of the first four decades are colored by (1) the human relations approach, which was quite popular until recently; (2) a related preoccupation with effective management; (3) treatment of communication either in terms of the visible, easily measured aspects of information flow or in terms of simple perceptions; and (4) an accompanying bias toward positivistic research methodologies. In an informative essay, Jablin (1978b) crystallizes the priorities and concerns of organizational communication researchers during each decade. We reprint his table (see Table 1) to help visualize the progress of the field.

In the 1980s the study of organizational communication is rapidly expanding to include a variety of theoretical and methodological approaches. For ease of presentation, we identify four "families" of related, but not necessarily compatible, research efforts. In each case, the "family resemblance" is based on a shared general conception of how to look at organizations; yet members of the same family may be oriented toward different methods and goals. Thus, we urge the reader to consider the family names as heuristics, or perhaps as loosely-defined perspectives. The four families of emerging research are (1) the information-processing, (2) the rhetorical, (3) the cultural, and (4) the political perspectives. Each is discussed in terms of its actual and potential contribution to organizational communication research.

The Information-Processing Perspective

Treating organizations as information-processing systems has gained widespread appeal outside the speech-communication field. The essence of organizing, in this perspective, is the gathering, transmitting, storing, and using of information (Galbraith, 1973; O'Reilly & Pondy, 1979). Information refers to messages and data, often treated as energy

Table I	PAST RESEARCH PRIORITIES IN ORGANIZATIONAL COMMUNICATION
Era	*Predominant Research Questions*
1940s	What effects do downward directed mass media communications have upon employees?
	Is an informed employee a productive one?
1950s	How do small-group communication networks affect organizational performance and members' attitudes and behaviors?
	What are the relationships between organizational members' attitudes and perceptions of their communication behavior (primarily upward and downward communication) and their on-the-job performance?
	What is the relationship between the attitudes and performance of workers and the feedback they receive?
	Is a well-informed employee a satisfied employee?
1960s	What do organizational members perceive to be the communication correlates of "good" supervision?
	In what ways do actual and perceived communicative behaviors of liaison and nonliaison roles within organizational communication networks differ?
	What is the relationship between subordinates' job-related attitudes and productivity and the extent to which they perceive they participate in decision-making?
1970s	What are the communicative components and correlates of organizational communication climates?
	What are the characteristics and distribution of "key" communication roles within organizational networks?

Reprinted by permission from Fredric M. Jablin, "Past, Present, and Future Research Priorities in Organizational Communication." Revision of a paper presented at the annual convention of the Speech Communication Association, Minneapolis, Minnesota, November 1978.

that reduces uncertainty and aids predictability. Consistent with a systemic view of organizations, information processing pervades all activities, from decision making and control to organizational design and conflict management (Huber, 1982). Initiated by organizational design theorists (Galbraith, 1973), studies of information processing center on microlevel activities, such as communication between work groups, coordination among group members, and the impact of task structure on information flow and on macro-issues, such as decision making and adaptation to organizational environments.

The Rhetorical Perspective

The study of symbolic influence, while only of recent concern to information-processing researchers, has its roots in ancient Greco-Roman writings on rhetoric and persuasion. Today, communication scholars are applying classical and modern rhetorical theory to the study of complex organizations. This section reviews four lines of rhetorically informed organizational research. The first approach, known as "symbolic convergence theory," is being carved out by Ernest G. Bormann (1972, 1982, 1983) and his colleagues at the University of Minnesota. Symbolic convergence theory derives from "fantasy theme" analysis, a form of rhetorical criticism that highlights the way groups construct shared symbolic realities. Fantasy themes are creative and imaginative interpretations of events that are "chained out" in social settings. When a number of fantasy themes merge, they form a "rhetorical vision" that sustains formal and informal groups. Symbolic convergence theory attends to the dramatic aspects—for example, sagas, narratives, heroes, villains, inside jokes—that foster common understandings within work groups, departments, and entire organizations (Cragan & Shields, 1981).

A second rhetorically grounded program, under the direction of Phillip K. Tompkins at Purdue University (Cheney, 1983; Tompkins & Cheney, 1982; P.K. Tompkins, Fisher, Infante & Tompkins, 1975) is tentatively labeled "communication and unobtrusive organizational control." This approach attempts to blend Aristotle's (1954) "enthymeme" and Kenneth Burke's (1969) "identification" to interpret, explain, and critique how organizational members are influenced and controlled. The theory posits two "enthymemic" models: enthymeme, which resembles Aristotle's rhetorical syllogism in that members bring with them to the organization the major premises necessary for making "appropriate" responses through organizationally desired decisions; and enthymeme, where conclusions are drawn from premises inculcated by controlling members of the organization (Tompkins & Cheney, 1982).

A third area, the study of "corporate issue advocacy," has attracted interest at the University of Houston and at Purdue University. Corporate advocacy aims to introduce, change, or reinforce public attitudes on issues of importance to organizations. As a form of purposive "external" organizational communication, corporate advocacy is amenable to analysis through traditional sender-oriented argumentation methods and through contemporary process-oriented approaches.

A final area of rhetorically oriented research draws from the public address literature, but applies it to organizational settings. As businesses increase their participation in public affairs, Knapp (1970) argues for a concomitant growth in the study of "business rhetoric," that is, field research on the public speeches of business executives.

The Cultural Perspective

A more popular approach to the study of organizational communication is known by the catchwords, "organizational cultures." The diversity of ways that organizational culture is examined is not surprising given the ambiguities that surround "culture" itself. Thus, we view the concept's usefulness to organizational study as "a family of concepts" (Pettigrew, 1979, p. 574), rather than as a unitary perspective. As an anthropological concept, culture refers to a social unit's collective sense of what reality is, what it means to be a member of a group, and how a member ought to act. Although students of "organizational culture" approach their subject in a variety of ways, most of them stress the achievement of intersubjective meaning, understanding, and common pursuits among organizational members.

The Political Perspective

The political perspective, as developed in this essay, subsumes a number of diverse yet related orientations to organizational communication; namely, studies of power, politics, conflict, bargaining, and deviance. Drawing from Cyert and March's (1963) view of organizations as political coalitions, this perspective treats organizations as sets of different interest groups, "fractured by subcultures" (Baldridge, 1971, p. 25). In this view decisions emerge through an influence process frequently characterized by compromise and bargaining among groups with competing interests. However, one school within this perspective, critical theory, contends that this competition is not among equals because "dominant coalitions" or power groups control most organizational actions.

PRACTICAL APPLICATIONS OF ORGANIZATIONAL COMMUNICATION RESEARCH

Social scientists and organizational practitioners exist in an inseparable bond that stems from the bridge between theory and practice and from the dual roles of researcher and consultant (Albrow, 1980; Zey-Ferrell & Aiken, 1981). Just as academicians shape practice with theoretical models and research findings, practitioners influence research through sharing their "personal theories" of organizational life. This section examines the links between research and practice with special attention to the history of this relationship, communication training and consulting, organizational communication audits, and implications of the emerging approaches for communication practice.

Organizational communication grew out of a concern for developing managerial skills, improving the effectiveness of various media, and discovering why communication fails (Sexton & Staudt, 1959). Early efforts to address these issues applied simple solutions to complex problems and virtually ignored developments in communication theory (Redding, 1966; Van Voorhis, 1974). In the 1950s communication training, evaluation, and consulting began to flourish. To ascertain the need for these programs, researchers surveyed employees on the amount of time they spent communicating (Klemmer & Snyder, 1972) and on the importance of such skills as listening, persuading, and interviewing for different organizational roles (DiSalvo, Larsen & Seiler, 1976; Hanna, 1978). To understand the nature and extent of organizational training programs, researchers investigated the frequency, content, and materials used in public speaking training (Hicks, 1955; Knapp, 1968, 1969; Zelko, 1951); the importance, goals, and attitudes toward communication training (Wasylik, Sussman, & Leri, 1976); the frequency, targets, and methods of training (Meister & Reinsch, 1978); and the role functions and conflicts of communication trainers and consultants (Putnam, 1979).

Training activities and problem-solving consultation are often combined in practice by organizational trainers. External consultants, who are not members of the organization, serve primarily as ''trouble shooters'' to diagnose problems and determine appropriate intervention techniques. Redding (1979a) defines communication consulting as a broad-ranged ''helping'' activity and indicates that the role requires ''a thorough grounding'' in rhetorical, interpersonal, and mass communication theories. Approximately one-third of 200 respondents in a survey on communication consulting employ intervention techniques associated with organizational development, a system of planned organizational change (Eich, 1977). In a literature review on the role of communication in organizational development, Axley (1980) concludes that the goals of such techniques as team building, process consultation, T-groups, and participatory decision making include improving communication, without careful attention to the repercussions these improvements will have on other organizational behaviors.

The organizational communication audit, as a type of consulting, provides an evaluation of a corporation's entire communication system. Initiated by Odiorne (1954) as a concept for the study of information flow, the communication audit now refers to a multi-instrument procedure for collecting, analyzing, and feeding back data on communication climate, networks, media usage, information flow, and communication satisfaction (Goldhaber et al., 1978; Goldhaber & Rogers, 1979). Audit systems provide standardized data-gathering techniques and a normative data bank for comparison of research results. The International Communication Audit represents a joint effort of over 100 scholars ''to provide organizations with reliable, factual data about their internal communication'' (Greenbaum, Hellweg & Falcione, 1983, p. 89). Richetto (1977) recaps the history of this process, and Greenbaum et al. (1983) present a very comprehensive review of studies that evaluate organizational communication systems, including research that employs the ICA Audit and the Organizational Communication Development audit developed in Finland under the leadership of Osmo Wiio (Wiio, Goldhaber & Yates, 1980). As of 1979 researchers and practitioners had administered the ICA Audit to over 5,000 employees in 19 organizations.

In many respects, theory and practice in organizational communication have taken diverse turns. Emerging areas of theory and research appear less concerned with problems that managers face and more concerned with understanding the complexities of organizational life. Communication trainers who adhere to emerging approaches might concentrate less on media usage and presentational skills and more on developing problem-solving skills for analyzing messages and organizational symbols (Smircich, 1983b). As Johnson and Shaw (1978) propose, ''consultant-heroes,'' as opposed to ''trainer technicians,'' deal in ideas, inspire clients to think, strive for impartiality, and have a vision for what is being done and why. From the political perspective, organizational members would need to intensify their training in bargaining and strategic decision making (Tushman, 1977).

Communication consulting, while primarily a tool of management, might be used for organizational reflection to expose repressive actions and unnecessary bureaucratic controls. While it is unlikely that consultants will become critical theorists, they might increase their awareness of the political implications of their interventions (Tushman, 1977; Browning, 1977); the value and ethical dilemmas of consulting (Redding, 1979a); and the managerial bias inherent in projects commissioned and directed by "elite" organizational members (Zey-Ferrell & Aiken, 1981).

CONCLUSION

What we have tried to do in this review is to paint, with broad strokes, a "mural" of organizational communication as a subunit of the speech communication field. We have depicted the emergence of "organizational communication" as an identifiable area of study—how it has borrowed from other fields and how its research foci have shifted during its short history. Because of the nature of this effort, we have had to organize and "color" bodies of research in ways that may make them seem too sharply distinguished; indeed a "true" painting of organizational communication would be rather impressionistic. Nevertheless, we have offered what we think is a useful schema for viewing the field now.

As organizational communication progresses, we expect it to follow the strong lines already being sketched in the 1980s. Organizational communication researchers will probably emphasize message content and process even more, striving to capture meaning, context, and changes in symbolic activity among organizational actors. We see researchers continuing to explore to a much greater extent the multiple perspectives of organizational actors, rather than looking at the world solely through a managerial lens. . . . Along similar lines, we anticipate that the meaning of "practice" or "application" will continue to broaden, as researchers attempt not only to help "the organization" (that is, upper management) but also individuals and groups within it, often through critique of the existing order. . . . We expect that researchers will continue to employ a pluralism of methods in order to view organizational life from a variety of angles. . . . and perhaps most important for the student of organizational commu-

nication, we anticipate that the field will eventually move toward a clearer image of itself, a coherent identity embracing preferred concepts, theories, methods, and interventions.

REFERENCES

Albrecht. T.L. (1979). The role of communication in perceptions of organizational climate. In D. Nimmo (Ed.), *Communication yearbook 3.* New Brunswick, N.J.: ICA / Transaction Books.

Albrecht, T. L., & Ropp, V. A. (1982). The study of network structuring in organizations through the use of method triangulation. *WJSC, 46,* 162–178.

Albrow, M. (1980). The dialectic of science and values in the study of organizations. In G. Salaman and K. Thompson (Eds.), *Control and ideology in organizations.* Cambridge, Mass.: MIT Press.

Aristotle. (1954). [*The rhetoric & poetics*] (W. R. Roberts, trans.). New York: Modern Library.

Athanassiades, J. C. (1973). The distortion of upward communication in hierarchical organizations. *AMJ, 16,* 207–226.

Axley, S. R. (1980, May). *Communication's role in organizational change: A review of relevant literature.* Paper presented at the annual conference of the International Communication Association, Acapulco.

Axley, S. R. (1983, May). *Managerial philosophy in organizational house organs: Two case studies.* Paper presented at the annual conference of the ICA, Dallas.

Baldridge, J. V. (1971). *Power and conflict in the university.* New York: Wiley.

Barnard, C. (1938). *The functions of the executive.* Cambridge, Mass.: Harvard University Press.

Bavelas, A. (1950). Communication patterns in task-oriented groups. *Acoustical Society of America Journal, 22,* 727–730.

Beach, B. (1950). Employee magazines build morale. *Personnel Journal, 29,* 216–220.

Blau, P. M. (1954). Patterns of interaction among a group of officials in a government agency. *HR, 7,* 337–348.

Bormann, E. G. (1972). Fantasy and rhetorical vision: The rhetorical criticism of social reality. *QJS, 58,* 396–407.

Bormann, E. G. (1982). Symbolic convergence theory of communication: Applications and implications for teachers and consultants. *JACR, 10,* 50–61.

Bormann, E. G. (1983). Symbolic convergence: Organizational communication and culture. In L. L. Putnam

& M. E. Pacanowsky (Eds.), *Communication and organization: An interpretive approach.* Beverly Hills: Sage.

Boyd, B. B., & Jensen, J. M. (1972). Perceptions of the first-line supervisor's authority: A study in superior-subordinate communication. *AMJ, 15,* 331–342.

Bradley, P. H. (1978). Power, status, and upward communication in small decision-making groups. *CM, 45,* 35–43.

Bradley, P. H., & Baird, J. E., Jr. (1977). Management and communicator style: A correlational analysis. *CSSJ, 28,* 194–203.

Bradley, P. H., & Baird, J. E., Jr. (1980). *Communication for business and the professions.* Dubuque, Iowa: William C. Brown.

Browning, L. (1977, December). *Applied communication within our field: The politics of change.* Paper presented at the annual meeting of the SCA, Washington, D.C.

Burke, K. (1969). *A rhetoric of motives.* Berkeley: University of California Press.

Cheney, G. (1983). The rhetoric of identification and the study of organizational communication. *QJS, 69,* 143–158.

Cohen, A. R. (1959). Situational structure, self-esteem, and threat-oriented reactions to power. In D. Cartwright (Ed.), *Studies in social power.* Ann Arbor: Institute for Social Research.

Collins, G. R. (1924). Public speaking in colleges of Business Administration and United YMCA Schools. *QJSE, 10,* 374–379.

Cragan, J. F., & Shields, D. C. (1981). *Applied communication research: A dramatistic approach.* Prospect Heights, Ill.: Waveland Press.

Cusella, L. P. (1982). The effects of source expertise and feedback valence on intrinsic motivation. *HCR, 9,* 17–32.

Cusella, L. P. On the need for conceptual authenticity in organizational communication research. *CQ,* in press.

Cyert, R. M., & March, J. G. (1963). *A behavioral theory of the firm.* Englewood Cliffs, N.J.: Prentice-Hall.

Dahle, T. L. (1954). An objective and comparative study of five methods for transmitting information to business and industrial employees. *SM, 21,* 21–28.

Daly, J. A., McCroskey, J. C., & Falcione, R. A. (1976, April). *Communication apprehension, supervisor communication receptivity and satisfaction with supervisors.* Paper presented at the annual convention of the ECA, Philadelphia.

Danowski, J. A. (1980). Group attitude uniformity and connectivity of organizational communication networks for production, innovation, and maintenance content. *HCR, 6,* 299–308.

Danowski, J. A. (1983, May). *Automated network analysis: A survey of different approaches to the analysis of human communication relationships.* Paper presented at the annual conference of the ICA, Dallas.

Davis, K. (1953). Management communication and the grapevine. *HBR, 31,* 43–49.

Davis, K. (1978). Methods for studying informal communication. *JC, 28,* 112–116.

Dennis, H. S., Goldhaber, G. M., & Yates, M. P. (1978). Organizational communication theory and research: An overview of research methods. In B. D. Ruben (Ed.), *Communication yearbook 2.* New Brunswick, N.J.: ICA / Transaction Books.

Derry, J. O. (1969). *The effects of a public relations speech on five Chicago audiences.* Unpublished master's thesis, University of Wisconsin-Milwaukee.

DiSalvo, V., Larsen, D. C., & Seiler, W. J. (1976). Communication skills needed by persons in business organizations. *CE, 25,* 269–275.

Dover, C. J. (1959). The three eras of management communication. *JC, 9,* 168–172.

Downs, C., Berg, D., & Linkugel, W. (1977). *The organizational communicator.* New York: Harper & Row.

Downs, C. W., & Hazen, M. D. (1977). A factor analytic study of communication satisfaction. *JBC, 14,* 63–73.

Eich, R. K. (1977). *Organizational communication consulting: A descriptive study of consulting practices and prescriptions.* Unpublished doctoral dissertation, University of Michigan.

Eilon, S. (1968). Taxonomy of communications. *ASQ, 13,* 266–288.

Ellis, D. G. (1979). Relational control in two group systems. *CM, 46,* 153–166.

Erbe, W. (1962). Gregariousness, group membership, and the flow of information. *AJS, 67,* 502–516.

Falcione, R. L., & Werner, E. (1978, April). *Organizational climate and communication climate: A state-of-the-art.* Paper presented at the annual conference of the ICA, Chicago.

Farace, R. V., & MacDonald, D. (1974). New directions in the study of organizational communication. *PP, 27,* 1–15.

Farace, R. V., Monge, P. R., & Russell, H. M. (1977). *Communicating and organizing.* Reading, Mass.: Addison-Wesley.

Festinger, L. (1950). Informal social communication. *Psychological Review, 57,* 271–282.

Fisher, R. M. (1965). Modern business speaking: A rhetoric of conventional wisdom. *SSJ, 30,* 326–327.

Fowler, G. D., & Wackerbarth, M. E. (1980). Audio teleconferencing versus face-to-face conferencing: A synthesis of the literature. *WJSC, 44,* 236–252.

Galbraith, J. R. (1973). *Designing complex organizations.* Reading, Mass.: Addison-Wesley.

Giddens, A. (1979). *Central problems in social theory.* Berkeley: University of California Press.

Given, W. (1949). *Bottom-up management.* New York: Harper.

Goldhaber, G. M., & Rogers, D. P. (1979). *Auditing organizational communication systems: The ICA communication audit.* Dubuque, Iowa: Kendall/Hunt.

Goldhaber, G. M., Yates, M. P., Porter, D. T., & Lesniak, R. (1978). Organizational communication: 1978 *HCR, 5,* 76–96.

Greenbaum, H. M., Hellweg, S. A., & Falcione, R. L. (1983, May). *Evaluation of communication in organizations: An analysis of current and past methodologies.* Paper presented at the annual conference of the ICA, Dallas.

Guetzkow, H. (1965). Communication in organizations. In J. G. March (Ed.), *Handbook of organizations.* Chicago: Rand McNally.

Haney, W. V. (1973). *Communication and organizational behavior.* Homewood, Ill.: Richard D. Irwin.

Hanna, M. S. (1978). Speech communication training needs in the business community. *CSSJ, 29,* 163–172.

Hawes, L. C. (1974). Social collectivities as communication: Perspectives on organizational behavior. *QJS, 60,* 497–502.

Hay, R. D. (1974). A brief history of internal organizational communication through the 1940's. *JBC, 11,* 6–11.

Heron, A. (1942). *Sharing information with employees.* Palo Alto, Calif.: Stanford University Press.

Hicks, M. A. (1955). Speech training in business and industry. *JC, 5,* 161–168.

Hintz, R. A., & Couch, C. J. (1978). Mediated messages and social coordination. *JC, 28,* 117–123.

Hoffman, W. G. (1923). *Public speaking for business men.* New York: McGraw-Hill.

Howell, W. S., & Bormann, E. G. (1971). *Presentational speaking for business and the professions.* New York: Harper & Row.

Huber, G. (1982). Organizational information systems: Determinants of their performance and behavior. *Management Science, 28,* 138–155.

Infante, D. A., & Gordon, W. I. (1979). Subordinate and superior perceptions of self and one another: Relations, accuracy and reciprocity of liking. *WJSC, 43,* 212–223.

Ireland, R. D., Van Auken, P. M., & Lewis, P. V. (1978). An investigation of the relationship between organization climate and communication climate. *JBC, 16,* 3–10.

Irwin, J. V., & Brockhaus, H. H. (1963). The 'Teletalk project': A study of the effectiveness of two public relations speeches. *SM, 30,* 359–368.

Jablin, F. M. (1978). Message-response and "openness" in superior-subordinate communication. In B. D. Ruben (Ed.), *Communication yearbook 2.* New Brunswick, N.J.: ICA / Transaction Books. (a)

Jablin, F. M. (1978, November). *Research priorities in organizational communication.* Paper presented at the annual meeting of the SCA, Minneapolis. (b)

Jablin, F. M. (1979). Superior-subordinate communication: The state of the art. *Psychological Bulletin, 86,* 1201–1222.

Jablin, F. M. (1980). Organizational communication theory and research: An overview of communication climate and network research. In D. Nimmo (Ed.), *Communication yearbook 4.* New Brunswick, N.J.: ICA / Transaction Books. (a)

Jablin, F. M. (1980). Superior's upward influence, satisfaction, and openness in superior-subordinate communication: A reexamination of the "Pelz Effect." *HCR, 6,* 210–220. (b)

Jablin, F. M. (1982). Formal structural characteristics of organizations and superior-subordinate communication. *HCR, 8,* 338–347.

Jacobson, E., & Seashore, S. (1951). Communication practices in complex organizations. *Journal of Social Issues, 7,* 28–40.

Johnson, B. M., & Shaw, M. R. (1978, November). *Preparing the communication consultant.* Paper presented at the annual meeting of the SCA, Minneapolis.

Katz, D., & Kahn, R. L. (1978). *The social psychology of organizations* (2nd ed.). New York: Wiley.

Kelly, L. (1982, May). *A critical review of the literature on superior-subordinate communication.* Paper presented at the annual conference of the ICA, Boston.

Klemmer, E. T., & Snyder, F. W. (1972). Measurement of time spent communicating, *JC, 22,* 142–158.

Knapp, M. L. (1968). Public speaking in business and industry: Policies, publications, and publicity. *JBC, 5,* 3–10.

Knapp, M. L. (1969). Public speaking training programs in American business and industrial organizations. *ST, 18,* 129–134.

Knapp, M. L. (1970). Business rhetoric: Opportunity for research in speech. *SSJ, 35,* 244–255.

Koehler, J. W., Anatol, K. W. E., & Applbaum, R. L.

(1981). *Organizational communication: Behavioral perspectives* (2nd ed.). New York: Holt.

Lazarsfeld, P., Berelson, B., & Gaudet, H. (1948). *The people's choice.* New York: Columbia University Press.

Leavitt, H. J. (1951). Some effects of certain communication patterns on group performance. *Journal of Abnormal and Social Psychology, 46,* 38–50.

Lewin, K. (1951). *Field theory in social science.* New York: Harper.

Litwin, G., & Stringer, R. (1968). *Motivation and organizational climate.* Cambridge, Mass.: Harvard University Press.

MacDonald, D. (1976). Communication roles and communication networks in a formal organization. *HCR, 2,* 365–375.

Mahoney, T. A. (1954). How management communicates with employees. *Personnel, 31,* 109–114.

McGregor, D. (1960). *The human side of enterprise.* New York: McGraw-Hill.

McMurray, R. N. (1965). Clear communication for chief executives. *HBR, 43,* 131–147.

Meister, J. E., & Reinsch, N. L., Jr. (1978). Communication training in manufacturing firms. *CE, 27,* 235–244.

Miller, J. G. (1960). Information input, overload, and psychopathology. *American Journal of Psychiatry, 116,* 695–704.

Monge, P. R. (1982). Systems theory and research in the study of organizational communication: The correspondence problem. *HCR, 8,* 245–261.

Monge, P. R., Edwards, J. A., & Kiriste, K. K. (1978). The determinants of communication and communication structure in large organizations: A review of research. In B. Ruben (Ed.), *Communication yearbook 2.* New Brunswick, N.J.: ICA / Transaction Books.

Moreno, J. L. (1953). *Who shall survive? Foundations of sociometry, group psychotherapy and sociodrama.* New York: Beacon House.

Muchinsky, P. M. (1977). An intraorganizational analysis of the Roberts and O'Reilly organizational communication questionnaire. *JAP, 62,* 184–188.

Odiorne, G. (1954). An application of the communication audit. *PP, 1,* 235–243.

O'Reilly, C. A. (1978). The intentional distortion of information in organizational communication: A laboratory and field investigation. *HR, 31,* 173–193.

O'Reilly, C. A. (1980). Individuals and information overload in organizations: Is more necessarily better? *AMJ, 23,* 684–696.

O'Reilly, C. A., & Anderson, J. C. (1980). Trust and the communication of performance appraisal information: The effect of feedback on performance and job satisfaction. *HCR, 6,* 290–298.

O'Reilly, C. A., & Pondy, L. R. (1979). Organizational communication. In S. Kerr (Ed.), *Organizational behavior.* Columbus, Ohio: Grid.

O'Reilly, C. A., & Roberts, K. H. (1974). Information filtration in organization: Three experiments. *Organizational Behavior and Human Performance, 11,* 253–265.

Paterson, D., & Jenkins, J. (1948). Communication between management and workers. *JAP, 32,* 71–80.

Pelz, D. C. (1952). Influence: A key to effective leadership in the first-line supervisor. *Personnel, 29,* 3–11.

Peters, R. W. (1950). *Communication within industry.* New York: Harper & Row.

Pettigrew, A. M. (1979). On studying organizational cultures. *ASQ, 24,* 570–581.

Pfeffer, J. (1981). Management as symbolic action: The creation and maintenance of organizational paradigms. In L. L. Cummings and B. M. Staw (Eds.), *Research in Organizational Behavior* (Vol. 3). Greenwich, Conn.: JAI Press.

Pietri, P. H. (1974). Organizational communication: The pioneers, *JBC, 11,* 3–6.

Pigors, P. (1949). *Effective communication in industry.* New York: National Association of Manufacturers.

Plain, H. G. (1980, May). *Computer-linked memo systems, expectations and utilization: A case study.* Paper presented at the annual conference of the ICA, Acapulco.

Planty, E., & Machaver, W. (1952). Upward communications: A project in executive development using the syndicate method. *Personnel, 28,* 304–318.

Poole, M. S., & McPhee, R. D. (1983). A structurational analysis of organizational climate. In L. L. Putnam & M. E. Pacanowsky (Eds.), *Communication and organization: An interpretive approach.* Beverly Hills: Sage.

Porter, L. W., & Roberts, K. H. (1976). Communication in organizations. In M. D. Dunnette (Ed.), *Handbook of industrial and organizational psychology.* Chicago: Rand McNally.

Porterfield, C. D. (1974). Organizational communication: Developments from 1960 to the present. *JBC, 11,* 18–24.

Putnam, L. L. (1979). Role functions and role conflicts of communication trainers. *JBC, 17,* 37–52.

Putnam, L. L. (1982). Paradigms for organizational communication research: An overview and synthesis. *WJSC, 46,* 192–206. (a)

Putnam, L. L. (1982, April). *Understanding the unique characteristics of groups within organizations*. Paper presented at the Conference on Research in Small Group Communication, State College, Pa. (b)

Putnam, L. L. (1983). Organizational communication amendment. *Spectra, 19,* 1–2. (a)

Putnam, L. L. (1983). The interpretive perspective: An alternative to functionalism. In L. L. Putnam & M. E. Pacanowsky (Eds.), *Communication and organization: An interpretive approach*. Beverly Hills: Sage. (b)

Putnam, L. L., & Cheney, G. (1983). A critical review of research traditions in organizational communication. In M. Mander (Ed.), *Communication in transition*. New York: Praeger.

Read, W. H. (1962). Upward communication in industrial hierarchies. *HR, 15,* 3–15.

Redding, W. C. (1966). The empirical study of human communication in business and industry. In P. E. Reid (Ed.), *The frontiers in speech-communication research*. Syracuse: Syracuse University Press.

Redding, W. C. (1972). *Communication within the organization: An interpretive review of theory and research*. New York: Industrial Communication Council, Inc.

Redding, W. C. (1979). Graduate education and the communication consultant: Playing God for a fee. *CE, 28,* 346–352. (a)

Redding, W. C. (1979). Organizational communication theory and ideology: An overview. In D. Nimmo (Ed.), *Communication yearbook 3*. New Brunswick, N.J.: ICA / Transaction Books. (b)

Rice, R. E. (1982). Communication networking in computer-conferencing systems: A longitudinal study of group roles and system structure. In M. Burgoon (Ed.), *Communication yearbook 6*. Beverly Hills: Sage. (a)

Rice, R. E. (1982). *Human communication networking in a teleconferencing environment*. Unpublished doctoral dissertation, Stanford University. (b)

Richards, W. D. (1974, May). *Network analysis in large complex systems: Techniques and methods—tools*. Paper presented at the annual conference of the ICA, New Orleans. (a)

Richards, W. D. (1974, May). *Network analysis in large complex systems: Theoretical basis*. Paper presented at the annual conference of the ICA, New Orleans. (b)

Richetto, G. M. (1977). Organizational communication theory and research: An overview. In B. D. Ruben (Ed.), *Communication yearbook 1*. New Brunswick, N.J.: ICA / Transaction Books.

Richmond, V. P., & McCroskey, J. C. (1979). Management communication style, tolerance for disagreement, and innovativeness as predictors of employee satisfaction: A comparison of single-factor, two-factor, and multiple-factor approaches. In D. Nimmo (Ed.), *Communication yearbook 3*. New Brunswick, N.J.: ICA / Transaction Books.

Richmond, V. P., McCroskey, J. C., & Davis, L. M. (1982). Individual differences among employees, management communication style, and employee satisfaction: Replication and extension. *HCR, 8,* 170–188.

Roberts, K. H., & O'Reilly, C. A. (1974). Failures in upward communication in organizations: Three possible culprits. *AMJ, 17,* 205–215. (a)

Roberts, K. H., & O'Reilly, C. A. (1974). Measuring organizational communication. *JAP, 59,* 321–326. (b)

Roberts, K. H., & O'Reilly, C. A. (1978). Organizations as communication structures. *HCR, 4,* 283–293.

Roberts, K., O'Reilly, C., Bretton, G. E., & Porter, L. (1974). Organizational theory and organizational communication: A communication failure. *HR, 27,* 501–524.

Roethlisberger, F. J., & Dickson, W. J. (1939). *Management and the worker*. Cambridge, Mass.: Harvard University Press.

Rogers, E. M. (1962). *Diffusion of innovations*. New York: Free Press.

Rogers, E. M., & Agarwala-Rogers, R. (1976). *Communication in organizations*. New York: Free Press.

Sanborn, G. A. (1961). *An analytical study of oral communication practices in a nationwide retail sales organization*. Unpublished doctoral dissertation, Purdue University.

Sanborn, G. A. (1964). Communication in business: An overview. In W. C. Redding & G. A. Sanborn (Eds.), *Business and industrial communication: A source book*. New York: Harper & Row.

Sanford, W. P. & Yeager, W. H. (1929). *Business and professional speaking*. New York: McGraw-Hill.

Schwartz, M. M., Stark, H. F., & Schiffman, H. R. (1970). Responses of union and management leaders to emotionally toned industrial relations terms. *PP, 23,* 361–367.

Sexton, R., & Staudt, V. (1959). Business communication: A survey of the literature. *Journal of Social Psychology, 50,* 101–118.

Shaw, M. (1964). Communication networks. In L. Berkowitz (Ed.), *Advances in experimental social psychology* (Vol. 1). New York: Academic Press.

Smircich, L. (1983). Implications for management theory. In L. L. Putnam & M. E. Pacanowsky (Eds.), *Communication and organization: An interpretive approach.* Beverly Hills: Sage.

Smircich, L., & Chesser, R. J. (1981). Superiors' and subordinates' perceptions of performance: Beyond disagreement. *AMJ, 24,* 198–205.

Spiker, B. K., & Daniels, T. D. (1981). Information adequacy and communication relationships: An empirical examination of 18 organizations. *WJSC, 45,* 342–354.

Thayer, L. O. (1961). *Administrative communication.* Homewood, Ill.: Richard D. Irwin.

Thayer, L. O. (1967). Communication and organization theory. In F. Dance (Ed.), *Human communication theory.* New York: Holt.

Tichy, N. M., Tushman, M. L., & Fombrun, C. (1979). Social network analysis for organizations. *Academy of Management Review, AMR, 4,* 507–519.

Tompkins, P. K. (1962). *An analysis of communication between headquarters and selected units of a national labor union.* Unpublished doctoral dissertation, Purdue University.

Tompkins, P. K. (1967). Organizational communication: A state-of-the-art review. In G. Richetto (Ed.), *Conference on organizational communication.* Huntsville, Ala.: George C. Marshall Space Flight Center, NASA.

Tompkins, P. K. (1977). Management qua communication in rocket research and development. *CM, 44,* 1–26.

Tompkins, P. K. (1978). Organizational metamorphosis in space research and development. *CM, 45,* 110–118.

Tompkins, P. K. (1984). Functions of communication in organizations. In C. Arnold & J. W. Bowers (Eds.), *Handbook of rhetorical and communication theory.* New York: Allyn & Bacon.

Tompkins, P. K., & Cheney, G. (1982, November). *Toward a theory of unobtrusive control in contemporary organizations.* Paper presented at the annual meeting of the SCA, Louisville, Ky.

Tompkins, P. K., Fisher, J. Y., Infante, D. A., & Tompkins, E. V. (1975). Kenneth Burke and the inherent characteristics of formal organizations. *SM, 42,* 135–142.

Triandis, H. C. (1959). Categories of thought, of managers, clerks, and workers about jobs and people in an industry. *JAP, 43,* 338–344. (a)

Triandis, H. C. (1959). Cognitive similarity and interpersonal communication in industry. *JAP, 43,* 321–326. (b)

Trujillo, N. (1983). ''Performing'' Mintzberg's roles: The nature of managerial communication. In L. Putnam & M. Pacanowsky (Eds.), *Communication and organization: An interpretive approach.* Beverly Hills: Sage.

Tushman, M. L. (1977). Special boundary roles in the innovation process. *ASQ, 22,* 587–605.

Tushman, M. L., & Scanlan, T. J. (1981). Boundary spanning individuals: Their role in information transfer and their antecedents. *AMJ, 24,* 289–305. (a)

Tushman, M. L., & Scanlan, T. J. (1981). Characteristics and external orientations of boundary spanning individuals. *AMJ, 24,* 83–98. (b)

Van Voorhis, K. R. (1974). Organizational communication: Advances made during the period from WW II through the 1950s. *JBC, 11,* 11–18.

Wasylik, J. E., Sussman, L., & Leri, R. P. (1976). Communication training as perceived by training personnel. *CQ, 24,* 32–38.

Watson, K. (1982). A methodology for the study of organizational behavior at the interpersonal level of analysis. *AMR, 7,* 392–402. (a)

Watson, K. M. (1982). An analysis of communication patterns: A method for discriminating leader and subordinate roles. *AMJ, 25,* 107–120. (b)

Weaver, C. H. (1958). The quantification of the frame of reference in labor-management communication. *JAP, 42,* 1–9.

Webber, R. A. (1970). Perceptions of interactions between superiors and subordinates. *HR, 23,* 235–248.

Weick, K. (1979). *The social psychology of organizing* (2nd ed.). Reading, Mass.: Addison-Wesley.

Wiio, O. A., Goldhaber, G. M., & Yates, M. P. (1980). Organizational communication research: Time for reflection? In D. Nimmo (Ed.), *Communication yearbook 4.* New Brunswick, N.J.: ICA / Transaction Books.

Williams, F., & Sundene, B. (1965). A field study in effects of a public relations speech. *JC, 15,* 161–170.

Zelko, H. P. (1951). Adult speech training: Challenge to the speech profession. *QJS, 37,* 55–62.

Zelko, H. P. (1953). Information racks: New frontier in industrial communication. *Management Review, 42,* 75–76.

Zelko, H. P., & Dance, F. E. X. (1965). *Business and professional speech communication.* New York: Holt.

Zey-Ferrell, M., & Aiken, M. (1981). Introduction to critiques of dominant perspectives. In M. Zey-Ferrell & M. Aiken (Eds.), *Complex organizations: Critical perspectives.* Glenview, Ill.: Scott, Foresman.

2 PERSPECTIVES

When focusing attention on one thing, you are not attending to something else. This is a truism of our everyday life—a truism reinforced by those times we have been "blind-sided" by events because we were attending to problems in the other direction. It is also a truism that underlies the study of organizations. In approaching organizations we adopt *perspectives*—the perspective of a particular theory, the perspective of management, the perspective of a customer, the perspective of an economic theory (e.g., capitalism). In adopting a perspective, we become sensitive to certain aspects of an organization, but we also become insensitive to other aspects.

In an obvious example, if you approach an organization from a customer's point of view, you are less likely to be concerned about the organization's profit than about your own finances (when was the last time you felt you should pay an extra 10% for a hamburger just to help out McDonald's?). On the other hand, if you are a member of a cooperative organization (one in which the customers are the owners—e.g., large farm cooperatives like Land-O-Lakes—the people who make all that butter), your perspective as an owner-member-customer will focus your attention on both sides of the customer-company transaction.

We approach any organization we study from a point of view; that is, we take a perspective on organizations that helps define what we see and do not see when we study organizations. In everyday life, those perspectives are often taken for granted (we assume a perspective without much conscious thought). But when studying an organization, we should adopt a perspective more consciously since a perspective will profoundly affect our practical, theoretical, methodological, and even philosophical assumptions.

The Corman article in Part I demonstrated how general communication theories can help shape a person's view of communication. This section focuses on how specific perspectives on organizations shape a person's understanding of organizations. We present six different perspectives on organizations, beginning with classical theory and concluding with critical theory. There is a great deal of consensus as to the importance of at least four of these perspectives—classical, human relations, systems, and organizational culture—while there is less consensus about the remaining two—Weick's theory and critical theory. We present all six approaches here so you have the opportunity to study both the more established and the less established perspectives.

The perspectives are ordered historically, by the sequence in which they assumed importance in organizational studies. We start with classical theory developed at the end of the nineteenth century and the beginning of the twentieth century and begin with famous articles by Taylor and Follett, followed by a more recent but equally famous chapter by Bernard, and close with a contemporary essay by Booth.

The second group of articles focuses on human relations theories of organization, which were stimulated by the Hawthorne studies in the 1920s. Roethlisberger's chapter explicitly discusses the nature of communication and illustrates the shift from classical theory's view of people as parts of mechanisms to an emphasis on *humans* in organizations. That emphasis on human beings is also exemplified by Herzberg's article, as he presents his two-factor theory of motivation, and by Roy's ethnographic account of how production workers informally organize their time and social relations.

The third perspective on organizations, systems theory, became dominant in the 1960s with the publication of Katz and Kahn's *The Social Psychology of Organizations*. We include here a chapter from the second edition (1978) as well as Hardin's (1970) pointed illustration of systems principles.

In 1969, Karl Weick published the *Social Psychology of Organizing,* titled to contrast *organizing* with Katz and Kahn's emphasis on *organizations*. By focusing on *organizing* as an activity, Weick offered scholars a creative and unique approach to organizations. To illustrate his approach, we include both a chapter from the second edition of the *Social Psychology of Organizing* (1979) and Bantz's explication and application of Weick's perspective.

In the late 1970s, studying organizations as cultures emerged and became popular in many disciplines. Pacanowsky and O'Donnell-Trujillo published the first article presenting a cultural method for studying organizational communication. By studying two rock bands, Scheibel illustrates how analyzing organizational cultures provides a rich interpretation of organizational life.

Critical theory, while of importance in other disciplines for more than 30 years, has assumed importance in the study of organizational communication only in the 1980s. Stephen Banks' essay takes on the task of explaining critical theory and illustrating its use in organizational analysis.

In each of these sections we present readings that illustrate the basic perspective and its application. In reading the selections, look for the assumptions that the writer makes about the purpose of organizations, the role of management and workers in organizations, the role of an outsider observer/consultant in organizations, whether organizations can be changed by their members, whether or how an organization connects to other organizations, and, most importantly, what the role of communication is in that perspective.

When you answer these questions, also consider what is being excluded in each of the perspectives. For example, if you note that classical theory places management in a particularly important position, is someone else placed in a particularly unimportant position?

5 THE PRINCIPLES OF SCIENTIFIC MANAGEMENT
FREDERICK W. TAYLOR

In general, classical views of organization and organizational communication present a very idealized and rational perspective. Frederick Winslow Taylor's "scientific management" approach to organizational behavior at first appears to foster just such a mechanistic view of workers who can be tuned up like machines for the dastardly purpose of increasing productivity, all to the benefit of factory owners. This common interpretation of Taylor's work is understandable, in light of his efforts to improve production processes through "time and motion" studies. However, Taylor's view of worker motivation and his objectives for instituting scientific management are theoretically grounded in a search for economic gains for *both* labor and management, coupled with improved job relationships and working conditions—a very modern sentiment.

Although Taylor is often labeled the "father of scientific management," several contradictions in this essay highlight the key conceptual problems in the classical approach that led later theorists to investigate other approaches to understanding organizational behavior. For example, what are Taylor's claims about the benefits and beneficiaries of scientific management, and how are these claims borne out in the examples he presents? What role do Taylor's economic ideas play in giving scientific management a theoretical foundation, and how are those ideas manifested in his view of the work process and worker motivation?

By far the most important fact which faces the industries of our country, the industries, in fact, of the civilized world, is that not only the average worker, but nineteen out of twenty workmen throughout the civilized world firmly believe that it is for their best interests to go slow instead of to go fast. They firmly believe that it is for their interest to give as little work in return for the money that they get as is practical. The reasons for this belief are two-fold, and I do not believe that the workingmen are to blame for holding these fallacious views.

If you will take any set of workmen in your own town and suggest to those men that it would be a good thing for them in their trade if they were to double their output in the coming year, each man turn out twice as much work and become twice as efficient, they would say, "I do not know anything about other people's trades; what you are saying about increasing efficiency being a good thing may be good for other trades, but I know that the only result if you come to our trade would be that half of us would be out of a job before the year was out." That to the average workingman is an axiom; it is not a matter subject to debate at all. And even among the average business men of this country that opinion is almost universal. They firmly believe that

Adapted from Frederick Taylor, "The Principles of Scientific Management." Reprinted from *The Bulletin of the Taylor Society*, II, 5, December 1916, 13–23. Copyright 1916 by The Taylor Society.

that would be the result of a great increase in efficiency, and yet directly the opposite is true.

THE EFFECT OF LABOR-SAVING DEVICES

Whenever any labor-saving device of any kind has been introduced into any trade—go back into the history of any trade and see it—even though that labor-saving device may turn out ten, twenty, thirty times that output that was originally turned out by men in that trade, the result has universally been to make work for more men in that trade, not work for less men.

Let me give you one illustration. Let us take one of the staple businesses, the cotton industry. About 1840 the power loom succeeded the old hand loom in the cotton industry. It was invented many years before, somewhere about 1780 or 1790, but it came in very slowly. About 1840 the weavers of Manchester, England, saw that the power loom was coming, and they knew it would turn out three times the yardage of cloth in a day that the hand loom turned out. And what did they do, these five thousand weavers of Manchester, England, who saw starvation staring them in the face? They broke into the establishments into which those machines were being introduced, they smashed them, they did everything possible to stop the introduction of the power loom. And the same result followed that follows every attempt to interfere with the introduction of any labor-saving device, if it is really a labor-saving device. Instead of stopping the introduction of the power loom, their opposition apparently accelerated it, just as opposition to scientific management all over the country, bitter labor opposition today, is accelerating the introduction of it instead of retarding it. History repeats itself in that respect. The power loom came right straight along.

And let us see the result in Manchester. Just what follows in every industry when any labor-saving device is introduced. Less than a century has gone by since 1840. The population of England in that time has not more than doubled. Each man in the cotton industry in Manchester, England, now turns out, at a restricted estimate ten yards of cloth for every yard of cloth that was turned out in 1840. In 1840 there were 5,000 weavers in Manchester. Now there are 265,000. Has that thrown men out of work? Has the introduction of labor-saving machinery, which has multiplied the output per man by tenfold, thrown men out of work?

What is the real meaning of this? All that you have to do is to bring wealth into this world and the world uses it. That is the real meaning. The meaning is that where in 1840 cotton goods were a luxury to be worn only by rich people when they were hardly ever seen on the street, now every man, woman and child all over the world wears cotton goods as a daily necessity.

Nineteen-twentieths of the real wealth of this world is used by the poor people, and not the rich, so that the workingman who sets out as a steady principle to restrict output is merely robbing his own kind. That group of manufacturers which adopts as a permanent principle restriction of output, in order to hold up prices, is robbing the world. The one great thing that marks the improvement of this world is measured by the enormous increase in output of the individuals in this world. There is fully twenty times the output per man now that there was three hundred years ago. That marks the increase in the real wealth of the world; that marks the increase of the happiness of the world, that gives us the opportunity for shorter hours, for better education, for amusement, for art, for music, for everything that is worthwhile in this world—and it all goes right straight back to this increase in the output of the individual. The workingmen of today live better than the king did three hundred years ago. From what does the progress the world has made come? Simply from the increase in the output of the individual all over the world.

THE DEVELOPMENT OF SOLDIERING

The second reason why the workmen of this country and of Europe deliberately restrict output is a very simple one. They, for this reason, are even less to blame than they are for the other. If, for example, you are manufacturing a pen, let us assume for simplicity that a pen can be made by a single man. Let us say that the workman is turning out ten pens per day, and that he is receiving $2.50 a day for his wages. He has a progressive foreman who is up to date, and that foreman goes to the workman and suggests, "Here, John, you are getting $2.50 a day, and you are turning out ten pens. I would suggest that I pay you 25 cents for making that pen." The man takes the job, and through the help of his foreman, through his own ingenuity, through his increased work, through his interest in his business, through the help of his friends, at the end of the year he finds himself turning out twenty pens instead of ten. He is happy, he is making $5, instead of $2.50 a day. His foreman is happy because, with the same room, with the same men he had before, he has doubled the output of his department, and the manufacturer himself is sometimes happy, but not often. Then someone on the board of directors asks to see the payroll, and he finds that we are paying $5 a day where other similar mechanics are only getting $2.50, and in no uncertain terms he announces that we must stop ruining the labor market. We cannot pay $5 a day when the standard rate of wages is $2.50; how can we hope to compete with surrounding towns? What is the result? Mr. Foreman is sent for, and he is told that he has got to stop ruining the labor market of Cleveland. And the foreman goes back to his workman in sadness, in depression, and tells his workman, "I am sorry, John, but I have got to cut the price down for that pen; I cannot let you earn $5 a day; the board of directors has got on to it, and it is ruining the labor market; you ought to be willing to have the price reduced. You cannot earn more than $3 or $2.75 a day, and I will have to cut your wages so that you will only get $3 a day." John, of necessity accepts the cut, but he sees to it that he never makes enough pens to get another cut.

CHARACTERISTICS OF THE UNION WORKMAN

There seem to be two divergent opinions about the workmen of this country. One is that a lot of the trade unions' workmen, particularly in this country, have become brutal, have become dominating, careless of any interests but their own, and are a pretty poor lot. And the other opinion which those same trade unionists hold of themselves is that they are

pretty close to little gods. Whichever view you may hold of the workingmen of this country, and my personal view of them is that they are a pretty fine lot of fellows, they are just about the same as you and I. But whether you hold the bad opinion or the good opinion, it makes no difference. Whatever the workingmen of this country are or whatever they are not, they are not fools. And all that is necessary is for a workingman to have but one object lesson, like that I have told you, and he soldiers for the rest of his life.

There are a few exceptional employers who treat their workmen differently, but I am talking about the rule of the country. Soldiering is the absolute rule with all workmen who know their business. I am not saying it is for their interest to soldier. You cannot blame them for it. You cannot expect them to be large enough minded men to look at the proper view of the matter. Nor is the man who cuts the wages necessarily to blame. It is simply a misfortune in industry.

THE DEVELOPMENT OF SCIENTIFIC MANAGEMENT

There has been, until comparatively recently, no scheme promulgated by which the evils of rate cutting could be properly avoided, so soldiering has been the rule.

Now the first step that was taken toward the development of those methods, of those principles, which rightly or wrongly have come to be known under the name of scientific management—the first step that was taken in an earnest endeavor to remedy the evils of soldiering; an earnest endeavor to make it unnecessary for workmen to be hypocritical in this way, to deceive themselves, to deceive their employers, to live day in and day out a life of deceit, forced upon them by conditions—the very first step that was taken toward the development was to overcome that evil. I want to emphasize that, because I wish to emphasize the one great fact relating to scientific management, the greatest factor: namely, that scientific management is no new set of theories that has been tried on by any one at every step. Scientific management at every step has been an evolution, not a theory. In all cases the practice has preceded the theory, not succeeded it. In every case one measure after another has been tried out, until the proper remedy has been found. That series of proper eliminations, that evolution, is what is called scientific management. Every element of it has had to fight its way against the elements that preceded it, and prove itself better or it would not be there tomorrow.

All the men that I know of who are in any way connected with scientific management are ready to abandon any scheme, any theory in favor of anything else that could be found that is better. There is nothing in scientific management that is fixed. There is no one man, or group of men, who have invented scientific management.

What I want to emphasize is that all of the elements of scientific management are an evolution, not an invention. Scientific management is in use in an immense range and variety of industries. Almost every type of industry in this country has scientific management working successfully. I think I can safely say that on the average in those establishments in which scientific management has been introduced, the average workman is turning out double the output he was before. I think that is a conservative statement.

THE WORKMAN THE CHIEF BENEFICIARIES

Three or four years ago I could have said there were about fifty thousand men working under scientific management, but now I know there are many more. Company after company is coming under it, many of which I know nothing about. Almost universally they are working successfully. This increasing of the output per individual in the trade, results, of course, in cheapening the product; it results, therefore, in larger profit usually to the owners of the business; it results also, in many cases, in a lowering of the selling price, although that has not come to the extent it will later. In the end the public gets the good. Without any question, the large good which so far has come from scientific management has come to the worker. To the workman has come, practically right off as soon as scientific management is introduced, an increase in wages amounting from 33 to 100 per cent, and yet that is not the

greatest good that comes to the workmen from scientific management. The great good comes from the fact that, under scientific management, they look upon their employers as the best friends they have in the world; the suspicious watchfulness which characterizes the old type of management, the semi-antagonism, or the complete antagonism between workmen and employers is entirely superseded, and in its place comes genuine friendship between both sides. That is the greatest good that has come under scientific management. As a proof of this in the many businesses in which scientific management has been introduced, I know of not one single strike of workmen working under it after it had been introduced, and only two or three while it was in process of introduction. In this connection I must speak of the fakers, those who have said they can introduce scientific management into a business in six months or a year. That is pure nonsense. There have been many strikes stirred up by that type of man. Not one strike has ever come, and I do not believe ever will come, under scientific management.

WHAT SCIENTIFIC MANAGEMENT IS

What is scientific management? It is no efficiency device, nor is it any group of efficiency devices. Scientific management is no new scheme for paying men, it is no bonus system, no piecework system, no premium system of payment; it is no new method of figuring costs. It is no one of the various elements by which it is commonly known, by which people refer to it. It is not time study nor man study. It is not the printing of a ton or two of blanks and unloading them on a company and saying, ''There is your system, go ahead and use it.'' Scientific management does not exist and cannot exist until there has been a complete mental revolution on the part of the workmen working under it, as to their duties toward themselves and toward their employers, and a complete mental revolution in the outlook for the employers, toward their duties, toward themselves, and toward their workmen. And until this great mental change takes place, scientific management does not exist. Do you think you can make a great mental revolution in a large group of workmen in a year, or do you think you can make it in a large group of foremen and superintendents in a year? If you do, you are very much mistaken. All of us hold mighty close to our ideas and principles in life, and we change very slowly toward the new, and very properly too.

Let me give you an idea of what I mean by this change in mental outlook. If you are manufacturing a hammer or a mallet, into the cost of that mallet goes a certain amount of raw materials, a certain amount of wood and metal. If you will take the cost of the raw materials and then add to it that cost which is frequently called by various names— overhead expenses, general expense, indirect expense; that is, the proper share of taxes, insurance, light, heat, salaries of officers and advertising—and you have a sum of money. Subtract that sum from the selling price, and what is left over is called the surplus. It is over this surplus that all of the labor disputes in the past have occurred. The workman naturally wants all he can get. His wages come out of that surplus. The manufacturer wants all he can get in the shape of profits, and it is from the division of this surplus that all the labor disputes have come in the past—the equitable division.

The new outlook that comes under scientific management is this: The workmen, after many object lessons, come to see and the management come to see that this surplus can be made so great, providing both sides will stop their pulling apart, will stop their fighting and will push as hard as they can to get as cheap an output as possible, that there is no occasion to quarrel. Each side can get more than ever before. The acknowledgement of this fact represents a complete mental revolution.

INTELLIGENT OLD-STYLE MANAGEMENT

There is one more illustration of the new and great change which comes under scientific management. I can make it clearer, perhaps, by contrasting it with what I look upon as the best of the older types of management. If you have a company employing five hundred or a thousand men, you will have in that company perhaps fifteen different trades. The workmen in those trades have learned absolutely all that they know, not from books, not by being taught, but they have learned it traditionally. It has been handed

down to them, not even by word of mouth in many cases, but by seeing what other men do. One man stands alongside of another man and imitates him. That is the way the trades are handed down, and my impression is that trades are now picked up just as they were in the Middle Ages.

The manufacturer, the manager, or the foreman who knows his business realizes that his chief function as a manager—I am talking now of the old-fashioned manager—ought to be to get the true initiative of his workman. He wants the initiative of the workman, their hard work, their good will, their ingenuity, their determination to do all they can for the benefit of his firm. If he knows anything about human nature, if he has thought over the problems, he must realize that in order to get the initiative of his workman, in order to modify their soldiering, he must do something more for his men than other employers are doing for their men under similar circumstances. The wise manager, under the old type of management, deliberately sets out to do something better for his workmen than his competitors are doing, better than he himself has ever done before. It takes a good while for the workmen to stop looking for that [snake in the grass], but if the manager keeps at them long enough he will get the confidence of the men, and when he does workmen of all kinds will respond by giving a great increase in output. When he sets out to do better for his men than other people do for theirs, the workmen respond liberally when that time comes. I refer to this case as being the highest type of management, the case in which the managers deliberately set out to do something better for their workmen than other people are doing, and to give them a special incentive of some kind, to which the workmen respond by giving a share at least of their initiative.

WHAT SCIENTIFIC MANAGEMENT WILL DO

I am going to try to prove to you that the old style of management has not a ghost of a chance in competition with the principles of scientific management. Why? In the first place, under scientific management, the initiative of the workmen, their hard work, their good-will, their best endeavors are obtained with absolute regularity. There are cases all the time where men will soldier, but they become the exception, as a rule, and they give their true initiative under scientific management. That is the least of the two sources of gain. The greatest source of gain under scientific management comes from the new and almost unheard-of duties and burdens which are voluntarily assumed, not by the workmen, but by the men on the management side. These are the things which make scientific management a success. These new duties, these new burdens undertaken by the management have rightly or wrongly been divided into four groups, and have been called the principles of scientific management.

The first of the great principles of scientific management, the first of the new burdens which are voluntarily undertaken by those on the management side is the deliberate gathering together of the great mass of traditional knowledge which, in the past, has been in the heads of the workmen, recording it, tabulating it, reducing it in most cases to rules, laws, and in many cases to mathematical formulae, which, with these new laws, are applied to the cooperation of the management to the work of the workmen. This results in an immense increase in the output, we may say, of the two. The gathering in of this great mass of traditional knowledge, which is done by the means of motion study, time study, can be truly called the science.

Let me make a prediction. I have before me the first book, so far as I know, that has been published on motion study and on time study. That is, the motion study and time study of the cement and concrete trades. It contains everything relating to concrete work. It is of about seven hundred pages and embodies the motions of men, the time and the best way of doing that sort of work. It is the first case in which a trade has been reduced to the same condition that engineering data of all kinds have been reduced, and it is this sort of data that is bound to sweep the world.

I have before me something which has been gathering for about fourteen years, the time or motion study of the machine shop. It will take probably four or five years more before the first book will be ready to publish on that subject. There is a collection of sixty or seventy thousand elements affecting machine-shop work. After a few years, say three,

four or five years more, some one will be ready to publish the first book giving the laws of the movements of men in the machine shop—all the laws, not only a few of them. Let me predict, just as sure as the sun shines, that is going to come in every trade. Why? Because it pays, for no other reason. That results in doubling the output in any shop. Any device which results in an increased output is bound to come in spite of all opposition, whether we want it or not. It comes automatically.

THE SELECTION OF THE WORKMAN

The next of the four principles of scientific management is the scientific selection of the workman, and then his progressive development. It becomes the duty under scientific management of not one, but of a group of men on the management side, to deliberately study the workmen who are under them; study them in the most careful, thorough and painstaking way; and not just leave it to the poor, overworked foreman to go out and say, ''Come on, what do you want? If you are cheap enough I will give you a trial.''

This is the old way. The new way is to take a great deal of trouble in selecting the workmen. The selection proceeds year after year. And it becomes the duty of those engaged in scientific management to know something about the workmen under them. It becomes their duty to set out deliberately to train the workmen in their employ to be able to do a better and still better class of work than ever before, and to then pay them higher wages than ever before. This deliberate selection of the workmen is the second of the great duties that devolve on the management under scientific management.

BRINGING TOGETHER THE SCIENCE AND THE MAN

The third principle is the bringing together of this science of which I have spoken and the trained workmen. I say bringing because they don't come together unless some one brings them. Select and train your workmen all you may, but unless there is some one who will make the men and the science come together, they will stay apart. The "make" involves a great many elements. They are not all disagreeable elements. The most important and largest way of "making" is to do something nice for the man whom you wish to make come together with the science. Offer him a plum, something that is worthwhile. There are many plums offered to those who come under scientific management—better treatment, more kindly treatment, more consideration for their wishes, and an opportunity for them to express their wants freely. That is one side of the "make." An equally important side is, whenever a man will not do what he ought, to either make him do it or stop it. If he will not do it, let him get out. I am not talking of any mollycoddle. Let me disabuse your minds of any opinion that scientific management is a mollycoddle scheme.

I have a great many union friends. I find they look with especial bitterness on this word "make." They have been used to doing the "making" in the past. That is the attitude of the trade unions, and it softens matters greatly when you can tell them the facts, namely, that in our making the science and the men come together, nine-tenths of our trouble comes with the men on the management side in making them do their new duties. I am speaking of those who have been trying to change from the old system to the new. Nine-tenths of our troubles come in trying to make the men on the management side do what they ought to do, to make them do the new duties, and take on these new burdens, and give up their old duties. That softens this word "make."

THE PRINCIPLE OF THE DIVISION OF WORK

The fourth principle is the plainest of all. It involves a complete re-division of the work of the establishment. Under the old scheme of management, almost all of the work was done by the workmen. Under the new, the work of the establishment is divided into two large parts. All of that work which formerly was done by the workmen alone is divided into two large sections, and one of those sections is handed over to the management. They do a whole division of the

work formerly done by the workmen. It is this real cooperation, this genuine division of the work between the two sides, more than any other element which accounts for the fact that there never will be strikes under scientific management. When the workman realizes that there is hardly a thing he does that does not have to be preceded by some act of preparation on the part of management, and when that workman realizes when the management falls down and does not do its part, that he is not only entitled to a kick, but that he can register that kick in the most forcible possible way, he cannot quarrel with the men over him. It is team work. There are more complaints made every day on the part of the workmen that the men on the management side fail to do their duties than are made by the management that the men fail. Every one of the complaints of the men have to be heeded, just as much as the complaints from the management that the workmen do not do their share. That is characteristic of scientific management. It represents a democracy, cooperation, a genuine division of work which never existed before in this world.

THE PROOF OF THE THEORY

I am through now with the theory. I will try to convince you of the value of these four principles by giving you some practical illustrations. I hope that you will look for these four elements in the illustrations. I shall begin by trying to show the power of these four elements when applied to the greatest kind of work I know of that is done by man. The reason I have heretofore chosen pig-iron for an illustration is that it is the lowest form of work that is known.

A pig of iron weighs about ninety-two pounds on an average. A man stoops down and, with no other implement than his hands, picks up a pig of iron, walks a few yards with it, and drops it on a pile. A large part of the community has the impression that scientific management is chiefly handling pig-iron. The reason I first chose pig-iron for an illustration is that, if you can prove to any one the strength, the effect, of those four principles when applied to such rudimentary work as handling pig-iron, the presumption is that it can be applied to something better. The only way to prove it is to start at the bottom and show those four principles all along the line. I am sorry I cannot, because of lack of time, give you the illustration of handling pig-iron. Many of you doubt whether there is much of any science in it. I am going to try to prove later with a high class mechanic that the workman who is fit to work at any type of work is almost universally incapable of understanding the principles without the help of some one else. I will use shoveling because it is a shorter illustration, and I will try to show what I mean by the science of shoveling, and the power which comes to the man who knows the science of shoveling. It is a high art compared with pig-iron handling.

THE SCIENCE OF SHOVELING

When I went to the Bethlehem Steel Works, the first thing I saw was a gang of men unloading rice coal. They were a splendid set of fellows, and they shoveled fast. There was no loafing at all. They shoveled as hard as you could ask any man to work. I looked with the greatest of interest for a long time, and finally they moved off rapidly down into the yard to another part of the yard and went right at handling iron ore. One of the main facts connected with that shoveling was that the work those men were doing was that, in handling the rice coal, they had on their shovels a load of 3¾ pounds, and when the same men went to handling ore with the same shovel, they had over 38 pounds on their shovels. Is it asking too much of anyone to inquire whether 3¾ pounds is the right load for a shovel, or whether 38 pounds is the right load for a shovel? Surely if one is right the other must be wrong. I think that is a self-evident fact, and yet I am willing to bet that that is what workmen are doing right now in Cleveland.

Under scientific management every little trifle—there is nothing too small—becomes the subject of experiment. The experiments develop into a law; they save money; they increase the output of the individual and make the thing worthwhile. How is this done? What we did in shoveling experiments was to deliberately select two first class shovelers, the best we knew how to get. We brought them into the office and said, "Jim and Mike, you two fellows are both good shovelers. I have a proposition to make to you. I am going to pay you double wages if you fellows will go out and do what I want you to do. There will be a young chap go along with you with a pencil and a piece of paper, and he will tell you to do a lot of fool things, and you will do them, and he will write down a lot of fool things, and you will think it is a joke, but it is nothing of the kind. Let me tell you one thing: if you fellows think that you can fool that chap you are very much mistaken, you cannot fool him at all. Don't get it through your heads you can fool him. If you take this double wages, you will be straight and do what you are told." They both promised and did exactly what they were told. What we told them was this: "We want you to start in and do whatever shoveling you are told to do, and work at just the pace, all day long, that when it comes night you are going to be good and tired, but not tired out. I do not want you exhausted or anything like that, but properly tired. You know what a good day's work is. In other words, I do not want any loafing business or any overwork business. If you find yourself overworked and getting too tired, slow down." Those men did that and did it in the most splendid kind of way day in and day out. We proved their cooperation because they were in different parts of the yard, and they both got near enough the same results. Our results were duplicated.

I have found that there are a lot of schemes among my working friends, but no more among them than among us. They are good, straight fellows if you only treat them right, and put the matter up squarely to them. We started in at a pile of material, with a very large shovel. We kept innumerable accurate records of all kinds, some of them useless. Thirty or forty different items were carefully observed about the work of those two men. We counted the number of shovelfuls thrown in a day. We found with a weight of between thirty-eight and thirty-nine pounds on the shovel, the man made a pile of material of a certain height. We then cut off the shovel, and he shoveled again and with a thirty-four pound load his pile went up and he shoveled more in a day. We again cut off the shovel to thirty pounds, and the pile went up again. With twenty-six pounds on the shovel, the pile again went up, and at twenty-one and one-half pounds the men could do their best. At twenty pounds the pile went down, at eighteen it went down, and at fourteen it went down. So that they were at the peak of twenty-one and one-half pounds. There is a scientific fact. A first class shoveler ought to take twenty-one and one-half pounds on his shovel in order to work to the best possible advantage. You are not giving that man a chance unless you give him a shovel which will hold twenty-one pounds.

The men in the yard were run by the old fashioned foreman. He simply walked about with them. We at once took their shovels away from them. We built a large labor tool room which held ten to fifteen different kinds of shoveling implements so that for each kind of material that was handled in that yard, all the way from rice coal, ashes, coke, all the way up to ore, we would have a shovel that would just hold twenty-one pounds, or average twenty-one. One time it would hold eighteen, the next twenty-four, but it will average twenty-one.

One of the first principles we adopted was that no man in that labor gang could work on the new way unless he earned sixty per cent higher wages than under the old plan. It is only just to the workman that he shall know right off whether he is doing his work right or not. He must not be told a week or month after, that he fell down. He must know it the next morning. So the next slip that came out of the pigeon hole was either a white or yellow slip. We used the two colors because some of the men could not read. The yellow slip meant that he had not earned his sixty per cent higher wages. He knew that he could not stay in that gang and keep on getting yellow slips.

TEACHING THE MEN

I want to show you again the totally different outlook there is under scientific management by illustrating what happened when that man got his yellow slips. Under the old scheme, the foreman could say to him, "You are no good, get out of this; no time for you, you cannot earn sixty per cent higher wages; get out of this! Go!" It was not done politely, but the foreman had no time to palaver. Under the new scheme what happened? A teacher of shoveling went down to see that man. A teacher of shoveling is a man who is handy with a shovel, who

has made his mark in life with a shovel, and yet who is a kindly fellow and knows how to show the other fellow what he ought to do. When that teacher went there he said, "See here, Jim, you have a lot of those yellow slips, what is the matter with you? What is up? Have you been drunk? Are you tired? Are you sick? Anything wrong with you? Because if you are tired or sick we will give you a show somewhere else." "Well, no, I am all right." "Then if you are not sick, or there is nothing wrong with you, you have forgotten how to shovel. I showed you how to shovel. You have forgotten something, now go ahead and shovel and I will show you what is the matter with you." Shoveling is a pretty big science, it is not a little thing.

If you are going to use the shovel right you should always shovel off an iron bottom; if not an iron bottom, a wooden bottom; and if not a wooden bottom a hard dirt bottom. Time and again the conditions are such that you have to go right into the pile. When that is the case, with nine out of ten materials it takes more trouble and more time and more effort to get the shovel into the pile than to do all the rest of the shoveling. That is where the effort comes. Those of you again who have taught the art of shoveling will have taught your workmen to do this. There is only one way to do it right. Put your forearm down onto the upper part of your leg, and when you push into the pile, throw your weight against it. That relieves your arm of work. You then have an automatic push, we will say, about eighty pounds, the weight of your body thrown on to it. Time and again we would find men whom we had taught to shovel right were going at it in the old way, and of course they could not do a day's work. The teacher would simply stand over that fellow and say, "There is what is the matter with you, Jim, you have forgotten to shovel into the pile."

You are not interested in shoveling, you are not interested in whether one way or the other is right, but I do hope to interest you in the difference of the mental attitude of the men who are teaching under the new system. Under the new system, if a man falls down, the presumption is that it is our fault at first, that we probably have not taught the man right, have not given him a fair show, have not spent time enough in showing him how to do his work.

Let me tell you another thing that is characteristic

of scientific management. In my day, we were smart enough to know when the boss was coming, and when he came up we were apparently really working. Under scientific management, there is none of that pretense. I cannot say that in the old days we were delighted to see the boss coming around. We always expected some kind of roast if he came too close. Under the new, the teacher is welcomed; he is not an enemy, but a friend. He comes there to try to help the man get bigger wages, to show him how to do something. It is the great mental change, the change in the outlook that comes, rather than the details of it.

DOES SCIENTIFIC MANAGEMENT PAY?

It took the time of a number of men for about three years to study the art of shoveling in that yard at the Bethlehem Steel Works alone. They were carefully trained college men, and they were busy all the time. That costs money, the tool room costs money, the clerks we had to keep there all night figuring up how much the men did the day before cost money, the office in which the men laid out and planned the work cost money. The very fair and proper question, the only question to ask is "Does it pay?" because if scientific management does not pay, there is nothing in it; if it does not pay in dollars and cents, it is the rankest kind of nonsense. There is nothing philanthropic about it. It has got to pay, because business which cannot be done on a profitable basis ought not to be done on a philanthropic basis, for it will not last. At the end of three and one-half years we had a very good chance to know whether or not it paid.

Fortunately in the Bethlehem Steel works they had records of how much it cost to handle the materials under the old system, where the single foreman led a group of men around the works. It costs them between seven and eight cents a ton to handle materials, on an average throughout the year. After paying for all this extra work I have told you about, it cost between three and four cents a ton to handle materials, and there was a profit of between seventy-five and eighty thousand dollars a year in that yard by handling those materials in the new way. What the men got out of it was this: Under the old system there were between four and six hundred men handling the material in that yard, and when we got through there were about one hundred and forty. Each one was earning a great deal more money. We made careful investigation and found they were almost all saving money, living better, happier; they are the most contented set of laborers to be seen anywhere. It is only by this kind of justification, justification of a profit for both sides, an advantage to both sides, that scientific management can exist.

THE EFFECT ON THE WORKMAN

Almost every one says, "Why, yes, that may be a good thing for the manufacturer, but how about the workmen? You are taking all the initiative away from that workman, you are making a machine out of him; what are you doing for him? He becomes merely a part of the machine." That is the almost universal impression. Again let me try to sweep aside the fallacy of that view by an illustration. The modern surgeon without a doubt is the finest mechanic in the world. He combines the greatest manual dexterity with the greatest knowledge of the implements and the greatest knowledge of the materials on which he is working. He is a true scientist, and he is a very highly skilled mechanic.

How does the surgeon teach his trade to the young men who come to the medical school? Does he say to them, "Now, young men, we belong to an older generation than you do, but the new generation is going to far outstrip anything that has been done in our generation; therefore, what we want of you is your initiative. We must have your brains, your thought, with your initiative. Of course, you know we old fellows have certain prejudices. For example, if we were going to amputate a leg, when we come down to the bone we are accustomed to take a saw, and we use it in that way and saw the bone off. But, gentlemen, do not let that fact one minute interfere with your originality, with your initiative, if you prefer an axe or a hatchet." Does the surgeon say this? He does not. He says, "You young men are going to outstrip us, but we will show you how. You shall not use a single implement in a single way until you know just which one to use, and we will tell you which one to use, and until you know how to use it, we will tell you how to use that implement, and after you have learned to use that implement our way, if you then see any defects in the implements, any defects in the method, then invent; but, invent so that you can invent upwards. Do not go inventing things which we discarded years ago.''

That is just what we say to our young men in the shops. Scientific Management makes no pretense that there is any finality in it. We merely say that the collective work of thirty or forty men in this trade through eight or ten years has gathered together a large amount of data. Every man in the establishment must start that way, must start our way, then if he can show us any better way, I do not care what it is, we will make an experiment to see if it is better. It will be named after him, and he will get a prize for having improved on one of our standards. There is the way we make progress under scientific management. There is your justification for all this. It does not dwarf initiative, it makes true initiative. Most of our progress comes through our workmen, but it comes in a legitimate way.

6 BIG BROTHER IS COUNTING YOUR KEYSTROKES
William Booth

William Booth gives a modern-day example of Taylorism at a detailed level of application. He reminds us in 1987 that Frederick Taylor's emphasis on recording events at work to improve productivity can easily be turned into an obsession by some organizations. Computer and telecommunications technologies permit the recording of minute details of an individual's work day. Booth points out that this recording goes beyond simple interests in "quality control." Organizations may in fact monitor employees' behavior so closely that employees suffer stress-related illness. Is this level of monitoring simply the kind of good business practice that Frederick Taylor would endorse, or is it an unreasonable invasion of individual privacy?

This article also validates once again the claim that classical organizational principles provide a powerful perspective for explaining modern organizational phenomena (cf. Perrow reading, Part I).

Frederick W. Taylor, the father of ''scientific management,'' would be pleased. At the turn of the century, Taylor warned that management needed to exercise greater control over workers, even down to choreographing the smallest movements performed on the shop floor. The road to efficiency, Taylor argued, must be lined with monitoring gadgets and constant supervision. *The Electronic Supervisor,* a report issued by the Congressional Office of Technology Assessment (OTA) on 21 September, concludes that employers today have extremely sophisticated tools at their disposal for monitoring workers through their use of computers and telephones, counting, for example, the number of times per hour a clerk strokes a letter on his keyboard.

Alan Westin, a professor of public law and government at Columbia University who compiled information for the OTA report, interviewed 1100 workers and 650 supervisors at 110 organizations between 1982 and 1986. Of the corporations and government agencies which monitor individual employees, Westin found that roughly two-thirds follow a model that is more "Tayloresque" than not. A Taylor model, according to Westin, would include such practices as constant monitoring of employees by a machine; a standardized pace; individual quotas; and work paid per piece.

OTA notes that in the worst of cases, the office could become an Orwellian nightmare, a brand of "electronic sweatshop," in which employees must do "boring, repetitive, fast-paced work that requires constant alertness and attention to detail," where "the supervisor isn't even human" but an "unwinking computer taskmaster."

Westin estimates that between 20 and 35 percent of all U.S. clerical workers—or between 4 million and 6 million people—are currently being monitored. Who gets monitored? Word processors, data transcribers, and telemarketers, among others. The clerical work force is predominately female and disproportionately composed of minorities.

Monitoring employees is not a new trick. What is new is the sophistication brought to the practice, OTA notes. "The technology is much more refined and elaborate now than it was even in the early 1980s," says Westin. Robert E. Nolan, a work-study specialist who consulted for OTA's study, sells software to companies that want to increase worker productivity. One package, the Auto-AOC (for Advanced Office Controls), contains 223 blocks of time, each block representing a part of a task. If an employer, for example, wants to know how many envelopes a worker should open in an hour, he would enter into Auto-AOC the letters "GRSF," for Gather, Receive, Sealed envelope, Folded contents. GRSF is allotted 185 time units, or about 7.5 seconds per envelope. Stapling sheets together is awarded 41 time units, or about 2.9 seconds. These time standards did not come out of thin air, but from the Methods-Time Measurement system, which since the 1940s has been tabulating time values for every motion performed by the human body "in a productive setting." Software designed to monitor employees is an area of great growth. "We're finding that everybody is trying to be as mean and lean as possible," says Nolan.

In addition, employers are using the telephone to monitor workers. For example, most of the country's 226,000 telephone operators are subjected to "service observation," meaning their boss gets on the line and listens to them assist customers. Today, operators hear no telltale click or drop in volume to indicate that someone else is on the line listening. According to OTA, "telephone accounting is one of the fastest growing segments of the telecommunications market." No wonder. A recent audit by the Office of the Inspector General found that 20% of calls made on the government's commercial lines were personal. Analysis by various private companies and government agencies of frequently called numbers revealed many calls to off-track betting establishments, the weather report, and so-called "Dial-a-Porn" numbers.

Stress-related illnesses and absenteeism are just two problems that might arise from compulsive monitoring. According to an earlier OTA report, stress-related illnesses cost businesses $50 to $75 billion a year. Constantly monitoring workers with computerized standards and listening in on private phone calls—even to Dial-a-Porn—raises some tricky ethical and legal questions. But as OTA notes, "there are no legal requirements in U.S. law that monitoring be fair, that jobs be well designed, or that employees be consulted about work standards." The future, it seems, holds more in store. The OTA report mentions the possibility of widespread use of polygraph testing (already 2 million are given to job applicants and employees every year), drug testing, genetic screening, and brainwave testing. As OTA puts out, the technologies are "controversial because they point out a basic tension between an employer's right to control or manage the work process and an employee's right to autonomy, dignity, and privacy."

7   HOW MUST BUSINESS MANAGEMENT DEVELOP IN ORDER TO POSSESS THE ESSENTIALS OF A PROFESSION?

M. P. FOLLETT

Like Taylor, Follett uses "science" as the basis of business management. But she applies these principles to managers instead of workers. Her writings continue to be relevant in part because of her emphasis on information as a foundation of effective management. She argues that a scientific approach will help managers deal with limitations of natural resources, competition, and scarcity of labor, while raising ethical standards and serving the public. Follett suggests management could benefit by using scientific techniques such as the systematic recording of decisions and their results.

By such careful record keeping, management can indeed assess successes and failures and avoid making the same mistake twice. But in this day of information overload, what are the limits of recording and *using* information in organizations? What types of information about you and your work would you not want recorded by your employer? Should managers be subject to the same kind of scrutiny described in the previous article by Booth?

The word "profession" connotes for most people a foundation of *science* and a motive of *service*. That is, a profession is said to rest on the basis of a proved body of knowledge, and such knowledge is supposed to be used in the service of others rather than merely for one's own purposes. Let us ask ourselves two questions: (1) How far does business management rest on scientific foundations? (2) What are the next steps to be taken in order that business management shall become more scientific?

PRESENT SIGNS OF A SCIENTIFIC BASIS FOR BUSINESS MANAGEMENT

We have many indications that scientific method is being more and more applied to business management. First, of course, is the development of so-called "scientific management" which, after its early stages, began to concern itself with the technique

Adapted from M. P. Follett, "How Must Business Management Develop in Order to Possess the Essentials of a Profession?" Reprinted from Henry C. Metcalf (editor), *Business Management as a Profession*, pages 73 through 88, Chicago: A. W. Shaw. Copyright 1927 by A. W. Shaw.

of management as well as with the technique of operating.

Secondly, there is the increasing tendency toward specialized, or what is being called functionalized, management. Functionalized management has, indeed, not yet been carried far. In some cases the only sign we see of it, beyond the recognition that different departments require different kinds of knowledge, different kinds of ability, is the employing of experts for special problems. In other cases a further step is taken and a planning department is created; but the powers given to planning departments vary greatly from plant to plant—some take up only occasional problems as they are asked, some are only advisory bodies. Yet in most plants the functionalization of management is a process which in one way or another has gained a good deal of ground recently. That is, the fact is very generally accepted that different types of problems require different bodies of knowledge.

In the third place, arbitrary authority is diminishing, surely an indication that more value is being put on scientific method. The tendency today is to vest authority in the person who has most knowledge of the matter in question and most skill in applying that knowledge. Hiring, for instance, is now based on certain principles and special knowledge. The job of hiring is given to those who have that knowledge. It is not assumed by some one by virtue of a certain position.

Finally, management, not bankers nor stockholders, is now seen to be the fundamental element in industry. It is good management that draws credit, that draws workers, that draws customers. Moreover, whatever changes come, whether industry is owned by individual capitalists or by the state or by the workers, it will always have to be managed. Management is a permanent function of business.

There are many circumstances which are impelling us toward a truly scientific management: (1) efficient management has to take the place of that exploitation of our natural resources whose day is now nearly over; (2) keener competition; (3) scarcity of labor; (4) a broader conception of the ethics of human relations; (5) the growing idea of business as a public service which carries with it a sense of responsibility for its efficient conduct.

WHAT ARE THE NEXT STEPS TOWARD MAKING BUSINESS MANAGEMENT MORE SCIENTIFIC?

Recognizing that business management is every day coming more and more to rest on scientific foundations, what has it yet to do? First, the scientific standard must be applied to the whole of business management; it is now often applied to only one part. Business management includes: (1) on the technical side, as it is usually called, a knowledge of production and distribution, and (2) on the personnel side, a knowledge of how to deal fairly and fruitfully with one's fellows. While the first has been recognized as a matter capable of being taught, the latter has been often thought to be a gift which some men possess and some do not. That is, one part of business management rested on science; the other part, it was thought, never could. Oliver Sheldon says: "Broadly, management is concerned with two primary elements—things and men. The former element is susceptible to scientific treatment, the latter is not."[1] And again: "Where human beings are concerned, scientific principles may be so much waste paper."[2] Let us take that statement—that human relations are not susceptible of scientific treatment—and ask what scientific treatment is. Science has been defined as "knowledge gained by systematic observation, experiment, and reasoning; knowledge coordinated, arranged and systematized." Can we not accumulate in regard to human relations knowledge gained by systematic observation, experiment, and reasoning? Can we not coordinate, arrange, and systematize that knowledge? I think we can.

Sheldon says further: "There may be a science of costing, of transportation, of operation, but there can be no science of cooperation."[3] The reason we are here studying human relations in industry is that we believe there can be a science of cooperation. By this I mean that cooperation is not, and this I insist on, merely a matter of good intentions, of kindly feeling. It must be based on these, but you cannot have successful cooperation until you have worked out the methods of cooperation—by experiment after experiment, by a comparing of experiments, by a pooling of results. Not everyone who cries "Cooperation, cooperation!" . . . It is my plea above everything else that we learn *how* to cooperate. Of course, one may have a special aptitude for dealing with men as others may have for dealing with machines, but there is as much to learn in the one case as in the other.

In all our study of personnel work, however, we should remember that we can never wholly separate the human and the mechanical problem. This would seem too obvious to mention if we did not so often see that separation made. Go back to that sentence of Sheldon's: "There may be a science of costing, of transportation, of operation, but there can be no science of cooperation." But take Sheldon's own illustration, that of transportation. The engineering part of transportation is not the larger part. Please note that I do not say it is a small part. It is a large part, and it is the dramatic part, and it is the part we have done well, and yet the chief part of transportation is the personal thing. Every one knows that the main difficulty about transportation is that there have not always been sensible working arrangements between the men concerned. But you all see every day that the study of human relations in business and the study of technique of operating are bound up together. You know that the way the worker is treated affects output. You know that the routing of materials and the maintenance of machines is a matter partly of human relations. You know, I hope, that there is danger in "putting in" personnel work if it is superadded instead of being woven through the plant. You remember the man who wanted to know something about Chinese metaphysics and so looked up China in the encyclopedia and then metaphysics, and put them together. We shall not have much better success if we try merely to add personnel work. Even although there is, as I certainly believe there should be, a special personnel department run by a trained expert, yet it seems to me that every executive should make some study of personnel work a part of that broad foundation which is today increasingly felt to be necessary for the business man.

If, then, one of the first things to be done to make business management more scientific is to apply scientific methods to those problems of management which involve human relations, another requirement is that we should make an analysis of managers' jobs somewhat corresponding to the analysis of workers' jobs in the Taylor system. We need to get away from tradition, prejudice, stereotypes, guesswork, and find the factual basis for managerial jobs. We know, for instance, what has been accomplished in elimination of waste by scientific methods of research and experiment applied to operating, to probable demand for commodities, and so on. I believe that this has to be carried further, and that managerial waste, administrative waste, should be given the same research and experiment. How this can be done, I shall take up later.

The next step business management should take is to organize the body of knowledge on which it should rest. We have defined science as an organized body of exact knowledge. That is, scientific method consists of two parts: (1) research, and (2) the organization of the knowledge obtained by research. The importance of research, of continued research, receives every year fuller and fuller appreciation from business men; but methods of organizing the results of such research have not kept pace with this appreciation. While business management is collecting more and more exact knowledge, while it is observing more keenly, experimenting more widely, it has not yet gone far in organizing this knowledge. We have drawn a good many conclusions, have thought out certain principles, but have not always seen the relation between these conclusions or these principles.

I have not time to speak here of more than one way of organizing in industrial plants our accumulating knowledge in regard to executive technique. There should be, I think, in every plant, an official, one of whose duties should be to classify and interpret managerial experience with the aid of the carefully kept records which should be required of every executive. From such classification and interpretation of experience—this experience which in essentials repeats itself so often from time to time, from department to department, from plant to plant—it would be possible to draw useful conclusions. The importance of this procedure becomes more obvious when we remember that having experience and profiting by experience are two different matters. Experience may leave us with mistaken notions, with prejudice or suspicion.

A serious drawback to a fuller understanding of and utilization of executive experience is that we have at present (1) no systematic follow-up of decisions, of new methods, of experiments in managing; and (2) no carefully worked out system of recording. Poorly kept records, or the absence of any systematic recording, are partly responsible for what seems in some plants like a stagnant management, and in all plants for certain leaks in management. For instance, the fact that we have no follow-up for executive decisions with a comparing of results—a procedure necessary before business management can be considered fully on a scientific basis—is partly a deficiency in recording. The fact that an executive, if he wishes to introduce a certain method (not in operating but in management itself), cannot find in any records whether that method has been tried before or anything like it, and what the results have been, is a serious deficiency in recording. If an executive is facing a certain problem, he should be able to find out: (1) whether other executives have had to meet similar problems, (2) how they met them, (3) what the results were. It seems to me very unfortunate that it is possible for one man to say to another, as I heard some one say at the suggestion of a new method, ''I believe our department tried that a few years ago, but I've forgotten what we thought of it.''

I have heard it said that the Harvard football team was put on its feet when Percy Haughton introduced the system of recording football experience. After that, if some one thought he had a brilliant idea that such and such a play could be tried on Yale, the first thing done was to examine the records; and it might be found that that play had been tried two years before and failed. It might even be discovered why it had failed. This system of recording—I believe it already existed at Yale—was Mr. Haughton's great contribution to Harvard football. Because of it, the team could not, at any rate, go on making the *same* mistakes.

The recording of executive experience, which will probably need a technique somewhat different from that used for the rest of business recording, should have, I think, our immediate attention. The system of both recording and reporting should be such that records and reports can be quickly mas-

tered, and thus be practically useful to all, instead of buried underneath their own verbiage, length, and lack of systematization. And there should be required from every executive, training in the technique of keeping records and making reports.

But we need more than records. We need a new journal, or a new department in some present journal; we need sifted bibliographies of reports; ways of getting information from other parts of the country, from other countries; above all, we need executive conferences with carefully worked out methods for comparing experience which has been scientifically recorded, analyzed, and organized. When many different plants are willing to share with one another the results of their experience, then we shall have business policies based on wider data than those of the present.

The Graduate School of Business Administration and the Bureau of Business Research of Harvard University are now collecting cases of business policy, thus opening the way for classifying and crossindexing. Harvard has, of course, been able to get hold of a very small number of cases, but this seems to be a valuable and significant undertaking.

I have been interested also in what a certain recent committee, with representatives from various firms, deliberately stated as its object: ''the comparison of experience.'' I should like to know how frank and full their exchange of experience was; but any attempt of this kind is interesting, indicating, as it does, the attitude on the part of those participating that they expect to gain more by working together than they will lose (the old idea) by allowing other firms to gain any intimate knowledge of their affairs.

Moreover, not only should we analyze and compare our experience, but we should deliberately experiment. We should make experiments, observe experiments, compare and discuss these with each other, and see what consensus we can come to in our conclusions. For this we should be wholly frank with one another. If we have the scientific attitude toward our work, we shall be willing to tell our failures. I heard of a man who made an ice machine which did not work, and the following conversation took place between him and a friend he met:

FRIEND: ''I was sorry to hear your experiment was a failure!''

MAN: "Who told you it was a failure?"

FRIEND: "Why, I heard your ice machine wouldn't work."

MAN: "Oh, that was true enough, but it was a great success as an experiment. You can learn as much from your failures as from your successes."

From such experimenting and from the comparison of experience, I think certain standards would emerge. But we should remember that, as no Taylorite thinks there is anything final in "standardization," so we should not aim at a static standardization of managerial method, executive technique. We should make use of all available present experience, knowing that experience and our learning from it should be equally continuous matters.

If science gives us research and experimentation as its two chief methods, it at the same time shows us that nothing is too small to claim our attention. There is nothing unimportant in business procedure. For instance, I spoke above of record keeping. I know a firm where they tell me that they are not getting nearly so much advantage as they should from their records because they have not yet worked out a system of cross-indexing. Yet to some, cross-indexing may not seem to be of great importance. I know a man who says frequently about this detail or that, "Oh, that doesn't matter." Everything matters to the scientist. The following incident seems to me to have some significance. I told a man that I was working at the technique of the business interview, at which he seemed rather amused and said, "I guess most business men know how to conduct interviews." It was evident that he thought he did—but he is a man who has never risen above a small position. Later, I said the same thing to a clever man in a good position, a New York man, by the way. I said it a little hesitatingly, for I thought he too might consider it beneath his notice, but he was much interested and asked if he might see my paper when finished.

I have spoken of the classification of experience, the organizing of knowledge, as one of the necessary preliminaries to putting business management on a scientific basis. This organized body of knowledge tends at first to remain in the hands of a few. Measures should be taken to make it accessible to the whole managerial force. There should be opportunities for the training of executives through talks, suggested readings (including journals on management), through wisely led discussion groups and conferences, through managers' associations, foremen's associations, and the like. The organized knowledge of managerial methods which many of the higher officials possess should spread to the lower executives. In some cases, the higher official does not even think of this as part of his responsibility. He will say to a subordinate, "Here is what I want done; I don't care how you do it, that's up to you." Indeed, many an official has prided himself on this way of dealing with subordinates. But this is changing. It is part of the Taylor system that standards and methods for each worker's job are made accessible to the worker; also knowledge of the quality of work expected, which is shown him by specifications or drawings. Some such system should be developed for management. To develop it might be made part of that analysis of managerial jobs which I spoke of a few moments ago. Indeed, more and more of the higher executives are seeing now that managers' jobs as well as workers' jobs are capable of carrying with them accepted standards and methods.

Of course, it is recognized that many of these standards and methods need the sanction of custom rather than of authority, that they should be indicated rather than prescribed, also that much more elasticity should be allowed than in the detailed instructions of the Taylor system—but this is all part of that large subject, the method of training executives. Possibly in time, as business organization develops, we shall have an official for executives corresponding to the functional foreman who is sometimes known as the "methods instructor," an official whose duty it will be to see that certain managerial methods are understood and followed, as it is the duty of the functional foreman to see that certain operating methods are understood and followed. But I should not advocate this unless the executives were allowed fullest opportunity for contributing to such prescribed methods. The development of managerial technique has been thought by some to involve the risk of crushing originality, the danger of taking away initiative. I think that, rightly managed, it should give executives increased opportunity for the fruitful exercise of initiative and originality, for it is they themselves who must develop this technique even if helped by experts. The choice here presented is not that between originality and a mechanical system, but between a haphazard, hit-or-miss way of performing executive duties and a scientifically determined procedure.

Yet when business management has gained something of an accepted technique, there still remains, as part of the training of executives, the acquiring of skill in its application. Managerial skill cannot be painted on the outside of executives; it has to go deeper than that. Like manual workers, managerial workers have to acquire certain habits and attitudes. And just as in the case of manual workers, for the acquisition of these habits and attitudes three conditions must be given: (1) detailed information in regard to a new method; (2) the stimulus to adopt this method; and (3) the opportunity to practice it so that it may become a habit.

A business man tells me that I should emphasize the last point particularly. He says that his firm has been weak just here; that they have done more preaching than giving opportunity for practice. He says: "We've given them a lecture on piano playing and then put them on the concert stage. This winter we are going to try to invent ways of giving real practice to foremen so that a set of habits can be formed." No subject is more important than the training of executives, but it is a subject which would require an evening for even the most superficial consideration. If you wish to train yourself for higher executive positions, the first thing for you to decide is what you are training for. Ability to dominate or manipulate others? That ought to be easy enough, since most of the magazines advertise sure ways of developing something they call "personality." But I am convinced that the first essential of business success is the capacity for organized thinking.

In conclusion: What does all this imply in regard to the profession of business management? It means that men must prepare themselves as seriously for this profession as for any other. They must realize that they, as all professional men, are assuming grave responsibilities, that they are to take a creative part in one of the large functions of society, a part which, I believe, only trained and disciplined men can in the future hope to take with success.

NOTES

1. Oliver Sheldon, *Bulletin of Taylor Society*, Vol. 8, No. 6, December, 1913, p. 211.
2. Oliver Sheldon, *The Philosophy of Management* (London, Sir Isaac Pitman & Sons, Ltd., 1923), p. 36.
3. *Ibid.*, p. 35.

8 THE THEORY OF FORMAL ORGANIZATION
CHESTER I. BARNARD

Though he was the Chief Executive Officer of a telephone company by profession, Chester Barnard might be thought of as one of the first widely known organizational communication theorists. He is usually thought of as a classical theorist, but Barnard's book, *The Functions of the Executive*, gives some of the first indications of the human relations approach that was emerging during the 1930s.

He rejects the classical notion that compliance with orders is a function of managers' formal authority over their subordinates. Instead he argues for a view of compliance as a result of voluntary cooperation that managers create through communication with subordinates.

In the following, a chapter from his book, Barnard outlines his formal theory of organization. He says in order for organization to occur, members must be willing to cooperate. This cooperation must also be directed toward some common purpose. Barnard sees communication as the means by which organization is accomplished: Cooperation and a sense of common purpose are literally *created* through communication. Communication is therefore also at the very heart of issues like organizational effectiveness and efficiency.

An organization comes into being when (1) there are persons able to communicate with each other (2) who are willing to contribute action (3) to accomplish a common purpose. The elements of an organization are therefore (1) communication; (2) willingness to serve; and (3) common purpose. These elements are necessary and sufficient conditions initially, and they are found in all such organizations. The third element, purpose, is implicit in the definition. Willingness to serve, and communication, and the interdependence of the three elements in general, and their mutual dependence in specific cooperative systems, are matters of experience and observation.

For the continued existence of an organization either *effectiveness* or *efficiency* is necessary; and the longer the life, the more necessary both are. The vitality of organizations lies in the willingness of individuals to contribute forces to the cooperative system. This willingness requires the belief that the purpose can be carried out, a faith that diminishes to the vanishing point as it appears that it is not in fact in process of being attained. Hence, when effectiveness ceases, willingness to contribute disappears. The continuance of willingness also depends upon the satisfactions that are secured by individual contributors in the process of carrying out the purpose. If the satisfactions do not exceed the sacrifices required, willingness disappears, and the condition is one of organization inefficiency. If the satisfactions exceed the sacrifices, willingness persists, and the condition is one of efficiency of organization.

In summary, then, the initial existence of an organization depends upon a combination of these elements appropriate to the external conditions at the moment. Its survival depends upon the maintenance of an equilibrium of the system. This equilibrium is primarily internal, a matter of proportions between the elements, but it is ultimately and basically an equilibrium between the system and the total situation external to it. This external equilibrium has two terms in it: first, the effectiveness of the organization, which comprises the relevance of its purpose to the environmental situation; and, second, its efficiency, which comprises the interchange between the organization and individuals. Thus the elements stated will each vary with external factors, and they are at the same time interdependent; when one is varied compensating variations must occur in the other if the system of which they are components is to remain in equilibrium, that is, is to persist or survive.

We may now appropriately consider these elements and their interrelations in some detail, having in mind the system as a whole.

I

I. Willingness to Cooperate

By definition there can be no organization without persons. However, as we have urged that it is not persons, but the services or acts or action or influences of persons, which should be treated as constituting organizations, it is clear that *willingness* of persons to contribute efforts to the cooperative system is indispensable.

There are a number of words and phrases in common use with reference to organization that reach back to the factor of individual willingness. "Loyalty," "solidarity," "*esprit de corps*," "strength" of organization, are the chief. Although they are indefinite, they relate to intensity of attachment to the "cause," and are commonly understood to refer to something different from effectiveness, ability, or value of personal contributions. Thus "loyalty" is regarded as not necessarily related either to position, rank, fame, remuneration, or ability. It is vaguely recognized as an essential condition of organization.

Willingness, in the present connection, means self-abnegation, the surrender of control of personal conduct, the depersonalization of personal action. Its effect is cohesion of effort, a sticking together. Its immediate cause is the disposition necessary to "sticking together." Without this there can be no sustained personal effort as a contribution to cooperation. Activities cannot be coordinated unless there is first the disposition to make a personal act a contribution to an impersonal system of acts, one in which the individual gives up personal control of what he does.

The outstanding fact regarding willingness to contribute to a given specific formal organization is the indefinitely large range of variation in its intensity among individuals. If all those who may be considered potential contributors to an organization are arranged in order of willingness to serve it, the scale gradually descends from possibly intense willingness through neutral or zero willingness to intense unwillingness or opposition or hatred. The *preponderance of persons in a modern society always lies on the negative side* with reference to any particular existing or potential organization. Thus of the possible contributors only a small minority actually have a positive willingness. This is true of the largest and most comprehensive formal organizations, such as the large nations, the Catholic Church, etc. Most of the persons in existing society are either indifferent to or positively opposed to any single one of them; and if the smaller organizations subordinate to these major organizations are under consideration the minority becomes of course a much smaller proportion, and usually a nearly negligible proportion, of the conceivable total.

A second fact of almost equal importance is that the willingness of any individual cannot be constant in degree. It is necessarily intermittent and fluctuating. It can scarcely be said to exist during sleep, and is obviously diminished or exhausted by weariness, discomfort, etc., a conception that was well expressed by the saying "The spirit is willing, but the flesh is weak."

A corollary of the two propositions just stated is that for any given formal organization the number of persons of positive willingness to serve, but near the neutral or zero point, is always fluctuating. It follows that the aggregate willingness of potential contributors to any formal cooperative system is unstable—a fact that is evident from the history of all formal organizations.

Willingness to cooperate, positive or negative, is the expression of the net satisfactions or dissatisfactions experienced or anticipated by each individual in comparison with those experienced or anticipated through alternative opportunities. These alternative opportunities may be either personal and individualistic or those afforded by other organizations. That is, willingness to cooperate is the net effect, first, of the inducements to do so in conjunction with the sacrifices involved, and then in comparison with the practically available net satisfactions afforded by alternatives. The questions to be determined, if they were matters of logical reasoning, would be, first, whether the opportunity to cooperate grants any advantage to the individual as compared with independent action; and then, if so, whether that advantage is more or less than the advantage obtainable from some other cooperative opportunity. Thus, from the viewpoint of the individual, willingness is the joint effect of personal desires and reluctances; from the viewpoint of organization it is the joint effect of objective inducements offered and burdens imposed. The measure of this net result, however, is entirely individual, personal, and subjective. Hence, organizations depend upon the motives of individuals and the inducements that satisfy them.

II. Purpose

Willingness to cooperate, except as a vague feeling or desire for association with others, cannot develop without an objective of cooperation. Unless there is such an objective it cannot be known or anticipated what specific efforts will be required of individuals, nor in many cases what satisfactions to them can be in prospect. Such an objective we denominate the "purpose" of an organization. The necessity of having a purpose is axiomatic, implicit in the words "system," "coordination," "cooperation." It is something that is clearly evident in many observed systems of cooperation, although it is often not formulated in words, and sometimes cannot be so formulated. In such cases what is observed is the direction or effect of the activities, from which purpose may be inferred.

A purpose does not incite cooperative activity unless it is accepted by those whose efforts will constitute the organization. Hence there is initially something like simultaneity in the acceptance of a purpose and willingness to cooperate.

It is important at this point to make clear that every cooperative purpose has in the view of each cooperating person two aspects which we call (a) the cooperative and (b) the subjective aspect, respectively.

(a) When the viewing of the purpose is an *act of cooperation,* it approximates that of detached observers from a special position of observation; this position is that of the interests of the organization; it is largely determined by organization knowledge, but is personally interpreted. For example, if five men are cooperating to move a stone from A to B, the moving of the stone is a different thing in the organization view of each of the five men involved. Note, however, that what moving the stone means to each man personally is not here in question, but what he thinks it means to the organization *as a whole.* This includes the significance of his own effort as an element in cooperation, and that of all others, in his view; but it is not at all a matter of satisfying a personal motive.

When the purpose is a physical result of simple character, the difference between the purpose as objectively viewed by a detached observer and the purpose as viewed by each person cooperating *as an act of cooperation* is ordinarily not large or important, and the different cooperative views of the persons cooperating are correspondingly similar. Even in such cases the attentive observer will detect differences that result in disputes, errors of action, etc., even though no *personal* interest is implicated. But when the purpose is less tangible—for example, in religious cooperation—the difference between objective purpose and purpose as cooperatively viewed by each person is often seen ultimately to result in disruption.

We may say, then, that a purpose can serve as an element of a cooperative system only so long as the participants do not recognize that there are serious divergences of their understanding of that purpose as the object of cooperation. If in fact there is important difference between the aspects of the purpose as objectively and as cooperatively viewed, the divergencies become quickly evident when the purpose is concrete, tangible, physical; but when the purpose is general, intangible, and of sentimental character, the divergencies can be very wide yet not be recognized. Hence, an objective purpose that can serve as the basis for a cooperative system is one that is *believed* by the contributors (or potential contributors) to it to be the determined purpose of the organization. The inculcation of belief in the real existence of a common purpose is an essential executive function. It explains much educational and so-called morale work in political, industrial, and religious organizations that is so often otherwise inexplicable.

(b) Going back to the illustration of five men moving a stone, we have noted "that what moving the stone means to each man personally is not here in question, but what he thinks it means to the *organization as a whole.*" The distinction emphasized is of first importance. It suggests the fact that every participant in an organization may be regarded as having a dual personality—an organization personality and an individual personality. Strictly speaking, an organization purpose has directly no meaning for the individual. What has meaning for him is the organization's relation to him—what burdens it imposes, what benefits it confers. In referring to the aspects of purpose as cooperatively viewed, we are alluding to the *organization* personality of individuals. In many cases the two personalities are so clearly developed that they are quite apparent. In military action individual conduct may be so dominated by organization personality that it is utterly contradictory of what personal motivation would require. It has been observed of many men that their private conduct is entirely inconsistent with official conduct, although they seem completely unaware of the fact. Often it will be observed that participants in political, patriotic, or religious organizations will accept derogatory treatment of their personal conduct, including the assertion that it is inconsistent with their organization obligations, while they will become incensed at the slightest derogation of the tenets or doctrines of their organization, even though they profess not to understand them. There are innumerable other cases, however, in which almost no organization personality may be said to exist. These are cases in which personal relationship with the cooperative system is momentary or at the margin of willingness to participate.

In other words we have clearly to distinguish between organization purpose and individual motive. It is frequently assumed in reasoning about organizations that common purpose and individual motive are or should be identical. With the exception noted below, this is never the case; and under modern conditions it rarely even appears to be the case. Individual motive is necessarily an internal, personal, subjective thing; common purpose is necessarily an external, impersonal, objective thing even though the individual interpretation of it is subjective. The one exception to this general rule, an important one, is that the accomplishment of an organization purpose becomes itself a source of personal satisfaction and a motive for many individuals in many organizations. It is rare, however, if ever, and then I think only in connection with family, patriotic, and religious organizations under special conditions, that organization purpose becomes or can become the *only* or even the major individual motive.

Finally it should be noted that, once established, organizations change their unifying purposes. They tend to perpetuate themselves; and in the effort to survive may change the reasons for existence. I shall later make clearer that in this lies an important aspect of executive functions.

III. Communication

The possibility of accomplishing a common purpose and the existence of persons whose desires might constitute motives for contributing toward such a common purpose are the opposite poles of the system of cooperative effort. The process by which these potentialities become dynamic is that of communication. Obviously a common purpose must be commonly known, and to be known must be in some way communicated. With some exceptions, verbal communication between men is the method by which this is accomplished. Similarly, though under crude and obvious conditions not to the same extent, inducements to persons depend upon communication to them.

The method of communication centers in language, oral and written. On its crudest side, motions or actions that are of obvious meaning when observed are sufficient for communication without deliberate attempt to communicate; and signaling by various methods is an important method in much cooperative activity. On the other side, both in primitive and in highly complex civilization "observational feeling" is likewise an important aspect of communication.[1] I do not think it is generally so recognized. It is necessary because of the limitations of language and the differences in the linguistic capacities of those who use language. A very large element in special experience and training and in continuity of individual association is the ability to understand without words, not merely the situation or conditions, but the *intention*.

The techniques of communication are an important part of any organization and are the preeminent problems of many. The absence of a suitable technique of communication would eliminate the possibility of adopting some purposes as a basis for organization. Communication technique shapes the form and the internal economy of organization. This will be evident at once if one visualizes the attempt to do many things now accomplished by small organizations if each "member" spoke a different language. Similarly, many technical functions could hardly be carried on without special codes; for example, engineering or chemical work. In an exhaustive theory of organization, communication would occupy a central place, because the structure, extensiveness, and scope of organization are almost entirely determined by communication techniques. Moreover, much specialization in organization originates and is maintained essentially because of communication requirements.

II

I. Effectiveness of Cooperation

The continuance of an organization depends upon its ability to carry out its purpose. This clearly depends jointly upon the appropriateness of its action and upon the conditions of its environment. In other words, effectiveness is primarily a matter of technological[2] processes. This is quite obvious in ordinary cases of purpose to accomplish a physical objective, such as building a bridge. When the objective is non-physical, as is the case with religious and social organizations, it is not so obvious.

It should be noted that a paradox is involved in this matter. An organization must disintegrate if it cannot accomplish its purpose. It also destroys itself by accomplishing its purpose. A very large number of successful organizations come into being and then disappear for this reason. Hence most continuous organizations require repeated adoption of new purposes. This is concealed from everyday recognition by the practice of generalizing a complex series of specific purposes under one term, stated to be "*the* purpose" of this organization. This is strikingly true in the case of governmental and public utility organizations when the purpose is stated to be a particular kind of service through a period of years. It is apparent that their real purposes are not abstractions called "service" but specific acts of service. A manufacturing organization is said to exist to make, say, shoes; this is its "purpose." But it is evident that not making shoes in general but making specific shoes from day to day is its series of purposes. This process of generalization, however, provides in advance for the approximate definition of new purposes automatically—so automatically that the generalization is normally substituted in our minds for the concrete performances that are the real purposes. Failure to be effective is, then, a real cause of disintegration; but failure to provide for the decisions resulting in the adoption of new purposes would have the same result. Hence the generalization of purpose which can only be defined concretely by day-to-day events is a vital aspect of permanent organization.

II. Organization Efficiency

It has already been stated that "efficiency" as conceived in this treatise is not used in the specialized and limited sense of ordinary industrial practice or in the restricted sense applicable to technological processes. So-called "practical" efficiency has little meaning, for example, as applied to many organizations such as religious organizations.

Efficiency of effort in the fundamental sense with which we are here concerned is efficiency relative to the securing of necessary personal contributions to

the cooperative system. The life of an organization depends upon its ability to secure and maintain the personal contributions of energy (including the transfer of control of materials or money equivalent) necessary to effect its purposes. This ability is a composite of perhaps many efficiencies and inefficiencies in the narrow senses of these words, and it is often the case that inefficiency in some respect can be treated as the cause of total failure, in the sense that if corrected success would then be possible. But certainly in most organization—social, political, national, religious—nothing but the absolute test of survival is significant objectively; there is no basis for comparison of the efficiencies of separate aspects.

The emphasis here is on the view that efficiency of organization is its capacity to offer effective inducements in sufficient quantity to maintain the equilibrium of the system. It is efficiency in this sense and not the efficiency of material productiveness which maintains the vitality of organizations. There are many organizations of great power and permanency in which the idea of productive efficiency is utterly meaningless because there is no material production. Churches, patriotic societies, scientific societies, theatrical and musical organizations, are cases where the original flow of *material* inducements is toward the organization, not from it—a flow necessary to provide resources with which to supply material inducements to the small minority who require them in such organizations.

In those cases where the primary purpose of organization is the production of material things, insufficiency with respect to the non-material inducements leads to the attempt to substitute material inducements for the non-material. Under favorable circumstances, to a limited degree, and for a limited time, this substitution may be effective. But to me, at least, it appears utterly contrary to the nature of men to be sufficiently induced by material or monetary considerations to contribute enough effort to a cooperative system to enable it to be productively efficient to the degree necessary for persistence over an extended period.

If these things are true, then even in purely economic enterprises efficiency in the offering of non-economic inducements may be as vital as productive efficiency. Perhaps the word efficiency as applied to such non-economic inducements as I have given for illustration will seem strange and forced. This, I think, can only be because we are accustomed to use the word in a specialized sense.

The non-economic inducements are as difficult to offer as others under many circumstances. To establish conditions under which individual pride of craft and of accomplishment can be secured without destroying the material economy of standardized production in cooperative operation is a problem in real efficiency. To maintain a character of personnel that is an attractive condition of employment involves a delicate art and much insight in the selection (and rejection) of personal services offered, whether the standard of quality be high or low. To have an organization that lends prestige and secures the loyalty of desirable persons is a complex and difficult task in efficiency—in all-round efficiency, not one-sided efficiency. It is for these reasons that good organizations—commercial, governmental, military, academic, and others—will be observed to devote great attention and sometimes great expense of money to the non-economic inducements, because they are indispensable to fundamental efficiency, as well as to effectiveness in many cases.

The theory of organization set forth in this chapter is derived from the study of organizations which are exceedingly complex, although it is stated in terms of ideal simple organizations. The temptation is to assume that, in the more complex organizations which we meet in our actual social life, the effect of complexity is to modify or qualify the theory. This appears not to be the case. Organization, simple or complex, is always *an impersonal system of coordinated human efforts;* always there is purpose as the coordinating and unifying principle; always there is the indispensable ability to communicate, always

the necessity for personal willingness, and for effectiveness and efficiency in maintaining the integrity of purpose and the continuity of contributions. Complexity appears to modify the quality and form of these elements and of the balance between them; but fundamentally the same principles that govern simple organizations may be conceived as governing the structure of complex organizations, which are composite systems.

NOTES

1. The phrase "observational feeling" is of my coining. The point is not sufficiently developed, and probably has not been adequately studied by anyone. I take it to be at least in part involved in group action not incited by any "overt" or verbal communication. The cases known to me from the primitive field are those reported by W. H. R. Rivers on pages 94–97 of his *Instinct and the Unconscious* (2nd edition Cambridge University Press, 1924), with reference to Polynesia and Melanesia. One case is summarized by F. C. Bartlett, in *Remembering* (Cambridge University Press, 1932), at p. 297. Rivers states in substance that in some of the relatively small groups decisions are often arrived at and acted upon without having ever been formulated by anybody.
   I have observed on innumerable occasions apparent unanimity of decision of equals in conferences to quit discussion without a word to that effect being spoken. Often the action is initiated apparently by someone's rising; but as this frequently occurs in such groups *without* the termination of the meeting, more than mere rising is involved. "Observational feeling," I think, avoids the notion of anything "occult."
2. Using "technological" in the broad sense.

9   OF WORDS AND MEN
F. J. ROETHLISBERGER

In moving beyond scientific management's concern with the structure of the job, the human relations perspective focuses on human interaction and group life. In focusing on how human beings working together accomplish tasks, the human relations perspective raises a very difficult question: How do people come to understand one another? This question and the problem it represents for human relations scholars makes communication important to organizational life (for one answer is that people come to understand each other by communicating).

In this chapter from one of the most famous books associated with the human relations perspective, Fred Roethlisberger confronts the task of explaining why both understanding and misunderstanding occur in communication, thus providing an explanation for how organizational members sometimes succeed and also sometimes fail when working together. Roethlisberger disputes the notion that managers should interpret language as objective fact. Instead he argues that a single word can mean different things, depending on circumstances. Further, since communication has a strong emotional component that on the surface does not appear to exist in most conversations or discussions, managers may often find themselves misunderstanding messages from their employees. Roethlisberger argues, therefore, that language is always problematic and therefore human relations managers must consider how people are making sense of language in their particular organization.

The thesis of this chapter will consist of two points: (1) a good portion of the executive's environment is verbal, far more than he sometimes seems to realize; (2) little attention has been explicitly given, either by the executive or by students of administration, to the skills required in handling the verbal environment. The executive often has no conceptual framework in terms of which he can deal with it, nothing comparable at least to the explicit skills with which he handles his external nonhuman environment.

THE EXECUTIVE'S ENVIRONMENT IS VERBAL

That a good portion of the executive's environment is verbal seems hardly open to question. In discussions, meetings, and conferences the verbal atmosphere is thick. The executive is dealing largely with words, symbols, and abstractions. Of course, this applies to any one of us. We are all responding to words and other stimuli involving meaning. It seems to me obvious, however, that the higher the executive goes in an organization the more important it becomes for him, if he is to handle effectively one aspect of his job, to deal competently with his verbal environment.

On the one hand, he has to become skillful in using words that will appeal to his listeners' sentiments. In trying to secure the cooperation of individuals in the common purposes of the enterprise the executive often has to practice the art of persuasion. He uses words that he hopes will produce the appropriate efforts on his listeners. In statements to stockholders, employees, and customers, the executive has to resort to words, both oral and written. In handling complaints and grievances, the executive is using, as well as listening to, words.

On the other hand, the executive has to be able to interpret skillfully what people say, for in so far as his work involves the interactions of human beings his data come from what he hears as well as from what he sees and does.[1] Whether he likes it or not, he has to practice this difficult art; yet he has no explicit tools for doing it. He either picks up the skill intuitively or tries to organize his work so that the need for exercising it is at a minimum. This latter method is likely to be unsuccessful because it leads him to busy himself more and more with logical, statistical, and oversimplified abstractions or lofty principles about human motivation and conduct. In doing so he loses touch with the concrete situation before him.

In short, words play an important role in all the major functions of the executive. If this proposition is true, it seems sensible to ask what the executive needs to know about words and their functions and what skills he can explicitly develop in interpreting what people say.

THE FUNCTIONS OF LANGUAGE OR WORDS

Let us consider some of the different functions of language or words.[2] In the first place, words can be used to refer to events and happenings outside of our skin: this can be called the logico-experimental function of language. In this way words are used by scientists or by two or more people engaged in a discussion of matters with which they have first-hand, familiar, and intuitive acquaintance, as well as a common background of systematic knowledge. The words and symbols used by the speaker refer to events, and uniformities among events, which occur primarily outside of him or the listener, and to which they can go for observation and check in case of disagreement. Most of us spend only a very small portion of our day using words in this strict sense. We are much more likely to be engaged in less arduous and more pleasant verbal practices.

In a social conversation, for example, the situation is likely to be quite different. When two or more people are talking together, what is primarily happening is an interaction of sentiments rather than anything strictly logical. One person is using words to express certain sentiments, to which the other responds with similar or opposing sentiments; or one person tries to influence the other by using symbols that will have a favorable reaction on the latter's sentiments. This can be called the "emotive"[3] function of language, as opposed to the logico-experimental. The skillful politician is a good example of a person using words in this way.

There is a third function of language which has received considerable attention during the past two or three decades. Through words man not only communicates but satisfies his desires. I refer to the day-dreaming, revery, and air-castle building in which we all indulge and from which we obtain considerable satisfaction. A good portion of our day is spent in using words to satisfy our desires in this way.

That "Language serves a man not only to express something but also to express himself,"[4] every executive should realize and explicitly take into account. The fact that language has different functions and that these functions, except under special circumstances are rarely distinguished complicates our problem. Words refer not only to things happening outside our skins, but also to our attitudes, feelings, and sentiments toward these objects and events. This means that many statements are expressed which have little or no meaning apart from the personal situation of the person who makes them. This not only makes the interpretation of what people say difficult, it also makes it imperative to do a skillful job, because if we refer words to a wrong context we are likely to misunderstand what a person is telling us. The channels of communication in a business organization often become clogged because words are referred to wrong contexts.

The problem would be simple if when people spoke they labeled what it was they were telling us. . . . . Unfortunately (or fortunately, depending upon our point of view), this is not often true. We very seldom express our sentiments *as sentiments*. One of the most time-consuming pastimes of the human mind is to rationalize sentiments and to disguise sentiments as logic.

THE SKILL OF INTERPRETING WHAT PEOPLE SAY

All I have said so far shows clearly that the interpretation of what people say is a difficult business. There is nothing to be gained by pretending that the job is simple. It is something that some people learn from experience and at which some people— physicians, lawyers, and businessmen—become exceedingly skillful. (These skillful people, however, often cannot communicate their skill.) The technique cannot be learned without practice but, again, for some people practice is not enough. No matter how much experience they have in listening to or in using words, they never acquire any great ability in this field. They continue to deal with words as constants rather than as variables, as if they had universal meanings rather than different meanings for different people under different conditions and situations. Some academic people are the worst offenders in this respect. Some scientists and engineers can never learn that words outside of the limited area of their specialty have different uses and important social functions.

Dr. Henderson has said: "Effective rules of procedure in interpreting what men say have not yet been developed . . . Therefore we are in respect of this kind of work still more or less in the master-apprentice stage."[5] However, in the past twelve years the research group with which I am associated has had considerable experience in trying to interpret what people say. It may be of some interest, therefore, if I try to state more explicitly some of the rules or discriminations which we have worked out. It may seem rather absurd to try to communicate a skill which, like any other, is in certain respects ineffable. However, inasmuch as all of us are practicing it, some more successfully than others, it can do no harm and perhaps some good to try to state more explicitly its nature. What I shall say, of course, can be only very rough, approximate, and tentative.

Getting People to Talk about Matters Important to Them

When I am confronted with a complex situation involving the interactions of people, what people say is necessarily an important part of the data from which I have to make a diagnosis. Therefore, my first object is to get people to talk freely and frankly about matters which are important to them. This situation in which I try to get people to talk I shall call the interview. In the interview I use a number of simple rules or ideas: I listen. I do not interrupt. I do not give advice. I avoid leading questions. I refrain from making moral judgments about the opinions expressed. I do not express my own opinions, beliefs, or sentiments. I avoid argument at all cost. I do this by seeing to it that the speaker's sentiments do not react on my own. Inasmuch as these rules have been stated elsewhere, I shall not elaborate on them here.[6]

Orientation to Speaker

Although it is sometimes difficult to get people to talk freely about matters of importance to them, it is not nearly so difficult as the next part of my job. While I am listening intently and sympathetically to what the person is saying, my mind is not just a blank. I am listening for something; there is some framework in which my thought is set. I am oriented to the speaker in a certain way. To take an example, let us assume that an employee in a large factory is speaking to me: he says, "The supervisors in this company are a bunch of goddam slavedrivers." What is my attitude toward such a remark?

First, I am not interested in the verbal definition of the word "slavedriver." Secondly, I do not allow my sentiments to be acted upon by this word, nor do I try to argue the speaker out of his belief. Thirdly, I am not assuming that there exists one particular quality in some supervisors to which this word refers; that is, I do not assume that because there is a word "slavedriver" there is only one thing to which it refers. Finally, I am not assuming that truth or falsity has anything to do with the statement.[7]

How, then, am I oriented to such a remark? In the first place, I assume that this person is expressing his feelings and sentiments. I assume that these feelings and sentiments are not "words," although words are being used to express them. I assume that I shall not be able to understand the feelings and sentiments expressed until I find the context to which they refer. In order to find the context, I am thinking of those events in the life of the employee to which his statement may refer, and also of the social situations in which they occurred. In other words, I am hunting for the referents of the statement. Therefore, I try to get the employee to talk about the particular supervisors (Supervisor 1, Supervisor 2, etc.) with whom he has been associated—when, where, how often, under what conditions, and so on. I am listening for what these particular supervisors did and under what conditions they did it, what meanings the employee assigned to their behavior, what the employee did and under what conditions he did it, and so on.

But more than this, I am also thinking of, and trying to get the employee to talk about, events in his previous history or in his associations with people outside the factory to which events involving interactions with people within the factory may be related *for the employee*. I do this because I assume that this particular employee's unpleasant feelings about a particular supervisor are a resultant of two sets of factors: (1) what he (the employee) is bringing to the situation in terms of hopes and expectations (sentiments), and (2) the social demands which the situation is making of him.

(1) In order to find out what the employee is bringing to the situation in terms of sentiments, I need to know something about the meaningful associations he has had with other people and groups before coming to the factory. I assume that from these previous associations he has been conditioned to a certain way of life and to certain hopes, fears, and expectations. In terms of this kind of data, I can see more clearly what sentiments of the employee are being violated, disregarded, or misunderstood by a particular supervisor. I may find, for example, that the employee's attitude toward supervision is rooted somewhere in his attitude toward authority as conditioned by his early family situation; on anyone in authority he may be projecting the parental image.

(2) But if I stopped here I might still be missing an important context to which his statement may refer. This worker is not an isolated individual. He has relations with other people. He is part of a social system called the factory. He is part of a smaller social system called the department. He is part of a still smaller social system called the work group—those people with whom he is associating daily at work. It may be that in the small work group this employee is an informal leader. The workers respect him as a craftsman; they go to him for help about their work; they go to him with their troubles. He instructs them about difficult jobs and he listens to their grievances. Perhaps the foreman of his department does not recognize this employee's status in the informal work situation or, if he does, has not seen to it that his superiors also recognize it. Perhaps through ignorance of the situation he has recently promoted a younger and shorter-service man to a supervisory job in this department, a man whose efficiency record is good, and who is therefore easier to recommend to his superiors for promotion, but who is looked upon by his own work associates as a "rate buster," "chiseler," or "squealer." Perhaps it is the disturbances within this social situation to which the employee's statement, "The supervisors in this company are a bunch of goddam slave-drivers," refers.

I need not emphasize that it is important to know what a person is really complaining about before trying to act on the verbal manifestation of his complaint. Otherwise, we shall be dealing with words, or symptoms, rather than with the situation determining the grievance.

So far, I have told you of my attitude in an interview toward a person when he is complaining about another person, but my attitude is very similar if he is complaining about nonhuman objects and events in his experience. (I say "in an interview" because this is not my ordinary social attitude.) If a person tells me, for example, that his desk is too small, I do not try to convince him that the size of his desk is sufficient for his purposes; I am thinking of the social setting in which desks appear in his work situation. What human relationship does the desk symbolize for him? It may be that in his organization the higher in the business structure the person goes, the bigger the desk becomes. It may be that the person who is talking to me is a college man with a burning desire to succeed. He may be indulging in a little wishful thinking; by getting a bigger desk he may think he is elevating himself in the company. When he complains that his desk is too small, he may really be telling me about his dissatisfaction with his advancement in the company. If so, I get him to talk about that.

DIAGNOSING HUMAN SITUATIONS

In discussing how I interpret what people say, I have also been describing how I go about diagnosing a personal situation, that is, how I go from what people say to what their situation is. Obviously, it is the situation to which the words refer that is important and not the words themselves. *It is the situation and not the words that we want to understand.* I assume here that just as control of our physical environment came when we were able to control the objects and events to which words refer, so human control begins when we can control the human situations to which words refer.

In diagnosing human situations I try to avoid two tricks which words can play: (1) The danger of treating alike by words things that are different and unique, and (2) the danger of separating by words things that are inseparable in fact.[8]

Treating Alike by Words Situations That Are Different

In our ordinary language we often use one word to refer to many unique objects in many different settings and in many different stages of process. For example, we have one word "chair" to refer to many unique objects, such as Chair 1, Chair 2, Chair 3, etc. We have one word "chair" to refer to Chair 1, which Smith 1 (the boss) occupies, and Chair 2, which Smith 2 (the secretary) occupies. The behavior of people toward the person who occupies Chair 1 is quite different from their behavior toward the person using Chair 2. The duties, obligations, and privileges of the occupant of Chair 1 are quite different from those of the occupant of Chair 2. Very seldom, at least in large business organizations, does Smith 1 sit on Chair 2. Even less often does Smith 2 sit on Chair 1, at least if Smith 1 is present; it would be considered inappropriate behavior if she did, if not by Smith 1 then by Smith 3

(Smith 1's boss). Moreover, we have the same word "chair" to refer to Chair 3 when it was in the boss's office ten years ago and Chair 3 when it has become old and dilapidated and is being used by the janitor in the basement.

Thus, our ordinary language tends to make the objects and events in our experience appear in isolation, that is, apart from their context. This is particularly true of common objects, such as chairs and desks, which occur in events involving human interactions. They appear in a certain time setting, that is, they are preceded by certain events and followed by others; moreover, they appear in a certain social setting. Therefore, if we pay exclusive attention to words and exclude the situations to which the words refer we miss very important differences of context. We fall into the error of assuming that because the same word can be applied to many different objects and events in different situations they are in some way the same. As a result, we fail to notice differences, and we read into our experience similarities where differences exist. Therefore, whenever I am concerned with overt or verbal behavior involving the interactions of human beings I am alert to differences in situation and I look for differences before I look for uniformities.

Let me give an example of what I mean. Let us assume that we have been called in to study a large company which has had in operation for a number of years a bonus plan for its executives; the management is interested to know whether or not the bonus is acting as an incentive. How do we approach such a problem? Can we assume that because there is one word "executive" all the persons to whom this label applies are the same and the "bonus" means the same thing to each of them? Can we assume that because there is one word "incentive" there is one thing to which this word applies? Can we determine the effects of the bonus on something before we diagnose what that something is? Or do we look first at the particular people, the particular interrelations among them, and the particular situations in which the words "executive," "incentive," and "bonus" appear?

If we follow this last procedure, what do we find? We find Executive 1 with a particular background and social conditioning (private hopes, fears, sentiments) in association with people in a particular department and a particular division, i.e., a member of a particular social system.[9]

After studying the executives in the company from this point of view, let us ask what effects the bonus might be expected to have. We might expect to find, first, that there are as many different effects from the bonus as there are different executives or different kinds of executive situations. Secondly, we might find that there are as many different effects from the bonus as there are different social systems. We might find that a bonus plan is in fact a different system as applied to different social organizations. Only after we have broken down our data into these differences, however, do we look for uniformities. Only in this way can we avoid reading verbal similarities into things that are different.

With this kind of approach, what happens to our original question of whether or not the bonus acts as an incentive? Like many questions that the human mind can devise, it becomes meaningless, and like many meaningless questions, such as "How many angels can sit on the point of a needle?" it has no meaningful answer. Some of us find it difficult to throw a question overboard. We feel that *because we can frame a simple question there must be a simple answer*, and to give up such a question is like parting with our best friend or our favorite hat. To those who can free themselves from sentimental attachments to words, however, it becomes apparent that by giving up the question nothing is lost—at least, nothing is lost from the point of view of knowledge; indeed, there is something gained. We know in fact some of the effects the bonus is now having on particular persons in particular positions in a particular organization. In these terms new questions can be raised by means of which we may learn more; and from this new knowledge the bonus plan may be better evaluated.

Separating by Words Things That Are Inseparable in Fact

In diagnosing human situations there is also the danger of separating by words things that are inseparable in fact. It is important, in tracing expressions of sentiment to the events in a person's experience to which they refer, to keep the events in their context;

in other words, it is important to keep together those things which are together when experienced.

For example, the executive is kept together with the social system to which he is contributing his services, and together with his social conditioning. These things are kept together because they are together in his experience. An executive apart from a personal history would be something no one has seen anywhere, any time. An executive apart from a cooperative system ceases to be an executive. He may be an executive out of a job; but this is a different context from that of our illustration.

THREE DIFFERENT PERSONAL SITUATIONS

So far, we have considered how to get a person to talk freely about things that are important to him and how the listener is oriented to the speaker in order to interpret skillfully what he says. We have seen some of the ways in which words can prevent us from understanding a concrete situation. We have seen the necessity of looking for differences in our data before searching for simple uniformities. Although each human situation is unique, there are certain uniformities which begin to emerge after a large number of people have been interviewed. There are three uniformities which I have found among a number of persons I have interviewed and in terms of which I make my first rough diagnosis. As I listen to a person in the manner I have described, I am roughly asking three questions and I am roughly expecting three answers:

1. Am I listening to a person who is well related to the work group of which he is a member; and, therefore, am I listening essentially to the sentiments of the social system to which he belongs— the routines of collaboration of his group—the norms and codes of behavior of his group—the organizational way of thinking and the customary way of doing things? Or am I listening to a person who in practically everything he says is expressing a lack of relationship, or a defective relationship, to his work group? In the latter case,

2. Am I listening to the ''obsessive thinking'' of a person who, outside of the family, has never achieved in all his experience an effective or intimate relationship with his contemporaries or with his own age group, or

3. Am I listening to a person whose disequilibrium, or lack of orientation to his social surrounding, is not so much due to his early social conditioning as to his inability to adjust readily and without assistance to changes in his present environment? Is this a man who has lost his way because his customary and routine relations with people were altered too rapidly by demotion, promotion, transference, or some technical change in his work?

People in these three quite different human situations will respond to the systems, policies, and practices about them in three quite different ways. In any business organization (if there is not a strike in process) there will probably be a large proportion of Class 1. Wherever there is a great deal of discontent, one can probably find a number of the Class 3 group. In any large concern, however, no matter how well run, there are likely to be Class 3 situations which need attention, although some of them recover their equilibrium without any help. Class 2 people will probably not stay very long in a business organization without considerable attention being given them; they are likely to be found among the newcomers.

THE EXECUTIVE NOT ONLY LISTENS; HE ALSO USES WORDS

We have considered the executive as a listener who is trying to interpret skillfully what people say in order that he may be better able to understand and control the human situations about him. But the executive not only listens; he speaks and uses words in written and oral statements to other members of the organization. As a result, other people in the organization are in a position of understanding or misunderstanding, correctly interpreting or misinterpreting, what he says. This raises a number of problems concerning the communication of matters that are related to the feelings and sentiments of

people. Executives are not always communicating strictly logical propositions.

It is interesting to note that in business today, particularly in manufacturing organizations, it is not considered quite appropriate for the executive to indulge in statements of sentiment when talking to his employees and fellow associates. This form of behavior is the province of his salesforce when appealing to a particular customer, or when talking to the public on the air, or through other mediums of advertising. With regard to employer-employee relations, however, the executive code dictates that employers should interact with their employees merely on the basis of fact. This code has led to a curious state of affairs. It has blinded some executives to what is going on around them. It has forced some into a position of trying to handle matters of sentiments as if they were matters of fact. And when matters of sentiment so blatantly arise that even the most obtuse cannot fail to label them for what they are, they have no techniques for dealing with them.

Skills Involved in Handling Matters of Sentiment

This latter case was forcibly brought to my attention the other day by the captain of a ship in the merchant marine. He had gone to sea as a boy and had been brought up in the tradition that the captain is master of the ship: his word at sea is law. Although he was kindly toward his crew, all his reflexes had been conditioned to this tradition. As a result, for years he failed to see that his authority depended only upon the fact that his junior officers and crew also accepted and upheld the tradition. And then things at sea began to change. People who had not been so well conditioned for coöperation, and particularly for coöperation on the basis of this tradition, began to join his crew. The code began to change. The captain had to meet with his crew and listen to some of their complaints and grievances. In one instance he was confronted with a long list of complaints about the food. One item on this list was to the effect that the crew did not get ''seconds on jello.'' Now, it was at this point in the captain's story that his face became flushed and speech failed him. But his gestures of exasperation and frustration expressed only too well what he could not say in words. Imagine him—the captain—having to deal with people who made such ridiculous charges! Moreover, the actual fact was that they *could* get "seconds on jello." In the face of this problem, the captain was helpless. All his conditioned reflexes could do was to produce sputtering noises. He had no skills for handling this ridiculous situation. His sense of humor was gone; his ordinary social insight was gone. He could not remember the social mechanisms he had used when he was a boy to "get somebody's goat." In the face of this situation, the captain could only talk about "communism," "fifth-column activities," "agitators," "aliens," and then, as the story developed, get sick with a case of shingles.[10]

This is not intended as a funny story, nor to cast any aspersions on the captain. None of us would want to be in his position. He was up against a difficult human problem, even though it manifested itself at the level of "seconds on jello." The only point I want to make is to show the state of affairs into which we can get when we try to handle matters of sentiment as if they were matters of fact. For the captain, a difficult problem of human diagnosis was involved which entailed going from the symptoms to the underlying human situation among his crew. But for this he received no help; he had no skills, and his conditioned reflexes could only make matters worse both for himself and for the crew.

The Tendency to Deal with Employees on a Basis of Facts Alone

In the past several years, considerable emphasis has been placed upon providing information to employees about the economic conditions of the business. Many concerns have prepared interesting, attractive, graphic reports which would be intelligible to the layman. Underlying this tendency to communicate simple economic facts to employees has been the assumption that labor difficulties primarily arose because the employees were not sufficiently acquainted with the economic purposes and problems of the company. That there is some truth in this assumption may be granted; the interesting thing to note, however, is again the tendency to deal with employees on a basis of facts alone. It happens, however, that loyalty and confidence are matters of feeling and sentiment and are not necessarily se-

cured by this approach, as any skillful politician knows.

In collective bargaining activities the same tendency prevails in many organizations. Elaborate charts and diagrams are prepared to show that the charges or demands made by the union are not accurate or reasonable in terms of the facts, sometimes even to show that in fact they are served "seconds on jello." In the battle to decide who is right and who is wrong, human situations involving simple matters of sentiment are ignored.

THE EXERCISE OF HUMAN CONTROL BY LISTENING BEFORE TALKING

That the executive in dealing with human beings should take on some of the behavior patterns of the politician is not being suggested by these observations. Nor is it being recommended that the executive should make Fourth of July speeches, although in this connection it is interesting to note the bifurcation in our modern industrial society: on the one hand, the industrial leader is supposed to secure the loyalty of his employees by appealing to facts, while, on the other hand, the political leader is allowed to secure the loyalty of his constituents by appealing to emotion. What is being suggested is more simple and is of this order:

1. There are many words used by executives that not only communicate information, they convey sentiments.
2. The persons to whom the words are addressed also have sentiments; their sentiments vary with age, sex, personal situation, official rank and informal position in the organization.
3. Because these sentiments in part relate to the different positions which people occupy in the organization, then it follows that some words which are very meaningful to some members, or some parts of the organization, may have little or no meaning or different meanings to other members and other parts of the organization.
4. This problem demands serious consideration. It is the problem of the effect on different members, and on different parts of an organization of

words used by the executive when he gives an instruction or order, when he announces a policy, or when he prepares a statement addressed to employees or to stockholders. This point is very simple. The legal jargon of a lawyer may give aesthetic satisfaction to him and his fellow brethren, but it may send shivers down the spine of the layman. The exact and precise jargon of the engineer may not be communicating "facts" to the employees who are being addressed; it may be transmitting feelings of apprehension. Sometimes also, symbols may lose their customary and traditional significance, as our example of the captain in relation to his crew well illustrated. For seamen who demand "seconds on jello" symbols evoking the traditions of the sea have lost their power to motivate.

5. Therefore, when talking to an individual or group, it is important to address oneself to their sentiments, so that on the one hand what one says will not be misunderstood, and on the other hand it will have the effect on the listeners that the speaker intends. But how does one address oneself to the listeners' sentiments? How does one know what they are? Here is where the "skill of listening" previously described comes in. This skill allows one to go from the words to the sentiments being expressed; but still more important, it allows one to go from the sentiments being expressed to the human situations underlying them. Words addressed to concrete human situations are likely to be more appropriate.

6. Therefore, it is important for the executive *to listen* before talking. By this means he comes to understand the sentiments and situations of the person or group before he practices the art of persuasion or assurance in order to secure their loyalty, confidence, and cooperation. In any large-scale organization, where many layers of supervision separate the top from the bottom, these dual skills are needed. Only when the people at the top of the organization understand better the feelings and sentiments of the people at the bottom can they communicate to the bottom what to top management is important, in a manner which will obtain the understanding and ac-

ceptance of those at the bottom. This is the exercise of human control by "understanding" and not by "verbal magic."

NOTES

1. These statements are similar to those made about the social scientist by Professor L. J. Henderson in *Three Lectures on Concrete Sociology* (privately distributed), p. 13.
2. For the purposes of this paper it would be inappropriate to discuss the many different theories of language. Only three well-recognized functions of language will be mentioned to illustrate some of the problems involved in interpreting what people say.
3. Taken from C. K. Ogden and I. A. Richards, *The Meaning of Meaning* (New York: Harcourt, Brace and Company, 1925), p. 257.
4. *Ibid.*, p. 261 (statement by G. von der Gabelentz, quoted by Ogden and Richards).
5. Henderson, *Three Lectures on Concrete Sociology*, p. 19.
6. These rules for interviewing are described more fully in the following publications: L. J. Henderson, "Physician and Patient as a Social System," *The New England Journal of Medicine*, vol. 212, no. 18, May, 1935, pp. 819–823; Elton Mayo, *The Human Problems of an Industrial Civilization* (New York: Macmillan, 1933), pp. 91–92; F. J. Roethlisberger and W. J. Dickson, *Management and the Worker* (Cambridge: Harvard University Press, 1939), pp. 270–291.
7. Perhaps I should say, "I try not to let myself take these customary attitudes toward words," but this is often easier said than done.
8. For the ideas expressed in this section I am greatly indebted to A. Korzybski, *Science and Sanity* (New York: The Science Press Printing Co., 1933).
9. This is, of course, an oversimplified representation. The executive is a member of more than one social system. However, for the present purposes of illustration, this representation of the executive's situation is sufficient.
10. It may be well to point out that the captain is a Class 3 situation as above described. His customary ways of dealing with people were no longer adequate in the new situation in which he found himself.

10   ONE MORE TIME: HOW DO YOU MOTIVATE EMPLOYEES?

FREDERICK HERZBERG

In this article, Frederick Herzberg epitomizes the reaction of human *resources* theorists to the popular tenets of the human *relations* movement. He says that typical attempts by managers to motivate their employees through rewards and conditioning—benefits programs, wage increases, counseling, communication training, and so forth—do little to produce motivation or job satisfaction. These kinds of rewards service *deficiency needs*, which, if not satisfied, result in dissatisfaction among employees. However, he argues that once these basic deficiency needs have been met, smart managers should turn to characteristics of the work itself to motivate employees. By enhancing the challenge and sense of accomplishment in an employee's job, managers fulfill *growth needs*. This produces motivation that is self-sustaining and produces true job satisfaction.

We also note that in making this argument, Herzberg draws on his *two factor theory of job satisfaction*, for which he is well known. It expands on traditional one-dimensional views by arguing that job *dissat*isfaction and job *sat*isfaction are different phenomena that are related, respectively, to deficiency and growth needs.

How many articles, books, speeches, and workshops have pleaded plaintively, "How do I get an employee to do what I want him to do?"

The psychology of motivation is tremendously complex, and what has been unraveled with any degree of assurance is small indeed. But the dismal ratio of knowledge to speculation has not dampened the enthusiasm for new forms of snake oil that are constantly coming on the market, many of them with academic testimonials. Doubtless this article will have no depressing impact on the market for snake oil, but since the ideas expressed in it have been tested in many corporations and other organizations, it will help—I hope—to redress the imbalance in the aforementioned ratio.

"MOTIVATING" WITH KITA

In lectures to industry on the problem, I have found that the audiences are anxious for quick and practi-

cal answers, so I will begin with a straightforward, practical formula for moving people.

What is the simplest, surest, and most direct way of getting someone to do something? Ask him? Tell him? Give him a monetary incentive? Show him? We need a simple way. Every audience contains the "direct action" manager who shouts, "Kick him!" And this type of manager is right. The surest and least circumlocuted way of getting someone to do something is to kick him in the pants—give him what might be called the KITA.

There are various forms of KITA, and here are some of them: *Negative physical KITA* is a literal application of the term and was frequently used in the past. It has, however, three major drawbacks: (1) it is inelegant; (2) it contradicts the precious image of benevolence that most organizations cherish; and (3) since it is a physical attack, it directly stimulates the autonomic nervous system, and this often results in negative feedback—the employee may just kick you in return. These factors give rise to certain taboos against negative physical KITA.

Negative psychological KITA has several advantages over negative physical KITA. First, the cruelty is not visible; the bleeding is internal and comes much later. Second, since it affects the higher cortical centers of the brain with its inhibitory powers, it reduces the possibility of physical backlash. Third, since the number of psychological pains that a person can feel is almost infinite, the direction and site possibilities of the KITA are increased many times. Fourth, the person administering the kick can manage to be above it all and let the system accomplish the dirty work. Fifth, those who practice it receive some ego satisfaction (one-upmanship), whereas they would find drawing blood abhorrent. Finally, if the employee does complain, he can always be accused of being paranoid, since there is no tangible evidence of an actual attack.

Now, what does negative KITA accomplish? If I kick you in the rear (physically or psychologically), who is motivated? *I* am motivated; *you* move! Negative KITA does not lead to motivation, but to movement.

Let us consider motivation. If I say to you, "Do this for me or the company, and in return I will give you a reward, an incentive, more status, a promotion, all the quid pro quos that exist in the industrial organization," am I motivating you? The overwhelming opinion I receive from management people is, "Yes, this is motivation."

I have a year-old Schnauzer. When it was a small puppy and I wanted it to move, I kicked it in the rear and it moved. Now that I have finished its obedience training, I hold up a dog biscuit when I want the Schnauzer to move. In this instance, who is motivated—I or the dog? The dog wants the biscuit, but it is I who want it to move. Again, I am the one who is motivated, and the dog is the one who moves. In this instance all I did was apply KITA frontally; I extended a pull instead of a push. When industry wishes to use such positive KITAs, it has available an incredible number and variety of dog biscuits (jelly beans for humans) to wave in front of the employee to get him to jump.

But positive KITA is not motivation. If I kick my dog (from the front or the back), he will move. And when I want him to move again, what must I do? I must kick him again. Similarly, I can charge a man's battery, and then recharge it, and recharge it

again. But it is only when he has his own generator that we can talk about motivation. He then needs no outside stimulation. He *wants* to do it.

HYGIENE VS. MOTIVATORS

Let me rephrase the perennial question this way: How do you install a generator in an employee? A brief review of my motivation-hygiene theory of job attitudes is required before theoretical and practical suggestions can be offered. The theory was drawn from investigations using a wide variety of populations (including some in the Communist countries). The findings of these studies, along with corroboration from many other investigations using different procedures, suggest that the factors involved in producing job satisfaction (and motivation) are separate and distinct from the factors that lead to job dissatisfaction.

Since separate factors need to be considered, depending on whether job satisfaction or job dissatisfaction is being examined, it follows that these two feelings are not opposites of each other. The opposite of job satisfaction is not job dissatisfaction but, rather, *no* job satisfaction; and, similarly, the opposite of job dissatisfaction is not job satisfaction, but *no* job dissatisfaction.

Two different needs of man are involved here. One set of needs can be thought of as stemming from his animal nature—the built-in drive to avoid pain from the environment, plus all the learned drives which become conditioned to the basic biological needs. For example, hunger, a basic biological drive, makes it necessary to earn money, and then money becomes a specific drive. The other set of needs relates to that unique human characteristic, the ability to achieve and, through achievement, to experience psychological growth. The stimuli for the growth needs are tasks that induce growth; in the industrial setting, they are the *job content*. Contrariwise, the stimuli inducing pain-avoidance behavior are found in the *job environment*.

The growth or *motivator* factors that are intrinsic to the job are: achievement, recognition for achievement, the work itself, responsibility, and growth or advancement. The dissatisfaction-avoidance or *hygiene* (KITA) factors that are extrinsic to the job include: company policy and administration, supervision, interpersonal relationships, working conditions, salary, status, and security.

A composite of the factors that are involved in causing job satisfaction and job dissatisfaction, drawn from samples of 1,685 employees, is shown in Exhibit I. The results indicate that motivators were the primary cause of satisfaction, and hygiene factors the primary cause of unhappiness on the job. As the lower right-hand part of the exhibit shows, of all the factors contributing to job satisfaction, 81% were motivators. And of all the factors contributing to the employees' dissatisfaction over their work, 69% involved hygiene elements.

Job Loading

In attempting to enrich an employee's job, management often succeeds in reducing the man's personal contribution, rather than giving him an opportunity for growth in his accustomed job. Such an endeavor, which I shall call horizontal job loading (as opposed to vertical loading, or providing motivator factors), has been the problem of earlier job enlargement programs. This activity merely enlarges the meaninglessness of the job. Some examples of this approach, and their effects, are:

- Challenging the employee by increasing the amount of production expected of him. If he tightens 10,000 bolts a day, see if he can tighten 20,000 bolts a day. The arithmetic involved shows that multiplying zero by zero still equals zero.

- Adding another meaningless task to the existing one, usually some routine clerical activity. The arithmetic here is adding zero to zero.

Exhibit I   FACTORS AFFECTING JOB ATTITUDES, AS REPORTED IN 12 INVESTIGATIONS

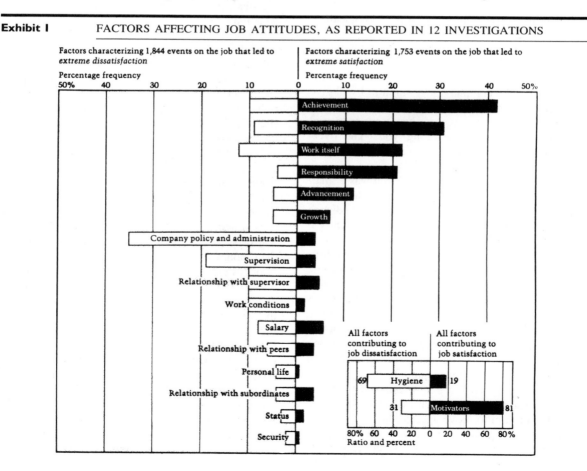

Exhibit II   PRINCIPLES OF VERTICAL JOB LOADING

Principle	Motivators Involved
A. Removing some controls while retaining accountability	Responsibility and personal achievement
B. Increasing the accountability of individuals for own work	Responsibility and recognition
C. Giving a person a complete natural unit of work (module, division, area, and so on)	Responsibility, achievement, and recognition
D. Granting additional authority to an employee in his activity; job freedom	Responsibility, achievement, and recognition
E. Making periodic reports directly available to the worker himself rather than to the supervisor	Internal recognition
F. Introducing new and more difficult tasks not previously handled	Growth and learning
G. Assigning individuals specific or specialized tasks, enabling them to become experts	Responsibility, growth, and advancement

- Rotating the assignments of a number of jobs that need to be enriched. This means washing dishes for a while, then washing silverware. The arithmetic is substituting one zero for another zero.

- Removing the most difficult parts of the assignment in order to free the worker to accomplish more of the less challenging assignments. This traditional industrial engineering approach amounts to subtraction in the hope of accomplishing addition.

These are common forms of horizontal loading that frequently come up in preliminary brain storming sessions on job enrichment. The principles of vertical loading have not all been worked out as yet, and they remain rather general, but I have furnished seven useful starting points for consideration in Exhibit II.

STEPS TO JOB ENRICHMENT

Now that the motivator idea has been described in practice, here are the steps that managers should take in instituting the principle with their employees:

1. Select those jobs in which (a) the investment in industrial engineering does not make changes too costly, (b) attitudes are poor, (c) hygiene is

becoming very costly, and (d) motivation will make a difference in performance.
2. Approach these jobs with the conviction that they can be changed. Years of tradition have led managers to believe that the content of the jobs is sacrosanct and the only scope of action that they have is in ways of stimulating people.
3. Brainstorm a list of changes that may enrich the jobs, without concern for their practicality.
4. Screen the list to eliminate suggestions that involve hygiene, rather than actual motivation.
5. Screen the list for generalities, such as "give them more responsibility," that are rarely followed in practice. This might seem obvious, but the motivator words have never left industry; the substance has just been rationalized and organized out. Words like "responsibility," "growth," "achievement," and "challenge," for example, have been elevated to the lyrics of the patriotic anthem for all organizations. It is the old problem typified by the pledge of allegiance to the flag being more important than contributions to the country—of following the form, rather than the substance.
6. Screen the list to eliminate any *horizontal* loading suggestions.
7. Avoid direct participation by the employees whose jobs are to be enriched. Ideas they have expressed previously certainly constitute a valu-

able source for recommended changes, but their direct involvement contaminates the process with human relations *hygiene* and, more specifically, gives them only a *sense* of making a contribution. The job is to be changed, and it is the content that will produce the motivation, not attitudes about being involved or the challenge inherent in setting up a job. That process will be over shortly, and it is what the employees will be doing from then on that will determine their motivation. A sense of participation will result only in short-term movement.

8. In the initial attempts at job enrichment, set up a controlled experiment. At least two equivalent groups should be chosen, one an experimental unit in which the motivators are systematically introduced over a period of time, and the other one a control group in which no changes are made. For both groups, hygiene should be allowed to follow its natural course for the duration of the experiment. Pre- and post-installation tests of performance and job attitudes are necessary to evaluate the effectiveness of the job enrichment program. The attitude test must be limited to motivator items in order to divorce the employee's view of the job he is given from all the surrounding hygiene feelings that he might have.

9. Be prepared for a drop in performance in the experimental group the first few weeks. The changeover to a new job may lead to a temporary reduction in efficiency.

10. Expect your first-line supervisors to experience some anxiety and hostility over the changes you are making. The anxiety comes from their fear that the changes will result in poorer performance for their unit. Hostility will arise when the employees start assuming what the supervisors regard as their own responsibility for performance. The supervisor without checking duties to perform may then be left with little to do.

After a successful experiment, however, the supervisor usually discovers the supervisory and managerial functions he has neglected, or which were never his because all his time was given over to checking the work of his subordinates. For example, in the R&D division of one large chemical company I know of, the supervisors of the laboratory assistants were theoretically responsible for their training and evaluation. These functions, however, had come to be performed in a routine, unsubstantial fashion. After the job enrichment program, during which the supervisors were not merely passive observers of the assistants' performance, the supervisors actually were devoting their time to reviewing performance and administering thorough training.

What has been called an employee-centered style of supervision will come about not through education of supervisors, but by changing the jobs that they do.

CONCLUDING NOTE

Job enrichment will not be a one-time proposition, but a continuous management function. The initial changes, however, should last for a very long period of time. There are a number of reasons for this:

- The changes should bring the job up to the level of challenge commensurate with the skill that was hired.

- Those who have still more ability eventually will be able to demonstrate it better and win promotion to higher-level jobs.

- The very nature of motivators, as opposed to hygiene factors, is that they have a much longer-term effect on employees' attitudes. Perhaps the job will have to be enriched again, but this will not occur as frequently as the need for hygiene.

Not all jobs can be enriched, nor do all jobs need to be enriched. If only a small percentage of the time and money that is now devoted to hygiene, however, were given to job enrichment efforts, the return in human satisfaction and economic gain would be one of the largest dividends that industry and society have ever reaped through their efforts at better personnel management.

The argument for job enrichment can be summed up quite simply: If you have someone on a job, use him. If you can't use him on the job, get rid of him, either via automation or by selecting someone with lesser ability. If you can't use him and you can't get rid of him, you will have a motivation problem.

NOTE

Author's Note: I should like to acknowledge the contributions that Robert Ford of the American Telephone and Telegraph Company has made to the ideas expressed in this article, and in particular to the successful application of these ideas in improving work performance and the job satisfaction of employees.

---

11   BANANA TIME: JOB SATISFACTION AND INFORMAL INTERACTION
Donald F. Roy

Donald F. Roy's classic description of life at the clicking machines of a plastic goods factory gives a personal and detailed illustration of issues that concern human relations theorists. Imagine standing 12 or 14 hours a day at a die-punch machine in a room the size of a small classroom with barred windows endlessly performing a repetitive, mechanical task day after monotonous day. Roy interpreted his own ethnographic account as evidence that job satisfaction is derived in large part from informal interaction among work group members. Moreover, Roy's failure to detect any positive influence of group interaction on productivity has been vindicated by later researchers. One of his key observations, however, often is overlooked by readers of "Banana Time": The intended function for the workers of the informally designated "times" and "themes" was to establish meaningful social activities in an otherwise meaningless work life. Look for other evidence that members of the clicking room group created their own meanings in their work situation. Why did the group develop roles and rules that were not dictated by management?

My fellow operatives and I spent our long days of simple, repetitive work in relative isolation from other employees of the factory. Our line of machines was sealed off from other work areas of the plant by the four walls of the clicking room. The one door of this room was usually closed. Even when it was kept open, during periods of hot weather, the consequences were not social; it opened on an uninhabited storage room of the shipping department. Not even the sounds of work activity going on elsewhere in the factory carried to this isolated work place. There were occasional contacts with "outside" employees, usually on matters concerned with the work; but, with the exception of the daily calls of one fellow who came to pick up finished materials for the next step in processing, such visits were sporadic and infrequent.

Moreover, face-to-face contact with members of the managerial hierarchy were few and far between. No one bearing the title of foreman ever came around. The only company official who showed himself more than once during the two-month obser-

Reproduced by permission of Society for Applied Anthropology from *Human Organization*, volume 18 (Winter), 1959–1960.

vation period was the plant superintendent. Evidently overloaded with supervisory duties and production problems which kept him busy elsewhere, he managed to pay his respects every week or two. His visits were in the nature of short, businesslike, but friendly exchanges. Otherwise he confined his observable communications with the group to occasional utilization of a public address system. During the two-month period, the company president and the chief chemist paid one friendly call apiece. One man, who may or may not have been of managerial status, was seen on various occasions lurking about in a manner which excited suspicion. Although no observable consequences accrued from the peculiar visitations of this silent fellow, it was assumed that he was some sort of efficiency expert, and he was referred to as "The Snooper."

As far as our work group was concerned, this was truly a situation of laissez-faire management. There was no interference from staff experts, no hounding by time-study engineers or personnel men hot on the scent of efficiency or good human relations. Nor were there any signs of industrial democracy in the form of safety, recreational, or production committees. There was an international union, and there was a highly publicized union-management cooperation program; but actual interactional processes of cooperation were carried on somewhere beyond my range of observation and without participation of members of my work group. Furthermore, these union-management get-togethers had no determinable connection with the problem of "toughing out" a twelve-hour day at monotonous work.

Our work group was thus not only abandoned to its own resources for creating job satisfaction, but left without that basic reservoir of ill-will toward management which can sometimes be counted on to stimulate the development of interesting activities to occupy hand and brain. Lacking was the challenge of intergroup conflict, that perennial source of creative experience to fill the otherwise empty hours of meaningless work routine.

The clicking machines were housed in a room approximately thirty by twenty-four feet. They were four in number, set in a row, and so arranged along one wall that the busy operator could, merely by raising his head from his work, freshen his reveries with a glance through one of three large barred windows. To the rear of one of the end machines sat

a long cutting table; here the operators cut up rolls of plastic materials into small sheets manageable for further processing at the clickers. Behind the machine at the opposite end of the line sat another table which was intermittently the work station of a female employee who performed sundry scissors operations of a more intricate nature on raincoat parts. Boxed in on all sides by shelves and stocks of materials, this latter locus of work appeared a cell within a cell.

THE WORK GROUP

Absorbed at first in three related goals of improving my clicking skill, increasing my rate of output, and keeping my left hand unclicked, I paid little attention to my fellow operatives save to observe that they were friendly, middle-aged, foreign-born, full of advice, and very talkative. Their names, according to the way they addressed each other, were George, Ike, and Sammy.[1] George, a stocky fellow in his late fifties, operated the machine at the opposite end of the line; he, I later discovered, had emigrated in early youth from a country in Southeastern Europe. Ike, stationed at George's left, was tall, slender, in his early fifties, and Jewish; he had come from Eastern Europe in his youth. Sammy, number three man in the line, and my neighbor, was heavy set, in his late fifties, and Jewish; he had escaped from a country in Eastern Europe just before Hitler's legions had moved in. All three men had been downwardly mobile as to occupation in recent years. George and Sammy had been proprietors of small businesses; the former had been "wiped out" when his uninsured establishment burned down; the latter had been entrepreneuring on a small scale before he left all behind him to flee the Germans. According to his account, Ike had left a highly skilled trade which he had practiced for years in Chicago.

I discovered also that the clicker line represented a ranking system in descending order from George to myself. George not only had top seniority for the group, but functioned as a sort of leadman. His superior status was marked in the fact that he received five cents more per hour than the other clickermen, put in the longest workday, made daily contact, outside the workroom, with the superintendent on work matters which concerned the entire line, and communicated to the rest of us the directives which he received. The narrow margin of superordination was seen in the fact that directives were always relayed in the superintendent's name; they were on the order of, ''You'd better let that go now, and get on the green. Joe says they're running low on the fifth floor.'' or, ''Joe says he wants two boxes of the 3-die today.'' The narrow margin was also seen in the fact that the superintendent would communicate directly with his operatives over the public address system; and, on occasion, Ike or Sammy would leave the workroom to confer with him for decisions or advice in regard to work orders.

Ike was next to George in seniority, then Sammy. I was, of course, low man on the totem pole. Other indices to status differentiation lay in informal interaction, to be described later.

With one exception, job status tended to be matched by length of workday. George worked a thirteen-hour day, from 7 a.m. to 8:30 p.m. Ike worked eleven hours, from 7 a.m. to 6:30 p.m.; occasionally he worked until 7 or 7:30 for an eleven and a half- or a twelve-hour day. Sammy put in a nine-hour day, from 8 a.m. to 5:30 p.m. My twelve hours spanned from 8 a.m. to 8:30 p.m. We had a half hour for lunch, from 12 to 12:30.

The female who worked at the secluded table behind George's machine put in a regular plant-wide eight-hour shift from 8 to 4:30. Two women held this job during the period of my employment; Mable was succeeded by Baby. Both were Negroes, and in their late twenties.

A fifth clicker operator, an Arabian *emigré* called Boo, worked a night shift by himself. He usually arrived about 7 p.m. to take over Ike's machine.

THE WORK

It was evident to me, before my first workday drew to a weary close, that my clicking career was going to be a grim process of fighting the clock, the particular timepiece in this situation being an old-fashioned alarm clock which ticked away on a shelf near George's machine. I had struggled through many dreary rounds with the minutes and hours during the various phases of my industrial experience, but never had I been confronted with such a dismal combination of working conditions as the extra-long workday, the infinitesimal cerebral excitation, and the extreme limitation of physical movement. The contrast with a recent stint in the California oil fields was striking. This was no eight-hour day of racing hither and yon over desert and foothills with a rollicking crew of ''roustabouts'' on a variety of repair missions at oil wells, pipe lines, and storage tanks. Here there were no afternoon dallyings to search the sands for horned toads, tarantulas, and rattlesnakes, or to climb old wooden derricks for raven's nests, with an eye out, of course, for the telltale streak of dust in the distance which gave ample warning of the approach of the boss. This was standing all day in one spot beside three old codgers in a dingy room looking out through barred windows at the bare walls of a brick warehouse, leg movements largely restricted to the shifting of body weight from one foot to the other, hand and arm movements confined, for the most part, to a simple repetitive sequence of place the die, —— punch the clicker, —— place the die, —— punch the clicker, and intellectual activity reduced to computing the hours to quitting time. It is true that from time to time a fresh stack of sheets would have to be substituted for the clicked-out old one; but the stack would have been prepared by someone else, and the exchange would be only a minute or two in the making. Now and then a box of finished work would have to be moved back out of the way, and an empty box brought up; but the moving back and the bringing up involved only a step or two. And there was the half hour for lunch, and occasional trips to the lavatory or the drinking fountain to break up the day into digestible parts. But after each momentary respite, hammer and die were moving again: click, —— move die, —— click, —— move die.

Before the end of the first day, Monotony was joined by his twin brother, Fatigue. I got tired. My legs ached, and my feet hurt. Early in the afternoon I discovered a tall stool and moved it up to my machine to ''take the load off my feet.'' But the superintendent dropped in to see how I was ''doing'' and promptly informed me that ''we don't sit down on this job.'' My reverie toyed with the idea of quitting the job and looking for other work.

The next day was the same: the monotony of the work, the tired legs and sore feet and thoughts of quitting.

INFORMAL SOCIAL ACTIVITY OF THE WORK GROUP: TIMES AND THEMES

I began to take serious note of the social activity going on around me; my attentiveness to this activity came with growing involvement in it. What I heard at first, before I started to listen, was a stream of disconnected bits of communication which did not make much sense. Foreign accents were strong and referents were not joined to coherent contexts of meaning. It was just "jabbering." What I saw at first, before I began to observe, was occasional flurries of horseplay so simple and unvarying in pattern and so childish in quality that they made no strong bid for attention. For example, Ike would regularly switch off the power at Sammy's machine whenever Sammy made a trip to the lavatory or the drinking fountain. Correlatively, Sammy invariably fell victim to the plot by making an attempt to operate his clicking hammer after returning to the shop. And, as the simple pattern went, this blind stumbling into the trap was always followed by indignation and reproach from Sammy, smirking satisfaction from Ike, and mild paternal scolding from George. My interest in this procedure was at first confined to wondering when Ike would weary of his tedious joke or when Sammy would learn to check his power switch before trying the hammer.

But, as I began to pay closer attention, as I began to develop familiarity with the communication system, the disconnected became connected, the nonsense made sense, the obscure became clear, and the silly actually funny. And, as the content of the interaction took on more and more meaning, the interaction began to reveal structure. There were "times" and "themes," and roles to serve their enaction. The interaction had subtleties, and I began to savor and appreciate them. I started to record what hitherto had seemed unimportant.

Times

This emerging awareness of structure and meaning included recognition that the long day's grind was broken by interruptions of a kind other than the formally instituted or idiosyncratically developed

disjunctions in work routine previously described. These additional interruptions appeared in daily repetition in an ordered series of informal interactions. They were, in part, but only in part and in very rough comparison, similar to those common fractures of the production process known as the coffee break, the coke break, and the cigarette break. Their distinction lay in frequency of occurrence and in brevity. As phases of the daily series, they occurred almost hourly, and so short were they in duration that they disrupted work activity only slightly. Their significance lay not so much in their function as rest pauses, although it cannot be denied that physical refreshment was involved. Nor did their chief importance lie in the accentuation of progress points in the passage of time, although they could perform that function far more strikingly than the hour hand on the dull face of George's alarm clock. If the daily series of interruptions be likened to a clock, then the comparison might best be made with a special kind of cuckoo clock, one with a cuckoo which can provide variation in its announcements and can create such an interest in them that intervening minutes become filled with intellectual content. The major significance of the interactional interruptions lay in such a carryover of interest. The physical interplay which momentarily halted work activity would initiate verbal exchanges and thought processes to occupy group members until the next interruption. The group interactions thus not only marked off the time; they gave it content and hurried it along.

Most of the breaks in the daily series were designated as "times" in the parlance of the clicker operators, and they featured the consumption of food or drink of one sort or another. There was coffee time, peach time, banana time, fish time, coke time, and, of course, lunch time. Other interruptions, which formed part of the series but were not verbally recognized as times, were window time, pickup time, and the staggered quitting times of Sammy and Ike. These latter unnamed times did not involve the partaking of refreshments.

My attention was first drawn to this times business during my first week of employment when I was encouraged to join in the sharing of two peaches. It was Sammy who provided the peaches; he drew them from his lunch box after making the announcement, "Peach time!" On this first occasion I refused the proffered fruit, but thereafter regularly consumed my half peach. Sammy continued to provide the peaches and to make the ''Peach time!'' announcement, although there were days when Ike would remind him that it was peach time, urging him to hurry up with the mid-morning snack. Ike invariably complained about the quality of the fruit, and his complaints fed the fires of continued banter between peach donor and critical recipient. I did find the fruit a bit on the scrubby side but felt, before I achieved insight into the function of peach time, that Ike was showing poor manners by looking a gift horse in the mouth. I wondered why Sammy continued to share his peaches with such an ingrate.

Banana time followed peach time by approximately an hour. Sammy again provided the refreshments, namely, one banana. There was, however, no four-way sharing of Sammy's banana. Ike would gulp it down by himself after surreptitiously extracting it from Sammy's lunch box, kept on a shelf behind Sammy's work station. Each morning, after making the snatch, Ike would call out, ''Banana time!'' and proceed to down his prize while Sammy made futile protests and denunciations. George would join in with mild remonstrances, sometimes scolding Sammy for making so much fuss. The banana was one which Sammy brought for his own consumption at lunch time; he never did get to eat his banana, but kept bringing one for his lunch. At first this daily theft startled and amazed me. Then I grew to look forward to the daily seizure and the verbal interaction which followed.

Window time came next. It followed banana time as a regular consequence of Ike's castigation by the indignant Sammy. After ''taking'' repeated references to himself as a person badly lacking in morality and character, Ike would ''finally'' retaliate by opening the window which faced Sammy's machine, to let the ''cold air'' blow in on Sammy. The slandering which would, in its echolalic repetition, wear down Ike's patience and forbearance usually took the form of the invidious comparison: ''George is a good daddy! Ike is a bad man! A very bad man!'' Opening the window would take a little time to accomplish and would involve a great deal of verbal interplay between Ike and Sammy, both before and after the event. Ike would threaten, make feints toward the window, then finally open it. Sam-

my would protest, argue, and make claims that the air blowing in on him would give him a cold; he would eventually have to leave his machine to close the window. Sometimes the weather was slightly chilly, and the draft from the window unpleasant; but cool or hot, windy or still, window time arrived each day. (I assume that it was originally a cold season development.) George's part in this interplay, in spite of the ''good daddy'' laudations, was to encourage Ike in his window work. He would stress the tonic values of fresh air and chide Sammy for his unappreciativeness.

Following window time came lunch time, a formally designated half-hour for the midday repast and rest break. At this time, informal interaction would feature exchanges between Ike and George. The former would start eating his lunch a few minutes before noon, and the latter, in his role as straw boss, would censure him for malobservance of the rules. Ike's off-beat luncheon usually involved a previous tampering with George's alarm clock. Ike would set the clock ahead a few minutes in order to maintain his eating schedule without detection, and George would discover these small daylight saving changes.

The first ''time'' interruption of the day I did not share. It occurred soon after I arrived on the job, at eight o'clock. George and Ike would share a small pot of coffee brewed on George's hot plate.

Pickup time, fish time, and coke time came in the afternoon. I name it pickup time to represent the official visit of the man who made daily calls to cart away boxes of clicked materials. The arrival of the pickup man, a Negro, was always a noisy one, like the arrival of a daily passenger train in an isolated small town. Interaction attained a quick peak of intensity to crowd into a few minutes all communications, necessary and otherwise. Exchanges invariably included loud depreciations by the pickup man of the amount of work accomplished in the clicking department during the preceding twenty-four hours. Such scoffing would be on the order of ''Is that all you've got done? What do you boys do all day?'' These devaluations would be countered with allusions to the ''soft job'' enjoyed by the pickup man. During the course of the exchanges news items would be dropped, some of serious import, such as reports of accomplished or impending layoffs in the various plants of the company, or of gains or losses in orders for company products. Most of the new items, however, involved bits of information on plant employees told in a light vein. Information relayed by the clicker operators was usually told about each other, mainly in the form of summaries of the most recent kidding sequences. Some of this material was repetitive, carried over from day to day. Sammy would be the butt of most of this newscasting, although he would make occasional counter-reports on Ike and George. An invariable part of the interactional content of pickup time was Ike's introduction of the pickup man to George. "Meet Mr. Papeatis!" Ike would say in mock solemnity and dignity. Each day the pickup man "met" Mr. Papeatis, to the obvious irritation of the latter. Another pickup time invariably would bring Baby (or Mable) into the interaction. George would always issue the loud warning to the pickup man: "Now I want you to stay away from Baby! She's Henry's girl!" Henry was a burly Negro with a booming bass voice who made infrequent trips to the clicking room with lift-truck loads of materials. He was reputedly quite a ladies' man among the colored population of the factory. George's warning to "Stay away from Baby!" was issued to every Negro who entered the shop. Baby's only part in this was to laugh at the horseplay.

About mid-afternoon came fish time. George and Ike would stop work for a few minutes to consume some sort of pickled fish which Ike provided. Neither Sammy nor I partook of this nourishment, nor were we invited. For this omission I was grateful; the fish, brought in a newspaper and with head and tail intact, produced a reverse effect on my appetite. George and Ike seemed to share a great liking for fish. Each Friday night, as a regular ritual, they would enjoy a fish dinner together at a nearby restaurant. On these nights Ike would work until 8:30 and leave the plant with George.

Coke time came late in the afternoon, and was an occasion for total participation. The four of us took turns in buying the drinks and in making the trip for them to a fourth floor vending machine. Through George's manipulation of the situation, it eventually became my daily chore to go after the cokes; the straw boss had noted that I made a much faster trip to the fourth floor and back than Sammy or Ike.

Sammy left the plant at 5:30, and Ike ordinarily retired from the scene an hour and a half later. These quitting times were not marked by any distinctive interaction save the one regular exchange between Sammy and George over the former's "early wash-up." Sammy's tendency was to crowd his washing up toward five o'clock, and it was George's concern to keep it from further creeping advance. After Ike's departure came Boo's arrival. Boo's was a striking personality productive of a change in topics of conversation to fill in the last hour of the long workday.

Themes

To put flesh, so to speak, on this interactional frame of "times," my work group had developed various "themes" of verbal interplay which had become standardized in their repetition. These topics of conversation ranged in quality from an extreme of nonsensical chatter to another extreme of serious discourse. Unlike the times, these themes flowed one into the other in no particular sequence of predictability. Serious conversation could suddenly melt into horseplay, and vice versa. In the middle of a serious discussion on the high cost of living, Ike might drop a weight behind the easily startled Sammy, or hit him over the head with a dusty paper sack. Interaction would immediately drop to a low comedy exchange of slaps, threats, guffaws, and disapprobations which would invariably include a ten-minute echolalia of "Ike is a bad man, a very bad man! George is a good daddy, a very fine man!" Or, on the other hand, a stream of such invidious comparisons as followed a surreptitious switching-off of Sammy's machine by the playful Ike might merge suddenly into a discussion of the pros and cons of saving for one's funeral.

"Kidding themes" were usually started by George or Ike, and Sammy was usually the butt of the joke. Sometimes Ike would have to "take it," seldom George. One favorite kidding theme involved Sammy's alleged receipt of $100 a month from his son. The points stressed were that Sammy did not have to work long hours, or did not have to work at all, because he had a son to support him. George would always point out that he sent money to his daughter; she did not send money to him. Sammy received occasional calls from his wife, and his claim that these calls were requests to shop for groceries on the way home were greeted with feigned disbelief. Sammy was ribbed for being closely watched, bossed, and henpecked by his wife, and the expression "Are you man or mouse?" became an echolalic utterance, used both in and out of the original context.

Ike, who shared his machine and the work scheduled for it with Boo, the night operator, came in for constant invidious comparison on the subject of output. The socially isolated Boo, who chose work rather than sleep on his lonely night shift, kept up a high level of performance, and George never tired of pointing this out to Ike. It so happened that Boo, an Arabian Moslem from Palestine, had no use for Jews in general; and Ike, who was Jewish, had no use for Boo in particular. Whenever George would extol Boo's previous night's production, Ike would try to turn the conversation into a general discussion on the need for educating the Arabs. George, never permitting the development of serious discussion on this topic, would repeat a smirking warning, "You watch out for Boo! He's got a long knife!"

The "poom poom" theme was one that caused no sting. It would come up several times a day to be enjoyed as unbarbed fun by the three older clicker operators. Ike was usually the one to raise the question, "How many times you go poom poom last night?" The person questioned usually replied with claims of being "too old for poom poom." If this theme did develop a goat, it was I. When it was pointed out that I was a younger man, this provided further grist for the poom poom mill. I soon grew weary of this poom poom business, so dear to the hearts of the three old satyrs, and, knowing where the conversation would inevitably lead, winced whenever Ike brought up the subject.

I grew almost as sick of a kidding theme which developed from some personal information contributed during a serious conversation on property ownership and high taxes. I dropped a few remarks about two acres of land which I owned in one of the western states, and from then on I had to listen to questions, advice, and general nonsensical comment in regard to "Danelly's farm."[2] This "farm" soon became stocked with horses, cows, pigs, chickens, ducks, and the various and sundry domesticated beasts so tunefully listed in "Old McDonald Had a Farm." George was a persistent offender with this theme. Where the others seemed to be mainly interested in statistics on livestock, crops, etc., George's teasing centered on a generous offering to help with the household chores while I worked in the fields. He would drone on, *ad nauseam*, "when I come to visit you, you will never have to worry about the housework, Danelly. I'll stay around the house when you go out to dig the potatoes and milk the cows, I'll stay in and peel potatoes and help your wife do the dishes." Danelly always found it difficult to change the subject on George, once the latter started to bear down on the farm theme.

Another kidding theme which developed out of serious discussion could be labelled "helping Danelly find a cheaper apartment." It became known to the group that Danelly had a pending housing problem, that he would need new quarters for his family when the permanent resident of his temporary summer dwelling returned from a vacation. This information engendered at first a great deal of sympathetic concern and, of course, advice on apartment hunting. Development into a kidding theme was immediately related to previous exchanges between Ike and George on the quality of their respective dwelling areas. Ike lived in "Lawndale," and George dwelt in the "Woodlawn" area. The new pattern featured the reading aloud of bogus "apartment for rent" ads in newspapers which were brought into the shop. Studying his paper at lunchtime, George would call out, "Here's an apartment for you, Danelly! Five rooms, stove heat, $20 a month, Lawndale Avenue!" Later, Ike would read from his paper, "Here's one! Six rooms, stove heat, dirt floor. $18.50 a month! At 55th and Woodlawn." Bantering would then go on in regard to the quality of housing or population in the two areas. The search for an apartment for Danelly was not successful.

Serious themes included the relating of major misfortunes suffered in the past by group members. George referred again and again to the loss, by fire, of his business establishment. Ike's chief complaints centered around a chronically ill wife who had undergone various operations and periods of hospital care. Ike spoke with discouragement of the expenses attendant upon hiring a housekeeper for himself and his children; he referred with disappointment and disgust to a teen-age son, an inept lad who "couldn't even fix his own lunch. He couldn't even make himself a sandwich!" Sammy's reminiscences centered on the loss of a flourishing business when he had to flee Europe ahead of Nazi invasion.

But all serious topics were not tales of woe. One favorite serious theme which was optimistic in tone could be called either "Danelly's future" or "getting Danelly a better job." It was known that I had been attending "college," the magic door to opportunity, although my specific course of study remained somewhat obscure. Suggestions poured forth on good lines of work to get into, and these suggestions were backed with accounts of friends, and friends of friends, who had made good via the academic route. My answer to the expected question, "Why are you working here?" always stressed the "lots of overtime" feature, and this explanation seemed to suffice for short-range goals.

There was one theme of especially solemn import, the "professor theme." This theme might also be termed "George's daughter's marriage theme"; for the recent marriage of George's only child was inextricably bound up with George's connection with higher learning. The daughter had married the son of a professor who instructed in one of the local colleges. This professor theme was not in the strictest sense a conversation piece; when the subject came up. George did all the talking. The two Jewish operatives remained silent as they listened with deep respect, if not actual awe, to George's accounts of the Big Wedding which, including the wedding pictures, entailed an expense of $1,000. It was monologue, but there was listening, there was communication, the sacred communication of a temple, when George told of going for Sunday afternoon walks on the Midway with the professor, or of joining the professor for a Sunday dinner. Whenever he spoke of the professor, his daughter, the wedding, or even of the new son-in-law, who remained for the most part in the background, a sort of incidental like the wedding cake, George was complete master of the interaction. His manner, in speaking to the rank-

and-file of clicker operators, was indeed that of master deigning to notice his underlings. I came to the conclusion that it was the professor connection, not the straw-boss-ship or the extra nickel an hour, which provided the fount of George's superior status in the group.

If the professor theme may be regarded as the cream of verbal interaction, the "chatter themes" should be classed as the dregs. The chatter themes were hardly themes at all; perhaps they should be labelled "verbal states," or "oral autisms." Some were of doubtful status as communication; they were like the howl or cry of an animal responding to its own physiological state. They were exclamations, ejaculations, snatches of song or doggerel, talkings-to-oneself, mutterings. Their classification as themes would rest on their repetitive character. They were echolalic utterances, repeated over and over. An already mentioned example would be Sammy's repetition of "George is a good daddy, a very fine man! Ike is a bad man, a very bad man!" Also, Sammy's repetition of "Don't bother me! Can't you see I'm busy? I'm a very busy man!" for ten minutes after Ike had dropped a weight behind him would fit the classification. Ike would shout "Mamariba!" at intervals between repetition of bits of verse, such as:

Mama on the bed,
Papa on the floor,
Baby in the crib
Says giver some more!

Sometimes the three operators would pick up one of these simple chatterings in a sort of chorus. "Are you man or mouse? I ask you, are you man or mouse?" was a favorite of this type.

So initial discouragement with the meagerness of social interaction I now recognized as due to lack of observation. The interaction was there, in constant flow. It captured attention and held interest to make the long day pass. The twelve hours of "click, —— move die, —— click, ——move die" became as easy to endure as eight hours of varied activity in the oil fields or eight hours of playing the piecework game in a machine shop. The "beast of boredom" was gentled to the harmlessness of a kitten.

CONCLUSIONS

Speculative assessment of the possible significance of my observations on information interaction in the clicking room may be set forth in a series of general statements.

Practical Application

First, in regard to possible practical application to problems of industrial management, these observations seem to support the generally accepted notion that one key source of job satisfaction lies in the informal interaction shared by members of a work group. In the clicking-room situation the spontaneous development of a patterned combination of horseplay, serious conversation, and frequent sharing of food and drink reduced the monotony of simple, repetitive operations to the point where a regular schedule of long work days became livable. This kind of group interplay may be termed "consumatory" in the sense indicated by Dewey, when he makes a basic distinction between "instrumental" and "consumatory" communication.[3] The enjoyment of communication "for its own sake" as "mere sociabilities," as "free, aimless social intercourse," brings job satisfaction, at least job endurance, to work situations largely bereft of creative experience.

In regard to another managerial concern, employee productivity, any appraisal of the influence of group interaction upon clicking-room output could be no more than roughly impressionistic. I obtained no evidence to warrant a claim that banana time, or any of its accompaniments in consumatory interaction, boosted production. To the contrary, my diary recordings express an occasional perplexity in the form of "How does this company manage to stay in business?" However, I did not obtain sufficient evidence to indicate that, under the prevailing conditions of laissez-faire management, the output of our group would have been more impressive if the playful cavorting of three middle-aged gentlemen about the barred windows had never been. As far as achievement of managerial goals is concerned, the most that could be suggested is that leavening the deadly boredom of individualized work routines with a concurrent flow of group festivities had a negative effect on turnover. I left the group, with sad reluctance, under the pressure of strong urgings to accept a research fellowship which would involve no factory toil. My fellow clickers stayed with their machines to carry on their labors in the spirit of banana time.

Theoretical Considerations

Secondly, possible contribution to ongoing sociological inquiry into the behavior of small groups, in general, and factory work groups, in particular, may lie in one or more of the following ideational products of my clicking-room experience:

1. In their day-long confinement together in a small room spatially and socially isolated from other work areas of the factory the Clicking Department employees found themselves ecologically situated for development of a "natural" group. Such a development did take place; from worker intercommunications did emerge the full-blown sociocultural system of consumatory interactions which I came to share, observe, and record in the process of my socialization.

2. These interactions had a content which could be abstracted from the total existential flow of observable doings and sayings for labelling and objective consideration. That is, they represented a distinctive sub-culture, with its recurring patterns of reciprocal influencings which I have described as times and themes.

3. From these interactions may also be abstracted a social structure of statuses and roles. This structure may be discerned in the carrying out of the various informal activities which provide the content of the sub-culture of the group. The times and themes were performed with a system of roles which formed a sort of pecking hierarchy. Horseplay had its initiators and its victims, its amplifiers and its chorus; kidding had its attackers and attacked, its least attacked and its most attacked, its ready acceptors of attack and its strong resistors to attack. The fun went on with the participation of all, but within the controlling frame of status, a matter of who can say or do what to whom and get away with it.

4. In both the cultural content and the social structure of clicker group interaction could be seen the permeation of influences which flowed from the various multiple group memberships of the participants. Past and present ''other-group'' experiences or anticipated ''outside'' social connections provided significant materials for the building of themes and for the establishment and maintenance of status and role relationships. The impact of reference group affiliations on clicking-room interaction was notably revealed in the sacred, status-conferring expression of the professor theme. This impact was brought into very sharp focus in developments which followed my attempt to degrade the topic, and correlatively, to demote George.

5. Stability of the clicking-room social system was never threatened by immediate outside pressures. Ours was not an instrumental group, subject to disintegration in a losing struggle against environmental obstacles or oppositions. It was not striving for corporate goals; nor was it faced with the enmity of other groups. It was strictly a consumatory group, devoted to the maintenance of patterns of self-entertainment. Under existing conditions, disruption of unity could come only from within.

Potentials for breakdown were endemic in the interpersonal interactions involved in conducting the group's activities. Patterns of fun and fooling had developed within a matrix of frustration. Tensions born of long hours of relatively meaningless work were released in the mock aggressions of horseplay. In the recurrent attack, defense, and counter-attack there continually lurked the possibility that words or gestures harmless in conscious intent might cross the subtle boundary of accepted, playful aggression to be perceived as an assault. While such an occurrence might incur displeasure no more lasting than necessary for the quick clarification or creation of kidding norms, it might also spark a charge of hostility sufficient to disorganize the group.

A contributory potential for breakdown from within lay in the dissimilar ''other group'' experiences of the operators. These other-group affiliations and identifications could provide differences in tastes and sensitivities, including appreciation of humor, differences which could make maintenance of consensus in regard to kidding norms a hazardous process of trial and error adjustments. . . .

NOTES

1. All names used are fictitious.
2. This spelling is the closest I can come to the appellation given me in George's broken English and adopted by other members of the group.
3. John Dewey, *Experience and Nature*, Open Court Publishing Co., Chicago, 1925, pp. 202–206.

12   ORGANIZATIONS AND THE SYSTEMS CONCEPT
Daniel Katz and Robert L. Kahn

In this classic article, Katz and Kahn begin with the premise that the popular tendency toward explaining organizational phenomena based on the organization's location in the environment and its stated purposes is fallacious. With only this information, we cannot understand how the organization actually operates or how it relates to its environment. As an answer to this shortcoming, Katz and Kahn invoke the basic principles of systems theory. This perspective focuses on organizations as hierarchically "nested" entities that actively communicate with their environment.

The use of systems theory to study human behavior radically altered the types of questions studied in organizational communication and the methods used to study these questions. The focus shifted from a physics model in which few variables were studied in isolation to a model in which the relationships among large numbers of variables were studied simultaneously. The effect of the systems framework can be seen in the Putnam and Cheney article in Part I. Their tracking of organizational communication research indicates that researchers before the 1970s studied relationships among isolated sets of two or three variables, but that researchers in the 1970s shifted to the study of many systemic variables at once. Pacanowsky and O'Donnell-Trujillo also note this shift in research focus in their justification of the organizational culture paradigm later in this section.

The aims of social science with respect to human organizations are like those of any other science with respect to the events and phenomena of its domain. Social scientists wish to understand human organizations, to describe what is essential in their form, aspects, and functions. They wish to explain cycles of growth and decline, to predict organizational effects and effectiveness. Perhaps they wish as well to test and apply such knowledge by introducing purposeful changes into organizations—by making them, for example, more benign, more responsive to human needs.

Such efforts are not solely the prerogative of social science, however; common-sense approaches to understanding and altering organizations are ancient and perpetual. They tend, on the whole, to rely heavily on two assumptions: that the location and nature of an organization are given by its name; and that an organization is possessed of built-in goals—because such goals were implanted by its founders, decreed by its present leaders, or because they emerged mysteriously as the purposes of the organizational system itself. These assumptions scarcely provide an adequate basis for the study of organizations and at times can be misleading and even fallacious. We propose, however, to make use of the information to which they point.

THE DEFINITION AND IDENTIFICATION OF ORGANIZATIONS

The first problem in understanding an organization or a social system is its location and identification. How do we know that we are dealing with an organization? What are its boundaries? What behavior belongs to the organization and what behavior lies outside it? Who are the individuals whose actions are to be studied and what segments of their behavior are to be included?

The common-sense answer to such questions begins with the organizational name. The fact that popular names exist to label social organizations, however, is both a help and a hindrance. These labels represent socially accepted stereotypes about organizations and do not specify their role structure, their psychological nature, or their boundaries. On the other hand, these names help in locating the area of behavior in which we are interested. Moreover, the fact that people both within and without an organization accept stereotypes about its nature and functioning is one determinant of its character.

The second key characteristic of the common-sense approach to understanding an organization is to regard it simply as the epitome of the purposes of its designer, its leaders, or its key members. The teleology of this approach is again both a help and a hindrance. Since human purpose is deliberately built into organizations and is specifically recorded in the social compact, the by-laws, or other formal protocol of the undertaking, it would be inefficient not to utilize these sources of information. In the early development of a group, many processes are generated that have little to do with its rational purpose, but over time there is a cumulative recognition of the devices for ordering group life and a deliberate use of these devices.

Apart from formal protocol, the primary mission of an organization as perceived by its leaders furnishes a highly informative set of clues, for the researcher seeking to study organizational functioning. Nevertheless, the stated purposes of an organization as given by its by-laws or in the reports of its leaders can be misleading. Such statements of objectives may idealize, rationalize, distort, omit, or even conceal some essential aspects of the functioning of the organization. Nor is there always agreement about the mission of the organization among its leaders and members. The university president may describe the purpose of the institution as turning out national leaders; the academic dean sees it as imparting the cultural heritage of the past, the academic vice-president as enabling students to move toward self-actualization and development, the graduate dean as creating new knowledge, the dean of students as training young people in technical and professional skills which will enable them to earn their living, and the editor of the student newspaper as inculcating the conservative values that will preserve the status quo of an outmoded capitalistic society.

The fallacy here is equating the purposes or goals of organizations with the purposes and goals of individual members. The organization as a system has an output, a product or an outcome, but this is not necessarily identical with the individual purposes of group members. Though the founders of the organization and its key members do think in teleological terms about organizational objectives, we should not accept such practical thinking, useful as it may be, in place of a theoretical set of constructs for purposes of scientific analysis. Social

science, too frequently in the past, has been misled by such shortcuts and has equated popular phenomenology with scientific explanation.

It would be much better theoretically, however, to start with concepts that do not call for identifying the purposes of the designers and then correcting for them when they do not seem to be fulfilled. The theoretical concepts should begin with the input, output, and functioning of the organization as a system and not with the rational purposes of its leaders. We may want to employ such purposive notions to lead us to sources of data or as subjects of special study, but not as our basic theoretical constructs for understanding organizations.

Our theoretical model for the understanding of organizations is that of an energic input-output system in which the energic return from the output reactivates the system. Social organizations are flagrantly open systems in that the input of energies and the conversion of output into further energic input consist of transactions between the organization and its environment.

All social systems, including organizations, consist of the patterned activities of a number of individuals. Moreover, these patterned activities are complementary or interdependent with respect to some common output or outcome; they are repeated, relatively enduring, and bounded in space and time. If the activity pattern occurs only once or at unpredictable intervals, we could not speak of an organization. The stability or recurrence of activities can be examined in relation to the *energic input* into the system, the *transformation of energies within the system*, and the *resulting product or energic output*. In a factory the raw materials and the human labor are the energic input, the patterned activities of production the transformation of energy, and the finished product the output. To maintain this patterned activity requires a continued renewal of the inflow of energy. This is guaranteed in social systems by the energic return from the product or outcome. Thus the outcome of the cycle of activities furnishes new energy for the initiation of a renewed cycle. The company that produces automobiles sells them and by doing so obtains the means of securing new raw materials, compensating its labor force, and continuing the activity pattern.

In many organizations outcomes are converted

into money and new energy is furnished through this mechanism. Money is a convenient way of handling energy units both on the output and input sides, and buying and selling represent one set of social rules for regulating exchange. Indeed, these rules are so effective and so widespread that there is some danger of mistaking the business of buying and selling for the defining cycles of organization. It is a commonplace executive observation that businesses exist to make money, and the observation is usually allowed to go unchallenged. It is, however, a very limited statement about the purposes of business.

Some human organizations do not depend on the cycle of selling and buying to maintain themselves. Universities and public agencies depend rather on bequests and legislative appropriations, and in so-called voluntary organizations the output reenergizes the activity of organization members in a more direct fashion. Member activities and accomplishments are rewarding in themselves and tend therefore to be continued without the mediation of the outside environment. A society of bird watchers can wander into the hills and engage in the rewarding activities of identifying birds for their mutual edification and enjoyment. Organizations thus differ on this important dimension of the source of energy renewal, with the great majority utilizing both intrinsic and extrinsic sources in varying degree. Most large-scale organizations are not as self-contained as small voluntary groups and are very dependent upon the social effects of their output for energy renewal.

Our two basic criteria for identifying social systems and determining their functions are (1) tracing the pattern of energy exchange or activity of people as it results in some output and (2) ascertaining how the output is translated into energy that reactivates the pattern. We shall refer to organizational functions or objectives not as the conscious purposes of group leaders or group members but as the outcomes that are the energic source for maintenance of the same type of output.

The problem of identifying the boundaries of an organization is solved by following the energic and informational transactions as they relate to the cycle of activities of input, throughput, and output. Behavior not tied to these functions lies outside the system. Many factors are related to the intake of materials into a structure but only those activities concerned with the actual importation of energy or information are part of that structure. Similarly, many processes are associated with the reception of outputs by the environment, but only those activities having to do with export of products are behavioral patterns of the organization. Obviously there is less difficulty in identifying the patterns of behavior responsible for the throughput of the system than for the boundary subsystems that deal with the environment. These subsystems do not always have clearly identifiable borders. Nor can the problems be handled by regarding any behavior of an organizational member as organizational behavior. A person in a boundary role may interact with members of another system as if he or she belonged to that system. Even the production worker's behavior, although physically taking place within the factory, at times may be social interaction with friends unrelated to the work role. In searching for criteria to define the boundaries of a system one looks for some qualitative break in the nature of the behavior pattern under scrutiny or some sudden quantitative change. These changes can be noted as the same people step out of their organizational roles and behave in radically different fashion or as we move to different people operating in different role systems.

This model of an energic input-output system is taken from the open system theory as promulgated by von Bertalanffy (1956). Theorists have pointed out the applicability of the system concepts of the natural sciences to the problems of social science. It is important, therefore, to examine in more detail the constructs of system theory and the characteristics of open systems.

System theory is basically concerned with problems of relationships, of structure, and of interdependence rather than with the constant attributes of objects. In general approach it resembles field theory except that its dynamics deal with temporal as well as spatial patterns. Older formulations of system constructs dealt with the closed systems of the physical sciences, in which relatively self-contained structures could be treated successfully as if they were independent of external forces. But living systems, whether biological organisms or social organizations, are acutely dependent on their external environment and so must be conceived of as open systems.

The essential difference between closed and open systems can be seen in terms of the concept of entropy and the second law of thermodynamics. According to the second law of thermodynamics, a system moves toward equilibrium; it tends to run down, that is, its differentiated structures tend to move toward dissolution as the elements composing them become arranged in random disorder. For example, suppose that a bar of iron has been heated by the application of a blowtorch on one side. The arrangement of all the fast (heated) molecules on one side and all the slow molecules on the other is an unstable state, and over time the distribution of molecules becomes in effect random, with the resultant cooling of one side and heating of the other, so that all surfaces of the iron approach the same temperature. A similar process of heat exchange will also be going on between the iron bar and its environment, so that the bar will gradually approach the temperature of the room in which it is located, and in so doing will elevate somewhat the previous temperature of the room. More technically, entropy increases toward a maximum and equilibrium occurs as the physical system attains the state of the most probable distribution of its elements. In social systems, however, structures tend to become more elaborated rather than less differentiated. The rich may grow richer and the poor may grow poorer. The open system does not run down, because it can import energy from the world around it. Thus the operation of entropy is counteracted by the importation of energy and the living system is characterized by negative rather than positive entropy.

COMMON CHARACTERISTICS OF OPEN SYSTEMS

Though the various open systems have common characteristics by virtue of being open, they differ in other characteristics. If this were not the case, we would be able to obtain all our basic knowledge about social organizations through studying biological organisms or even through the study of a single cell.

The following ten characteristics seem to define all open systems.

1. *Importation of energy.* Open systems import some form of energy from the external environment. The cell receives oxygen from the bloodstream; the body similarly takes in oxygen from the air and food from the external world. The personality depends on the external world for stimulation.

2. *The throughput.* Open systems transform the energy available to them. The body converts starch and sugar into heat and action. The personality converts chemical and electrical stimuli into sensory qualities, and information into thought patterns. The organization creates a new product, or processes materials, or trains people, or provides a service. These activities entail some reorganization of input. Some work gets done in the system.

3. *The output.* Open systems export some product into the environment, whether it be the invention of an inquiring mind or a bridge constructed by an engineering firm. Even the biological organism exports physiological products such as carbon dioxide from the lungs, which helps to maintain plants in the immediate environment. Continuing to turn out a system product depends on the receptivity of the environment. The stuff that is pumped into the environment may not be absorbed—either the primary product which surfeits the market or the secondary product which pollutes the surrounding air and water.

4. *Systems as cycles of events.* The pattern of activities of the energy exchange has a cyclic character. The product exported into the environment furnishes the sources of energy for the repetition of the cycle of activities. The energy reinforcing the cycle of activities can derive from some exchange of the product in the external world or from the activity itself. In the former instance, the industrial concern utilizes raw materials and human labor to turn out a product which is marketed, and the monetary return is used to obtain more raw materials and labor to perpetuate the cycle of activities. In the latter instance, the voluntary organization can provide expressive satisfactions to its members so that the energy renewal comes directly from the organizational activity itself.

System structure, or the relatedness of parts, can be observed directly when the system itself is physically bounded and its subparts are also bounded within the larger structure. The human body and its various organs constitute such a system. But how do we deal with social structures, where physical boundaries in this sense do not exist? The genius of F. H. Allport (1962) contributed the answer, namely that the structure is to be found in an interrelated set of events that return upon themselves to complete and renew a cycle of activities. It is events rather than things which are structured, so that social structure is a dynamic rather than a static concept. Activities are structured so that they comprise a unity in their completion or closure. A simple linear stimulus-response exchange between two people would not constitute social structure. To create structure, the responses of A would have to elicit B's reactions in such a manner that the responses of the latter would stimulate A to further responses. Of course the chain of events may involve many people, but their behavior can be characterized as showing structure only when there is some closure to the chain by a return to its point of origin, with the probability that the chain of events will then be repeated. The repetition of the cycle does not have to involve the same set of phenotypical happenings. It may expand to include more subevents of exactly the same kind or it may involve similar activities directed toward the same outcomes. In the individual organism the eye may move in such a way as to have the point of light fall upon the center of the retina. As the point of light moves, the movements of the eye may also change but to complete the same cycle of activity, that is, to focus upon the point of light.

A single cycle of events of a self-closing character gives us a simple form of structure. But such single cycles can also combine to give a larger structure of events or an event system. An event system may consist of a circle of smaller cycles or hoops, each one of which makes contact with several others. Cycles from other types of subsystems may also be tangential to one another. The basic method for the identification of social structures is to follow the energic chain of events from the input of energy through its transformation to the point of closure of the cycle.

5. *Negative entropy.* To survive, open systems must reverse the entropic process; they must acquire negative entropy. The entropic process is a universal law of nature in which all forms of organization move toward disorganization or death. Complex physical systems move toward simple random distribution of their elements and biological organisms also run down and perish. In the long run all open systems are subject to the law of entropy; they lose inputs or the ability to transform them, and die. While they live, however, the entropic process is arrested or reversed. The cycle of input, transformation, and output is essential to system life, and it is a cycle of negative entropy.

Open systems vary in their ability to survive even brief interruptions in this cycle. Some storage capacity, however, is characteristic. By importing more energy from its environment than it expends, the open system can store energy and acquire negative entropy. Within the limits of its storage capacity, an open system tends to maximize its ratio of imported to expended energy, to survive and, even during periods of crisis, to live on borrowed time. Prisoners in concentration camps on a starvation diet will carefully conserve the expenditure of energy, in order to make the limited food go as far as possible (Cohen, 1954). Social organizations will seek to improve their survival position and to acquire in their reserves a comfortable margin of operation.

The entropic process asserts itself in all biological systems as well as in closed physical systems. The energy replenishment of the biological organism cannot maintain indefinitely the complex organizational structure of living tissue. Social systems, however, are not anchored in the same physical constancies as biological organisms and so are capable of almost indefinite arresting of the entropic process. Nevertheless the number of organizations that go out of existence every year is large.

6. *Information input, negative feedback, and the coding process.* The inputs into living systems do not consist only of energic materials that become transformed or altered in the work that gets done. Inputs are also informative in character and furnish signals to the structure about the environment and about its own functioning in relation to the environment. Just as we recognize the distinction between cues and drives in individual psychology, so must we distinguish between informational and energic inputs for all living systems.

The simplest type of informational input found in all systems is negative feedback. Information feedback of a negative kind enables the system to correct its deviations from course. The working parts of the machine feed back information about the effects of their operation to some central mechanism or subsystem which acts on such information to keep the system on target. The thermostat that controls the temperature of the room is a simple example of a regulatory device which operates on the basis of negative feedback. The automated power plant would furnish more complex examples. Miller (1955) emphasizes the critical nature of negative feedback in his proposition: *"When a system's negative feedback discontinues, its steady state vanishes, and at the same time its boundary disappears and the system terminates"* (p. 529). If there is no corrective device to get the system back on its course, it will expend too much energy or it will ingest too much energic input and no longer continue as a system.

The reception of inputs into a system is selective. Not all energic inputs can be absorbed into every system. The digestive system of living creatures assimilates only those inputs to which it is adapted. Similarly, systems can react only to those information signals to which they are attuned. The general term for the selective mechanisms of a system by which incoming materials are rejected or accepted and translated for the structure is coding. Through the coding process the "blooming, buzzing confusion" of the world is simplified into a few meaningful and basic categories for a given system. The nature of the functions performed by the system determines its coding mechanisms, which in turn perpetuate this type of functioning.

7. *The steady state and dynamic homeostasis.* The importation of energy to arrest entropy operates to maintain some constancy in energy exchange, so that open systems that survive are characterized by a steady state. A steady state is not a motionless or true equilibrium. There is a continuous inflow of energy from the external environment and a continuous export of the products of the system, but the character of the system, the ratio of the energy exchanges and the relations between parts, remains the same. The catabolic and anabolic processes of tissue breakdown and restoration within the body preserve a steady state so that the organism from time to time is not the identical organism it was but a highly similar organism. The steady state is seen in

clear form in the homeostatic processes for the regulation of body temperature; external conditions of humidity and temperature may vary, but the temperature of the body remains the same. The endocrine glands are a regulatory mechanism for preserving an evenness of physiological functioning. The general principle here is that of Le Châtelier (see Bradley and Calvin, 1956), who maintains that any internal or external factor that threatens to disrupt the system is countered by forces which restore the system as closely as possible to its previous state. Krech and Crutchfield (1948) similarly hold, with respect to psychological organization, that cognitive structures will react to influences in such a way as to absorb them with minimal change to existing cognitive integration. The initial adjustment to such disturbances is typically approximate rather than precise. If it is insufficient, further adjustment in the same direction will follow. If it is excessive, it will be followed by a counteradjustment. The iterative process will then continue to the point of equilibrium or until the process is broken by some further disruptive event. A temporal chart of activity will thus show a series of ups and downs instead of a smooth curve. Moreover, the system itself is in motion. Its equilibrium, as Lewin (1947) put it, is quasi-stationary, more like the constant depth of a flowing river than a still pond. *The basic principle is the preservation of the character of the system.*

The homeostatic principle must be qualified in one further respect in its application to complex living systems: in counteracting entropy these systems move toward growth and expansion. This apparent contradiction can be resolved, however, if we recognize the complexity of the subsystems and their interaction in anticipating changes necessary for the maintenance of an overall steady state.

Growth is one form of this tendency toward equilibria of increasing complexity and comprehensiveness. In preserving its character, the system tends to import more energy than is required for its output, as we noted in discussing negative entropy. To insure survival, systems operate to acquire some margin of safety beyond the immediate level of existence. The body will store fat, the social organization will build up reserves, the society will increase its technological and cultural base. Miller (1955) has formulated the proposition that the rate of growth of a system—

within certain ranges—is exponential if it exists in a medium that makes available unrestricted amounts of energy for input.

Thus, the steady state, which at the simple level is one of homeostasis over time, at more complex levels becomes one of preserving the character of the system through growth and expansion. The basic system does not change directly as a consequence of expansion. The most common growth pattern is a multiplication of the same type of cycles or subsystems—a change in quantity rather than in quality. Animal and plant species grow by multiplication. A social system adds more units of the same essential type as it already has. Haire (1959) has studied the ratio between the sizes of different subsystems in growing business organizations. He found that though the number of people increased in both the production subsystem and the subsystem concerned with the external world, the ratio of the two groups remained constant. Qualitative change does occur, however, in two ways. In the first place, quantitative growth calls for supportive subsystems of a specialized character not necessary when the system was smaller. In the second place, there is a point where quantitative changes produce a qualitative difference in the functioning of a system. A small college that triples its size is no longer the same institution in terms of the relation between its administration and faculty, relations among the various academic departments, or the nature of its instruction.

In short, living systems exhibit a growth or expansion dynamic in which they maximize their basic character. They react to change or they anticipate change through growth which assimilates the new energic inputs to the nature of their structure. In terms of Lewin's quasi-stationary equilibrium, the ups and downs of the adjustive process do not always result in a return to the old level. Under certain circumstances a solidification or freezing occurs during one of the adjustive cycles. A new base line is thus established and successive movements fluctuate around this level, which may be either above or below the previous plateau of operation.

8. *Differentiation.* Open systems move in the direction of differentiation and elaboration. Diffuse global patterns are replaced by more specialized functions. The sense organs and the nervous system evolved as highly differentiated structures from the primitive nervous tissues. The growth of the personality proceeds from primitive, crude organizations of mental functions to hierarchically structured and well-differentiated systems of beliefs and feelings. Social organizations move toward the multiplication and elaboration of roles with greater specialization of function. In the United States today medical specialists now outnumber the general practitioners.

One type of differentiated growth in systems is what von Bertalanffy (1956) terms *progressive mechanization.* It finds expression in the way in which a system achieves a steady state. The early method is a process that involves an interaction of various dynamic forces, whereas the later development entails the use of a regulatory feedback mechanism.

9. *Integration and Coordination.* As differentiation proceeds, it is countered by processes that bring the system together for unified functioning. Von Bertalanffy (1956) spoke of progressive mechanization in the regulatory processes of organic systems, the replacement of dynamic interaction by fixed control arrangements. In social systems, in contrast to biological systems, there are two different paths for achieving unification, which Georgopoulos (1975) calls coordination and integration.[1] Coordination is analogous to von Bertalanffy's fixed control arrangements. It is the addition of various devices for assuring the functional articulation of tasks and roles—controlling the speed of the assembly line, for example. Integration is the achievement of unification through shared norms and values.

In organisms, hormonal and nervous subsystems provide the integrating mechanisms. In social systems, without built-in physical mechanisms of regulation, integration is often achieved at the small group level through mutually shared psychological fields. For large social organizations, coordination, rather than integration, is the rule for providing orderly and systematic articulation—through such devices as priority setting, the establishment and regulation of routines, timing and synchronization of functions, scheduling and sequencing of events.

10. *Equifinality.* Open systems are further characterized by the principle of equifinality, a principle suggested by von Bertalanffy in 1940. According to this principle, a system can reach the same final

state from differing initial conditions and by a variety of paths. The well-known biological experiments on the sea urchin show that a normal creature of that species can develop from a complete ovum, from each half of a divided ovum, or from the fusion product of two whole ova. As open systems move toward regulatory mechanisms to control their operations, the amount of equifinality may be reduced.

SOME CONSEQUENCES OF VIEWING ORGANIZATIONS AS OPEN SYSTEMS

Like most innovations in scientific theory, the open system approach was developed in order to deal with inadequacies in previous models. The inadequacies of closed system thinking about organizations became increasingly apparent during the midcentury decades of rapid societal change. The limitations of empirical research based on closed system assumptions also pointed up the need for a more comprehensive theoretical approach. The consequences, or rather the potentialities, of dealing with organizations as open systems can best be seen in contrast to the limitations and misconceptions of closed system thinking. The most important of these misconceptions, almost by definition, is the failure to recognize fully the dependence of organizations on inputs from their environment. That inflow of materials and energy is neither constant nor assured, and when it is treated as a constant much of organizational behavior becomes unexplainable. The fact that organizations have developed protective devices to maintain stability and that they are notoriously difficult to change or reform should not be allowed to obscure their dynamic relationships with the social and natural environment. Changes in that environment lead to demands for change in the organization, and even the effort to resist those demands results in internal change.

It follows that the study of organizations should include the study of organization-environment relations. We must examine the ways in which an organization is tied to other structures, not only those that furnish economic inputs and support but also structures that can provide political influence and societal legitimation. The open-system emphasis on such relationships implies an interest in properties of the environment itself. Its turbulence or placidity, for example, limits the kinds of relationships that an organization can form with systems in the environment and indicates also the kinds of relationships that an organization will require to assure its own survival.

The emphasis on openness is qualified, however. There is a duality to the concept of open system; the concept implies openness but it also implies system properties, stable patterns of relationships and behavior within boundaries. Complete openness to the environment means loss of those properties; the completely open organization would no longer be differentiated from its environment and would cease to exist as a distinct system. The organization lives only by being open to inputs, but selectively; its continuing existence requires both the property of openness and of selectivity.

The open system approach requires study of these selective processes, analysis of those elements in the environment that are actively sought, those disregarded, and those kept out or defended against. The basis of these choices, the means employed for their implementation, and the consequences for organizational effectiveness and survival becomes topics for research. In well-established organizations the internal arrangements for making and implementing such choices are highly developed, a fact that often allows such organizations to withstand environmental turbulence better than the reform or revolutionary movements that seek to displace them. Sustained supportive inputs are less predictable for groups attempting social change.

A second serious deficiency in closed system thinking, both theoretical and pragmatic, is overconcentration on principles of internal functioning. This could be viewed as merely another aspect of disregard for the environment, but it has consequences of its own. Internal moves are planned without regard for their effects on the environment and the consequent environmental response. The effects of such moves on the maintenance inputs of motivation and morale tend not to be adequately considered. Stability may be sought through tighter integration and coordination when flexibility may be the more important requirement. Coordination and control become ends in themselves, desirable states within a closed system rather than means of attaining an adjustment between the system and its environment. Attempts to introduce coordination in kind and degree not functionally required tend to produce new internal problems.

Two further errors derive from the characteristic closed system disregard of the environment and preoccupation with internal functions—the neglect of equifinality and the treatment of disruptive external events as error variance. The equifinality principle simply asserts that there are more ways than one of producing a given outcome. In a completely closed system, the same initial conditions must lead to the same final result; nothing has changed and therefore nothing changes. In open systems, however, the principle of equifinality applies; it holds true at the biological level, and it is more conspicuously true at the social level. Yet in practice most armies insist that there is one best way for all recruits to assemble their guns; most coaching staffs teach one best way for all baseball players to hurl the ball in from the outfield. And in industry the doctrine of scientific management as propounded by Taylor and his disciples begins with the assumption of the one best way: discover it, standardize it, teach it, and insist on it. It is true that under fixed and known conditions there is one best way, but in human organizations the conditions of life are neither fixed nor fully known. Such organizations are better served by the general principle, characteristic of all open systems, that there need not be a single method for achieving an objective.

The closed system view implies that irregularities in the functioning of a system due to environmental influences are error variances and should be treated accordingly. According to this conception, they should be controlled out of studies of organizations. From the organization's own operations they should be excluded as irrelevant and should be guarded against. The decisions of officers to omit a consideration of external factors or to guard against such influences in a defensive fashion, as if they would go away if ignored, is an instance of this type of thinking. So is the now outmoded "public be damned" attitude of business executives toward the clientele upon whose support they depend. Open system theory, on the other hand, would maintain

that environmental influences are not sources of error variance but are integral to the functioning of a social system, and that we cannot understand a system without a constant study of the forces that impinge upon it.

Finally, thinking of organizations as closed systems results in failure to understand and develop the feedback or intelligence function, the means by which the organization acquires information about changes in the environment. It is remarkable how weak many industrial companies are in their market research departments when they are so dependent on the market. The prediction can be hazarded that organizations in our society will increasingly move toward the improvement of the facilities for research in assessing environmental forces. We are in the process of correcting our misconception of the organization as a closed system, but the process is slow.

Open system theory, we believe, has potentialities for overcoming these defects in organizational thinking and practice. Its potentialities, however, cannot be realized merely by acknowledging the fact of organizational openness; they must be developed. Open is not a magic word, and pronouncing it is not enough to reveal what has been hidden in the organizational cave. We have begun the process of specification by discussing properties shared by all open systems. We turn next to the special properties of human organizations, as one category of such systems.

NOTE

1. This distinction is similar to the one formulated by Nancy Morse on *binding-in* and binding-*between* functions—the binding-in referring to the involvement of people in the system, the binding-between referring to the ties between system parts. (Unpublished manuscript.)

REFERENCES

Allport, F. H. 1962. A structuronomic conception of behavior: individual and collective. I. Structural theory and the master problem of social psychology. *Journal of Abnormal and Social Psychology, 64*, 3–30.

Bradley, D. F. and Calvin, M. 1956. Behavior: imbalance in a network of chemical transformations. *General Systems*. Yearbook of the Society for the Advancement of General System Theory, 1, 56–65.

Cohen, E. 1954. *Human behavior in the concentration camp*. London: Jonathan Cape.

Georgopoulos, B. S. 1975. *Hospital organization research: review and source book*. Philadelphia: W. B. Saunders.

Haire, M. 1959. Biological models and empirical histories of the growth of organizations. In Haire, M. (ed). *Modern organization theory*. New York: Wiley, 272–306.

Lewin, K. 1947. Frontiers in group dynamics. *Human Relations, 1*, 5–41.

Krech, D. and Crutchfield, R. 1948. *Theory and problems of social psychology*. New York: McGraw-Hill.

Miller, J. G. 1955. Toward a general theory for the behavioral sciences. *American Psychologist, 10*, 513–531.

Morse, N. 1953. *Satisfactions in the white collar job*. Ann Arbor, Mich.: Survey Research Center.

von Bertalanffy, L. 1940. Der organismus als physikalisches system betrachtet. *Naturwissenschaften, 28*, 521 ff.

von Bertalanffy, L. 1956. General system theory. *General systems*. Yearbook of the Society for General Systems Theory, 1, 1–10.

13   THE COST OF INTERVENTION IN NATURE
Garrett Hardin

Despite being somewhat dated, Professor Hardin's illustrations of systems theory clearly demonstrate its most fundamental premise that everything is connected to everything else and that therefore you cannot do just one thing. Both his fanciful (and possibly sexist) example of the consequences of introducing the cat into rural England and his poignant listing of the consequences of building the world's largest earth-filled dam show that those who seek to intervene in systems—whether made by people or nature—must realize there will be many consequences they do not intend and cannot foresee. Hardin's lesson can be extended to students of organizational communication: do not assume messages mean only one thing, nor that they will produce only one consequence.

Rachel Carson started a revolution when she published "Silent Spring" in 1962. True to form, this revolutionary work was widely misunderstood at first. Some critics complained that Miss Carson had not presented all of the evidence—which was true. Others said that pesticides were not necessarily so bad as her horrendous examples implied—which also was true. But most of the nit-picking critics missed entirely the revolutionary meaning of "Silent Spring."

What Miss Carson was trying to tell us was simply this: The world can no longer afford to ignore what has been called the "ecologic ethic." The ethical system under which we operated in the past was possibly adequate for an uncrowded world, though even this is debatable. But it is not adequate for a world that is already critically overcrowded, a world in which it is increasingly difficult for anyone to do anything at all without seriously affecting the well-being of countless other human beings. In castigating pesticide sprayers as monomaniacs, Rachel Carson was alerting the world to what has been called the fundamental principle of ecology, namely: *We can never do merely one thing.* A monomaniac, by definition, is someone who thinks he can do just one thing, whether it be killing pests with pesticides, creating law and order with naked force or bringing Utopia into being with uninstructed love.

NOTHING STANDS ALONE

We can never do merely one thing, because the world is a system of fantastic complexity. Nothing stands alone. No intervention in nature can be focused exclusively on but one element of the system. More than 100 years ago, Charles Darwin gave an amusing example of an ecologic system in his classic discussion of the consequences of introducing a cat into rural England:

"The number of humble-bees in any district depends in a great measure upon the number of field-mice which destroy their combs and nests; and Col. Newman who has long attended to the habits of humble-bees, believes that 'more than two-thirds of them are thus destroyed all over England.' Now the number of mice is largely dependent, as everyone knows, on the number of cats; and Col. Newman says, 'Near villages and small towns I have found the nests of humble-bees more numerous than elsewhere, which I attribute to the number of cats that destroy the mice.' Hence it is quite credible that the presence of a feline animal in large numbers in a district might determine, through the intervention first of mice and then of bees, the frequency of certain flowers in that district!"

This story, from "The Origin of Species," was later embroidered upon by others, who pointed out that, on the one hand, it is well known that old maids keep cats, and that on the other, red clover (which requires humble-bees as pollinators) is used to make the hay that nourishes the horses of the British cavalry. From all this, "it logically follows" that the continuance of the British Empire is depen-

dent on a bountiful supply of old maids. (Should a Ph.D. thesis be done on the relation between the marriage rate in England from 1920–60 and the loss of India, Suez and the African colonies? Worse topics have served.)

Everyone has heard of the Aswan Dam in Egypt. It has been built high up in the Nile for two purposes: to generate electricity and to provide a regular flow of water for irrigation of the lower Nile basin. Ecology tells us that we cannot do merely one thing; neither can we do merely two things. What have been the consequences of the recently built Aswan Dam?

First, the replacement of periodic flooding by controlled irrigation is depriving the flood plains of the annual fertilization it has depended on for 5,000 years. (The fertile silt is now deposited behind the dam, which will eventually have to be abandoned.) Consequently, artificial fertilizers will soon have to be imported into the Nile valley.

Second, controlled irrigation without periodic flushing salinates the soil, bit by bit. There are methods for correcting this, but they cost money. This problem has not yet been faced in Egypt.

Third, the sardine catch in the eastern Mediterranean has diminished from 18,000 tons a year to 500 tons, a 97 per cent loss, because the sea is now deprived of flood-borne nutrients. No one has reimbursed the fishermen for their losses.

Fourth, schistosomiasis (a fearsomely debilitating disease) has greatly increased among Egyptians. The disease organism depends on snails, which depend on a steady supply of water, which constant irrigation furnishes but annual flooding does not. Of course, medical control of the disease is possible—but that, too, costs money.

Is this all? By no means. The first (and perhaps only a temporary) effect of the Aswan Dam has been to bring into being a larger population of Egyptians, of whom a greater proportion than before are chronically ill. What will be the political effects of this demographic fact? This is a most difficult question—but would anyone doubt that there will be many political consequences, for a long time to come, of trying to do "just one thing," like building a dam on the Nile? The effects of any sizable intervention in an ecosystem are like ripples spreading out on a pond from a dropped pebble; they go on and on.

14   AN INTRODUCTION TO ORGANIZING
KARL WEICK

Karl Weick is one of the most original thinkers and oft-quoted writers in organizational theory. He takes life in work institutions not as static sets of functions and relationships (organization) but as interactive processes of creating and rationalizing collective action (organizing). His ideas are wide-ranging, and their complexity makes his work all but impossible to summarize in brief. The best way to introduce yourself to Weick's approach is to read *The Social Psychology of Organizing* (all 264 pages) and to spend much time thinking about Weick's ideas.

As an alternative (not a substitute), we present the beginning of the beginning—the first part of Chapter 1, where Weick tells the reader ten stories illuminating ten concepts that form the basis of his notion of organizing. In reading these pages, read the stories as parables, as stories designed to suggest ideas beyond themselves, and read them with joy and appreciation—these may be outrageous stories, but one can learn from the outrageous.

A professor, named Alex Bavelas, often plays golf with other professors. "Once, he took the foursome down to the golf course, and they were going to draw straws for partners. He said, 'Let's do this after *the game.'"*
Brand 1975, p. 47

"The story goes that three umpires disagreed about the task of calling balls and strikes. The first one said, 'I calls them as they is.' The second one said, 'I calls them as I sees them.' The third and cleverest umpire said, 'They ain't nothin' till I calls them.'"
Simons 1976, p. 29

"A police officer with a special ability for resolving sticky situations in unusual ways, often involving a disarming use of humor, was in the process of issuing a citation for a minor traffic violation when a hostile crowd began to gather around him. By the time he had given the offender his ticket, the mood of the crowd was ugly and the sergeant was not certain he would be able to get back to the relative safety of his patrol car. It then occurred to him to announce in a loud voice: 'You have just witnessed the issuance of a
traffic ticket by a member of your Oakland Police Department.' And while the bystanders were busy trying to fathom the deeper meaning of this all too obvious communique, he got into his cruiser and drove off."
Watzlawick, Weakland, and Fisch 1974, pp. 108–9

In 1938 the Fort Motor Car Co. tried to reach a new group of customers by introducing a car that was smaller than their V8 in size and power. After several years of development they produced a car (dubbed 92A) that was narrower, shorter, and 600 pounds lighter than the regular Ford. However, the small motor cost only $3 less to manufacture and the entire car could be built for only $36 less than the big car. By mid-April the project was abandoned, signifying that the company would not expand the range of its models downward.
Nevins and Hill 1963, p. 118

Farmers have been buying heavier and more advanced machinery to save labor. The heavier machines have caused problems. "They pack the soil and sometimes

Karl Weick, *The Social Psychology of Organizations* (Random House, 1979). Reprinted by permission.

harden the subsoil and keep water from penetrating to the plant's roots. The subsoil then must be tilled with an even larger, deeper plow which, of course, requires a more powerful tractor to pull it.''

Reed 1975

''*Uruguayan conductor Jose Serebrier stabbed himself through the hand with his baton when he became 'over-passionate' while leading 180 members of a brass-percussion ensemble and chorus through a special Easter musical festival in Mexico City recently. 'The baton broke into pieces,' Serebrier said. 'One piece was sticking through my hand. I guess I was more surprised than anybody. Ironically I never use a baton. But I decided to use one for this performance because I thought it would help achieve greater musical control. That was a mistake because I got over-passionate. All of a sudden I had stabbed myself. But I didn't stop conducting. I managed to pull the piece of baton out of my hand without stopping the music.' The band played on and the chorus sang for another 20 minutes until the finale. Afterwards Serebrier was taken to a local hospital for treatment.''*

''*Suicide attempts?'' April 10, 1975*

''*Time-motion and eye-movement studies confirm my observation that conductors are able to fix visually different performers at precisely defined times and then make sweeping gestures in their direction. In a previous study I found that successful quarterbacks do the same thing, singling one player out of many after a precise number of counts and, with a precise overhand motion, projecting a score object in that player's direction. Since plots of quarterback and conductor ages show little overlap, it is evident that one could quite successfully become the other. This concept, called Sequential Career Commonality Utilization; is now being applied in many other fields, and the Sequential Career Commonality Utilization Branch is slated to achieve bureau status in a few years. The greatest breakthrough achieved by this branch was the finding of politician-night watchman commonalities, such as random walking, peering into darkness, and lack of a requirement for intelligent conversation suggesting that either could serve as the other.''*

Anderson 1974, p. 727

''*Secretary of the Army Howard H. Callaway is asking that his 'Glad You Asked' policy be considered throughout the Army. Secretary Callaway explained the*

'*Glad You Asked' concept this way: suppose that tomorrow morning someone calls you and asks about your stickiest problem—the last thing in the world you wanted anyone to call about. You answer. 'Glad You Asked,' and mean it. This is possible when your attitude and actions result from an open, candid, honest evaluation of the facts at hand.''*

''*Glad you asked,'' 1975*

''*If the National Hockey League has been wondering why it cannot keep expanding indiscriminately, the final round of the Stanley Cup playoffs between the Buffalo Sabers and the Philadelphia Flyers may have provided one big reason: fog. . . . Last night the temperature was about 76 degrees at game time, but near the 90 mark inside the rink. For the last 33 minutes, including 18½ minutes of overtime, the contest was halted 12 times by referee Lloyd Gilmour when the clouds of steam made it impossible to see the puck. . . . Rene Roberts of Buffalo burst out of one fogbank in sudden death to tally the gamewinning goal.''*

Keese 1975

''*Computer simulations [of organizations] have a propensity for luring researchers into Bonini's paradox—the more realistic and detailed one's model, the more the model resembles the modeled organization, including resemblance in the directions of incomprehensibility and indescribability.''*

Starbuck 1976, p. 1101

All ten of those episodes illustrate *organizing,* which is defined as a *consensually validated grammar for reducing equivocality by means of sensible interlocked behaviors.* To organize is to assemble ongoing interdependent actions into sensible sequences that generate sensible outcomes.

Two contrasting definitions will help the reader understand what is being asserted:

Organizations are ''structures of mutual expectation, attached to roles which define what each of its members shall expect from others and from himself'' (Vickers 1967, pp. 109–10).

An organization is ''an identifiable social entity pursuing multiple objectives through the coordinated activities and relations among members and objects. Such a social system is open-ended and dependent for survival on other individuals and sub-systems in the larger entity—society (Hunt 1972, p 4).

Organizing is first of all grounded in agreements concerning what is real and illusory, a grounding that is called *consensual validation*. This term was coined by Harry Stack Sullivan; Ruth Munroe, in describing Sullivan's work, captures the phrase's nuance that we wish to incorporate into organizing:

> In my glossary of Sullivanese, consensual validation seems to be "common sense" of a high order—the things people agree upon because their common sensual apparatus and deeply common interpersonal experiences make them seem objectively so. It is a critical and cautious term for the "reality" so often used by other psychological schools (Munroe 1955, p. 356, f.n.).

The important issues of consensus in organizing concern rules for building social processes out of behaviors and interpretations that can be imposed on the puzzling inputs to these processes.

Organizing is like a grammar in the sense that it is a systematic account of some rules and conventions by which sets of interlocked behaviors are assembled to form social processes that are intelligible to actors. It is also a grammar in the sense that it consists of rules for forming variables and causal linkages into meaningful structures (later called cause maps) that summarize the recent experience of the people who are organized. The grammar consists of recipes for getting things done when one person alone can't do them and recipes for interpreting what has been done.

Organizing is directed initially at any input that is not self-evident. Happenings that represent a change, a difference, or a discontinuity from what has been going on, happenings that seem to have more than one meaning (they are equivocal) are the occasion for sizable collective activity. Once these inputs have become less equivocal, there is a decrease in the amount of collective activity directed at them.

Finally, the substance of organizing, the raw material that supplies the stable elements for the grammar, is interlocked behaviors (Buckley 1967, chap. 4). This interlocking is circular and was described by Allport:

> When individuals respond to one another in a direct, face-to-face manner, a social stimulus, given, for example, by the behavior of individual A, is likely to evoke from individual B a response which serves in turn as a stimulus to A causing him to react further. The direction of the stimuli and of their effects is thus *circular*, the response of each person being reevoked or increased by the reactions which his own responses called forth from others" (1924, pp. 148–49).

The sequence Allport describes is called a double-interact throughout this book and is analyzed in Chapter 4.

For the moment, it is sufficient to say that Bavelas's golfers, Callaway's colonels, Serebrier's musicians, and the other characters depicted in the initial examples are all engaged in the same organizing that we associate with General Motors, NASA, IBM, and McDonald's. In every case there is a shared sense of appropriate procedures and appropriate interpretations, an assemblage of behaviors distributed among two or more people, and a puzzle to be worked on. The conjunction of these procedures, interpretations, behaviors, and puzzles describes what organizing does and what an organization is (see Fig. 1).

With this preliminary understanding in hand we can review the relevance of each example for the arguments to be presented.

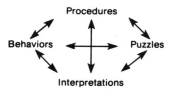

Figure 1

BAVELAS AND RETROSPECT

Bavelas's crazy foursome is interesting because for 18 holes they participate in a puzzle. What they've been doing for those 18 holes won't be known until the match is finished and they find who their partner is (was?). For example, the putt that I worry about on the 16th hole is worth the worry if my partner turns out to be Professor Bavelas, but if my partner is either Professor Webb or Professor Leavitt, then my worry is inappropriate.

But chronic and enduring puzzles like this aren't confined to the golf course. Organizations run into them all the time. But organizations are often reluctant to admit that a good deal of their activity consists of reconstructing plausible histories after-the-fact to explain where they are now, even though no such history actually got them to precisely this place. "How can I know how I've played until I see who my partner was?" On the 18th green that's the puzzle that has to be managed within Bavelas's foursome. But in the form of the related assertion, "How can I know what I think until I see what I say?" that puzzle has to be managed day after day by everybody who deals with organizations. The consequences of that reality will unfold as we proceed.

With a touch of regret we also note that Bavelas's world gains relevance for organizations because he was unable to get any takers for his proposal. In the actual match where this innovation was proposed, people found the prospect so strange that they all refused to try it. Collectivities such as the ones we will explore in this book also have their aversions to risk. Thus, we become much more interested in the question of when they will take chances, foster mutations, become playful.

UMPIRES AND ENACTMENT

The umpire who correctly asserts "They ain't nothin' till I calls them" rather neatly fingers a key element in organizational life: the important role that people play in creating the environments that impose on them. Organizations, despite their apparent pre-

occupation with facts, numbers, objectivity, concreteness, and accountability, are in fact saturated with subjectivity, abstraction, guesses, making do, invention, and arbitrariness . . . just like the rest of us. Much of what troubles organizations is of their own making; before completion of this essay, the ways in which organizations figure prominently in their own landscapes will become more evident.

COPS AND EQUIVOCALITY

The puzzle posed by Bavelas and the puzzle that faces the umpire who creates the reality of baseball both pale in comparison to the equivocal puzzle posed for an unruly crowd by the Oakland policeman. In their attempts to get "behind" the meaning of the remarks about writing tickets and to discover what input produced that output, members of the crowd probably turned to one another, sought some kind of help in figuring out what was up, and in their mixture of puzzlement and social activity proceeded to inattend the sergeant long enough for him to leave.

The basic raw materials on which organizations operate are informational inputs that are ambiguous, uncertain, equivocal. Whether the information is embedded in tangible raw materials, recalcitrant customers, assigned tasks, or union demands, there are many possibilities or sets of outcomes that *might* occur. Organizing serves to narrow the range of possibilities, to reduce the number of "might occurs." The activities of organizing are directed toward the establishment of a workable level of certainty. An organization attempts to transform equivocal information into a degree of unequivocality with which it can work and to which it is accustomed. This means that absolute certainty is seldom required. It also means that there can be enormous differences among organizations and industries with respect to the level of clarity that they regard as sufficient for action.

Members of organizations spend considerable time negotiating among themselves an acceptable version of what is going on. The activity itself is preserved by the phrase *consensual validation* and the content of the activity is preserved by the phrase *reducing equivocality.* The policeman's utterance could be interpreted to have two or more meanings (he's giving a ticket, he's nuts, he's signaling an accomplice, he's acting on TV, he's a clown, it's a trick, etc), and the true meaning can't be determined. That's what makes the scene equivocal. As the cop might have said, "We aim to police." When any outcome, such as the word *police* in the preceding sentence, could have been produced by two or more inputs ("We aim to keep law and order," "We aim to please"), the display is equivocal and people turn to their similar associates for help in sorting through the meanings and for help in stabilizing one of them (Festinger 1954).

FORDS AND MEMORIES

The troubles that the Ford Motor Car Company had in the 1930s producing a compact car suggest that one of their problems resulted from the fact that they presumed small cars are made the same way as large cars: take a big car and shrink it. Since Ford knew how to make large cars, they thought there was no problem. Suppose, however, that the Ford people had entertained some doubts about their expertise. Suppose they said both "Yes, we know how to make small cars," and "No, we don't know how to make small cars." The latter doubt suggests that small cars might not be simply scaled-down large cars. After all, shrinking a clock into a watch is neither easy nor cheap. Furthermore, even the belief among watchmakers that they can make watches is proving troublesome as the electronic watches built by firms who never before made watches begin to grab a sizable share of the market ("Seiko's smash" 1978).

The expensive Ford compact provides a handy summary of the possibility we will explore later, namely, that an ambivalent stance toward past wisdom makes adaptive sense. Organizations that both believe and doubt their past experience retain more flexibility and adaptive capacity.

Repeatedly, we will look at organizational practices for their relevance to the theme that adaptation precludes adaptability. Specialization in the production of large cars with technology, tasks, and skills devoted solely toward this production makes the organization profitable and efficient in the short run, but vulnerable in the long run. The biological version of this point is described by Dunn:

> Environmental changes often transform earlier adaptive specializations into cruel traps. As a changing environment passes beyond the range of a gene pool narrowed and made less versatile through specialization, it often forces the extinction of whole species. Just as in species formation those individual organisms fail to survive whose genetic range is inadequate to match the requirements of a changing environment, a species that generates a narrower genetic range (genetic pool of the population) through specialization may, when faced with environmental change, fail to support a dynamic adaptation and thus bring about extinction of the biotype (1971, p. 45).

TRACTORS AND VICIOUS CIRCLES

The problem created when heavy machinery packed the soil and necessitated heavier machinery to break it up is an eloquent example of feedback loops that sometimes turn into vicious circles. The cause-effect relationships that exist in organizations are dense and often circular. Sometimes these causal circuits cancel the influences of one variable on another, and sometimes they amplify the effects of one variable on another. It is the network of these causal relationships that impose many of the controls in organizations and that stabilize or disrupt the organization. It is the patterns of these causal links that account for much of what happens in organizations. Though not directly visible, these causal patterns account for more of what happens in organizations than do some of the more visible elements such as machinery, time clocks, and pollution equipment.

CONDUCTORS AND CONTROL

A glimpse of misplaced beliefs about control is found in the tragically charming anecdote about the enthusiastic conductor. The problem of coordinating

180 musicians *is* immense, but the idea that a mere baton ''would help achieve greater musical control'' seems pathetically heroic. Under these circumstances, again it is the patterns of alliances, causal loops, and norms that exist *between* people that accomplish or defeat efforts at control. Mutual influence between pairs of people is at the root of most control observed in much larger aggregations. While the conductor may presume that he and the baton produce an ordered performance, in actuality they probably are minor contributors to the outcome. Of more importance are the bonds and mutually supportive relationships that have been built up among small subsets of the musicians. It is these interpersonal bonds that hold the organization together and that become activated in response to the conductor, whether he stabs himself in the process or not.

QUARTERBACKS AND INTERCHANGEABILITY

The quarterback-conductor episode illustrates some possible consequences that occur when activity becomes overrationalized, overmanaged, overorganized. A recurrent theme in this book is that managers often get in the way of activities that have their own self-regulation, form, and self-correction tendencies.

These natural control circuits frequently are disrupted by managerial meddling. Management intervenes in the mistaken belief that single individuals do the controlling and that control is not implicit in causal circuits and inter-personal influence processes. Failure to acknowledge these sources of control, coupled with interventions that actively disrupt them, are the occasions for much mismanagement in organizations.

Although the theme is introduced with tongue-in-cheek by Anderson (1974), the issue of interchangeability of persons and positions is also a crucial one within organizations, and we shall refer to it frequently. If making hand motions at people really is the core of conducting, and if this is the only crucial activity involved in conducting, then it *is* true that aged quarterbacks might be substitutable for conductors . . . Sonny Jurgenson conducts Bruckner.

CALLAWAY AND OPENNESS

''Glad you asked'' is an uncommonly rich summary of much that goes on in large organizations. The necessity to invoke this slogan and to push for its acceptance suggests a prior history of nasty surprises when outsiders started poking around. Incidentally, at the time Callaway first enunciated this policy he also went on record as saying that women would never enter West Point. (''Why are women now at West Point? Glad you asked.'')

If it worked the way it was supposed to, the ''Glad you asked'' campaign should lead to more openness, more willingness to admit poor judgment in prior decisions, and a more candid and honest evaluation of the facts at hand. These outcomes are valued by many organizational theorists who try to enhance the authenticity with which organizational actors deal with one another (e.g., Argyris 1964). ''Glad you asked,'' followed up by honest answers, would certainly seem to be a way to enhance authenticity. If this policy really did have the effect of making people relax in the belief that there was nothing to hide, then it might be the case that confidence and pride in work would result and that dealings with the public would be less deceptive.

Whenever policies such as ''Glad you asked'' are introduced, it is valuable to examine the internal consequences of such policies. ''Glad you asked'' seems to be a policy designed to manage external dealings. Historically the ''Glad you asked'' policy was articulated soon after the Watergate revelations. But to view ''Glad you asked'' as a policy that is responsive to the public is to miss much of its potential for *internally* organizing the actions of organizational members.

Think, for example, of the internal implications of ''We're only number two—we try harder.'' If customers who have been alerted by this advertising ''send back'' to Avis workers cues that allow the Avis workers to try harder or to demonstrate that they are trying harder, if those slogans help Avis workers to make their work activities more sensible (e.g., ''I wasn't sure before what I was doing, but now I know: I'm trying harder so that we can become number one''), and if the recognition of that symbol by the public has the effect of making Avis workers feel more pride in their organization, then a policy that looks as if it is directed mainly outward may in fact have its largest effect on actions of those insiders about whom the policy comments.

In short, when "Glad you asked" is implemented effectively, organizations become more open, candid, and trusting. However, the felt need to introduce this policy in the first place suggests that organizations have other values that supercede openness—one of them being managing the indicators that the public is responsive to.

HOCKEY FOG AND CAUSAL CHAINS

The fog-clouded Stanley Cup playoffs in Buffalo are an excellent illustration of the point that causal chains within organizations are lengthy as well as dense (Reynolds 1974). It seems hard to imagine that expanding the number of teams would result in a controversial playoff due to fog. Nevertheless, there is a kind of inevitability once some of these small beginnings of expansion are set in motion. As you sign more teams, it takes a longer season for all teams to play all other teams; the playoffs also last longer. This means that hockey, normally a cold-weather sport, now spills over into the spring for the playoffs and into the early fall for exhibition games. Both of these encroachments on warmer seasons raise the odds that hot air will mix with cold air coming from the ice and that the mixture will form clouds of vapor on the surface.

Notice that this long chain of causes also has the potential for being self-defeating. Not only does the fog cut down visibility for spectators, television cameras, and news photographers, but it also contains the potential for some genuine feuds over whether scores should be allowed.

The presence of fog is even self-defeating for players because it lessens the quality of play:

What made last night's action even more bizarre was the spectacle of nearly exhausted players being asked to skate around the rink to stir up air currents and make the fog rise, with the game tied 4-4, and at its tensest in the sudden death. . . . "It was brutal out there,"

said Jerry Korab, the big Buffalo defenseman. "Not only did I lose at least 10 pounds, but I couldn't breathe. The fog smelled like gas or ammonia and got in my eyes, too" (Keese 1975).

In analyzing organizations we will want to examine the density of causal linkages and their circular patterns, but we will also want to examine the length of these chains of interdependence. Immediate activities can have remote consequences.

The ludicrous playoff might also look like a classic case of poor planning. That may be. But it's not obvious that even more planning is the answer: plans have been overrated as a crucial component for accomplishment of effective actions.

Plans are important in organizations, but not for the reasons people think. Cohen and March (1974) argue that plans are symbols, advertisements, games, and excuses for interactions. They are *symbols* in the sense that when an organization does not know how it is doing or knows that it is failing, it can signal a different message to observers. If the organization does not have a compact car in its line, it can announce plans to have one. On the basis of this announcement the firm may be valued more highly than an organization that makes no such announcement. It is less crucial that the organization is actually planning to make the car than that all concerned imagine this to be the case. It is in this sense that plans are symbols and that they negotiate a portion of the reality that then comes back and rearranges the organization.

Plans are *advertisements* in the sense that they often are used to attract investors to the firm. Plans show the organization at its best; they are documents designed to persuade, but again, they are more valuable externally than internally. One earmark of a plan that advertises is that it lacks relevant information about the organization. "Real" plans, those that bind the energies and time of people, contain a maximum of relevant information; plans that pass as advertisements are deficient on information.

Plans are *games* because they often are used to test how serious people are about the programs they advocate. If departments want programs badly enough, then they should be willing to spend the effort necessary to justify the program and to embed it in a plan. "If an administrator wishes to avoid saying 'yes' to everything, but has no basis for saying 'no' to anything, he tests the commitment of the department by asking for a plan" (Cohen and March 1974, p. 115).

Finally, plans become *excuses for interaction* in the sense that they induce conversations among diverse populations about projects that may have been low-priority items. The interaction may yield immediate positive results, but such outcomes are usually incidental. Much of the power of planning is explained by the people that it puts into contact and the information that these people exchange about *current* circumstances. When people meet to plan for contingencies five years away, contingencies that seldom materialize, they may modify one another's ideas about what should be done today. But that is about all that can be accomplished.

Plans are a pretext under which several valuable activities take place in organizations, but one of those activities is not forecasting. As Ambrose Bierce said, to plan is to "bother about the best method of accomplishing an accidental result" (1946, p. 327).

STARBUCK AND CLUTTER

Starbuck's summarization of the dilemma faced by Bonini (1963) when he tried to simulate an organization holds true for a much bigger set of inquiry procedures than computer simulations. Thick descriptions (Geertz 1973) of organizations may well be disorganized because that's the way organizations are. Organizations deal with equivocality, but their ways of dealing are often themselves equivocal and subject to many interpretations.

Cohen and March (1974) have suggested, for example, that university organizations have *goals* that are inconsistent, ill-defined, and loosely coupled; *technology* that no one understands; and *participants* who vary in how much time and effort they invest in the organization. If that's partially what a university organization is like, then a thick description of that organization will be confusing when it starts to comment about goals (e.g., Friday they wanted to discourage graduate students, but Thursday they wanted to encourage them), technology

(e.g., they don't have the foggiest idea how people get educated), or participants (e.g., the president didn't realize her provost was on sabbatical for the year). The irony is that this confusion in the observer's report testifies to its authenticity and not to its sloppiness.

Confusion as an indicator of validity is a crucial nuance because many of the ways of thinking about organizing that will be introduced in this book will portray organizations as superimposed structures. This imagery implies that there is not an underlying "reality" waiting to be discovered. Rather, organizations are viewed as the inventions of people, inventions superimposed on flows of experience and momentarily imposing some order on these streams. Notice, however, that many portions of the streams of experience will remain unorganized, and those portions being temporarily organized by imposed ideologies will remain equivocal. These enduring equivocalities should be detected by scrupulous observers, but since that which is noticed is partially indescribable and partially incomprehensible, the efforts at description will appear flawed. Such are the dilemmas that face those who choose as their topic of interest phenomena that are complex, fluid, collective.

SUMMARY

We stated at the outset that this was a book about organizing and about the appreciating of organizing. Through examination of a diverse set of events, the reader has been exposed to both appreciating and organizing.

The activity of appreciating was implicit in the approach taken to each incident. Brief attempts were made to embellish each example, to examine it from a variety of angles, and to add to its richness.

A significant portion of the existing organizational literature is steeped in criticism (Lumsden 1973). Less often do we see analyses patterned after those found in such fields as rhetoric, literary criticism, and aesthetics (Elbow 1973; March 1976; Wimsatt 1976; Gass 1975; Silverman 1975). I feel there is a need for a dialectic between criticism and affirmation as modes of apprehending organizations. At the moment we are heavily into criticism. A balancing of this with more emphasis on affirmation would lead to more activity of this kind:

> The critic (of poetry or art) more commonly looks for interpretations that discover aspects of an artistic expression making it more interesting or more beautiful than when first observed, or developing the uncertainties of simultaneous attraction and repulsion. Truly distinguished pieces of criticism are almost always ones in which a critic enlarges our appreciation of the beauties and complexities of art that is loved (March 1976, p. 18).

In the process of embellishing, reworking, and contemplating each prior example, we began to identify some elements associated with organizing. In each example some portion of a stream of experience was bracketed, and efforts were made to turn the stream into information and then to do something about the information that had been constructed. The raw data which people tried to make sensible consisted of such diverse displays as packed dirt, a moving baseball, a pierced hand, a fog-shrouded puck, opponentless golf, a cryptic policy, an even more cryptic traffic citation, and an expensive cheap car. In each case our interest was in the genesis of the puzzling raw data, attempts by groups of people to transform those puzzles into information, and what was done as a result of the momentary imposing of meaning on those puzzles (e.g., the car project was abandoned, skaters created a human fan, the conductor conducted for another 20 minutes).

This very general picture of organizing was supplemented by brief mention of some elements that compose it; those elements will be discussed further in subsequent chapters. These elements include suggestions such as these:

1. Equivocal information triggers organizing.
2. Efforts to stabilize meanings for equivocal displays typically involve the efforts of two or more people.
3. Most efforts at sensemaking involve interpretation of previous happenings and of writing plausible histories that link these previous happenings with current outcomes.

4. Interdependencies among people are the substance of organizations, but these interdependencies are fluid and shifting.
5. Organizations have a major hand in creating the realities which they then view as "facts" to which they must accommodate.
6. An ambivalent stance with respect to "lessons of experience" is a major way in which organizations preserve some adaptability to cope with changed contingencies.
7. Events in organizations are held together and regulated by dense, circular, lengthy strands of causality perceived by members.
8. Networks of self-regulating causal links are realized in the form of coordinated behaviors between two or more people.
9. Organizations frequently use only parts of persons, and those portions used vary in the ease with which they can be replaced.
10. Most policies within organizations have both internal and external consequences, whether intended or not, and these consequences may work in opposite directions.
11. There is ambivalence within organizations toward being open and closed and toward being suspicious and trusting.

Additional properties of organizations will be developed as we proceed. However, we have already hinted at some of the directions that will be taken. To gain some perspective on how these hints mesh with and play off existing ideas about organizations we can examine a stunning example of the organizing process *in vivo*.

REFERENCES

Allport, F. H. 1924. *Social psychology*. Cambridge, Mass.: Houghton Mifflin.

Anderson, N. G. 1974. Science and management techniques. *Science* 183: 726–727.

Argyris, C. 1964. *Integrating the individual and the organization*. New York: Wiley.

Bierce, A. 1946. *The collected writings of Ambrose Bierce*. New York: Citadel.

Bonini, C. P. 1963. *Simulation of information and decision systems in the firm*. Englewood Cliffs, N.J.: Prentice-Hall.

Brand S. 1975. Caring and clarity: Conversations with Gregory Bateson and Edmund G. Brown, Jr. *CoEvolution Quarterly*, Sept. 23, 1975, pp. 32–47.

Buckley, W. 1967. *Sociology and modern systems theory*. Englewood Cliffs, N.J.: Prentice-Hall.

Cohen, M. D., and J. G. March. 1974. *Leadership and ambiguity*. New York: McGraw-Hill.

Dunn, E. S., Jr. 1971. *Economic and social development*. Baltimore: Johns Hopkins University Press.

Elbow, P. 1973. *Writing without teachers*. London: Oxford.

Festinger, L. 1954. A theory of social comparison processes. *Human Relations 7*: 117–140.

Gass, W. 1965. *On being blue*. Boston: Godine.

Geertz, C. 1973. *The interpretation of cultures*. New York: Basic Books.

Glad you asked. *Depot Dispatch*, January 20, 1975, p. 2.

Hunt, J. W. 1972. *The restless organization*. Sydney: Wiley and Sons Australasia Pty. Ltd.

Keese, P. 1975. Fog clouds NHL expansion. *New York Times*, May 22, 1975, pp. 47, 50.

Lumsden, J. 1973. On criticism. *Australian Psychologist 8*, No. 3: 186–192.

March, J. G. 1976. Susan Sontag and heteroscedasticity. Paper presented at the Annual Meeting of the American Educational Research Association, San Francisco, April 19, 1976.

Munroe, R. L. 1955. *Schools of psychoanalytic thought*. New York: Holt.

Nevins, A., and F. E. Hill. 1963. *Ford: Decline and rebirth, 1938–1962*. New York: Scribner.

Reed, R. 1975. Farmers angry over doubling of machinery costs. *New York Times*, August 31, 1975, p. 33.

Reynolds. W. E. 1974. The analysis of complex behavior: A qualitative systems approach. *General Systems 19*: 73–89.

Seiko's smash. *Business Week*, June 5, 1978, pp. 86–97.

Silverman, D. 1975. *Reading Castenada*. London: Routledge and Kegan Paul.

Simons, H. W. 1976. *Persuasion*. Reading, Mass.: Addison-Wesley.

Starbuck, W. H. 1976. Organizations and their environments. In M. D. Dunnette (ed.), *Handbook of industrial and organizational psychology*. Chicago: Rand, pp. 1069–1123.

Suicide attempts? *Ithaca New Times*, April 10, 1975, p. 2.

Vickers, G. 1967. *Towards a sociology of management*. New York: Basic Books.

Watzlawick, P., J. Weakland, and R. Fisch. 1974. *Change*. New York: Norton.

Wimsatt, W. K. 1976. *Day of the leopards*. New Haven, Conn.: Yale University Press.

15 ORGANIZING AND ENACTMENT: KARL WEICK AND THE PRODUCTION OF NEWS

Charles Bantz

In the following chapter, Charles Bantz provides an interpretation and application of Karl Weick's theory of organizing. Bantz directs our attention to the ways that human action and creativity generate the environments in which organizations operate. This "enactment" of the organizational world is a central feature of Weick's model and the basis for Bantz's analysis of the production of news. News organizations produce news stories on a regularly recurring, routine basis; consequently, "newswork" functions to make the nonroutine events of social life into routines of news production. In the process, the newsworthy events are, in

Weick's terms, "enacted" as relevant aspects of the newswork environment. Notice how Bantz uses Weick's theory to account for pseudoevents and for the similarity among news accounts from different news organizations.

Karl Weick's *The Social Psychology of Organizing* (1969, 1979) is a creative and joyous book that provides its readers with an alternative view of what we usually call *organizations*. Weick argues that organization theory needs to be reshaped by more careful attention to what people actually do in organizational life. That argument was significantly revised and expanded in the second edition (1979), leading to a stronger emphasis on the meaning-making nature of organizing. In 1979, Weick defined organizing as "a consensually validated grammar for reducing equivocality by means of sensible interlocked behaviors" (p. 3). That definition, elaborated in the preceding article, focuses attention on how organizational members coordinate their action for making sense together.

This essay sketches Weick's organizing perspective and model, then applies the model to the production of news.[1] To provide a manageable focus, I will emphasize several aspects of Weick's model (enactment, the environment, and the influence of retention on subsequent organizing). The first part of the essay outlines Weick's overall perspective on organizing, suggests the concept of an evolutionary model, then reviews Weick's model of organizing. The second part of the essay uses Weick's thinking to extend theorizing about the production of news (what I call *newswork theory*).

WEICK'S PERSPECTIVE AND MODEL

Even a casual reading of the first chapter of *The Social Psychology of Organizing* suggests Weick is not a staid traditionalist. He tells stories and suggests interpretations of those stories, provoking the reader's thought more than explaining his own thoughts. Weick's writing seeks to involve the reader in the process of organizing—that is, a collaborative making sense of the world. Instead of an organization being a fixed object that can be "handled," Weick suggests organizing is an *activity* in which persons engage. That activity is making sense—where we try to reduce the multitude of potential or

possible meanings (which Weick labels equivocality) in the messages and objects with which we deal. Weick conceives of sense-making as a collective activity, as an intersubjective process; hence, organizing is a communicative process, as people acting together exchange messages in order to process equivocality.

Fundamental to Weick's perspective is his argument that persons develop patterns of making sense. Thus, members of a basketball team develop a collective set of patterns (Weick calls this a grammar) to interpret each other's moves, so they can play *together*. These collective patterns of interpretation help explain how two members of the same team realize they will pass the ball between them, while the opponents are completely surprised by the pass. The two players share a group grammar for interpreting not only each other's actions but also the actions of the opponents. Such organizing occurs not only with small groups of people but also with large groups and among groups of groups. Thus, a large computer manufacturer, such as IBM, not only has enormous amounts of information about its competitors' products, marketing strategies, and pricing but also has patterns of interpreting that information (e.g., ignore some, store some, analyze some).

An Evolutionary Model

Weick not only outlines a conceptual perspective on organizing, he also proposes the organizing model. Building on Donald T. Campbell's work (1965), Weick suggests that organizing is accomplished in an evolutionary fashion. The metaphor of evolution is based on an image of progression—one moves from stage to stage across time. It should be noted, however, that evolution does not inherently mean the social group evolves to a "higher level" or that evolution means the social group will be "longer-lasting." Rather, evolution refers to a three-stage process repeated across time.

Evolution, as described both by Campbell and biological evolutionary theory, involves three processes: variation, selection, and retention. In sociocultural evolution, variation occurs when a new behavior occurs within a sociocultural group. For example, a member of an organization may begin communicating through electronic mail in addition to written mail. The use of an innovation in a group is a variation on prior patterns of communication. The second stage of sociocultural evolution involves the selection of some of the varied behaviors. Thus, in the organization the group may select electronic communicating and a number of members will try out electronic mail. The third stage in sociocultural evolution involves the social group affirming its selection by retaining it as part of the group process. Thus, in the organization, electronic mail moves beyond the experimental use by a number of members to a regularized pattern of communicating.

Sociocultural evolution, then, involves innovation, choice, and persistence. Examining social groups for the development of new activities and new patterns helps identify the variations in behavior that may or may not be selected for incorporation into the group's social fabric. By assessing whether those innovations in social activity are single occurrences or more widespread, the observer can note which variations are selected by members. And, finally, by following the group across time, it is possible to note which of those variations, once selected, are retained in subsequent activities.

An evolutionary model, by virtue of its form, views activity as occurring across time and is based on collective activity. An evolutionary model is a developmental model of process, viewing a social group as something that develops across time—

much as a model of child development views the child as going through a process of personal and social change. The developmental, processual emphasis inherent in evolutionary thinking made Campbell's sociocultural model a logical source for Weick's development of a model of organizing as a collective process.

Weick's Model

If Weick's model of organizing were a simple application of the sociocultural evolutionary model, this section would be very brief. In order to use the sociocultural model to describe the process of organizing as sense-making, however, Weick made a significant modification of the sociocultural model by reconceptualizing the variation process as *enactment*. Weick's organizing model, presented as Figure 1, replaces variation with enactment. The concept of variation presumes an objective character of the changes in a system—as when humans developed a thumb that works in opposition to the fingers. Such an objective character fails to consider the role of the human in introducing change into systems. By reconceptualizing variation as enactment, Weick's model places *humans* at the center of organizing. Understanding enactment is essential to understanding Weick's model and to my later discussion of newswork.

Enactment. Enactment suggests that in acting, human beings in effect create the inputs to organiz-

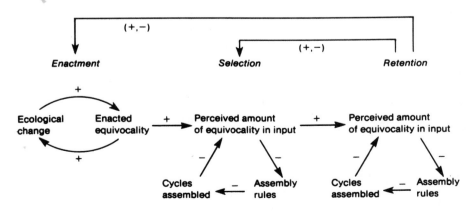

Figure 1 Weick's Model of Organizing

ing, that is, through their actions organizational members en-act those "things" that they then process. For example, by deciding to "notice" the scheduled news conference, by deciding to send a reporter to cover it, by processing the information brought back, that is, by paying attention to it, a news organization is involved in enacting aspects of its environment. By sending a reporter to cover a news conference, a news organization enacts information with several different meanings that the organization then processes. The reporter may bring back to the news organization a rich and complex set of information involving stories of mistakes in presentation, surprising turns of events, and difficult-to-comprehend claims, thus presenting the organizing process with inputs that are highly equivocal by virtue of the multiple meanings of the information. In contrast, the reporter could bring back a relatively simple set of information of low equivocality ("The news conference was cancelled because of a power failure"). In either case, it is the organization that chooses to enact the news conference.

Organizations, then, literally constitute information by acting upon and in their environment. Thus, colleges and universities in the late 1970s "discovered" that there were people in their environment who were over 25 years old and interested in attending college. These people were constituted as "nontraditional students" and significant efforts were (and are) made to make sense of those students—their needs, values, and resources. Acting in their environment by doing demographic surveys, marketing surveys, listening to corporate requests for educational programs, and so forth, educational organizations "created" a new input to organizing: the nontraditional student. It is crucial to recognize that there were potential students over 25 in the environment before the late 1970s, yet most colleges and universities did not "notice" them, did not gather information about them, did not—in Weick's term—enact them. Only when nontraditional students were enacted did they become input to the organizing of universities.

Weick's emphasis on enactment is central to his conception of organizing, for it makes organizing a *human* process (humans enact, objects cannot), it makes organizing an *active* process (someone must do something for enactment to occur), and it makes

organizing *creative* within its environment (it is not simply reactive to its environment). By emphasizing that organizations are creative within their environment, Weick allows for an explanation of why organizations do not enact prominent features of their environment. For example, why were the Detroit automakers caught by surprise when small cars began selling rapidly in the early 1970s? An organizing explanation would suggest that by failing to survey trend setters such as California auto buyers (see Brown, 1985) and because executives were insulated from purchasing and maintaining their own cars (Wright, 1979), U.S. manufacturers failed to enact new consumer trends (small is beautiful, energy efficiency is important, buying Japanese is socially acceptable).

Organizing Processes. For Weick, once information is enacted, organizing involves organizational participants collectively reducing the number of different meanings of the information (its equivocality) by selecting an interpretation of that information and then retaining the causal patterns in that interpretation. These two processes parallel Campbell's sociocultural evolutionary model in their labels—selection and retention.

Weick's basic argument is that "organizations are presumed to talk to themselves over and over to find out what they're thinking" (1979, pp. 133–134). The collective activity of organizing involves talking, interpreting, and remembering. He expresses his argument in what he calls a "recipe for sense-making": "How can I know what I think until I see what I say?" (p. 133). While this recipe could be interpreted as humorous play, it plays an important role in explicating what Weick means when he suggests that organizing is collective sense-making. Furthermore, the recipe locates saying as the center of organizing and in so doing communication is central to organizing.

In that recipe, the activity of saying is enactment. The environment external to organizing is not simply an "objective" environment, it is also an environment enacted by organizing. The enactment of the environment is a consequence of actors imposing order on their world through their actions (Weick, 1979, pp. 164–169). That is, organizing tends to construct or enact the environment in which it takes place. In doing so, enactment produces information with equivocality (having multiple meanings) rather than reducing equivocality (p. 133).

In the recipe, the activity of seeing what one says is selection. Following the enactment of equivocality, the input is available for the selection process. In selection, actors must first register the amount of equivocality in the inputs, then retrospectively choose an interpretation of the inputs and extrapolate a sensible pattern in the interpretation (Weick, 1979, ch. 7).

In the recipe, knowing what one thinks is retention. In retention the interpretation and extrapolation are retained as "enacted environments stored in the form of labeled variables that are causally connected" (p. 187). These patterns of causally connected variables are called causal maps (Maruyama, 1963). For example, an organization's causal maps might include a map that shows that higher production leads to higher pay and higher pay leads to higher morale. However, retention is not a simple storage process, as previously recorded maps and the new maps interact in ways that emphasize the importance of the previously stored maps (p. 211). Thus, if a new map (e.g., higher morale leads to fewer resignations) is retained, it may interact with and perhaps be joined to a previous map. We could, therefore, retain a map that connects higher production to higher pay to higher morale to fewer resignations.

To show that what is retained in organizing can influence subsequent organizing, Weick's model includes lines between retention and selection and between retention and enactment. Those lines are feedback or causal loops that connect retention to selection and retention to enactment. Thus, feedback from retention can affect both those processes.

The causal loop between retention and enactment means that "the environment is viewed as an output rather than an input" to organizing (p. 228). The causal connection between retention and selection means the retained causal maps can affect the process of sense-making by influencing which interpretations are selected. In the model, the causal links between retention and enactment and selection can be either positive or negative. That means actors organizing can either credit (+) or discredit (−) the causal maps stored in retention. If, in enactment, actors continually credit the retained causal maps,

they will continually enact environments as they have before. Conversely, if in enactment actors continually discredit retained causal maps, they will continually enact environments in new ways. Weick argues that the optimal compromise is ambivalence, where in the process of organizing actors either: (1) alternately credit and discredit retained causal maps or (2) simultaneously credit retained causal maps in one portion of organizing, while discrediting retained causal maps in other portions of organizing. This ambivalence toward retention means that memory is available for guidance, but is not the only guide to organizing.

Subprocesses of Organizing.   In the lower part of the organizing model, Weick presents the elements of the processes of enactment, selection, and retention. Since those are not central to the discussion below, a brief description will suffice.

In the *enactment* process, by acting upon their environment, members of the organization enact aspects of their environment ("ecological change"). Through enactment, information is brought into the organizing process. Those inputs of information have varying levels of equivocality ("enacted equivocality"). Enactment thus produces the equivocal information that will be processed by the members in the remaining organizing processes (Weick, 1979, p. 133).

Both *selection* and *retention* are constituted by members first perceiving the level of equivocality in the input (e.g., high, moderate, low), then, based on the level of equivocality, selecting a number of rules for proceeding ("assembly rules"), and then again, based on those assembly rules, engaging in behavior cycles ("cycles assembled") that reduce the equivocality in the input. The subprocesses of organizing thus involve collectives assessing inputs for equivocality, identifying rules for behaving with such inputs, engaging in the behavior so specified, and thus reducing the equivocality in the inputs.

Weick specifies that if an input has a high number of possible meanings (high equivocality), there are fewer assembly rules for processing it (small number of rules), which leads to many behavior cycles being followed (large number of behaviors), which in turns leads to large reduction in the number of meanings and less equivocality remaining (low equivocality remaining). These inverse relationships are indicated by the negative signs beside the arrows. In cases where the input is low equivocality, there are many assembly rules to follow, few behavior cycles are assembled, and little equivocality is removed from the initial input. To illustrate these principles, consider checking out in a discount store. If a person steps up and places a pack of gum and a dollar bill on the checkout counter, the cashier is presented with a low equivocal event and has a large set of rules that direct her to a few actions (e.g., enter amount, take cash, give change, bag purchase with receipt). On the other hand, if a deaf and mute person steps up with a pack of gum and a bag of gold dust, the cashier is presented with a more equivocal event and has fewer rules that direct her, which leads to more actions to try to make collective sense of an event.

Weick argues that as collectives select an interpretation of the inputs to organizing, they seek to reduce the number of meanings in those inputs. If the inputs they are are processing are highly equivocal (many meanings), they will have few rules to follow, leading to many attempts at interpetation, leading to a dramatic reduction in the number of meanings in the input. In a corollary fashion, when retaining the interpretation, the collective will have few rules to follow a highly equivocal interpretation, will need to engage in many behaviors, which will lead to greater reduction in equivocality of the interpretation being retained.

The subprocesses of Weick's model and the specific relationships among equivocality, assembly rules, and behaviors have generated much interest by organizational communication researchers. The three separate studies that have assessed whether Weick's predictions are upheld in organizing provide a much more detailed discussion of these issues and the interested reader is referred to them (Bantz & Smith, 1977; Kreps, 1980; Putnam & Sorenson, 1982).

The final two aspects of the organizing formulation I will mention are minor but useful for understanding the production of news. First, Weick suggests that organizing processes need to be examined relative to their external environment (1979, p. 167). Weick's rationale is that if an organization is very tightly interconnected (what he calls tightly coupled), it is less likely to be influenced by the external, objective environment. For example, a cell of revolutionaries, who have sworn a blood oath to each other, are less likely to be influenced by the environment than a group of students who have never met before and do not expect to work together again, but who are assigned to work together for an hour. Thus, the internal strength of relationships within an organization will affect how resistant the organization is to environmental influence: Tightly coupled organizations are more resistant to the environment than loosely coupled organizations.

Second, Weick argues that larger organizations are likely to be larger contributors to their environment than smaller organizations (1979, p. 167). To take an easy example, General Motors contributed to its environment more than the no-longer-independent American Motors ever did. If we extend the concept of size to include importance, then when examining clusters of organizations (such as an industry), the "important" organizations will have a greater impact on the industry's environment than organizations of lesser importance. Thus, extending my example, General Motors had a greater impact on the environment of the entire auto industry than did American Motors.

These two points can be combined, suggesting that tightly coupled, large or important organizations will have more influence on their environment and be less influenced by their environment than loosely coupled, small or unimportant organizations.

AN APPLICATION OF WEICK'S THEORY

To illustrate Weick's approach to organizing, I show how organizing can contribute to developing theory about the production of news. First, I briefly describe newswork research; then Weick's concepts are used to extend newswork theorizing.

Newswork Research

The term *newswork* is used to describe the process of producing news—whether television news, newspapers, magazine, or radio news. Newswork research explores this process through a variety of approaches, including theoretical work (e.g., Molotch & Lester, 1974; Park, 1940; Roscho, 1975; Tuchman, 1978), studies of the economic, regulatory, and organizational factors influencing news production (Dimmick, 1979; Epstein, 1973; Gans, 1979; Schudson, 1978; Turow, 1984), and close study of the people and organizations producing the news (Altheide, 1976; Bantz, McCorkle, & Baade, 1980; Ericson, Baranek, & Chan, 1987; Johnstone, Slawski, & Bowman, 1976; Scheslinger, 1978; Tuchman, 1978). For those newswork researchers who study the organizations that produce the news, Weick's conception of organizing can contribute significantly to understanding the production process.

Organizing Newswork Theory

The most pervasive conception of newswork is that news organizations establish routines of behavior that permit their newsworkers to process nonroutine events as if they were actually routine (Altheide, 1976; Bantz et al., 1980; Tuchman, 1972, 1973, 1978). The development of routines explains how news organizations can so easily present an unusual event (e.g., an assassination attempt) as if it were just like covering a daily news conference. News organizations develop patterns of work that turn the unusual into the ordinary (just as hospitals turn what is rare and unusual for me—minor surgery—into an event so routine it is boring for the hospital workers).

Within this conception of newswork, the general assumption is that newsworkers take *events* and turn them into stories (Altheide, 1976). The events are taken for granted, and the stories are constructed using an "angle"("the framework to which specific content will be nailed in order to tell a story," p. 76). Tuchman's early work describes "events" (happenings in the everyday world), . . . news (accounts and explanations of events presented by news organizations), and . . . events-as-news . . . (events not only as happenings in the everyday world, but also as potentially newsworthy materials)" (Tuchman, 1973, p. 112).

Enacting Events. Weick's formulation provides an excellent refinement of newswork theorizing by emphasizing that the environment and even events are not simply existent, but are *enacted* by news organizations. By framing any aspect of the social world, newsworkers enact that aspect of the world as equivocal information. That equivocality (information with multiple meanings) is then interpreted as it is structured into a news story. Thus, newsworkers enact their news environment. In so doing, they enact events that they then structure into news stories. Weick's concept of enactment broadens the theoretical conception of newswork by showing how newsworkers create the news they report.

Two examples show how much Weick's concept adds to traditional ideas about newswork. First, as was often discussed in the 1960s, the presence of television cameras appeared to incite or enlarge civil disorders into full-blown riots. The presence of newsworkers literally enacted an environment, including specific events like trashing, that could be then reported on or ignored as selection proceeded to make reasonable sense of the environment. Much of the discussion of the effect of cameras on events involved trying to make sense of the enactment; that is, was the riot "news" or was it a "pseudo-event" occurring only to be covered (Boorstin, 1962). Tom Wolfe's recent novel *The Bonfire of Vanities* (1987) satirically exposes how a demonstration may exist only for the television cameras—not even for the newspapers.

My second example is a more common occurrence for news organizations and was mentioned when describing the concept of enactment. A common element in newswork is going to news conferences. The appearance of newsworkers at a conference constitutes enactment of the conference as a news event. A news conference without newsworkers is not part of news organizations' environment. Weick's formulation provides a theoretically important understanding of the common attack on news conferences as pseudo-events (Boorstin, 1962).

Pack Journalism. Two aspects of Weick's theory provide a theoretical explanation for the development of "pack journalism" (that is, when journalists appear to join together, finding similar stories and interpreting those stories in a similar fashion). Those two aspects are (1) the disproportionate effect of large organizations on their environment and (2) the effect of following retained causal maps when enacting new inputs.

Weick suggests that large organizations may be more influential in their environment than others. By extending his notion of size to include importance, organizing can contribute to understanding pack journalism. News organizations operate within an environment populated by other news organizations; however, some organizations are more important to the environment's definition than others.

Within the news environment, certain organizations function as opinion leaders—being seen as more important, knowledgeable, or influential than other organizations. The most obvious example of this is the *New York Times*, which functions to guide and legitimize stories in other newspapers and media (see Halberstam, 1979). The *Times* is not alone in its disproportionate effect on the news environment— the *Washington Post* has moved to an influential national position, the *Los Angeles Times* may well be there, the *Wall Street Journal* holds that position in business news, and CBS used to be acknowledged as the most influential in broadcast news. Even in local media markets, news directors and editors read and watch competitors' product to see if the stories they deemed important were so labeled by the other outlets. The process is especially important with continuing stories, such as trials (see Tuchman, 1973), where journalists have the opportunity to monitor each other's work across time.

Weick's concept of organizing provides an appealing explanation for this process. As opinion leaders organizations enact the environment for themselves; they literally construct portions of the environment for all news organizations within their realm. Thus, as the elite national newspaper, the *New York Times* is more influential on other national news organizations, whereas the leading local media outlet is more influential in its local market.

The second aspect of Weick's theory is his notion that retention involves saving a selected interpretation as a pattern of relationships, which Weick labels a *causal map*. It is likely that news organizations retain causal maps of at least two types (1) the relationships of variables concerning how the story was produced (e.g., send an assertive reporter to interview a reluctant interviewee and a good story results, for example, Mike Wallace on *60 Minutes*) and (2) maps of the content variables of stories (e.g., as an election nears, candidates are more likely to make unfounded claims against their opponents). A map that records the causal pattern of how a story was produced is a map that influences enactment. When a news organization continually follows (credits) such established causal maps, it is likely that news stories will become repetitive as the organization repeatedly enacts events in the same manner. (It also may interpret those inputs as in the past and thus retain a similar interpretation, e.g., Patterson and McClure, 1976, found all three U.S. television networks treated the election as a horse race.) Such repetitive enactment processes will likely lead to repetitious coverage.

If we combine these two aspects—the influence of opinion leader organizations on the environment and following retained causal maps concerning enactment—Weick's formulation provides a theoretical explanation of pack journalism. If a leading news organization continually credits its past practices, it will not only produce stories that are repetitive when compared with previous stories it produced, it will also encourage (through its opinion leadership) the same repetitive stories among the lesser organizations in its environment. Thus, it is not surprising that studies find astonishing similarities in the news stories reported on independent news organizations such as ABC, NBC, and CBS (Bantz & Robinson, 1985; Hofsetter, 1976). Those three organizations, along with several newspapers, are operating within the same news environment, being influenced by the same opinion leader organizations, and replicating their past practices in story selection.

CONCLUSION

Weick's approach to organizing has directly or indirectly stimulated much of the theorizing in organizational communication during the past 20 years. The richness of his work means that there are are many other aspects of Weick's theory that can be applied to newswork theorizing as well as other theoretical issues in organizational communication. By focusing on the concept of enactment in the context of newswork, I hope I've suggested the value of Weick's contribution.

NOTE

1. Portions of this essay are based on my paper "Organizing the news: Extending newswork theorizing through Weick's organizing formulation," presented at the Speech Communication Association Annual Conference in New York, November 1980.

REFERENCES

Altheide, D. L. (1976). *Creating reality: How tv news distorts events.* Beverly Hills: Sage Publications.

Bantz, C. R., McCorkle, S., & Baade, R. C. (1980). The news factory. *Communication Research, 7,* 45–68.

Bantz, C. R., & Robinson, D. C. (1985, November). Events without context: The use of historical context in U.S. television news stories. Paper presented at the Speech Communication Association Annual Conference, Denver, CO.

Bantz, C. R., & Smith, D. H. (1977). A critique and experimental test of Weick's model of organizing. *Communication Monographs, 44,* 45–68.

Boorstin, D. J. (1962). *The image or what happened to the American dream.* New York: Atheneum.

Brown, W. (1985, February 18). GM envoy monitors tastes of California trend-setters in auto styling. *Minneapolis Star and Tribune,* Section S, p. 13.

Campbell, D. T. (1965). Variation and selective retention in socio-cultural evolution. In H. R. Barringer, G. I. Blanksten, and R. Mack (Eds.), *Social change in developing areas* (pp. 19–49). Cambridge, MA: Schenkman.

Dimmick, J. W. (1979). The gatekeepers: Media organizations as political coalitions. *Communication Research, 6,* 203–222.

Epstein, E. J. (1973). *News from nowhere: Television and the news.* New York: Random House.

Ericson, R. V., Baranek, P. M., & Chan, J. B. L. (1987). *Visualizing deviance: A Study of news organization.* Milton Keynes, UK: Open University Press.

Gans, H. J. (1979). *Deciding what's news: A study of CBS Evening News, NBC Nightly News, Newsweek, and Time.* New York: Pantheon.

Halberstam, D. (1979). *The powers that be.* New York: Knopf.

Hofstetter, C. R. (1976). *Bias in the news: Network television coverage of the 1972 Presidential campaign.* Columbus: Ohio State University Press.

Johnstone, J. W. C., Slawski, E. J., & Bowman, W. W. (1976). *The news people: A sociological portrait of American journalists and their work.* Urbana: University of Illinois Press.

Kreps, G. L. (1980). A field experimental test of Weick's model of organizing. In D. Nimmo (Ed.), *Communication yearbook 4* (pp. 389–398). New Brunswick, NJ: Transaction Books.

Maruyama, M. The second cybernetics: Deviation-amplifying mutual causal processes. *American Scientist,* 1963, *51,* 164–179.

Molotch, H., & Lester, M. (1974). News a purposive behavior: On the strategic use of routine events, accidents, and scandals. *American Sociological Review, 39,* 101–112.

Park, R. E. (1940). News as a form of knowledge: A chapter in the sociology of knowledge. *American Journal of Sociology, 45,* 669–686.

Patterson, T. E., & McClure, R. D. (1976). *The unseeing eye: The myth of television power in national elections.* New York: G. P. Putnam's Sons.

Putnam, L. L., & Sorenson, R. (1982). Equivocal messages in organizations. *Human Communication Research, 8,* 114–132.

Roscho, B. (1975). *Newsmaking.* Chicago: University of Chicago Press.

Schlesinger, P. (1978). *Putting "reality" together: BBC news.* London: Constable.

Schudson, M. (1978). *Discovering the news: A social history of American newspapers.* New York: Basic Books.

Tuchman, G. (1972). Objectivity as strategic ritual: An examination of newsmen's notions of objectivity. *American Journal of Sociology, 77,* 660–679.

Tuchman, G. (1973). Making news by doing work: Routinizing the unexpected. *American Journal of Sociology, 79,* 110–131.

Tuchman, G. (1978). *Making news: A Study in the construction of reality.* New York: Free Press.

Turow, J. (1984). *Media industries: The production of news and entertainment.* New York: Longman.

Weick, K. E. (1969). *The social psychology of organizing.* Reading, MA: Addison-Wesley.

Weick, K. E. (1979). *The social psychology of organizing* (2nd ed.). New York: Random House.

Wolfe, T. (1987). *The bonfire of the vanities.* New York: Farrar Straus Giroux.

Wright, J. P. (1979). *On a clear day you can see General Motors: John Z. DeLorean's look inside the automotive giant.* Grosse Point, MI: Wright Enterprises.

16   COMMUNICATION AND ORGANIZATIONAL CULTURES

MICHAEL E. PACANOWSKY
AND NICK O'DONNELL-TRUJILLO

Pacanowsky and O'Donnell-Trujillo argue that most organizational research has been oriented toward meeting the needs of management rather than understanding the organization itself. To balance such a "managerial bias" in research, they propose the organizational culture paradigm, with its focus on how the members of an organization construct organizational reality. The organizational culture paradigm sees organizations as symbolic realities created by members through communication. To understand organizations, therefore, researchers should examine the communication of members and analyze the constructs, facts, practices, vocabularies, metaphors, stories, rites, and rituals to identify the organization's culture. For example, in "Banana Time" (Chapter 11), Donald Roy notes vocabulary such as "lunch time," "banana time," and "break time" in the ticking machine room and details the workers' stories, especially the "professor" stories. Through his careful analysis of the communication in the machine room, Roy demonstrates the type of insight Paconowsky and O'Donnell-Trujillo believe can come from organizational cultural analysis.

In *Communication Yearbook I* and *II*, there are two articles that review the state of theory and methodology in organizational communication. In both articles, organizational communication is presented as a virtual jungle of variables, theoretical perspectives, and measurement techniques. In *Communication Yearbook I*, Richetto walks us through the conceptual legacy (debris?) of the 20s, 30s, 40s, 50s, and 60s, only to present what loom as the skeletons of the future: supervisor-subordinate homophily-heterophily, communication networks, quality of working life, communication apprehension and occupational communication demand, interorganizational communication, and communication climate.[1] In *Communication Yearbook II*, Dennis, Goldhaber, and Yates present the quest for the sufficient methodology in a series of debates so often heard in other realms of communication research that we are cha-

grined to see them again: laboratory versus field settings for research, descriptive versus predictive research designs, behavioral versus nonbehavioral data bases, quantitative versus qualitative research, and so on.[2] In both articles, the authors bemoan the immaturity of the discipline and the lack of a comprehensive, unified paradigm for organizational communication research. A key point in these articles, made explicit by Richetto and left more implicit by Dennis and others, is that the overwhelming diversity of theoretical and methodological perspectives is largely responsible for impeding the development of such a paradigm.

We have two quarrels with this conclusion. First, pre-paradigmatic research is not inherently a waste of time, and so we question the need to rush toward a comprehensive unified paradigm for organizational communication research. Perhaps our academic enterprise is not sufficiently mature at this time to warrant such a commitment.[3] Moreover, many in our field challenge the feasibility and utility of such a paradigm.[4] In fact, some philosophers of science go so far as to argue that pre-paradigmatic or multi-paradigmatic research is even healthy for any developing area of inquiry.[5]

Second, and more to the point of this paper, the notion that there is too much diversity in approaches to the study of organizational communication is questionable. To those who practice them, such things as communication climate analysis or network analysis may seem worlds apart; but for all the differences that exist among these and most other approaches, there are substantial similarities among them.

At the very least, virtually all of these approaches presuppose a similar notion of organizations. Regardless of conceptual definition (organization as system, organization as interlocked behaviors), the archetypal organization operationally and pragmatically is the business firm or the government agency. Moreover, most of these approaches presuppose that the purpose of organizational communication theory is to provide a causal understanding of how organizations work and thus render the ultimate task of the communication researcher to be the linking of communication variables to organizational outcome variables, such as productivity, survival, or effectiveness.[6] And lastly, these approaches generally presuppose (sometimes explicitly, usually implicitly) that the relevant audience for organizational communication research must include the organizational communication practitioner–and the manager he or she works for.

This paper presents an alternative approach for doing organizational communication research that begins with a different set of presuppositions about organizations. The jumping-off point for this approach is the mundane observation that more things are going on in organizations than getting the job done. People do get the job done, true (though probably not with the singleminded task-orientation that organizational communication texts would have us believe); but people in organizations also gossip, joke, knife one another, initiate romantic involvements, cue new employees to ways of doing the least amount of work that still avoids hassles from a supervisor, talk sports, arrange picnics.

Now it seems to us quite a presumption that work activities should have some kind of ascendant hold on our attention, whereas picnic-arranging should not. And it seems even more of a presumption that before we might legitimately begin looking at picnic-arranging, we need to have some glimmer of a theoretical rationale which causally links picnic-arranging to organizational effectiveness.

From our point of view, organizations are placed where people work and do a whole lot of other things, and all of these work things and other things constitute life in that organization. We believe that organizational life is interesting in its own right, irrespective of its relationship to organizational outcomes. Moreover, we embrace the argument that organizational life, *as constituted by communication*, is a legitimate area of inquiry for organizational communication scholars.[7]

So that our intentions are not misunderstood, let us make explicit what claims we are *not* making for the organizational culture perspective. First, we do not claim that the organizational culture perspective is ''better'' than any of the traditional perspectives. We do not suppose it to be more useful, nor more effective as a consulting tool. We see it as an alternative, not as a competing perspective.

Second, we do not see the organizational culture perspective in any way correcting those flaws in the traditional perspectives identified by traditional researchers.[8] So far as we can tell, the organizational culture perspective will not lead to the ready collection of a bank of normative organizational data, nor will it help standardize data-gathering and analysis procedures, nor will it move us away from small unrepresentative samples, nor will it tie communication variables to existing managerially-oriented social-psychological theories of organizations. Finally, we doubt that the organizational culture perspective will soon lead to a comprehensive, unified theory of organizational communication.

Our intention is not to ''improve'' on existing approaches. Our intention is to mark a new path of inquiry that will allow us to ask radically different, yet interesting, questions about organizations. As has been hinted at already, the organizational culture perspective begins by liberating our conceptions of what counts as an organization and what counts as organizational behavior. These conceptual shifts allow us to refocus our notions of the role of communication in organizations and thus liberate the kinds of questions that we as organizational communication researchers can legitimately ask.

We would like to do several things in the remainder of this paper. First, we want to explore the ways in which the theory, methods, and practice of organizational communication research combine to constrain the kinds of questions traditionally asked by organizational researchers. Second, we want to describe in preliminary detail the notion of organizational culture—to discuss briefly the nature of theory in the organizational culture approach, to posit types of questions about organizational communication the perspective enjoins us to ask, and to describe the requirements for methods of doing organizational culture research. Finally, we want to discuss the potential utilities of the organizational culture approach.

THE TRADITIONAL APPROACH

Traditionally, researchers in organizational communication have adopted what is commonly viewed as the ''scientific'' approach. These researchers argue for (or assume) the superiority of science, invoking such adjectives as ''objective,'' ''controlled,'' and ''detached'' to describe its methods.[9] Those doing organizational communication research from this position often call for the systematic and cumulative development of theory so that we can explain more organizational phenomena and, in so doing, provide evidence that organizational communication is indeed a legitimate area of inquiry.

In recent years, however, many researchers have come to recognize, sometimes reluctantly, that scientific methods are not as ''objective'' as we once believed. Indeed, some have proposed that research is always constrained by assumptions, values, and biases and that results will always reflect these.[10] The result is that research inevitably requires a taking of sides and, as Becker says, ''the question is not whether we should take sides, since we inevitably will, but rather, whose side are we on.''[11] Critics of organizational research have argued that organizational researchers typically take the side of management. Sociologists, especially, have pointed out a distinct ''managerial bias'' in organizational re-

search.[12] Moreover, this managerial orientation is as prevalent in organizational communication research as in other areas of organizational research.[13]

We believe that the managerial orientation in organizational research can be traced largely to the pragmatics of doing organizational research: organizational research is typically done *for* managers. Not surprisingly, then, a pragmatic motive *underlies* virtually all organizational research; and a pragmatic rhetoric *surrounds* virtually all organizational research: *we talk about our desire to understand organizations better so that organizations can be made to run better.* And, because of the peculiar pragmatics of doing organizational research, what has come to count as ''better organizational functioning'' are notions with a distinctly managerial flavor. As Perrow has noted, organizational research is better understood when ''effectiveness'' is recognized in terms of the preferences of those who hold power in the organization.[14]

Managerial Requirements for Organizational Theory

The research questions of traditional organizational research derive from the pragmatic motive to understand how organizations work—so that managers can make them work better. Thus, traditional researchers are prompted to ask questions that presuppose the legitimacy of such notions as ''the organization is functioning well'' or ''the organization is not meeting its goals.'' Typically, an understanding of organizational functioning is related to effectiveness variables, such as productivity or profitability or other measures of organizational output.[15] The task of traditional organizational scholars is to isolate the variables instrumental in determining the values of outcome variables, and relate them in some sort of causal theory, so that managers can manipulate organizational effectiveness by bringing their administrative powers to bear on those crucial instrumental variables. Communication researchers often plug into organizational theorizing by creating communication variables that are related to those psychological or sociological variables related to effectiveness. Thus, whereas psychologists and sociologists have tried to develop a causal theoretical relationship between job satisfaction and productivity (though without unequivocal success), communication researchers have tried to show that communication satisfaction is an instrumental part of job satisfaction.[16]

In any case, organizational theorizing is (managerially) constrained by a need to develop a set of theoretical links between variables of interest and organizational outcomes. Although these links ideally ought to be demonstrated empirically, the acceptance of theoretical relationships as worthy of investigation is often based on "good rhetoric" which establishes merely the plausibility of causal links between instrumental variables and organizational effectiveness.[17] The important point here is that, because organizational theorizing is constrained by a managerial emphasis on the bottom line, the research questions prompted by traditional perspectives and the rhetoric of their phrasings are similarly and necessarily constrained.

Managerial Requirements for Methods

The development of traditional research methodologies has been directed by both theoretical and pragmatic concerns. Because traditional organizational theory tends to be causal, the methods employed must be able to permit claims of causality. At the same time, because organizational research is done *in* organizations, methods must be devised that intrude as little as possible on organization efforts to get the job done. We believe that both of these concerns are responsible for the movement in recent years away from observational or case study approaches to more quantitatively-oriented survey methods.

As anyone versed in research methodology will affirm, case study methods are not particularly well-suited to establish causal relationships among variables. Case studies do not permit control of mediating or confounding variables, nor are they typically generalizable. Case studies thus do not provide ways of ruling out plausible rival hypotheses, and thus the case study approach makes establishing and verifying causal relationships impossible.[18]

Quantitative survey methods, especially as they are replicated over a large number of organizations, surmount these problems (and thus the enthusiasm with which many organizational communication

scholars have felt for the ICA audit). Even more to their advantage (from a managerial point of view), they permit the *quantification* of causal relationships, increasing the efficiency with which managers can tweak instrumental variables to achieve certain levels of outcome variables (that is, for example, managers like to know exactly how much job satisfaction will have to be raised to achieve certain increases in production).

Survey methods also have some pragmatic advantages over case study methods. Survey methods do not tie up as many key organizational resources as case study methods might. If a survey is administered, it takes so many people so long to fill it out, and that ends the data-gathering. Whatever results are arrived at, it is with a known commitment of organizational resources (a very real consideration if a manager as sponsor of organizational research has to "sell" the project to higher-ups).

Also important from the managerial point of view is that survey methods constrain the kind of information that will be yielded about an organization. That is, the results of a survey may be flattering, or the results of the survey may indicate difficulties; but because the manager knows what questions will be asked, the management at least knows the boundaries around the kind of news he or she will hear. The case study approach suffers from the possibility that the researcher may come up with some real surprises—e.g., love affairs impeding rational decision-making—that the manager would just as soon not be made public or semi-public knowledge.[19]

Thus, for theoretical and pragmatic reasons, survey methods are widely used in organization communication research. But, in spite of these advantages, we believe they do have some real disadvantages. First, survey methods cannot match the richness of detail that can be achieved via case study methods. Second, and even more of a problem, survey methods presume that we know what questions we want to ask *before* we go into an organization. The research task becomes essentially one of measurement, not of discovery.

If a researcher is sure of exactly what questions need to be asked, then measurement and not discovery is very much the task, and sufficient detail replaces rich detail as a research goal. Thus, for most researchers the theoretical, methodological, and pragmatic considerations to the traditional study of organizations seem no burden. For them, these constraints are necessary for the development of a research paradigm and provide guidance in selecting coherent sets of research questions. But for those whose commitment to the managerial orientation is minimal at best, these same theoretical, methodological, and pragmatic considerations constrain too severely the kinds of questions they would like to ask about organizations.

THE ORGANIZATIONAL CULTURE APPROACH

Our orientation is not managerial; it is communication-based (and perhaps peculiarly communication-based at that). We believe that an intriguing thing about communication is the way in which it creates and constitutes the taken-for-granted reality of the world.[20] Social activity, as we see it, is primarily the communicative accomplishment of interrelated actions. So whereas the underlying motive of traditional research is coming to an understanding of how to make organizations work better, the underlying motive of the organizational culture approach is coming to understand how organizational life is accomplished communicatively. To understand how organizational life is brought into being, we cannot let ourselves be limited to asking questions that require some implicit or explicit link to organizational productivity for their legitimacy. What we hope to do in the remainder of this paper is lay a preliminary foundation for a research approach that will allow us to legitimately ask provocative questions about the relationship between communication and organizational life.

Organizations Preliminarily Defined

We believe our conception of organizations needs to be cut loose from its managerial moorings. And once cut loose, it should be allowed to drift free until research itself indicates to us the auspicious spot for anchoring. So for now, we choose a definition of organization that is as broad as possible; an organization is the interlocked actions of a collectivity.[21]

By this definition, IBM would be an organization, but so would a regular Friday night poker group, the Jones family, or even a crowd of people who get on an elevator together. What we mean to imply is, that at this stage of thinking about organizations, we ought not be restrictive in our presuppositions about the beasts. Organizations can be large, or organizations can be small. Organizations can be long-lived, or organizations can be short-lived. Organizations can be concerned with outputs, or they need not be concerned with outputs. Although this definition may seem absurdly inclusive to some (those who already "know" organizations are systems, or are rational, or strive to maximize profits), it is well-suited for those who wish to take seriously the idea that organizations are accomplished communicatively. Moreover, such an inclusive definition may render organization phenomena more visible and more amenable to concept formation and hypothesis generation.[22] So for now, it seems appropriate to construe organizations as places where people do things together, to the extent that what they do together involves communication.

Some Notions of Organizational Culture

We have labelled our approach the "organizational culture" approach because we want to indicate that what constitutes the legitimate realm of inquiry is everything that constitutes organizational life. Just as an anthropologist might be interested in the workways, folk tales, and ritual practices of a culture, we are interested in the workways, folk tales, and ritual practices of an organization.

But our interest is not simply in listing or documenting aspects of organizational life. We are interested in understanding how that organizational life is accomplished communicatively. We take as a guiding tenet for the development of the organizational culture approach the stance of Clifford Geertz: "man is an animal suspended in webs of significance he himself has spun . . . culture [is] those webs, and the analysis of it [is] therefore not an experimental science in search of law but an interpretive one in search of meaning."[23] Three features of this pronouncement undergird our understanding of organizational culture research.

First, the web is a well-considered metaphor for culture. Webs are confining. Spider webs, for example, limit a spider's range of movement to that particular slice of universe traversed by the web. At the same time, spider webs are the very things that make movement for the spider possible. So the ''webs of significance'' are our cultures. Membership in any one culture generally comes at the cost of non-membership in all other cultures (at least momentarily). We inhabit ''a'' reality, not all realities. Yet our particular reality—constructed as it is of particular jokes, stories, songs, myths, polite exchanges, and so forth—is that which gives substance and meaning to what would otherwise be insensate behavior. And so our research consciously avoids evaluating one organizational culture in light of others (including our own), but rather seeks to understand the culture in terms of what it makes possible.

Second, as Geertz suggests, culture is to be studied not so much as a system of kins, or a collection of artifacts, or as a corpus of myths, but as sense-making, as a reality constructed and displayed by those whose existence is embedded in a particular set of webs. But the web not only exists, it is spun. It is spun when people go about the business of construing their world as sensible—that is, when they communicate. When they talk, write a play, sing, dance, fake an illness, they are communicating; and they are constructing their culture. The web is the residue of the communication process. It is the resultant structure—the sense that is made or the account of reality—that body of knowledge that is drawn upon as a resource for explaining and making sense of new experiences. If these two components of culture are to be studied—culture as structure and culture as process—then the methodological implication is that researchers must not be content simply with accounts, but must also be present during occasions of naturally-occurring discourse.

Third, we agree with Geertz that the aim of cultural analysis is not the discovery of law. ''Culture is not a power, something to which social events, behaviors, institutions, or processes can be causally attributed.''[24] Culture no more ''causes'' behavior than spider webs ''cause'' spiders to move. Culture and spider webs are ''contexts.'' As a context, culture is amenable not to causal analysis but to interpretation—as Geertz would have it, ''thick description''—that reveals the nuances of sense-making displayed in the discourse of cultural members. An interpretation, an account of organizational culture begs not for an assessment of its reliability and validity, but for an assessment of its plausibility and its insight. The reader is asked to ask: Has a good story been told that takes you to the heart of the matter?

Given that organizational sense-making is accomplished communicatively and displayed communicatively, research from an organizational culture position must then attempt to answer the twin questions: (1) What are the key communication activities, the unfolding of which are occasions when sense-making is accomplished? and (2) What is the sense members of any particular organization have made of their experiences? In order to make sense of members' sense-making—to uncover an organization's culture—a researcher can begin by focusing on the following (not exhaustive) set of indicators and displayers of organizational sense-making.

Relevant Constructs.   Each culture has its set of relevant constructs (objects, individuals, processes) used by organizational members. These constructs, such as ''committee meeting,'' ''seminar,'' and ''*WJSC*,'' for a communication professor identify the generic aspects of organizational understandings and serve as global indicators of how members structure their experiences. Hawes' study of ''information'' in a regional planning commission is one example of research which displays the nature of organizational constructs.[25]

Facts.   Each organizational culture has its own system of facts which members use to explain how and why the organization operates the way it does. These facts make up what might be viewed as the ''social knowledge'' of the organization. As Farrell argues, ''social knowledge comprises conceptions of symbolic relationships among problems, persons, interests, and action, which imply (when accepted) certain notions of preferable public behavior.''[26] This social knowledge is based on attributed rather than actualized consensus, is dependent upon the assumptions of particular organizational audiences, and is transitional and generative rather than fixed or permanent. An organizational culture's social knowledge typically concretizes and qualifies its relevant constructs.

Practices. Organizational members continually reveal the practices for accomplishing organizational activities, for "getting the job done." Practices known as "tasks" are often initially expressed formally by a supervisor, but come to be realized in the particular performances of organizational members as they become competent in the ways of their situated activities. Thus, organizational members come to practice tasks such as record keeping,[27] intake processing,[28] criminal prosecuting,[29] and gynecological examinations,[30] not as formally prescribed but as practically accomplished. Other practices, such as "looking busy when there's nothing to do," are typically never expressed formally but are nearly always disclosed informally.

Vocabulary. Another distinguishing feature of any organizational culture is the particular vocabulary used by its members. This specialized vocabulary, sometimes called vernacular or argot, often provides clues as to what are the relevant constructs, facts, and practices of organizational life. As Folb has suggested, "Because vocabulary is the part of language that is most immediately under the conscious manipulation and control of its users, it provides the most accessible place to begin exploration of their experiences."[31] An organizational argot is sometimes so extensive that researchers feel compelled to include a glossary of the lexical system in their research reports.[32] Research from an organizational culture approach might, in addition to providing such a resource, benefit from indicating "the methods by which it was located or recognized as an instance of argot in the first place."[33]

Metaphors. Useful displays of organizational culture related to vocabulary are the metaphors used by organizational members. As Lakoff and Johnson have argued, one's conception of reality is largely constituted in interlocking systems of metaphors.[34] Organizational metaphors, when used by organizational members, may be helpful in understanding a sense of how members structure their experiences. Koch and Deetz have recently explored how two organizational metaphors, "machine" and "organism," serve a constitutive function in organizational reality.[35]

Stories. Each organizational culture also contains stories which members exchange on a regular basis. And, as Labov and Waletsky have pointed out, stories "recapitulate experience verbally,"[36] and allow members to share their organizational experiences with other members or outsiders. These stories, when exchanged with other members, typify and anonymize organizational experience in that they reveal how, in principle, the experience narrated could be duplicated by any organizational member.[37] Thus, stories about the personal successes or "screw-ups" of organizational members are not merely entertaining narratives but constitute organizational reality insofar as they signify possible future scenarios of organizational life. Other stories take on folkloric qualities which are used to substantiate organizational knowledge or pass on the unrecorded traditions or customs of organizational life. These stories include personal legends about individual members, such as "how the president used to be a mail clerk," and local legends pertaining to specific periods in the organization's history, such as "how the business almost went down the tubes the day Bennett was left in charge.[38] These legends weave an historical texture into the organization, a texture which members come to recognize and reshape in their continual narration.

Rites and Rituals. Finally, each organizational culture develops various rites and rituals which orient members temporally and serve as occasions for sense-making. Semi-annual reviews, weekly staff meetings, and daily coffee breaks all constitute organizational rites and rituals which members regularly or occasionally participate in. Participation in such events provides access for members to a particular shared sense of reality. "These events," Abrahams writes, "have a sense of wholeness and potential to them; they invoke special ways of acting, special language, rules, and even boundaries."[39] The annual company picnic, for example, although not as overtly dramatic as a Balinese cockfight, is a culturally formalized event in which participants make evident their cultural membership and display their organizational sense-making. Donald Roy's "Banana Time" illustrates the constitutive and integrative features of everyday organizational rituals in a group of factory workers.[40]

As members constitute their relevant constructs, practices, rituals, and so forth, they are also constituting parts of their organizational culture. These constructs, practices, and rituals are mini-accomplishments embedded in the larger ongoing accomplishment of organizational culture. As Weider formulated it, these mini-accomplishments represent "indexical expressions which operate as 'parts' of a Gestalt-contextual."[41] That is, each part, each accomplishment, is one constitutive indexical "piece" of the larger contextual whole of organizational culture. Thus, a *reflexivity* is implicated in which these indexical accomplishments and the context of organizational culture mutually elaborate one another. The task then, in organizational culture research, is to work back and forth between parts and wholes, between constructs and cultures, and unravel the webs of significance and their patterning that give particular meaning to organizational life.

Requirements for Organizational Culture Methods

Clearly, given the different purposes for conducting the research and the different questions driving the research, the methods for studying organizational cultures are likely to differ from the methods of traditional organizational communication research. In order to build a plausible interpretation of how organizational members communicatively make sense of their interlocked actions, it is necessary to have recourse to instances of members communicatively making sense, and recourse to the body of knowledge that members draw upon in order to make sense. What is required then are details— detailed observations of organizational members "in action" and detailed interviews (formal or informal) of organizational members accounting for their actions. Surveys that measure climate, networks, and so forth do not provide sufficient (nor the right kind of) detail for building a plausible interpretation of organizational sense-making. Nor do case study

methods, employed from the managerial orientation, necessarily insure the gathering of the kind of data we think is required for telling a "good organizational story."

What we envision as sufficient procedures for gathering organizational culture data require the researcher to place himself or herself in something of a dilemma. The researcher must become intimately familiar with the organizational life he or she is interpreting, so that the organizational experiences are understood in terms of the understandings of organizational members.[42] At the same time, the researcher must not "go native," but maintain a posture of radical naivete and allow himself or herself to experience organizational life as "strange," so that he or she will be sure to prompt organizational members for the resources (or knowledge) they are drawing upon which allow them to take for granted those very same organizational experiences.

Getting sufficiently detailed data, through observations and interviews, and becoming intimately familiar with organizational experiences require time, and lots of it. They require lots of note-taking, tape recording, transcribing, picture-taking, and collecting of organizational documents. They also require perceptiveness and sensitivity to nuance. The researcher must become intensively immersed in organizational experience both to have a source of data, and to come to understand that experience the way organizational members do.

At the same time, the researcher must not fall into the trap of failing to recognize the taken-for-granted assumptions about organizational experience that make it possible for organizational members to deal with their world as nonproblematic. The researcher must constantly make organizational experience "strange." This chore is extremely difficult, especially as the researcher becomes more and more familiar with organizational routines.

We have found three techniques especially helpful in maintaining the "strangeness" of an organizational culture. First, the researcher should train himself or herself to constantly ask organizational members "Why?", as in "Why did you do that?" or "Why did you say that?" Responses to why questions from organizational members are often varied and often intriguing, and will encourage the researcher to keep digging. Second, the researcher can take the advice of Weick to "mutate metaphors."[43] By looking at organizations as though they were something very different than our ordinary or our academic conceptions of them—as though they were, for example, garbage cans[44] or see-saws[45]—the researcher may be led to consider everyday organizational practices in an unusual and revealing light.

Finally, we have found collaborative research to be especially effective. Members of a research team will usually pick up on different nuances of the organizational culture, providing what Douglas calls "multiperspectival checks" on the field setting.[46] Moreover, we have found it particularly helpful if some researchers do the field work, while other researchers agree never to set foot in the organization being studied. The role of these outside researchers is to react to the data collected by the inside researchers, and to strive constantly to make the interpretation of this data problematic. The outside researchers can do this by continually asking why questions of the data, or by offering naive interpretations of the data (which usually seem "wrong" to the inside researchers, who are then pushed to articulate the grounds for their own understanding). Through this differentiation of research postures by collaborators on the research project, the dilemma of seeing organizational experience as simultaneously nonproblematic and problematic is resolved.

The Potential Utilities of the Organizational Culture Approach

The result of using the organizational culture approach ought to be a non-managerially oriented account of sense-making in a particular organization. This account should not be a compendium of problems and solutions; rather, it should be a story of organizational life in all its fullness. Of what use is such an account? There are several possibilities.

First, an organizational culture study can serve as necessary, pre-quantitative description for those researchers interested in devising quantitative measures for further research in that same organization.[47] An organizational culture study could also be used in conjunction with a quantitative study to help interpret or place in context results from a statistical analysis of an organization. And, in rare cases, an organizational culture study may even have the capacity to "reject" theories. As Campbell has argued:

> In a case study done by an alert social scientist who has thorough local acquaintance, the theory he uses to explain the focal difference also generates predictions or expectations on dozens of other aspects of the culture, and he does not retain the theory unless most of these are also confirmed. In some sense, he has tested the theory with degrees of freedom coming from multiple implications of any one theory.[48]

In short, organizational culture research has theory-generative, theory-contextualizing, and even theory-testing possibilities.

Second, each organizational culture study can provide any member (manager, worker, volunteer) with an overall picture of the organization. In any organization, a member's perception of that organization is typically limited by its perspective. The larger the organization, the more insulated members become from that which constitutes the entirety of organizational experience. As a result of such insulation, organizational life can be experienced as alienating. The overall picture that an organizational culture study presents may or may not have utility (from a managerial point of view). But, like the first time one sees an artist's rendition of one's self, organizational culture pictures are usually seen by members as interesting, informative, and thought-provoking.[49]

Third, each organizational culture study reaffirms the centrality of communicative behaviors in organizational inquiry. Communication researchers and even organizational theorists have long argued that communication is the central process in organizations. Yet, despite such arguments, our research has often failed to look at communication itself. Instead, we ignore the very phenomena we allege to explain. Instead, most researchers still seem to prefer paper and pencil tests that purport to measure attitudes toward, recollections of, or aggregations of communicative activity. One strength of the organizational culture position is its invitation—or more accurately, its directive—to observe, record, and make sense of the communicative behavior of organizational members. The call of the organizational culture perspective is simple: at long last, to attend to and interpret what we have been trying for so long to explain.

Fourth, each organizational culture study stands as a critique of the assumptions of traditional organizational communication research. The maturity of any discipline depends, in part, on its members' ability to rigorously examine the basic assumptions of their research. Unfortunately, researchers in organizational communication have not critically reflected on the managerial constraints underlying their research. Every organizational culture study manifestly denies the taken-for-granted managerial assumptions that would have us define as characteristics of "real" organizations their goal-orientation, or their rationality, or the presumed cooperation of members, or their likeness as systems. Thus, the organizational culture position provides at least one contrast to traditional organizational communication research which may stimulate others to reflect and take stock of their work.

Finally, each organizational culture study serves, in Geertz's terms, to "expand the universe of discourse."[50] This last utility is perhaps the most important. The ubiquity of organizations in modern life is often commented on in organizational communication textbooks. But our understanding of organizational life is very much glossed. Actual descriptions of what goes on in organizations are very rare. (One could read numerous organizational communication textbooks, for example, and not discover that people in organizations often swear.) Some might say in apology that our textbooks operate at a very high level of abstraction. We could counter that our textbooks are very out of touch with reality. Before we make truly insightful comments about communication and organizations, we are going to have to know the beasts a bit more intimately. We believe that the organizational culture approach can go a long way to putting us in touch.

NOTES

1. Gary M. Richetto, "Organizational Communication Theory and Research: An Overview," in *Communication Yearbook I*, ed. Brent D. Ruben (New Brunswick, N.J.: Transaction Books 1977), pp. 331–346.
2. Harry S. Dennis III, Gerald M. Goldhaber, and Michael P. Yates, "Organizational Communication Theory and Research: An Overview of Research Methods," in *Communication Yearbook II*, ed. Brent D. Ruben (New Brunswick, N.J.: Transaction Books, 1978), pp. 243–269.
3. Ian I. Mitroff suggests the use of delayed judgment in scientific research to protect from the premature and often unquestioned allegiance to pet paradigms and practices in *The Subjective Side of Science* (New York: Elsevier, 1974).
4. Porter and Roberts conclude that the search for such a framework is "likely to prove fruitless." Others, including Weick and Redding, argue for less grand "middle range" theories of organizational behavior. See, Lyman W. Porter and Karlene Roberts, "Communication in Organizations," in *Handbook of Industrial and Organizational Psychology*, ed. M. D. Dunnette (Chicago: Rand McNally, 1976), p. 1554; Karl E. Weick, "Middle Range Theories of Social Systems," *Behavioral Science*, 19 (1974), 357–367; and W. Charles Redding, "Organizational Communication Theory and Ideology: An Overview," in *Communication Yearbook III*, ed. Dan Nimmo (New Brunswick, N.J.: Transaction Books, 1979), pp. 309–341.
5. See Karl Popper, *The Logic of Scientific Discovery* (London: Hutchinson, 1959), and Paul Feyerabend, "Problems of Empiricism," in *Beyond the Edge of Certainty*, ed. R. Colodny (Englewood Cliffs, N.J.: Prentice-Hall, 1965), pp. 145–260.
6. Richetto makes this argument in his review article in *Communication Yearbook I*. A similar call for tying communication variables to sociological, psychological, and managerial theories of organization is made by Karlene Roberts, Charles O'Reilly, G. Bretton, and Lyman Porter, "Organizational Theory and Organizational Communication: A Communication Failure?" Technical Report #2, Contract #N000314-69-A-0222, Washington, D.C., Office of Naval Research, 1973.

7. Leonard C. Hawes, "Social Collectivities as Communication: Perspectives on Organizational Behavior," *Quarterly Journal of Speech*, 60 (1974), 497–502. Note that from this point of view, the *outcome* of organizational communication is not productivity, but the *organization* itself.

8. Richetto, 341–342.

9. Fred N. Kerlinger, *Foundations of Behavioral Research*, 2nd. ed. (New York: Holt, Rinehart and Winston, 1973), pp. 2–15.

10. Daniel J. O'Keefe, "Logical Empiricism and the Study of Human Communication," *Speech Monographs*, 42 (1975), 169–183, and B. Aubrey Fisher, *Perspectives on Human Communication* (New York: MacMillan, 1978).

11. Howard S. Becker, "Whose Side Are We On?" in *Qualitative Methodology*, ed. William J. Filstead (Chicago: Markham, 1970), p. 15. See Also Gideon Sjoberg, ed., *Ethics, Politics, and Social Research* (Cambridge, Mass.: Schenkman, 1967).

12. This argument has been made by David Silverman, *The Theory of Organizations* (New York: Basic Books, 1971) and by J. Kenneth Benson, "Innovation and Crisis in Organizational Analysis," *The Sociological Quarterly*, 18 (1977), 3–16.

13. We understand that Phillip K. Tompkins, Department of Communication, Purdue University, has prepared a monograph in which these sociological critiques are applied to organizational communication.

14. Charles Perrow, "Three Types of Effectiveness Studies," in *New Perspectives on Organizational Effectiveness*, eds. Paul S. Goodman, Johannes M. Pennings, and Associates (San Francisco: Jossey-Bass, 1977), pp. 96–105. Perrow notes, for example, that "high morale means that people find it gratifying to do what the organization wants them to do" (p. 102).

15. For a discussion of the problems in defining organizational effectiveness, see Paul S. Goodman, Johannes M. Pennings, and Associates, eds., *New Perspectives on Organizational Effectiveness*.

16. See Michael L. Hecht, "The Conceptualization and Measurement of Interpersonal Communication Satisfaction," *Human Communication Research*, 4 (1978), 253–264, and Paul M. Machinsky, "Organizational Communication: Relationships to Organizational and Job Satisfaction," *Academy of Management Journal*, 20 (1977), 592–607.

17. So far as we know, no organizational intervention has been subjected to sufficiently rigorous evaluation that can be claimed unequivocally to effect successful organizational outcomes.

18. Matthew B. Miles, "Qualitative Data as an Attractive Nuisance: The Problems of Analysis," *Administrative Science Quarterly*, 24 (1979), 590–601. For a discussion in support of the case study as a limited method for hypothesis testing, see Donald T. Campbell, "Degrees of Freedom and the Case Study," *Comparative Political Studies*, 8 (1975), 178–193.

19. Miles also makes this point in "Qualitative Data."

20. Peter Berger and Thomas Luckmann, *The Social Construction of Reality* (Garden City, N.Y.: Anchor Doubleday, 1967).

21. This definition has been appropriated from Karl E. Weick, *The Social Psychology of Organizing* (Reading, Mass.: Addison-Wesley, 1969), 43–53. However, where Weick uses the term "behavior" we choose the word "action" to express our understanding that these activities stand as meaningful, interpretable, and accountable by their performers.

22. See Karl E. Weick, "Amendments to Organizational Theorizing," *Academy of Management Journal*, 17 (1974), 487–502. Weick's conception of organization in this essay includes: (1) everyday events (e.g. escalator rides), (2) everyday places (e.g. college campuses), (3) everyday questions (e.g. one says "my that's changed" when driven around in a strange area by a local who subsequently supplies information which tells the one what he was referring to), (4) micro-organizations (e.g. jazz orchestra), and (5) absurd organizations (e.g. an organization "that does not know what it is doing").

23. Clifford Geertz, *The Interpretation of Cultures* (New York: Basic Books, 1973), p. 5.

24. Geertz, p. 5

25. See Leonard C. Hawes, "Toward a Hermeneutic Phenomenology of Communication," *Communication Quarterly*, 25 (1977), 38–41.

26. Thomas B. Farrell, "Knowledge, Consensus, and Rhetorical Theory," *Quarterly Journal of Speech*, 62 (1976), 4.

27. Don H. Zimmerman, "Record Keeping and the Intake Process in a Public Welfare Organization," in *On Record*, ed. Stanton Wheeler (New York: Russell Sage Foundation, 1969), pp. 319–354.

28. Harold Garfinkel, " 'Good' Organizational Reasons for 'Bad' Clinic Records," in *Studies in Ethnomethodology*, ed. Harold Garfinkel (Englewood Cliffs, N.J.: Prentice-Hall, 1967), pp. 186–207.

29. David Sudnow, "Normal Crimes: Sociological Features of the Penal Code in a Public Defender Office," *Social Problems*, 12 (1965), 225–276.

30. Joan P. Emerson, "Behavior in Private Places," in

Recent Sociology, vol 2, ed. H. P. Dreitzel (New York: MacMillan, 1970), pp. 35–49.

31. Edith A. Folb, "Vernacular Vocabulary: A View of Interracial Perceptions and Experiences," in *Intercultural Communication: A Reader*, eds. Larry A. Samovar and Richard Porter (Belmont, Cal.: Wadsworth, 1976), p. 194.

32. See, for example, E. Sutherland, *The Professional Thief* (Chicago: University of Chicago Press, 1937).

33. Kenneth Stoddard, "Pinched: Notes on the Ethnographer's Location of Argot," in *Ethnomethodology*, ed. Roy Turner (Middlesex, England: Penguin Books, 1974), pp. 173–179.

34. G. Lakoff and M. Johnson, *Metaphors We Live By* (Chicago: University of Chicago Press, in press).

35. Susan Koch and Stanley Deetz, "Metaphor Analysis of Social Reality in Organizations," paper presented to the Speech Communication Association/International Communication Association Conference on Interpretive Approaches to Organizational Communication, Alta, 1981.

36. William Labov and J. Waletsky, "Narrative Analysis: Oral Versions of Personal Experiences," in *Essays on the Verbal and Visual Arts*, ed. J. Helm (Seattle: University of Washington Press, 1967), pp. 12–44.

37. Berger and Luckmann, p. 39. Robert A. Georges discusses other social uses of storytelling, such as teaching a lesson, in "Toward an Understanding of the Storytelling Event," *Journal of American Folklore*, 82 (1969), 313–328.

38. Jan H. Brunvand makes this distinction between personal and local legends in *The Study of American Folklore*, 2nd ed. (New York: W. W. Norton and Company, 1978), pp. 99–124.

39. Roger D. Abrahams, "Toward an Enactment Theory of Folklore," in *Frontiers of Folklore*, ed. William R. Bascom (Boulder, Colorado: Westview Press, 1977), p. 100.

40. Donald F. Roy, " 'Banana Time': Job Satisfaction and Informal Interaction," *Human Organization*, 18 (1960), 158–168.

41. Lawrence Weider, "Telling the Code," in *Ethnomethodology*, ed. Roy Turner (Middlesex, England: Penguin Books, 1974), p. 161.

42. John Lofland, *Doing Social Life* (New York: Wiley and Sons, 1976). Becoming intimately familiar with one's data, though often associated with qualitative research, is useful in quantitative research as well. It seems to us that those quantitative researchers most familiar with their data can more plausibly reveal the nuance of meaning embedded in their statistical analyses.

43. Weick, The *Social Psychology of Organizing*, 2nd ed., p. 47.

44. M. D. Cohen, James G. March, and J. P. Olsen, "A Garbage Can Model of Organizational Choice," *Administrative Science Quarterly*, 17 (1972), 1–25.

45. B. L. T. Hedberg, P. C. Nystrom, and W. H. Starbuck, "Camping on See-Saws: Prescriptions for a Self-Designing Organization," *Administrative Science Quarterly*, 21 (1976), 41–65.

46. Jack D. Douglas, *Investigative Social Research* (Beverly Hills: Sage Publications, 1976), p. 218.

47. This is sometimes called a "grounded theory" approach to research. See Barney G. Glaser and Anselm L. Strauss, *The Discovery of Grounded Theory* (Chicago: Aldine, 1976), and Larry D. Browning, "A Grounded Organizational Communication Theory Derived From Qualitative Data," *Communication Monographs*, 45 (1978), 93–109.

48. Campbell, "Degrees of Freedom," 181–182.

49. These reactions describe the responses we are familiar with from employees in a family health clinic, an advertising agency, a print shop, a workshop for the handicapped, and a police department where we and our colleagues have done organizational culture studies.

50. Geertz, p. 14.

17   THE EMERGENCE OF ORGANIZATIONAL CULTURES
DEAN SCHEIBEL

Dean Scheibel's study of two rock bands illustrates how examining the interrelationship of three types of symbolic forms (organizational metaphors, stories, and fantasy themes) can yield a sophisticated analysis of organizational culture. Scheibel applies the culture perspective advocated by Pacanowky and O'Donnell-Trujillo; he explains metaphors, stories, and fantasy themes, then uses them in understanding two rock bands—*The Grind* and *Charm*. Scheibel's analysis demonstrates that the metaphors, stories, and fantasy themes in everyday talk are powerful contributors to the culture of that organization. In comparing the organizational cultures of the two bands, ask yourself: How difficult would it be for a member of *The Grind* to become a member of *Charm*? Why? Would you rather be a member of one band or the other? Why?

It is evident that there are a variety of approaches to organizational culture (cf. Frost, Moore, Louis, Lundberg, & Martin, 1985; Pondy, Frost, Morgan, & Dandridge, 1983; Putnam & Pacanowsky, 1983). In this sense, the organizational culture perspective is not monolithic. Organizational culture may be seen from a functionalist perspective, where interest may focus on the role or functions of cultural objects in terms of organizational maintenance. Conversely, organizational culture can be seen from an interpretive perspective, where interest may focus on the communicative processes through which organizational realities are constructed. Thus, functionalist and interpretive perspectives to the study of organizational culture vary in terms of how each approaches the study of organizational culture and the types of questions asked (cf. Morgan, Frost, & Pondy, 1983; Putnam, 1983; Smircich & Calas, 1987).

This research deals with organizational culture from an interpretive perspective that focuses on organizational symbolism as communicative sensemaking (cf. Bantz, 1983; Morgan, Frost, & Pondy, 1983; Putnam, 1983). I briefly overview the per-

spective, present a rationale culminating in several research questions, and provide empirical data that support a particular interpretation of organizational symbolism.

From an interpretive perspective, organizational cultures are the processes through which the social realities that constitute organizational life are produced and reproduced. In this sense, communication practices serve as the means by which organizational realities are situationally constituted (cf. Pacanowsky & O'Donnell-Trujillo, 1982; Smircich & Calas, 1987).

A focus on organizational symbolism centralizes the interpretation of organizational members' use of symbols and the communicative processes by which shared meanings are produced and reproduced. That is, communication refers to the use of symbols:

> Symbols are not proxy for their objects but are *vehicles for the conception of objects*. To conceive a thing or a situation is not the same thing as to "react to it" overtly, or to be aware of its presence. In talking *about* things we have conceptions of them, not the things

themselves; and *it is the conceptions, not the things, that symbols directly "mean."* (Langer, 1957, pp. 60–61)

In this sense, interpretations of organizational cultures seek descriptions of shared symbols and meanings that are produced and reproduced as patterns of discourse by organizational members (cf. Geertz, 1973; Pacanowsky & O'Donnell-Trujillo, 1982; Smircich & Calas, 1987). To this end organizational symbolism researchers examine such symbolic forms as myths (e.g., Abravanel, 1983), rituals (e.g., Pacanowsky & O'Donnell-Trujillo, 1983), rites (e.g., Trice & Beyer, 1984), stories (e.g., Brown, 1985), fantasy (e.g., Bormann, Pratt, & Putnam, 1978), ceremonies (e.g., Rosen, 1985), and metaphors (e.g., Pepper, 1987). However, such research typically focuses on examining individual symbolic forms rather than examining relationships between and/or among symbolic forms. In this sense, studying organizational symbolism as discrete symbolic forms may mask a more complex process.

In investigating the interaction of symbolic forms, the current study examines metaphor, story, and fantasy. Metaphor is conceptualized as "understanding and experiencing one kind of thing in terms of another" (Lakoff & Johnson, 1980, p. 5). Metaphors serve as sense-making devices that are displayed in the vocabulary of organizational members. As such, members' use of metaphors produces and reproduces organizational culture (cf. Koch & Deetz, 1981; Pacanowsky & O'Donnell-Trujillo, 1982).

Stories have been examined by various organizational culture researchers (e.g., Brown, 1985; Martin, Feldman, Hatch, & Sitkin, 1983; Pacanowsky & O'Donnell-Trujillo, 1982, 1983; Scheibel, 1986). Stories allow members to typify organizational experiences for other members (Berger & Luckmann, 1966, p. 39) and "signify possible future scenarios of organizational life" (Pacanowsky & O'Donnell-Trujillo, 1982, p. 126). Thus, stories serve to reflect and create culturally-related meanings.

Finally, fantasy is a symbolic form that Bormann (1986) defines as "the creative and imaginative shared interpretation of events that fulfills a group psychological or rhetorical need" (p. 221). Bales (1950, cited in Bormann, 1972) found that fantasy is used to develop common group culture. Typically, a fantasy theme involves dramatizing messages and exacting incidents in a setting removed from the here-and-now of the group situation (Bormann, 1983, p. 107).

Rock groups are an excellent context for studying communication activities in that the role of communication among members of a group is crucial. Members must coordinate their actions when selecting, learning, and rehearsing songs for their repertoire, when coordinating technology and resources to support a performance, and when performing. Such research is valuable not only for understanding the organizational processes of rock groups, but also the organization of people, social knowledge, resources, and technology within a wide variety of social contexts (Scheibel, 1986, p. 2)

Within the current study, the symbolic forms of metaphor, story, and fantasy, are examined in three ways: (1) how the various symbolic forms create and reflect socially constructed realities within the context of the rock bands, (2) to compare and contrast how the use of symbolic forms differs between the two rock bands, and (3) to examine the relationship of symbolic forms to each other in terms of how they are manifested within the context of the rock bands.

RESEARCH METHOD

The data of the current study was collected over a two-year period. The two rock groups, "The Grind" and "Charm," were, individually, the subjects of previous case studies (Scheibel 1984, 1986). The sources of data included audiotaped observations of the two groups' rehearsals, informal interviews with members of the bands, attendance at the bands' public performances, and the researcher's tacit and intuitive knowledge of rock bands. In addition, photographs, publicity stills, flyers, and a newspaper advertisement were collected.

THE BANDS

There are different types of rock bands. Within the genre of rock music, some bands specialize in playing songs that have been previously popularized by other bands. Such groups are typically referred to as "Top 40" or "copy" bands, depending on the songs that comprise the group's repertoire; such groups are concerned with, in part, the accurate replication of what is already known. However, another type of group plays group-generated compositions, generically recognized as "originals." Groups that play original music are not concerned with replication, but rather, with creativity and innovation.[1] The current study examines two bands: one is "original" and the other is "Top 40."

The Grind

The band's repertoire is original. The group's members are blue-collar workers, male, 26–34 years of age, and have been playing music together for almost three years. Individually, each of the members has been playing in rock groups for over ten years. Some of the members have played together in other rock bands. The group is composed of five individuals: Darryl, Curt, Ed, Allan, and Bob. Darryl alternately plays guitar and keyboard; Curt is the lead singer, and also alternately plays guitar and keyboard; Ed sings harmonic accompaniment to Curt's lead vocals, and also alternates on guitar and keyboard; Allan plays bass guitar; Bob plays drums. Darryl, Curt, and Ed all write songs. The songwriting is occasionally done together, but more often, they write independently of each other.

Within the band, Darryl, Curt, and Ed all "double" on guitar and keyboard. However, although each owns his own guitar, they share keyboard duties on the same instrument and, in fact, own the instrument jointly. The fact that the three members all play the same instruments, as well as the fact that each composes songs for the group, is important in terms of the roles each member enacts within the group. This is compounded by the fact that individuals' perceptions of self within music groups is heavily influenced by individuals' identification with the instrument(s) they play.

Charm

The band's repertoire is primarily Top 40, with a few other songs form the 1960s and 1970s. The group's members are primarily blue-collar workers,

four males and one female, 21–32 years of age, and have been playing music together for under a year. The group consists of Gary, Ian, Hans, Karla, and Joey. Gary alternates between keyboard and guitar and sings some lead vocals, but primarily sings harmonic accompaniment; Ian plays lead guitar and sings harmony; Hans plays keyboard and synthesizer and sings harmony; Karla is the primary lead singer; Joey plays drums. Although each of the members has played in rock bands before, Gary has the widest range of experience and is the only member who makes a living from music; during the day, Gary teaches music at a local guitar shop.

In contrast with The Grind, Charm is still in a state of growth, both in terms of the group's repertoire and in terms of the group's membership. Charm's drummer, Joey, has not attended a rehearsal for several weeks. Hans, frustrated at the group's inability to "get it together," suddenly quit the band. These two incidents lead to the decision by the remaining members to audition two new members, Frank, a drummer, and Larry, a bassist.

THE SYMBOLIC TRIAD

Within music theory, a triad is recognized as three different notes that can be played together; in playing the notes together, a chord is formed. Similar to a chord, the interaction among group members and the manifestation of symbolic forms that arise are creatively interactive; thus, metaphors, stories, and fantasies can be expected to arise in an overlapping, blending manner.

In the current study, the metaphor of culture serves as an "umbrella metaphor" in which other symbolic forms reside (Frost, Moore, Louis, Lundberg, & Martin 1985). Although each of the symbolic forms—metaphor, story, and fantasy—has been associated with the culture approach, the forms are often studied discretely. Brown (1985) examines stories in terms of organizational socialization. Bormann, Pratt, and Putnam (1978) concentrate on fantasies and emergent leadership. Hartman and Gibbard (1974) examine fantasy in terms of the evolution of group culture. Although symbolic forms have been studied, profitably, as individual forms within the context of a given collective, it is possible that the use of symbolic forms is not clear cut. Thus, the current study is also interested in the manner in which symbolic forms arise and influence each other, in addition to their place as creative, sense-making apparatuses.

In the following exchange, the use of similes serves as a locus of meaning about a particular quality of group-life (i.e., what is it like to be a member of a band).

FRANK: It's like a marriage. . . .

KARLA: Yeah.

FRANK: . . . it *can* be

GARY: Yeah.

FRANK: Yeah.

KARLA: Like a family.

LARRY: Yeah.

GARY: Yeah.

The notion that a band is "like a family" reflects an interpretation about the nature of the social reality within bands. To band members, the familial quality of group-life stems from the interdependent and synergistic nature of playing music together. The connotative value of the metaphor reflects a consensual understanding that the relationships that may exist within the context of a rock band are complex, multifaceted, and personal. In some sense, the family metaphor reflects various aspects of members' social knowledge that permeate the social reality of group-life.

Of similar relevance is the metaphor of marriage. In equating relations within the band with a marriage, the social reality is perceived by members as possessing an intimate quality. Among musicians, the metaphor of marriage is not uncommon, not only in terms of relationships among members, but also in terms of music. The nature of rock bands tends to create a social reality that fosters such perceptions. The blending of individuals' voices and instruments into a single sound, a single image, fosters a sense of intimacy. The metaphor of marriage seems most applicable in terms of auditioning. The auditioning process, if successful, results in a reformation of the group's membership. It is an evaluative process by which the fitness or suitability of individual(s) is

judged. A prominent aspect of auditioning is that it is an inherently two-way street; it is a courtship ritual in which individuals determine whether a merging will be beneficial in terms of respective goals (Scheibel, 1986).

GARY: Well, I hope that you're having a good enough time that you don't wanna go home.

LARRY: Oh, absolutely! This is what we've been looking for . . . somebody who already knows their end of it and that we don't have to train them.

KARLA: Yeah.

IAN: That's what we're looking for.

GARY: We're looking for the same thing.

LARRY: Yeah, it'll take a certain amount to tighten up our ends together but. . . .

GARY: Yeah.

LARRY: . . . but at least we know the songs.

The courtship of the audition can be viewed as a prelude to enculturation, or the process by which members of a collectivity "acquire the social knowledge and skills necessary to behave as competent members" (Pacanowsky & O'Donnell-Trujillo, 1983, p. 143). However, within rock bands, the sense of "who is enculturating whom?" becomes problematic. The reformation of Charm is a mutual enculturation, more a blending of formerly separate and distinctive cultural structures.

Within the process of auditioning, stories are shared by members. These stories, which typify and "recapitulate experience verbally" (Labov & Waletsky, 1967, p. 12–44), serve as cultural bonding; they are expressions of social knowledge that all members have experienced. In telling the following story during the initial meeting of the two factions, Larry's recapitulation of his and Frank's past experiences serves as typifications of experiences that the members of Charm recognize as knowledge that is not dissimilar to their own:

LARRY: We've [he and Frank] been working together most of this year. We did all the work getting the sets together; we did a couple of gigs; and we recorded a tape, took pictures, and then everybody bailed out [laughs]. We done all the work and then, *boom*, they're gone, you know?

Larry's story represents a sharing of social knowledge that is typical of many bands. It represents things that the members of Charm have previously experienced. The members of Charm interpret the story as evidence that Larry and Frank possess knowledge and experience similar to their own, even though specifics are different. The fact that Larry can laugh-off the adverse experience gains him credibility—it is interpreted as a testament to a resilient nature—adversity will not deter him.

The story also reveals various elements of social knowledge that are reflected in the vocabulary[2] of the story; "sets," "gigs" or public performances, "tape" or demonstration tape, which is played for prospective employers in order to be hired for gigs, and "pictures" or publicity photographs, which are also shown to prospective employers.

Stories also serve as adjunctive communicative organizing activities that reflect and create culturing within the group. For example, when Karla forgets some lyrics when Charm rehearsed a song entitled "No More Words," Gary tells the following stories:

GARY: Yeah . . . you're freaking out 'cause I'm mimicking the words after you. Have you ever had that happen with someone in the audience? I was singing something I wasn't real sure of one night, I think it was at the Duke [a club] . . . anyway, there's this guy sitting there across the bar . . . and I was singing a Cars' song . . . I think it was "Best Friend's Girl" or something . . . but the guy was sitting there singing every word and I'm going, "I better not blow this . . . this guy *knows* this song. He knows every word and he's singing it with me."

KARLA: I'd just look away . . . I don't look at people.

GARY: Yeah, but he's right in front of you . . . what do you do? After singing a wrong word in "Gimme Three Steps" . . . some sailor came up . . . after I'd been singing this for about a month that way . . . some sailor comes up and says, "I know that song real good and it's one of my favorite songs and I gotta tell you . . . there's this one spot where you're singing it wrong" . . . he corrected this *one* word. Every night he'd come in and see the same band for about three months and finally after about a month he got up the nerve to say, "fix it!"

The theme of both of Gary's stories mirrors what has just occurred within the group; Gary's stories are generated in response to Karla, who had forgotten some lyrics of the song the band was rehearsing. In addition, both of Gary's stories serve as more than entertaining narratives. The stories constitute a possible future reality for members of the group. In describing his own experiences with audience members during live performances, Gary signifies "possible future scenarios of organizational life" (Pacanowsky & O'Donnell-Trujillo, 1982, p. 126). In the telling of the stories, Gary implicitly states his beliefs concerning role enactment for a singer; both stories deal with the idea that the singer should know every word of every song in the band's performance repertoire. In addition, both stories portray something about the nature of the audiences. Rather than being static entities, Gary's stories reflect his belief that audiences interact with and influence a band's performance experience.

Although the marriage/family metaphor may be suitable for rock bands, it is problematic that a single image of marriage and family exists, either for all rock groups, or for all occasions within a single rock group. In this sense, the metaphor is dynamic rather than static. Differences in individuals' perceptions of the social reality, and the existence of conflict stemming from various sources, are reflected in the ongoing process of group-life. Within rock groups, the marriage metaphor is flexible enough to encompass social realities that parallel marriage in everyday life; that is, not all of them are made in heaven. The late John Lennon, commenting on the breakup of the Beatles, stated, ''It feels like a divorce'') Coleman, 1984, p. 332).

The remainder of the current study examines the use of fantasy in terms of reflecting, dealing with, and creating conflict within rock groups. The connection between fantasy and conflict has been posited by various researchers (Bales, 1970; Hartman & Gibbard, 1974) and has surfaced in various studies, including Bormann et al. (1978) and Scheibel (1984).

There has been some controversy surrounding fantasy.[3] Variously, fantasy has been defined as ''a mode of psychological action not subject to the same restraints as more consciously controlled forms of thought'' (Bales, 1970, p. 136), ''the creative and imaginative shared interpretation of events that fulfills a group psychological or rhetorical need'' (Bormann, 1986, p. 221), and ''conscious, nontask-directed thoughts, beliefs, or assumptions held by individuals'' (Hartman & Gibbard, 1974, p. 316). These conceptualizations of fantasy reflect differences in terms of the locus of fantasy. However, the idea that fantasy is related to group culture is explicitly recognized (Bormann, 1983, 1986; Hartman & Gibbard). The current study conceptualizes fantasy as a creative mode of psychological action that is initiated by individuals, yet may serve group as well as individual needs.

HANS: I knew their personalities were rubbing against . . . cause I could see what he feels . . . but she's not *quite* as abrasive on me as probably with you . . . but see, I've been with so many female singers that I'm automatically . . . like . . . it's hard to get somebody good who's just going to kick back and just let things happen . . . everybody is thinking about their own career and everything.

IAN: It's like waiting for Mrs. Right to come through the door . . .

GARY: Yeah.

IAN: . . . she ain't coming.

GARY: Right.

HANS: Exactly . . . and once you realize that, you decide on what you can live with.

The marriage metaphor is very much in evidence in the above exchange. Ian expresses exasperation over his dealings with Karla. Ian's comment about ''waiting for Mrs. Right'' metaphorically casts a generic female band member as a prospective marriage partner or wife. In this instance, the metaphor is ''chained out''[4] as a fantasy theme through Hans, who, in commiserating with Ian, states that ''you decide what you can *live* with'' [emphasis added]. The fantasy takes place in the ''here-and-now'' symbolic domain of group interaction.[5] The exchange demonstrates the interrelatedness of symbolic forms. In this case, the metaphor of marriage is enacted within a specific situation as a fantasy, which then chains out through other members.

The social reality of rock groups is too complex to be represented by a single metaphor. Although the metaphor of family may serve to frame a general pattern of meanings, situations arise that require metaphors that more accurately depict the constructed social realities within rock groups. Krefting and Frost (1985) state that ''extended, multiple, or mixed metaphors may be necessary to capture the important aspects of such situations'' (pp. 162–163).

Charm's conversation reflects a social reality in which conflict threatens the stability of the family. However, as will be seen, the metaphor of family, while applicable to particular situations, must be extended for other situations.

A Dirge[6] in the Family

IAN: One thing we've got to decide on is . . . are we gonna eighty-six Joey?

GARY: I think Joey has committed suicide.

HANS: Yeah, I think he has.

KARLA: Yeah.

GARY: I don't know . . . I'll talk to him tomorrow.

HANS: If he hasn't, man, we cannot go on . . . the band cannot go on without a drummer here . . . it's to that point

. . . we will never fly without it . . . without a guy here like we're here . . . all the time. I think if we get somebody else, we should really get somebody who could sing some harmony and really help . . . what do you think we should do, Ian? . . . as far as . . . think we should look at a lot of different drummers . . . or what?

IAN: We need one that sings.

Gary responds to Ian's point-blank question about getting rid of Joey with a fantasy that ". . . Joey has committed suicide." Gary's symbolic metaphor of death by suicide is readily seized by other group members. Such an interpretation allows the group to believe they cannot be held responsible for Joey's "death"; this allows the group to avoid being symbolically cast as murderers. In solving the problem of a family member who has failed to fulfill role expectations, the fantasy of death by suicide has an appealing rationale for other members of Charm. Because bands tend to be close-knit groups, getting rid of a group member, even when justifiable, is not something done lightly. The fantasy serves to justify actions deemed necessary for the benefit of the group. Similarly, Hans' dramatic comment that "we cannot go on without a drummer here . . ." posits that the band's very existence rests on finding a new drummer who can be "here like we're here . . . all the time." In conjoining symbolic meaning of the exchange, the death of one member is juxtaposed with death of the group. Thus the group uses symbolic forms to create meaning by which a problematic situation can be dealt with. The survival of the family takes precedence over a symbolic death.

Conflict within The Grind stems from various sources: rivalry over band leadership, artistic squabbles over how particular songs should be played, which songs should be learned, and some hostile feelings surrounding past conflicts that have occurred during the three years the group has been together. The intensity exhibited during the rehearsal exemplifies Coser's (1956) thoughts on the intensity of conflict within a group:

a conflict is more passionate and more radical when it arises out of close relationships. The coexistence of union and opposition in such relations makes for the peculiar sharpness of the conflict. Enmity calls forth deeper and more violent reactions, the greater the involvement of the parties among whom it originates. (p. 71)

In the following exchange, an argument takes place regarding the treatment of The Grind's keyboard. The incident is interesting in terms of the interlocking use of fantasy and metaphor.

DARRYL: I don't know how to impress this upon you. I know you've never read the manual *Curt*, but this mem . . . this memory protect button has got to stay *on* on either side. The . . . this was just off!

CURT: Is that a fact?

DARRYL: Yeah, it was just off!

CURT: Gosh.

ED: How did it get that way?

DARRYL: I guess it doesn't

CURT: I turn that off . . .

DARRYL: . . . matter; just keep it out on the porch . . .

CURT: . . . every . . . every night. I switch a different button every night . . .

DARRYL: Yeah, well this was just on.

CURT: . . . I had a screwdriver . . .

DARRYL: This was *on*. Memory Protect *on*.

CURT: . . . I had the thing all apart. I was lookin' inside of it . . . it was bitchin.

DARRYL: That means every . . . program we got is . . . up!

CURT: . . . you did it again man . . . I tell ya.

DARRYL: Yeah, you did.

CURT: That's a nice story. He's gonna tell that story, uh, Sunday night . . . I wrecked the Juno [name of keyboard] . . . anyway, and then we're gonna play Geisha Girl [name of a song].

BOB: Don't take the Juno, you'll kill yourself.

CURT: And then, I better turn around and look and double-check . . .

DARRYL: You'd think he'd . . . read the manual . . . no, it's in . . . English and . . .

CURT: . . . that the keyboard player, like, hasn't left the stage . . .

DARRYL: . . . that . . . blows my mind!

CURT: . . . because he might have found out that I ruined his guitar two weeks before I wrecked the Juno . . .

DARRYL: Well, you keep it out in the rain and you know you . . .

CURT: I wonder if he knows about the time that I, like, was playing catch with the Marshall [name of guitar amplifier]?

DARRYL: God! I own part of this thing [the keyboard] . . . why don't we like just chop it in thirds!

The exchange demonstrates the compelling nature of fantasy. During the exchange between Darryl and Curt, Curt repeatedly uses fantasy, while Darryl does not. However, in the end, Darryl is drawn into the fantasy of the destruction of the keyboard. Curt's initial fantasy sequence of responses is an inversion of Darryl's charges that Curt has treated the keyboard shabbily. Curt attempts to ridicule Darryl's charges by creating the fantasy that he (Curt) is mentally unbalanced, and had, in the past, disassembled the keyboard every night with a screwdriver. Curt's fantasy moves to the future as he fantasizes about Darryl telling the story in front of the live audience on "Sunday night." Moving from

a defensive posture to an offensive one, Curt fantasizes about actually being on stage and having to make sure "the keyboard player [Darryl] like hasn't left the stage . . ." This is probably in reference to Darryl's numerous sojourns to the refrigerator for beer. Finally, Curt returns to the theme of the destruction of musical instruments.

The fantasy of destroying various musical instruments can be interpreted as a metaphor for the conflict within the band. Darryl's chaining out of Curt's fantasy of destroying instruments leaves little doubt about this. Darryl's comment about chopping the keyboard into thirds is a reference to the fact that the keyboard is jointly owned by Darryl, Curt, and Ed. The parcelling out of the fantasized "thirds" of the keyboard is the symbolic destruction of the band.

Bob also participates in the fantasy; his joke, "Don't take the Juno, you'll kill yourself" is a takeoff on a drunk-driving commercial. It is possible that Bob's fantasy is the result of a free association to Curt's use of the word "wrecked," which he connects with wrecked cars, and then couples that association with his perception that Darryl is inebriated. However, as opposed to a fantasized destruction of instruments, Bob's joke includes the symbolic death of a group member.

The fantasy episode is noteworthy for several reasons. Curt's use of fantasy is expressively rhetorical; Curt uses fantasy as a rhetorical device to stultify Darryl's angry criticisms. The conflict within the fantasy reflects various aspects of the group's social realities. Substantively, the focus on instruments points to the magnitude to which individuals identify with instruments and technology. Within rock groups, ownership of technology is an expensive proposition. Darryl, Curt, and Ed jointly claim ownership of the keyboard; however, this joint ownership is out of necessity, not convenience. Although the theme of instrument destruction continues throughout the rehearsal, it is likely that the focus on instruments belies affective conflict pertaining to issues relating to status, leadership, and norms. Curt, in refusing to answer Darryl's charges directly, uses fantasy to insulate himself from Darryl's aggressive anger.

The fact that fantasy did not chain out through the whole group during the conflict can be interpreted in various ways. First, it is possible that individuals not directly concerned in the conflict would choose to stay out of it, not wishing to get involved in a conflict they perceived as being intense and interpersonal. Thus, although Ed also owned part of the keyboard, he did not become involved in the conflict. Second, during intense interpersonal conflict between two individuals, other group members may choose to keep quiet rather than risk getting involved and being perceived by those in conflict as taking sides in the conflict.

The exchange between Darryl and Curt over the treatment of the keyboard hints at the importance of musical instruments and technology as integral cultural artifacts to rock groups. All group members interact with such devices. In fact, the relationship between a group member's role as a musician and the instrument is a unique one. Because group members have spent a considerable amount of time and energy to become proficient at playing their respective instrument(s), there is an element of identification with the instrument(s); part of this identification can be attributed to the fact that during much of the time spent with the group, the instruments will, in a sense, be the group members' means of interacting with each other (Scheibel, 1984).

CODA[7]

Within the current study, the culture approach provides an interpretative framework for describing the social realities constructed by the members of two rock bands, The Grind and Charm. Such an approach facilitates an understanding of how the everyday existence of group-life is accomplished communicatively (Pacanowsky & O'Donnell-Trujillo, 1982).

Analyzing organizational culture through a variety of symbolic forms reveals not only the structures and processes of culture, but also the interrelated nature of the symbolic forms. Within the current study, communicative activities of the two bands reveal various metaphors that influence individuals' cognitive sense-making of the social realities that comprise group-life. Within the framework of particular metaphors, stories and fantasies serve as sense-making apparatuses by which individuals construct meaning in dealing with the events of everyday group-life.

The marriage and family metaphors reflect band members' understanding and expectations about the roles that individuals' enact, and the intimate and intense qualities that pervade group-life. At a lower level, individuals use death and destruction metaphors and fantasy themes to deal with problematic situations within the here-and-now of group life. Fantasies may serve as pressure-release for conflicts that members do not wish to deal with in an open and direct manner. Thus, although violent fantasies may reflect hostility and conflict that exists between individuals, the expression of violent fantasies may well allow the group to continue. Such an interpretation would seem to fit Coser's (1956) notion of "unrealistic" conflict, which is occasioned "by the need for tension release by individuals engaged in conflict" (p. 49).

Stories reveal various culturally-relevant structures and processes that exist within the group-life of rock bands. They serve to typify organizational experiences among members and reveal, through their content, elements of the social knowledge that musicians possess.

Finally, the use of overlapping symbolic forms by individuals within the two rock bands seems to indicate that a rethinking may be in order in terms of how researchers study symbolic forms. That is, if the occurrence of overlapping symbolic forms is found to be a common feature of social interaction, then the practice of studying symbolic forms as discrete entities may be an oversimplification of a more complex process.

NOTES

1. Denisoff and Bridges' (1982) hierarchy of types of music performers, "starting bands," "working acts," and "recording artists," implicitly subsumes the types of rock bands discussed in the current study.
2. According to Bantz (1981), the analysis of vocabulary "emphasizes the importance of understanding both the denotative and connotative meanings of words in organizations" (p. 4). Thus, a researcher studying a rock band who does not know the referent

for "sets," lacks information necessary for a cultural analysis.

3. Mohrmann (1982a, 1982b) criticizes fantasy theme analysis on the basis that fantasy theme analysis, as conceptualized by Bormann (1972), lacks substantial theoretical moorings. In response, Bormann (1982) contends that fantasy theme analysis is not dependent on a Freudian or Balesian conception of fantasy as a prerequisite for theoretical validity.

4. Bales' (1970) notion of a fantasy chain is that of a "chain reaction of associations *enacted* by the persons" involved. The fantasy chains out as "people are forced into the roles portrayed by the fantasy, by projection, seduction, or manipulation" (p. 138).

5. Bales (1970) posits three overlapping symbolic and emotional domains. These include: (a) "the domain of the manifest content," (b) "the domain of the 'here-and-now,' " and (c) "the domain of past experience" (p. 141). Bormann's (1983) conceptualization of fantasy in symbolic convergence theory is primarily concerned with the domain of manifest content.

6. *Webster's New World Dictionary* (1970) defines dirge as "a slow, sad song, poem, or musical composition expressing grief or mourning" (p. 399).

7. *Webster's New World Dictionary* (1970) defines coda as "a passage formally ending a composition or section" [of music] (p. 274).

BIBLIOGRAPHY

Abravanel, H. (1983). Mediatory myths in the service of organizational ideology. In L. R. Pondy, P. J. Frost, G. Morgan, & T. C. Dandridge (Eds.), *Organizational symbolism* (pp. 273–293). Greenwich, CT: JAI Press.

Bales, R.F. (1970). *Personality and interpersonal behavior*. New York: Holt, Rinehart & Winston.

Bantz, C.R. (1981, August). *Interpreting organization cultures: A proposed procedure, criteria for evaluation, and consideration of research methods*. A paper prepared for the Speech Communication Association-International Communication Association summer conference on interpretive approaches to the study of organizational communication. Alta, UT.

Bantz, C.R. (1983). Naturalistic research traditions. In L.L. Putnam & M. E. Pacanowsky (Eds.), *Communication and organizations: An interpretive approach* (pp. 55–71). Beverly Hills: Sage.

Bormann, E.G. (1972). Fantasy and rhetorical vision: The rhetorical criticism of social reality. *Quarterly Journal of Speech, 58*, 396–407.

Bormann, E.G. (1982). Fantasy and rhetorical vision: Ten years later. *Quarterly Journal of Speech, 68*, 288–305.

Bormann, E.G. (1983). Symbolic convergence: Organizational communication and culture. In L.L. Putnam & M.E. Pacanowsky (Eds.), *Communication and organizations: An interpretive approach* (pp. 99–122). Beverly Hills: Sage.

Bormann, E.G. (1986). Symbolic convergence theory and communication in group decision making. In R.Y. Hirokawa & M.S. Poole (Eds.), *Communication and group decision-making* (pp. 219–236). Beverly Hills: Sage.

Bormann, E.G., Pratt, J., & Putnam, L.L. (1978). Power, authority, and sex: Male response to female leadership. *Communication Monographs, 45*, 119–155.

Brown, M.H. (1985). That reminds me of a story: Speech action in organizational socialization. *Western Journal of Speech Communication, 49*, 27–42.

Coleman, R. (1984). *Lennon*. New York: McGraw-Hill.

Coser, L.A. (1956). *The functions of social conflict*. New York: The Free Press.

Denisoff, S.R., & Bridges J. (1982). Popular music: Who are the recording artists? *Journal of Communication, 32*(1), 132–142.

Frost, P.J., Moore, L.F., Louis, M.R., Lundberg, C.C., & Martin, J. (1985). *Organizational culture*. Beverly Hills: Sage.

Geertz, C. (1973). *The interpretation of cultures*. New York: Basic Books.

Hartman, J.J., & Gibbard, G.S. (1974). A note on fantasy themes in the evolution of group culture. In J.J. Hartman, G.S. Gibbard, & R.D. Mann (Eds.), *Analysis of groups* (pp. 315–335). San Francisco: Jossey-Bass.

Koch, S., & Deetz, S. (1981). Metaphor analysis of social reality in organizations. *Journal of Applied Communication Research, 9*, 1–15.

Krefting, L.A., & Frost, P.J. (1985). Untangling webs, surfing waves, and wildcatting: A multiple-metaphor perspective on managing organizational culture. In P.J. Frost, L.F. Moore, M.R. Louis, C.C. Lundberg, & J. Martin (Eds.), *Organizational culture* (pp. 155–168). Beverly Hills: Sage.

Labov, W., & Waletsky, J. (1967). Narrative analysis: Oral versions of personal experiences. In J. Helm (Ed.), *Essays on the verbal and visual arts* (pp. 12–44). Seattle: University of Washington Press.

Lakoff, G., & Johnson, M. (1980). *Metaphors we live by.* Chicago: University of Chicago Press.

Langer, S. K. (1957). *Philosophy in a new key* (3rd ed.) Cambridge: Harvard University Press.

Martin, J., Feldman, M.S., Hatch, M.H., & Sitkin, S.B. (1983). The uniqueness paradox in organizational stories. *Administrative Science Quarterly, 28,* 438–453.

Mohrmann, G.P. (1982a). An essay on fantasy theme criticism. *Quarterly Journal of Speech, 68,* 109–132.

Mohrmann, G.P. (1982b). Fantasy theme criticism: A peroration. *Quarterly Journal of Speech, 68,* 306–313.

Morgan, G., Frost, P. J., & Pondy, L. R. (1983). Organizational symbolism. In L.R. Pondy, P. J. Frost, G. Morgan, T. C. Dandridge (Eds.), *Organizational symbolism* (pp. 3–35) Greenwich, CT: JAI Press.

Pacanowsky, M.E., & O'Donnell-Trujillo, N. (1982). Communication and organizational cultures. *Western Journal of Speech Communication, 46,* 115–130.

Pacanowsky, M.E., & O'Donnell-Trujillo, N. (1983). Organizational communication as cultural performance. *Communication Monographs, 50,* 126–147.

Pepper, G. L. (1987). *A procedure for assisting and contrasting the metaphoric and literal perceptions of leadership within an organization.* Unpublished doctoral dissertation, University of Minnesota, Minneapolis.

Pondy, L.R., Frost, P.J., Morgan, G. & Dandridge, T.C. (Eds.). (1983). *Organizational symbolism* (pp. 3–35). Greenwich, CT: JAI Press.

Putnam, L.L. (1983). The interpretive perspective: An alternative to functionalism. In L.L. Putnam & M.E. Pacanowsky (Eds.), *Communication and organizations: An interpretive approach* (pp. 99–122). Beverly Hills: Sage.

Putnam, L.L., & Pacanowsky, M.E. (Eds.). (1983). Communication and organizations: An interpretive approach (pp. 99–122). Beverly Hills: Sage.

Rosen, M. (1985). Breakfast at Spiro's: Dramaturgy and dominance. *Journal of Management, 11,* 31–48.

Scheibel, D.F. (1984). *Bashing and clanging: A fantasy theme analysis of conflict during a rock group's rehearsal.* Unpublished manuscript. Northridge: California State University, Department of Speech Communication.

Scheibel, D.F. (1986). *Communicative organizing activities and the organizational culture of a rock and roll band.* Unpublished master's thesis. California State University, Northridge.

Smircich, L., & Calas, M.B. (1987). Organizational culture: A critical assessment. In F.M. Jablin, L.L. Putnam, K. H. Roberts, & L. W. Porter (Eds.), *Handbook of organizational communication* (pp. 228–263). Newbury Park, CA: Sage.

Trice, H. M., & Beyer, J. M. (1984). Studying organizational cultures through rites and ceremonials. *Academy of Management Review, 9,* 653–669.

Webster's new world dictionary. (1980). (2nd college ed.). New York: Simon & Schuster.

3 ORGANIZATIONAL COMMUNICATION CONCEPTS AND ISSUES

Most handbooks and texts on organizational communication devote significant attention to applying the theories described in Part II to circumstances encountered in organizational life. This reader follows that pattern. What makes organizational communication "communicational" is the concern scholars and practitioners have for learning about the relationships among the countless interactions in organizations and the principles of communication. What makes it "organizational" is the focus on applying communication theory and research to the unique dynamics of complex organizations. Part III presents readings that reflect this intersection of communication concepts and organizational circumstances. What follows is a collection of original research and practical applications that illustrate some of the major issues and problems addressed by organizational communication. Key issues represented in Part III are leadership and the roles and relationships of managers, minorities, and women in the workplace; organizational ethics; personal and institutional power; decision making; and organizational networks.

We cannot do justice here to the long history and varied literature of leadership research. Throughout much of the tradition, most theories and research about leadership generally have acknowledged communication but treated it as a peripheral factor. More recently communication has emerged as a focal concern in leadership studies; however, the focus has been primarily on supervisor-subordinate interaction. Chapters in this part by Herbert A. Simon, Frederic M. Jablin, Henry Mintzberg, and Warren Bennis reflect this emphasis.

Among the key questions scholars have asked about leadership are: How do persons in leadership positions influence followers in order to obtain desired behaviors? What is the role of speech and writing skills in effective leadership? And, how does communication contribute to the maintenance of order, stability, and change in organizational relationships?

Since the rise of the human resources movement and the progressive social agenda of the 1960s that pressed for equal employment opportunity, the concerns of women and minorities in the workplace have been of special interest to organizational researchers. Moving beyond analyses of the structural factors that influence these workers' lives, communication scholars have begun developing useful theories and defining pertinent research issues and problems related to differences among organizational members. Among the key concerns are: What are the implications of rapid changes in the composition of work forces in terms of sex, race, ethnicity, nationality, and age? How does communication facilitate or inhibit the effective integration of a heterogeneous work population? What communication strategies can foster such integration and the achievement of equality in the work place? Some answers are suggested in the chapters by Rosabeth Moss Kanter and Edward W. Jones, Jr., included here.

These are crucially important ethical questions for our times, but they are not the only ethical issues that involve organizational communication. Organizations of all types increasingly are being named as culprits in the pollution of the environment, deception of consumers, purveying of "dirty tricks," violation of individual civil rights, and on and on. In such a social context, the communication of values is critical. Currently, scholars are asking: What is ethical communication and how can it be made practical in a competitive environment? What communication strategies mask unethical behavior and how can they be detected and brought to task? And, how is communication implicated in commercial and industrial disasters such as the tragedies at Three Mile Island and Chernobyl or the mistaken shootdowns of commercial airliners? The chapters by Gerald F. Cavanagh, Dennis J. Moberg, and Manuel Velasquez and by Sissela Bok are concerned directly with the ethics of organizational communication.

Ethical problems abound as well in matters involving the distribution and use of power and the struggles for resources and influence in organizational settings. A unique social feature of organizational life is its official sanctioning of different orders of power and control within the group. The John R.P. French and Bertrand Raven chapter addresses the bases of power in such social orders. Formal and informal hierarchies of power and control frequently set the stage for conflict. Many perspectives have been offered on the nature and management of power and conflict; however, all views acknowledge that they are transacted fundamentally in communicative behavior. Stephen P. Bank's chapter directs research and theory attention toward power as interaction. Power and conflict researchers in general seek answers to questions such as, What are the ways that power is enacted through communication? What are the communicative sources and functions of conflict? How is communication involved in the resolution of conflict episodes? And how does communication contribute to the creation and maintenance of power relationships?

Researchers have studied how communication dynamics are related to the achievement of group consensus and how the communication procedures of leaders can facilitate followers' participation in decision processes. While most communication research on decision making has focused on the social psychology of groups, some interesting newer trends investigate how decisions are rationalized through communicative behavior and how situational contexts, including relations of power and influence, may frame decision premises. Irving Janis and Leon Mann's chapter is foundational for this trend.

In addition, in studying decision making, scholars have examined the ways that group development—and the nature of the group and its social context—influence the effectiveness of decisions. These issues are apparent in the chapter by John McCormick.

Finally, network research—represented here in the contributions by Everett Rogers and R. Argawala Rogers and by Bruce Kapferer—continues to generate findings about the perceived patterns of interaction among organizational members. Some recent studies have attempted to link network data with levels of worker satisfaction and commitment and with organizational culture; others have looked for conditions that instigate or block incidents of interaction. Network research has contributed to the identification of informal opinion leaders, cliques, and isolated individuals; however, it is in the efforts to relate network data to other areas, such as interpersonal relationships, that its future direction seems to lie.

Integration of issues and applications is key to reading the selections in Part III. Although each section represents work in a specific research area, the issues dealt with are conceptually and pragmatically linked to issues in the other sections. Decision making, for example, has ethical dimensions because it often appeals to institutional power arrangements, and it is influenced by the leadership climate of the group. Furthermore, the decision procedure can be analyzed profitably by use of network research techniques. Consequently, it is important to bear in mind while reading these selections that they represent interrelated issues and problems in organizational communication. The epilogue is a chapter by Harland Cleveland that looks into the future of organizational life. Cleveland makes the key linkages among information, power, and values in an open society, which exemplifies the integrated nature of Part III.

18 THE FINE ART OF ISSUING ORDERS

Herbert A. Simon

Here is an example of the classic leadership concern about how best to influence followers to obtain desired results. This essay was originally published in 1945, but it contains advice based on a remarkably contemporary idea. Simon argues that orders should be thought of as events that activate some kind of preexisting potential for action in an organization rather than as proclamations of the will of managers that create order from chaos. Note ways in which communication concerns are central to Simon's idea of effective order giving. He advocates thinking about orders in ways readers of this book probably consider basic: adaptation to audience, distinctions between message and meaning, and considerations about credibility.

The art of issuing orders consists largely in knowing when *not* to issue them. In any organization the executive must issue orders from time to time, but the more effective the organization scheme, and the more effective the planning procedures, the fewer will be the number of specific orders required. Orders issued by the chief executive will relate not only to the specific procedures which should govern the activities of departments but particularly to the procedures governing contacts between different departments. A number of cities have found it desirable to codify the more permanent administrative orders governing procedures and to issue them as administrative codes or manuals. Administrative codes and manuals are more fully discussed later in this article.

Of a somewhat different nature are orders issued in response to emergency needs for action. Such orders may secure the removal of a dead animal or may bring the report of a burglary to the attention of the proper police officer. Similar orders may be needed to deal with more serious emergencies: a windstorm, a flood or a conflagration.

Though the particular occasion when such orders will be needed cannot be anticipated, whenever a matter requiring official attention occurs with a sufficient degree of frequency, regular methods can be worked out for dealing with it. Thus the handling of the most common types of citizen complaints and reports of criminal acts can be regularized so as to require little or no attention of the chief executive.

ORDERS AND WISHES

An order is not, or should not be, simply a wish. Its purpose and function is to bring about or to confirm some change in the activity of the operating personnel. Unless it accomplishes this, it is useless.

Order issuing should be sharply distinguished from executive wish-thinking. Perhaps the chief administrator, while on an inspection tour of the city hall, is impressed by the dinginess of departmental offices. When he returns to his office, he dictates the following "order" to his secretary:

"To all departments: The physical appearance of offices in the city hall is such as to create a decidedly unfavorable impression on citizens who transact business in city offices. Each department is hereby explicitly instructed that its offices must be kept at

H. A. Simon, "The Fine Art of Issuing Orders." Reprinted with permission from *Public Management*, July, 1945, published by International City Management Association.

all times in good order, that desks must be neat, floors well swept and varnished, walls and ceilings clean and painted. All departments will henceforth be held strictly accountable for the appearance and condition of their offices.''

This "order" expresses a very laudable aim: the city hall should be kept in a neat and attractive condition. But is the order the method best calculated to bring about the desired result? Do the departments have budget authorizations adequate to keep floors swept and varnished, and walls and ceilings painted? Is this matter within their jurisdiction at all, or is there a separate maintenance department which must at least share the responsibility? For how long a period of time will the order produce any visible effect on the behavior of the staffs of city departments?

That such an order would be issued without previous consideration of the questions just raised might seem improbable; yet the above example is based upon an actual occurrence in an administrative organization. It well illustrates the typical characteristics of executive "wish-thinking": "Something needs to be done! Very well, I will order it done— and then consider it as good as done." Every executive has lapses in which he mistakes the wish for the deed, an error for which he must be constantly alert when he is issuing orders. If the chief administrator keeps the following principles in mind in issuing orders, this particular difficulty can be minimized:

1. No order should be issued until it has been determined that the recipient of the order has the authority and the means at his disposal to carry it out without neglecting other duties which have been imposed on him.

2. Every order must be written in the language best calculated to impress it on the minds (and habits!) of its recipients. An order to day laborers should not be expressed in department-head language. Usually it is impossible to express an order too simply.

3. Every order must be communicated in some fashion which will bring it forcibly to the attention of the persons who are expected to obey it. A bulletin board may be a satisfactory place for certain orders, if the persons affected read that board regularly. Orders should not be expected to simply trickle down through department heads to their subordi-

nates. If they are intended for all employees, all should generally be supplied with copies.

4. There is a limit (and a very low limit) to the rate at which employees can absorb new orders. Case workers in welfare departments have often been swamped with piles of eligibility rules and "interpretations" of rules, which have remained unread on their desks. An unread order will not be obeyed.

5. If an order is expected to have more than temporary effect, it must be incorporated in some kind of permanent manual available to the persons affected by it, and must be made the subject of periodic inservice training procedures.

6. An order is a "last resort." Before issuing an order, the executive should explore all other possible means of bringing about the desired change— particularly inservice training.

7. An order should be thought of as a product to be "sold," and full use should be made of modern advertising techniques. An attractive poster with a three word caption often proves more effective than a precisely worded "directive." The language of soap ads may lack legal precision, but it sells soap.

Evidence of the validity of these principles is provided by the development during the past generation of accident prevention methods. Experts in the field of industrial safety have learned by experience that the order: "You are forbidden to operate this machine without first placing the guard in position" is an ineffectual way of bringing about the desired result. Hence, they now concentrate their efforts on training programs and advertising programs in place of orders. Military administrators, too, have long been aware of the limits of order giving. Military field orders specify *what* the subordinate is to do: he is expected to know *how* to do it. The "how to" is imparted to him in the training he receives before he is placed in the field.

THE USE OF AUTHORITY

Another point must be kept constantly in mind when issuing orders: the executive must not lean too heavily on his authority to put his orders across—he must not too frequently "pull rank" on his subordinates. Mary Follett, in her stimulating writings on management, has suggested the ideal to be aimed at.[1] She insists that an order should be obeyed not because of the *authority* of the order-giver, but because the order is recognized as *correct* by the persons to whom it is issued. Every administrative problem has a "best" solution, the merits of which will be recognized by almost everyone concerned once it has been discovered and analyzed. The task of the administrator, under this conception, is to help his subordinates discover the "best" solution, to reach with them an agreement on it, and to translate it into an order.

While this conception of order-giving may reflect an ideal of friendly, cooperative, intelligent administration which cannot always be attained fully in practice, still it sets a goal at which the administrator may well aim. In the first place, subordinate status creates in most men a certain amount of resentment—often in direct proportion to the subordinate's intelligence and initiative. This resentment is minimized when the superior and his subordinates focus their attention on carrying out a joint task—on

finding the right solution—instead of concerning themselves with questions of authority and status. This has an equally favorable effect on the superior, for under these circumstances he is not likely to issue a hasty or ill-advised order merely to "show who's boss."

In so far as the chief administrator can educate his staff to this "best single solution" idea he will find that he has lightened not only his task of direction, but that of coordination as well. For when employees are concentrating on getting a job done, they are in a frame of mind to coordinate their activities spontaneously without indulging in jurisdictional disputes to assert authority and maintain prestige.

NOTE

1. See, particularly, *Dynamic Administration* (New York: Harper and Brothers, 1942), Chapters 2, 7, 12, and 13.

---

19 TASK/WORK RELATIONSHIPS: A LIFE-SPAN PERSPECTIVE
Fredric M. Jablin

Leadership occurs in a rich interpersonal context that includes organization members' ideas about their relationships with others as well as the relationships themselves. The following article by Jablin recognizes this fact, starting with a discussion of the forces that shape people's ideas about work relationships. Jablin then reviews the literature on relationships at work, most of which occur between superiors and subordinates and between co-workers.

This article encourages a broad approach to leadership and superior-subordinate communication. It helps us view these phenomena as everyday activities that occur

Adapted from F. Jablin, "Task/Work Relationships: A Life-Span Perspective." Reprinted with permission from M. L. Knapp and G. R. Miller (eds.), *Handbook of Interpersonal Communication*, pp. 615–649, Beverly Hills, Calif: Sage. Copyright 1985 by Sage Publications, Inc.

in an ongoing mileu of organizational relationships rather than special instances of communication that occur in special circumstances. It also points to the importance of individual attitudes and backgrounds in shaping leadership and vertical communication.

From childhood through retirement task-oriented relationships are an omnipresent part of our lives. Moreover, whether it is performing one's chores as a member of the family unit, participating in classroom or extracurricular school activities, working in a part- or full-time job, or serving as a volunteer member of a community action group, the effective completion of task-oriented activities usually involves some degree of interpersonal communication. Given the invariable presence of task-oriented activities in our lives, and the correspondingly important role interpersonal communication plays in facilitating the completion of these tasks, it is not surprising to discover that the nature, functions, and constraints associated with interpersonal communication in task settings have received a considerable amount of research attention. In particular, the great majority of studies in this area have focused on exploring the dynamics of interpersonal communication in the *work/organizational setting*. Consistent with this trend, the primary goal of this chapter is to organize, review, and interpret interpersonal communication research that has attempted to examine task relationships in work/organizational settings.

While a variety of schemes might have been used to organize and review the literature on interpersonal communication in task/organizational relationships, the developmental, life-span approach was chosen in this case for the following reasons: (1) the life-span approach recognizes the developmental nature of interpersonal and organizational relationships/processes; (2) the approach incorporates the notion that interpersonal and organizational communication processes are dynamic versus static in nature; and (3) the life-span framework allows us to explore interpersonal communication in task relationships within work/organizational settings, as well as within other task environments.

In summary, this review will examine the roles, functions, and characteristics of interpersonal communication in work/organizational settings. However, unlike most traditional treatments of this subject, in this analysis the work/organizational setting will be construed in very broad terms—from a life-span perspective. Consequently, the first part of this chapter will explore processes through which people learn about or anticipate interpersonal communication in work/organizational settings. This section will then be followed by an examination of the nature of interpersonal communication within the work/organizational context itself.

ANTICIPATION OF INTERPERSONAL COMMUNICATION AT WORK

Vocational/Occupational Development

Prior to ever entering into work relationships, most of us have developed certain beliefs and expectations about how people communicate and interact in the job setting. As Drucker (1973, p. 184) observes, "By the time a human being has reached the age of four or five he has been conditioned to work." To a large extent this conditioning and development of attitudes are byproducts of the process of vocational development, which for most people occurs during maturation from childhood to "young adulthood" (Crites, 1969). Vocational development is the process by which a person chooses (deliberately or accidentally) a career direction and develops expectations about what that profession or career will be like. There are probably five basic sources from which we obtain information that affects our vocational development and perceptions of how people communicate at work: (1) family, (2) educational institutions, (3) the mass media, (4) peers, and (5) part-time jobs (see Leifer & Lesser, 1976; Van Maanen, 1975). Research related to each of these sources of information is reviewed briefly below.

Family. Probably the first "significant others" we observe in a set of coordinated task relationships are the members of our families, and in particular our parents. Studies indicate that by the time most children enter the first grade they are already integrally involved in the performance of routine household chores on a regular basis (for example, see Goldstein & Oldham, 1979). Not unexpectedly, it has also been found that even at this very young age children have already developed perceptions about the behaviors of leaders and followers in task relationships. Specifically, Goldstein and Oldham (1979, p. 53) report that by the time children begin to attend school they already perceive that a "boss tells others what to do and how to do it." Relatedly, other studies have shown that as early as three years of age children have developed sex stereotypes of occupational roles (see Beuf, 1974; Kirchner & Vondracek, 1973; Schlossberg & Goodman, 1972). However, despite the apparent importance of parents and family in early vocational development, at present we still know little about what children learn from their familial ties concerning interaction and communication in task relationships.

Educational Institutions. To date, only one study has attempted to explore what students learn as they progress through school about the *communication* behaviors of persons in work roles and occupations. In this investigation Jablin (1985) sought to discover what occupations students (as reported by their teachers) talk and read about in school, and the types of interpersonal communicator styles (Norton, 1978) they attribute to persons in these roles. Results of the study indicate that as students progress from elementary through secondary school, their classroom discussions and texts increasingly depict the communication styles of persons in work relationships as "inactive" and "unresponsive-unreceptive." Though this trend was consistent across all occupations, findings also revealed that students (as reported by their teachers) perceived distinctions in the interpersonal communicator styles across persons in different occupations.

Media. A considerable amount of evidence exists suggesting that the mass media, and in particular television, often transmit an inaccurate, stereotypic image of how people behave/communicate in various occupations (for example, see Nobel, 1975). Specifically, there is a tendency to represent successful role occupants as fairly "aggressive" communicators who spend a majority of their time giving orders or advice to others (DeFleur, 1964; Turow, 1974, 1980). Thus it is not surprising that when DeFleur (1964) interviewed 237 children about the occupational characteristics they most admired, "power" (ability to "boss" others) consistently ranked highest. It is also interesting to observe that content analyses of television representations of "talk" at work reveal that most conversations have little to do with work; rather, conversations are focused on "social" topics (Katzman, 1972; Turow, 1974).

In general, the research evidence concerning the effects of television representations of occupational behavior/communication on children is somewhat limited, and very difficult to draw causal relationships from. However, several studies have reported findings suggesting that children may generalize mass media content of interpersonal interaction to work to their expectations of how such persons actually behave (Bogatz & Ball, 1971; DeFleur & DeFleur, 1967; Dominick, 1974; Siegel, 1958). In particular, the available evidence indicates that this may be especially true for occupations that children do not often come into contact with in their everyday lives.

Peers and Part-Time Jobs. Of the five sources that are likely to affect one's vocational development and beliefs about communication at work, the least is probably known about the effects of peer influences and part-time jobs. Yet, with respect to peer influences, research in related areas suggests that friends influence adolescents' career aspirations (Bain & Anderson, 1974) and that it is not unusual for peers to discuss and compare their career aspirations with one another (Duncan, Haller, & Portes, 1968; Simpson, 1962; Woelfel & Haller, 1971). Further, Brown (1980), in a study of adolescent peer group communication and decisions about occupations, proposes that peers have a strong influence on what young adults perceive as "proper" interaction attitudes and behaviors. If this is the case, then it is also likely that peers are concomitantly influencing one another's perceptions of the communication characteristics of persons in work roles. As noted above, the influence of peers on perceptions of interpersonal communication in task/work relationships is an area sorely in need of future research.

Organizational Choice

Once an individual has chosen (consciously or unconsciously) an area to pursue for a career, and has received the requisite training to perform the tasks associated with that job, he or she typically will seek an organizational position in which to enact the role. For the job seeker a concomitant of the job search process is the formation of expectations about the jobs and organizations in which he or she has applied for employment. Typically, recruits acquire expectations about specific jobs and organizations from organizational literature (annual reports, advertisements, training brochures, and the like), interpersonal interactions with organizational representatives, or both. In particular, one of the most frequent and critical methods of information exchange between organization and applicant is the selection interview (Arvey & Campion, 1982; Schmidt, 1976).

Selection Interview.   The importance of the interview as a selection and recruitment device is epitomized by the fairly large number of literature reviews that have been published over the last twenty years summarizing research in this area (for example, see Arvey & Campion, 1982; Jablin & McComb, 1984; Mayfield, 1964; Schmidt, 1976; Ulrich & Trumbo, 1965; Wright, 1969). It is also important to note that communication-related behavior has been a major focus of this research tradition. For example, Jablin and McComb (1984) report that of the 53 employment interviewing studies they found conducted between 1976 and 1982, 30 (57 percent) explored communication-related variables.

Several generalizations about interpersonal communication in the selection interview can be drawn from recent reviews and empirical studies:

1. Generally, applicants' interview outcome expectations (including likelihoods of accepting job offers) often appear related to their perceptions of their recruiters as trustworthy, competent, composed, and well-organized communicators (see Alderfer & McCord, 1970; Fisher, Ilgen, & Hoyer, 1979; Jablin, Tengler, & Teigen, 1982; Teigen, 1983).

2. Applicants do not particularly like or trust inter-

viewers and appear hesitant to accept job offers if their only sources of information are recruiters (see Fisher et al., 1979).

3. Interviewee satisfaction appears related to the quality and amount of organizational and job information the recruiter provides, the degree to which the recruiter shows interest in the applicant, and the extent to which the recruiter asks the interviewee open-ended questions and allows him or her sufficient "talk time" (Karol, 1977; Tengler, 1982).

4. Most questions applicants ask their interviewers are closed-ended, singular in form, typically not phrased in the first person, asked after interviewers ask for applicants' inquiries, and seek job-related information (Babbitt, 1983).

5. Applicants' perceptions of their interviewers as empathic listeners appear to be negatively related to the degree to which interviewers interject "interruptive statements" while the interviewees are speaking (McComb & Jablin, 1984).

6. Interviewees who display "high" versus "low" levels of nonverbal immediacy (operationalized by eye contact, smiling, posture, interpersonal distance, and body orientation), are "high" in vocal activity, and engage their interviewers in "response-response" versus primarily "question-response" conversations tend to be favored by interviewers (Byrd, 1979; Einhorn, 1981; Imada & Hakel, 1977; McGovern & Tinsley, 1978; Tengler & Jablin, 1983; Trent, 1978).

7. Recruiters find interviewees more acceptable if they receive favorable information about them prior to or during their interviews; however, recruiters do not necessarily adopt confirmatory question strategies to validate their expectancies (Constantin, 1976; Sackett, 1979).

8. Interviewers tend to employ inverted funnel question sequences (they begin with closed questions and then progress to more open-ended questions), thus limiting applicant "talk time" during the crucial opening "decision-making" minutes of interviews (Tengler & Jablin, 1983).

9. Applicants and recruiters tend to have differential perceptions of numerous communication behaviors evidenced in interviews, such as talk-

ativeness, listening, and questioning (Cheatham & McLaughlin, 1976).

10. The great majority of communication-related selection interview studies have concentrated solely on exploring the communication perceptions and behaviors of interviewers versus interviewees, and generally have failed to examine the two parties in dynamic interaction (Daly, 1978; Jablin & McComb, 1984).

Job/Organizational Expectations. The interview is important not only as an interpersonal communication event, but also because of the role it plays in communicating job/organizational expectations to potential employees. For example, Teigen (1983) recently discovered that about 38 percent of the "talk" (operationalized by word count) and 18 percent of the topics discussed in selection interviews are devoted to information exchanges about organizational climate issues (job duties and responsibilities, advancement potential, pay/benefits, supervision, coworker relations). Additionally, he concludes from some of his results that "interviewees who recruiters consider attractive candidates may be provided with certain kinds of climate information not given to less attractive candidates" (Teigen, 1983, p. 188).

At the same time, however, it is essential to observe that research indicates that regardless of the mode of information exchange between employer and applicant the "typical outcome of this process is the emergence of inflated expectations by the recruit of what his or her potential job and organization will be like (Wanous, 1977, 1980)" (Jablin, 1982a, p. 264). In fact, recent evidence suggests that new recruits may often have extremely inflated expectations of the communication climates of their jobs and organizations, including the amounts of information they will receive from and send to others, from whom they will receive information, the timeliness of the information they will receive, and the channels that will be used for communication (Jablin, 1984). Obviously, it is probably not very desirable for recruits to possess such inflated expectations of the interpersonal communication environments of their jobs and organizations because these inflated expectations will be very difficult to meet. And, "as a result of large discrepancies between

expectations and reality, recruits with inflated communication climate expectations may have a higher probability of job turnover and/or less job satisfaction" (Jablin, 1981a, p. 2).

Summary.   The study of how and what people learn about interpersonal communication in work relationships prior to entering their chosen occupations and/or job settings is still a relatively new area of communication research. However, it seems evident that individuals *do* anticipate the interpersonal communication environments of work settings they may enter, and that these expectations are likely to affect their communication behaviors and perceptions once on the job. The specific nature and effects of this interaction of expectations and "reality" obviously should be a focus of future research.

INTERPERSONAL COMMUNICATION IN THE ORGANIZATIONAL SETTING

Upon entry into an organization, a recruit formally begins the organizational assimilation process. "Organizational assimilation refers to the process by which organizational members become a part of, or are absorbed into, the culture of an organization" (Jablin, 1982a, p. 256). This process is typically considered to contain two reciprocal components: the organization's planned and unplanned attempts to "socialize" the recruit, and the new employee's efforts to "individualize" his or her role. Each of these components of assimilation will be reviewed briefly below, followed by a discussion of the role of interpersonal communication in the organizational assimilation process.

According to Van Maanen (1975, p. 67), organizational socialization is the "process by which a person learns the values and norms and required behaviors that permit him to participate as a member of the organization." Or, as Schein (1968, p. 2) has proposed, it is the "process of 'learning the ropes,' the process of being indoctrinated and trained, the process of being taught what is important in the organization." It should also be noted that while the organizational socialization process may appear to have its greatest impact during one's initial tenure in an organization, it is a *continuous* process that will "change and evolve as the individual remains longer with the organization" (Porter, Lawler, & Hackman, 1975, p. 161). Moreover, it is essential to keep in mind that at the same time that the organization is trying to socialize the new employee, the new organizational member is striving to individualize his or her role by modifying the organization so that it can better satisfy his or her needs, values, and ideas (for example, see Schein, 1968).

When viewed concurrently, the employee individualization and organizational socialization processes characterize the fundamental elements of organizational "role taking" (Katz and Kahn, 1966) or "role making" (Graen, 1976). As has often been noted in the research literature, a role "is at once the building block of social systems and the summation of the requirements with which the system confronts the individual member" (Katz & Kahn, 1966, p. 171). Moreover, roles are learned, have content and stylistic dimensions, possess formal and informal duties, rights, and privileges, and, perhaps most important, can be understood by scrutinizing the role expectations that are communicated to and from an individual by members of his or her "role set" (task-related relevant others). Thus it is as " a result of the communication of expectations by members of the role set that the new employee 'encounters' his or her organizational role and learns the values, behaviors, and patterns of thinking that are considered acceptable to the organizational system" (Jablin, 1982a, p. 259). At the same time, however, it is important to realize that new employees are not merely passive receivers of role sendings, but can proactively negotiate or "make" their roles by attempting to alter the expectations of members of their role sets (Graen, 1976).

As is evident from the above discussion, communication is essential to the organizational assimilation/role-making process. Generally speaking, there are three sources of information available to assist new recruits (as well as existing organizational members) in the role-making process: (1) "official" media-related management sources (such as handbooks, manuals, official house magazines and newsletters), (2) superiors and subordinates, and (3) members of one's work group (coworkers). Of these sources, interpersonal interactions with superiors/subordinates and other work group members are probably most influential in the assimilation/role-making process. This is due largely to the general inability of media-related (typically written), downward management messages to alter employee behavior; rather, most research suggests that such types of documents serve to inform employees of desired behaviors, but rarely by themselves can cause changes in behavior (Redding, 1972; Weiss, 1969). In addition, interpersonal communication with superiors/subordinates and coworkers plays an important role in the organizational assimilation process for several other reasons, as outlined below.

Superior-subordinate communication is generally perceived as crucial to an employee's assimilation into the organization for the following reasons:

(1) the supervisor frequently interacts with the subordinate and thus may serve as a role model (Weiss, 1977), (2) the supervisor has the formal power to reward and punish the employee, (3) the supervisor mediates the formal flow of downward communication to the subordinate (for example, the supervisor serves as an interpreter/filter of management messages), and (4) the supervisor usually has a personal as well as formal role relationship with the recruit. (Jablin, 1982a, p. 269)

In addition, it is important to observe that an employee's superior is of critical importance to his or her individualization efforts. As Graen (1976, p. 1206) suggests, "Although other members of the new person's role set can enter the negotiation of the definition of the new person's role . . . only the leader is granted the authority to impose formal sanctions to back up his negotiations."

On the other hand, formal and informal interactions with coworkers in one's task group also appear to perform an important function in the organizational assimilation process. As Feldman (1981, p. 314) notes, "New recruits turn to other members of the work group to get help in interpreting rules, and to learn the informal networks." Further, group members can serve as a normative referent for "appropriate" behavior, and as a source of emotional support against the organization's socialization attempts (Becker, Geer, Hughes, & Strauss, 1961; Burns, 1955; Feldman, 1977). Additionally, recent evidence suggests that in the uncertain environment of a new job recruits may model and/or assume the attitudes and behaviors of their coworkers (Crawford, 1974; Katz, 1980; Rakestraw & Weiss, 1981; Weiss, 1977; White & Mitchell, 1979). The vital role of communication with coworkers to successful organizational assimilation is epitomized in the following research anecdote from Feldman (1981, p. 314):

> I have found that many recruits report feeling that until such time as they became friendly with co-workers and could trust them, they could not find out information that was essential to doing their jobs well. Moreover, until incumbent employees felt they could trust recruits, they withheld information about supervisors' preferences and personalities, making the recruits less competent in the eyes of the supervisors.

In summary, a considerable amount of evidence exists suggesting that new recruits, as well as continuing members of organizations, make "sense of" (Louis, 1980) and understand their work environments primarily as a result of their interpersonal communication interactions with (1) superior/ subordinates and (2) work group members/ coworkers. Given the apparent importance of these types of communication relationships to becoming assimilated into (and remaining assimilated in) organizations, the following two sections of this chapter provide extensive reviews of these respective research literatures. Since few studies in either of these areas have utilized longitudinal or time-series research designs, these literature reviews have been organized topically rather than in a developmental fashion.

Superior-Subordinate Communication

As has often been observed, within work organizations there are always subordinates and superiors "even though these terms may not be expressly used, and even though there may exist fluid arrangements whereby superior and subordinate roles may

be reversible" (Redding, 1972, p. 18). Generally research concerning superior-subordinate communication has focused "on those exchanges of information and influence between organizational members, at least one of whom has formal (as defined by official organizational sources) authority to direct and evaluate the activities of other organizational members" (Jablin, 1979, p. 1202). With respect to the types of messages that tend to be exchanged between superiors and subordinates, Katz and Kahn (1966, pp. 239–241) suggest that superior-to-subordinate communications usually focus on information concerning organizational procedures and practices, indoctrination of goals, job instructions and rationale, or feedback about performance. Relatedly, subordinates' communications to superiors tend to be concerned with information about the subordinates themselves, their coworkers and their problems, information about tasks that need to be done, or information about organizational policies and practices (Katz & Kahn, 1966, p. 245).

An extensive multidisciplinary review of empirical research exploring the nature and functions of superior-subordinate communication was recently published by Jablin (1979). In this review the empirical literature on superior-subordinate communication was classified into nine topical categories: (1) interaction patterns and related attitudes, (2) openness in communication, (3) upward distortion, (4) upward influence, (5) semantic-information distance, (6) effective versus ineffective superiors, (7) personal characteristics, (8) feedback, and (9) systemic variables. The following discussion briefly summarizes Jablin's analysis of the research in each of these categories. In addition, several investigations in a new category, "conflict," are also reviewed. Selective studies relevant to each of the original nine categories but conducted subsequent to Jablin's 1979 review are also discussed.

Interaction Patterns and Related Attitudes. Probably one of the most consistent findings in superior-subordinate communication research is that supervisors spend from one-third to two-thirds of their time communicating with subordinates. Further, the majority of this communication concerns task-related issues and is conducted in face-to-face meetings. It is also interesting to note that superiors and subordinates tend to have differential perceptions about (1) the amount of time they spend communicating with one another, and (2) who initiates these communication contacts. Research conducted since 1979 lends further support to this interaction profile (Volard & Davies, 1982).

Openness in Communication. Redding (1972, p. 330) distinguishes two basic dimensions of openness in superior-subordinate communication: openness in message sending ("candid disclosure of feelings, or 'bad news,' and important company facts"), and openness in message receiving ("encouraging, or at least permitting, the frank expression of views divergent from one's own"). Moreover, Jablin (1979, p. 1204), in his review of the empirical research in this area, concludes that

> in an open communication relationship between superior and subordinate, both parties perceive the other interactant as a willing and receptive listener and refrain from responses that might be perceived as providing negative relational or disconfirming feedback. Moreover, these inquiries suggest that what distinguishes an open from a closed relationship may not be the types of messages exchanged but how the interactants evaluate the appropriateness of these communications.

In addition, a substantial amount of research exists indicating that subordinates are more satisfied with their jobs when they have an "open" versus "closed" communication relationship with their superiors. However, it should be noted that a recent study has revealed that the degree to which a superior is involved in "organizational politics" may moderate perceptions of openness in superior-subordinate communication. "Specifically, it appears that subordinates feel comfortable being open in communication with superiors who are minimally or moderately involved in politics, but not with superiors who are highly involved in political activities" (Jablin, 1981b, p. 273).

Upward Distortion. A long tradition of laboratory and field research has investigated the frequent phenomenon of upward distortion that occurs when persons of lower hierarchical rank in organizations communicate with persons of higher hierarchical rank (who also typically have power over the advancement of the persons of lower rank). Moreover, numerous variables have been found to moderate the occurrence of upward distortion, including subordinates' mobility aspirations, ascendancy and security needs, trust in superiors, gender, and motivation.

With respect to the types of messages that are most frequently distorted, studies generally have found that subordinates are most reluctant to communicate information to their superiors that is negative or unfavorable. On the other hand, superiors seem to compensate for the positive "halo" often associated with the messages they receive from subordinates by viewing them as less accurate than messages that are unfavorable to subordinates. However, Downs, and Conrad (1982), in a rather unique study of the characteristics of effect subordinacy, suggest that "effective" subordinates are perceived as willing to "confront" their superiors with challenging or unwanted information. These authors conclude that perhaps subordinates *in general* tend to avoid passing on negative or unfavorable information to their superiors, but that "*effective* subordinates do—and they avoid some communication problems by doing so" (Downs & Conrad, 1982, p. 34.).

Upward Influence. As Jablin (1979) notes, studies of influence in superior-subordinate communication have focused on two of its basic dimensions: (1) the effects a superior's influence in the organizational hierarchy has on his or her relationships with subordinates, and (2) the transmission of influence by subordinates to superiors (which is often closely associated with research on upward distortion). With respect to the former category of research, studies have basically concentrated on what is often termed the "Pelz Effect" (Pelz, 1952). Essentially, this effect suggests that subordinate satisfaction with supervision is a by-product not only of an open, supportive relationship between the two parties, but also of the supervisor's ability to satisfy his or her subordinates' needs by possessing influence with those higher in the organizational hierarchy.

Several recent studies have been directed at exploring the generalizability of the Pelz Effect. Much of this research has been stimulated by the House, Filley, and Gujarati (1971) assertion that for subordinates who perceive their supervisors as supportive leaders, there exists a curvilinear rather than positive linear association between supervisors' upward influence and subordinates' openness and satisfaction with supervision. Specifically, House et al. (1971, p. 429) argue that

> where supervisors are seen to have such high influence, it is likely that there will be a greater status separation between them and their subordinates, and that such status differentiation will result in a restriction of upward information flow, less willingness on the part of subordinates to approach superiors, and less satisfaction with the social climate of the work unit.

Results of studies exploring the House et al. (1971) hypothesis, however, have not generally supported this revisionist position (Daniels & Logan, 1983; Jablin, 1980a, 1980b). Moreover, findings suggest that the Pelz Effect holds for strategic (personnel and administrative policy decisions) and *work-related* influence, and appears to exist under conditions of high and low leader supportiveness, though it has its greatest impact in situations where subordinates perceive their superiors as supportive leaders.

The message strategies subordinates employ to influence their superiors' decisions have also been a focus of recent research (Allen & Porter, 1983; Kipnis, Schmidt, & Wilkinson, 1980; Krone, 1984; Mowday, 1978; Porter, Allen, & Angle, 1981; Schilit & Locke, 1982; Weinstein, 1979). Generally, these studies suggest nine basic strategies that subordinates employ to influence their superiors' decisions: logical or rational presentation of ideas; informal or non-performance-specific exchanges (for example, ingratiation); formal exchange (exchanging desired work behaviors for rewards); adherence to rules (essentially a form of negative influence); upward appeal (bypassing one's direct superior and appealing to a person of higher authority); threats or sanctions; manipulation (arguing such that the target is not aware of the influence attempt); formal coalitions (power equalization); and persis-

tence or assertiveness ("wearing down" the other party's resistance) (Schilit & Locke, 1982, p. 305). However, as Krone (1984) has observed, from a communication perspective these nine strategies can essentially be categorized into one of three types of messages: (1) open persuasion (the influence attempt is overt and the desired outcome stated), (2) manipulative persuasion (the use of either covert means of influence and open expression of desired outcomes or open means of influence and undisclosed desired outcomes), and (3) manipulation (disguising both the influence means and desired outcome—deception).

Results of research exploring the frequencies with which these different types of message strategies are used in influence attempts are mixed. Specifically, some studies have found that subordinates use logical presentations (open persuasion) more often than the other strategies (Kipnis et al., 1980; Schilit & Locke, 1982), while the results of other investigations suggest that forms of covert messages are most commonly used in upward influence attempts (Porter et al., 1981; Weinstein, 1979). These findings would seem to indicate that a subordinate's selection and use of a message strategy in an influence attempt may be dependent on a wide array of situational factors (such as decision type, organizational climate and structure, and perceived power of the target). Obviously, future research should focus on delineating the factors that mediate choice of message strategy, as well as the impact/effectiveness of these influence attempts on superiors' decision making.

Semantic-Information Distance. The term "semantic-information distance" was coined by Tompkins (1962) to describe the gap in agreement and/or understanding that often exists between subordinates and superiors on specified issues. In the research literature a number of other terms have often been used analogously, such as "disparity," "congruence," "semantic agreement," and "categorical and syndectic similarity." Research in this area has clearly demonstrated numerous areas and topics in which large gaps in understanding exist between superiors and subordinates, including subordinates' basic job duties and supervisors' authority. As Jablin (1979, p. 1208) concludes in his review of this research literature, "Incessantly, we find the existence of semantic-information distance in superior-subordinate relations, often at levels that would appear to seriously obstruct organizational effectiveness." However, it should also be recognized that perceptual incongruence in the superior-subordinate dyad is, within limits, a natural consequence of role structuration in organizations and thus may be dysfunctional for the relationship only if "it impairs the productivity, stability or adaptability of the dyad" (Sussman, 1975, p. 198).

Several recent studies of semantic-information distance have focused on differences in "meta-perceptions" (Laing, Phillipson, & Lee, 1966), that is, superiors' and subordinates' views of the other person's views. Thus, rather than exploring agreement and disagreement between superiors and subordinates on specified issues (the typical orientation of previous studies), these investigations have been concerned with perceptions of understanding or misunderstanding between members of the dyad. Results of these studies suggest that superiors and subordinates not only have different "direct" perspectives on specified issues, but also do not understand one another's meta-perspectives (Infante & Gordon, 1979; Smircich & Chesser, 1981). In addition, recent research (Hatfield & Huseman, 1982; Richmond, Wagner, & McCroskey, 1983) indicates that perceptual congruence (direct perspectives) about various aspects of superior-subordinate communication is to some degree positively associated with subordinates' general job satisfaction.

Effective versus Ineffective Superiors. In his review of the literature, Jablin (1979, p. 1208) suggests that "over the years the identification of effective as compared to ineffective communication behaviors of superiors has received more investigation than any other area of organizational communication." Yet, he also notes in his analysis that two basic and somewhat contradictory perspectives/conclusions can be drawn from the literature: (1) a common profile of the communication characteristics of "effective" supervisors exists, and (2) the communication qualities of "effective" leaders varies and is contingent on numerous situational factors.

Redding (1972, p. 443) provides a fairly complete compendium of the communication characteristics often considered to be indicative of "good" supervisors:

1. The better supervisors tend to be more "communication-minded"; they enjoy talking and speaking up in meetings; they are able to explain instructions and policies; they enjoy conversing with subordinates.

2. The better supervisors tend to be willing, empathic listeners; they respond understandingly to so-called "silly" questions from employees; they are approachable; they will listen to suggestions and complaints with an attitude of fair consideration and willingness to take appropriate action.

3. The better supervisors tend (with some notable exceptions) to "ask" or "persuade" in preference to "telling" or "demanding."

4. The better supervisors tend to be sensitive to the feelings and ego-defense needs of their subordinates; e.g., they are careful to reprimand in private rather than in public.

5. The better supervisors tend to be more open in their passing along of information; they are in favor of giving advance notice of impending changes, and of explaining the "reasons why" behind policies and regulations.

On the other hand, as noted above, a considerable amount of research also exists suggesting that "effective" leadership behaviors are contingent on a host of situational factors including gender, task type, organizational climate, and work-unit size. For example, Bednar (1982) found recently that the "communicator style" (Norton, 1978) characteristics associated with "effective" managerial performance seem to vary depending on organizational context and setting (in this case an insurance agency versus a hospital). Moreover, in recent years the general assumption that leaders manifest one stable supervisory style in their interactions with *all* subordinates has come under attack by Graen and his colleagues (Dansereau, Graen, & Haga, 1975;

Graen & Cashman, 1975). According to their Vertical Dyad Linkage (VDL) model of leadership, because of their competence, trustworthiness, and motivation certain subordinates are chosen by supervisors to receive "preferential treatment." Further,

> these selected subordinates (in-group members) make contributions that go beyond their formal job duties and take on responsibility for the completion of tasks that are most critical to the success of the unit. In return, they receive greater attention, support, and sensitivity from their supervisors. Subordinates who are not chosen by the supervisor (out-group members) perform the more routine, mundane tasks of the unit and experience a more formal exchange with the supervisor. (Liden & Graen, 1980)

In summary, the research of Graen and others is beginning to bring into question the assumption that supervisors or managers possess an "average" communication style. Rather, these investigations suggest that the dyadic communication exchange patterns that exist between superiors and subordinates be viewed as somewhat unique to each dyad. In conclusion, a decisive answer to the question of whether or not an "ideal" communication style exists that is "effective" in all supervisory situations still remains to be provided. As Jablin observed in his 1979 review, "the only way we will be able to resolve this question is by research that investigates the effects situational variables have on superior-subordinate communication" (Jablin, 1979, p. 1211).

Personal Characteristics. The mediating effects of the personal characteristics of superiors and subordinates on their communicative behavior historically have been of interest to researchers. Traits that have been examined include locus of control, dogmatism, and communication apprehension, as well as the gender composition of the dyad. More recent research has focused attention on the effects of attributional models and schemas on communicative behavior (see the section below on feedback), measurement of communicator competence

(Monge, Bachman, Dillard, & Eisenberg, 1982), and different types of "managerial communication styles" (Richmond, McCroskey, & Davis, 1982; Richmond, McCroskey, Davis, & Koontz, 1980). With respect to this latter research, findings suggest that subordinates perceive the communication of coercive power with a "boss-centered," tell-type managerial communication style, and that subordinate satisfaction with supervision increases as managerial communication style becomes more "employee centered."

Feedback. Of all the categories of research reviewed here, feedback has been one of the most popular topics of research since 1979. This research interest is probably a result of the extensive incorporation of theories of social cognition (particularly attribution theory) into feedback studies, as well as several excellent reviews and models of feedback processes that have been published in the last few years (Arvey & Ivancevich, 1980; Ashour & Johns, 1983, Cusella, 1980; Ilgen, Fisher, & Taylor, 1979; Larson, 1984; Sims, 1980). At the same time, however, one should note that this more recent research has been generally supportive of the two major conclusions that Jablin drew from his review of the literature through 1979; (1) "Feedback from superiors to subordinates appears related to subordinate performance and satisfaction," and (2) "a subordinate's performance to a large extent controls the nature of his/her superior's feedback" (Jablin, 1979, p. 1214).

More recent studies also suggest the following additional conclusions: (1) Feedback from supervisors high in credibility (trust and expertise) can positively influence subordinates' levels of satisfaction and/or motivation (Cusella, 1982; O'Reilly & Anderson, 1980); (2) supervisors tend to give negative feedback sooner to poorly-performing subordinates than they give positive feedback to well-performing subordinates (Fisher, 1979; Pavett, 1983); (3) when required to give unfavorable feedback to subordinates, superiors tend to distort the feedback by positively inflating it (Fisher, 1979; Ilgen & Knowlton, 1980); (4) supervisors tend to overestimate the value subordinates place on supervisory feedback (Greller, 1980; Ilgen, Peterson, Martin, & Boeschen, 1981); (5) when subordinates perform poorly, superiors tend to attribute this poor performance to factors internal rather than external to the subordinates; as a result, superiors tend to direct their responses toward the subordinates (for example, in the form of reprimands) rather than attempting to alter the work situation (Green & Mitchell, 1979; Kipnis et al., 1981; Mitchell & Wood, 1980); (6) "managers will tend to influence trusted employees with persuasion and will use coercion with untrusted employees" (Riccillo & Trenholm, 1983, p. 336); and (6) superior and subordinate relational feedback responses (dominance, structuring, equivalence, deference, and submissiveness) are somewhat constrained by the interactants' formal organizational roles (Watson, 1982).

Conflict. Within the last ten years the study of the role of communication in superior-subordinate conflict has received a considerable amount of research attention. Working from earlier conceptualizations of superior-subordinate conflict advance by Blake, Shepard, and Mouton (1964) and Kilmann and Thomas (1977), a number of investigations have been directed at developing coding schemes and/or scales to measure and analyze conflict strategies (Bullis, Cox, & Bokeno, 1982; Putnam & Wilson, 1982; Riggs, 1983; Ross & DeWine, 1982; Sillars, 1980). Results from these and other studies suggest that supervisors generally use "controlling" or "forcing" strategies when managing conflicts with subordinates. However, several factors have been discovered to affect a superior's choice of conflict management mode, including the supervisor's level of self-confidence, perceptions of skill, and organizational level (Conrad, 1983; Putnam & Wilson, 1982). Relatedly, Richmond et al. (1983) report that subordinates and superiors have difficulty agreeing on how "active" supervisors actually are in managing conflict.

Systemic Variables. In his 1979 review Jablin notes that less empirical, as opposed to theoretical, research had been pursued exploring the effects systemic organizational variables (technology, structure, environment, and so on) have on superior-subordinate communication. Unfortunately, this conclusion still holds true today. However, two studies have recently been published reporting rela-

tionships between the characteristics of superior-subordinate communication and different types of organizational structures and technologies.

In the first of these investigations Jablin (1982b) collected data from fifteen organizations in an attempt to determine the effects of several structural characteristics of organizations (organizational size, organizational level, and span of control) on subordinates' perceptions of openness in superior-subordinate communication. Findings of the study revealed that "subordinates in the lowest levels of their organizational hierarchies perceived significantly less openness in superior-subordinate communication than subordinates at the highest levels of their hierarchies" (Jablin, 1982b, p. 338). However, Jablin also observes that organizational level did not account for much variance in perceptions of openness in communication.

On the other hand, Klauss and Bass (1982), exploring the effects of organizational size and technology (in two organizations) on subordinates' perceptions of managerial communication behavior, report results indicating that in "high-technology" versus "traditional-technology" settings managers are perceived as less "careful" message transmitters and listeners. In summary, the failure of this study and that of Jablin (1982b) to find any significant relationships between perceptions of superior-subordinate communication and work-group or organizational size suggests that size may not be a moderator of quality of superior-subordinate communication in organizations.

Summary. The preceding section has attempted to provide an overview of results of contemporary empirical research exploring the communication dynamics of probably the most common interpersonal task relationship found in organizations: the interaction of superiors/leaders and subordinates/followers. As Jablin noted in his 1979 review of this literature, three items seem to be studied consistently as factors affecting interpersonal communication between superiors and subordinates—power and status, trust, and semantic-information distance. Moreover, given that investigations of superior-subordinate communication have traditionally focused on power- and status-related issues, it is not surprising to discover that a considerable amount of recent research has concentrated on exploring the message strategies that each member of the dyad utilizes to influence the behavior and attitudes of the other party (see research reviewed in the sections on upward influence and feedback above). In addition, it appears evident that the current popularity of research examining the cognitive processes that superiors and subordinates use to interpret messages from one another is largely a result of the endemic presence of semantic-information distance in superior-subordinate communication. Finally, it is important to note that the degree of trust that exists between superiors and subordinates continues to be shown frequently to moderate their message-encoding and message decoding behaviors.

Work Group and Coworker Communication

As suggested earlier, new recruits to organizations (as well as continuing members) receive information from their coworkers that assists them in discovering and adapting to what are considered to be "normal" and "acceptable" behaviors and attitudes in their organizations (Feldman, 1981; Van Maanen,1975). In particular, members of the work group "help the new employee decode and interpret the scripts and schemas that prevail in the organization as well as cushion the impact of the recruit's organizational encounter" (Jablin, 1982a, p. 272). However, as evidenced earlier in the research anecdote presented by Feldman (1981), coworkers will usually serve these functions only after the initiate has become a trusted and accepted member of the work group.

The interpersonal messages that employees receive from other members of their work groups are essentially of two types: "ambient" and "discretionary" (Hackman, 1976). Ambient messages are nonselective, often unintentional, and directed to all members of the work group, while discretionary messages are intentionally and somewhat contingently communicated to specific group members.

Recent research on "social information processing" in organizations (Caldwell & O'Reilly, 1982; O'Reilly & Caldwell, 1979; Roberts & Glick, 1981; Salancik & Pfeffer, 1978; Weiss & Nowicki, 1981; White & Mitchell, 1979) exemplifies the effects ambient communication among coworkers can have

on their job attitudes. Specifically, the social information processing framework proposes that a worker's job attitudes are socially constructed and are largely a result of normative and informational cues communicated to the worker by others in the work environment, particularly coworkers. Thus this approach suggests that the job attitudes a recruit develops arise in part from the elements of the work environment that coworkers somewhat unconsciously call attention to in their "everyday" talk. In other words, by frequently talking about and evaluating certain aspects of the work context group members cue one another about the importance and "meaning" of elements in the work environment. In fact, recent studies indicate that perhaps the critical factor in a worker's satisfaction with his or her job is working in an environment where coworkers express positive job/work attitudes (O'Reilly & Caldwell, 1979; White & Mitchell, 1979). And, as Rakestraw and Weiss (1981, p. 341) have suggested, "Social influences on the development of goals and performance standards may be most pronounced for new workers or individuals approaching an unfamiliar task."

On the other hand, a long tradition of research also exists indicating that discretionary communications from the members of one's work group can have important effects on the development of job attitudes and behavior (Feldman, 1984; Hackman, 1976). These communications are most often sent from coworkers to the new member to educate or socialize the individual to *selective* group norms and values, as well as preferred task behaviors (Feldman, 1984). For example, a number of "classic" studies have demonstrated the powerful effects of the communication of group norms on such phenomena as group cohesiveness (Schachter, Ellertson, McBride, & Gregory, 1951; Seashore, 1954), production restrictions (Trist & Bamforth, 1951; Whyte, 1955), decision making (Janis, 1972), and conformity (Asch, 1951; Sherif, 1936). Moreover, through their communications with recruits coworkers provide new employees with information concerning rewards and costs present in the group and organizational environments, who controls the allocation of rewards, and the behaviors that lead to receiving rewards (Hackman, 1976). At the same time, however, it is important to recognize that recruits upon first entering new work settings often *proactively* send messages to coworkers through which they seek information about the above types of issues (Feldman & Brett, 1983).

From a more general perspective communication among members of organizational work groups can be thought of as serving formal-organizational and psychological-individual functions (Jablin & Sussman, 1983; Schein, 1980). Specifically,

> *formal* organizational group communication generally occurs to: (a) generate information, (b) process information, (c) share information necessary for the coordination of interdependent organizational tasks, (d) disseminate decisions, or (e) reinforce a group's perspective/consensus. On the other hand, psychological, *individual*-oriented organizational group communication functions to: (a) provide members with feedback about their self-concepts, (b) gratify needs for affiliation, (c) share and test perspectives about social reality, (d) reduce organization-related uncertainty and concomitant feelings of anxiety, insecurity, and powerlessness, or (e) accomplish employee-related (versus organization-related) tasks and resolve individual or group-related problems. (Jablin & Sussman, 1983)

Research exploring the interpersonal communication behavior of workers in organizational task groups has recently been reviewed by Jablin and Sussman (1983). Selective findings from their examination of the literature are summarized briefly below.

Task Characteristics.   Probably one of the most consistent conclusions that can be drawn from research on the communication behavior of members of task groups is that task type and task technology significantly affect workers' interpersonal interaction patterns (Hackman, Brousseau, & Weiss, 1976; Hackman & Vidmar, 1970; Shiflett, 1972; Sorenson, 1971). As Jablin and Sussman (1983, p. 34) conclude after reviewing recent laboratory and field studies of group communication networks, it is apparent that "groups when given the opportunity

generally adapt their communication structures to the nature of the work or task at hand.''

With respect to task type (production, problem solving, discussion), research results suggest that distinct patterns of interaction and perceptions evolve among group members as a function of the "intellective" nature of the task. In discussing the findings of their research, Hackman and Vidmar (1970, p. 50) outline several of these distinctions:

> Production tasks resulted in more reports of tensions and conflict among members than did other types, . . . discussion tasks led to a somewhat more "relaxed" atmosphere, and . . . problem-solving tasks resulted in perceptions that members were working together relatively effectively.

Similarly, investigations probing the effects of technology (the combination of task variability and analyzability) on group interaction suggest that technology affects the information processing demands of the group, such that as task certainty increases the group coordinates itself more through impersonal (rules, plans) than through personal communication modes (Penley & Alexander, 1979; Randolph, 1978, Van de Ven, Delbecq, & Koening, 1976).

Group Problem Solving.   Of the various types of tasks that groups perform, the communication dynamics of problem-solving or decision-making groups have probably received the most research attention. In particular, studies have focused on testing explanations for the "risky shift" phenomenon (the tendency for decisions resulting from group discussions to be more risky than the averaged individual decisions of a group's members) (Cecil, Cummings, & Chertkoff, 1973; Pruitt, 1971a, 1971b) and the relative merits of direct interaction among group members during problem solving (Jablin & Seibold, 1978; Van de Ven & Delbecq, 1974).

In reference to the risky shift phenomenon, recent studies indicate that degree of choice shift is affected by quantity (versus quality) of arguments presented by group members (Bishop & Myers, 1974; Morgan & Beatty, 1976), and patterns of agreement/disagreement by group members (Levine, Skroka, & Snyder, 1977). On the other hand, findings from studies exploring problem-solving strategies suggest that for short-lived task groups working on applied fact-finding problems, *nominal* (individuals initially work alone and later join together to discuss their ideas) and *delphi* (members complete sets of sequential questionnaires but never meet in face-to-face discussion) strategies are more effective than conventional interacting groups (Huber & Delbecq, 1972; Van de Ven & Delbecq, 1971, 1974). In contrast, for ongoing, long-term groups choice of interaction strategy is more complex and contingent on numerous factors, "including group motivation, time limitations, distribution of problem solving information, the nature of the problem, status differences among group members, and socio-emotional variables related to the group's development" (Jablin & Seibold, 1978, pp. 351–352). In addition, it has been found that an individual's communication predisposition may affect his or her relative effectiveness in interacting problem-solving groups (see Jablin, 1981c).

Moderators.   A number of other factors have also been shown to affect the communication behavior of task group members in problem-solving or decision-making situations. For example, results of studies have frequently found that trust-destroying communication negatively affects interaction processes and problem-solving effectiveness. Specifically, with the destruction of trust, feedback responses among group members often become "tense, inflexible and personal" (Leathers, 1970, p. 186), verbal fluency decreases (Prentice, 1975), communication distortions occur (Zand, 1972), and group performance diminishes (Klimoski & Karol, 1976). Further, other studies have found that the degree of "orientation behavior" that is displayed by group members (messages directed at resolving conflicts, facilitating achievement of group goals, making helpful suggestions, or lessening tension) is associated with the probability that members will reach consensus decisions (Kline, 1970, 1972; Knutson, 1972). Relatedly, research exploring feedback responses in task groups suggests that the impact of feedback on group members is contingent on several variables, including individual differences among group mem-

bers (for example, achievement motivation), group task structure, the ways in which members process feedback, as well as the nature of the feedback information—evaluative content, task/process focus, aggregation level and so on (see Nadler, 1979, for a complete review of this literature).

Group Development.   Finally, research exploring the interpersonal communication patterns that emerge among members of work groups as the groups develop over time warrants discussion (Ellis & Fisher, 1975; Fisher, 1970; Gouran & Baird, 1972; Heinen & Jacobson, 1976; Mabry, 1975). Of particular importance are a series of investigations recently conducted by Poole (1981, 1983). The findings of Poole's research are of relevance because they bring into question the generally held assumption that decision-making groups follow uniform sequences of phases of development (generally depicted as an initial orientation phase, followed by a period of evaluation, and concluding with a control phase; see Bales & Strodtbeck, 1951). Specifically, findings from Poole's studies suggest that over time the sequence of communication phases of decision-making groups are not necessarily uniform, and that different groups may have different sequences of phases. Accordingly, Poole (1981, p. 20) suggests that a contingency theory of group development may be required, though the traditional "unitary sequence" model might serve "as a 'baseline' which is altered and diversified in different ways by different groups."

Summary.   The preceding section has attempted to provide an overview of recent research exploring the nature, functions, and effects of interpersonal communication among coworkers in organizational task groups. Results of this analysis suggest that recruits' communication relationships with their coworkers play important informational and socioemotional functions in the assimilation of newcomers into organizations. Further, it was noted that for both new and continuing employees the "ambient" and "discretionary" messages they exchange with one another often have considerable impact on their work attitudes and behaviors. However, given that employees (especially new recruits) are likely to receive these types of massages from multiple sources (often presenting conflicting perspectives) within their task environments, research exploring the message characteristics that lead workers to attend to and accept certain of these communications and not others is needed (Weiss & Nowicki, 1981). In summary, findings from this literature review suggest that probably the most influential factors affecting interpersonal communication patterns and relationships among group members are the characteristics of the task on which they are working.

Outcomes of Assimilation

As frequently noted in findings from studies reviewed here, employees' communication relationships with their superiors/subordinates and coworkers may affect a number of outcomes of the organizational assimilation process. Among the outcomes that have been mentioned in studies considered to this point are workers' levels of job satisfaction, motivation, and work performance. However, from a communication perspective there are at least two other important outcomes of the organizational assimilation process that merit consideration: (1) the emergence within employees of perceptions of the communication climates of the organizations in which they work, and (2) some degree of participation by workers in their organizations' emergent communication networks.

Communication Climate. It is generally assumed that as an employee is assimilated into an organization, "she/he develops an evolving set of perceptions about what the organization is like as a communication system" (Jablin, 1982a, p. 273), that is, the communication "climate" of the organization. Though numerous factors constitute an individual's perceptions of the communication climate of his or her organization, most conceptualizations of the climate construct place heavy emphasis on perceptions of interpersonal communication with superiors/subordinates and coworkers (Albrecht, 1979; Dennis, 1974; Goldhaber & Rogers, 1979; Jablin, 1980c; Roberts & O'Reilly, 1974). Thus there seems to be a fair amount of agreement among researchers that an individual's communication relationships with his or her superiors/subordinates

and coworkers play key roles in the development of overall organizational communication climate perceptions. Unfortunately, little research exists exploring *how* perceptions of overall (or superior-subordinate, or peer) communication climates develop over time.

However, one recently completed study does provide some exploratory data concerning the development of communication climate perceptions. In this longitudinal investigation, Jablin (1984) examined recruits' (newly hired nursing assistants) perceptions of the communication climates of their new jobs and organizations on their first days of work (expectations) and after six, twelve, and eighteen weeks of employment. In addition, a sample of recruits completed communication logs/diaries during their third and ninth weeks of employment. Results of the research revealed that after six weeks of work recruits' communication climate perceptions (including all scales measuring attributes of superior-subordinate and peer communication) were significantly deflated from their initial expectations, but, rather than increasing or decreasing over the remaining months of the study, remained at the six-week level. Somewhat similarly, the communication log data indicated that between their third and ninth weeks of work the recruits became less positive toward their interactions with superiors, peers, and patients.

In summary, the communication climate perceptions of the recruits in Jablin's (1984) study were (1) sharply influenced by their initial "encounters" in their organizations, and (2) evidenced this "encounter effect" for at least their first six months of work. Whether or not this is a typical pattern of development of communication climate perceptions obviously should be a focus of future research. Moreover, inquiries aimed at exploring relationships between communication with superiors/subordinates and coworkers and the development of climate perceptions that evolve as recruits remain in their organizations for longer periods of time need to be conducted.

Communication Networks. To a large extent employee participation in emergent organizational communication networks (a process concurrent to the development of climate perceptions; see Jablin,

1980c) is also an outcome of the organizational assimilation process. Specifically, it is likely that as a result of the regular communication that a new organizational member has with his or her superiors/subordinates and coworkers that he or she will become a "link" in a number of overlapping sets of stable interaction patterns or structures that exist in the organization. For example, the recruit might become a "link" in authority, information exchange, friendship, and status networks in the organization (Farace, Monge, & Russell, 1977; Guetzkow, 1965; Katz & Kahn, 1966).

Further, as an employee is assimilated into an organization it is likely not only that he or she will become a link in several networks, but that he or she will also assume certain specific communication network roles, such as "group member" (a participant in a group within a network), "intergroup linker" (liaison—a person who links two or more groups but is not a member of a group him- or herself; bridge—a group member who links his or her group to another group), or an "isolate" (a person who maintains no linkages with other network members; see Farace et al., 1977; Monge, Edwards, & Kirste, 1978). Moreover, it should be noted that the types of network roles an individual performs will probably affect his or her communication attitudes and behaviors (Albrecht, 1979; Monge et al., 1978).

To date there has been only a limited amount of research exploring how emergent networks and/or network roles in organizations develop over time (for example, see Rogers & Kincaid, 1981). However, based upon recent research that suggests possible relationships between the degrees to which individuals are "connected" or "integrated" into the communication networks of their organizations and their group attitude uniformity, morale, and organizational commitment (Danowski, 1980; Eisenberg, Monge & Miller, 1983; McLaughlin & Cheatham, 1977), two propositions appear tenable. First, it seems reasonable to hypothesize that organizational members who frequently are "isolates" in communication networks have not been very effectively assimilated into their organizations (though there may be exceptions to this; for instance, Granovetter's [1973] discussion of "weak ties" in networks). Second, and in contrast, it seems likely that recruits

who eventually assume intergroup linker or group member roles have been effectively (at least relative to isolates) assimilated into their organizations. Van Maanen's (1975) typology of individual adjustment approaches to organizational socialization (assumption of "team player," isolate," "warrior," or "outsider" roles) would also seem to lend support to these assertions. However, the validity of these propositions should be viewed as tentative until they are tested by future research.

Summary.   The preceding section has suggested two closely interrelated *communication* outcomes of the organizational assimilation process: (1) the development of perceptions of organizational communication climate, and (2) participation in organizational communication networks. Moreover, as indicated in this discussion, interpersonal communication with superiors/subordinates and coworkers is intrinsic to both of these outcomes/processes. At the same time, however, it is clearly evident that to date few empirical studies have been conducted exploring how organizational members' perceptions of communication climate and involvement in communication networks emerge/develop over time. Both of these areas represent fruitful foci for research and beg further investigation.

CONCLUSION

Within work organizations numerous types of interpersonal relationships exist. The great majority of these relationships, however, can be categorized as involving interactions either with superiors/subordinates or with coworkers (and in particular fellow members of one's task group). Based upon the research reviewed in the preceding pages, it also appears evident that these two types of communication relationships play instrumental roles in the organizational assimilation process—the *continuous* process by which workers share in and become cognitively and behaviorally a part of their organizations' "realities."

Throughout this discussion of the functions and roles of interpersonal communication in organizational task relationships, research summaries, conclusions, and recommendations for future research have been provided. However, an assessment of the research examined in these sections suggests several additional more general conclusions. First, it is obvious that the great majority of studies that have explored interpersonal communication relationships in work organizations have failed to consider adequately the (positive and negative) constraints that the *embeddedness* of these relationships within a larger organizational system has upon communication processes. Such systemic factors as organizational structures, organizational technologies, and relevant external organizational environments are likely to affect interpersonal communication relationships in organizations, and consequently should be considered as potential moderating variables in the creating of research designs (Jablin & Sussman, 1983).

Second, and closely related to the above concern, is the tendency of most studies to consider the relationships of people in various organizational roles independent of the other roles they perform, both within the organization and external to it. For example, at a very basic level an employee within an organization is likely to perform at least three roles: superior, subordinate, and coworker (peer). Yet when we conduct studies of communication relationships in organizations we typically focus upon a person in only one of his or her roles. Moreover, most of our research tends to concentrate on the intraorganizational communication associated with individual roles, rather than with how organizational actors assimilate information from sources external to the organization (boundary spanning; see Tushman, 1977; Tushman & Scanlon, 1981), integrate this information, and then communicate it to their superiors, subordinates, and coworkers. Consequently, we generally are remiss in considering how an individual's communicative behavior is affected by the domain of his or her task-relevant role relationships, that is, the "role set" (see Schuler, 1979).

Similarly most investigations of communication behavior in organizational task relationships ignore the fact that employees often assume task roles in other settings (family, community) and that these other roles may affect their communicative behavior in their organizational relationships (especially if role conflicts exist; see Feldman, 1981). In essence, it is suggested that in the future our research needs to show greater concern for the effects intra- and extra-organizational task role sets have on communicative behavior and attitudes among organizational members.

Third, and as noted repeatedly in this chapter, it is apparent that out knowledge of the dynamics of interpersonal communication in task/organizational relationships is severely constrained by the paucity of longitudinal, as well as cross-sectional research that has been conducted in this area. Thus we are in the interesting position of being able to identify and describe various communicative "states" that exist in task/organizational relationships, while knowing little of what causes them to develop in these ways. Moreover, our understanding of the "life cycles" that communication in task relationships follow is extremely limited, and essentially nonexistent with respect to the dynamics of their deterioration. In summary, it is recommended that future research exploring communication processes in task/organizational relationships be directed at examining these relationships from a more developmental perspective.

Finally, although the present discussion has focused on communication processes in task relationships within work organizations, it is probably fair to conclude that similar processes and characteristics would exist in other types of task-related collectivities. In other words, while recognizing that there will always be some variability due to situation-specific factors, it is suggested that the assimilation-communication processes that have been outlined here are inherent to most ongoing relationships that occur within task-related groups/collectivities.

This chapter has attempted to examine the roles, functions, and characteristics of interpersonal communication in work/organizational relationships. However, unlike most traditional treatments of this subject, this analysis approached work/organizational relationships and settings from a very broad orientation—from a "life-span" perspective. Consequently, this chapter explored (1) the processes by which people anticipate and learn about interpersonal communication in work/organizational relationships, (2) the roles and characteristics of interpersonal communication in the organizational assimilation process, and (3) the functions of interpersonal communication in disengagement from work/organizational settings.

An analysis of the literature reviewed in this chapter indicates that the majority of our knowledge of interpersonal communication in task relationships is concentrated within the period when individuals are employed in work organizations. In other words, our understanding of how and what people learn about interpersonal communication in work/organizational relationships prior to ever entering them, as well as processes associated with interpersonal communication and disengagement from work/organizational relationships, is extremely limited. While numerous reasons can be posited for this bias in our research, it seems evident that until we recognize the *developmental* nature of how people learn to communicate in task settings even our understanding of interpersonal communication in the organizational assimilation process will remain constrained. It is hoped that the research recommendations provided in the preceding pages can stimulate and provide direction for future investigations of interpersonal communication in task/work relationships from a developmental perspective.

In closing, a relatively new focus of research in interpersonal communication in task/work relationships is deserving of discussion, especially since it is perceived by many to be the "wave of the future" (Toffler, 1980). Specifically, this emerging research area concerns the effects of innovations in *communication/information technology* (electronic mail, teleconferencing, computer conferencing, desk-top personal computers, videotext, satellite communications, cable television, and so on) on interpersonal communication in task/work relationships (see Hiemstra, 1983; Rice & Associates, 1984). In considering this research, however, it should be noted that while there has been an enormous growth in the number of studies exploring the adoption, use, and impact of these new technologies on interpersonal communication in work/organizational settings in the last decade, generalizable conclusions are still difficult to draw from this literature. On the other hand, it does seem apparent that the adoption of these new technologies by both individuals and organizations is rapidly expanding, and that in certain task contexts they can affect interpersonal communication processes (Keen, 1981; Kerr & Hiltz, 1982; Rice, 1980). However, whether or not the adoption and use of these new technologies in task/work settings moderates or even negates interpersonal communication patterns and relationships established by previous research remains to be determined.

REFERENCES

Albrecht, T. L. (1979). The role of communication in perceptions of organizational climate. In D. Nimmo (Ed.), *Communication yearbook 3* (pp. 343–357). New Brunswick, NJ: Transaction.

Alderfer, C. P., & McCord, C. G. (1970). Personal and situational factors in the recruitment interview. *Journal of Applied Psychology, 54*, 377–385.

Allen, R. W., & Porter, L. W. (1983). *Organizational influence processes.* Glenview, IL: Scott, Foresman.

Arvey, R. D., & Campion, J. E. (1982). The employment interview: A summary and review of recent research. *Personnel Psychology, 35*, 281–322.

Arvey, R. D., & Ivancevich, J. M. (1980). Punishment in organizations: A review, propositions and research suggestions. *Academy of Management Review, 5*, 123–132.

Asch, S. (1951). Effects of group pressure upon the modification and distortion of judgments. In H. Guetzkow (Ed.), *Groups, leadership, and men* (pp. 117–190). Pittsburgh: Carnegie.

Ashour, A. S., & Johns, G. (1983). Leader influence through operant principles: A theoretical and methodological framework. *Human Relations, 36*, 603–626.

Babbitt, L. V. (1983). *Effects of applicants' questions on interview outcomes in naturally occurring employment screening interviews.* Unpublished master's thesis, University of Texas at Austin.

Bain, R. K., & Anderson, J. G. (1974). School context and peer influences on educational plans of adolescents. *Review of Educational Research, 44*, 429–445.

Bales, R. F., & Strodtbeck, F. (1951). Phases in group problem-solving. *Journal of Abnormal and Social Psychology, 46*, 485–495.

Becker, H. S., Geer, B., Hughes, E. C., & Strauss, A. (1961). *Boys in white: Student culture in medical school.* Chicago: University of Chicago Press.

Bednar, D. A. (1982). Relationships between communicator style and managerial performance in complex organizations: A field study. *Journal of Business Com-muinication, 19,* 51–76.

Beuf, A. (1974). Doctor, lawyer, household drudge. *Journal of Communication, 24,* 142–145.

Bishop, G. D., & Myers, D. G. (1974). Informational influences in group discussion. *Organizational Behavior and Human Performance, 12,* 92–104.

Blake, R. R., Shepard, H., & Mouton, J. S. (1964). *Managing intergroup conflict in industry.* Houston: Gulf.

Bogatz, G. A., & Ball, S. J. (1971), *The second year of Sesame Street: A continuing evaluation.* Princeton, NJ: Educational Testing Service.

Brown, J. D. (1980). *Adolescent peer group communication, sex-role norms and decisions about occupations.* Paper presented at the annual meeting of the International Communication Association, Acapulco.

Bullis, C. B., Cox, M. C., & Bokeno, S. L. (1982). *Organizational conflict management: The effects of socialization, type of conflict, and sex on conflict management strategies.* Paper presented at the annual meeting of the International Communication Association, Boston.

Burns, T. (1955). The reference of conduct in small groups: Cliques and cabals in occupational milieux. *Human Relations, 8,* 467–486.

Byrd, M. L. V. (1979). *The effects of vocal activity and race of applicant on the job selection interview decision.* Unpublished doctoral dissertation, University of Missouri–Columbia.

Caldwell, D. F., & O'Reilly, C. A. (1982). Task perceptions and job satisfacton: A question of causality. *Journal of Applied Psychology, 67,* 361–369.

Cecil, E. A., Cummings, L. L., & Chertkoff, J. M. (1973). Group composition and choice shift: Implications for administration. *Academy of Management Journal, 16,* 412–422.

Cheatham, T. R., & McLaughlin, M. (1976). A comparison of co-participant perceptions of self and others in placement center interviews. *Communication Quarterly, 24,* 9–13.

Conrad, C. (1983). Power and performance as correlates of supervisors' choice of modes of managing conflict: A preliminary investigation. *Western Journal of Speech Communication, 47,* 218–228.

Constantin, S. W. (1976). An investigation of information favorability in the employment interview. *Journal of Applied Psychology, 61,* 743–749.

Crawford, J. L. (1974). Task uncertainty, decision impor-tance, and group reinforcement as determinants of communication processes in groups. *Journal of Personality and Social Psychology, 29,* 619–627.

Crites, J. O. (1969). *Vocational psychology.* New York: McGraw-Hill.

Cusella, L. P. (1980). The effects of feedback on intrinsic motivation: A propositional extension of cognitive evaluation theory from an organizational communication perspective. In D. Nimmo (Ed.), *Communication yearbook 4* (pp. 367–387). New Brunswick, NJ: Transaction.

Cusella, L. P. (1982). The effects of source expertise and feedback valence on intrinsic motivation. *Human Communication Research, 9,* 17–32.

Daly, J. A. (1978). *The personal selection interview: A state of the art review.* Paper presented at the annual meeting of the International Communication Association, Chicago.

Daniels, T. D., & Logan, L. L. (1983). Communication in women's career development relationships. In R. N. Bostrom (Ed.), *Communication yearbook 7* (pp. 532–552). Beverly Hills, CA: Sage.

Danowski, J. A. (1980). Group attitude-belief uniformity and connectivity of organizational communication networks for production, innovation, and maintenance content. *Human Communication Research, 6,* 299–308.

Dansereau, F., Graen, G., & Haga, W. J. (1975). A vertical dyad linkage approach to leadership within formal organizations. *Organizational Behavior and Human Performance, 13,* 46–78.

DeFleur, M. L. (1964). Occupational roles as portrayed on television. *Public Opinion Quarterly, 28,* 57–74.

DeFleur, M. L., & DeFleur, L. B. (1967). The relative contribution of television as a learning source for children's occupational knowledge. *American Sociological Review, 32,* 777–789.

Dennis, H. S. (1974). *A theoretical and empirical study of managerial communication climate in complex organizations.* Unpublished doctoral dissertation, Purdue University.

Dominick, J. R. (1974). Children's viewing of crime shows and attitudes on law enforcement. *Journalism Quarterly, 51,* 5–12.

Downs, C. W., & Conrad, C. (1982). Effective subordinancy. *Journal of Business Communication, 19,* 27–37.

Drucker, P. (1973). *Management: Tasks, responsibilities, practices.* New York: Harper & Row.

Duncan, O. D., Haller, A. D., & Portes, A. (1968). Peer influences on aspirations: A reinterpretation. *American Journal of Sociology, 74*, 119–137.

Einhorn, L. J. (1981). An inner view of the job interview: An investigation of successful communicative behaviors. *Communication Education, 30*, 217–228.

Eisenberg, E. M., Monge, P. R., & Miller, K. I. (1983). Involvement in communication networks as a predictor of organizational commitment. *Human Communication Research, 10*, 179–201.

Ellis, D. G., & Fisher, B. A. (1975). Phases of conflict in small group development: A Markov analysis. *Human Communication Research, 1*, 195–212.

Farace, R. V., Monge, P. R., & Russell, H. M. (1977). *Communicating and organizing.* Reading, MA: Addison-Wesley.

Feldman, D. C. (1977). The role of initiation activities in socialization. *Human Relations, 30*, 977–990.

Feldman, D. C. (1981). The multiple socialization of organization members. *Academy of Management Review, 6*, 309–318.

Feldman, D. C. (1984). The development and enforcement of group norms. *Academy of Management Review, 9*, 47–53.

Feldman, D. C., & Brett, J. M. (1983). Coping with new jobs: A comparative study of new hires and job changers. *Academy of Management Journal, 26*, 258–272.

Fisher, B. A. (1970). Decision emergence: Phases in group decision-making. *Speech Monographs, 37*, 53–66.

Fisher, C. D. (1979). Transmission of positive and negative feedback to subordinates: A laboratory investigation. *Journal of Applied Psychology, 64*, 533–540.

Fisher, C. D., Ilgen, D. R., & Hoyer, W. D. (1979). Source credibility, information favorability, and job offer acceptance. *Academy of Management Journal, 22*, 94–103.

Goldhaber, G. M., & Rogers, D. P. (1979). *Auditing organizational communication systems: The ICA communication audit.* Dubuque, IA: Kendall/Hunt.

Goldstein, B., & Oldham, J. (1979). *Children and work: A study of socialization.* New Brunswick, NJ: Transaction.

Gouran, D. S., & Baird, J. E. (1972). An analysis of distributional and sequential structure in problem-solving and informal group discussions. *Speech Monographs, 39*, 18–22.

Graen, G. (1976). Role-making processes within complex organizations. In M. D. Dunnette (Ed.), *Handbook of industrial and organizational psychology* (pp. 1201–1245). Chicago: Rand McNally.

Graen, G., & Cashman, J. (1975). A role-making model of leadership in formal organizations: A developmental approach. In J. G. Hunt & L. L. Larson (Eds.), *Leadership frontiers* (pp. 143–165). Kent, OH: Kent State University Press.

Granovetter, M. S. (1973). The strength of weak ties. *American Journal of Sociology, 78*, 1360–1380.

Green, S. G., & Mitchell, T. R. (1979). Attributional processes of leaders in leader-member interactions. *Organizational Behavior and Human Performance, 23*, 429–458.

Greller, M. M. (1980). Evaluation of feedback sources as a function of role and organizational level. *Journal of Applied Psychology, 65*, 16–23.

Guetzkow, H. (1965). Communication in organizations, In J. G. March (Ed.), *Handbook of organizations (pp. 534–573). Chicago: Rand McNally.*

Hackman, J. R. (1976). Group influences on individuals. In M. D. Dunnette (Ed.), *Handbook of industrial and organizational psychology* (pp. 1455–1525). Chicago: Rand McNally.

Hackman, J. R., Brousseau, K. R., & Weiss, J. A. (1976). The interaction of task design and group performance strategies in determining group effectiveness. *Organizational Behavior and Human Performance, 16*, 350–365.

Hackman, J. R., & Vidmar, N. (1970). Effects of size and task type on group performance and member reactions. *Sociometry, 33*, 37–54.

Hatfield, J. D., & Huseman, R. C. (1982). Perceptual congruence about communication as related to satisfaction: Moderating effects of individual characteristics. *Academy of Management Journal, 25*, 349–358.

Heinen, J. S., & Jacobson, E. (1976). A model of task group development in complex organizatons and a strategy of implementation. *Academy of Management Review, 1*, 98–111.

Hiemstra, G. (1983). You say you want a revolution? ''Information Technology'' in organizations. In R. N. Bostrom (Ed.), *Communication yearbook 7* (pp. 802–827). Beverly Hills, CA: Sage.

House, R. L., Filley, A. C., & Gujarati, D. W. (1971). Leadership style, hierarchical influence, and the satisfaction of subordinate role expectations: A test of Likert's influence proposition. *Journal of Applied Psychology, 55*, 422–432.

Huber, G. P., & Delbecq, A. L. (1972). Guidelines for combining the judgments of individual members in decision conferences. *Academy of Management Journal, 15,* 161–174.

Ilgen, D. R., Fisher, C. D., & Taylor, M. S. (1979). Consequences of individual feedback on behavior in organizations. *Journal of Applied Psychology, 64,* 349–371.

Ilgen, D. R., & Knowlton, W. A. (1980). Performance attributional effects on feedback from superiors. *Organizational Behavior and Human Performance, 25,* 441–456.

Ilgen, D. R., Peterson, R. B., Martin, B. A., & Boeschen, D. A. (1981). Supervisor and subordinate reactions to performance appraisal sessions. *Organizational Behavior and Human Performance, 28,* 311–330.

Imada, A. S., & Hakel, M. D. (1977). Influence of nonverbal communication and rater proximity on impressions and decisions in simulated employment interviews. *Journal of Applied Psychology, 62,* 295–300.

Infante, D. A., & Gordon, W. I. (1979). Subordinate and superior perceptions of self and one another: Relations, accuracy, and reciprocity of liking. *Western Journal of Speech Communication, 43,* 212–223.

Jablin, F. M. (1979). Superior-subordinate communication: The state of the art. *Psychological Bulletin, 86,* 1201–1222.

Jablin, F. M. (1980a). Superior's upward influence, satisfaction, and openness in superior-subordinate communication: A reexamination of the "Pelz Effect." *Human Communication Research, 6,* 210–220.

Jablin, F. M. (1980b). Subordinate's sex and superior-subordinate status differentiation as moderators of the Pelz Effect. In D. Nimmo (Ed.), *Communication yearbook 4* (pp. 349–366). New Brunswick, NJ: Transaction.

Jablin, F. M. (1980c). Organizational communication theory and research: An overview of communication climate and network research. In D. Nimmo (Ed.), *Communication yearbook 4* (pp. 327–347). New Brunswick, NJ: Transaction.

Jablin, F. M. (1981a). *Organizational entry and organizational communication: Job retrospections, expectations, and turnover.* Paper presented at the annual meeting of the Academy of Management, San Diego.

Jablin, F. M. (1981b). An exploratory study of subordinates' perceptions of supervisory politics. *Communication Quarterly, 29,* 269–275.

Jablin, F. M. (1981c). Cultivating imagination: Factors that enhance and inhibit creativity in brainstorming groups. *Human Communication Research, 7,* 245–258.

Jablin, F. M. (1982a). Organizational communication: An assimilation approach. In M. E. Roloff & C. R. Berger (Eds.), *Social cognition and communication* (pp. 255–286). Beverly Hills, CA: Sage.

Jablin, F. M. (1982b). Formal structural characteristics of organizations and superior-subordinate communication. *Human Communication Research, 8,* 338–347.

Jablin, F. M. (1984). Assimilating new members into organizations. In R. N. Bostrom (Ed.), *Communication yearbook 8* (pp. 594–626). Beverly Hills, CA: Sage,

Jablin, F. M. (1985). An exploratory study of vocational organizational communication socialization. *Southern Speech Communication Journal, 50,* 261–282.

Jablin, F. M., & McComb, K. B. (1984). The employment screening interview: An organizational assimilation and communication perspective. In R. N. Bostrom (Ed.), *Communication yearbook 8* (pp. 137–163). Beverly Hills, CA: Sage.

Jablin, F. M., & Seibold, D. R. (1978). Implications for problem-solving groups of empirical research on "brainstorming": A critical review of the literature. *Southern Speech Communication Journal, 43,* 327–356.

Jablin, F. M., & Sussman, L. (1983). Organizational group communication: A review of the literature and model of the process. In H. H. Greenbaum, R. L. Falcione, & S. A. Hellweg (Eds.), *Organizational communication: Abstracts, analysis and overview* (Vol. 8, pp. 11–50). Beverly Hills, CA: Sage.

Jablin, F. M., Tengler, C. D., & Teigen, C. W. (1982). *Interviewee perceptions of employment screening interviews: Relationships among perceptions of communication satisfaction, interviewer credibility and trust, interviewing experience, and interview outcomes.* Paper presented at the annual meeting of the International Communication Association, Boston.

Janis, I. (1972). *Victims of groupthink: A psychological study of foreign policy decisions and fiascos.* Boston: Houghton Mifflin.

Karol, B. L. (1977). *Relationship of recruiter behavior, perceived similarity, and prior information to applicants' assessments of the campus recruitment interview.* Unpublished doctoral dissertation, Ohio State University.

Katz, R. (1980). Time and work: Toward an integrative

perspective. In B. M. Staw & L. L. Cummings (Eds.), *Research in organizational behavior* (Vol. 2, pp. 81–127). Greenwich, CT: JAI.

Katz, D., & Kahn, R. L. (1966). *The social psychology of organizations.* New York: John Wiley.

Katzman, N. I. (1972). Television soap operas: What's been going on anyway? *Public Opinion Quarterly, 36,* 200–212.

Keen, P. (1981). Information systems and organizational change. *Communications of the ACM, 24* (1), 24–33.

Kerr, E., & Hiltz, S. R. (1982). *Computer-mediated communication systems.* New York: Academic Press.

Kilmann, R. H., & Thomas, K. W. (1977). Developing a forced-choice measure of conflict-handling behavior: The MODE instrument. *Educational and Psychological Measurement, 37,* 309–325.

Kipnis, D., Schmidt, S. M., & Wilkinson, I. (1980). Intraorganizational influence tactics: Explorations in getting one's way. *Journal of Applied Psychology, 65,* 440–452.

Kipnis, D., Schmidt, S. M., Price, K., & Stitt, C. (1981). Why do I like thee: Is it your performance or my orders? *Journal of Applied Psychology, 66,* 324–328.

Kirchner, E. P., & Vondracek, S. I. (1973). *What do you want to be when you grow up? Vocational choice in children aged three to six.* Paper presented at the meeting of the Society for Research in Child Development, Philadelphia.

Klauss, R., & Bass, B. M. (1982). *Interpersonal communication in organizations.* New York: Academic Press.

Klimoski, R. J., & Karol, B. L. (1976). The impact of trust on creative problem solving groups. *Journal of Applied Psychology, 61,* 630–633.

Kline, J. A. (1970). Indices of orienting and opinionated statements in problem-solving discussions. *Speech Monographs, 37,* 282–286.

Kline, J. A. (1972). Orientation and group consensus. *Central States Speech Journal, 23,* 44–47.

Knapp, M. L. (1978). *Social intercourse: From greeting to goodbye.* Boston: Allyn & Bacon.

Knutson, T. J. (1972). An experimental study of the effects of orientation behavior on small group consensus. *Speech Monographs, 39,* 159–165.

Krone, K. J. (1984). *A framework for studying upward influence messages in decision making contexts.* Paper presented at the annual meeting of the International Communication Association, San Francisco.

Laing, R. D., Phillipson, H., & Lee, A. R. (1966). *Interpersonal perception: A theory and method of research.* New York: Springer.

Larson, J. R. (1984). The performance feedback process: A preliminary model. *Organizational Behavior and Human Performance, 33,* 42–76.

Leathers, D. G. (1970). The process effects of trust-destroying behavior in small groups. *Speech Monographs, 37,* 180–187.

Leifer, A. D., & Lesser, G. S. (1976). *The development of career awareness in young children.* Washington, DC: National Institute of Education.

Levine, J. M., Skroka, K. R., & Snyder, H. N. (1977). Group support and reaction to stable and shifting agreement/disagreement. *Sociometry, 40,* 214–224.

Liden, R. C., & Graen, G. (1980). Generalizability of the vertical dyad linkage model of leadership. *Academy of Management Journal, 23,* 451–465.

Mabry, E. A. (1975). Exploratory analysis of a developmental model for task-oriented small groups. *Human Communication Research, 2,* 66–74.

Mayfield, E. C. (1964). The selection interview: A reevaluation of published research. *Personnel Psychology, 17,* 234–260.

McComb, K. B., & Jablin, F. M. (1984). Verbal correlates of interviewer empathic listening and employment interview outcomes. *Communication Monographs, 51,* 353–371.

McGovern, T. V., & Tinsley, H. E. A. (1978). Interviewer evaluations of interviewee nonverbal behavior. *Journal of Vocational Behavior, 13,* 163–171.

McLaughlin, M. L., & Cheatham, T. R. (1977). Effects of communication isolation on job satisfaction of bank tellers: A research note. *Human Communication Research, 3,* 171–175.

Mitchell, T. R., & Wood, R. E. (1980). Supervisors' responses to subordinate poor performance: A test of an attributional model. *Organizational Behavior and Human Performance, 25,* 123–138.

Monge, P. R., Bachman, S. G., Dillard, J. P., & Eisenberg, E. M. (1982). Communicator competence in the workplace: Model testing and scale development. In M. Burgoon, (Ed.), *Communication yearbook 5* (pp. 505–527). New Brunswick, NJ: Transaction.

Monge, P. R., Edwards, J. A., & Kirste, K. K. (1978). The determinants of communication and communication structure in large organizations: A review of research. In B. Ruben (Ed.), *Communication yearbook 2* (pp. 311–331). New Brunswick, NJ: Transaction.

Morgan, C. P., & Beatty, R. W. (1976). Information relevant to the task in the risky shift phenomenon. *Academy of Management Journal, 19,* 304–308.

Mowday, R. T. (1978). The exercise of upward influence

in organizations. *Administrative Science Quarterly, 23,* 137–156.

Nadler, D. A. (1979). The effects of feedback on task group behavior: A review of the experimental research. *Organizational Behavior and Human Performance, 23,* 309–338.

Noble, G. (1975). *Children in front of the small screen.* Beverly Hills, CA: Sage.

Norton, R. W. (1978). Foundation of a communicator style construct. *Human Communication Research, 4,* 99-112.

O'Reilly, C. A., & Anderson, J. C. (1980). Trust and the communication of performance appraisal information: The effect of feedback on performance and job satisfaction. *Human Communication Research, 6,* 290–298.

O'Reilly, C. A., & Caldwell, D. (1979). Informational influence as a determinant of task characteristics and job satisfaction. *Journal of Applied Psychology, 64,* 157–165.

Pavett, C. M. (1983). Evaluation of the impact of feedback on performance and motivation. *Human Relations, 36,* 641–654.

Pelz, D. (1952). Influence: A key to effective leadership in the first line supervisor. *Personnel, 29,* 209–217.

Penley, L. E., & Alexander, E. R. (1979). The communication and structure of work groups: A contingency perspective. In R. C. Huseman (Ed.), *Academy of Management Proceedings* (pp. 331–335). Mississippi State: Academy of Management.

Poole, M. S. (1981). Decision development in small groups I: A comparison of two models. *Communication Monographs, 48,* 1–24.

Poole, M. S. (1983). Decision development in small groups II: A study of multiple sequences in decision making. *Communication Monographs, 50,* 206–232.

Porter, L. W., Allen, R. W., & Angle, H. L. (1981). The politics of upward influence in organizations. In L. L. Commings & B. Staw (Eds.), *Research in organizational behavior* (Vol. 3, pp. 109–149). Greenwich, CT: JAI.

Porter, L. W., Lawler, E. E., & Hackman, J. R. (1975). *Behavior in organizations.* New York: McGraw-Hill.

Prentice, D. S. (1975). The effect of trust-destroying communication on verbal fluency in the small group. *Speech Monographs, 42,* 262–270.

Pruitt, D. G. (1971a). Choice shifts in group discussion: An introductory review. *Journal of Personality and Social Psychology, 20,* 339–360.

Pruitt, D. G. (1971b). Conclusion: Toward an understanding of choice shifts in group decisions. *Journal of Personality and Social Psychology, 20,* 495–510.

Putnam, L. L., & Wilson, C. E. (1982). Communicative strategies in organizational conflicts: Reliability and validity of a measurement scale. In M. Burgoon (Ed.), *Communication yearbook 6* (pp. 629–652). Beverly Hills, CA: Sage.

Rakestraw, T. L., & Weiss, H. M. (1981). The interaction of social influences and task experience on goals, performance, and performance satisfaction. *Organizational Behavior and Human Performance, 27,* 326–344.

Randolph, W. A. (1978). Organization technology and the media and purpose dimensions of organizational communications. *Journal of Business Research, 6,* 237–259.

Redding, W. C. (1972). *Communication within the organization: An interpretive review of theory and research.* New York: Industrial Communication Council.

Riccillo, S. C., & Trenholm, S. (1983). Predicting managers' choice of influence mode: The effects of interpersonal trust and worker attributions on managerial tactics in a simulated organizational setting. *Western Journal of Speech Communication, 47,* 323–339.

Rice, R. E. (1980). The impacts of computer-mediated organizational and interpersonal communication. In M. Williams (Ed.), *Annual review of information science and technology* (Vol. 15, pp. 221–249). White Plains, NY: Knowledge Industries.

Rice, R. E., & Associates. (1984). *The new media: Communication, research, and technology.* Beverly Hills, CA: Sage.

Richmond, V. P., McCroskey, J. C., & Davis, L. M. (1982). Individual differences among employees, management communication style, and employee satisfaction: Replication and extension. *Human Communication Research, 8,* 170–188.

Richmond, V. P., McCroskey, J. C., Davis, L. M., & Koontz, K. A. (1980). Perceived power as a mediator of management communication style and employee satisfaction: A preliminary investigation. *Communication Quarterly, 28,* 37–46.

Richmond, V. P., Wagner, J. P., & McCroskey, J. C. (1983). The impact of perceptions of leadership style, use of power, and conflict management style on organizational outcomes. *Communication Quarterly, 31,* 27–36.

Riggs, C. J. (1983). Communication dimensions of conflict tactics in organizational settings: A functional analysis. In R. Bostrom (Ed.), *Communication yearbook 7* (pp. 517–531). Beverly Hills, CA: Sage.

Roberts, K. H., & Glick, W. (1981). The job characteristics approach to task design: A critical review. *Journal of Applied Psychology, 66,* 193–217.

Roberts, K. H., & O'Reilly, C. A. (1974). Measuring organizational communication. *Journal of Applied Psychology, 59,* 321–326.

Rogers, E. M., & Kincaid, L. (1981). *Communication networks: A paradigm for research.* New York: Macmillan.

Ross, R., & DeWine, S. (1982). *Interpersonal conflict: Measurement and validation.* Paper presented at the annual meeting of the Speech Communication Association, Louisville.

Sacket, P. R. (1979). *The interviewer as hypothesis tester: The effects of impressions of an applicant on subsequent interviewer behavior.* Unpublished doctoral dissertation, Ohio State University.

Salancik, G. R., & Pfeffer, J. (1978). A social information processing approach to job attitudes and task design. *Administrative Science Quarterly, 23,* 224–253.

Schachter, S.,Ellertson, N., McBride, D., & Gregory, D. (1951). An experimental study of cohesiveness and productivity. *Human Relations, 4,* 229–238.

Schein, E. H. (1968). Organizational socialization and the profession of management. *Industrial Management Review, 9,* 1–16.

Schein, E. H. (1978). *Career dynamics: Matching individual and organizational needs.* Reading, MA: Addison-Wesley.

Schein, E. H. (1980). *Organizational psychology* (3rd ed.). Englewood Cliffs, NJ: Prentice-Hall.

Schilit, W. K., & Locke, E. A. (1982). A study of upward influence in organizations. *Administrative Science Quarterly, 27,* 304–316.

Schlossberg, N. K., & Goodman, J. (1972). A woman's place: Children's sex stereotypes of occupations. *Vocational Guidance Quarterly, 20,* 266–270.

Schmidt, N. (1976). Social and situational determinants of interview decisions: Implications for the employment interview. *Personnel Psychology, 29,* 79–101.

Schuler, R. S. (1979). A role perception transactional process model for organizational communication-outcome relationships. *Organizational Behavior and Human Performance, 23,* 268–291.

Seashore, S. (1954). *Group cohesiveness in the industrial work group.* Ann Arbor, MI: University of Michigan, Institute for Social Research.

Sherif, M. (1936). *The psychology of social norms.* New York: Harper & Row.

Shiflett, S. C. (1972). Group performance as a function of task difficulty and organizational interdependence. *Organizational Behavior and Human Performance, 7,* 442–456.

Siegel, A. E. (1958). The influence of violence in the mass media upon children's role expectations. *Child Development, 29,* 35–56.

Sillars, A. L. (1980). The stranger and the spouse as target persons for compliance-gaining strategies: A subjective expected utility model. *Human Communication Research, 6,* 265–279.

Simpson, R. L. (1962). Parental influence, anticipatory socialization, and social mobility. *American Sociological Review, 17,* 754–761.

Sims, H. P. (1980). Further thoughts on punishment in organizations. *Academy of Management Review, 5,* 133–138.

Smircich, L., & Chesser, R. J. (1981). Superiors' and subordinates' perceptions of performance: Beyond disagreement. *Academy of Management Journal, 24,* 198–205.

Sorenson, J. R. (1971). Task demands, group interaction, and group performance. *Sociometry, 34,* 483–495.

Sussman, L. (1975). Communication in organizational hierarchies: The fallacy of perceptual congruence. *Western Speech Communication, 39,* 191–199.

Teigen, C. W. (1983). *Communication of organizational climate during job screening interviews: A field study of interviewee perceptions, ''actual'' communication behavior and interview outcomes.* Unpublished doctoral dissertation, University of Texas at Austin.

Tengler, C. D. (1982). *Effects of question-type and question orientation on interview outcomes in naturally occurring employment interviews.* Unpublished master's thesis, University of Texas at Austin.

Tengler, C. D., & Jablin, F. M. (1983). Effects of question type, orientation, and sequencing in the employment screening interview. *Communication Monographs, 50,* 245–263.

Toffler, A. (1980). *The third wave.* New York: William Morrow.

Tompkins, P. K. (1962). *An analysis of communication between headquarters and selected units of a national labor union.* Unpublished doctoral dissertation, Purdue University.

Trent, L. W. (1978). *The effect of varying levels of interviewee nonverbal behavior in the employment interview.* Unpublished doctoral dissertation, Southern Illinois University.

Trist, E. L., & Bamforth, K. W. (1951). Some social and psychological consequences of the longwall method of coal-getting. *Human Relations, 4,* 1–38.

Turow, J. (1974). Advising and ordering in daytime, primetime. *Journal of Communication, 24,* 138–141.

Turow, J. (1980). Occupation and personality in television dramas: An industry view. *Communication Research, 7,* 295–318.

Tushman, M. (1977). Communication across organizational boundaries: Special boundary roles in the innovation process. *Administrative Science Quarterly, 22,* 587–605.

Tushman, M., & Scanlon, T. (1981). Boundary spanning individuals: Their role in information transfer and their antecedents. *Academy of Management Journal, 24,* 289–305.

Ulrich, L., & Trumbo, D. (1965). The selection interview since 1949. *Psychological Bulletin, 63,* 100–116.

Van de Ven, A. H., & Delbecq, A. L. (1971). Nominal versus interacting group processes for committee decision-making effectiveness. *Academy of Management Journal, 14,* 203–212.

Van de Ven, A. H., & Delbecq, A. L. (1974). The effectiveness of nominal, delphi, and interacting group decision making processes. *Academy of Management Journal, 17,* 605–621.

Van de Ven, A. H., Delbecq, A. L., & Koenig, R. (1976). Determinants of coordination modes within organizations. *American Sociological Review, 41,* 332–338.

VanMaanen, J. (1975). Breaking in: Socialization to work. In R. Dubin (Ed.), *Handbook of work, organization and society* (pp. 67–120). Chicago: Rand McNally.

Volard, S. V., & Davies, M. R. (1982). Communication patterns of managers. *Journal of Business Communication, 19,* 41–53.

Wanous, J. P. (1977). Organizational entry: Newcomers moving from outside to inside. *Psychological Bulletin, 84,* 601–618.

Watson, K. M. (1982). An analysis of communication patterns: A method for discriminating leader and subordinate roles. *Academy of Management Journal, 25,* 107–120.

Weinstein, D. (1979). *Bureaucratic opposition: Challenging abuses of the workplace.* New York: Pergamon.

Weiss, H. M. (1977). Subordinate imitation of supervisor behavior: The role of modeling in organizational socialization. *Organizational Behavior and Human Performance, 19,* 89–105.

Weiss, H. M., & Nowicki, C. E. (1981). Social influence on task satisfaction: Model competence and observer field dependence. *Organizational Behavior and Human Performance, 27,* 345–366.

Weiss, W. (1969). Effects of the mass media of communication. In G. Lindzey & E. Aronson (Eds.), *Handbook of social psychology* (Vol. 5, pp. 77–195). Reading, MA: Addison-Wesley.

White, S. E., & Mitchell, T. R. (1979). Job enrichment versus social cues: A comparison and competitive test. *Journal of Applied Psychology, 64,* 1–9.

Whyte, W. F. (1955). *Money and motivation.* New York: Harper & Row.

Woelfel, J., & Haller, A. O. (1971). Significant others, the self-reflective act and the attitude formation process. *American Sociological Review, 36,* 74–87.

Wright, O. R. (1969). Summary of research on the selection interview since 1964. *Personnel Psychology, 22,* 391–413.

Zand, D. E. (1972). Trust and managerial problem solving. *Administrative Science Quarterly, 17,* 229–239.

20   THE MANAGER'S JOB: FOLKLORE AND FACT

HENRY MINTZBERG

Henry Mintzberg challenged the conventional wisdom of classical and human relations theorists that what managers *do* is planning, organizing, coordinating, and controlling. He made his case by examining his own and others' research that observed the actual behavior of executives, managers, and other leaders. Here, Mintzberg identifies four folk beliefs about managerial work and presents the facts that discredit those conventional notions. He then distills the research on the manager's job by describing managers' behavior in terms of functional roles. Mintzberg showed all later leadership theorists the wisdom of focusing on actual leader behaviors. Notice, too, the prominence of self-understanding and social information in Mintzberg's prescriptions for improving managerial performance.

If you ask a manager what he does, he will most likely tell you that he plans, organizes, coordinates, and controls. Then watch what he does. Don't be surprised if you can't relate what you see to these four words.

When he is called and told that one of his factories has just burned down, and he advises the caller to see whether temporary arrangements can be made to supply customers through a foreign subsidiary, is he planning, organizing, coordinating, or controlling? How about when he presents a gold watch to a retiring employee? Or when he attends a conference to meet people in the trade? Or on returning from that conference, when he tells one of his employees about an interesting product idea he picked up there?

The fact is that these four words, which have dominated management vocabulary since the French industrialist Henri Fayol first introduced them in 1916, tell us little about what managers actually do. At best, they indicate some vague objectives managers have when they work.

The field of management, so devoted to progress and change, has for more than half a century not seriously addressed *the* basic question: What do managers do? Without a proper answer, how can we teach management? How can we design planning or information systems for managers? How can we improve the practice of management at all?

My intention in this article is simple: to break the reader away from Fayol's words and introduce him to a more supportable, and what I believe to be a more useful, description of managerial work. This description derives from my review and synthesis of the available research on how various managers have spent their time.

In some studies, managers were observed intensively ("shadowed" is the term some of them used); in a number of others, they kept detailed diaries of their activities; in a few studies, their records were analyzed. All kinds of managers were studied—foremen, factory supervisors, staff managers, field sales managers, hospital administrators, presidents of companies and nations, and even street gang leaders. These ''managers'' worked in the United States, Canada, Sweden, and Great Britain.

A synthesis of these findings paints an interesting picture, one as different from Fayol's classical view as a cubist abstract is from a Renaissance painting. In a sense, this picture will be obvious to anyone who has ever spent a day in a manager's office, either in front of the desk or behind it. Yet at the same time, this picture may turn out to be revolutionary, in that it throws into doubt so much of the folklore that we have accepted about the manager's work.

I first discuss some of this folklore and contrast it with some of the discoveries of systematic research—the hard facts about how managers spend their time. Then I synthesize these research findings in a description of ten roles that seem to describe the essential content of all manager's jobs. In a concluding section, I discuss a number of implications of this synthesis for those trying to achieve more effective management, both in classrooms and in the business world.

SOME FOLKLORE
AND FACTS
ABOUT MANAGERIAL WORK

There are four myths about the manager's job that do not bear up under careful scrutiny of the facts.

1

Folklore: The manager is a reflective, systematic planner. The evidence on this issue is overwhelming, but not a shred of it supports this statement.

Fact: Study after study has shown that managers work at an unrelenting pace, that their activities are characterized by brevity, variety, and discontinuity, and that they are strongly oriented to action and dislike reflective activities. Consider this evidence:

- Half the activities engaged in by the five chief executives of my study lasted less than nine minutes, and only 10% exceeded one hour.[1] A study

of 56 U.S. foremen found that they averaged 583 activities per eight-hour shift, an average of 1 every 48 seconds.[2] The work pace for both chief executives and foremen was unrelenting. The chief executives met a steady stream of callers and mail from the moment they arrived in the morning until they left in the evening. Coffee breaks and lunches were inevitably work related, and ever-present subordinates seemed to usurp any free moment.

- A diary study of 160 British middle and top managers found that they worked for a half hour or more without interruption only about once every two days.[3]

- Of the verbal contacts of the chief executives in my study, 93% were arranged on an ad hoc basis. Only 1% of the executives' time was spent in open-ended observational tours. Only 1 out of 368 verbal contacts was unrelated to a specific issue and could be called general planning. Another researcher finds that ''in *not one single case* did a manager report the obtaining of important external information from a general conversation or other undirected personal communication.''[4]

- No study has found important patterns in the way managers schedule their time. They seem to jump from issue to issue, continually responding to the needs of the moment.

Is this the planner that the classical view describes? Hardly. How, then, can we explain this behavior? The manager is simply responding to the pressures of his job. When the manager must plan, he seems to do so implicitly in the context of daily actions, not in some abstract process reserved for two weeks in the organization's mountain retreat. The plans of the chief executives I studied seemed to exist only in their heads—as flexible, but often specific, intentions. The traditional literature notwithstanding, the job of managing does not breed reflective planners; the manager is a real-time responder to stimuli, an individual who is conditioned by his job to prefer live to delayed action.

2

Folklore: The effective manager has no regular duties to perform. Managers are constantly being told to spend more time planning and delegating, and less time seeing customers and engaging in negotiations. These are not, after all, the true tasks of the manager. To use the popular analogy, the good manager, like the good conductor, carefully orchestrates everything in advance, then sits back to enjoy the fruits of his labor, responding occasionally to an unforeseeable exception.

Fact: In addition to handling exceptions, managerial work involves performing a number of regular duties, including ritual and ceremony, negotiations, and processing of soft information that links the organization with its environment. Consider some evidence from the research studies:

- A study of the work of the presidents of small companies found that they engaged in routine activities because their companies could not afford staff specialists and were so thin on operating personnel that a single absence often required the president to substitute.[5]

- One study of field sales managers and another of chief executives suggest that it is a natural part of both jobs to see important customers, assuming the managers wish to keep those customers.[6]

- Someone, only half in jest, once described the manager as that person who sees visitors so that everyone else can get his work done. In my study, I found that certain ceremonial duties—meeting visiting dignitaries, giving out gold watches, presiding at Christmas dinners—were an intrinsic part of the chief executive's job.

- Studies of managers' information flow suggest that managers play a key role in securing "soft" external information (much of it available only to them because of their status) and in passing it along to their subordinates.

3

Folklore: The senior manager needs aggregated information, which a formal management information system best provides. Not too long ago, the words *total information system* were everywhere in the management literature. In keeping with the classical view of the manager as that individual perched on the apex of a regulated, hierarchical system, the literature's manager was to receive all his important information from a giant, comprehensive MIS.

But lately, as it has become increasingly evident that these giant MIS systems are not working—that managers are simply not using them—the enthusiasm has waned. A look at how managers actually process information makes the reason quite clear. Managers have five media at their command—documents, telephone calls, scheduled and unscheduled meetings, and observational tours.

Fact: Managers strongly favor the verbal media—namely, telephone calls and meetings. The evidence comes from every single study of managerial work. Consider the following:

- In two British studies, managers spent an average of 66% and 80% of their time in verbal (oral) communication.[7] In my study of five American chief executives, the figure was 78%.

- These five chief executives treated mail processing as a burden to be dispensed with. One came in Saturday morning to process 142 pieces of mail in just over three hours, to "get rid of all the stuff." This same manager looked at the first pieces of "hard" mail he had received all week, a standard cost report, and put it aside with the comment, "I never look at this."

- These same five chief executives responded immediately to 2 of the 40 routine reports they received during the five weeks of my study and to four items in the 104 periodicals. They skimmed most of these periodicals in seconds, almost ritualistically. In all, these chief executives of good-sized organizations initiated on their own—that is, not in response to something else—a grand total of 25 pieces of mail during the 25 days I observed them.

An analysis of the mail the executives received reveals an interesting picture—only 13% was of specific and immediate use. So now we have another piece in the puzzle: not much of the mail provides live, current information—the action of a competitor, the mood of a government legislator, or the rating of last night's television show. Yet this is the information that drove the managers, interrupting their meetings and rescheduling their workdays.

Consider another interesting finding. Managers seem to cherish "soft" information, especially gossip, hearsay, and speculation. Why? The reason is its timeliness; today's gossip may be tomorrow's fact. The manager who is not accessible for the telephone call informing him that his biggest customer was seen golfing with his main competitor may read about a dramatic drop in sales in the next quarterly report. But then it's too late.

Consider the words of Richard Neustadt, who studied the information-collecting habits of Presidents Roosevelt, Truman, and Eisenhower.

It is not information of a general sort that helps a President see personal stakes; not summaries, not surveys, not the *bland amalgams*. Rather . . . it is the odds and ends of *tangible detail* that pieced together in his mind illuminate the underside of issues put before him. To help himself he must reach out as widely as he can for every scrap of fact, opinion, gossip, bearing on his interests and relationships as President. He must become his own director of his own central intelligence.[8]

The manager's emphasis on the verbal media raises two important points:

First, verbal information is stored in the brains of people. Only when people write this information down can it be stored in the files of the organization—whether in metal cabinets or on magnetic tape—and managers apparently do not write down much of what they hear. Thus the strategic data bank of the organization is not in the memory of its computers but in the minds of its managers.

Second, the manager's extensive use of verbal media helps to explain why he is reluctant to delegate tasks. When we note that most of the manager's important information comes in verbal form and is stored in his head, we can well appreciate his reluctance. It is not as if he can hand a dossier over to someone; he must take the time to "dump memory"—to tell that someone all he knows about the subject. But this could take so long that the manager may find it easier to do the task himself. Thus the manager is damned by his own information system to a "dilemma of delegation"—to do too much himself or to delegate to his subordinates with inadequate briefing.

4

Folklore: Management is, or at least is quickly becoming, a science and a profession. By almost any definitions of *science* and *profession*, this statement is false. Brief observation of any manager will quickly lay to rest the notion that managers practice a science. A science involves the enaction of systematic, analytically determined procedures or programs. If we do not even know what procedures managers use, how can we prescribe them by scientific analysis? And how can we call management a profession if we cannot specify what managers are to learn? For after all, a profession involves "knowledge of some department of learning or science" (*Random House Dictionary*).[9]

Fact: The managers' programs—to schedule time, process information, make decisions, and so on—remain locked deep inside their brains. Thus, to describe these programs, we rely on words like *judgement* and *intuition*, seldom stopping to realize that they are merely labels for our ignorance.

I was struck during my study by the fact that the executives I was observing—all very competent by any standard—are fundamentally indistinguishable from their counterparts of a hundred years ago (or a thousand years ago, for that matter). The information they need differs, but they seek it in the same way—by word of mouth. Their decisions concern modern technology, but the procedures they use to make them are the same as the procedures of the nineteenth-century manager. Even the computer, so important for the specialized work of the organization, has apparently had no influence on the work procedures of general managers. In fact, the manager is in a kind of loop, with increasingly heavy work pressure but no aid forthcoming from management science.

But the pressures of the manager's job are becoming worse. Where before he needed only to respond to owners and directors, now he finds that subordinates with democratic norms continually reduce his freedom to issue unexplained orders and a growing number of outside influences (consumer groups, government agencies, and so on) expect his attention. And the manager has had nowhere to turn for help. The first step in providing the manager with some help is to find out what his job really is.

BACK TO A BASIC DESCRIPTION OF MANAGERIAL WORK

Now let us try to put some of the pieces of this puzzle together. Earlier, I defined the manager as that person in charge of an organization or one of its subunits. Besides chief executive officers, this definition would include vice presidents, bishops, foremen, hockey coaches, and prime ministers. Can all of these people have anything in common? Indeed they can. For an important starting point, all are vested with formal authority over an organizational unit. From formal authority comes status, which leads to various interpersonal relations, and from these comes access to information. Information, in turn, enables the manager to make decisions and strategies for his unit.

The manager's job can be described in terms of various "roles," or organized sets of behaviors identified with a position. My description comprises ten roles. As we shall see, formal authority gives rise to the three interpersonal roles, which in turn give rise to the three informational roles; these two sets of roles enable the manager to play the four decisional roles.

Interpersonal Roles

Three of the manager's roles arise directly from his formal authority and involve basic interpersonal relationships.

1

First is the *figurehead* role. By virtue of his position as head of an organizational unit, every manager must perform some duties of a ceremonial nature. The president greets the touring dignitaries, the foreman attends the wedding of a lathe operator, and the sales manager takes an important customer to lunch.

The chief executives of my study spent 12% of their contact time on ceremonial duties; 17% of their incoming mail dealt with acknowledgments and requests related to their status. For example, a letter to a company president requested free merchandise for a crippled schoolchild; diplomas were put on the desk of the school superintendent for his signature.

Duties that involve interpersonal roles may sometimes be routine, involving little serious communication and no important decision making. Nevertheless, they are important to smooth functioning of an organization and cannot be ignored by a manager.

2

Because he is in charge of an organizational unit, the manager is responsible for the work of the people of that unit. His actions in this regard constitute the *leader* role. Some of these actions involve leadership directly—for example, in most organizations the manager is normally responsible for hiring and training his own staff.

In addition, there is the indirect exercise of the leader role. Every manager must motivate and encourage his employees, somehow reconciling their individual needs with the goals of the organization. In virtually every contact the manager has with his employees, subordinates seeking leadership clues probe his actions: "Does he approve?" "How would he like the report to turn out?" "Is he more interested in market share than high profits?"

The influence of the manager is most clearly seen in the leader role. Formal authority vests him with great potential power, leadership determines in large part how much of it he will realize.

3

The literature of management has always recognized the leader role, particularly those aspects of it related to motivation. In comparison, until recently it has hardly mentioned the *liaison* role, in which the manager makes contacts outside his vertical chain of command. This is remarkable in light of the finding of virtually every study of managerial work that managers spend as much time with peers and other people outside their units as they do with their own subordinates—and, surprisingly, very little time with their own superiors.

In Rosemary Stewart's diary study, the 160 British middle and top managers spent 47% of their time with peers, 41% of their time with people outside their unit, and only 12% of their time with their superiors. For Robert H. Guest's study of U.S. foremen, the figures were 44%, 46%, and 10%. The chief executives of my study averaged 44% of their contact time with people outside their organizations, 48% with subordinates, and 7% with directors and trustees.

As we shall see shortly, the manager cultivates such contacts largely to find information. In effect, the liaison role is devoted to building up the manager's own external information system—informal, private, verbal, but, nevertheless, effective.

Informational Roles

By virtue of his interpersonal contacts, both with his subordinates and with his network of contacts, the manager emerges as the nerve center of his organizational unit. He may not know everything, but he typically knows more than any member of his staff.

Studies have shown this relationship to hold for all managers, from street gang leaders to U.S. presidents. In *The Human Group*, George C. Homans explains how, because they were at the center of the information flow in their own gangs and were also in close touch with other gang leaders, street gang leaders were better informed than any of their followers.[10]

The processing of information is a key part of the manager's job. In my study, the chief executives spent 40% of their contact time on activities devoted exclusively to the transmission of information; 70% of their incoming mail was purely informational (as opposed to requests for action). The manager does not leave meetings or hang up the telephone in order to get back to work. In large part, communication *is* his work. Three roles describe these informational aspects of managerial work.

1

As *monitor*, the manager perpetually scans his environment for information, interrogates his liaison contacts and his subordinates, and receives unsolicited information, much of it as a result of the network of personal contacts he has developed. Remember that a good part of the information the manager collects in his monitor role arrives in verbal form, often as gossip, hearsay, and speculation. By virtue of his contacts, the manager has a natural advantage in collecting this soft information for his organization.

2

He must share and distribute much of this information. Information he gleans from outside personal contacts may be needed within his organization. In his *disseminator* role, the manager passes some of his privileged information directly to his subordinates, who would otherwise have no access to it. When his subordinates lack easy contact with one another, the manager will sometimes pass information from one to another.

3

In his *spokesman* role, the manager sends some of his information to people outside his unit—a president makes a speech to lobby for an organization cause, or a foreman suggests a product modification to a supplier. In addition, as part of his role as spokesman, every manager must inform and satisfy the influential people who control his organizational unit. For the foreman, this may simply involve keeping the plant manager informed about the flow of work through the shop.

The president of a large corporation, however, may spend a great amount of his time dealing with a host of influences. Directors and shareholders must be advised about financial performance; consumer groups must be assured that the organization is fulfilling its social responsibilities; and government officials must be satisfied that the organization is abiding by the law.

Decisional Roles

Information is not, of course, an end in itself; it is the basic input to decision-making. One thing is clear in the study of managerial work: the manager plays the major role in his unit's decision-making system. As its formal authority, only he can commit the unit to important new courses of action; and as its nerve center, only he has full and current information to make the set of decisions that determines the unit's strategy. Four roles describe the manager as decision-maker.

1

As *entrepreneur*, the manager seeks to improve his unit, to adapt it to changing conditions in the environment. In his monitor role, the president is constantly on the lookout for new ideas. When a good one appears, he initiates a development project that he may supervise himself or delegate to an employee (perhaps with the stipulation that he must approve the final proposal).

There are two interesting features about these development projects at the chief executive level.

First, these projects do not involve single decisions or even unified clusters of decisions. Rather, they emerge as a series of small decisions and actions sequenced over time. Apparently, the chief executive prolongs each project so that he can fit it bit by bit into his busy, disjointed schedule and so that he can gradually come to comprehend the issue, if it is a complex one.

Second, the chief executives I studied supervised as many as 50 of these projects at the same time. Some projects entailed new products or processes; others involved public relations campaigns, improvement of the cash position, reorganization of a weak department, resolution of a morale problem in a foreign division, integration of computer operations, various acquisitions at different stages of development, and so on.

The chief executive appears to maintain a kind of inventory of the development projects that he himself supervises—projects that are at various stages of development, some active and some in limbo. Like a juggler, he keeps a number of projects in the air; periodically, one comes down, is given a new burst of energy, and is sent back into orbit. At various intervals, he put new projects on-stream and discards old ones.

2

While the entrepreneur role describes the manager as the voluntary initiator of change, the *disturbance handler* role depicts the manager involuntarily responding to pressures. Here change is beyond the manager's control. He must act because the pressures of the situation are too severe to be ignored: strike looms, a major customer has gone bankrupt, or a supplier reneges on his contract.

In effect, every manager must spend a good part of his time responding to high-pressure disturbances. No organization can be so well run, so standardized, that it has considered every contingency in the uncertain environment in advance. Disturbances arise not only because poor managers ignore situations until they reach crisis proportions, but also because good managers cannot possibly anticipate all the consequences of the actions they take.

3

The third decisional role is that of *resource allocator*. To the manager falls the responsibility of deciding who will get what in his organizational unit. Perhaps the most important resource the manager allocates is his own time. Access to the manager constitutes exposure to the unit's nerve center and decision-maker. The manager is also charged with designing his unit's structure, that pattern of formal relationships that determines how work is to be divided and coordinated.

Also, in his role as resource allocator, the manager authorizes the important decisions of his unit before they are implemented. By retaining this power, the manager can ensure that decisions are interrelated; all must pass through a single brain. To fragment this power is to encourage discontinuous decision making and a disjointed strategy.

There are a number of interesting features about the manager's authorizing others' decisions. First, despite the widespread use of capital budgeting procedures—a means of authorizing various capital expenditures at one time—executives in my study made a great many authorization decisions on an ad hoc basis. Apparently, many projects cannot wait or simply do not have the quantifiable costs and benefits that capital budgeting requires.

Second, I found that the chief executives faced incredibly complex choices. They had to consider the impact of each decision on other decisions and on the organization's strategy. They had to ensure that the decision would be acceptable to those who influence the organization, as well as ensure that resources would not be overextended. They had to understand the various costs and benefits as well as the feasibility of the proposal. They also had to consider questions of timing. All this was necessary for the simple approval of someone else's proposal. At the same time, however, delay could lose time, while quick approval could be ill considered and quick rejection might discourage the subordinate who had spent months developing a pet project.

One common solution to approving projects is to pick the man instead of the proposal. That is, the manager authorizes those projects presented to him by people whose judgment he trusts. But he cannot always use this simple dodge.

4

The final decisional role is that of *negotiator*. Studies of managerial work at all levels indicate that managers spend considerable time in negotiations: the president of the football team is called in to work out a contract with the holdout superstar; the corporation president leads his company's contingent to negotiate a new strike issue; the foreman argues a grievance problem to its conclusion with the shop steward. As Leonard Sayles puts it, negotiations are a "way of life" for the sophisticated manager.

These negotiations are duties of the manager's job; perhaps routine, they are not to be shirked. They are an integral part of his job, for only he has the authority to commit organizational resources in "real time," and only he has the nerve center information that important negotiations require.

The Integrated Job

It should be clear by now that the ten roles I have been describing are not easily separable. In the terminology of the psychologist, they form a gestalt, an integrated whole. No role can be pulled out of the framework and the job be left intact. For example, the manager without liaison contacts lacks external information. As a result, he can neither disseminate the information his employees need nor make decisions that adequately reflect external conditions. (In fact, this is a problem for the new person in a managerial position, since he cannot make effective decisions until he has built up his network of contacts.)

Here lies a clue to the problems of team management.[11] Two or three people cannot share a single managerial position unless they can act as one entity. This means that they cannot divide up the ten roles unless they can very carefully reintegrate them. The real difficulty lies with the informational roles. Unless there can be full sharing of managerial information—and, as I pointed out earlier, it is primarily verbal—team management breaks down. a single managerial job cannot be arbitrarily split, for example, into internal and external roles, for information from both sources must be brought to bear on the same decisions.

To say that the ten roles form a gestalt is not to say that all managers give equal attention to each role. In fact, I found in my review of the various research studies that

. . . sales managers seem to spend relatively more of their time in their interpersonal roles, presumably a reflection of the extrovert nature of the marketing activity;

. . . production managers give relatively more attention to the decisional roles, presumably a reflection of their concern with efficient work flow;

. . . staff managers spend the most time in the informational roles, since they are experts who manage departments that advise other parts of the organization.

Nevertheless, in all cases the interpersonal, informational, and decisional roles remain inseparable.

TOWARD MORE EFFECTIVE MANAGEMENT

What are the messages for management in this description? I believe, first and foremost, that this description of managerial work should prove more important to managers than any prescription they might derive from it. That is to say, *the manager's effectiveness is significantly influenced by his insight into his own work.* His performance depends on how well he understands and responds to the pressures and dilemmas of the job. Thus managers who can be introspective about their work are likely to be effective at their jobs.

Let us take a look at three specific areas of concern. For the most part, the managerial logjams—the dilemma of delegation, the data base centralized in one brain, the problems of working with the management scientist—revolve around the verbal nature of the manager's information. There are great dangers in centralizing the organization's data bank in the minds of its managers. When they leave, they take their memory with them. And when subordinates are out of convenient verbal reach of the manager, they are at an informational disadvantage.

1

The manager is challenged to find systematic ways to share his privileged information. A regular debriefing session with key subordinates, a weekly memory dump on the dictating machine, the maintaining of a diary of important information for limited circulation, or other similar methods may ease the logjam of work considerably. Time spent disseminating this information will be more than regained when decisions must be made. Of course, some will raise the question of confidentiality. But managers would do well to weigh the risks of exposing privileged information against having subordinates who can make effective decisions.

If there is a single theme that runs through this article, it is that the pressures of his job drive the manager to be superficial in his actions—to overload himself with work, encourage interruption, respond quickly to every stimulus, seek the tangible and avoid the abstract, make decisions in small increments, and do everything abruptly.

2

Here again, the manager is challenged to deal consciously with the pressures of superficiality by giving serious attention to the issues that require it, by stepping back from his tangible bits of information in order to see a broad picture, and by making use of analytical inputs. Although effective managers have to be adept at responding quickly to numerous and varying problems, the danger in managerial work is that they will respond to every issue equally

(and that means abruptly) and that they will never work the tangible bits and pieces of informational input into a comprehensive picture of their world.

As I noted earlier, the manager uses these bits of information to build models of his world. But the manager can also avail himself of the models of the specialists. Economists describe the functioning of markets, operations researchers simulate financial flow processes, and behavioral scientists explain the needs and goals of people. The best of these models can be searched out and learned.

In dealing with complex issues, the senior manager has much to gain from a close relationship with the management scientists of his own organization. They have something important that he lacks—time to probe complex issues. An effective working relationship hinges on the resolution of what a colleague and I have called "the planning dilemma."[12] Managers have the information and the authority; analysts have the time and the technology. A successful working relationship between the two will be effected when the manager learns to share his information and the analyst learns to adapt to the manager's needs. For the analyst, adaptation means worrying less about the elegance of the method and more about its speed and flexibility.

It seems to me that analysts can help the top manager especially to schedule his time, feed in analytical information, monitor projects under his supervision, develop models to aid in making choices, design contingency plans for disturbances that can be anticipated, and conduct "quick-and-dirty" analysis for those that cannot. But there can be no cooperation if the analysts are out of the mainstream of the manager's information flow.

3

The manager is challenged to gain control of his own time by turning obligations to his advantage and by turning those things he wishes to do into obligations. The chief executives of my study initiated only 32% of their own contacts (and another 5% by mutual agreement). And yet to a considerable extent they seemed to control their time. There were two key factors that enabled them to do so.

First, the manager has to spend so much time discharging obligations that if he were to view them as just that, he would leave no mark on his organization. The unsuccessful manager blames failure on the obligations; the effective manager turns his obligations to his own advantage. A speech is a chance to lobby for a cause; a meeting is a chance to reorganize a weak department; a visit to an important customer is a chance to extract trade information.

Second, the manager frees some of his time to do those things that he—perhaps no one else—thinks important by turning them into obligations. Free time is made, not found, in the manager's job; it is forced into the schedule. Hoping to leave some time open for contemplation or general planning is tantamount to hoping that the pressures of the job will go away. The manager who wants to innovate initiates a project and obligates others to report back to him; the manager who needs certain environmental information establishes channels that will automatically keep him informed; the manager who has to tour facilities commits himself publicly.

No job is more vital to our society than that of the manager. It is the manager who determines whether our social institutions serve us well or whether they squander our talents and resources. It is time to strip away the folklore about managerial work, and time to study it realistically so that we can begin the difficult task of making significant improvements in its performance.

NOTES

1. All the data from my study can be found in Henry Mintzberg, *The Nature of Managerial Work* (New York: Harper & Row, 1973).

2. Robert H. Guest, "Of Time and the Foreman," *Personnel*, May 1956, p. 478.

3. Rosemary Stewart, *Managers and Their Jobs* (London: Macmillan, 1967); see also Sune Carlson, *Executive Behaviour* (Stockholm: Strombergs, 1951), the first of the diary studies.

4. Francis J. Aguilar, *Scanning the Business Environment* (New Yokr: Macmillan, 1967), p. 102.

5. Unpublished study by living Choran, reported in Mintzberg, *The Nature of Managerial Work*.

6. Robert T. Davis, *Performance and Development of Field Sales Managers* (Boston: Division of Research, Harvard Business School, 1957); George H. Copeman, *The Role of the Managing Director* (London: Business Publications, 1963).

7. Stewart, *Managers and Their Jobs*; Tom Burns, "The Directions of Activity and Communication in a Departmental Executive Group," *Human Relations* 7, no. 1 (1954): 73.

8. Richard E. Neustadt, *Presidential Power* (New York: John Wiley, 1960), pp. 153-154; italics added.

9. For a more thorough, though rather different, discussion of this issue, see Kenneth R. Andrews, "Toward Professionalism in Business Management," HBR March-April 1969, p. 49.

10. George C. Homans, *The Human Group* (New York: Harcourt, Brace & World, 1950), based on the study by William F. Whyte entitled *Street Corner Society*, rev. ed. (Chicago: University of Chicago Press, 1955).

11. See Richard C. Hodgson, Daniel J. Levinson and Abraham Zaleznik, *The Executive Role Constellation* (Boston: Divison of Research, Harvard Business School, 1965), for a discussion of the sharing of roles.

12. James S. Hekimian and Henry Mintzberg, "The Planning Dilemma," *The Management Review*, May 1968, p. 4.

21 THE DOPPLEGANGER EFFECT
Warren Bennis

Warren Bennis has been a leading organizational researcher, prominent university administrator, and prolific author. He has written authoritatively about topics as diverse as the differences between managers and leaders and the psychopathology of work institutions. In the selection that follows, he points out that powerful leaders inevitably spawn clones among their lieutenants—the "doppleganger effect"—and that these "ghostly doubles" can cause devastating problems. Bennis sounds a warning that leaders must seek out information and opinions contrary to their own, a warning that, sadly, has been too often ignored since this article first appeared.

Why is it that most of the younger Watergate witnesses look and act alike? The answer is that they are spiritual or ghostly doubles—*doppelgangers*. This doppelganger phenomenon is by no means accidental, nor is it confined to the White House. If the Watergate cameras could zoom in on the headquarters of any huge bureaucracy—government, corporation, university, hospital—we would see it repeated more often than we should like to imagine. By and large, people at the top of massive organizations tend to select as key assistants people who resemble them.

In my graduate-student days, specializing in organizational theories and problems, I found that many such leaders tended to select key assistants who resembled them, not only in ideas and attitudes, but down to such characteristics as height, stature, dress—even the cigarettes they smoked.

Of course, this is perfectly human and understandable—up to a point. The huge size of such organizations and the enormous overload burdening every top leader make it impossible for him to verify all his own information, analyze all of his own problems, or always decide who should or should not have his ear or time. Since he must rely for much of this upon his key assistants, he would not feel comfortable in so close and vital a relationship with men who were not at least of kindred minds and of compatible enough personalities.

SCREENED PEOPLE

This means, of course, that the leader is likely to see only that highly selective information, or those carefully screened people, that his key assistants decide he should see. In a very crucial situation, he may discover only too late that he has acted on information that was inadequate or inaccurate, or that he has been shielded from "troublesome" visitors who had something to tell him he should have known, or protected from some problem that should have been his primary concern. The corollary danger is that doppelgangers anxious to be more royal than the king may take actions they feel sure he wants but keep from him lest they burden or, possibly, embarrass him.

People in power have to work very hard at getting people to tell them the truth. The right people will, and the right bosses will hear it.

The whole Vietnam mess that has almost wrecked the country flows from people not telling the truth, or failing to tell what they did know, or lacking the courage to act in situations they knew to be wrong. The deliberate faking of the 1969 and 1970 bombing of Cambodia is only the latest instance of official lying to emerge. Even George Ball, that prophet with most honor for his internal predictions of where the fatal chain of actions would

Warren Bennis, "The Doppleganger Effect." Published in *Newsweek* (September 17, 1973). Reprinted by permission of Warren Bennis.

lead, never let the public itself in on his dismay, and justified this later by saying mordantly, "After all, we're just hired hands of the President."

There is a fine point to Khrushchev's answer to one of the written, anonymous questions handed up to him at a New York press conference during his 1959 visit. The question: what was he, an important figure, doing during all those crimes of Stalin he had retroactively exposed and denounced? Khrushchev was livid with rage. "Who asked that question?" he demanded. "Let him stand up!" Nobody did. "That's what I was doing," said Khrushchev.

STEREOTYPES

The staff around a President develops stereotypes about people: "The boss wouldn't want to see him—he's the fellow who went to the wedding in tennis shoes." The President himself may say, "Jesus, did you see what So and So told the Post?" And down through assistant through secretary to people taking down phone calls, go the reverberations. So suddenly a very few people are implicitly skewing, selecting information that gives an inaccurate picture on which decisions may be based.

A President's assistant should give him complete loyalty. The problem is that if the subordinate is your person, and your person *only*, he has a personal stake in perpetuating himself in that role, and for that reason may, unconsciously, not tell you the whole truth. Thus, the vulnerability that comes from being totally dependent on one man.

President Nixon's present problems, it seems to me, stem in considerable part from the fact that his Orange County doppelgangers were in precisely that position of vulnerability. None had ever been elected to any office, so they had little or no concept of what was politically realistic and what was politically dangerous, perhaps even mortally so. Having no previous constituency, none had something to fall back upon, and all were completely dependent on the approval or disapproval of one man. As we have seen, this skewed not only the information they got and gave, but also their personal concepts of what was ethically, morally or legally permissible. Whatever responsibility the President may have for the mess he is now in, there is no question that his

own doppelgangers put him there. As a French saying has it, "It is worse than a crime; it is a blunder."

SUGGESTIONS

How could the President, or future Presidents, avoid such humiliation and entrapment by overeager spiritual and ghostly doubles? I would urge:

- As much as possible, he should put his key assistants on temporary duty, at most for two years, with the advance knowledge they would be so rotated. This would make them less likely to overreach to consolidate their own power positions. It would also make for less arrogance, greater humility, more openness to countervailing ideas and counsel.

- He should see that some, not all, of these men should have had at some time relationships with some important constituency. They could then know the limits of politics, and the limits of power. Obviously, neither Haldeman nor Ehrlichman had the faintest idea about either. Melvin Laird, a former congressman, has; so does ex-Governor Connally.

- Run, don't walk, from the doppelganger syndrome. If a President is, like Nixon, naturally reclusive, he should not surround himself with men who are even more so. He should seek to surround himself with the utmost diversity of view still capable of being orchestrated harmoniously. I don't mean that he should bring in revolutionaries or radicals, or even devil's advocates. He does need people who are different from each other in experience, attitudes, approaches and philosophies.

- He ought to read at least one newspaper. A man who relies for his news on a daily summary by doppelgangers may not discover the truth until long after the whole nation knows it. Far from assuming that the press is out to "get" him, he could do worse than heed a wise old editor's credo that the best maxim for a good reporter is, "Beware of finding what you're looking for."

A leader—of any sort of organization—who hears only what he wants to hear, and finds only what he wants to find, will find himself in trouble.

22 NUMBERS: MINORITIES AND MAJORITIES

ROSABETH MOSS KANTER

The following chapter from Rosabeth Moss Kanter's (1977) *Men and Women of the Corporation* is considered by many to be a landmark in theory dealing with majority/minority relations. Kanter explains how, in one organization, normal cognitive and communication processes created conditions that keep members of token groups in the minority.

These processes were not *intended* to do this. For example, there are few tokens in the organization to observe, so each one gets a larger share of the attention than does any nontoken. This increased attention means that tokens are very visible organization members. Kanter reasons that this greater visibility increases pressure to perform, and this pressure probably increases chances that tokens will perform poorly. Thus, even in the absence of intentional discrimination, the sheer numerical "disadvantage" of tokens creates conditions that tend to inhibit their success.

Whether the process Kanter describes is generally valid or not (and there is some debate about this), this chapter is important because it demonstrates a *systemic* approach to explaining intergroup relations: Feedback mechanisms that work against underrepresented groups can be unintended consequences of complex interdependencies between different parts of organizations. The chapter also suggests a central role for communication in discriminatory processes. When reading, think about how communication theory might be used to enhance Kanter's theory or resolve the problem discussed above.

"Indsco" is a pseudonym for the organization in which Kanter did her research.

The token woman stands in the Square of the Immaculate Exception blessing pigeons from a blue pedestal. . . . The token woman is placed like a scarecrow in the long haired corn: her muscles are wooden. Why does she ride into battle on a clothes horse?

Marge Piercy, Living in the Open

Up the ranks in Industrial Supply Corporation, one of the most consequential conditions of work for women was also among the simplest to identify: there were so few of them. On the professional and managerial levels, Industrial Supply Corporation was nearly a single-sex organization. Women held less than 10 percent of the exempt (salaried) jobs starting at the bottom grades—a 50 percent rise from a few years earlier—and there were no women at the level reporting to officers. When Indsco was asked to participate in a meeting on women in business by bringing their women executives to a civic luncheon, the corporate personnel committee had no difficulty selecting them. There were only five sufficiently senior women in the organization.

The numerical distributions of men and women at the upper reaches created a strikingly different interaction context for women than for men. At local and regional meetings, training programs, task forces, casual out-of-the office lunches with colleagues, and career review or planning sessions with managers, the men were overwhelmingly likely to find themselves with a predominance of people of their own type—other men. For men in units with no exempt women, there would be, at most, occasional events in which a handful of women would be present alongside many men. Quite apart from the content of particular jobs and their location in the hierarchy, the culture of corporate administration and the experiences of men in it were influenced by this fact of numerical dominance, by the fact that men were the *many*.

Women, on the other hand, often found themselves alone among male peers. The twenty women in a three hundred-person sales force were scattered over fourteen offices. Their peers, managers, and customers were nearly all men. Never more than two women at a time were found in twelve-person personnel training groups. There was a cluster of professional women on the floor at corporate headquarters housing employee administration and training, but all except three were part of different groups where they worked most closely with men.

The life of women in the corporation was influenced by the proportions in which they found themselves. Those women who were few in number among male peers and often had "only woman" status became tokens: symbols of how-women-can-do, stand-ins for all women. Sometimes they had the advantages of those who are "different" and thus were highly visible in a system where success is tied to becoming known. Sometimes they faced the loneliness of the outsider, of the stranger who intrudes upon an alien culture and may become self-estranged in the process of assimilation. In any case, their turnover and "failure rate" were known to be much higher than those of men in entry and early grade positions; in the sales function, women's turnover was twice that of men. What happened around Indsco women resembled other reports of the experiences of women in politics, law, medicine, or management who have been the few among many men.

At the same time, they also echoed the experiences of people of any kind who are rare and scarce: the lone black among whites, the lone man among women, the few foreigners among natives. Any situation where proportions of significant types of people are highly skewed can produce similar themes

and processes. It was rarity and scarcity, rather than femaleness *per se*, that shaped the environment for women in the parts of Indsco mostly populated by men.

The situations of Industrial Supply Corporation men and women, then, point to the significance of numerical distributions for behavior in organizations: how many of one social type are found with how many of another.[1] As proportions begin to shift, so do social experiences.

THE MANY AND THE FEW: THE SIGNIFICANCE OF PROPORTIONS FOR SOCIAL LIFE

Georg Simmel's classic analysis of the significance of numbers for social life argued persuasively that numerical shifts transform social interaction, as in the differences between two-person and three-person situations or between small and large groups.[2] But Simmel, and then later investigations in this tradition, dealt almost exclusively with the impact of absolute numbers, with group size as a determinant of form and process. We have no vocabulary for dealing with the effects of *relative* numbers, of *proportional* representation: the difference for individuals and groups that stem from particular numerical distributions of categories of people.

Yet questions of how many and how few confound any statements about the organizational behavior of special kinds of people. For example, certain popular conclusions and research findings about male-female relations or role potentials may turn critically on the issue of proportions. One study of mock jury deliberations found that men played proactive, task-oriented leadership roles, whereas women in the same groups tended to take reactive, emotional and nurturant postures—supposed proof that traditional stereotypes reflect behavior realities. But, strikingly, *men far outnumbered women in all of the groups studied.* Perhaps it was the women's scarcity that pushed them into classical positions and the men's numerical superiority that encouraged them to assert task superiority. Similarly, the early kibbutzim, collective villages in Israel that theoretically espoused equality of the sexes but were unable to fully implement it, could push women into traditional service positions because there were *more than twice as many men as women*. Again, relative numbers interfered with a fair test of what men or women can "naturally" do, as it did in the case of the relatively few women in the upper levels of Indsco. Indeed, recently Marcia Guttentag has found sex ratios in the population in general to be so important that they predict a large number of behavioral phenomena, from the degree of power women and men feel to the ways they cope with the economic and sexual aspects of their lives.[3]

To understand the dramas of the many and the few in the organization requires a theory and a vocabulary. Four group types can be identified on the basis of different proportional representations of kinds of people, as Figure 1 shows. *Uniform* groups have only one kind of person, one significant social type. The group may develop its own differentiations, of course, but groups called uniform can be considered homogeneous with respect to salient external master statuses such as sex, race, or ethnicity. Uniform groups have a typological ratio of 100:0. *Skewed* groups are those in which there is a large preponderance of one type over another, up to a ratio of perhaps 85:15. The numerically dominant types also control the group and its culture in enough

ways to be labeled "dominants." The few of another type in a skewed group can appropriately be called "tokens," for, like the Indsco exempt women, they are often treated as representatives of their category, as symbols rather than individuals. If the absolute size of the skewed group is small, tokens can also be solos, the only one of their kind present; but even if there are two tokens in a skewed group, it is difficult for them to generate an alliance that can become powerful in the group, as we shall see later. Next, *tilted* groups begin to move toward less extreme distributions and less exaggerated effects. In this situation, with ratios of perhaps 65:35, dominants are just a "majority" and tokens become a "minority." Minority members have potential allies among each other, can form coalitions, and can affect the culture of the group. They begin to become individuals differentiated from each other as well as a type differentiated from the majority. Finally, at about 60:40 and down to 50:50, the group becomes *balanced*. Culture and interaction reflect this balance. Majority and minority turn into potential subgroups that may or may not generate actual type-based identifications. Outcomes for individuals in such a balanced peer group, regardless of type, will depend more on other structural and personal factors, including formation of subgroups or differentiated roles and abilities.

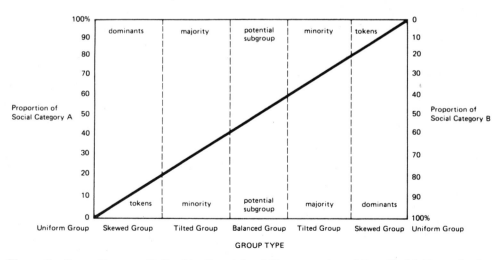

Figure 1 Group Types as Defined by Proportional Representation of Two Social Categories in the Membership

It is the characteristics of the second type, the skewed group, that underlay the behavior and treatment of professional and managerial women observed at Indsco. If the ratio of women to men in various parts of the organization begins to shift, as affirmative action and new hiring and promotion policies promised, forms of relationships and peer culture should also change. But as of the mid-1970s, the dynamics of tokenism predominated in Indsco's exempt ranks, and women and men were in the positions of token and dominant. Tokenism, like low opportunity and low power, set in motion self-perpetuating cycles that served to reinforce the low numbers of women and, in the absence of external intervention, to keep women in the position of token.

VIEWING THE FEW: WHY TOKENS FACE SPECIAL SITUATIONS

The proportional rarity of tokens is associated with three perceptual tendencies: visibility, contrast, and assimilation. These are all derived simply from the ways any set of objects are perceived. If one sees nine X's and one 0:

X X x x X X 0 X x X

the 0 will stand out. The 0 may also be overlooked, but if it is seen at all, it will get more notice than any X. Further, the X's may seem more alike than different because of their contrast with the 0. And it will be easier to assimilate the 0 to generalizations about all 0's than to do the same with the X's, which offer more examples and thus, perhaps, more variety and individuation. The same perceptual factors operate in social situations, and they generate special pressures for token women.

First, tokens get attention. One by one, they have higher visibility than dominants looked at alone; they capture a larger awareness share. A group member's awareness share, averaged over other individuals of the same social type, declines as the proportion of total membership occupied by the category increases, because each individual becomes less and less surprising, unique, or noteworthy. In

Gestalt psychology terms, those who get to be common more easily become ''ground'' rather than ''figure''; as the group moves from skewed to tilted, tokens turn into a less individually noticed minority. But for tokens, there is a ''law of increasing returns'': as individuals of their type represent a *smaller* numerical proportion of the overall group, they each potentially capture a *larger* share of the awareness given to that group.

Contrast—or polarization and exaggeration of differences—is the second perceptual tendency. In uniform groups, members and observers may never become self-conscious about the common culture and type, which remain taken for granted and implicit. But the presence of a person or two bearing a different set of social characteristics increases the self-consciousness of the numerically dominant population and the consciousness of observers about what makes the dominants a class. They become more aware both of their commonalities and their difference from the token, and to preserve their commonality, they try to keep the token slightly outside, to offer a boundary for the dominants. There is a tendency to exaggerate the extent of the differences between tokens and dominants, because as we see next, tokens are, by definition, too few in numbers to defeat any attempts at generalization. It is thus easier for the commonalities of dominants to be defined in contrast to the token than in tilted or balanced groups. One person can be perceptually isolated and seen as cut off from the core of the group more than many, who begin to represent too great a share of what is called the group.

Assimilation, the third perceptual tendency, involves the use of stereotypes, or familiar generalizations about a person's social type. The characteristics of a token tend to be distorted to fit the generalization. Tokens are more easily stereotyped than people found in greater proportion. If there were enough people of the token's type to let discrepant examples occur, it is eventually possible that the generalization would change to accommodate the accumulated cases. But in skewed groups, it is easier to retain the generalization and distort the perception of the token. It is also easier for tokens to find an instant identity by conforming to the preexisting stereotypes. So tokens are, ironically, both highly visible as people who are different and yet not permitted the individuality of their own unique, non-stereotypical characteristics.

All of these phenomena occurred around the proportionally scarce women in Indsco, but there was, of course, no way to compare these same women's behavior and treatment when they were not in the token position. However, a clever and suggestive laboratory experiment showed that the same person may be perceived differently depending on whether he or she is a token in a skewed group or one of many in a balanced group. (Because the categories used in the experiment were black-white rather than male-female, it also demonstrated the generality of such perceptual tendencies beyond token women.) Shelley Taylor and Susan Fiske played a tape of a group discussion to subjects while showing them pictures of the "group," and then asked them for their impressions of group members on a number of dimensions. The tape was the same for all subjects, but the purported composition of the group varied. The pictures illustrated either an otherwise all-white male group with one black man (the "token" condition) or a mixed black-white male group. In the token condition, disproportionate attention was paid to the token, his prominence in the group was overemphasized, and his attributes were exaggerated. Similarly, the token was perceived as playing out special roles in the group, often highly stereotypical ones. By contrast, in "integrated" groups, subjects recalled no more about blacks than whites, and their attributes were evaluated about the same.[4]

Visibility, contrast, and assimilation are each associated with particular forces and dynamics that, in turn, generate typical token responses. These dynamics are, again, similar regardless of the category from which the tokens come, although the specific kinds of people and their history of relationships with dominants provide cultural content for specific communications. Visibility tends to create *performance pressures* on the token. Contrast leads to heightening of *dominant culture boundaries*, including isolation of the token. And assimilation results in the token's *role encapsulation*.

The experiences of exempt women at Industry Supply Corporation took their shape from these processes.

PERFORMANCE PRESSURES: LIFE IN THE LIMELIGHT

Indsco's upper-level women, especially those in sales, were highly visible, much more so than their male peers. Even those who reported they felt ignored and overlooked were known in their immediate divisions and spotted when they did something unusual. But the ones who felt ignored also seemed to be those in jobs not enmeshed in the interpersonal structure of the company: for example, a woman in public relations who had only a clerical assistant reporting to her and whose job did not occupy a space in the competitive race to the top.

In the sales force, where peer culture and informal relations were most strongly entrenched, everyone knew about the women. They were the subject of conversation, questioning, gossip, and careful scrutiny. Their placements were known and observed through the division, whereas those of most men typically were not. Their names came up at meetings, and they would easily be used as examples. Travelers to locations with women in it would bring back news of the latest about the women, along with other gossip. In other functions, too, the women developed well-known names, and their characteristics would often be broadcast through the system in anticipation of their arrival in another office to do a piece of work. A woman swore in an elevator in an Atlanta hotel while going to have drinks with colleagues, and it was known all over Chicago a few days later that she was a "radical." And some women were even told by their managers that they were watched more closely than the men. Sometimes the manager was intending to be helpful, to let the woman know that he would be right there behind her. But the net effect was the same as all of the visibility phenomena. Tokens typically performed their jobs under public and symbolic conditions different from those of dominants.

The Two-Edged Sword of Publicity

The upper-level women became public creatures. It was difficult for them to do anything in training programs, on their jobs, or even at informal social affairs that would not attract public notice. This provided the advantage of an attention-getting edge at the same time that it made privacy and anonymity impossible. A saleswoman reported: "I've been at sales meetings where all the trainees were going up to the managers—'Hi, Mr. So-and-So'—trying to make that impression, wearing a strawberry tie, whatever, something that they could be remembered by. Whereas there were three of us [women] in a group of fifty, and all we had to do was walk in and everyone recognized us."

But their mistakes or their intimate relationships were known as readily as other information. Many felt their freedom of action was restricted, and they would have preferred to be less noticeable, as these typical comments indicated: "If it seems good to be noticed, wait until you make your first major mistake." "It's a burden for the manager who gets asked about a woman and has to answer behind-the-back stuff about her. It doesn't reach the woman unless he tells her. The manager gets it and has to deal with it." "I don't have as much freedom of behavior as men do; I can't be as independent."

On some occasions, tokens were deliberately thrust into the limelight and displayed as showpieces, paraded before the corporation's public but in ways that sometimes violated the women's sense of personal dignity. One of Indsco's most senior women, a staff manager finally given two assistants (and thus managerial responsibilities) after twenty-six years with the company, was among the five women celebrated at the civic lunch for outstanding women in business. A series of calls from high-level officers indicated that the chairman of the board of the corporation wanted her to attend a lunch at a large hotel that day, although she was given no information about the nature of the event. When she threatened not to go unless she was given more information, she was reminded that the invitation had come down from the chairman himself, and of course she would go. On the day of the luncheon, a corsage arrived and, later, a vice-president to escort her. So she went, and found she was there to represent the corporation's "prize women," symbolizing the strides made by women in business. The program for the affair listed the women executives from participating companies, except in the case of Indsco, where the male vice-presidential escorts were

listed instead. Pictures were taken for the employee newsletter and, a few days later, she received an inscribed paperweight as a memento. She told the story a few weeks after the event with visible embarrassment about being "taken on a date. It was more like a senior prom than a business event." And she expressed resentment at being singled out in such a fashion, "just for being a woman at Indsco, not for any real achievement." Similar sentiments were expressed by a woman personnel manager who wanted a pay increase as a sign of the company's appreciation, not her picture in a newspaper, which "gave the company brownie points but cost nothing."

Yet the senior woman had to go, the personnel manager had to have her picture taken, and they had to be gracious and grateful. The reaction of tokens to their notice was also noticed. Many of the tokens seemed to have developed a capacity often observed among marginal or subordinate peoples: to project a public persona that hid inner feelings. Although some junior management men at Indsco, including several fast trackers, were quite open about their lack of commitment to the company and dissatisfaction with aspects of its style, the women felt they could not afford to voice any negative sentiments. They played by a different set of rules, one that maintained the split between public persona and private self. One woman commented, "I know the company's a rumor factory. You must be careful how you conduct yourself and what you say to whom. I saw how one woman in the office was discussed endlessly, and I decided it would be better to keep my personal life and personal affairs separate." She refused to bring dates to office parties when she was single, and she did not tell anyone at work that she got married until several months later—this was an office where the involvement of wives was routine. Because the glare of publicity meant that no private information could be kept circumscribed or routine, tokens were forced into the position of keeping secrets and carefully contriving a public performance. They could not afford to stumble.

Symbolic Consequences

The women were visible as category members, because of their social type. This loaded all of their acts with extra symbolic consequences and gave them the burden of representing their category, not just themselves. Some women were told outright that their performances could affect the prospects of other women in the company. In the men's informal conversations, women were often measured by two yardsticks: how *as women* they carried out the sales or management role; and how *as managers* they lived up to images of womanhood. In short, every act tended to be evaluated beyond its meaning for the organization and taken as a sign of 'how women perform.'' This meant that there was a tendency for problematic situations to be blamed on the woman—on her category membership—rather than on the situation, a phenomenon noted in other reports of few women among many men in high-ranking corporate jobs. In one case of victim-blaming, a woman in sales went to her manager to discuss the handling of a customer who was behaving seductively. The manager jumped to the assumption that the woman had led him on. The result was an angry confrontation between woman and manager in which she thought he was incapable of seeing her apart from his stereotypes, and he said later he felt misunderstood.

Women were treated as symbols or representatives on those occasions when, regardless of their expertise or interest, they would be asked to provide the meeting with "the woman's point of view" or to explain to a manager why he was having certain problems with his women. They were often expected to be speaking for women, not just for themselves, and felt, even in my interviews, that they must preface personal statements with a disclaimer that they were speaking for themselves rather than for women generally. Such individuality was difficult to find when among dominants. But this was not always generated by dominants. Some women seized this chance to be a symbol as an opportunity to get included in particular gatherings or task forces, where they could come to represent all women at Indsco. "Even if you don't want *me* personally," they seemed to be saying to dominants, "you can want me as a symbol." Yet, if they did this, they would always be left with uncertainty about the grounds for their inclusion; they were failing to distinguish themselves as individuals.

Woman also added symbolic consequences to each other's affairs. Upper-level women were scru-

tinized by those on a lower level, who discussed the merits of things done by the higher-ranking women and considered them to have implications for their own careers. One woman manager who was passed over for a promotion in her department was the subject of considerable discussion by other women, who felt as she should have pushed to get the opening and complained when she did not.

The extension of consequences for those in token statuses may increase their self-consciousness about their self-presentation and about their decisions, and can change the nature of the decisions that get made. Decisions about what to wear and who to sit with at lunch are not casual. One executive woman knew that her clothing and leisure choices would have impact. She deliberately wore pants one day as she walked through an office—not her own—of female clerks supervised by a man who wanted them to wear dresses, and she noted that a few women cautiously began to wear pants occasionally. She decided to let it be known that she was leaving at four p.m. for ballet lessons once a week, arguing that the men at her level did the same thing to play golf, but also knowing that ballet was going to have a very different meaning from golf. Her act was a gesture performed with an audience in mind as much as an expression of preference. The meaning of "natural" in such situations is problematic, for in doing what they might find natural as private beings, tokens as public personae are also sending messages to the organization.

Business as well as personal decisions were handled by tokens with an awareness of their extended symbolic consequences. One woman manager was faced with the dilemma of deciding what to do about a woman assistant who wanted to go back to the secretarial ranks from which she had recently been promoted. The manager felt she jeopardized her own claims for mobility and the need to open the system to more women if she let her assistant return and had to admit that a woman who was given opportunity had failed. She spent much more time on the issue than a mere change of assistants would have warranted, going privately to a few men she trusted at the officer level to discuss the situation. She also kept the assistant on much longer than she felt was wise, but she thought herself trapped.

Sometimes the thought of the symbolic as well as

personal consequences of acts led token women to outright distortions. One was an active feminist in a training staff job who, according to her own reports, "separated what I say for the cause from what I want for myself." Her secret ambition was to leave the corporation within a year or two to increase her own professional skills and become an external consultant. But when discussing her aspirations with her own manager in career reviews or with peers on information occasions, she always smiled and said, "Chairman of the board of Industrial Supply Corporation." Every time a job at the grade level above her became vacant, she would inquire about it and appear to be very interested, making sure that there was some reason at the last minute she could not take it. "They are watching me," she explained, "to see if women are really motivated or if they will be content to stay in low-level jobs. They are expecting me to prove something one way or the other."

The Tokenism Eclipse

The token's visibility stemmed from characteristics—attributes of a master status—that threatened to blot out other aspects of a token's performance. Although the token captured attention, it was often for her discrepant characteristics, for the auxiliary traits that gave her token status. The token does not have to work hard to have her presence noticed, but she does have to work hard to have her achievements noticed. In the sales force, the women found that their technical abilities were likely to be eclipsed by their physical appearances, and thus, an additional performance pressure was created. The women had to put in extra effort to make their technical skills known, and said they worked twice as hard to prove their competence.

Both male peers and customers could tend to forget information women provided about their experiences and credentials while noticing and remembering such secondary attributes as style of dress. For example, there was this report from a salesman: "Some of our competition, like ourselves, have women sales people in the field. It's interesting that when you go in to see a purchasing agent, what he has to say about the woman sales person. It is

always what kind of a body she had or how good-looking she is or "Boy, are you in trouble on this account now." They don't tell you how good-looking your competitors are if they're males, but I've never heard about a woman's technical competence or what kind of a sales person she was—only what her body was like." And a saleswoman complained in an angry outburst, "There are times when I would rather say to a man, 'Hey, listen, you can have our bodies and look like a female and have the advantage of walking in the room and being noticed.' But the noticeability also has attached to it that surprise on the part of men that you can talk and talk intelligently. Recognition works against you as well as for you." And another: "Some of the attention is nice, but some of it is demeaning to a professional. When a man gets a job, they don't tell him he's better looking than the man who was here before—but they say that to me." The focus on appearance and other non-ability traits was an almost direct consequence of the presence of very few women.

Fear of Retaliation

The women were also aware of another performance pressure: not to make the dominants look bad. Tokenism sets up a dynamic that can make tokens afraid of being too outstanding in performance on group events and tasks. When a token does well enough to "show up" a dominant, it cannot be kept a secret, since all eyes are upon the token, and therefore, it is more difficult to avoid the public humiliation of a dominant. Thus, paradoxically, while the token women felt they had to do better than anyone else in order to be seen as competent and allowed to continue, they also felt, in some cases, that their successes would not be rewarded and should be kept to themselves. They needed to toe the fine line between doing just well enough and too well. One woman had trouble understanding this and complained of her treatment by managers. They had fired another woman for not being aggressive enough, she reported; yet she, who succeeded in doing all they asked and brought in the largest amount of new business during the past year, was criticized for being "too aggressive, too much of a hustler."

The fears had some grounding in reality. In a corporate bureaucracy like Indsco, where "peer acceptance" held part of the key to success in securing promotions and prized jobs, it was known how people were received by colleagues as well as by higher management. Indeed, men down the ranks resented the tendency for some top executives to make snap judgments about people after five minutes' worth of conversation and then try to influence their career reviews and create instant stars. So the emphasis on peer acceptance in performance evaluations, a concept known to junior managers, was one way people lower down the managerial hierarchy retained some control over the climbing process, ensured themselves a voice, and maintained a system they felt was equitable, in which people of whom they approved had a greater chance for success. Getting along well with peers was thus not just something that could make daily life in the company more pleasant; it was also fed into the formal review system.

At a meeting of ten middle managers, two women who differed in peer acceptance were contrasted. One was well liked by her peers even though she had an outstanding record because she did not flaunt her successes and modestly waited her turn to be promoted. She did not trade on her visibility. Her long previous experience in technical work served to certify her and elicit colleague respect, and her pleasant but plain appearance and quiet dress minimized disruptive sexual attributes. The other was seen very differently. The mention of her name as a "star performer" was accompanied by laughter and these comments: "She's infamous all over the country. Many dislike her who have never met her. Everyone's heard of her whether or not they know her, and they already have opinions. There seems to be no problem with direct peer acceptance from people who see her day-to-day, but the publicity she has received for her successes has created a negative climate around her." Some thought she was in need of a lesson for her cockiness and presumption. She was said to be aspiring too high, too soon, and refusing to play the promotion game by the same rules the men had to use: waiting for one's turn, the requisite years' experience and training. Some men at her level found her overrated and were concerned

that their opinions be heard before she was automatically pushed ahead. A common prediction was that she would fail in her next assignment and be cut down to size. The managers, in general, agreed that there was backlash if women seemed to advance too fast.

And a number of men were concerned that women would jump ahead of them. They made their resentments known. One unwittingly revealed a central principle for the success of tokens in competition with dominants: to always stay one step behind, never exceed or excel. "It's okay for women to have these jobs," he said, "as long as they don't go zooming by *me*."

One form peer retaliation against success took was to abandon a successful woman the first time she encountered problems. A dramatic instance involved a confrontation between a very dignified woman manager, the only woman in a management position in her unit, who supervised a large group of both male and female workers, and an aggressive but objectively low-performing woman subordinate, who had been hired by one of the other managers and was unofficially "sponsored" by him. The woman manager had given low ratings to the subordinate on her last performance appraisal, and another review was coming up; the manager had already indicated that the rating would still be low, despite strong protests of unfairness from the worker. One day after work, the manager walked through a public lounge area where several workers were standing around, and the subordinate began to hurl invectives at her, accusing her of being a "bitch, a stuck-up snob," and other unpleasant labels. The manager stood quietly, maintaining her dignity, then left the room, fearing physical violence. Her feelings ranged from hurt to embarrassment at the public character of the scene and the talk it would cause. The response over the next few days from her male peers ranged from silence to comments like, "The catharsis was good for X. She needed to get that off her chest. You know, you never *were* responsive to her." A male friend told the manager that he heard two young men who were passed over for the job she was eventually given commenting on the event: "So Miss High-and-Mighty finally got hers!" The humiliation and the thought that colleagues supported the workers rather than her was enough to make this otherwise-successful woman consider leaving the corporation.

Tokens' Responses to Performance Pressures

A manager posed the issue for scarce women this way: "Can they survive the organizational scrutiny?" The choices for those in the token position were either to over-achieve and carefully construct a public performance that minimized organizational and peer concerns, to try to turn the notoriety of publicity to advantage, or to find ways to become socially invisible. The first course means that the tokens involved are already outstanding and exceptional, able to perform well under close observation where others are ready to notice first and to attribute any problems to the characteristics that set them apart—but also able to develop skills in impressions management that permit them to retain control over the extra consequences loaded onto their acts. This choice involved creating a delicate balance between always doing well and not generating peer resentment. Such dexterity requires both job-related competence and political sensitivity that could take years to acquire. For this reason, young women just out of college had the greatest difficulty in entering male domains like the Indsco sales force and were responsible for much of the high turnover among women in sales. Women were successful, on the other hand, who were slightly older than their male peers, had strong technical backgrounds, and had already had previous experiences as token women among male peers. The success of such women was most likely to increase the prospects for hiring more women in the future; they worked for themselves and as symbols.

The second strategy, accepting notoriety and trading on it, seemed least likely to succeed in a corporate environment because of the power of peers. A few women at Indsco flaunted themselves in the public arena in which they operated and made a point out of demonstrating their "difference," as in refusing to go to certain programs, parading their high-level connections, or bypassing the routine authority structure. Such boldness was usually accompanied by top management sponsorship. But this

strategy was made risky by shifting power alliances at the top; the need to secure peer cooperation in certain jobs where negotiation, bargaining, and the power of others to generate advantage or disadvantage through their use of the rules were important; and the likelihood that some current peers would eventually reach the top. Furthermore, those women who sought publicity and were getting it in part for their rarity developed a stake in not sharing the spotlight. They enjoyed their only-women status, since it gave them an advantage, and they seemed less consciously aware than the other women of the attendant dangers, pressures, psychic costs, and disadvantages. In a few instances, they operated so as to keep other women out by excessive criticism of possible new-hires or by subtly undercutting a possible woman peer (who eventually left the company), something that, we shall see later, was also pushed for by the male dominants. Thus, this second strategy eventually kept the numbers of women down both because the token herself was in danger of not succeeding and because she might keep other women out. This second strategy, then, serves to reinforce the dynamics of tokenism by ensuring that, in the absence of external pressures like affirmative action, the group remains skewed.

The third choice was more often accepted by the older generation of corporate women, who predated the women's movement and had years ago accommodated to token status. It involved attempts to limit visibility, to become "socially invisible." This strategy characterizes women who try to minimize their sexual attributes so as to blend unnoticeably into the predominant male culture, perhaps by adopting "mannish dress," as in reports by other investigators. Or it can include avoidance of public events and occasions for performance—staying away from meetings, working at home rather than in the office, keeping silent at meetings. Several of the saleswomen deliberately took such a "low profile," unlike male peers who tended to seize every opportunity to make themselves noticed. They avoided conflict, risks, or controversial situations. They were relieved or happy to step into assistant or technical staff jobs such as personnel administration or advertising, where they could quietly play background roles that kept men in the visible forefront— or they at least did not object when the corporation put them into low-visibility jobs, since for many years the company had a stake in keeping its "unusual" people hidden.

Those women preferring or accepting social invisibility also made little attempt to make their achievements publicly known or to get credit for their own contributions to problem-solving or other organizational tasks, just like other women reported in the research literature who have let men assume visible leadership or take credit for accomplishments that the women really produced—the upper corporate equivalent of the achieving secretary. In one remarkable laboratory experiment, women with high needs for dominance, paired with a man in a situation where they had to choose a leader, exercised their dominance by *appointing him* the leader.[5] Women making this choice, then, did blend into the background and control their performance pressures, but at the cost of limited recognition of their competence. This choice, too, involved a psychic splitting, for rewards for such people often came with secret knowledge—knowing what they had contributed almost anonymously to an effort that made someone else look good. In general, this strategy, like the last, also reinforces the existence of tokenism and keeps the numbers of women down, because it leads the organization to conclude that women are not very effective: low risk-takers who cannot stand on their own.

The performance pressures on people in token positions generate a set of attitudes and behaviors that appear sex-linked, in the case of women, but can be understood better as situational responses, true of any person in a token role. Perhaps what has been called in the popular literature "fear of success in women," for example, is really the token woman's *fear of visibility*. The original research that identified the fear of success concept created a hypothetical situation in which a woman was at the top of her class in medical school—a token woman in a male peer group. Such a situation is the kind that exacts extra psychic costs and creates pressures for some women to make themselves and their achievements invisible—to deny success. Replication of this research using examples of settings in which women were not so clearly proportionately scarce produced very different results and failed to confirm the sex-linked nature of this construct. Seymour

Sarason also pointed out that minorities of any kind, trying to succeed in a culturally alien environment, may fear visibility because of retaliation costs and, for this reason, may try to play down any recognition of their presence, as did Jews at Yale for many years.[6] Fear of visibility, then, is one response to performance pressures in a token's situation. The token must often choose between trying to limit visibility—and being overlooked—or taking advantage of the publicity—and being labeled a "troublemaker."

BOUNDARY HEIGHTENING AND MEMBERSHIP COSTS: TOKENS IN DOMINANTS' GROUPS

Contrast, or exaggeration of the token's differences from dominants, sets a second set of dynamics in motion. The presence of a token or two makes dominants more aware of what they have in common at the same time that it threatens that commonality. Indeed, it is often at those moments when a collectivity is threatened with change that its culture and bonds become exposed to itself; only when an obvious "outsider" appears do group members suddenly realize aspects of their common bond as insiders. The "threat" a token poses is twofold. First, the token represents the danger of challenge to the dominants' premises, either through explicit confrontation by the token or by a disaffected dominant who, through increased awareness, sees the culture for what it is and sees the possibility of alternatives. Second, the self-consciousness created by the token's presence is uncomfortable for people who prefer to operate in casual, superficial, and easygoing ways, without much psychological self-awareness and without the strain of reviewing habitual modes of action—a characteristic stance in the corporate environment.

Furthermore, as Everett Hughes pointed out, part of the hostility peer groups show to new kinds of people stems from uncertainty about their behavior when non-structured, non-routine events occur. Tokens cannot be assumed to share the same unspoken understandings that the rest of the members share, because of their common membership in a social category, one basis for closing ranks against those who are different. For smooth interaction, groups require both discretion (the ability to put statements in their proper perspective) and a shared vocabulary of attitudes (the ability to take feelings and sentiments for granted) so that they can avoid the time-consuming process of translation. At best, then, members of the dominant category are likely to be uncomfortable and uncertain in the presence of a member of a different category. Other analysts have also shown that people with "incongruent statuses," like women in male jobs, strain group interaction by generating ambiguity and lack of social certitude.[7] It is not only the first of a kind that arouses discomfort. People who are usually not found in that setting and come from a category with a history of special forms of interaction with the numerical dominants, as rare women among men, are also potentially disruptive of peer interaction.

The token's contrast effect, then, can lead dominants to exaggerate both their commonality and the token's "difference." They move to heighten boundaries of which, previously, they might even have been aware. They erect new boundaries that at some times exclude the token or at others let her in only if she proves her loyalty.

Exaggeration of Dominants' Culture

Indco men asserted group solidarity and reaffirmed shared in-group understandings in the presence of token women, first, by emphasizing and exaggerating those cultural elements they shared in contrast to the token. The token became both occasion and audience for the highlighting and dramatizing of those themes that differentiated her as the outsider. Ironically, tokens, unlike people of their type represented in greater proportion, are thus instruments for under*lining* rather than under*mining* majority culture. At Indsco, this phenomenon was most clearly in operation on occasions that brought together people from many parts of the organization who did not necessarily know each other well, as in training programs and at dinners and cocktail parties during meetings. Here the camaraderie of men, as in other work and social settings,[8] was based in part on tales of sexual adventures, ability with respect to "hunting" and capturing women, and off-color jokes.

Other themes involved work prowess and sports, especially golf and fishing. The capacity for and enjoyment of drinking provided the context for displays of these themes. They were dramatized and acted out more fervently in the presence of token women than when only men were present.[9] When the men were alone, they introduced these themes in much milder form and were just as likely to share company gossip or talk of domestic matters such as a house being built. This was also in contrast to more equally mixed male-female groups in which there were a sufficient number of women to influence and change group culture and introduce a new hybrid of conversational themes based on shared male-female concerns.[10]

Around token women, then, men sometimes exaggerated displays of aggression and potency: instances of sexual innuendos, aggressive sexual teasing, and prowess-oriented "war stories." When a woman or two were present, the men's behavior involved "showing off," telling stores in which "masculine prowess" accounted for personal, sexual, or business success. They highlighted what they could do, as men, in contrast to the women. In a set of training situations for relatively junior salespeople, these themes were even acted out overtly in role plays in which participants were asked to prepare and perform demonstrations of sales situations. In every case involving a woman, the men played the primary, effective roles, and the women were objects of sexual attention. Sexual innuendos were heightened and more obvious and exaggerated than in all-male role plays, as in these two examples:

1. Two men and a woman simulated a call on a buyer; the woman was introduced as the president of the company, but the sales manager and his assistant did all the talking. The company was in the business of selling robots. The sales manager brought in a male "robot" to demonstrate the product. The sales manager leered at him, saying "Want a little company?" He then revealed that the woman introduced as the president was actually one of the female robots.

2. The two-man, one woman team was selling wigs; the woman was the wig stylist. The buyer on whom they were calling adopted an exaggerated homosexual caricature, which broadened

considerably during the "sales call." Toward the end of the role play, one of the men, trying to wrap up the sale, said, "We have other special services along with wigs. Other women who work with our stylist will come to your store to work for you." The buyer's response made it clear that he would be interested in those women sexually (though he was simulating homosexuality). Said the seller, "They'll be on your payroll; you can use them any way you want." Said the buyer, leering, "*Any* way I want?" The seller answered, "We might offer other services like a massage along with the wig." Said the buyer, "That sounds interesting. Can I have one right now?"

After these role plays, the group atmosphere seemed quite tense, and the women especially appeared highly uncomfortable.

The women themselves reported other examples of "testing" to see how they would respond to the "male" culture. They said that many sexual innuendos or displays of locker-room humor were put on for their benefit, especially by the younger men. (The older men tended to parade their business successes.) One woman was a team leader at a workshop (and the only woman), when her team decided to use as its slogan, "The [obscenity] of the week," looking at her for a reaction. By raising the issue and forcing the woman to choose not to participate, the men in the group created an occasion for uniting against the outsider and asserting dominant group solidarity. Such events, it must be pointed out, were relatively rare and occurred only at those informal occasions outside of the business routine in which people were unwinding, letting themselves go, or, as in the training role plays, deliberately creating unreal situations. Most behavior at Indsco was more businesslike in tone. But the fact that such interaction ever occurred, even infrequently, around women served to isolate them and make them uncomfortable at those very moments when, ironically, people were supposed to be relaxing and having fun.

A sales meeting at Indsco provided an interesting example of how the dominant culture could simultaneously acknowledge the presence of tokens and retain its own themes and flavor. It was traditional for salesmen to tell traveling salesman/farmer's

daughter jokes at informal gatherings. On this occasion, four years after women first entered the sales force, a raunchy traveling sales*woman*/farmer's *son* joke was told, a story currently going around the company. The form was the same, but the content reflected the presence of women.

Tokens' functions as audience for dominant cultural expressions also played a part in the next set of processes.

Interruptions as Reminders of "Difference"

On more formal occasions, as in meetings, members of the numerically dominant category underscored and reinforced differences between tokens and dominants, ensuring that tokens recognized their outsider status, by making the token the occasion for "interruptions" in the flow of group events. Dominants prefaced acts with apologies or questions about appropriateness directed at the token; they then invariably went ahead with the act, having placed the token in the position of interrupter or interloper, of someone who took up the group's time. This happened often in the presence of the saleswomen. Men's questions or apologies represented a way of asking whether the old or expected cultural rules were still operative—the words and expressions permitted, the pleasures and forms of release indulged in. (Can we still swear? Toss a football? Use technical jargon? Go drinking? Tell "in" jokes?)[11] Sometimes the questions seemed motivated by a sincere desire to put the women at ease and treat them appropriately, but the net effect was the same regardless of dominants' intentions. By posing these questions overtly, dominants made the culture clear to tokens, stated the terms under which tokens enter the relationship, and reminded them that they were special people. It is a dilemma of all cross-cultural interaction that the very act of attempting to learn what to do in the presence of the different kind of person so as to integrate him can reinforce differentiation.

The answers about conduct almost invariably affirmed the understandings of the dominants. The power of sheer numbers means that an individual rarely feels comfortable preventing a larger number of peers from engaging in an activity they consider normal. Most women did not want to make a fuss, especially about issues they considered trivial and irrelevant to their job status, like saying "god-damn" or how to open doors. Their interest in not being signaled out for special treatment made them quickly agree that things should proceed as they would if women were not present, and to feel embarrassment about stopping the flow of conversation. None wanted to be a "wet blanket"! As one said, "They make obscene suggestions for slogans when kidding around, looking to me for a reaction. Then they jump on me for not liking it."

Secondly, the tokens have been put on notice that interaction will not be "natural," that dominants will be "holding back," unless they agree to acknowledge and permit (and even encourage) majority cultural expressions in their presence. (It is important that this be stated, of course, for one never knows that another is holding back unless the other lets a piece of the suppressed material slip out.) At the same time, tokens have also been given the implicit message that majority members do *not* expect those forms of expression to be "natural" to the tokens' home culture; otherwise, majority members would not need to raise the question. (This is a function of what Judith Long Laws called the "double deviance" of tokens: deviant first because they are women in a man's world and second because they inappropriately aspire to the privileges of the dominants.)[12] Thus, the saleswomen were often in the odd position of reassuring peers and customers that they could go ahead and do something in the women's presence, like swearing, that the women themselves would not be permitted to do. They listened to dirty jokes, for example, but reported that they would not dare tell one themselves. In fact, whether or not to go drinking or tell jokes was a major question for women: "You can't tell dirty jokes. Clean jokes would go over like a lead balloon. So I sit there like a dummy and don't tell jokes."

Via difference-reminding interruptions, then, dominants both affirm their own shared understandings and draw the cultural boundary between themselves and tokens. The tokens learned that they caused interruptions in "normal" communication, and that their appropriate position was more like that of audience than that of full participant. But the

women also found the audience position frustrating or wearying, as these statements indicated: "I felt like one of the guys for a while. Then I got tired of it. They had crude mouths and were very immature. I began to dread the next week because I was tired of their company. Finally, when we were all out drinking, I admitted to myself, this is not me; I don't want to play their game." And: "I was at a dinner where the men were telling dirty jokes. It was fun for a while; then it got to me. I moved and tried to have a real conversation with a guy at the other end of the table. The dinner started out as a comrade thing, but it loses its flavor, especially if you're the only woman. I didn't want them to stop on my account, but I wish I had had an alternative conversation."

Overt Inhibition: Informal Isolation

In some cases, dominants did not wish to have tokens around all the time; they had secrets to preserve or simply did not know how far they could trust the women, especially those who didn't seem to play by all the rules. They thus moved the locus of some activities and expressions from public settings to which tokens had access to more private settings from which they could be excluded. When information potentially embarrassing or damaging to dominants is being exchanged, an outsider-audience is not desirable, because dominants do not know how far they can trust the tokens. As Hughes has pointed out, colleagues who rely on unspoken understandings may feel uncomfortable in the presence of "odd kinds of fellows" who cannot be trusted to interpret information in just the same way or to engage in the same relationships of trust and reciprocity.[13] There was a sense that it was not possible to level with a woman or be real with her, as one could with other men.

The result was sometimes "quarantine"—keeping tokens away from some occasions. Informal pre-meeting meetings were sometimes held. Some topics of discussion seemed rarely raised by men in the presence of many of their women peers, even though they discussed them among themselves: admissions of low commitment to the company or concerns about job performance, ways of getting around formal rules, political plotting for mutual advantage, strategies for impressing certain corporate executives. Many of the women did not tend to be included in the networks by which informal socialization occurred and politics behind the formal system were exposed, as researchers have found in other settings. One major project found that people with incongruent statuses, like the Indsco exempt women, were likely to become isolates in peer groups and to have less frequent interaction with the group than other members, outside of formally structured occasions.[14] Toward the upper levels of the corporation, any tendency for peer groups to quarantine women was reinforced by men-only social establishments; a senior personnel administrator committed to placing more women in top executive jobs was concerned about whether they could overcome the limitation on their business effectiveness placed by exclusion from informal exchanges at male clubs.

In a few cases, overt inhibition worked directly against women in their jobs. They missed out on important informal training by peers.[15] There were instances in which women trainees did not get direct criticism in time to improve their performance and did not know they were the subjects of criticism in the company until told to find jobs in other divisions. They were not part of the buddy network that uncovered such information quickly, and their managers were reluctant to criticize a women out of uncertainty about how she would receive the information. (One man put quite simply how he felt about giving negative feedback to a woman: "I'm chicken.") Here feelings that it was impossible to level with a different kind of person stood in the way.

Loyalty Tests

At the same time that tokens may be kept on the periphery of colleague interaction, they may also be expected to demonstrate loyalty to their dominant peers. Failure to do so could result in further isolation; signs of loyalty, on the other hand, permitted the token to come closer to being included in more of the dominants' activities. Through loyalty tests, the group sought reassurance that the tokens would not turn against the dominants or use any of the information gained through their viewing of the dominants' world to do harm to the group. In the normal course of peer interactions, people learn all sorts of things about each other that could be turned against the other. Indeed, many colleague relationships are often solidified by the reciprocal knowledge of potentially damaging bits of information and the understanding that they both have an interest in preserving confidentiality. Tokens, however, pose a different problem and raise uncertainties, for their membership in a different social category could produce loyalties outside the peer cadre.

This was a quite rational concern on occasion. With government pressures and public interest mounting, Indsco women were often asked to speak to classes or women's groups or to testify before investigating committees. One woman was called in by her manager before her testimony at hearings on discrimination against women in business; he wanted to hear her testimony in advance and have censorship rights. She refused, but then made only very general and bland statements at the hearing anyway.

Peers seek reassurance about embarrassing as well as damaging disclosures. There is always the possibility that tokens will find some of what the dominants naturally do silly or ridiculous and will insult them where they feel vulnerable. Dominants also want to know that tokens will not use their inside information to make the dominants look bad or turn them into figures of fun to members of the token's category outside with whom they must interact. The joking remarks men made when seeing women colleagues occasionally eating with the secretaries (e.g., "What do you 'girls' find so interesting to talk about?") revealed some of their concerns.

Assurance could be gained by asking tokens to join with or identify with the dominants against those who represented competing loyalties; in short, dominants pressured tokens to turn against members of their own category, just as occurred in other situations where women were dominants and men tokens.[16] If tokens colluded, they made themselves psychological hostages to the majority group. For token women, the price of being "one of the boys" was a willingness to occasionally turn against "the girls."

There were three ways token women at Indsco could demonstrate loyalty and qualify for a closer relationship with dominants. First, they could let slide (or even participate in) statements prejudicial to other members of their category. They could allow themselves to be viewed as "exceptions" to the "general rule" that others of their category have a variety of undesirable or unsuitable characteristics; Hughes recognized this as one of the "deals" token blacks might make for membership in white groups.[17] Women who did well were sometimes told they were "exceptions" and exceptional, not like a "typical woman." It is an irony of the token situation that women could be treated as both representatives of their type and exceptions to it, sometimes by the same people.

At meetings and training sessions, women were occasionally the subjects of ridicule or joking remarks about their incompetence. Some of the women who were insulted by such innuendos found it easier to appear to agree than to start an argument. A few accepted the dominants' view fully. One of the first saleswomen denied in interviews having any special problems because she was a woman, calling herself "skilled at coping with a man's world," and said the company was right not to hire more women. Women, she said, were unreliable and likely to quit; furthermore, young women might marry men who would not allow them to work. (She herself quit a few years later.) In this case, a token woman was taking over "gatekeeping" functions for dominants, letting them appear free of prejudice while a woman acted to exclude other women.[18]

Tokens could also demonstrate loyalty by allowing themselves and their category to provide a source of humor for the group. Laughing with others, as Rose Coser indicated, is a sign of a common definition of the situation; to allow oneself or one's kind to be the object of laughter signals a further willingness to accept the others' culture on their terms.[19] Just as Hughes found that the initiation of blacks into white groups might involve accepting the role of comic inferior,[20] Indsco women faced constant pressures to allow jokes at the expense of women, to accept "kidding" from the men around them. When a woman objected, the men denied any hostility or unfriendly intention, instead accusing the women, by inference, of "lacking a sense of humor." In order to cope, one woman reported, she "learned to laugh when they try to insult you with jokes, to let it roll off your back." Tokens could

thus find themselves colluding with dominants through shared laughter.

Thirdly, tokens could demonstrate their gratitude for being included by not criticizing their situation or pressing for any more advantage. One major taboo area involved complaints about the job or requests for promotion. The women were supposed to be grateful for getting as far as they had (when other women clearly had *not*) and thus expected to bury dissatisfaction or aspirations.

Responses of Tokens to Boundary Heightening

The dilemma posed here for tokens was how to reconcile their awareness of difference generated by information interaction with dominants with the need, in order to belong, to suppress dominants' concerns about the difference. As with performance pressures, peer group interaction around the tokens increased the effort required for a satisfactory public appearance, sometimes accompanied by distortions of private inclinations.

Of course, not all men participated in the dynamics noted. And some tokens managed to adapt very well. They used the same kind of language and expressed the same kinds of interests as many of the men. One woman loved fishing, she said, so when she came on as a manger and her office was concerned that that would end fishing trips, she could show them they had nothing to fear. Another had a boat on which she could take customers (along with her husband and their wives). A professional woman joined the men on "woman hunts," taking part in conversations in which the pro's and con's of particular targets were discussed. There were women known to be able to "drink the men under the table." It was never clear what the psychic toll of such accommodation was—whether, for example, such people would have made different choices in a balanced context—for they were also unlikely to talk about having any problems at all in their situation; they assumed they were full members.

Numerical skewing and polarized perceptions left tokens with little choice about accepting the culture of dominants. There were too few other people of the token's kind to generate a "counterculture" or to develop a shared intergroup culture. Tokens had to approach the group as single individuals. They thus had two general response possibilities. They could accept isolation, remaining only an audience for certain expressive acts of dominants. This strategy sometimes resulted in friendly but distant peer relations, with the risk of exclusion from occasions on which informal socialization and political activity took place. Or they could try to become insiders, proving their loyalty by defining themselves as exceptions and turning against their own social category.

The occurrence of the second response on the part of tokens suggests a reexamination of the popularized "women-prejudiced-against-women" hypothesis, also called the "Queen Bee syndrome," for possible structural (numerical) rather than sexual origins. Not only has this hypothesis not been confirmed in a variety of settings,[21] but the analysis offered here of the social psychological pressures on tokens to side with the majority provides a more compelling explanation for the kinds of situations most likely to produce this effect. To turn against others of one's kind (and thus risk latent self-hatred) can be a psychic cost of membership in a group dominated by another culture.

ROLE ENCAPSULATION

Tokens can never really be seen as they are, and they are always fighting stereotypes, because of a third tendency. The characteristics of tokens as individuals are often distorted to fit preexisting generalizations about their category as a group—what I call "assimilation." Such stereotypical assumptions about what tokens "must" be like, such mistaken attributions and biased judgments, tend to force tokens into playing limited and caricatured roles. This constrains the tokens but is useful for dominant group members. Whatever ambiguity there might be around a strange person is reduced by providing a stereotyped and thus familiar place for tokens in the group, allowing dominants to make use of already-learned expectations and modes of action, like the traditional ways men expect to treat women. Familiar roles and assumptions, further, can serve to keep tokens in a bounded place and out of the mainstream of interaction where the uncertainties they arouse

might be more difficult to handle. In short, tokens become encapsulated in limited roles that give them the security of a "place" but constrain their areas of permissible or rewarded action.

Status Leveling

Tokens were often initially misperceived as a result of their numerical rarity. That is, an unusual woman would be treated as though she resembled women on the average—a function of what has been called "statistical discrimination" rather than outright prejudice.[22] Since people make judgments about the role being played by others on the basis or probabilistic reasoning about what a particular kind of person will be doing in a particular situation, such misperceptions are the result of statistical mistakes. Thus, women exempts at Indsco, like other tokens, encountered many instances of "mistaken identitiy"—first impressions that they were occupying a *usual female* position rather than their *unusual* (for a woman) job. In the office, they were often taken for secretaries; on sales trips on the road, especially when they traveled with a male colleague, they were often taken for wives or mistresses; with customers, they were first assumed to be temporarily substituting for a man who was the "real" salesperson; with a male peer at meetings, they were seen as the assistant; when entertaining customers, they were assumed to be the wife or date. (One woman sales trainee accompanied a senior salesman to call on a customer, whose initial reaction was laughter: "What won't you guys think up next? A woman!" She had the last laugh, however, for that company's chief engineer happened to be a woman with whom she had instant rapport.)

Mistaken first impressions can be corrected, although they give tokens an extra burden of spending more time untangling awkward exchanges and establishing accurate and appropriate role relations. But meanwhile, status leveling occurs. Status leveling involves making adjustments in perception of a token's professional role to fit with the expected position of the token's category—that is, bringing situational status in line with what has been called "master status," the token's social type. Even when others knew that the women were not secretaries, for example, there was still a tendency to treat them like secretaries or to make secretary-like demands on them. In one blatant case, one woman was a sales trainee along with three men, all four of whom were to be given positions as summer replacements. The men were all assigned to replace salesmen; the woman was asked to replace a secretary—and only after a long and heated discussion with the manager was she given a more professional assignment. Similarly, when having professional contacts with customers and managers, the women felt themselves to be treated in more wife-like or date-like ways than a man would treat another man, even though the occasion was clearly professional. A professional woman at Indsco asked for a promotion and talked about looking for a better job; her manager's first assumption was that she did not feel "loved" and it was his fault for failing to give love to a woman. (She wanted challenge and more money.) In all these instances, it was easier for others to fit the token woman to their preexisting generalizations about women than to change the category; numerical rarity provided too few examples to contradict the generalization. (Instances of status leveling have also been noted around other kinds of tokens, such as male nurses;[23] in the case of tokens whose master status is higher than their situational status, leveling can work to their advantage, as when male nurses are called "Dr.")

The Woman's Slot

There was also a tendency to encapsulate women and to maintain generalizations by defining special roles for women, even on the managerial and professional levels, that put them slightly apart as colleagues. Again, it was easy to do this with a small number and would have been much harder with many more women spilling over the bounds of such slots. A woman could ensure her membership by accepting a special place but then find herself confined by it. Once women began to occupy certain jobs, those jobs sometimes gradually came to be defined as "women's slots." One personnel woman at Indsco pointed this out. In her last career review, she had asked to be moved, feeling that, in another six months, she would have done and learned all she could in her present position and was ready to be upgraded. "They [the managers] told me to be pa-

tient; if I waited a year or two longer, they had just the right job for me, three grades up. I knew what they had in mind. Linda Martin [a senior woman] would be retiring by then from a benefits administration job, and they wanted to give it to me because it was considered a place to put a woman. But it had no *real* responsibilities despite its status; it was all routine work."

Affirmative action and equal employment opportunity jobs were also seen as "women's jobs." Many women, who would otherwise be interested in the growth and challenge they offered, said that they would not touch such a position: "The label makes it a dead end. It's a way of putting us out to pasture." There was no way to test the reality of such fears, given the short time the jobs had been in existence, but it could be observed that women who worked on women's personnel or training issues were finding it hard to move out into other areas. These women also found it hard to interest some other, secretly sympathetic managerial women in active advocacy of upward mobility for women because of the latter's own fears of getting too identified with a single issue. (Others, though, seized on it as a way to express their values or to get visibility.)

Committees, task forces, and other ad hoc events had a tendency, too, to develop a woman's slot for those women selected to participate. Sometimes it would take the form of giving the women areas of responsibility that were stereotypically "female" concerns, or, as mentioned earlier, giving them the role in the group of "expert on women." This posed major dilemmas for the women seriously interested in being women's advocates but who were also aware of how the role encapsulation process could undercut their effectiveness and limit their organizational mobility. They had to carefully balance the time spent as woman-symbols with other activities and with attention to the technical/professional aspects of their jobs.

Stereotyped Informal Roles

Dominants can incorporate tokens and still preserve their generalizations by inducting tokens into stereotypical roles that preserve familiar forms of interaction between the kinds of people represented by the token and the dominants. In the case of token women in colleague groups at Indsco, four informal role traps were observed, all of which encapsulated the tokens in a category the men could respond to and understand. Each was formed around one behavioral tendency of the token, building this into an image of the token's place in the group and forcing her to continue to live up to the image; each defined for dominants a single response to the token's sexuality. Two of the roles are classics in Freudian theory: the "mother" and the "seductress." Freud wrote of the need for men to handle women's sexuality by envisioning them either as "madonnas" or "whores"— as either asexual mothers or overly sexual, debased seductresses, perhaps as a function of Victorian family patterns, which encouraged separation of idealistic adoration toward the mother and animalistic eroticism.[24] The others, termed the "pet" and the "iron maiden," also have family counterparts in the kid sister and the virgin aunt.

Mother

A token woman sometimes found that she became a "mother" to men in the group. One by one, they brought her their private troubles, and she was expected to comfort them. The assumption that women are sympathetic, good listeners and easy to talk to about one's problems was common, even though, ironically, men also said it was hard to level with women over task-related issues. One saleswomen was constantly approached by her all-male peers to listen to their problems with their families. In a variety of residential training groups, token women were observed acting out other parts of the traditional nurturant-maternal role: doing laundry, sewing on buttons for men.

The mother role was comparatively safe. A mother is not necessarily vulnerable to sexual pursuit (for Freud it was the very idealization of the madonna that was in part responsible for men's ambivalence toward women), nor do men need to compete for her favors, since they are available to everyone. However, the typecasting of women as nurturers can have three negative consequences for the woman's task performance: (1) The mother is rewarded primarily for service and not for independent action. (2) The dominant, powerful aspects of the maternal image may be feared, and thus the mother is expected to keep her place as a non-

critical, accepting "good mother" or lose her rewards. Since the ability to differentiate and be critical is often an indicator of competence in work groups, the mother is prohibited from exhibiting this skill. (3) The mother becomes an emotional specialist. This provides her with a place in the life of the group and its members. Yet, at the same time one of the stereotypically "feminine" characteristics men in positions of authority in industry most often criticize in women is excess "emotionality." Although the mother herself might not ever cry or engage in emotional outbursts in the group, she remains identified with emotional matters. As long as she is in the scarce position of token, however, it is unlikely that nurturance, support, and expressivity will be valued or that a mother can demonstrate and be rewarded for critical, independent, task-oriented behaviors.

Seductress

The role of seductress or sexual object is fraught with more tension that the maternal role, for it introduces an element of sexual competition and jealousy. The mother can have many sons; it is more difficult for the sexually attractive to have many swains. Should the woman cast as sex object (that, is, seen as sexually desirable and potentially available—seductress is a perception, and the woman herself may not be consciously behaving seductively) share her attention widely, she risks the debasement of the whore. Yet, should she form a close alliance with any man in particular, she arouses resentment, particularly so because she represents a scarce resource; there are just not enough women to go around.

In several situations I observed, a high status male allied himself with the seductress and acted as her "protector," partly because of his promise of rescue from sex-charged overtures of the rest of the men as well as because of his high status *per se*. The powerful male (staff member, manager, sponsor, etc.) could easily become the "protector" of the still "virgin" seductress, gaining through masking his own sexual interest what the other men could not gain by declaring theirs. However, this removal of the seductress from the sexual marketplace contained its own problems. The other men could resent the high-status male for winning the prize and resent the woman for her ability to get an "in" with the high-status male that they could not obtain as men. Although the seductress was rewarded for her femaleness and insured attention from the group, then, she was also the source of considerable tension; and needless to say, her perceived sexuality blotted out all other characteristics.

Men could adopt the role of protector toward an attractive woman, regardless of her collusion, and by implication cast her as sex object, reminding her and the rest of the group of her sexual status. In the guise of "helping" her, self-designated protectors may actually put up further barriers to the solitary woman's full acceptance by inserting themselves, figuratively speaking, between the woman and the rest of the group. A male management trainer typically offered token women in management assessment groups extra help and sympathetic attention to the problems their male peers might cause, taking them out alone for drinks at the end of daily sessions. But this kind of "help" also preserved the sex object role.

Pet

The "pet" was adopted by the male group as a cute, amusing little thing and symbolically taken along on group events as mascot—a cheerleader for shows of prowess. Humor was often a characteristic of the pet. She was expected to admire the male displays but not to enter into them; she cheered from the sidelines. Shows of competence on her part were treated as special and complimented just because they were unexpected (and the compliments themselves can be seen as reminders of the expected rarity of such behavior). One woman reported that when she was alone in a group of men and spoke at length on an issue, comments to her by men after the meeting often referred to her speech-making ability rather than the content of what she said (e.g., "You talk so fluently"), whereas comments the men made to one another were almost invariably content- or issue-oriented. Competent acts that are taken for granted when performed by males were often unduly "fussed over" when performed by exempt women, considered precocious or precious—a kind of look-what-she-did-and-she's-only-a-woman attitude. Such attitudes on the part of men encouraged self-effacing, girlish responses on the part of solitary

women (who may be genuinely relieved to be included and petted) and prevented them from realizing or demonstrating their own power and competence.

Iron Maiden

The "iron maiden" is a contemporary variation of the stereotypical roles into which strong women are placed. Women who failed to fall into any of the first three roles and, in fact, resisted overtures that would trap them in a role (such as flirtation) might consequently be responded to as "tough" or dangerous. (One woman manager developed such a reputation in company branches throughout the country.) If a token insisted on full rights in the group, if she displayed competence in a forthright manner, or if she cut off sexual innuendos, she could be asked, "You're not one of those women's libbers, are you?" Regardless of the answer, she was henceforth regarded with suspicion, undue and exaggerated shows of politeness (by inserting references to women into conversations, by elaborate rituals of *not* opening doors), and with distance, for she was demanding treatment as an equal in a setting in which no person of her kind had previously been an equal. Women inducted into the "iron maiden" role were stereotyped as tougher than they are (hence the name) and trapped in a more militant stance than they might otherwise take. Whereas seductresses and pets, especially, incurred protective responses, iron maidens faced abandonment. They were left to flounder on their own and often could not find peers sympathetic to them when they had problems.

Responses of Tokens to Role Encapsulation

The dynamics of role entrapment tended to lead tokens to a variety of conservative and low-risk responses. The time and awkwardness involved in correcting mistaken impressions led some tokens to a preference for already-established relationships, for minimizing change and stranger-contact in the work situation. It was also often easier to accept stereotyped roles than to fight them, even if their acceptance meant limiting the tokens' range of expressions or demonstrations of task competence, because they offered a comfortable and certain position. The personal consequence for tokens, of course, was a measure of self-distortion. John Athanassiades, though not taking into account the effects of numerical representation, found that women in organizations tended to distort upward communication more than men, especially those with low risk-taking propensity, and argued that many observed work behaviors of women may be the result of such distortion and acceptance of organizational images. Submissiveness, frivolity, or other attributes may be feigned by people who feel they are prescribed by the dominant organizational culture.[25] This suggests that accurate conclusions about work attitudes and behavior cannot be reached by studying people in the token position, since there may always be an element of compensation or distortion involved.

The analysis also suggests another way in which tokenism can be self-perpetuating: acceptance of role encapsulation and attendant limitations on demonstration of competence may work to keep down the numbers of women in the upper ranks of the organization, thus continuing to put people in token positions. Role encapsulation confirms dominants' stereotypes and proves to them how right they were all along. On the other hand, some women try to stay away from the role traps by bending over backwards not to exhibit any characteristics that would reinforce stereotypes. This strategy, too, is an uneasy one, for it takes continual watchful effort, and it may involve unnatural self-distortion. Finally, token women must steer a course between protectiveness and abandonment. Either they allow other people to take over and fight their battles for them, staying out of the main action in stereotypical ways, or they stand much too alone. They may be unable by virtue of scarcity even to establish effective support systems of their own.

HOW MANY ARE ENOUGH? THE TWO-TOKEN SITUATION

The examination of numerical effects leads to the additional question of tipping points: How many of a category are enough to change a person's status from token to full group member? When does a group move from skewed to tipped to balanced?

What is the impact for a woman of the presence of another?

In the exempt ranks of Indsco, there were a number of instances of situations in which two rather than one woman were found among male peers, but still constituted less than 20 percent of the group. Despite Solomon Asch's classic laboratory finding that one potential ally can be enough to reduce the power of the majority of secure conformity,[26] in the two-token situation in organizations, dominants several times behaved in ways that defeated an alliance between the two women. This was done through setting up invidious comparisons. One woman was characteristically set up as superior, and the other as inferior—exaggerating traits in both cases. One was identified as the success, the other as the failure. The one given the success label felt relieved to be included and praised, recognizing that alliance with the identified failure would jeopardize her acceptance. The consequence, in one office, was that the identified success stayed away from the other woman and did not give her any help with her performance, withholding criticism she had heard that might have been useful, and the second woman soon left. In another case, a layer of the hierarchy was inserted between two women who were at the same level: one was made the boss of the other, causing great strain between them. Dominants also could defeat alliances, paradoxically, by trying to promote them. Two women in a training group of twelve were treated as though they were an automatic pair, and other group members felt that they were relieved of responsibility for interacting with or supporting the women. The women reacted to this forced pairing by trying to create difference and distance between them and becoming extremely competitive. Thus, structural circumstances and pressures from the majority could further produce what appeared to be intrinsically prejudicial responses of women to each other. There were also instances in which two women developed a close alliance and refused to be turned against each other. Strong identification with the feminist cause or with other women was behind such alliances. Allied, two tokens could reduce some of the pressures and avoid some of the traps in their position. They could share the burden of representing womankind, and they could each be active on some pieces of "the woman's slot" while leaving time free to demonstrate other abilities and interests. Two women personnel trainers, for example, on a six-person staff, could share responsibility for programs on women without either of them becoming over-identified with it.

A mere shift in *absolute* numbers, then, as from one to two tokens, could potentially reduce stresses in a token's situation even while *relative* numbers of women remained low. But two were also few enough to be rather easily divided and kept apart. It would appear that larger numbers are necessary for supportive alliances to develop in the token context.

EFFECTS ON TOKENS AS INDIVIDUALS: STRESSES AND COSTS IN THE TOKEN SITUATION

The point is not that all of these things happen to token women, or that they happen only to people who are tokens. Some young men at Indsco complained that as new-hires they, too, felt performance pressures, uncertainties about their acceptance, and either over-protected or abandoned. But these issues were part of a transitional status out of which new-hires soon passed, and, in any event, men did not so routinely or dramatically encounter them. Similarly, age and experience helped women make a satisfactory accommodation, and over time, many women settled into comfortable and less token-like patterns. Some said that there was no problem they could not handle with time and that the manifestations of discrimination in their jobs were trivial. But still, the issues stemming from rarity and scarcity arose for women in every new situation, with new peers, and at career transitions. Even successful women who reported little or no discrimination said that they felt they had to "work twice as hard" and expend more energy than the average man to succeed. It is also clear that not all women in the token situation behave alike or engender the same responses in others. There was variety in the individual choices, and there were alternative strategies for managing the situation. But a system characteristic—the numerical proportion in women and men were found—set limits on behavioral possibilities and defined the context for peer interaction.

The token position contains a number of dilemmas and contradictions:[27]

- Tokens are simultaneously representatives and exceptions. They serve as symbols of their category, especially when they fumble, yet they also are seen as unusual examples of their kind, especially when they succeed.

- They are made aware of their differences from the numerical dominants, but then must often pretend that the differences do not exist, or have no implications.

- Tokens are among the most visible and dramatized of performers, noticeably on stage, yet they are often kept away from the organizational backstage where the dramas are cast.

- Tokens are the quintessential "individuals" in the organization, since they stand apart from the mass of peer group members; yet they lose their individuality behind stereotyped roles and carefully constructed public personae that can distort their sense of self.

- Those situations in which organizational peers are supposedly "relaxing" (after-work drinks, celebratory dinners, sports events) are often the most stressful for tokens, for on such occasions the protection of defined positions and structured interaction disappears. So tokens, paradoxically, may be most relaxed and feel the most "natural" during the official parts of the business day when other people are the most constrained by formal roles.

- Tokens suffer from their loneness, yet the dynamics of interaction around them create a pressure for them to seek advantage by dissociating themselves from others of their category and, hence, to remain alone.

- As long as numbers are low, disruptions of interaction around tokens (and their personal problems) are seen by the organization as a huge deflection from its central purposes, a drain of energy, leading to the conclusion that it is not worth having people like the tokens around. Yet the disruptions are primarily a function of the numbers being low and could be remedied by proportional increases.

In short, organizational, social, and personal ambivalence surrounds people in token situations. It is likely that the burdens carried by tokens in the management of social relations take their toll in psychological stress, even if the tokens succeed in work performance. Research on people with inconsistent or poorly crystallized statuses has identified a number of psycho-social difficulties, including unsatisfactory social relationships, unstable self-images, frustration from dealing with contradictory demands from others as well as the self), and insecurity. More serious physical and mental stress has also been found to be associated with status incongruities and from role pressures at work.[28]

Even the best coping strategy is likely to have some internal repercussions, ranging from inhibition of self-expression to feelings of inadequacy and, perhaps, self-hatred. Sidney Jourard hypothesized that one of the ''lethal'' aspects of the male role (that literally kills men off at an early age) is the inhibition of self-disclosure.[29] Self-repression and refraining from certain kinds of expressiveness are, as we have seen, part of the culture in large organizations. But tokens of any kind are especially in a position where true disclosure to peers is not possible, and tokens may not even easily join work peers in their characteristic modes of tension release. Finally, to the extent that tokens accept their exceptional status, dissociate themselves from others of their category, and turn against them, tokens may be denying parts of themselves and engaging in self-hatred. This can produce inner tension.

There is a small positive psychological side to tokenism: the self-esteem that comes from mastering a difficult situation and from getting into places that traditionally exclude others of one's kind. If the token can segregate conflicting expectations and has strong outside support groups with which to relax, then perhaps a potentially stress-producing situation can be turned into an opportunity for ego enhancement. Indeed, one study showed that people whose racial ethnic statuses were ''lower'' than their occupational ranks on social prestige scales (the up-

wardly mobile) did not report the physical symptoms otherwise associated with inconsistent statuses.[30] But, on balance, token situations seem more stressful than beneficial.

EXTENSIONS AND ORGANIZATIONAL IMPLICATIONS

What have been identified as the major issues in the situation of the numerically few at Industrial Supply Corporation are also characteristic of the token position in general. The same pressures and processes can occur around people of any social category who find themselves few of their kind among others of a different social type, as a few examples indicate. Bernard Segal studied the male token situation in a hospital in which 22 out of 101 nurses were men. He found that male nurses were isolates in the hospital social structure—not because the men dissociated themselves from their women peers but because the women felt the men were out of place and should not be nurses. The male and female nurses had the same objective rank, but people of both sexes felt that the men's subjective status was lower. The women placed the men in stereotypical positions, expecting them to do the jobs the women found distasteful or considered ''men's work.''[31] One male nursing student whom I interviewed reported that he thought he would enjoy being the only man in a group of women. Then he found that he engendered a great deal of hostility and that he was teased every time he failed to live up to a manly image—e.g., if he was vague or subjective in speech. The *content* of interaction when men are tokens may appear to give them an elevated position, but the process is still one of role encapsulation and treating tokens as symbols. Deference can be a patronizing reminder of difference, too.

Similarly, a blind man indicated that when he was the only blind person among sighted people, he often felt conspicuous and attended to more than he would like, creating pressure for him to work harder to prove himself. In the solo situation, he was never sure that he was getting the same treatment as other members of the group (first fellow students, later fellow members of an academic situation), and he suspected that people tended to protect him. When he was a token, compared with balanced situations in which other blind people were present, sighted people felt free to grab his arm and pull him along and were more likely to apologize for references to visual matters, reinforcing his sense of being different and being cast in the role of someone who is more helpless than he, in fact, perceived himself to be.

People's treatment, then, is not automatically fixed by inflexible characteristics but depends on their numbers in a particular situation. Change in the behavior and treatment of women in token positions is strongly tied to shifting proportions. But to argue for the importance of numbers smacks of advocacy of quotas, and many Americans object to quotas. Quantitative limits on expansion (which is how quotas are seen: not as more jobs for women, but fewer for men) have always seemed objectionable to some in the United States, especially when ''individual rights'' for the advantaged are involved, as shown in concerns over gasoline rationing or income ceilings. Yet, it seems clear that numbers, especially relative numbers, can strongly affect a person's fate in an organization. This is a *system* rather than an individual construct—located not in characteristics of the person but in how many people, like that person in significant ways, are also present. *System phenomena* require *system-level intervention* to make change.

In the absence of external pressures for change, *tokenism is a self-perpetuating system*. Tokens of Type O who are successful in their professional roles face pressures and inducements to dissociate themselves from other O's, and thus they may fail to promote, or even actively block, the entry of more O's. At the same time, tokens who are less than successful and appear less than fully competent confirm the organization's decision not to recruit more O's, unless they are extraordinarily competent and not like most O's. And since just a few O's can make the X-majority people feel uncomfortable, X's will certainly not go out of their way to include more O's. In short, outside intervention is required to break the cycles created by the social composition of groups.

Most arguments made in favor of numerical guidelines in hiring and job placement limit their own effectiveness by making only part of the case.

They say that *equality of opportunity* is the goal, but that this goal is hard to measure without *proof of outcome*. Therefore, numbers hired serve as a shorthand for, a measure of, non-discrimination in selection. However, there is also a strong case that can be made for number-balancing as a worthwhile goal in itself, because, inside the organization, relative numbers can play a large part in further outcomes—from work effectiveness and promotion prospects to psychic distress.

NOTES

1. There are two questions that must be answered, of course, in any analysis of the effects of proportional representation: first, the circumstances under which a given characteristic is ''salient'' for differentiating group members; and second, the nature of the boundaries defining the extent and limits of the ''group'' within which proportional representation is measured. Here I am defining ascribed characteristics with a physical manifestation (such as sex) as salient, and the ''group'' as work peers in equivalent statuses.
2. Kurt H. Wolff, *The Sociology of Georg Simmel* (Glencoe, Illinois: Free Press, 1950).
3. On juries: Fred L. Strodtbeck and Richard d. Mann, ''Sex Role Differentiation in Jury Deliberations,'' *Sociometry*, 19 (March 1956): pp. 3–11; and Fred L. Strodtbeck, Rita M. James, and Charles Hawkins, ''Social Status in Jury Deliberations,'' *American Sociological Review*, 22 (1957): pp. 713–19. On the kibbutz: Lionel Tiger and Joseph Shepher, *Women in the Kibbutz* (New York: Harcourt, Brace Jovanovich, 1975), and my critique in terms of sex ratios, Rosabeth Moss Kanter, ''Interpreting the Results of a Social Experiment,'' *Science*, 192 (14 May 1976): pp. 662–63. ''Behavioral demography'' as the study of population ratios: Marcia Guttentag, *Too Many women* (New York: Basic Books, in press).
4. Shelley E. Taylor and Susan Fiske, ''The Token in the Small Group: Research Findings and Theoretical Implications,'' in *Psychology and Politics*, J. Sweeney, ed. (New Haven, Yale University Press, 1976).
5. Margaret Hennig, *Career Development for Women Executives*, Unpublished Doctoral Dissertation, Harvard Business School, 1970, p. vi–21. The experimental study of high-dominance women was Edwin

I. Megaree, "Influence of Sex Roles on the Manifestation of Leadership," *Journal of Applied Psychology*, 53 (1969): pp. 377–82. Cynthia Epstein's book is *Woman's Place* (Berkeley: University of California Press, 1970). See also Edith M. Lynch, *The Executive Suite: Feminine Style* (New York: AMACOM, 1973); Margaret Cussler, *The Woman Executive* (New York: Harcourt, Brace, 1958)

6. See Adeline Levine and Janice Crumrine, "Women and the Fear of Success: A Problem in Replication," *American Journal of Sociology*, 80 (January 1975): pp. 967–74. Seymour Sarason's argument is in his "Jewishness, Blackness, and the Nature-Nurture Controversy," *American Psychologiest*, 28 (November 1973): pp. 962–71.

7. The Hughes citation is to Everett Hughes, *Men and Their Work* (Glencoe, Illinois: Free Press, 1958), p. 109. See also Hughes, "Dilemmas and Contradictions of Status," *American Journal of Sociology*, 50 (March 1944): pp. 353–59. Judith Lorber came to some similar conclusions in "Trust, Loyalty, and the Place of Women in the Informal Organization of Work," presented at the 1975 Meetings of the American Sociolgoical Association. On "status incongruence" as an explanatory variable in group member behavior, used in many of the same ways I use "tokenism" but without the explicit numerical connotations, see A. Zaleznik, C. R. Christensen, and F. J. Roethlisberger, *The Motivation, Productivity, and Satisfaction of Workers: A Prediction Study* (Boston: Harvard Business School Division of Research, 1958), especially pp. 56–68.

8. Jeane Kirkpatrick, *Political Woman* (New York: Basic Books, 1974), p. 113; Lionel Tiger, *Men in Groups* (New York: Random House, 1969).

9. Clearly I was limited in first-hand observations of how the men acted when alone, since, by definition, if I, as a female researcher, were present, they would not have been alone. For my data here I relied on tape recordings of several meetings in which the tape was kept running even during breaks, and on informants' reports immediately after informal social events and about meetings.

10. For supportive laboratory evidence, see Elizabeth Aries, *Interaction Patterns and Themes of Male, Female, and Mixed Groups*, Unpublished Doctoral Dissertation, Harvard University, 1973. Her work is discussed forther in Appendix II.

11. For examples in another context, see Marcia Greenbaum, "Adding 'Kenntnis' to 'Kirch, Kuche, und Kinder,' " *Issues in Industrial Society*, 2 (1971): pp. 61–68.

12. Judith Long Laws, 'The Psychology of Tokenism: An Analysis," *Sex Roles*, 1 (1975): pp. 51–67.

13. Hughes, "Men and Their Work" and "Dilemmas and Contradictions of Status"; Lorber, "Trust, Loyalty, and the Place of Women."

14. Zaleznik et al., *Motivation, Productivity and Satisfaction of Workers*; Hennig, *Career Development for Women Executives*; Epstein, *Woman's Place*; Brigid O'Farrell, "Affirmative Action and Skilled Craft Work," Unpublished Report, Cambridge, Mass., 1973 (available from Center for Research on Women, Wellesley College), Carol Wolman and Hal Frank, "The Solo Woman in a Professional Peer Group," *American Journal of Orthopsychiatry*, 45 (January 1975): pp. 164–71.

15. On secrecy and loyalty to peers in training, see Donald Roy, "Quota Restriction and Goldbricking in a Machine Shop," *American Journal of Sociology*, 57 (March 1952): pp. 427–42; Howard S. Becker and Anselm L. Strauss, "Careers, Personality, and Adult Socialization," *American Journal of Sociology*, 62 (November 1956): pp. 253–63.

16. Bernard E. Segal, "Male Nurses: A Study in Status Contradiction and Prestige Loss," *Social Forces*, 41 (October 1962): pp. 31–38. Personal interviews were used as a supplement.

17. Hughes, "Dilemmas and Contradictions of Status."

18. Laws, "Psychology of Tokenism."

19. Rose Laub Coser, "Laughter Among Colleagues: A Study of the Social Functions of Humor Among the Staff of a Mental Hosptial," *Psychiatry*, 23 (1960): pp. 81–95.

20. Everett C. Hughes, "Race Relations in Industry," in *Industry and Society*, W. F. Whyte, ed. (New York: McGraw-Hill, 1946), p. 115.

21. Marianne Abeles Ferber and Joan Althaus Huber, "Sex of Student and Instructor: A Study of Student Bias," *American Journal of Sociology*, 80 (January 1975): pp. 949–63.

22. *Annual Report of the Council of Economic Advisers* (Washington, D.C.: U.S. Government Printing Office, 1973), p. 106.

23. Segal, "Male Nurses," supplemented by my personal interviews.

24. Philip Rieff, ed., *Freud: Sexuality and the Psychology of Love* (New York: Collier Books, 1963); Bryan Strong, "Toward a History of the Experiential Family: Sex and Incest in the Nineteenth Century Fami-

ly,'' *Journal of Marriage and the Family*, 35 (August 1973): pp. 457–66.

25. John C. Athanassiades, ''An Investigation of Some Communication Patterns of Female Subordinates in Hierarchical Organizations,'' *Human Relations*, 27 (1974): pp. 195–209.

26. Solomon E. Asch, ''Effects of Group Pressure on the Modification and Distortion of Judgment,'' in *Group Dynamics*, second edition, D. Cartwright and A. Zander, eds. (Evanston, Illinois: Row Peterson, 1960), pp. 189–200.

27. Hughes used this phrase in a slightly different way in ''Dilemmas and Contradictions of Status.''

28. Gerhard Lenski, ''Status Crystallization: A Non-Vertical Dimension of Status,'' *American Sociological Review*, 19 (August 1954): pp. 405–13; Lenski, ''Social Participation and the Cyrstallization of Status,'' *American Sociolgoical Review*, 21 (August 1956): pp. 458–64; G. H. Fenchel, J. H. Monderer, and E. L. Hartley, ''Subjective Status and the Equilibirum Hypothesis,'' *Journal of Abnormal and So-cial Psychology*, 45 (October 1951): pp. 476–79; Elton F. Jackson, ''Status Consistency and Symptoms of Stress,'' *American Sociological Review*, 27 (August 1962): pp. 469–80. On role overload and coronary disease see Stephen M. Sales, ''Organizational Roles as a Risk Factor in Coronary Heart Disease,'' *Administrative Science Quarterly*, 14 (1969): pp. 235–336. For general reviews, see James S. House, ''The Effects of Occupational Stress on Physical Health,'' in *Work and the Quality of Life*, James O'Toole, ed. (Cambridge, Mass.: MIT Press, 1974), pp. 145–70; and Stanislav V. Kasl, ''Work and Mental Health,'' in *Work and the Quality of Life*, James O'Toole, ed. (Cambridge, Mass.: MIT Press, 1974), pp. 171–96.

29. Sidney M. Jourard, *The Transparent Self: Self-Disclosure and Well-Being* (Princeton: D. Van Nostrand, 1964).

30. Jackson, ''Status Consistency and Symptoms of Stress.''

31. Segal, ''Male Nurses.''

23 WHAT IT'S LIKE TO BE A BLACK MANAGER
Edward W. Jones, Jr.

Edward Jones writes of his own experiences as a new manager on the rise to middle management in a major corporation. He makes the case that differences of race in the work force may mean that the employer must account for differences in newcomers' expectations, preparation, and sensitivities. While new white managers go about the business of meeting employment objectives and tending to their careers, black managers often must expend efforts early in their careers learning new codes of behavior that might be unfamiliar. Notice how Jones links this requirement to the informal organization: How can employers improve the "fit" between new minority-group managers and the interpersonal norms that govern communication behavior?

When I was graduated from a predominantly black college, I was offered a job in one of the largest corporations in America. On reporting for work, I received a motivational speech from the personnel officer and acknowledged that I agreed with his opinion: the job was going to be challenging in its own right; however, the added burden of prejudice could make it unbearable. In a tone of bravado I said, "I promise you that I won't quit; you'll have to fire me."

At the time, I did not know how important that promise would become. For I was about to begin the most trying experience of my life—the rise to middle management in a white corporation. During those years, I found myself examining my actions, strategies, and emotional stability. I found myself trying desperately to separate fact from mental fiction. I found myself enveloped in almost unbearable emotional stress and internal conflict, trying to hold the job as a constant and evaluate my personal shortcomings with respect to it. At times I would look at myself in a mirror and wonder whether I had lost my mental balance. Somehow I always managed to answer positively, if not resolutely.

I think that my experiences should prove helpful to companies that are wrestling with the problem of how to move black employees from the entry level into positions of greater responsibility. I say this because the manner in which many companies are approaching the problem indicates to me that a number of well-intentioned efforts are doomed to failure.

Failure is likely because most companies merely substitute blacks in positions formerly filled by whites and then, acting as if the corporate environment is not color-sensitive, consider their obligation over. In short, U.S. business has failed to recognize the embryonic black manager's increased chances of failure due to the potentially negative impact of racially based prejudgments. Gaining acceptance in the organization, which the embryonic white manager takes for granted, can be a serious problem for his black counterpart.

THE JOB OFFER

My story begins when I happened to bump into a recruiter who was talking to a friend of mine. On

gathering that I was a college senior, the recruiter asked whether I had considered his company as an employer. I responded, "Are you kidding me—you don't have any black managers, do you?" He replied, "No, but that's why I'm here."

I did well in a subsequent interview procedure, and received an invitation for a company tour. Still skeptical, I accepted, feeling that I had nothing to lose. During a lunch discussion concerning the contemplated job and its requirements, I experienced my first reminder that I am black. After a strained silence, one of the executives at our table looked at me, smiled, and said, "Why is it that everyone likes Roy Campanella, but so many people dislike Jackie Robinson?"

I knew that this man was trying to be pleasant; yet I felt nothing but disgust at what seemed a ridiculous deterioration in the level of conversation. Here was the beginning of the games that I expected but dreaded playing. The question was demeaning and an insult to my intelligence. It was merely a rephrasing of the familiar patronizing comment, "One of my best friends is a negro." Most blacks recognize this type of statement as a thinly veiled attempt to hide bias. After all, if a person is unbiased, why does he make such a point of trying to prove it?

In the fragment of time between the question and my response, the tension within me grew. Were these people serious about a job offer? If so, what did they expect from me? I had no desire to be the corporate black in a glass office, but I did not wish to be abrasive or ungracious if the company was sincere about its desire to have an integrated organization.

There was no way to resolve these kinds of questions at that moment, so I gathered up my courage and replied, "Roy Campanella is a great baseball player. But off the field he is not an overwhelming intellectual challenge to anyone. Jackie Robinson is great both on and off the baseball field. He is very intelligent and therefore more of a threat than Roy Campanella. In fact, I'm sure that if he wanted to, he could outperform you in your job."

There was a stunned silence around the table, and from that point on until I arrived back at the employment office, I was sure that I had ended any chances of receiving a job offer.

I was wrong. I subsequently received an outstanding salary offer from the recruiter. But I had no intention of being this company's showcase black and asked seriously, "Why do you want me to work for you? Because of my ability or because you need a black?" I was reassured that ability was the "only" criterion, and one month later, after much introspection, I accepted the offer.

INITIAL EXPOSURE

I entered the first formal training phase, in which I was the only black trainee in a department of over 8,000 employees. During this period, my tension increased as I was repeatedly called on to be the in-house expert on anything pertaining to civil rights. I was proud to be black and had many opinions about civil rights, but I did not feel qualified to give "the" black opinion. I developed the feeling that I was considered a black first and an individual second by many of the people I came into contact with. This feeling was exacerbated by the curious executive visitors to the training class who had to be introduced to everyone except me. Everyone knew my name, and I constantly had the feeling of being on stage.

The next phase of training was intended to prepare trainees for supervisory responsibilities. The tension of the trainee group had risen somewhat because of the loss of several trainees and the increased challenges facing us. In my own case, an increasing fear of failure began to impact on the other tensions that I felt from being "a speck of pepper in a sea of salt." The result of these tensions was that I began behaving with an air of bravado. I wasn't outwardly concerned or afraid, but I was inwardly terrified. This phase of training was also completed satisfactorily, at least in an official sense.

At the conclusion of the training, I received a "yes, but" type of appraisal. For example: "Mr. Jones doesn't take notes and seems to have trouble using the reference material, but he seems to be able to recall the material." This is the type of appraisal that says you've done satisfactorily, yet leaves a negative or dubious impression. I questioned the subjective inputs but dropped the matter without any vehement objections.

Prior to embarking on my first management assignment, I resolved to learn from this appraisal and to use more tact and talk less. These resolutions were re-emphasized by my adviser, who was an executive with responsibility for giving me counsel and acting as a sounding board. He also suggested that I relax my handshake and speak more softly.

ON THE JOB

A warm welcome awaited me in the office where I was to complete my first assignment as a supervisor. I looked forward to going to work because I felt that subjectivity in appraisals would now be replaced by objectivity. Here was a situation in which I would either meet or fail to meet clearly defined numerical objectives.

There were no serious problems for three weeks, and I started to relax and just worry about the job. But then I had a conflict in my schedule. An urgent matter had to be taken care of in the office at the same time that I had an appointment elsewhere. I wrote a note to a supervisor who worked for another manager, asking him if he would be kind enough to follow up on the matter in the office for me.

I chose that particular supervisor because he had given me an embarrassingly warm welcome to the office and insisted that I "just ask" if there was anything at all that he could do to help me. I relied on the impersonality of the note because he was out on a coffee break and I had to leave immediately. The note was short and tactfully worded, and ended by giving my advance "thanks" for the requested help. Moreover, the office norms encouraged supervisory cooperation, so the fact that we worked under different managers did not seem to be a problem.

When I returned to the office, the manager I worked for called me in. He was visibly irritated. I sat down and he said, "Ed, you're rocking the boat." He stated that the supervisor I had asked for help had complained directly to the area manager that I was ordering him around and said he wasn't about to take any nonsense from a "new kid" in the office.

In a very calm voice, I explained what I had done and why I had done it. I then asked my manager,

"What did I do wrong?" He looked at me and said, "I don't know, but whatever it is, cut it out. Stop rocking the boat." When I asked why the note wasn't produced to verify my statements, he said that it "wasn't available."

I left my manager's office totally perplexed. How could I correct my behavior if I didn't know what was wrong with it? I resolved that I had no choice except to be totally self-reliant, since one thing was obvious: what I had taken at face value as friendliness was potentially a fatal trap.

The feelings aroused in this incident were indicative of those I was to maintain for some time. While I felt a need for closeness, the only option open to me was self-reliance. I felt that my manager should support and defend me, but it was obvious that he was not willing to take such a stance. Worst of all, however, was my feeling of disappointment and the ensuing confusion due to my lack of guidance. I felt that if my manager was not willing to protect and defend me, he had an increased responsibility to give me guidance on how to avoid future explosions of a similar nature.

For some months I worked in that office without any additional explosions, although I was continually admonished not to "rock the boat." During a luncheon with the area manager one day, I remember, he said, "Ed, I've never seen a guy try so hard. If we tell you to tie your tie to the right, you sure try to do it. But why can't you be like Joe [another trainee the area manager supervised]? He doesn't seem to be having any problems."

The Appraisal Incident

I directed my energies and frustrations into my work, and my supervisory section improved in every measured area of performance until it led the unit. At the end of my first six months on the job, I was slated to go on active duty to fulfill my military requirements as a lieutenant in the Army. Shortly before I left, my manager stated, "Ed, you've done a tremendous job. You write your own appraisal." I wrote the appraisal, but was told to rewrite it because "it's not good enough." I rewrote the appraisal four times before he was satisfied that I was not being too modest. As I indicated earlier, I had

resolved to be as unabrasive as possible, and, even though I had met or exceeded all my objectives, I was trying not to be pompous in critiquing my own performance.

Finally, on my next to last day on the job, my manager said, "Ed, this is a fine appraisal. I don't have time to get it typed before you go, but I'll submit this appraisal just as you have written it." With that, I went into the service, feeling that, finally, I had solved my problems.

Six months later, I took several days' leave from the Army to spend Christmas in the city with my family. On the afternoon of the day before Christmas, I decided to visit the personnel executive who had originally given me encouragement. So, wearing my officer's uniform, I stopped by his office.

After exchanging greetings and making small talk, I asked him if he had seen my appraisal. He answered, "yes," but when his face failed to reflect the look of satisfaction that I expected, I asked him if I could see it. The appraisal had been changed from the one that I had originally written to another "yes, but" appraisal. The numerical results said that I had met or exceeded all objectives, but under the section entitled "Development Program" the following paragraph had been inserted:

Mr. Jones's biggest problem has been overcoming his own impulsiveness. He has on occasion, early in his tour, jumped too fast with the result that he has incurred some resentment. In these cases his objectives have been good, but his method has ruffled feathers.

I asked the personnel executive to interpret my overall rating. He answered, "Well, we can run the business with people with that rating." I then asked him to explain the various ratings possible, and it became clear that I had received the lowest acceptable rating that wouldn't require the company to fire me. I could not see how this could be, since I had exceeded all my objectives. I explained how I had written my own appraisal and that this appraisal had been rewritten. The personnel officer could not offer an explanation; he recommended that I speak to my old area manager, who had had the responsibility to review and approve my appraisal, and ask him why I had been treated in that manner.

A Bleak Christmas

I tried to sort things out on my way to see my former area manager. My head was spinning, and I was disgusted. The appraisal was not just unfair—it was overtly dishonest. I thought of standing up in righteous indignation and appealing to higher authority in the company, but I had always resisted calling attention to my blackness by asking for special concessions and wanted to avoid creating a conflict situation if at all possible. While the 15-minute walk in the cold air calmed my anger, I still hadn't decided what I was going to do when I arrived at the area manager's office.

I walked into a scene that is typical of Christmas Eve in an office. People were everywhere, and discarded gift wrappings filled the wastebaskets. The area manager still had on the red Santa Claus suit. I looked around at the scene of merriment and decided that this was a poor time to "rock the boat."

The area manager greeted me warmly, exclaimed how great I looked, and offered to buy me a drink on his way home. I accepted, and with a feeling of disgust and disappointment, toasted to a Merry Christmas. I knew then that this situation was hopeless and there was little to be gained by raising a stink while we were alone. I had been naive, and there was no way to prove that the appraisal had been changed.

I was a very lonely fellow that Christmas Eve. My feelings of a lack of closeness, support, and protection were renewed and amplified. It became obvious that no matter how much I achieved, how hard I worked, or how many personal adjustments I made, this system was trying to reject me.

I didn't know which way to turn, whom to trust, or who would be willing to listen. The personnel executive had told me to expect prejudice, but when he saw that I was being treated unfairly, he sent me off on my own.

"What do they expect?" I thought. "They know that I am bound to run into prejudice; yet no one lifts a finger when I am treated unfairly. Do they expect a person to be stupid enough to come right out and say, 'Get out, blackie; we don't want your type here'? This surely wouldn't happen—such overt behavior would endanger the offending person's career."

After the Christmas Eve incident, I went off to finish the remaining time in the Army. During that period, I tossed my work problems around in my mind, trying to find the right approach. The only answer I came up with was to stand fast, do my best, ask for no special favors, and refuse to quit voluntarily.

NEW CHALLENGES

When I returned to the company, I was assigned as a supervisor in another area for five or six weeks, to do the same work as I had been doing prior to my departure for the military service. At the end of this uneventful refamiliarization period, I was reassigned as a manager in an area that had poor performance and was recognized as being one of the most difficult in the company. The fact that I would be responsible for one of three "manager units" in the area was exciting, and I looked forward to this new challenge.

I walked into my new area manager's office with a smile and an extended hand, anxious to start off on the right foot and do a good job. After shaking hands, my new boss invited me to sit down while he told me about the job. He began by saying, "I hope you don't but I am pretty sure you are going to fall flat on your face. When you do, my job is to kick you in the butt so hard that they'll have to take us both to the hospital."

I was shocked and angry. In the first place, my pride as a man said you don't have to take that kind of talk from anyone. I fought the temptation to say something like, "If you even raise your foot, you may well go the hospital to have it put in a cast."

As I held back the anger, he continued, "I don't know anything about your previous performance, and I don't intend to try to find out. I'm going to evaluate you strictly on your performance for me."

The red lights went on in my mind. This guy was making too much of an issue about his lack of knowledge concerning my previous performance.

Whom was he trying to kid? He had heard rumors and read my personnel records. I was starting off with two strikes against me. I looked at him and said, "I'll do my best."

More Appraisal Troubles

The area's results failed to improve, and John, the area manager, was replaced by a new boss, Ralph. Two weeks after Ralph arrived, he called me on the intercom and said, "Ed, John has your appraisal ready. Go down to see him in his new office. Don't worry about it; we'll talk when you get back." Ralph's words and tone of foreboding made me brace for the worst.

John rushed me into his office and began by telling me that I had been his worst problem. He then proceeded to read a list of every disagreement involving me that he was aware of. These ranged from corrective actions with clerks to resource-allocation discussions with my fellow managers. It was a strange appraisal session. John wound up crossing out half of the examples cited as I rebutted his statements. At the end of the appraisal, he turned and said, "I've tried to be fair, Ed. I've tried not to be vindictive. But if someone were to ask how you're doing, I would have to say you've got room for improvement."

Discussions with Ralph, my new boss, followed as soon as I returned to my office. He advised me not to worry, that we would work out any problems. I told him that this was fine, but I also pointed out the subjectivity and dishonesty reflected in previous and current appraisals and the circumstances surrounding them.

I was bitter that a person who had just been relieved for ineffectiveness could be allowed to have such a resounding impact on my chances in the company. My predecessor had been promoted; I had improved on his results; but there I was, back in questionable status again.

The Turning Point

About six weeks later, Ralph called me in and said, "Ed, I hope you make it on the job. But what are you going to do if you don't?"

At that moment, I felt as if the hands on the clock of life had reached 11:59. Time was running out very rapidly on me, and I saw myself against a wall, with my new boss about to deliver the coup de grâce. I felt that he was an honest and very capable person, but that circumstances had combined to give him the role of executioner. It seemed from his question that he was in the process of either wrestling with is own conscience or testing me to see how much resistance, if any, I would put up when he delivered the fatal blow. After all, while I had not made an issue of my ill treatment thus far in my career, no matter how unjustly I felt I had been dealt with, he was smart enough to realize that this option was still open to me.

I looked at Ralph and any thought about trying to please him went out of my mind. Sitting up straight in my chair, I met his relaxed smile with a very stern face. "Why do you care what I do if I don't make it?" I asked coldly.

"I care about you as a person," he replied.

"It's not your job to be concerned about me as a person," I said. "Your job is to evaluate my performance results. But since you've asked, it will be rough if I am fired, because I have a family and responsibilities. However, that's not your concern. You make your decision; and when you do, I'll make my decision." With that statement I returned to my office.

Several weeks after this discussion, a vice president came around to the office to discuss objectives and job philosophy with the managers. I noted at the time that while he only spent 15 or 20 minutes with the other managers, he spent over an hour talking with me. After this visit, Ralph and I had numerous daily discussions. Then Ralph called me into his office to tell me he had written a new appraisal with an improved rating. I was thrilled. I was going to make it. Later, he told me that he was writing another appraisal, stating I not only would make it but also had promotional potential.

After Ralph had changed the first appraisal, my tensions began to decrease and my effectiveness began to increase proportionately. The looser and more confident I became, the more rapidly the results improved. My assignment under Ralph became very fulfilling, and one of the best years I've spent in the company ensued. Other assignments followed, each more challenging than the previous, and each was handled satisfactorily.

LESSONS FROM EXPERIENCE

My point in relating these experiences is not to show that I was persecuted or treated unfairly by people in a large corporation. In fact, after talking to friends in the company who knew me during the period just described, I am convinced that many of the lack-of-tact and rock-the-boat statements were true. I am also convinced, however, that the problems I experienced were not uniquely attributable to me or my personality and that it is important for companies to understand what caused them.

The manager to whom I reported on my very first assignment made some information notes which help illustrate my conviction:

> I discussed each case with Ed. As might be expected, there is as much to be said in his defense as against him. He isn't all wrong in any one case. But the cumulative weight of all those unsolicited comments and complaints clearly shows that he is causing a lot of people to be unhappy, and I must see that it stops. I don't think it is a question of what he says and does or a question of objectives. It is a question of voice, manner, approach, method—or maybe timing. No matter what it is, he must correct whatever he does that upsets so many people.

These are not the words of a scheming bigot; they are the words of a man searching for an explanation to a phenomenon that neither he nor I understood at the time. I was not knowingly insensitive to other people or intent on antagonizing them. What this man and others failed to realize was that, being a black man in a unique position in a white company, I was extremely tense and ill at ease. Levels of sensitivity, polish, and tact which were foreign to me were now necessities of life. The world of white business presented me with an elaborate sociopolitical organization that required unfamiliar codes of behavior.

Abraham Zaleznik refers to this phenomenon in *The Human Dilemmas of Leadership*:

> The anxiety experienced by the upwardly mobile individual largely comes from internal conflicts generated within his own personality. On the one hand, there is the driving and pervasive need to prove himself as assurance of his adequacy as a person; on the other hand, the standards for measuring his adequacy come from sources somewhat unfamiliar to him.[1]

My personal pride and sense of worth were driving me to succeed. Ironically, the more determined I was to succeed, the more abrasive I became and the more critical my feedback became. This in turn impelled me to try even harder and to be even more uptight. As a result, I was vulnerable to prejudgments of inability by my peers and superiors.

The Lens of Color

What most white people do not understand or accept is the fact that skin color has such a pervasive impact on every black person's life that it subordinates considerations of education or class. Skin color makes black people the most conspicuous minority in America, and all blacks, regardless of status, are subjected to prejudice. I personally was not as disadvantaged as many other blacks, but to some extent all blacks are products of separate schools, neighborhoods, and subcultures. In short, black and white people not only look different but also come from different environments which condition them differently and make understanding and honest communication difficult to achieve.

Many whites who find it easy to philosophically accept the fact that blacks will be rubbing shoulders with them experience antagonism when they realize that the difference between blacks and whites goes deeper than skin color. They have difficulty adjusting to the fact that blacks really are different. It is critical that companies understand this point, for it indicates the need for increased guidance to help blacks adjust to an alien set of norms and behavioral requirements.

The Informal Organization

One of the phenomena that develops in every corporation is a set of behavioral and personal norms that facilitates communication and aids cohesiveness. Moreover, because this "informal organization" is built on white norms, it can reinforce the black-white differences just mentioned and thus reject or destroy all but the most persistent blacks.

The informal organization operates at all levels in a corporation, and the norms become more rigid the higher one goes in the hierarchy. While this phenomenon promotes efficiency and unity, it is also restrictive and very selective. It can preclude promotion or lead to failure on the basis of "fit" rather than competence.

Chester Barnard recognized the existence of the information organization in 1938. As he stated, "This question of fitness involves such matters as education, experience, age, sex, personal distinctions, prestige, race, nationality, faith. . . ."[2]

I believe that many of the problems I encountered were problems of fit with the informal organization. My peers and supervisors were unable to perceive me as being able to perform the job that the company hired me for. Their reaction to me was disbelief. I was out of the "place" normally filled by black people in the company; and since no black person had preceded me successfully, it was easy for my antagonists to believe I was inadequate.

I am not vacillating here from my previous statement that I was probably guilty of many of the subjective shortcomings noted in my appraisals. But I do feel that the difficulties I experienced were amplified by my lack of compatibility with the informal organization. Because of it, many of the people I had problems with could not differentiate between objective ability and performance and subjective dislike for me, or discomfort with me. I was filling an unfamiliar, and therefore uncomfortable, "space" in relation to them. Even in retrospect, I cannot fully differentiate between the problems attributable to me as a person, to me as a manager, or to me as a black man.

TOWARD FACILITATING "FIT"

Because of the foregoing problems, I conclude that business has an obligation to even out the odds for blacks who have executive potential. I am not saying that all blacks must be pampered and sheltered rather than challenged. Nor am I advocating the development of "chosen" managers. All managers must accept the risk of failure in order to receive the satisfactions of achievement.

I do, however, advocate a leveling out of these problems of "fit" with the informal organization that operate against black managers. Here are the elements vital to this process:

- *Unquestionable top management involvement and commitment*—The importance of this element is underscored by my discussions with the vice president who visited me during my crisis period. He disclosed that his objective was to see whether I was really as bad as he was being told. His conclusion from the visit was that he couldn't see any insurmountable problems with me. This high-level interest was the critical variable that gave me a fair chance. I was just lucky that this man had a personal sense of fair play and a desire to ensure equitable treatment.

But chance involvement is not enough. If a company is truly committed to equal opportunity, then it must set up reasoned and well thought-out plans for involvement of top management.

- *Direct two-way channels of communication between top management and black trainees*— Without open channels of communication, a company cannot ensure that it will recognize the need for a neutral opinion or the intercession of a disinterested party if a black trainee is having problems.

Clear channels of communication will also enable top management to provide empathetic sources of counsel to help the new black trainee combat the potentially crippling paranoia that I encountered. I didn't know whom to trust; consequently, I trusted no one. The counsel of mature and proven black executives will also help mitigate this paranoia.

- *Appraisal of managers on their contributions to the company's equal opportunity objectives*— The entire management team must be motivated to change any deep beliefs about who does and doesn't fit with regard to color. Accordingly, companies should use the appraisal system to make the welfare of the black trainee coincident with the well-being of his superior. Such action, of course, will probably receive considerable resistance from middle- and lower-level management. But managers are appraised on their ability to reach other important objectives; and, more significantly, the inclusion of this area in appraisals signals to everyone involved that a company is serious. Failure to take this step signals business as usual and adds to any credibility gap between the company and black employees.

The appraisal process also motivates the trainee's superior to "school" him on the realities of the political process in the corporation. Without this information, no one can survive in an organization. After upgrading my appraisal, Ralph began this process with me. The knowledge I gained proved to be invaluable in my subsequent decision making.

- *Avoid the temptation to create special showcase-black jobs.* They will be eyed with suspicion by the black incumbents, and the sincerity of the company will be open to question. Blacks realize that only line jobs provide the experience and reality-testing which develop the confidence required in positions of greater responsibility.
- *Select assignments for the new black managers which are challenging, yet don't in themselves increase his chances of failure.* My assignment with John was a poor choice. He was a top-rated area manager, but had a different job orientation and was struggling to learn his new responsibilities. So naturally he would resent any inexperienced manager being assigned to him. Moreover, the fact that he had never seen a successful black manager reinforced his belief that I could not do the job.

These basic steps need not be of a permanent nature, but they should be enacted until such time as the organizational norms accept blacks at all levels and in all types of jobs. The steps will help mitigate the fact that a black person in the organizational structure must not only carry the same load as a white person but also bear the burden attributable to prejudice and the machinations of the informal organization.

CONCLUSION

In relating and drawing on my own experiences, I have not been talking about trials and tribulations in an obviously bigoted company. At that time, my company employed a higher percentage of blacks than almost any other business, and this is still true today. I grant that there is still much to be done as far as the number and level of blacks in positions of authority are concerned, but I believe that my company has done better than most in the area of equal opportunity. Its positive efforts are evidenced by the progressive decision to sponsor my study at the Harvard Business School, so I would be prepared for greater levels of responsibility.

There are differences in detail and chronology, but the net effect of my experiences is similar to that of other blacks with whom I have discussed these matters. While prejudice exists in business, the U.S. norm against being prejudiced precludes an admission of guilt by the prejudiced party. Thus, in my own case, my first manager and John were more guilty of naïveté than bigotry—they could not recognize prejudice, since it would be a blow to their self images. And this condition is prevalent in U.S. industry.

My experience points out that a moral commitment to equal opportunity is not enough. If a company fails to recognize that fantastic filters operate between the entry level and top management, this commitment is useless. Today, integration in organizations is at or near the entry level, and the threat of displacement or the discomfort of having to adjust to unfamiliar racial relationships is the greatest for lower and middle managers, for they are the people who will be most impacted by this process. Therefore, companies must take steps similar to the ones I have advocated if they hope to achieve true parity for blacks.

Equal job opportunity is more than putting a black man in a white man's job. The barriers must be removed, not just moved.

NOTES

1. New York, Harper & Row, Publishers, 1966, p. 111.
2. *The Functions of the Executive* (Cambridge, Harvard University Press, 1938), p. 224.

24 THE ETHICS OF ORGANIZATIONAL POLITICS
GERALD F. CAVANAGH, DENNIS J. MOBERG, AND MANUEL VELASQUEZ

As we mentioned in the introduction to Part III, issues of communication ethics are becoming more and more important. Increasingly, too, these issues are being framed as issues of organizational politics. The reality of organizational politics has been written about since the days of Machiavelli, if not earlier. But organizational researchers have had much difficulty determining the ethicality of political behaviors. Cavanagh, Moberg, and Velasquez broach this subject by examining the strengths and weaknesses of the three most widely accepted ethical theories: utilitarianism, moral rights, and justice. They then propose a decision tree that incorporates all three theories to evaluate the ethics of a political behavior in organizations.

Power is the cornerstone of both management theory and management practice. Few concepts are more fundamental to the study of organizations, and power is a vital and ubiquitous reality in organizational life [Dahl, 1957; Zald, 1970; Zalesnik, 1970]. Our primary purpose here is to develop a framework for evaluating the ethical quality of certain uses of power within organizations. We will first distinguish political from nonpolitical uses of power and then canvass the literature of normative ethics in order to construct a model of ethical analysis that can be applied to political uses of power in organizations.

ORGANIZATIONAL POLITICS

The contemporary view of power in organizations is that it is the ability to mobilize resources, energy, and information on behalf of a preferred goal or

Adapted from Gerald F. Cavanagh, Dennis J. Moberg, and Manuel Velasquez, ''The Ethics of Organizational Politics.'' Reprinted with permission from *Academy of Management Review, 6,* 363–374. Copyright 1981 by the Academy of Business Management.

strategy [Tushman, 1977]. Thus, power is assumed to exist only when there is conflict over means or ends [Drake, 1979; Pfeffer, 1977]. More specifically, this view of power is based on two fundamental propositions:

1. Organizations are composed of individuals and coalitions that compete over resources, energy, information, and influence [Hickson, Hinings, Lee, Schneck, & Pennings, 1971; Thompson, 1967].
2. Individuals and coalitions seek to protect their interests through means that are unobtrusive when compared to existing controls, norms and sanctions [Allen, Madison, Porter, Renwick, & Mayes, 1979; Pfeffer & Salancik, 1974].

This perspective has led some authors to distinguish between political and nonpolitical uses of power [Gandz & Murray, 1980]. For example, Mayes and Allen [1977] draw the distinction in terms of organizational sanctions: nonpolitical uses of power are those that involve sanctioned means for sanctioned ends, and political uses involve unsanctioned means, or sanctioned means for unsanctioned ends. That is, when individuals and coalitions choose to move outside of their formal authority, established policies and procedures, or job descriptions in their use of power, that use is political. When they use power within these sanctions for ends that are not formally sanctioned through goal statements, this too is a political use of power, according to the Mayes and Allen definition.

Unlike more encompassing conceptualizations that equate politics with *any* use of power [e.g., Martin & Sims, 1956], *the Mayes and Allen definition underlines the discretionary nature of organizational politics.* In spite of formal systems designed to control the use of power, organizational members can and do exercise political power to influence their subordinates, peers, superiors, and others [Schein, 1977]. And coalitions may employ politics in their reaction to policy changes that threaten their own interests [Crozier, 1964; Pettigrew, 1973].

When individuals and coalitions move outside formal sanctions, the traditional authority/re-

sponsibility linkage is broken, and important ethical issues emerge. However, current treatments of organizational politics either beg the ethical issues entirely [e.g., Kotter, 1977] or offer simplistic ethical criteria. For example, Miles asserts that "it is . . . important to recognize that politics need not be bad, though common parlance uses the term in a pejorative sense. The survival of an organization may depend on the success of a unit or coalition in overturning a traditional but outdated formal organization objective or policy" [1980, p. 155]. However, there are a host of political actions that may be justified in the name of organizational survival that many would find morally repugnant. Among these are such Machiavellian techniques as "situational manipulation," "dirty tricks," and "backstabbing."

There is, then, a clear need for a normative theory of organizational politics that addresses ethical issues directly and from the standpoint of the exercise of discretion. Unfortunately, the business and society literature, where one might expect to find such issues discussed, offers little guidance in this regard. The emphasis in this literature is on institutional interactions (e.g., government regulations) and on broad human resource policy issues (e.g., affirmative action), and not on the day-to-day political decisions made in the organization.

Discussions of political tactics in the management literature also offer little guidance. The literature is, of course, rich with political guidelines: there are leadership theories, lateral relations prescriptions, notions about how to design and implement reward and control systems, conflict resolution strategies, and the like, all of which provide fodder for the development of political behavior alternatives (hereinafter PBA). However, the form of these theoretical notions tends to reduce decisions to *calculations based on effect*—that is, they provide the manager with an understanding and prediction of what PBAs are likely to evoke in terms of an outcome or set of outcomes. Armed with contemporary leadership theories, for example, managers can presumably determine the type of face-to-face direction that will result in the desired level of performance and satisfaction. This calculative emphasis defines theoretical debate over ethics in terms of the desirability of outcomes and tends to ignore the value of the activities, processes, and behaviors involved, independent of the outcomes achieved. What a manager *should do* is thus determined by the desirability of the outcomes and not by the quality of the behaviors themselves. Such an emphasis inevitably leads to a kind of ends-justify-the-means logic that fails to provide guidance for managers beyond linking alternatives to outcomes. Consider the following case.

Lorna is the production manager of a noncohesive work group responsible for meeting a deadline that will require coordinated effort among her subordinates. Believing that the members of the work group will pull together and meet the deadline if they have a little competition, Lorna decides in favor of a PBA. She tries to create the impression among her subordinates that members of the sales department want her group to fail to meet the deadline so that sales can gain an edge over production in upcoming budgetary negotiations.

How might we evaluate this PBA? Management theory tends to focus our attention on consequences. One might argue that if it works and Lorna's group pulls together and meets the deadline, it's okay. Or, a more critical observer might argue that even if the objective is accomplished, an important side effect could be the loss of a cooperative relationship between the sales and production departments. What we tend to lose sight of, though, is that "creating an impression" is a euphemism for lying, and lying may not be ethically acceptable in this situation.

This example illustrates what may be termed the teleological or goal-oriented form of management theory [Keeley, 1979; Krupp, 1961; Pfeffer, 1978]. This leads managers and management scholars alike to restrict normative judgments about organizational behavior to outcomes (e.g., performance, satisfaction, system effectiveness) rather than consider the ethical quality of the means employed.

In contrast, the field of normative ethics provides fertile ground on which to develop a normative theory of organizational politics. We will therefore turn to the literature of this field in order to draw out a set of principles that can provide the basis for a normative analysis of organizational politics that may reduce the ethical uncertainty surrounding the political use of power.

ETHICAL CRITERIA RELEVANT TO POLITICAL BEHAVIOR DECISIONS

Work in the field of normative ethics during this century has evolved from three basic kinds of moral theories: utilitarian theories (which evaluate behavior in terms of its social consequences), theories of rights (which emphasize the entitlements of individuals), and theories of justice (which focus on the distributional effects of actions or policies). Each of these has a venerable heritage. Utilitarian theory was precisely formulated in the eighteenth century [Bentham, 1789; Mill, 1863; Sidgwick, 1874]. Formulations of rights theories appeared in the seventeenth century [Hobbes, 1651; Locke, 1690; Kant, 1785]. Aristotle and Plato first formulated theories of justice in the fifth century B.C. This past decade has seen a continuing discussion of a subtle and powerful variant of utilitarianism called "rule utilitarianism" [Brandt, 1979; Sobel, 1970], an elaboration of several rights theories [Dworkin, 1978; Nozick, 1974], and the publication of sophisticated treatments of justice [Bowie, 1971; Rawls, 1971].

Utilitarian Theory

Utilitarianism holds that actions and plans should be judged by their consequences [Sidgwick, 1874; Smart, 1973]. In its classical formulation, utilitarianism claims that behaviors that are moral produce the greatest good for the greatest number [Mill, 1863]. Decision makers are required to estimate the effect of each alternative on all the parties concerned and to select the one that optimizes the satisfactions of the greatest number.

What can be said about the ethical quality of PBAs from a utilitarian standpoint? In its present form, utilitarianism requires a decision maker to select the PBA that will result in the greatest good for the greatest number. This implies not only considering the interests of all the individuals and groups that are affected by each PBA, but also selecting the PBA that optimizes the satisfactions of these constituencies. Obviously, this can amount to a calculative nightmare.

Accordingly, there are several shortcuts that may

be used to reduce the complexity of utilitarian calculations. Each of these involves a sacrifice of elegance for calculative ease. *First*, a decision maker can adopt some ideological system that reduces elaborate calculations of interests to a series of utilitarian rules. For example, some religious ideologies specify rules of behavior that, if followed, are supposed to result in an improved human condition (e.g., the Golden Rule). Certain organizational ideologies, like professionalism, allow complex utilitarian calculations to be reduced to a focus on critical constituencies [Schein, 1966]. *Second*, a decision maker can adopt a simplified frame of reference in evaluating the interests of affected parties. For example, an economic frame of reference presupposes that alternatives are best evaluated in terms of dollar costs and dollar benefits. In this way, utilitarian calculations can be quantified. And *third*, a decision maker can place boundaries on utilitarian calculation. For example, a decision maker can consider only the interests of those directly affected by a decision and thus exclude from analysis all indirect or secondary effects. Similarly, a decision maker can assume that by giving allegiance to a particular organizational coalition or set of goals (e.g., "official goals"), everyone's utilities will be optimized.

Calculative shortcuts like these do not automatically free decision makers from moral responsibility for their actions. Normative ethicians typically suggest that decision makers should periodically assess these simplifying strategies to assure themselves that certain interests are not being ignored or that decision rules do not lead to suboptimal outcomes [e.g., Bok, 1980].

Whatever form of utilitarianism is employed, two types of PBAs are typically judged unethical: (1) those that are consistent with the attainment of some goals (e.g., personal goals) at the expense of those that encompass broader constituencies (e.g., societal goals), and (2) those that constitute comparatively inefficient means to desired ends. Take the case of an employee of a company who uses personal power to persuade policy makers to grant unusually high levels of organizational resources to a project by systematically excluding important information about the progress of the project. This PBA is unethical if other resource allocation schemes would better satisfy a greater number of individuals or if persuasion of this kind is less efficient than being more open about how the project is progressing.

Theory of Rights

A theory of moral rights asserts that human beings have certain fundamental rights that should be respected in all decisions. Several fundamental rights have been incorporated into the American legal system in the form of the Constitutional Bill of Rights. In light of these Constitutional guarantees, advocates of moral rights have suggested the following:

1. *The right of free consent.* Individuals within an organization have the right to be treated only as they knowingly and freely consent to be treated [Bennis & Slater, 1968; Hart, 1955].
2. *The right to privacy.* Individuals have the right to do whatever they choose to do outside working hours and to control information about their private life, including information not intended to be made public [Miller, 1971; Mironi, 1974; Wasserstrom, 1978].
3. *The right to freedom of conscience.* Individuals have the right to refrain from carrying out any order that violates moral or religious norms to which they adhere [Ewing, 1977; Walzer, 1967].
4. *The right of free speech.* Individuals have the right to criticize conscientiously and truthfully the ethics or legality of the actions of others so long as the criticism does not violate the rights of other individuals [Bok, 1980; Eells, 1962; Walters, 1975].
5. *The right to due process.* Individuals have the right to a fair and impartial hearing when they believe their rights are being violated [Ewing, 1977, 1981; Evan, 1975].

Making decisions based on a theory of rights is much simpler than with utilitarian theory. One need only avoid interfering with the rights of others who might be affected by the decision. This can be complicated, of course, but generally a theory of rights does not involve the decision complexities that utilitarianism requires.

Theory of Justice

A theory of justice requires decision makers to be guided by equity, fairness, and impartiality. Canons of justice may specify three types of moral prescriptions: distributive rules, principles of administering rules, and compensation norms.

Distributive Rules. The basic rule of distributive justice is that differentiated treatment of individuals should not be based on arbitrary characteristics: individuals who are similar in the relevant respects should be treated similarly, and individuals who differ in a relevant respect should be treated differently in proportion to the differences between them [Perelman, 1963]. This rule is the basis for contentions that certain resource allocations are "fair." When applied to salary administration, for example, it would lead to a distribution of rewards such that those whose jobs are equal in terms of importance, difficulty, or some other criterion receive equal rewards.

A second distributive rule is that the attributes and positions that command differential treatment should have a clear and defensible relationship to goals and tasks [Daniels, 1978]. Clearly, it is unjust to distribute rewards according to differences unrelated to the situation at hand.

Principles of Administering Rules. Justice requires that rules should be administered fairly [Feinberg, 1973; Fuller, 1964]. Rules should be clearly stated and expressly promulgated. They should be consistently and impartially enforced. They should excuse individuals who act in ignorance, under duress, or involuntarily [Rawls, 1971].

Compensation Norms. A theory of justice also delineates guidelines regarding the responsibility for injuries [Brandt, 1959]. First, individuals should not be held responsible for matters over which they have no control. Second, individuals should be compensated for the cost of their injuries by the party responsible for those injuries.

While a theory of justice does not require the complicated calculations demanded by utilitarian theory, it is by no means easy to apply. There is the problem of determining the attributes on which differential treatment is to be based. There are factfinding challenges associated with administering rules. And there is the thorny problem of establishing responsibility for mistakes and injuries.

However, as applied to political behavior decisions, these canons of justice are useful in clarifying some ethical issues. First, PBAs for the purpose of acquiring an advantageous position in the distribution of resources are ethically questionable if there is no legitimate basis for the advantage. Second, PBAs based on an exchange of rule leniency for other favors are patently unethical unless everyone qualifies for the same level of leniency. Finally, political advantage should not be based on favorable attributions of responsibility or the compensation for injury [Allen et al., 1979]. In short, a theory of justice demands that inequality or advantage be determined fairly.

AN ANALYTICAL STRUCTURE FOR EVALUATING POLITICAL BEHAVIOR DECISIONS

Each of the three kinds of ethical theories has strong and weak points, as depicted in Table 1. Most important for our purposes, each can be shown to be inadequate in accounting for issues accounted for by another. Utilitarian theory cannot adequately account for rights and claims of justice [Lyons, 1965]. Rights theories proved deficient in dealing with social welfare issues [Singer, 1978]. And theories of justice have been criticized for both violating rights [Nozick, 1974] and diminishing incentives to produce goods and services [Okum, 1975]. One solution to the problem of theoretical inadequacy is to combine these three theories into a coherent whole.

To that end, we have incorporated all three normative theories in a decision tree, diagrammed in Figure 1. The three categories of ethical criteria that bear on a political behavior decision are arbitrarily arranged in the diagram. In addition to incorporating all three theories, the decision tree accounts for overwhelming factors that preclude the application of any of these criteria. These overwhelming factors

Table 1   ETHICAL THEORIES RELEVANT TO JUDGING POLITICAL BEHAVIOR DECISIONS

Theory	Strengths as an Ethical Guide	Weaknesses as an Ethical Guide
Utilitarianism (Bentham, Ricardo, Smith)	1. Facilitates calculative shortcuts (e.g., owing loyalty to an individual, coalition, or organization).	1. Virtually impossible to assess the effects of a PBA[a] on the satisfaction of all affected parties.
	2. Promotes the view that the interests accounted for should not be solely particularistic except under unusual circumstances (e.g., perfect competition).	2. Can result in an unjust allocation of resources, particularly when some individuals or groups lack representation or "voice."
	3. Can encourage entrepreneurship, innovation, and productivity.	3. Can result in abridging some persons' rights to accommodate utilitarian outcomes.
Theory of Rights (Kant, Locke)	1. Specifies minimal levels of satisfaction for all individuals.	1. Can encourage individualistic, selfish behavior—which, taken to an extreme, may result in anarchy.
	2. Establishes standards of social behavior that are independent of outcomes.	2. Reduces political prerogatives that may be necessary to bring about just or utilitarian outcomes.
Theory of Justice (Aristotle, Rawls)	1. Ensures that allocations of resources are determined fairly.	1. Can encourage a sense of entitlement that reduces entrepreneurship, innovation, and productivity.
	2. Protects the interests of those who may be underrepresented in organizations beyond according them minimal rights.	2. Can result in abridging some persons' rights to accommodate the canons of justice.

[a]*Political behavior alternative.*

will be specified after two cases illustrating the use of the decision tree have been presented.

Illustrative Cases

Sam and Bob are highly motivated research scientists who work in the new-product development lab at General Rubber. Sam is by far the most technically competent scientist in the lab, and he has been responsible for several patents that have netted the company nearly six million dollars in the past decade. He is quiet, serious, and socially reserved. In contrast, Bob is outgoing and demonstrative. While Bob lacks the technical track record Sam has, his work has been solid though unimaginative. Rumor has it that Bob will be moved into an administrative position in the lab in the next few years.

According to lab policy, a $300,000 fund is available every year for the best new-product development idea proposed by a lab scientist in the form of a competitive bid. Accordingly, Sam and Bob both prepare proposals. Each proposal is carefully constructed to detail the benefits to the company and to society if the proposal is accepted, and it is the

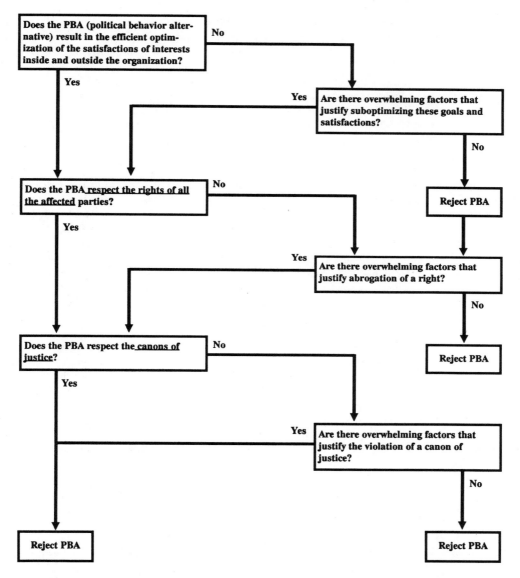

Figure 1   A Decision Tree for Incorporating Ethics into Political Behavior Decisions

consensus of other scientists from blind reviews that both proposals are equally meritorious. Both proposals require the entire $300,000 to realize any significant results. Moreover, the proposed line of research in each requires significant mastery of the technical issues involved and minimal need to supervise the work of others.

After submitting his proposal, Sam takes no fur-

ther action aside from periodically inquiring about the outcome of the bidding process. In contrast, Bob begins to wage what might be termed an open campaign in support of his proposal. After freely admitting his intentions to Sam and others, Bob seizes every opportunity he can to point out the relative advantages of his proposal to individuals who might have some influence over the decision. So effective is this open campaign that considerable informal pressure is placed on those authorized to make the decision on behalf of Bob's proposal. Bob's proposal is funded and Sam's is not.

An ethical analysis of Bob's action in this case could begin by using the decision tree shown in Figure 1. The first question in the sequence requires a utilitarian analysis. Clearly, Bob's interests are better served than Sam's. However, the nature of the two proposals seems to require one of the two to be disappointed. Moreover, the outcome in terms of broader interests (i.e., company, society) appears not to be suboptimal, since both proposals were judged equivalent in the blind reviews. Consequently, it is appropriate to answer the first question affirmatively.

The second question inquires into the rights respected by Bob's behavior. Here again, the evidence seems persuasive that no one's rights were violated. Sam did not have (did not create) the same opportunity to point out the advantages of his proposal to those at whom Bob directed his lobbying campaign, but Bob's open campaign involved no deceit, and Sam's inaction may be taken as implied consent.

It is in light of the third question that Bob's actions are most suspect. Justice would have best been served in this case if there had been a clear situation-relevant difference between the two proposals. The blind reviews found them equivalent, so some other basis for differentiating between the proposals presumably had to be found. Bob's efforts served to create irrelevant differences between them. If anything, Sam's superior technical track record would have been a more relevant factor than Bob's initiative and social skills in determining who should be favored to perform a technical task. Bob's actions in this regard were therefore unjust. Interestingly, had the proposals required supervision of others or the ability to persuade others, Bob's approach would have been justified.

Let us examine another case. Lee, 61, has been Director of Engineering for American Semiconductor for 14 years. He is very bright and a fine supervisor but he has not kept abreast of new developments in technology.

American Semiconductor's manufacturing process creates substantial quantities of toxic materials. Lee's rather casual attitude toward the disposal of these chemicals has resulted in a number of environmental citations. The firm is now tied up in court on two cases and will probably be forced to pay a considerable amount in damages. Yet, Lee still does not perceive the disposal problem as urgent. For three years, Charlie, the executive vice president, has tried to persuade Lee to make this a priority issue but has failed. Charlie has reluctantly concluded that Lee must be taken out of his position as Director of Engineering.

Charlie recognizes that it would demoralize the other managers if he were to fire Lee outright. So, Charlie decides that he will begin to tell selected individuals that he is dissatisfied with Lee's work. When there is open support for Lee, Charlie quietly sides with Lee's opposition. He casually lets Lee's peers know that he thinks Lee may have outlived his usefulness to the firm. He even exaggerates Lee's deficiencies and failures when speaking to Lee's coworkers. Discouraged by the waning support from his colleagues, Lee decides to take an early retirement.

In response to the first question in the decision tree, we can conclude that getting Lee out of his position may indeed bring about the "greatest good for the greatest number," presuming a suitable replacement can be found. Not only is Lee hindering the achievement of the apparent goals of the organization, but he is also causing external diseconomies in the disposal of the toxic wastes. Both of these problems, especially when taken together, bring us to the conclusion that Lee is hurting both American Semiconductor and many other people. Thus, Charlie's PBA seems to pass utilitarian criteria.

On the issue of rights, however, there are some difficulties with Charlie's PBA. Namely, Lee's right of free consent was violated. Lee has the right to be treated honestly and forthrightly and Charlie's attempt to destroy Lee's reputation behind his back failed to respect this right.

Overwhelming Factors

A still-unexplained qualification in the decision tree we have described is the concept of an "overwhelming factor"—i.e., a situational factor that may, in a given case, justify overriding one of the three ethical criteria: utilitarian outcomes, individual rights, or distributive justice. What counts as an overwhelming factor?

Conflicts between Criteria. As we have suggested, the three criteria are intended to systematically focus our attention on three kinds of decision factors: (1) the congruence between the decision and the efficient satisfaction of the greatest number of people, (2) the effect of the decision on individuals who have rights, and (3) the distributional consequences of the decision. Obviously, these three factors may come into conflict. As in the American Semiconductor case, the decision maker may be faced with a situation in which a choice must be made between, on the one hand, a course of action that achieves the greatest good for the greatest number but at the price of violating an individual's rights, and, on the other hand, a course of action that respects the individual's rights but at the price of a substantial reduction in the achievement of the greatest good.

There are no well-defined rules for solving the moral dilemmas that these conflicts pose. The dilemmas can be resolved only by making a considered judgment concerning which of the conflicting criteria should be accorded the most weight in the given situation. In some cases the judgment may be easier than in others. Suppose, for example, that violating an employee's right to privacy on the job is the only way to stopping continuing thefts that deprive thousands of customers from getting quality pharmaceutical products. Then the utilitarian criterion may be given greater weight than the rights criterion—employee's rights must be sacrificed for the "greatest good."

Although there are no hard and fast rules for resolving moral dilemmas of this sort, there is a systematic procedure for handling them—the *principle of double effect*. Stated simply, this principle holds that it is acceptable to make a decision that has two effects, one good and one bad, provided that the decision maker's dominant motivation is to achieve the good effect and provided that the good effect is important enough to permit the bad effect [Grisez, 1970].

Conflicts within Criteria. Not only may the three criteria conflict with each other, but each may

conflict with itself as well. *First*, there may be conflict between the utilitarian consequences of those involved or with the means chosen to accomplish the appropriate goals. This is probably typical in organizations that have coalitions with conflicting goals or where there is conflict among coalitions about the appropriate means to consensual goals. *Second*, there may be conflict between the rights of competing individuals. The decision maker may be forced to choose between permitting one person to preserve the right to privacy and allowing another person to exercise the right of free speech. *Third*, there may be a conflict between different canons of justice. Administering a rule with literal consistency, for example, may conflict with the principle that individuals who differ in relevant ways should be treated differently. Or there may be a conflict between individuals. A situation may, for example, call for hard choices between using seniority or using merit as the basis for deciding who is to be given preference.

As with conflicts between ethical criteria, there are no well-defined rules for resolving the dilemmas within ethical criteria. Again, the decision maker is forced to employ a weighting procedure. For example, when rights come into conflict, the decision maker must make a conscientious judgment concerning the relative importance of the interests protected by one right as compared to the interests protected by the conflicting right. Although sometimes easy and obvious, such judgments can also be exceedingly difficult to make.

Lack of Capacity to Employ the Criteria. Three kinds of factors might legitimately relieve the decision maker of the responsibility of adhering to the ethical criteria relevant to a certain decision. All three of these factors relate to the decision maker's personal incapacity to adhere to the relevant criteria.

First, the decision maker may legitimately lay aside a certain ethical criterion if there is no freedom to use it. For example, a manager may be so pressured by others that ethical criteria cannot be brought to bear on the decision. Or a decision maker may be only in partial control of a certain decision and thus unable to use a specific ethical criterion.

Second, the decision maker might legitimately fail to employ a certain ethical criterion owing to a lack of adequate information for using that criterion. As we have seen, this is more often the case with the utilitarian and justice criteria than with the rights criterion.

Third, the decision maker who has strong and reasonable doubts about the legitimacy of an ethical criterion can legitimately be excused from adhering to that criterion. There is nothing sacred about the specific ethical criteria proposed in this article. They represent a consensus among normative ethicians, but that does not preclude other, more or less constraining norms being employed, as long as they are arrived at conscientiously.

Faced with any of these three kinds of incapacitating factors, the decision maker may legitimately accord a lesser weight to one criterion. The underlying rationale for such systematic devaluation of ethical criteria is simple. Persons cannot be held responsible for matters they cannot control or for matters about which they are ignorant or sincerely in doubt. However, determining whether a decision maker's lack of freedom, lack of information, or lack of certitude is sufficient to abrogate ethical responsibility requires one to make some exceedingly difficult judgments.

IMPLICATIONS

An important implication of any research on ethics lies in the area of education and development. This is particularly true regarding the subject of organizational politics. Presented in an ethically bland fashion, theories of organizational politics tend to evoke an unfortunate combination of cynicism, defeatism, and paranoia. Without ethical paradigms, individuals too often infer that success is controlled by others or attained only by those who engage in unproductive behavior. In contrast, confronting the ethical issues in organizational politics leads individuals to assume responsibility for their political behavior decisions. It is unlikely that such an approach will enable individuals to solve all the ethical dilemmas they will face in their careers, but it may stimulate "moral" development [Kohlberg, 1973].

Several lines of research are also suggested by the foregoing analysis. First, there would be some value in further developing ethical paradigms for other areas of discretion faced by organizational members. For example, the areas of obedience, whistle blowing, self-promotion, and bottom-up social intervention all cry out for ethical guidance. Second, there is a need to conduct empirical research regarding what rights, canons of justice, and utilitarian rules are commonly accepted in general and in specific dilemmas. Third, the *process* of ethical judgment about politics and other issues needs empirical work. For example, what antecedent conditions are associated with ethical actions? Similarly, how do ethical codes formalized in an organization influence political behavior decisions?

CONCLUDING REMARKS

As should be clear from this discussion, reducing the ethical uncertainty surrounding political behavior decisions places significant cognitive burdens on the decision maker [Simon, 1976]. Judging the normative equality of PBAs can involve confronting complicated ethical dilemmas. Yet, there seems to be no satisfactory substitute for individual discretion that addresses these complexities directly and to the limits of one's cognitive capabilities.

As we have seen, management theory offers little guidance in this regard. Its calculative form influences us to be ethically myopic when we evaluate political behavior. Instead of determining whether human rights or standards of justice are violated, we are often content to judge political behavior according to its outcomes. This orientation invites cynicism about what are termed the political realities of organizational life [Nord, 1978]. For example, in describing a patently unethical political act, one writer asserted "many people think it is wrong to try to influence others in this way, even people who, without consciously recognizing it, use this technique themselves" [Kotter, 1977], as if to justify the action. We do not intend to replace cynicism of this kind with Polyanna assertions that ethical managers (politicians) will be more successful than unethical ones. They may or may not be, but that is really not the point. Ethics involves standards of conduct, not guidelines for personal gain. When it comes to the ethics of organizational politics, respect for justice and human rights should prevail for its own sake.

REFERENCES

Allen, R. W., Makison, D. L.; Porter, L. W.; Renwick, P. A.; & Mayes, B. T. Organizational politics: Tactics and characteristics of its actors. *California Management Review*, 1979, *22*(4), 77–83.

Aristotle. *The Nicomachean ethics* (J. A. K. Thomson, trans.). London: Allen & Unwin, 1953. (330 B.C.)

Bennis, W.; & Slater, P. *The temporary society.* New York: Harper & Row, 1968.

Bentham, J. *An introduction to the principles of morals and legislation.* New York: Hafner, 1948. (1789)

Bok, S. Whistleblowing and professional responsibilities. In D. Callahan & S. Bok (Eds.), *Ethics teaching in higher education.* New York: Plenum, 1980.

Bowie, N. E. *Toward a new theory of distributive justice.* Amherst: University of Massachusetts Press, 1971.

Brandt, R. B. *A theory of the good and the right.* New York: Oxford University Press, 1979.

Crozier, M. *The bureaucratic phenomena.* Chicago: University of Chicago Press, 1964.

Dahl, R. A. The concept of power. *Behavioral Science.* 1957, *2*, 201–205.

Daniels, N. Merit and meritocracy. *Philosophy & Public Affairs*, 1978, *7*, 206–223.

Drake, B. *Normative constraints on power in organizational decision making.* Unpublished manuscript, School of Business Administration, Wayne State University, Detroit, 1979.

Dworkin, R. *Taking rights seriously.* Cambridge: Harvard University Press, 1978.

Eells, R. *The government of corporations.* New York: Free Press, 1962.

Evan, W. M. Power, conflict, and constitutionism in organizations. *Social Science Information* 1975, *14*, 53–80.

Ewing, D. W. *Freedom inside the organization.* New York: McGraw-Hill, 1977.

Feinberg, J. *Social philosophy.* Englewood Cliffs, N.J.: Prentice-Hall, 1973.

Fuller, L. *The morality of law.* New Haven: Yale University Press, 1964.

Gandz, J.; & Murray, V. V. The experience of work place politics. *Academy of Management Journal*, 1980, *23*, 237–251.

Grisez, G. *Abortion: The myths, the realities, and the arguments.* New York: Corpus Book, 1970.

Hart, H. L. A. Are there any natural rights? *Philosophical Review*, 1955, *64*, 175–191.

Hickson, D. J.; Hinings, C. R.; Lee, C. A.; Schneck, R.

E.; & Pennings, J. M. A stragegic contingencies theory of intraorganizational power. *Administrative Science Quarterly.* 1971, *19*, 216–229.

Hobbes, T. *The leviathan.* New York: Bobbs-Merrill, 1958. (1651)

Kant, I. *The metaphysical elements of justice* (J. Ladd, trans.). New York: Library of Liberal Arts, 1965. (1797)

Keeley, M. *Justice versus effectiveness in organizational evaluation.* Paper presented at the annual meeting of the Academy of Management, Atlanta, 1979.

Kohlberg, L. *Collected papers on moral development and moral education.* Cambridge: Center for Moral Education, Harvard University, 1973.

Kotter, J. P. Power, dependence, and effective management. *Harvard Business Review*, 1977, *53*(3), 125–136.

Krupp, S. *Patterns of organization analysis.* New York: Holt, Rinehart & Winston, 1961.

Locke, J. *The second treatise of government.* New York: Liberal Arts Press, 1952. (1690)

Lyons, D. *The forms and limits of utilitarianism.* Oxford: Clarendon Press, 1965.

Martin, N. H.; & Sims, J. H. Power tactics. *Harvard Business Review*, 1956, *34*(3), 25–36.

Mayes, B. T.; & Allen, R. W. Toward a definition of organizational politics. *Academy of Management Review*, 1977, *2*, 672–678.

Mill, J. S. *Utilitarianism.* Indianapolis: Bobbs-Merrill, 1957. (1863)

Miller, A. R. *The assault on privacy.* Ann Arbor: University of Michigan Press, 1971.

Mironi, M. The confidentiality of personal records: A legal and ethical view. *Labor Law Journal*, 1974, *25*, 270–292.

Nord, W. R. Dreams of humanization and the realities of power. *Academy of Management Review*, 1978, *3*, 674–679.

Nozick, R. *Anarchy, state, and utopia.* New York: Basic Books, 1974.

Okum, A. M. *Equality and efficiency: The big trade-off.* Washington: Brookings Institution, 1975.

Perelman, C. *The idea of justice and the problem of argument.* New York: Humanities Press, 1963.

Pettigrew, A. M. *The politics of organizational decision making.* London: Tavistock, 1973.

Pfeffer, J. Power and resource allocation in organizations. In B. Staw & G. Salancik (Eds.), *New directions in organizational behavior.* Chicago: St. Clair Press, 1977, pp. 235–266.

Pfeffer, J. The micropolitics of organizatons. In M. W.

Meyer and associates (Eds.), *Environments and organizations*. San Francisco: Jossey-Bass, 1978, pp. 29–50.

Pfeffer, J.; & Salancik, G. Organizational decision making as a political process. *Administrative Science Quarterly*, 1974, *18,* 135–151.

Rawls, J. *A theory of justice*. Cambridge, Mass.: Belknap Press, 1971.

Schein, E. G. The problem of moral education for the business manager. *Industrial Management Review*, 1966, *7,* 3–11.

Schein, V. E. Individual power and political behaviors in organizations: An inadequately explored reality. *Academy of Management Review*, 1977, *2,* 64–72.

Sidgwick, H. *The methods of ethics*. New York: Dover, 1966. (1874)

Simon, H. A. *Administrative behavior* (3rd ed.). New York: Free Press, 1976.

Singer, P. Rights and the market. In J. Arthur & W. Shaw (Eds.), *Justice and economic distribution*. Englewood Cliffs, N.J.: Prentice-Hall, 1978, pp. 207–221.

Smart, J. J. C. An outline of a system of utilitarian ethics.

in J. C. C. Smart & B. Williams (Eds.), *Utilitarianism for and against*. New York: Cambridge University Press, 1973, 3–74.

Sobel, J. H. Utilitarianism: Simple and general. *Inquiry*, 1970, *13,* 394–449.

Thompson, J. D. *Organizations in action*. New York: McGraw-Hill, 1967.

Tushman, M. T. A political approach to organizations: A review and rationale. *Academy of Management Review*, 1977, *2,* 206–216.

Walters, K. D. Your employee's right to blow the whistle. *Harvard Business Review*, 1975, *53*(4), 26–34.

Walzer, M. The obligation to disobey. *Ethics*, 1967, *77*(3), 163–175.

Wasserstrom, R. Privacy and the law. In R. Bronaugh (Ed.), *Philosophical law*. Westport, Conn.: Greenwood Press, 1978.

Zald, M. N. (Ed.). *Power in organizations*. Nashville: Vanderbilt University Press, 1970.

Zalesnik, A. Power and politics in organizational life. *Harvard Business Review*, 1970, *48*(2), 47–60.

25 WHISTLEBLOWING AND LEAKS
Sissela Bok

In writing her books *Lying* and *Secrets*, Sissela Bok has explored ethical questions of communication that are more specific than the theoretical issues of Cavanagh, Moberg, and Velasquez. In this chapter from *Secrets*, Professor Bok considers the ethics of disclosing organizational information to outsiders. Bok suggests that there are viable rationales for secrecy (confidentiality and trade, research, administrative, and military secrecy), yet a sense of accountability may suggest organizational members disclose secrets to outsiders. One may disclose secrets either openly, in public, thus blowing the whistle on the organization, or surreptitiously, thus leaking information. Bok argues that to "blow the whistle" on one's own organization involves dissent, breach of loyalty, and an accusation. In deciding between secrecy and dissent, an individual has an ethical obligation to consider the seriousness of the problem, alternative solutions to the problem, and fairness.

REVELATION FROM WITHIN

*All that pollution up at Mølledal—all that reeking
waste from the mill—it's seeped into the pipes feeding
from the pump-room; and the same damn poisonous
slop's been draining out on the beach as well. . . .
I've investigated the facts as scrupulously as possible.
. . . There's irrefutable proof of the presence of
decayed organic matter in the water—millions of
bacteria. It's positively injurious to health, for either
internal or external use. Ah, what a blessing it is to
feel that you've done some service for your home town
and your fellow citizens.*

Dr. Thomas Stockman, in Henrik Ibsen,
An Enemy of the People, *Act 1*

Such was Dr. Stockman's elation, in Ibsen's play,
after having written a report on the contamination of
the town's newly installed mineral baths. As the
spa's medical director, he took it for granted that
everyone would be eager to learn why so many who
had come to the baths for health purposes the previous summer had been taken ill; and he assumed that
the board of directors and the taxpayers would glad-
ly pay for the extensive repairs that he recommended. By the fifth act of the play, he had been
labeled an "enemy of the people" at a public meeting, lost his position as the spa's medical director,
and suffered through the stoning of his house by an
angry crowd. But he held his ground: "Should I let
myself be whipped from the field by public opinion
and the solid majority and other such barbarities? No
thank you!"[1]

"Whistleblower" is a recent label for those who,
like Dr. Stockman, make revelations meant to call
attention to negligence, abuses, or dangers that
threaten the public interest. They sound an alarm
based on their expertise or inside knowledge, often
from within the very organization in which they
work. With as much resonance as they can muster,
they strive to breach secrecy, or else arouse an
apathetic public to dangers everyone knows about
but does not fully acknowledge.[2]

Few whistleblowers, however, share Dr. Stockman's initial belief that it will be enough to make
their message public, and that people who learn of
the danger will hasten to counter it. Most know,
rather, that their alarms pose a threat to anyone who

benefits from the ongoing practice and that their
own careers and livelihood may be at risk. The
lawyer who breaches confidentiality in reporting
bribery by corporate clients knows the risk, as does
the nurse who reports on slovenly patient care in a
hospital, the engineer who discloses safety defects
in the braking systems of a fleet of new rapid-transit
vehicles, or the industrial worker who speaks out
about hazardous chemicals seeping into a play-
ground near the factory dump.

For each of the rationales of shared secrecy that I
have discussed—confidentiality, trade secrecy, secrecy for research, and administrative and military
secrecy—concealment of negligence and abuses creates strong tensions for insiders. They must confront
questions of loyalty, conscience, and truthfulness,
and personal concerns about careers and peace of
mind. What should they consider revealing? And
which secrets must they at all costs bring to public
attention?

Would-be whistleblowers also face conflicting
pressures from without. In many professions, the
prevailing ethic requires above all else loyalty to
colleagues and to clients; yet the formal codes of
professional ethics stress responsibility to the public
in cases of conflict with such loyalties. Thus the
largest professional engineering society asks members to speak out against abuses threatening the
safety, health, and welfare of the public.[3] A number
of business firms have codes making similar requirements; and the United States Code of Ethics for
government servants asks them to "expose corruption wherever uncovered" and to "put loyalty to the
highest moral principles and to country above loyalty to persons, party, or Government department."[4]
Regardless of such exhortations, would-be whistleblowers have reason to fear the results of carrying
out the duty to reveal corruption and neglect. However strong this duty may seem in principle, they
know that in practice, retaliation is likely. They fear
for their careers and for their ability to support
themselves and their families.

Government service in the United States offers
insight into the variety of forms that retaliation can
take. A handbook issued during the Nixon era rec-
ommends reassigning "undesirables" to places so
remote that they would prefer to resign. Whistleblowers may also be downgraded or given work

without responsibility or work for which they are not qualified; or else they may be given more tasks than they can possibly perform.

Another risk to outspoken civil servants—devastating to their careers—is that they may be ordered to undergo a psychiatric "fitness for duty" examination. Congressional hearings in 1978 uncovered a growing tendency to resort to such mandatory examinations, and found that it frequently results from conflicts between supervisors and employees. A person declared unfit for service can then be "separated" and his assertions discredited. The chairman of the investigating subcommittee, Senator Edward Kennedy, concluded that "there was general agreement . . . that involuntary psychiatric examinations were not helpful to the Government, unfair to employees, and that the agencies placed psychiatrists in an impossible situation."[5]

Outright firing, finally, is the most direct institutional response to whistleblowers. Those who bring suit incur heavy legal expenses and have little assurance of prevailing in court. One civil servant, reflecting on her experience and on that of others, stated that their reactions, after speaking out about the agency in which they worked, had "ranged from humiliation, frustration, and helpless rage to complete despair about our democratic process."[6]

The plight of whistleblowers has been documented in the last decade by the press and by a growing number of books and scholarly articles.[7] Evidence of the hardships imposed on those who chose to act in the public interest has combined with a heightened awareness of professional malfeasance and corruption to produce a shift toward greater public support of whistleblowers. Public-service law firms and consumer groups have taken up their cause; institutional reforms and legislation have been enacted to combat illegitimate reprisals. Some would encourage even greater numbers of employees to ferret out and publicize improprieties in the agencies and organizations where they work.

Given the indispensable services performed by so many whistleblowers—as during the Watergate period and after—strong public support is often merited. But the new climate of acceptance makes it easy to overlook the dangers of whistleblowing: of work and reputations unjustly lost for those falsely accused, of privacy invaded and trust undermined. There comes a level of internal prying and mutual suspicion at which no institution can function. And it is a fact that the disappointed, the incompetent, the malicious, and the paranoid all too often make groundless accusations. Worst of all, ideological persecution throughout the world traditionally relies on insiders willing to inform on their colleagues or even on their family members, often through staged public denunciations or press campaigns.

The very societies that encourage such revelation from within of political or religious deviation are often least tolerant of whistleblowing concerning abuse or neglect in ruling circles. Such messages require some larger context where secrecy, corruption, and coercion are less solidly entrenched, some forum where an appeal to justice can still be made. They also require an avenue of concerted public response; for if the audience is not free to receive or to act on the information—as when censorship or fear of retribution stifles response—then the message only rebounds to injure the whistleblower. If protest within a nation is thus blocked, international appeals may be the only remaining possibility. Depending on the severity of the repression, only the most striking injustices may then filter through with sufficient strength to alert ordinarily indifferent foreigners. Alarms, like ripples in the water, weaken as they move away from their point of origin; if forced to go below the surface, they may be further attenuated.

No society can count itself immune from the risk that individuals or groups in power might use whistleblowing for their own purposes, and crush it when they see fit. A society that fails to protect the right to speak out even on the part of those whose warnings turn out to be spurious obviously opens the door to political repression. Given such protection, however, we still need to weigh the uses and the costs of whistleblowing, and to try to distinguish between its more and its less justifiable forms. From the moral point of view, there are important differences between the aims, messages, and methods of dissenters from within.

BLOWING THE WHISTLE

The alarm of the whistleblower is meant to disrupt the status quo: to pierce the background noise, perhaps the false harmony, or the imposed silence of "business as usual." Three elements, each jarring, and triply jarring when conjoined, lend acts of whistleblowing special urgency and bitterness: dissent, breach of loyalty, and accusation.*

Like all *dissent*, first of all, whistleblowing makes public a disagreement with an authority or a majority view. But whereas dissent can arise from all forms of disagreement with, say, religious dogma or government policy or court decisions, whistleblowing has the narrower aim of casting light on negligence or abuse, of alerting the public to a risk and of assigning responsibility for that risk.

It is important, in this respect, to see the shadings between the revelations of neglect and abuse which are central to whistleblowing, and dissent on grounds of policy. In practice, however, the two often come together. Coercive regimes or employers may regard dissent of any form as evidence of abuse or of corruption that calls for public exposure. And in all societies, persons may blow the whistle on abuses in order to signal policy dissent. Thus Daniel Ellsberg, in making his revelations about government deceit and manipulation in the Pentagon Papers, obviously aimed not only to expose misconduct and assign responsibility but also to influence the nation's policy toward Southeast Asia.

In the second place, the message of the whistleblower is seen as a *breach of loyalty* because it comes from within. The whistleblower, though he is neither referee nor coach, blows the whistle on his own team. His insider's position carries with it certain obligations to colleagues and clients. He may have signed a promise of confidentiality or a loyalty oath. When he steps out of routine channels to level accusations, he is going against these obligations. Loyalty to colleagues and to clients comes to be pitted against concern for the public interest and for those who may be injured unless someone speaks out. Because the whistleblower criticizes from within, his act differs from muckraking and other forms of exposure by outsiders. Their acts may arouse

anger, but not the sense of betrayal that whistleblowers so often encounter.

The conflict is strongest for those who take their responsibilities to the public seriously, yet have close bonds of collegiality and of duty to clients as well. They know the price of betrayal. They know, too, how organizations protect and enlarge the area of what is concealed, as failures multiply and vested interests encroach. And they are aware that they violate, by speaking out, not only loyalty but usually hierarchy as well.

It is the third element of *accusation*, of calling a "foul" from within, that arouses the strongest reactions on the part of the hierarchy. The charge may be one of unethical or unlawful conduct on the part of colleagues or superiors. Explicitly or implicitly, it singles out specific groups or persons as responsible: as those who knew or should have known what was wrong and what the dangers were, and who had the capacity to make different choices. If no one could be held thus responsible—as in the case of an impending avalanche or a volcanic eruption—the warning would not constitute whistleblowing. At times the whistleblower's greatest effort is expended on trying to show that someone *is* responsible for danger or suffering: that the collapse of a building, the derailment of a train, or a famine that the public may have attributed to bad luck or natural causes was in reality brought about by specific individuals, and that they can be held responsible, perhaps made to repair the damage or at least to avoid compounding it.

The whistleblower's accusation, moreover, concerns a present or an imminent threat. Past errors or misdeeds occasion such an alarm only if they still affect current practices. And risks far in the future usually lack the immediacy needed to render the alarm compelling, as well as the close connection to particular individuals that would justify accusations. Thus an alarm can be sounded about safety defects in a rapid-transit system that threaten or will shortly

---

*Consider the differences and the overlap between whistleblowing and civil disobedience with respect to these three elements. First, whistleblowing resembles civil disobedience in its openness and its intent to act in the public interest. But the dissent in whistleblowing, unlike that in civil disobedience, usually does not represent a breach of law; it is, on the contrary, protected by the right of free speech and often encouraged in codes of ethics and other statements of principle. Second, whistleblowing violates loyalty, since it dissents from within and breaches secrecy, whereas civil disobedience need not and can as easily challenge from without. Whistleblowing, finally, accuses specific individuals, whereas civil disobedience need not. A combination of the two occurs, for instance, when former CIA agents publish books to alert the public about what they regard as unlawful and dangerous practices, and in so doing openly violate, and thereby test, the oath of secrecy that they have sworn.

threaten passengers; but the revelation of safety defects in a system no longer in use, while of historical
interest, would not constitute whistleblowing. Nor
would the disclosure of potential problems in a system not yet fully designed and far from being implemented.

Not only immediacy but also specificity is
needed for the whistleblower to assign responsibility. A concrete risk must be at issue rather than
a vague foreboding or a somber prediction. The act
of whistleblowing differs in this respect from the
lamentation or the dire prophecy.

Such immediate and specific threats would normally be acted upon by those at risk. But the whistleblower assumes that his message will alert listeners to a threat of which they are ignorant, or
whose significance they have not grasped. It may
have been kept secret by members within the organization, or by all who are familiar with it. Or it may
be an ''open secret,'' seemingly in need only of
being pointed out in order to have its effect. In either
case, because of the elements of dissent, breach of
loyalty, and accusation, the tension between concealing and revealing is great. It may be intensified
by an urge to throw off the sense of complicity that
comes from sharing secrets one believes to be unjustly concealed, and to achieve peace of mind by
setting the record straight at last. Sometimes a desire
for publicity enters in, or a hope for revenge for
past slights or injustices. Colleagues of the whistleblower often suspect just such motives; they may
regard him as a crank, publicity-hungry, eager for
scandal and discord, or driven to indiscretion by his
personal biases and shortcomings.[8]

On the continuum of more or less justifiable acts
of whistleblowing, the whistleblower tends to see
more such acts as justified and even necessary than
his colleagues. Bias can affect each side in drawing
the line, so that each takes only some of the factors
into account—the more so if the action comes at the
end of a long buildup of acrimony and suspicion.

THE LEAK

When Otto Otepka sent classified documents and
names of persons he considered security risks to
''Red-hunter'' Julian Sourwine of the Senate Internal Subcommittee in the early 1960s, or when
''Deep Throat'' revealed facts about Watergate in
deepest secrecy, each was engaged in a practice that
has come to be called ''leaking.''[9] Each meant to
disclose information from within but to do so covertly, unlike the whistleblower or the official who
resigns in protest.*

Any kind of information can be leaked; but the
word ''leak'' is most often used in connection with
administrative secrets, such as the anonymous revelations in 1980 from within the Department of Justice concerning the ABSCAM investigations of
members of Congress, or with classified military
secrets.[10] The originator of a leak is usually unknown to the public and sometimes even to the
journalist or other intermediary. Anonymous messages may be sent by mail, dropped at doorsteps,
transmitted in coded form on computers.

Leaking has a symbiotic relationship with secrecy. Without secrecy there would be no need to
leak information. As government secrecy grows and
comes to involve more people, the opportunities to
leak from within expand; and with increased leaking, governments intensify their efforts to shore up
secrecy.

At the same time as they combat leaking, however, executives use it selectively to further their
own policies. With modern governments guarding
vast amounts of information, much of it inaccessible
to the public or actively kept secret, and with the
media eager to circulate newsworthy revelations to
vast audiences, the leak, unlike acts of whistleblowing, has become an important tool of governing.†
Administrators may leak stories as trial balloons, to
deflect attention from recent failures, or to smear

*The two cases differ in that Otepka's actions come much closer to informing than most efforts to leak. Leaks are generally directed to the
public via an intermediary, whereas informing is meant for the authorities. But Otepka considered those in charge of federal appointments
to be overly lenient, and so chose a different outlet for his revelations.

†Leaks are often seen as related to national, state, or local government affairs. But there is no reason not to use the word for analogous
revelations from international government bodies such as UN agencies or OPEC circles, or from nongovernmental ones such as IBM or
Nestlé.

political opponents. And civil servants who want to combat policies or particular decisions may leak selected compromising facts. If a secret plan is sufficiently sensitive, those who learn about it may, in this way, exercise a veto power over its execution. Thus the members of congressional committees overseeing CIA activities know that they need only leak details concerning any one of them to destroy its effectiveness.

Press and television reporters cooperate in bringing many of these leaks to public attention. They may discard pieces of information that cannot be verified or that seem of little interest; but at times they publish the flimsiest of rumors. Whether knowingly or not, they are also often the conduits for leaked disinformation. Because of their eagerness for news and "scoops," reporters become, as Francis Rourke has pointed out, "willing if not enthusiastic collaborators" with those who engage in leaking to influence public opinion.[11]

Unlike whistleblowing, leaking need not concern danger, negligence, or abuse, though both bring something that is secret or unnoticed into the open from within an organization. Thus a civil servant may leak secret documents in his agency's possession concerning another nation's military preparedness, or specifying steps in fragile diplomatic talks. But when a leak from within does concern misconduct, it is a variant of whistleblowing, undertaken surreptitiously because the revealer cannot or does not want to be known as its source.

Whether as a surreptitious form of whistleblowing, a tool for news management by administrators, or a means of bureaucratic maneuvering, leaking has become one of the main forms of communication about matters of public interest. But it is far from ideal from the point of view of the media or the public. For while it is preferable to complete secrecy, and offers one of the few ways of learning about risky policies and mismanagement otherwise shrouded in secrecy, it does so haphazardly and is ceaselessly used to manipulate public opinion.

Both leaking and whistleblowing can be used to challenge corrupt or cumbersome systems of secrecy—in government as in the professions, the sciences, and business. Both may convey urgently needed warnings, but they may also peddle false information and vicious personal attacks. How,

then, can one distinguish the many acts of revelation from within that are genuinely in the public interest from all the petty, biased, or lurid tales that pervade our querulous and gossip-ridden societies? Can we draw distinctions between different messages, different methods and motivations?

We clearly can, in a number of cases. Whistleblowing and leaks may be starkly inappropriate when used in malice or in error, or when they lay bare legitimately private matters such as those having to do with political belief or sexual life. They may, just as clearly, offer the only way to shed light on an ongoing practice such as fraudulent scientific research or intimidation of political adversaries; and they may be the last resort for alerting the public to a possible disaster. Consider, for example, the action taken by three engineers to alert the public to defects in the braking mechanisms of the Bay Area Rapid Transit System (BART):

> The San Francisco Bay Area Rapid Transit System opened in 1972. It was heralded as the first major breakthrough toward a safe, reliable, and sophisticated method of mass transportation. A public agency had been set up in 1952 to plan and carry out the project; and the task of developing its major new component, a fully automatic train control system, was allocated to Westinghouse.
>
> In 1969, three of the engineers who worked on this system became increasingly concerned over its safety. They spotted problems independently, and spoke to their supervisors, but to no avail. They later said they might well have given up their effort to go farther had they not found out about one another. They made numerous efforts to speak to BART's management. But those in charge were already troubled by costs that had exceeded all projections, and by numerous unforeseen delays. They were not disposed to investigate the charges that the control system might be unsafe. Each appeal by the three engineers failed.
>
> Finally, the engineers interested a member of BART's board of trustees, who brought the matter up at a board meeting. Once again, the effort failed. But in March 1973, the three

were fired once the complaint had been traced to them. When they wrote to ask why they had been dismissed, they received no answer.

Meanwhile, the BART system had begun to roll. The control system worked erratically, and at times dangerously. A month after the opening, one train overshot the last station and crashed into a parking lot for commuters. Claiming that some bugs still had to be worked out, BART began to use old-fashioned flagmen in order to avoid collisions.

The three engineers had turned, in 1972, to the California Society of Professional Engineers for support. The society, after investigating the complaint, agreed with their views, and reported to the California State legislature. It too had launched an investigation, and arrived at conclusions quite critical of BART's management.

The engineers filed a damage suit against BART in 1974, but settled out of court in 1975. They had difficulties finding new employment, and suffered considerable financial and emotional hardship in spite of their public vindication.[12]

The three engineers were acting in accordance with the law and with engineering codes of ethics in calling attention to the defects in the train control system. Because of their expertise, they had a special responsibility to alert the company, and if need be its board of directors and the public, to the risks that concerned them. If we take such a clear-cut case of legitimate whistleblowing as a benchmark, and reflect on what it is about it that weighs so heavily in favor of disclosure, we can then examine more complex cases in which speaking out in public is not so clearly the right choice or the only choice.

INDIVIDUAL MORAL CHOICE

What questions might individuals consider, as they wonder whether to sound an alarm? How might they articulate the problem they see, and weigh its seriousness before deciding whether or not to reveal it? Can they make sure that their choice is the right one?

And what about the choices confronting journalists or others asked to serve as intermediaries?

In thinking about these questions, it helps to keep in mind the three elements mentioned earlier: dissent, breach of loyalty, and accusation. They impose certain requirements: of judgment and accuracy in dissent, of exploring alternative ways to cope with improprieties that minimize the breach of loyalty, and of fairness in accusation. The judgment expressed by whistleblowers concerns a problem that should matter to the public. Certain outrages are so blatant, and certain dangers so great, that all who are in a position to warn of them have a *prima facie* obligation to do so. Conversely, other problems are so minor that to blow the whistle would be a disproportionate response. And still others are so hard to pin down that whistleblowing is premature. In between lie a great many of the problems troubling whistleblowers. Consider, for example, the following situation:

> An attorney for a large company manufacturing medical supplies begins to suspect that some of the machinery sold by the company to hospitals for use in kidney dialysis is unsafe, and that management has made attempts to influence federal regulatory personnel to overlook these deficiencies.
>
> The attorney brings these matters up with a junior executive, who assures her that he will look into the matter, and convey them to the chief executive if necessary. When she questions him a few weeks later, however, he tells her that all the problems have been taken care of, but offers no evidence, and seems irritated at her desire to learn exactly where the issues stand. She does not know how much further she can press her concern without jeopardizing her position in the firm.

The lawyer in this case has reason to be troubled, but does not yet possess sufficient evidence to blow the whistle. She is far from being as sure of her case as was Ibsen's Dr. Stockman, who had received laboratory analyses of the water used in the town spa, or as the engineers in the BART case, whose professional expertise allowed them to evaluate the risks of the faulty braking system. Dr. Stockman and the engineers would be justified in assuming that they had an obligation to draw attention to the dangers they saw, and that anyone who shared their knowledge would be wrong to remain silent or to suppress evidence of the danger. But if the attorney blew the whistle about her company's sales of machinery to hospitals merely on the basis of her suspicions, she would be doing so prematurely. At the same time, the risks to hospital patients from the machinery, should she prove correct in her suspicions, are sufficiently great so that she has good reason to seek help in looking into the problem, to feel complicitous if she chooses to do nothing, and to take action if she verifies her suspicions.

Her difficulty is shared by many who suspect, without being sure, that their companies are concealing the defective or dangerous nature of their products—automobiles that are firetraps, for instance, or canned foods with carcinogenic additives. They may sense that merely to acknowledge that they don't know for sure is too often a weak excuse for inaction, but recognize also that the destructive power of adverse publicity can be great. If the warning turns out to have been inaccurate, it may take a long time to undo the damage to individuals and organizations. As a result, potential whistleblowers must first try to specify the degree to which there is genuine impropriety, and consider how imminent and how serious the threat is which they perceive.

If the facts turn out to warrant disclosure, and if the would-be whistleblower has decided to act upon them in spite of the possibilities of reprisal, then how can the second element—breach of loyalty—be overcome or minimized? Here, as in the Pentagon Papers case, the problem is one of which set of loyalties to uphold. Several professional codes of ethics, such as those of engineers and public servants, facilitate such a choice as least in theory, by requiring that loyalty to the public interest should override allegiance to colleagues, employers, or clients whenever there is a genuine conflict. Accordingly, those who have assumed a professional responsibility to serve the public interest—as had both Dr. Stockman in Ibsen's play and the engineers in the BART case—have a special obligation not to remain silent about dangers to the public.

Before deciding whether to speak out publicly, however, it is important for them to consider whether the existing avenues for change within the organization have been sufficiently explored. By turning first to insiders for help, one can often uphold both sets of loyalties and settle the problem without going outside the organization. The engineers in the BART case clearly tried to resolve the problem they saw in this manner, and only reluctantly allowed it to come to public attention as a last resort. Dr. Stockman, on the other hand, acted much more impetuously and with little concern for discretion. Before the directors of the mineral baths had even received his report, he talked freely about it, and welcomed a journalist's request to publicize the matter. While he had every reason to try to remedy the danger he had discovered, he was not justified in the methods he chose; on the contrary, they were singularly unlikely to bring about corrective action.

It *is* disloyal to colleagues and employers, as well as a waste of time for the public, to sound the loudest alarm first. Whistleblowing has to remain a last alternative because of its destructive side effects. It must be chosen only when other alternatives have been considered and rejected. They may be rejected if they simply do not apply to the problem at hand, or when there is not time to go through routine channels, or when the institution is so corrupt or coercive that steps will be taken to silence the whistleblower should he try the regular channels first.

What weight should an oath or a promise of silence have in the conflict of loyalties? There is no doubt that one sworn to silence is under a stronger obligation because of the oath he has taken, unless it was obtained under duress or through deceit, or else binds him to something in itself wrong or unlawful. In taking an oath, one assumes specific obligations beyond those assumed in accepting employment. But even such an oath can be overridden with the public interest at issue is sufficiently strong. The fact that one has promised silence is no excuse for complicity in covering up a crime or violating the public trust.

The third element in whistleblowing—accusation—is strongest whenever efforts to correct a problem without going outside the organization have failed, or seem likely to fail. Such an outcome is especially likely whenever those in charge take part in the questionable practices, or have too much at stake in maintaining them. The following story relates the difficulties one government employee experienced in trying to decide whether to go public with accusations against superiors in his agency:

> As a construction inspector for a federal agency, John Samuels (not his real name) had personal knowledge of shoddy and deficient construction practices by private contractors. He knew his superiors received free vacations and entertainment, had their homes remodeled, found jobs for their relatives—all courtesy of a private contractor. These superiors later approved a multimillion no-bid contract with the same "generous" firm.
>
> Samuels also had evidence that other firms were hiring nonunion laborers at a low wage while receiving substantially higher payments from the government for labor costs. A former superior, unaware of an office dictaphone, had incautiously instructed Samuels on how to accept bribes for overlooking sub-par performance.
>
> As he prepared to volunteer this information to various members of Congress, he became tense and uneasy. His family was scared and the fears were valid. It might cost Samuels thousands of dollars to protect his job. Those who had freely provided him with information would probably recant or withdraw their friendship. A number of people might object to his using a dictaphone to gather information. His agency would start covering up and vent its collective wrath upon him. As for reporters and writers, they would gather for a few days, then move on to the next story. He would be left without a job, with fewer friends, with massive battles looming, and without the financial means of fighting them. Samuels decided to remain silent.[13]

Samuels could be sure of his facts, and fairly sure that it would not help to explore avenues within the agency in trying to remedy the situation. But was the method he envisaged—of volunteering his information to members of Congress and to the press—the one most likely to do so, and to provide a fair hearing for those he was charging with corruption and crime? Could he have gone first to the police? If he had been concerned to proceed in the fairest possible manner, he should at least have considered alternative methods of investigating and reporting the abuses he had witnessed.

These abuses were clearly such as to warrant attention. At other times, potential whistleblowers must also ask themselves whether their message, however accurate, is one to which the public is entitled in the first place or whether it infringes on personal and private matters that no one should invade. Here, the very notion of what is in the public interest is at issue: allegations regarding an official's unusual sexual or religious practices may well appeal to the public's interest without therefore being relevant to "the public interest." Those who regard such private matters as threats to the public voice their own religious and political prejudices in the language of accusation. Such a danger is never stronger than when the accusation is delivered surreptitiously; the anonymous allegations made during the McCarthy period regarding political beliefs and associations often injured persons who did not even know their accusers or the exact nature of the charges.

In fairness to those criticized, openly accepted responsibility for blowing the whistle should therefore be preferred to the secret denunciation or the leaked rumor—the more so, the more derogatory and accusatory the information. What is openly stated can be more easily checked, its source's motives challenged, and the underlying information examined. Those under attack may otherwise be hard put to it to defend themselves against nameless adversaries. Often they do not even know that they are threatened until it is too late to respond.

The choice between open and surreptitious revelation from within is admittedly less easy for the persons who intend to make them. Leaking information anonymously is safer, and can be kept up indefinitely; the whistleblower, on the contrary, shoots his bolt by going public. At the same time, those who leak know that their message may be taken less seriously, precisely because its source remains concealed. And because these messages go through several intermediaries before they appear in print, they may undergo changes along the way. At times, they are so adulterated that they lose their point altogether.

Journalists and other intermediaries must make choices of their own with respect to a leaked message. Should they use it at all, even if they doubt its accuracy? Should they pass it on verbatim or interpret it? Or should they seek to "plug" the leak? Newspaper and television bureaus receive innumerable leaks but act on only some of them. Unless the information is accompanied by indications of how the evidence can be checked, the source's anonymity, however safe, diminishes the value of the message.

In order to assure transmission of their message, yet be safe from retaliation, leakers often resort to a compromise: by making themselves known to a journalist or other intermediary, they make it possible to verify their credibility; by asking that their identity be concealed, they still protect themselves from the consequences they fear.

If anonymous sources can point to independent evidence of genuine risk or wrongdoing, the need for them to step forward is reduced and their motives are less important. For this reason, the toll-free numbers that citizens can use to report on government fraud, tax evasion, or police abuse serve an important purpose in protecting critics both from inside and from outside an organization without such evidence, accusations openly made by identifiable persons are preferable. The open charge is fairer to the accused, and allows listeners to weigh the motives and the trustworthiness of the whistleblowers.

Must the whistleblower who speaks out openly also resign? Only if staying on means being forced to participate in the objectionable activity, and thus to take on partial responsibility for its consequences. Otherwise, there should be no burden on whistleblowers to resign in voicing their alarm. In principle, at least, it is often their duty to speak out, and their positions ought not thereby to be at issue. In

practice, however, they know that retaliation, forced departure, perhaps blacklisting, may be sufficient risks at times so that it may be wise to resign before sounding the alarm: to resign in protest, or to leave quietly, secure another post, and only then blow the whistle.[14] In each case, those who speak out can then do so with the authority and knowledge of insiders, but without their vulnerability.

It is not easy to weigh all these factors, nor to compensate for the degree of bias, rationalization, and denial that inevitably influences one's judgment. By speaking out, whistleblowers may spark a re-examination of these forces among colleagues and others who had ignored or learned to live with shoddy or corrupt practices. Because they have this power to dramatize moral conflict, would-be whistleblowers have a special responsibility to ask themselves about biases in deciding whether or not to speak out: a desire for self-defense in a difficult bureaucratic situation perhaps, or unrealistic expectations regarding the likely effect of speaking out.*

As they weigh the reasons for sounding the alarm, or on the contrary for remaining silent, they may find it helpful to ask about the legitimacy of the rational for collective secrecy in the particular problem they face. If they are wondering whether or not to blow the whistle on the unnecessary surgery they have witnessed, for example, or on the manufacture of unsafe machinery, what weight should they place on claims to professional confidentiality or corporate secrecy?

Reducing bias and error in moral choice often requires consultation, even open debate; such methods force us to articulate the arguments at stake and to challenge privately held assumptions. But choices about whether or not to blow the whistle present special problems for such consultation. On the one hand, once whistleblowers sound their alarm publicly, their judgment *will* be subjected to open scrutiny; they will have to articulate their reasons for speaking out and substantiate their charges. On the other hand, it will then be too late to retract their

---

*If, for example, a government employee stands to make large profits from a book exposing the iniquities in his agency, there is danger that he might slant his report in order to cause more of a sensation. Sometimes a warning is so clearly justifiable and substantiated that it carries weight no matter what the motives of the speaker. But scandal can pay; and the whistleblower's motives ought ideally to be above suspicion, for his own sake as well as for the sake of the respect he desires for his warning. Personal gain from speaking out increases the need to check the accuracy of the speaker.

charges should they turn out to have been unfounded.

For those who are concerned about a situation within their organization, it is therefore preferable to seek advice *before* deciding either to go public or to remain silent. But the more corrupt the circumstances, the more dangerous it may be to consult colleagues, and the more likely it is that those responsible for the abuse or neglect will destroy the evidence linking them to it. And yet, with no one to consult, the would-be whistleblowers themselves may have a biased view of the state of affairs; they may see corruption and conspiracy where none exists, and choose not to consult others when in fact it would have been not only safe but advantageous to do so.

Given these difficulties, it is especially important to seek more general means of weighing the arguments for and against whistleblowing; to take them up in public debate and in teaching; and to consider changes in organizations, law, and work practices that could reduce the need for individuals to choose between blowing and "swallowing" the whistle.[15]

ORGANIZATIONAL CHANGE AND SOCIAL POLICY

What changes inside and outside organizations might protect the rights of dissenters and critics, and assure the public of needed information, while cutting down on undue breaches of loyalty and on false accusations?

An organization can reduce the need to resort to whistleblowing by providing mechanisms for evaluating criticism before it reaches the press or the courtroom. These mechanisms must work to counteract the blockages of information within an organization and the perennial pressures to filter out negative information before it reaches those who make decisions.[16] The filtering process may be simple or intricate, well-intentioned or malevolent, more or less consciously manipulated. Some abuses are covered up at the source; others are sidelined en route to department heads; still others are kept from reaching review boards or trustees.

Surveying the damage from such failures of communication, David Ewing has argued that managers

have much to gain by not discouraging internal criticism.[17] In recent survey, he found that over 60 per cent of the business firms responding to a questionnaire claimed that a senior executive's door is always open to anyone with a grievance.[18] A number of managers have other ways of encouraging the views of dissenters, and promise that no one will be unfairly dismissed or disciplined.

Such an "open-door" policy may suffice at times. When the policy is taken seriously by management, and its results are publicized, employees learn that they have nothing to lose from speaking out. But such policies are frequently inadequate. In the first place, the promises of protection given by top management cannot always be fulfilled. Though employees may keep their jobs, there are countless ways of making their position difficult, to the point where they may be brought to resign of their own volition or to stay while bitterly regretting that they had spoken out. Second, it would be naïve to think that abuses in industry or in government are always unknown to top management and perpetrated against their will by subordinates. If those in charge knowingly manufacture unsafe products or engage in corporate bribery, then the open-door policy is but a trap for the outspoken; even when employees suffer no reprisal for having voiced a criticism to management, they will usually find that it has simply been ignored.

For these reasons, proposals have been made to ensure independent internal consideration of the criticisms, while protecting those who voice them more formally. Internal review boards, ombudsmen, consumer or citizen representatives on boards of trustees, bills of rights for employees: these methods of protection spring up and die away with great rapidity. When they work, their usefulness is undeniable. They allow for criticism with much less need for heroism; give a way to deflect the crank or the witch-hunter *before* his message gains publicity, and a process of checking its accuracy; make it easier to distinguish between urgent alarms and long-range worries; and provide an arena for debating the moral questions of motive, loyalty, and responsibility to the public.

The methods fail when they are but window-dressing from the outset, meant only to please or exhaust dissenters; or when they change, no matter how independent at the start, into management tools. Such is the fate of many a patient representative in hospitals: their growing loyalty to co-workers and to the management and their distance from the patients they are meant to represent once again leave critics little choice between submission and open revolt. Still another reason for the failure of such intermediaries is that they often lack credibility. No matter how well-meaning, they will not be sought out if they cannot protect from retaliation those who turn to them for help. Even if they can give such protection, but cannot inspire confidence in their independence, their role will be largely ceremonial. Finally, they may protect the outspoken but not succeed in correcting the problem brought up; once again, they will quickly lose credence.

In the last decade, a growing number of laws have been enacted to protect employees against reprisals. First to be passed were laws covering federal and state employees; these, however, still work slowly and unevenly. In April 1981, Michigan became the first state to enact a "Whistleblowers Protection Act" covering corporate employees.[19] It allows courts to grant back pay, reinstatement in the job, and costs of litigation to employees who can demonstrate improper treatment.

Alan Westin points out that citizens of Michigan had special reason to support such legislation.[20] In the mid-1970s, a chemical company mistakenly shipped PBBs (polybrominated biphenyls) to state feed-grain cooperatives instead of their regular nutritional supplement. As a result, the health of residents was seriously injured, and a great many cattle died. The sponsor of the law stated that an official inquiry was begun when the farm animals began to die in large numbers. But it was seriously hampered by the reluctance of employees of the chemical company to come forth with information that might have given a clue to the link between the deaths of the animals and the accidental delivery of PBBs. Employees later testified that they had been threatened with dismissal if they told investigators that the PBB accident might have been the cause.

It is too early to tell whether laws such as that enacted in Michigan will become the rule rather than the exception, and whether they will succeed in protecting whistleblowers. The problem with such laws is that there are so many other ways to penalize employees without detection; and that it is not always easy for courts to tell the difference between legitimate and spurious complaints.* Nevertheless, such laws will continue to be needed to protect whistleblowers against the most egregious reprisals, and to encourage firms to set up more workable internal mechanisms for complaint.[21]

A different method for reducing the tension and risk of whistleblowing can complement laws that protect those who voice criticism. It is to state clear conditions under which those who learn about a certain kind of danger *must* report it. If such requirements to report are properly limited and if they succeed in deflecting reprisals, they can lessen the conflict of loyalties felt by would-be whistleblowers and strengthen their resolve. Such laws already exist in a number of places. One is the Toxic Substances Control Act, enacted in 1977, which requires companies to instruct employees that any person must report information about a chemical they take to present "a substantial risk of injury to health or to the environment."[22]

This type of law, like that protecting whistleblowers, can be undercut and circumvented in a number of ways; it is nevertheless useful insofar as it facilitates reporting of serious and documented dangers. Such laws must, however, be limited to clear-cut improprieties; and the lines must be firmly drawn against requiring reporting on political dissent or on purely personal matters. In many societies, citizens are asked to report "deviations," fellow workers encouraged to spy on one another, and students asked to expose the subversive views of their teachers and vice versa. No matter how great the need to eradicate unlawfulness and corruption, such parallels should not be ignored.

The alarms of whistleblowers would be unnecessary were it not for the many threats to the public

---

*In watching the evolution of such laws, their broader effect must also be kept in mind. To what extent might they contribute to making institutions more litigious? And to what extent will protection in one place put increased pressure on another? Is it not possible, for example, that the increasing difficulty in firing incompetent federal employees led to the growing resort to psychiatric fitness-for-duty examinations, and that these, in turn, have become a new weapon with which to fight outspoken critics within a bureaucracy?

interest shielded by practices of secrecy in such domains as law, medicine, commerce, industry, science, and government. Given these practices, whistleblowers perform an indispensable public service; but they do so at great human cost, and without any assurance that they uncover most, or even the worst, abuses. While they deserve strong support in their endeavors, every effort should therefore be made to combat the problems they signal by other means.

The most important task is to reduce the various practices of collective secrecy in order to permit the normal channels of public inquiry to take the place of whistleblowing and of leaking. The more encrusted a society becomes with unnecessary secrecy, confidential procedures, systems of classification, and means of corporate, professional, and administrative self-protection, the harder it is for the public to learn in time about risk and wrongdoing.

As I have argued, all secrecy cannot and should not be discarded. But even where limited secrecy fulfills an important function, as in protecting certain military secrets, controls are needed in order to reduce the dangers that arise when power and secrecy combine. And whatever the assumed benefits of secrecy, its role in damming up the usual alternatives to whistleblowing is a cost all too often forgotten.

NOTES

1. Henrik Ibsen, *An Enemy of the People*, (1882), in *Henrik Ibsen: The Complete Major Prose Plays*, trans, and ed. Rolf Fjelde (New York: New American Library, 1965), pp. 281–386; passage quoted on p. 384.

2. I draw, for this chapter, on my earlier essays on whistleblowing: ''Whistleblowing and Professional Responsibilities,'' in Daniel Callahan and Sissela Bok, eds., *Ethics Teaching in Higher Education* (New York: Plenum Press, 1980), pp. 277–95 (reprinted, slightly altered, in *New York University Educational Quarterly* 11 (Summer 1980):2–10; ''Blowing the Whistle,'' in Joel Fleishman, Lance Liebman, and Mark Moore, eds., *Public Duties: The Moral Obligations of Official* (Cambridge, Mass.: Harvard University Press, 1981), pp. 204–21.

3. Institute of Electrical and Electronics Engineers,

Code of Ethics for Engineers, art. 4, IEEE *Spectrum* 12 (February 1975):65.

4. Code of Ethics for Government Service, passed by the U.S. House of Representatives in the 85th Congress, 1958, and applying to all government employees and office holders.

5. U.S., Congress, House of Representatives, Committee on Post Office and Civil Service, Subcommittee on Compensation and Employee Benefits, *Forced Retirement/Psychiatric Fitness of Duty Exams*, 95th Cong, 2d sess., November 3, 1978, pp. 2–4. See also Subcommittee Hearings, February 28, 1978. Psychiatric referral for whistleblowers has become institutionalized in government service, but it is not uncommon in private employment. Even persons who make accusations without being employed in the organization they accuse, moreover, have been classified as unstable and thus as unreliable witnesses. See, for example, Jonas Robitscher, ''Stigmatization and Stone-walling: The Ordeal of Martha Mitchell,'' *Journal of Psychohistory* 6 (Winter 1979):393–407.

6. Carol S. Kennedy, ''Whistle-blowing: Contribution or Catastrophe?'' Address to the American Association for the Advancement of Science, February 15, 1978, p. 8.

7. For analyses and descriptions of whistleblowing, see: Rosemary Chalk and Frank von Hippel, ''Due Process for Dissembling 'Whistle-Blowers,' '' *Technology Review* 81 (June-July 1979):49–55; Louis Clark, ''The Sound of Professional Suicide,'' *The Barrister* 5 (Summer 1978):10–19; Helen Dudar, ''The Price of Blowing the Whistle,'' *New York Times Magazine*, October 30, 1977, pp. 41–54; John Edsall, *Scientific Freedom and Responsibility*; David W. Ewing, *Freedom Inside the Organization* (New York: E. P. Dutton & Co., 1977); Nader, Petkas, and Blackwell, *Whistle Blowing*; Charles Peters and Taylor Branch, *Blowing the Whistle* (New York: Praeger Publishers, 1972); Alan F. Westin and Stephan Salisbury, eds., *Individual Rights in the Corporation* (New York: Pantheon Books, 1980); Alan F. Westin, *Whistle Blowing! Loyalty and Dissent in the Corporation* (New York: McGraw-Hill Book Co., 1980).

8. Judith P. Swazey and Stephen R. Scheer suggest that when whistleblowers expose fraud in clinical research, colleagues respond *more* negatively to the whistleblowers who report the fraudulent research than to the person whose conduct has been reported. See ''The Whistleblower as a Deviant Professional: Professional Norms and Responses to Fraud in Clini-

cal Research,'' Workshop on Whistleblowing in Bio-
medical Research, Washington, D.C., September
1981, to be published.

9. See Peters and Branch, *Blowing the Whistle*; Carl
Bernstein and Robert Woodward, *All the President's
Men* (New York: Simon & Schuster, 1974).

10. On Leaking, see Bernstein and Woodward, *All the
President's Men*; Douglass Cater, *The Fourth Branch
of Government* (Boston: Houghton Mifflin Co.,
1959); Rourke, *Secrecy and Publicity*; David Wise,
''The President Leaks a Document,'' *The Politics of
Lying* (New York: Random House, 1973), pp. 117–
33; Halperin and Hoffman, *Top Secret*; and the works
cited above on whistleblowing and in note 14 on
resignation in protest.

11. Rourke, *Secrecy and Publicity*, p. 198.

12. See Robert J. Baum and Albert Flores, ed., *Ethical
Problems in Engineering* (Troy, N.Y.: Center for the
Study of the Human Dimensions of Science and
Technology, 1978), pp. 227–47; Chalk and von Hip-
pel, ''Due Process for Dissenting 'Whistle-
Blowers,' '' pp. 4–55.

13. This case is adapted from Clark, ''The Sound of
Professional Suicide.''

14. On resignation in protest, see Albert Hirschman,
Exit, Voice, and Loyalty (Cambridge, Mass.: Harvard University Press, 1970); Brian Barry, in a review of Hirschman's book in *British Journal of Political Science* 4 (1974):79–104, has pointed out that
''exit'' and ''voice'' are not alternatives but independent variations that may occur separately or together.
Both leaking and whistleblowing represent ''voice.''
They can be undertaken while staying on at work, or
before one's voluntary exit, or simultaneously with
it, or after it; they can also have the consequence of
involuntary or forced ''exit'' through dismissal or
being ''frozen out'' even though retained at work.
See also Edward Weisband and Thomas M. Franck,
Resignation in Protest (New York: Viking Press,

1975); James Thomson, ''Getting Out and Speaking
Out,'' *Foreign Policy*, no. 13 (Winter 1973–1974),
pp. 49–69; Joel L. Fleishman and Bruce L. Payne,
*Ethical Dilemmas and the Education of Policy-
makers* (Hastings-on-Hudson, N.Y.: Hastings Center, 1980).

15. Alan Westin discusses ''swallowing'' the whistle in
Whistle Blowing!, pp. 10–13. For a discussion of
debate concerning whistleblowing, see Rosemary
Chalk, ''The Miner's Canary,'' *Bulletin of the Atomic Scientists* 38 (February 1982): pp. 16–22.

16. John C. Coffee, in ''Beyond the Shut-eyed Sentry:
Toward a Theoretical View of Corporate Misconduct
and an Effective Legal Response,'' *Virginia Law
Review* 63 (1977): 1099–1278, gives an informed and
closely reasoned account of such ''information blockages,'' such ''filtering out,'' and of possible remedies. See also Christopher Stone, *Where the Law
Ends: The Social Control of Corporate Behavior*
(New York: Harper & Row, 1975), pp. 201–16.

17. David W. Ewing, ''The Employee's Right to Speak
Out: The Management Perspective,'' *Civil Liberties
Review* 5 (September–October 1978):10–15.

18. David W. Ewing, ''What Business Thinks About
Employee Rights,'' *Harvard Business Review* 55
(September–October 1977):81–94.

19. Alan Westin, ''Michigan's Law to Protect the Whistle Blowers,'' *Wall Street Journal*, April 31, 1981, p.
18.

20. Ibid.

21. For a discussion of legal approaches, see Alfred G.
Feliu, ''Discharge of Professional Employees: Protecting Against Dismissal for Acts Within a Professional Code of Ethics,'' *Columbia Human Rights
Law Review* 11 (1979–1980):149–87; Westin, *Whistle Blowing!*

22. Environmental Protection Agency, ''Toxic Substances Control Act,'' *Federal Register*, Thursday,
March 16, 1978, pt. 5.

26 THE BASES OF SOCIAL POWER
John R. P. French, Jr., and Bertram Raven

Most social theories conceive of power as involving a communication relationship. With their authority hierarchies, opportunities for political action, and communicatively rich relationships, work organizations are therefore natural sites for the study of power. But power is a complicated subject that requires a good descriptive foundation for further thought.

In an oft-cited article that we have abridged here, French and Raven define power as the ability to influence an individual's psychological field, including behavior, opinions, attitudes, goals, needs, and values. The article is best known for its identification of five sources of power: referent, expert, reward, coercive, and legitimate. French and Raven delineate the general circumstances when it is appropriate to use each source of power and describe how using power may have consequences for the person who holds the power.

The processes of power are pervasive, complex, and often disguised in our society. Accordingly one finds in political science, in sociology, and in social psychology a variety of distinctions among different types of social power or among qualitatively different processes of social influence (1, 7, 14, 20, 21, 24, 25, 29, 32). Our main purpose is to identify the major types of power and to define them systematically so that we may compare them according to the changes which they produce and the other effects which accompany the use of power.

Our theory of social influence and power is limited to influence on the person, P, produced by a social agent, O, where O can be either another person, a role, a norm, a group, or a part of a group. We do not consider social influence exerted on a group.

THE BASES OF POWER

By the basis of power we mean the relationship between O and P which is the source of that power. It is rare that we can say with certainty that a given empirical case of power is limited to one source.

Normally, the relation between O and P will be characterized by several qualitatively different variables which are bases of power (25). Although there are undoubtedly many possible bases of power which may be distinguished, we shall here define five which seem especially common and important. These five bases of O's power are: (*a*) reward power, based on P's perception that O has the ability to mediate rewards for him; (*b*) coercive power, based on P's perception that O has the ability to mediate punishments for him; (*c*) legitimate power, based on the perception by P that O has a legitimate right to prescribe behavior for him; (*d*) referent power, based on P's identification with O; (*e*) expert power, based on the perception that O has some special knowledge or expertness.

Reward Power

Reward power is defined as power whose basis is the ability to reward. The strength of the reward power of O/P increases with the magnitude of the rewards which P perceives that O can mediate for him. Reward power depends on O's ability to administer positive valences and to remove or decrease

J.R.P. French, Jr., and B. Raven, "The Bases of Social Power," pp. 150–167, in *Studies of Social Power*, edited by D. Cartwright, Ann Arbor, Michigan: Institute of Social Research, the University of Michigan. Reprinted with permission of the Institute for Social Research.

negative valences. The strength of reward power also depends upon the probability that O can mediate the reward, as perceived by P. A common example of reward power is the addition of a piece-work rate in the factory as an incentive to increase production.

The new state of the system induced by a promise of reward (for example, the factory worker's increased level of production) will be highly dependent on O. Since O mediates the reward, he controls the probability that P will receive it. Thus P's new rate of production will be dependent on his subjective probability that O will reward him for conformity minus his subjective probability that O will reward him even if he returns to his old level. Both probabilities will be greatly affected by the level of observability of P's behavior. Incidentally, a piece rate often seems to have more effect on production than a merit rating system because it yields a higher probability of reward for conformity and a much lower probability of reward for noncomformity.

The utilization of actual rewards (instead of promises) by O will tend over time to increase the attraction of P toward O and therefore the referent power of O over P. As we shall note later, such referent power will permit O to induce changes which are relatively independent. Neither rewards nor promises will arouse resistance in P, provided P considers it legitimate for O to offer rewards.

The range of reward power is specific to those regions toward within which O can reward P for conforming. The use of rewards to change systems within the range of reward power tends to increase reward power by increasing the probability attached to future promises. However, unsuccessful attempts to exert reward power outside the range of power would tend to decrease the power; for example, if O offers to reward P for performing an impossible act, this will reduce for P the probability of receiving future rewards promised by O.

Coercive Power

Coercive power is similar to reward power in that it also involves O's ability to manipulate the attainment of valences. Coercive power of O/P stems from the expectation on the part of P that he will be punished by O if he fails to conform to the influence attempt. Thus negative valences will exist in given regions of P's life space, corresponding to the threatened punishment by O. The strength of coercive power depends on the magnitude of the negative valence of the threatened punishment multiplied by the perceived probability that P can avoid the punishment by conformity, i.e., the probability of punishment for nonconformity minus the probability of punishment for conformity (11). Just as an offer of a piece-rate bonus in a factory can serve as a basis for reward power, so the ability to fire a worker if he falls below a given level of production will result in coercive power.

Coercive power leads to dependent change also, and the degree of dependence varies with the level of observability of P's conformity. An excellent illustration of coercive power leading to dependent change is provided by a clothes presser in a factory observed by Coch and French (3). As her efficiency rating climbed above average for the group the other workers began to "scapegoat" her. That the resulting plateau in her production was not independent of the group was evident once she was removed from the presence of the other workers. Her production immediately climbed to new heights.*

At times, there is some difficulty in distinguishing between reward power and coercive power. Is the withholding of a reward really equivalent to a punishment? Is the withdrawal of punishment equivalent to a reward? The answer must be a psychological one—it depends upon the situation as it exists for P. But ordinarily we would answer these questions in the affirmative; for P, receiving a reward is a positive valence as is the relief of suffering. There is some evidence (5) that conformity to group norms in order to gain acceptance (reward power) should be distinguished from conformity as a means of forestalling rejection (coercive power).

The distinction between these two types of power is important because the dynamics are different. The concept of "sanctions" sometimes lumps the two together despite their opposite effects. While reward power may eventually result in an independent system, the effects of coercive power will continue to

---

*Though the primary influence of coercive power is dependent, it often produces secondary changes which are independent. Brainwashing, for example, utilizes coercive power to produce many primary changes in the life space of the prisoner, but these dependent changes can lead to identification with the aggressor and hence to secondary changes in ideology which are independent.

be dependent. Reward power will tend to increase the attraction of P toward O; coercive power will decrease this attraction (11, 12). The valence of the region of behavior will become more negative, acquiring some negative valence from the threatened punishment. The negative valence of punishment would also spread to other regions of the life space. Lewin (23) has pointed out this distinction between the effects of rewards and punishment. In the case of threatened punishment, there will be a resultant force on P to leave the field entirely. Thus, to achieve conformity, O must not only place a strong negative valence in certain regions through threat of punishment, but O must also introduce restraining forces, or other strong valences, so as to prevent P from withdrawing completely from O's range of coercive power. Otherwise the probability of receiving the punishment, if P does not conform, will be too low to be effective.

Legitimate Power

Legitimate power is probably the most complex of those treated here, embodying notions from the structural sociologist, the group-norm and role oriented social psychologist, and the clinical psychologist.

There has been considerable investigation and speculation about socially prescribed behavior, particularly that which is specific to a given role or position. Linton (24) distinguishes group norms according to whether they are universals for everyone in the culture, alternatives (the individual having a choice as to whether or not to accept them), or specialties (specific to given positions). Whether we speak of internalized norms, role prescriptions and expectations (27), or internalized pressures (15), the fact remains that each individual sees certain regions toward which he should locomote, some regions toward which he should not locomote, and some regions toward which he may locomote if they are generally attractive for him. This applies to specific behaviors in which he may, should, or should not engage; it applies to certain attitudes or beliefs which he may, should, or should not hold. The feeling of "oughtness" may be an internalization from his parents, from his teachers, from his religion, or may have been logically developed from some idiosyncratic system of ethics. He will speak of such behaviors with expressions like "should," "ought to," or "has a right to." In many cases, the original source of the requirement is not recalled.

Legitimate power of O/P is here defined as that power which stems from internalized values in P which dictate that O has a legitimate right to influence P and that P has an obligation to accept this influence. We note that legitimate power is very similar to the notion of legitimacy of authority which has long been explored by sociologists, particularly by Weber (32), and more recently by Goldhammer and Shils (14). However, legitimate power is not always a role relation: P may accept an induction from O simply because he had previously promised to help O and he values his word too much to break the promise. In all cases, the notion of legitimacy involves some sort of code or standard, accepted by the individual, by virtue of which the external agent can assert his power. We shall attempt to describe a few of these values here.

Bases for Legitimate Power. Cultural values constitute one common basis for the legitimate power of one individual over another. O has characteristics which are specified by the culture as giving him the right to prescribe behavior for P, who may not have these characteristics. These bases, which Weber (32) has called the authority of the "eternal yesterday," include such things as age, intelligence, caste, and physical characteristics. In some cultures, the aged are granted the right to prescribe behavior for others in practically all behavior areas. In most cultures, there are certain areas of behavior in which a person of one sex is granted the right to prescribe behavior for the other sex.

Acceptance of the social structure is another basis for legitimate power. If P accepts as right the social structure of his group, organization, or society, especially the social structure involving a hierarchy of authority, P will accept the legitimate authority of O, who occupies a superior office in the hierarchy. Thus legitimate power in a formal organization is largely a relationship between offices rather than between persons. And the acceptance of an office as *right* is a basis for legitimate power—a judge has a right to levy fines, a foreman should assign work, a priest is justified in prescribing religious beliefs, and it is the management's prerogative to make certain decisions (10). However, legitimate power also involves the perceived right of the person to hold the office.

Designation by a legitimizing agent is a third basis for legitimate power. An influencer O may be seen as legitimate in prescribing behavior for P because he has been granted such power by a legitimizing agent whom P accepts. Thus a department head may accept the authority of his vice-president in a certain area because that authority has been specifically delegated by the president. An election is perhaps the most common example of a group's serving to legitimize the authority of one individual or office for other individuals in the group. The success of such legitimizing depends upon the acceptance of the legitimizing agent and procedure. In this case it depends ultimately on certain democratic values concerning election procedures. The election process is one of legitimizing a person's right to an office which already has a legitimate range of power associated with it.

Range of Legitimate Power of O/P. The areas in which legitimate power may be exercised are generally specified along with the designation of that power. A job description, for example, usually specifies supervisory activities and also designates the person to whom the job-holder is responsible for the duties described. Some bases for legitimate authority carry with them a very broad range. Culturally derived bases for legitimate power are often especially broad. It is not uncommon to find cultures in which a member of a given caste can legitimately prescribe behavior for all members of lower castes in practically all regions. More common, however, are instances of legitimate power where the range is specifically and narrowly prescribed. A sergeant in the army is given a specific set of regions within which he can legitimately prescribe behavior for his men.

The attempted use of legitimate power which is outside of the range of legitimate power will decrease the legitimate power of the authority figure. Such use of power which is not legitimate will also decrease the attractiveness of O (11, 12, 28).

Legitimate Power and Influence. The new state of the system which results from legitimate power usually has high dependence on O though it may become independent. Here, however, the de-

gree of dependence is not related to the level of observability. Since legitimate power is based on P's values, the source of the forces induced by O include both these internal values and O. O's induction serves to activate the values and to relate them to the system which is influenced, but thereafter the new state of the system may become directly dependent on the values with no mediation by O. Accordingly this new state will be relatively stable and consistent across varying environmental situations since P's values are more stable than his psychological environment.

We have used the term legitimate not only as a basis for the power of an agent, but also to describe the general behaviors of a person. Thus, the individual P may also consider the legitimacy of the attempts to use other types of power by O. In certain cases, P will consider that O has a legitimate right to threaten punishment for nonconformity; in other cases, such use of coercion would not be seen as legitimate. P might change in response to coercive power of O, but it will make a considerable difference in his attitude and conformity if O is not seen as having a legitimate right to use such coercion. In such cases, the attraction of P for O will be particularly diminished, and the influence attempt will arouse more resistance (11). Similarly the utilization of reward power may vary in legitimacy; the word "bribe," for example, denotes an illegitimate reward.

Referent Power

The referent power of O/P has its basis in the identification of P with O. By identification, we mean a feeling of oneness of P with O, or a desire for such an identity. If O is a person toward whom P is highly attracted, P will have a desire to become closely associated with O. If O is an attractive group, P will have a feeling of membership or a desire to join. If P is already closely associated with O he will want to maintain this relationship (31). P's identification with O can be established or maintained if P behaves, believes, and perceives as O does. Accordingly O has the ability to influence P, even though P may be unaware of this referent power. A verbalization of such power by P might be, "I am like O, and therefore I shall behave or believe as O does," or "I want to be like O, and I will be more like O if I behave or believe as O does.'' The stronger the identification of P with O the greater the referent power of O/P.

Similar types of power have already been investigated under a number of different formulations. Festinger (6) points out that in an ambiguous situation the individual seeks some sort of ''social reality'' and may adopt the cognitive structure of the individual or group with which he identifies. In such a case, the lack of clear structure may be threatening to the individual and the agreement of his beliefs with those of a reference group will both satisfy his need for structure and give him added security through increased identification with his group (16, 19).

We must try to distinguish between referent power and other types of power which might be operative at the same time. If a member is attracted to a group and he conforms to its norms only because he fears ridicule or expulsion from the group for nonconformity, we would call this coercive power. On the other hand if he conforms in order to obtain praise for conformity, it is a case of reward power. The basic criterion for distinguishing referent power from both coercive and reward power is the mediation of the punishment and the reward by O: to the extent that O mediates the sanctions (i.e., has means control over P) we are dealing with coercive and reward power; but to the extent that P avoids discomfort or gains satisfaction by conformity based on identification, regardless of O's responses, we are dealing with referent power. Conformity with majority opinion is sometimes based on a respect for the collective wisdom of the group, in which case it is expert power. It is important to distinguish these phenomena, all grouped together elsewhere as ''pressures toward uniformity,'' since the type of change which occurs will be different for different bases of power.

The concepts of ''reference group'' (30) and ''prestige suggestion'' may be treated as instances of referent power. In this case, O, the prestigeful person or group, is valued by P; because P desires to be associated or identified with O, he will assume attitudes or beliefs held by O. Similarly a negative reference group which O dislikes and evaluates negatively may exert negative influence on P as a result of negative referent power.

It has been demonstrated that the power which we designate as referent power is especially great when P is attracted to O (2, 6, 8, 9, 13, 21, 25). In our terms, this would mean that the greater the attraction, the greater the identification, and consequently the greater the referent power. In some cases, attraction or prestige may have a specific basis, and the range of referent power will be limited accordingly: a group of campers may have great referent power over a member regarding campcraft, but considerably less effect on other regions (25). However, we hypothesize that the greater the attraction of P toward O, the broader the range of referent power of O/P.

The new state of a system produced by referent power may be dependent on or independent of O; but the degree of dependence is not affected by the level of observability to O (7, 21). In fact, P is often not consciously aware of the referent power which O exerts over him. There is probably a tendency for some of these dependent changes to become independent of O quite rapidly.

Expert Power

The strength of the expert power of O/P varies with the extent of the knowledge or perception which P attributes to O within a given area. Probably P evaluates O's expertness in relation to his own knowledge as well as against an absolute standard. In any case expert power results in primary social influence on P's cognitive structure and probably not on other types of systems. Of course changes in the cognitive structure can change the direction of forces and hence of locomotion, but such a change of behavior is secondary social influence. Expert power has been demonstrated experimentally (9, 26). Accepting an attorney's advice in legal matters is a common example of expert influence; but there are many instances based on much less knowledge, such as the acceptance by a stranger of directions given by a native villager.

Expert power, where O need not be a member of P's group, is called ''information power'' by Deutsch and Gerard (4). This type of expert power must be distinguished from influence based on the content of communication as described by Hovland *et al.* (17, 18, 21, 22). The influence of the content of a communication upon an opinion is presumably a secondary influence produced after the *primary* influence (i.e., the acceptance of the information). Since power is here defined in terms of the primary changes, the influence of the content on a related opinion is not a case of expert power as we have defined it, but the initial acceptance of the validity of the content does seem to be based on expert power or referent power. In other cases, however, so-called facts may be accepted as self-evident because they fit into P's cognitive structure; if this impersonal acceptance of the truth of the fact is independent of the more-or-less enduring relationship between O and P, then P's acceptance of the fact is not an actualization of expert power. Thus we distinguish between expert power based on the credibility of O and informational influence which is based on characteristics of the stimulus such as the logic of the argument or the "self-evident facts."

Wherever expert influence occurs it seems to be necessary both for P to think that O knows and for P to trust that O is telling the truth (rather than trying to deceive him).

Expert power will produce a new cognitive structure which is initially relatively dependent on O, but informational influence will produce a more independent structure. The former is likely to become more independent with the passage of time. In both cases the degree of dependence on O is not affected by the level of observability.

The "sleeper effect" (18, 22) is an interesting case of a change in the degree of dependence of an opinion on O. An unreliable O (who probably had negative referent power but some positive expert power) presented "facts" which were accepted by the subjects and which would normally produce secondary influence on the opinions and beliefs. However, the negative referent power aroused resistance and resulted in negative social influence on their beliefs (i.e., set up a force in the direction opposite to the influence attempt), so that there was little change in the subjects' opinions. With the passage of time, however, the subjects tended to forget the identity of the negative communicator faster than they forgot the contents of his communications, so there was a weakening of the negative referent influence and a consequent delayed positive change in the subjects' beliefs in the direction of the influence attempt ("sleeper effect"). Later, when the identity of the negative communicator was experimentally reinstated, these resisting forces were reinstated, and there was another negative change in belief in a direction opposite to the influence attempt (22).

The range of expert power, we assume, is more delimited than that of referent power. Not only is it restricted to cognitive systems but the expert is seen as having superior knowledge or ability in very specific areas, and his power will be limited to these areas, though some "halo effect" might occur. Recently, some of our renowned physical scientists have found quite painfully that their expert power in physical sciences does not extend to regions involving international politics. Indeed, there is some evidence that the attempted exertion of expert power outside of the range of expert power will reduce that expert power. An undermining of confidence seems to take place.

SUMMARY

We have distinguished five types of power: referent power, expert power, reward power, coercive power, and legitimate power. These distinctions led to the following hypotheses.

1. For all five types, the stronger the basis of power the greater the power.
2. For any type of power the size of the range may vary greatly, but in general referent power will have the broadest range.
3. Any attempt to utilize power outside the range of power will tend to reduce the power.
4. A new state of a system produced by reward power or coercive power will be highly dependent on O, and the more observable P's conformity the more dependent the state. For the other three types of power, the new state is usually dependent, at least in the beginning, but in any case the level of observability has no effect on the degree of dependence.
5. Coercion results in decreased attraction of P toward O and high resistance; reward power results in increased attraction and low resistance.
6. The more legitimate the coercion the less it will produce resistance and decreased attraction.

REFERENCES

1. Asch, S. E. *Social psychology*. New York: Prentice-Hall, 1952.
2. Back, K. Influence through social communication. *Journal of Abnormal and Social Psychology*, 1951, **46**, 9–23.
3. Coch, L., & French, J. R. P., Jr. Overcoming resistance to change. *Human Relations*, 1948, **1**, 512–532.
4. Deutsch, M., & Gerard, H. A study of normative and informational influences upon individual judgment. *Journal of Abnormal and Social Psychology*, 1955, **51**, 629–636.
5. Dittes, J., & Kelley, H. Effects of different conditions of acceptance upon conformity to group norms. *Journal of Abnormal and Social Psychology*, 1956, **53**, 629–636.
6. Festinger, L. Informal social communication. *Psychological Review*, 1950, **57**, 271–282.
7. Festinger, L. An analysis of complaint behavior. In M. Sherif & M. O. Wilson (Eds.), *Group relations at the crossroads*. New York: Harper, 1953. Pp. 232–256.
8. Festinger, L., Schachter, S., & Back, K. *Social pressures in informal groups*. New York: Harper, 1950, Chap. 5.
9. Festinger, L., *et al.* The influence process in the presence of extreme deviates. *Human Relations*, 1952, **5**, 327–346.
10. French, J. R. P., Jr., Israel, J., & Ås, D. *Arbeidernes medvirkning i industribedriften: En eksperimentell undersøkelse*. Oslo, Norway: Institute for Social Research, 1957.
11. French, J. R. P., Jr., Morrison, H. W., & Levinger, G. Coercive power and forces affecting conformity. *Journal of Abnormal and Social Psychology*, 1960, **61**, 93–101.
12. Raven, B., & French, J. R. P., Jr. Legitimate power, coercive power, and observability in social influence. *Sociometry*, 1958, **21**, 83–97.
13. Gerard, H. The anchorage of opinions in face-to-face groups. *Human Relations*, 1954, **7**, 313–325.
14. Goldhammer, H., & Shils, E. Types of power and status. *American Journal of Sociology*, 1939, **45**, 171–178.
15. Herbst, P. Analysis and measurement of a situation. *Human Relations*, 1953, **2**, 113–140.
16. Hochbaum, G. Self-confidence and reactions to group pressures. *American Sociological Review*, 1954, **19**, 678–687.
17. Hovland, G., Lumsdaine, A., & Sheffield, F. *Experiments on mass communication*. Princeton, N. J.: Princeton Univ. Press, 1949.
18. Hovland, C., & Weiss, W. The influence of source credibility on communication effectiveness. *Public Opinion Quarterly*, 1951, **15**, 635–650.
19. Jackson, J., & Saltzstein, H. The effect of person-group relationships on conformity processes. *Journal of Abnormal and Social Psychology*, 1958, **57**, 17–24.
20. Jahoda, M. Psychological issues in civil liberties. *The American Psychologist*, 1956, **11**, 234–240.
21. Kelman, H. Three processes of acceptance of social influence: Compliance, identification, and internalization. Paper read at the meetings of the American Psychological Association, August, 1956.
22. Kelman, H., & Hovland, C. Reinstatement of the communicator in delayed measurement of opinion change. *Journal of Abnormal and Social Psychology*, 1953, **48**, 327–335.
23. Lewin, K. *Dynamic theory of personality*. New York: McGraw-Hill, 1935. Pp. 114–170.
24. Linton, R. *The cultural background of personality*. New York: Appleton-Century-Crofts, 1945.
25. Lippitt, R., *et al.* The dynamics of power. *Human Relations*, 1952, **5**, 37–64.
26. Moore, H. The comparative influence of majority and expert opinion. *American Journal of Psychology*, 1921, **32**, 16–20.
27. Newcomb, T. *Social psychology*. New York: Dryden, 1950.
28. Raven, B., & French, J. Group support, legitimate power, and social influence. *Journal of Personality*, 1958, **26**, 400–409.
29. Russell, B. *Power: A new social analysis*. New York: Norton, 1938.
30. Swanson, G., Newcomb, T., & Hartley, E. *Readings in social psychology*. New York: Holt, 1952.
31. Torrance, E., & Mason, R. Instructor effort to influence: An experimental evaluation of six approaches. Paper presented at USAF–NRC Symposium on Personnel, Training, and Human Engineering. Washington, D. C., 1956.
32. Weber, M. *The theory of social and economic organization*. Oxford: Oxford Univ. Press, 1947.

27 ORGANIZATIONAL POWER AS COMMUNICATIVE PRAXIS
Stephen P. Banks

In this chapter, Banks describes three popular perspectives on power and identifies some systemic problems that attend those views. As a response to these problems, he proposes an alternative way of considering power, one that focuses on the actions of individuals. A demonstration of organizational talk is presented that reveals how power can be generated in the discourse of workers, regardless of the authority levels of the persons involved. This chapter challenges traditional structural views of sources of power (cf. John R. P. French and Bertrand Raven, Chapter 26) because it substitutes actual instances of discourse as a source of power. Banks challenges readers to think of different ways that power can be conceived and analyzed in organizational settings and invites consideration of what kinds of evidence researchers rely on to support their claims about power. His point of view also locates communication at the center of power processes in organizations.

Discourse is not simply that which translates struggles or systems of domination, but is the thing for which and by which there is struggle, discourse is the power which is to be seized.
Michel Foucault

Power and its political implications are inescapable aspects of organizational life (Morgan, 1985). Brown and McMillan, for example, have asserted that power may be "one of the major determinants in each unique organizational configuration, capable of determining everything from the choosing of a technology to the establishment of a pecking order" (1988, p. 1). Moreover, with the emergence of the interpretive perspective and the culture metaphor in organizational communication research, scholars have made power relations central to their research (Conrad & Ryan, 1985; Dandridge, Mitroff & Joyce, 1980; Riley, 1983).

The concept of power, however, is not a simple and untroubled one. Many definitions and senses of power have been proffered (see, e.g., Pfeffer, 1981). Frost (1987, p. 505) points out the paradoxical situation in which every commentator seems to agree that power is a basic feature of organizational

life, yet remains "an inchoate and elusive concept, a 'messy' one, subject to much controversy and debate." Part of the elusiveness of power as a concept is due to its abstractness. Power typically is seen as an internal aspect of individuals, similar to attributes like intelligence and compassion, or as an attribute of relationships, like attraction or trust. Conrad and Ryan (1985) argue that traditional approaches conceive of power as a mental attribute of individuals that often is made tangible by researchers' inferences about peoples' behavior. On the other hand, critical-interpretive approaches also treat power as an abstraction, but the manifestations of power in behavior are analyzed as real to the persons being studied. As a consequence, power seems to be an objective factor in organizational life, susceptible to examination by traditional research methods. But it remains conceptually as an aspect of individuals or relationships that exist prior to instances of social interaction.

A second reason that power is an elusive concept is its relation to ideas of social structure. The very notion of power inevitably involves the positioning of individuals or groups relative to other individuals or groups—in exercises of authority, in contests for dominance, in conflicts about resources, in struggles for control. Without the positioning of persons or groups against one another, power would be undetectable; yet the positioning itself reflects a structure, an established order of social relations whose legitimacy is based on what is normally expected and experienced in institutions. Thus, the differing views researchers may have about norms and normativeness in institutional settings affect the way their research is conceived. In addition, their views about the nature of social structure and how it is produced and reproduced affect their approaches to power.

These sources of elusiveness comprise the basis of several conceptual problems that persist across all major approaches to power. This chapter presents three integrated problems in relation to organizational communication that persist in all studies of power. The problem areas are derived from a discussion of the primary theoretical and research approaches to power. To address these persistent problems, I propose a praxis perspective on power and communication in organizations. A praxis view focuses on the routine, everyday actions of individuals and groups and locates social phenomena, like power, in those actual instances of action. Then, to demonstrate the advantages of turning to a praxis perspective, I analyze the talk of a manager and workers in a corporate setting. Finally, some implications of a praxis approach for future research are set forth in the concluding section.

PERSPECTIVES ON POWER

Reviews of power in organizational settings (e.g., Astley & Sachdeva, 1984; Frost, 1987; Lukes, 1974) tend to partition studies into two general categories as approaches that are either basically functionalist or basically interpretivist. In some reviews, the distinction is not readily apparent, as in Frost's (1987) description of surface-level games and deep-level games in organizations; however, a common practice of setting up interpretivism as the opposite of functionalism prevails in recent analyses (Putnam, 1983). Conrad and Ryan (1985) display this tendency when they contrast "traditional" models to "symbological" models of power; but they ex-

pand the repertoire of categories by identifying "radical-critical" research as a relative of the symbological perspective that is nonetheless distinct from it in several ways. While I differ from them in the definitions and reasoning for separating symbological and radical-critical research, I adopt Conrad and Ryan's general view that three streams of thought and research comprise the major recent discussions about power and organizational communication. Accordingly, what follows is a brief description of the structural-functionalist view, the symbolic-interpretive view, and the critical-theoretic view of power.

The Structural-Functionalist View

By far the largest and longest-lived tradition conceives of power as an attribute an individual or group possesses and uses whenever they engage in some goal-directed social action. Power in this view is understood by knowing the bases from which it is obtained (Etzioni, 1961; French & Raven, 1959; Raven, 1974), the sources and opportunities from which the bases of power are derived (Bacharach & Lawler, 1980), and the social configurations—in terms of conflict and bargaining scenarios, coalitions, and interest groups—in which power is recognizable as political action (Putnam & Poole, 1987). A fundamental assumption of the structural-functionalist perspective is that power is instrumental in accomplishing organizational activities and goals; it is brought to bear, in communicative behavior, on decision making, allocating resources, and directing coordinated activity. This approach informs such communication research as Richmond et al.'s (1984) study of power strategies in superior-subordinate interaction and the relationship between workers' perceptions of power strategies and their own satisfaction with their positions. It also is the basis for Gudykunst's (1985) analysis of normative power and intergroup relations in intercultural settings. Even substantial numbers of organizational culture studies take power to be an attribute of members or institutional structures (e.g., Sathe, 1983; Schein, 1985).

The structural-functionalist approach has the advantage of rendering the concept of power measurable. Thus, if power is taken to be an organizational variable, it can be explicated in relation to other variables, including those that have become canons of communication research. It also benefits by coinciding substantially with folk notions of power; consequently, it is possible to ask individuals to reflect on their uses and bases of power without introducing a new vocabulary.

Among the problematic features of the structural-functionalist view, however, is the fact that power is assumed to exist a priori. It is inferred from observable data, yet because it is an abstract epiphenomenon, power is indistinguishable from conflict, bargaining, coalition activities, or other political engagements. Relatedly, the givenness of power extends to the assumption that power is a fundamental aspect of structural features of organizations—for example, the authority hierarchy and position power, unit segmentation, and resource distributions. Yet there are situations when power works against these structural features, such as a situation where higher level officials are controlled by subordinates; in such cases, power must be transformed into other concepts to maintain theoretical integrity. In this example, power is transformed into authority, which, unlike power, has the possibility of nonperformance. Similarly, when a worker slowdown forces managers to change policies, the explanatory concept must be transformed into ''counterpower'' (Yukl, 1981) or ''counteraction'' (Bacharach & Lawler, 1980).

The problem here is not only that power becomes conceptually ''impure'' but that it becomes remote: If institutional structures are powerful, then specifying their power and understanding its consequences, responsibilities, and possibilities for change also becomes removed from the individuals whose actions constitute the manifestations of such power. This is one of the ways our popular views of power promote cynical acceptance of ''the system'' and institutional inertia. We are powerless in the face of powerful institutional structures just because there are no identifiable agents of power.

The Symbolic-Interpretive View

A concern for members' meanings and the symbolic systems of codes through which meanings are generated in power relationships undergirds the symbolic-interpretive view. In this perspective, power is located in the privileged use of symbolic codes to advocate certain interpretations over others. Representative research thus include Brown's (1986) study of the rhetoric of social interventions, Rosen's (1985) analysis of a corporate breakfast meeting, and Brown and McMillan's (1988) grounded theory study of symbolic constructions in a nursing home.

The symbolic-interpretive view is particularly compatible with communication scholarship because it gives priority to communicative behavior as locus, content, and medium of power relationships. As Tompkins and Cheney (1985) point out, much symbolic-interpretive research emphasizes *verstehen*, an understanding of social conditions from the point of view of members of the social unit under study. A significant contribution of this perspective, then, is the attempt to understand power as persons in the social system understand it.

The symbolic view, however, still generally reflects a traditional conceptualization of power, because it assumes that power as an entity exists apart from and prior to palpable action. Tompkins (1985) argues that the concept of symbolism in organizational studies consistently is taken as an internal (that is, ''mental'') actuality, a set of ''interpretive schemes'' separate from and opposed to the external substance of organizational life. Organizational theorists, Tompkins points out, do not typically treat symbolism in the symbolic interactionist tradition, as the emergent creation of meaning in the moment of human interaction. Thus, concrete events and environments in organizations are secondary to members' ''interpretive schemes.'' Depictions of symbolic interaction, such as Rosen's (1985) retelling of a breakfast meeting at Spiro's, therefore, *reveal* power as a preexisting symbolic condition of both persons and social arrangements.

The Critical-Theoretic View

Critical theories inherently focus on power and domination and particularly seek to make people aware of hidden coercive forces that are either beneath normal consciousness or sedimented into institutional orders and routine, everyday practices (Geuss, 1981). Critical research in organizational communication involves a process of critique, which seeks to discover contradictions between what is routinely perceived and what are the actual, historical conditions of power and domination (Kersten, 1987). Moreover, a central task of the critical-theoretic view is to identify inconsistencies between the large-scale social structures of power and the microlevel instances of individuals' behavior (Conrad & Ryan, 1985). Typical of work in this perspective are studies by Clegg (1975, 1979), Deetz (1982), and Mumby (1987).

The signal contribution of the critical-theoretic view is its emphasis on the historically situated conditions of power relationships, including such structures of domination as social class, race, and sex biases. As Kersten (1985) points out, however, its problems in terms of communication research are many. Because its roots are decidedly Marxist, the critical approach is often politically unpopular. Also, the critical attitude that advocates emancipating presumedly beguiled populations of workers is often viewed as an arrogant stance toward research and its subjects. More important, researchers experience technical problems in their efforts to bridge concerns for both micro- and macrolevel phenomena: Meshing the need for critical self-reflection with analysis of action and social structural influences is a tall order. In terms of power theory, however, because the critical theoretic view paradigmatically addresses institutional dominance and power, it fosters the remoteness of power as a concept. Paradoxically, this view makes power more elusive while bringing it into a central and routine role in scholarship.

Each of these three perspectives, then, contributes useful theory and research to the understanding of power. All of these views, however, share major problems that obscure power and inhibit our understanding of how power is related to communication and social order. First, power is treated as a state of being or a capacity attributable to individuals or institutional entities. As such, power—as distinct from the bases, sources, and ramifications of power—is a static concept. Communication as a discipline, however, is fundamentally interested in process; by now it is practically a cliche to point out that communication research needs to be concerned with the dynamic aspects of social interaction. Thus, there is a conceptual incompatibility between popular notions of power and the basic nature of communication research.

That incompatibility is not fatal as long as researchers are not concerned with the abstractness and remoteness of power as a concept. Aiming, however, to make claims about the nature, genesis, and teleology of power brings one face to face with the second problem that is common to all three perspectives—the problem of conceptual abstraction. Gareth Morgan helps illustrate this problem with his caricature of how power works: "Power influences who gets what, when, and how" (Morgan, 1985, p. 158). Researchers within the three perspectives described above necessarily devote their studies to examining the "who, what, when, and how," assuming that power both motivates a priori what they observe and is the product of these elements acting together. The crucial term in Morgan's description of power is "influences," insofar as it partitions off power from its agents and effects. If power influences who gets what, etc., and power must be inferred from the getting of whatever by whomever, then addressing the true nature of power is doomed to an endlessly circular logic.

Taken together, the dual problems of the static nature and the abstract nature of power lead to a third issue of concern. I call this the unobtrusive control problem. Several scholars have noted that control in organizational settings need not be overt or even recognizable as such (e.g., Hardy, 1985; Hardy & Pettigrew, 1985; Pfeffer, 1981; Tompkins & Cheney, 1985). The extreme form of this interpretation of power and control links power to institutional entities, which Tompkins and Cheney label "juristic persons" (1985, p. 180). The traditional view of power as abstract and static facilitates these authors' account that power is increasingly separate from its sources as the world becomes more organizationally complex. Power thus becomes invested in institutional structures separate from the human actors who design, operate, and benefit from them, and individuals who are adversely affected by these "juristic persons" hear, in response to their complaints, "It's the system," or "You can't fight city hall." The assumptions underlying acceptance of unobtrusive control as a concept related to power are that it is inevitable, that institutional messages can be separated from human agents, and that social responsibility legitimately can be assigned to nonhuman entities.

POWER AS PRAXIS

The problem areas evident in the currently popular approaches to power are improved by applying praxis theories. Although there are many formulations of praxis theory reaching back to Aristotle's *praxis* and *phronesis* (Hoy, 1988), the emerging sense of the contemporary paradigm finds expression in the work of such scholars as Richard Rorty, George Lukacs, and Pierre Bourdieu. Modern praxis theory arose with early Marxism as a reaction against the passivity of positivism and its insistence on separating theory from practice. Praxis theory holds that the objectivity of the researcher is a fiction of positivism; praxis theorists "insist that we are a part of the world we study and cannot possibly be expected to theorize in some kind of detached, neutral manner" (Hoffman, 1975, p. 16). More fundamentally, the conjoining of theory and practice orients social science to the here-and-now, and to treat theory and practice, subject and object, micro and macro, as copresent in the social interaction of individuals. Praxis theory says, in essence, that the qualities of human relationships and social arrangements are knowable only through knowing the virtual everyday practices and individual histories of persons; those qualities are inscribed in personal and group histories in the very acts of performing practices that encompass shared cultural traditions. A fuller account of praxis and social reproduction also can be found in the works of Pierre Bourdieu (1977), Michel de Certeau (1984), Anthony Giddens (1984), and Fred Dallmayr (1984).

Praxis theory and the three perspectives discussed earlier are not totally incompatible; in fact, the critical-theoretic view is strongly dependent on a self-reflexive research attitude that acknowledges the researcher's influence on the practices being studied, and its data frequently are the historically situated habitual practices of groups and institutions. The significant difference here is that praxis theory generally holds that action and social structure are one—there is no social structure without identifiable practices in real time, and there are no practices that do not invoke and reproduce structure.

Since action—in the sense of ongoing virtual practices of actors and in the methodological sense that research is a practice that produces change—is fundamental to praxis theory, the first problem of traditional views of power, power as a static concept, is answered. Power as praxis is a way of doing, a mode of interaction among people. Barley (1986) presents a case for thinking of technological innovations as social objects and for seeing social structure as a form of process which is evident when technological changes are accompanied by changes in roles and interactions of persons. Similarly, power can be thought of as a process of interaction, evident in instances of "who is getting what, when, and how."

The praxis view of power also dissolves the problem of abstraction. Power has a dual nature, both as instantiated in social practices in the here-and-now and as the historical memory of such instances of practices. Coercion, deception, and other forms of practice become strategic subsets of power which inform us as to the "hows" of getting what one wants. No longer is it necessary to infer power as an abstract state or capacity; it is observable as a form of practice. In short, power is as power does.

A key contribution of the praxis perspective, then, is the reinterpretation of institutional power in terms of individuals' and groups' everyday practices. It demands evidence of concrete human actions—actual decisions made, discourses performed, social routines unconsciously repeated—to support a discussion of power. As such, the praxis view is inhospitable to the idea of juristic persons, texts without authors, social forces without practices of human agents. In behalf of citizens whose voting rights have been limited by "legislation" and travelers whose flights were cancelled because of "corporate instability" and immigrants who are refused entry because of "policy," praxis theorists would ask, "who decided what, when, and how?"

POWER IN CORPORATE DISCOURSE

What would a praxis theoretic study of organizational communication look like? There are already several pieces of research that display a bias toward praxis theory without explicitly acknowledging the connection. Tarla Rai Peterson's (1988) study of a Senate subcommittee hearing on proposed wilderness areas legislation is grounded in the actual talk among the senators and witnesses. Her approach is one of analyzing social structures as instantiated in the rhetorical practices of speakers rather than imposing structures from outside the observable action. Similarly, Nick Trujillo's (1983) study of interaction at the Lou Polito Dodge dealership grounds claims about power relationships directly in the observed conversations of workers at the dealership.

An example from my research in a large West Coast hotel illustrates how power is generated and perpetuated in routine talk of managers and workers. In this transcript excerpt,[1] the general manager of the hotel is talking with a select group of employees in a specially designated meeting called "Majortalks." The stated purpose of Majortalks is to afford rank-and-file employees an opportunity to discuss with the top manager any issues of concern in private and in strict confidence. The Majortalks are intended to be frank exchanges of views about problems and possible solutions, news and gossip, and they are seen as an opportunity to engage in personal social contact with the boss. This form of discussion is identified in company brochures and employee orientation training as one of many ways the company fosters full employee participation and a spirit of egalitarianism.

In this segment of the discussion, the general manager (MGR) has just made a long argument explaining why nonmanagerial workers are not cross-trained in jobs outside their work units. One of the reasons she has given is that with continuing high turnover, many employees are still being trained for their own jobs, and it is premature to cross-train them. At this point, a front desk clerk (KEN) says that he has been "pretty much thrown out there" without adequate task training. The general manager responds:

```
 1   MGR: Let me see if I understand you.
           You're s-you're
 2         telling me that in the front office (2)
           you learn
 3         only on the job and there's no
           pretraining time
```

```
 4         before you move out and do the job\.
 5   KEN: There is pretraining, but it is sit
           down and talk
 6         about what we're going to do. Not
           go through what
 7         we're going to do out of the public
           eye with less
 8         pressure. I mean ah ev-every trainee
           usually goes
 9         with the manager through the manual,
           and that's
10         great. But unless you actually have
           people in
11         front of you that are checking
           someone in that
12         isn't putting a lot of pressure on you
           but you can
13         ask questions of them (1) y'know,
           i-it's kinda-
14                              [         ]
15   MGR:                       Mm hm.
16   KEN: -hard.
17   MGR: So we should be doing role play,
           maybe
18         with play the cashiers kinda like a (1)
           a sample-
19         [                    ]
20   KEN: Role play'd be a great help.
21   MGR: -setup you can learn to feel
           comfortable with the
22         machine-you don't have to go . . .
23                              [
24   KEN:                       I like it. Yeah, So
                                you don't
25         feel like, well if I go out now that's
           it n y'know
26         I've lost money for the hotel,
           checking in guests
27         without credit-o:r I'll get the client
           mad at me
28         o:r any of the other things.
29   MGR: Good point. I like your attitude about
           making
30         money for the hotel.
```

31   //general laughter//

32   KEN: Th-that's what happens, y'know,
                 that's what,

33   that's what check-in's all about it
                 credit check

34   and the check-out program.

35   MGR: I must say that the cashiering at the
                 front office

36   has improved dramatically from some
                 time before.

37   We did have a, a period when we
                 lost (1) too much

38   money on (1) it. (2) Are you
                 through?

This excerpt of talk illustrates the instantiation of power by two speakers, one in a high-level position and one at the bottom of the organization's hierarchy. Although Ken does not enjoy the privileges or authorities of the general manager, he gets what he wants in this instance. Ken wants to inform the manager that a problem of inadequate task orientation is causing workers stress and is leading to possible client dissatisfaction and revenue losses. At the same time, he wants to appear loyal, supportive, and competent—in this corporation and industry, very rapid advancement is the norm, and Majortalks are an opportunity to be noticed. For her part, the general manager wants to identify problems and, if they are not critical issues, fashion remedies on the spot. She also wants to appear to the workers as approachable, competent, and in charge.

Both speakers display how they accomplish their ends, being powerful in a coordinated, harmonious way. Ken's power talk includes characterizing for others the nature of the problem and, more broadly, characterizing the significance of the check-in job functions (lines 32–34). Twice he overlaps his speech with MGR's talk—an act commonly attributed to dominance patterns of interaction. Moreover, he receives public confirmation from the general manager ("I like your attitude . . ."), and by inserting an evaluation (at line 24), he reframes the role-playing idea to appear as if MGR is floating a proposal for his approval ("I like it. Yeah.")

MGR's solution to the problem—role-playing—is a routine training technique in the hotel; her suggestion of the obvious is openly confirmed by the employee spokesperson. With Ken's enthusiastic public support for her solution (line 20), MGR avoids having to delve further into the issue of supervisors who are not training their workers properly—an issue she cannot resolve in the forum of Majortalks; in addition, she avoids having to schedule further action and followup, as often is the case with problem issues raised in such meetings. Further, MGR maintains an in-charge persona by issuing evaluative statements, not only about KEN's description of the problems that can result from poor training for check-in (line 20), but also about the quality of the cashiering unit (lines 35–38). The latter evaluation reminds the group of workers that MGR is authorized to determine standards of adequacy in the performance both of workers and of the hotel as a business. Her last utterance—"Are you through?"—instantiates her authority to manage the procedures of talk that occurs in this kind of discourse.

Not all interactions in the Majortalk meeting are as harmonious as the one just presented. In many instances, the talk creates asymmetries of power, reflecting asymmetries of authority, control, and privilege. The MGR–KEN segment, however, demonstrates how power can be conceived as action, in this case, talk. It illustrates the dynamic nature of power in the praxis perspective as well as its observable, concrete immediacy. To understand the discourse generated here, it is necessary to know the histories, purposes and sociocultural codes of the participants; to understand their power it is necessary—and nothing more is necessary—to observe their practices in the here-and-now.

CONCLUSION

I have attempted to isolate several conceptual problems in traditional notions of power—its static nature, its abstractness, and the unobtrusive control problem. A praxis perspective on power addresses these problems by discarding the abstractness of the concept and taking power to be what happens when persons get their way. It reveals power in its instants of becoming historical (remembered) fact and treats it as assignable to individual actors.

My adaptation of praxis theory is primitive and incomplete. Moreover, the discourse analysis presented here is an oversimplification, intended for illustration only. A number of conceptual problems wait to be worked out in the future. For example, what does a praxis perspective say about authority, control, domination, and so forth? How does praxis theory deal with nonroutine practices, that is, the highly irregular and strategic acts of managers and workers? And what is the precise relationship between practices, memory, history, and knowledge, and how do they change vis a vis one another? Despite these and other implications, a praxis view of power can stimulate new thinking about the sometimes "messy" and always problematic issue of power and organizational communication.

NOTE

1. The transcription conventions are based on those established by Gail Jefferson (see Atkinson & Heritage, 1984). I have added downward and upward slashes to indicate, respectively, falling and rising intonation.

REFERENCES

Astley, W.G., & Sachdeva, P.S. (1984). Structural Sources of Intraorganizational Power: A Theoretical Synthesis. *Academy of Management Review, 9*, 104–113.

Atkinson, J.M., & Heritage, J. (Eds.). (1984). *Structures of social action*. Cambridge: Cambridge University Press.

Bacharach, S.B., & Lawler, E.J. (1980). *Power and politics in organizations*. San Francisco: Jossey-Bass.

Barley, S.R. (1986). Technology as an occasion for structuring: Evidence from observations of CT scanners and the social order of radiology departments. *Administrative Science Quarterly, 31*, 78–108.

Bourdieu, P. (1977). *Outline of a theory of practice* (Trans. Richard Nice). Cambridge: Cambridge University Press.

Brown, M.H., & McMillan, J.J. (1988). *Constructions and counterconstructions: Organizational power revisited*. Paper presented to the annual conference of the International Communication, Association, New Orleans, LA.

Brown, W.R. (1986). Power and the rhetoric of social intervention. *Communication Monographs, 53*(2), 180–199.

Clegg, S. (1975). *Power, rule and domination: A critical and empirical understanding of power in sociological theory and everyday life*. London: Routledge and Kegan Paul.

Clegg, S. (1979). *The theory of power and organization*. London: Routledge and Kegan Paul.

Conrad, C., & Ryan, M. (1985). Power, praxis, and self in organizational communication theory. In R.D. McPhee & P.K. Tompkins (Eds.), *Organizational communication: Traditional themes and new directions* (pp. 235–258). Beverly Hills: Sage.

Dallmayr, F.R. (1984). *Polis and praxis: Exercises in contemporary political theory*. Cambridge, MA: The MIT Press.

Dandridge, T.C. Mitroff, I., & Joyce, W. (1980). Organization symbolism: A topic to expand organizational analysis. *Academy of Management Review, 5*, 77–82.

de Certeau, M. (1984). *The practice of everyday life*. Berkeley: The University of California Press.

Deetz, S. (1982). Critical interpretive research in organizational communication. *Western Journal of Speech Communication, 46*, 131–149.

Etzioni, A. (1961). *A comparative analysis of complex organizations*. New York: Free Press.

French, J.R.P., & Raven, B.H. (1959). The basis of social power. In D. Cartwright (Ed), *Studies in social power* (pp. 150–167). Ann Arbor: University of Michigan Press.

Frost, P.J. (1987). Power, politics, and influence. In F. Jablin, L. Putnam, K. Roberts, & L. Porter (Eds.), *Handbook of organizational communication: An interdisciplinary perspective* (pp. 503–548). Newbury Park, CA: Sage.

Guess, R. (1981). *The idea of a critical theory: Habermas and the Frankfurt school*. Cambridge: Cambridge University Press.

Giddens, A. (1984). *The constitution of society*. Berkeley: University of California Press.

Gudykunst, W.B. (1985). Normative power and conflict potential in intergroup relationships. In W.B. Gudykunst, L.P. Stewart, & S. Ting-Toomey (Eds.), *Communication, culture, and organizational processes* (pp. 155–173). Beverly Hills: Sage.

Hardy, C. (1985). *Managing organizational closure*. Epping, Essex: Gower Press.

Hardy, C., & Pettigrew, A.M. (1985). The use of power in managerial strategies for change. In R.S. Rosenbloom (Ed.), *Research, technological innovation, management and policy* (Vol. 2). Greenwich, CT: JAI Press.

Hoffman, J. (1975). *Marxism and the theory of praxis.* New York: International Publishers.

Hoy, T. (1988). *Praxis, truth, and liberation.* Lanham, MD: University Press of America.

Kersten, A. (1987). Multilevel analysis in critical research. In M. McLaughlin (Ed.), *Communication yearbook 10* (pp. 709–726). Beverly Hills: Sage.

Lukes, S. (1974). *Power: A radical view.* London: Macmillan.

Morgan, G. (1985). *Images of organization.* Beverly Hills: Sage.

Mumby, D.K. (1987). The political function of narrative in organization. *Communication Monographs, 54*(2), 113–127.

Peterson, T.R. (1988). The rhetorical construction of institutional authority in a Senate subcommittee hearing on wilderness legislation. *Western Journal of Speech Communication, 52*(4), 259–290.

Pfeffer, J. (1981). *Power in organizations.* Marshfield, MA: Pitman.

Putnam, L.L. (1983). The interpretive perspective: An alternative to functionalism. In L.L. Putnam & M.E. Pacanowsky (Eds.), *Communication and organizations: An interpretive approach* (pp. 31–53). Beverly Hills: Sage.

Putnam, L.L., & Poole, M.S. (1987). Conflict and negotiation. In F. Jablin, L.L. Putnam, K. Roberts, & L. Porter (Eds.), *Handbook of organizational communication: An interdisciplinary perspective* (pp. 549–599). Newbury Park, CA: Sage.

Raven, B.H. (1974). The comparative analysis of power and influence. In J.T. Tedeschi (Ed.), *Perspectives on social power* (pp. 172–198). Chicago: Aldine.

Richmond, J.P., Davis, L.M., Saylor, K., & McCroskey, J.C. (1984). Power strategies in organizations: Communication techniques and strategies. *Human Communication Research, 11*(1), 85–108.

Riley, P. (1983). A structurationist account of political culture. *Administrative Science Quarterly, 28,* 414–437.

Rosen, M. (1985). Breakfast at Spiro's: Dramaturgy and dominance. *Journal of Management, 11*(2), 31–48.

Sathe, V. (1983). Implications of corporate culture: A manager's guide to action. *Organizational Dynamics, 12*(2), 5–23.

Schein, E. (1985). *Organizational culture and leadership.* San Francisco: Jossey-Bass.

Tompkins, P.K. (1985). Organizational communications: Symbolism over substance. In R.D. McPhee & P.K. Tompkins (Eds.). *Organizational communication: Traditional themes and new directions.* Beverly Hills, CA: Sage.

Tomkins, P.K., & Cheney, G. (1985). Communication and unobtrusive control in contemporary organizations. In R.D. McPhee & P.K. Tomkins (Eds.), *Organizational communication: Traditional themes and new directions* (pp. 179–210). Beverly Hills, CA: Sage.

Trujillo, N. (1983). "Performing" Mintzberg's roles: The nature of managerial communication. In L.L. Putnam & M.E. Pacanowsky (Eds.), *Communication and organizations: An interpretive approach* (pp. 73–97). Beverly Hills: Sage.

Yukl, G. (1981). *Leadership in organizations.* Englewood Cliffs, NJ: Prentice-Hall.

28   DECISION-MAKING STRATEGIES
Irving Janis and Leon Mann

Surprisingly little research has been done on organizational decision making in general or on organizational decision-making communication specifically. This lack is undoubtedly because of the extreme complexity of the research problem. Imagine the difficulty of producing a specific explanation of how *you* make decisions. Multiply that project by, say, 100 members in a small organization, account for interactions between the different individual decision processes, add explanations of large-scale effects for organizational structure and history, and you begin to see what a complex phenomenon organizational decision making can be.

Some theoretical work has been done that begins to unravel this complexity, and the following article reviews it. Janis and Mann summarize concisely six different theoretical approaches to explaining decision making. These run the gamut from *optimizing*, which stresses a completely rational model of decision making, to *incrementalism*, which stresses a less rational approach. Although it was published in the late 1970s, this chapter covers most major approaches to decision making still being taken today.

When people are required to choose among alternative courses of action, what types of search, deliberation, and selection procedure do they typically use—that is, what decision-making strategy do they adopt? Unfortunately, this question has so far received relatively little attention in behavioral science research. Most of the pertinent observations of decision-making strategies consist of case studies, impressionistic surveys, and anecdotes reported by scholars in administrative science and related fields that deal with organizational policy making. Accordingly, we shall examine the answers they give concerning how "administrative man" typically carries out the tasks of decision making.

OPTIMIZING AND THE PERILS OF SUBOPTIMIZING

Specialists on organizational decision making describe the optimizing strategy as having the goal of selecting the course of action with the highest payoff. Such a strategy requires estimating the comparative value of every viable alternative in terms of expected benefits and costs (see Young, 1966, pp. 138–47). But, as Herbert Simon (1976) has pointed out, human beings rarely adopt this decision-making approach: people simply do not have "the wits to maximize" (p. xxviii). Part of the problem is that determining all the potentially favorable and unfavorable consequences of all the feasible courses of action would require the decision maker to process so much information that impossible demands would be made on his resources and mental capabilities. Moreover, so many relevant variables may have to be taken into account that they cannot all be kept in mind at the same time. Handicapped by the shortcomings of the human mind, the decision maker's attention, asserts Simon, "shifts from one value to another with consequent shifts in preference" (p. 83).

It is very costly in time, effort, and money to collect and examine the huge masses of information required when one uses an optimizing strategy to arrive at a decision. Furthermore, decision makers are often under severe pressure of time, which precludes careful search and appraisal. Managers in large companies, for example, seldom have time to engage in long-range planning because they are constantly occupied with current crises requiring emergency "fire fighting." The manager is likely to be "so busy solving immediate problems that he cannot effectively apply their solutions on a long-run recurrent basis; so busy manning the fire hose that he cannot devise a fire prevention program" (Young, p. 146).

As a result of personal limitations and various external constraints, a decision maker who does the best he can to use an optimizing strategy is still prone to such gross miscalculations that he ends up with an unsatisfactory *suboptimizing* solution, one that maximizes some of the utilities he expected to gain at the expense of losing other utilities.

The perils of suboptimization abound in large organizations, where different units and different types of personnel have incompatible objectives. The decisions made by policy makers in large organizations are, according to Young, "usually of a suboptimal nature, and only rarely can we assume that an ideal or unimprovable solution has been achieved" (p. 144). It needs to be emphasized, however, that a suboptimal policy is not necessarily unsatisfactory, even though it fails to attain all the policy makers' objectives; it may be a marked improvement over the former policy and constitute a step toward an optimizing solution.

Evidence from various social science disciplines indicates that, besides man's severe limitations as a processor of information, other recurrent conditions also militate against the use of an optimizing approach, even though it might often seem to be the ideal strategy for decisions (Brim et al., 1962; Etzioni, 1968; Johnson, 1974; Katona, 1953; Miller and Starr, 1967; Simmons et al., 1973; Steinbruner, 1974; Taylor, 1965; Vroom and Yetton, 1973).

Even in decisions made by business firms, where the overriding value would seem to be to make the greatest amount of profit, decision makers often do not orient themselves toward finding the course of action that will maximize profits and other tangible net gains. Without careful search and appraisal, corporation executives often make judgments about

a multiplicity of conflicting objectives, including "good will," "growth potential," "acceptability within the organization," and other intangible gains that are difficult to measure in any way (see Johnson, 1974).

Miller and Starr (1967) emphasize that there is no sound way to combine all the considerations involved in decision making into a single, objective utility measure, even though the decision maker might be capable of giving honest ratings of the subjective utility value of every consideration that enters into his choice.

> The utility an individual gains from a commodity or a service can be measured to some degree by observable market phenomena (e.g., how much of the commodity he will buy at different prices). But there is no convenient measuring unit for the utility of an intangible such as dignity. Therefore, even if these other factors can be theoretically expressed in terms of [subjective] utility, the difficulties involved in measuring the utilities prevent the theory [of maximization of utilities] from satisfactorily explaining observed behavior and decisions [pp. 25–26].

Many behavioral scientists regard the optimizing strategy as an excellent *normative* (or *prescriptive*) model—that is, a set of standards the decision maker *should* strive to attain when making vital decisions (to avoid miscalculations, wishful thinking, and vulnerability to subsequent disillusionment). Some, however, like Miller and Starr, question whether optimizing would very often prove to be the optimal strategy in view of its high costs and the usual constraints on the decision maker's resources; they strongly oppose prescriptive recommendations that might inadvertently encourage decision makers to strive blindly for optimizing solutions, regardless of the circumstances. Even more objections have been raised against the assumption that the optimizing strategy provides an accurate *descriptive* model of how people actually *do* make decisions. The numerous critiques we have just summarized pose a major problem for the psychology of decision making: if optimizing is *not* the dominant strategy actually used by most decision makers most of the time, then what is?

SATISFICING

The most influential hypothesis concerning the way administrative man arrives at a new policy has been formulated by Herbert Simon (1976). The decision maker, according to Simon, *satisfices*, rather than maximizes; that is, he looks for a course of action that is "good enough," that meets a minimal set of requirements. Businessmen, for example, often decide to invest in a new enterprise if they expect it to return a "satisfactory profit," without bothering to compare it with all the alternative investments open to them. Sometimes more than one criterion is used, but always it is a question of whether the given choice will yield a "good enough" outcome. The satisficing strategy involves more superficial search for information and less cognitive work than maximizing. All that the person has to do is consider alternative courses of action sequentially until one that "will do" is found.

Simon argues convincingly that the satisficing approach fits the limited information-processing capabilities of human beings. The world is peopled by creatures of "bounded or limited rationality," he says, and these creatures constantly resort to gross simplifications when dealing with complex decision problems. Man's limited ability to foresee future consequences and to obtain information about the variety of available alternatives inclines him to settle for a barely "acceptable" course of action that is "better than the way things are now." He is not inclined to collect information about all the complicated factors that might affect the outcome of his choice, to estimate probabilities, or to work out preference orderings for many different alternatives. He is content to rely on "a drastically simplified model of the buzzing, blooming confusion that constitutes the real world" (Simon, 1976, p. xxix).

According to Johnson (1974), executives often feel so uncertain about the outcome of what seems to be the best choice that they forego it in order to play safe: they gravitate toward a more conventional, "second-best" choice that will cause little immediate disturbance or disapproval because it will be seen as "acceptable" by superiors and peers who will review the decision and by subordinates who will implement it. Cyert and March (1963) suggest

that the more uncertainty there is about a long-term outcome, the greater the tendency to make a policy decision on the basis of its short-term acceptability within the organization.

The simplest variant of the satisficing strategy takes the form of relying upon a single formula as the sole decision rule, which comes down to using only one criterion for a tolerable choice. Simple decision rules are also prevalent in consumer behavior. Studies of consumer purchases indicate that people in shops and supermarkets sometimes buy on impulse, without any advance planning or deliberation (Engel, Kollat, and Blackwell, 1968; Hansen, 1972). The person notices something attractive that he would like to have, and, if the price is within the range he regards as "reasonable," he immediately decides to buy it. A similar decision rule may come into play when a customer impulsively decides to appropriate an attractive piece of merchandise if he sees that no one in the store is looking.

Quasi-satisficing

Some people use a simple moral precept as the sole rule when making a decision to help someone in trouble. Schwartz (1970), in his account of the psychological basis of altruism, describes this approach as "moral decision making." Once the person realizes that someone requires aid and that there is some obvious way help can be given, he promptly takes action without deliberating about alternatives. This use of a simple decision rule is similar to a satisficing approach in all respects except one: the helper does not share the full-fledged satisficer's belief that his choice is *minimally* satisfactory. Instead of regarding his action as merely "good enough," the moral decision maker is convinced that it is the *best*, that no other course would be morally justifiable.

Alexander George (1974) calls attention to the proclivity of national policy makers to rely on a simple formula rather than to attempt to master cognitively complex problems by means of careful search and analysis and weighing of alternatives. One type of decision rule frequently resorted to in a bureaucracy consists of using a simple criterion of "consensus," which requires only the single piece of information that could, in effect, be supplied by an opinion poll of the most powerful persons in the organization; thus, any policy is good enough to be adopted if the majority of influential people want it and will support it. Other simple decision rules sometimes used by policy makers consist of relying on, as a guide for action, a general ideological principle—e.g., "No appeasement of the enemy!"—or an operational code—e.g., the best tactic for dealing with an ultimatum from an enemy is to respond promptly with a more drastic ultimatum—(see George, 1974; Leites, 1953; Lindblom, 1965).

When making a major policy decision for which well-known historical precedents immediately come to mind, many national political leaders, according to historian Ernest May (1973) and political scientist Robert Jervis (1975), follow the simple decision rule "Do what we did last time if it worked and the opposite if it didn't."

There is always a grave danger, as George (1974) points out, that relying on a simple decision rule will lead to a premature choice that overlooks nonobvious negative consequences. Some of those consequences might be averted if the decision were delayed until more thorough deliberation and evaluation were carried out after obtaining information from available intelligence resources.

What Are the Variables?

Although it is not explicitly stated in most descriptive accounts of satisficing and quasi-satisficing, these strategies differ from optimizing in more than one important dimension. We find that at least four different variables are involved:

1. *Number of Requirements To Be Met.* One characteristic feature of the satisficing strategy is that the testing rule used to determine whether or not to adopt a new course of action specifies a *small number of requirements* that must be met, sometimes only one (e.g., that a personal choice should be acceptable to one's spouse or that a policy choice should be acceptable to the majority of a policy-making group). The decision maker ignores many other values and spheres of interest that he realizes might also be implicated by his decision. In contrast, when the decision maker is using an optimizing strategy he takes account of a large number of requirements or objectives, with the intention of

selecting the course of action that achieves the greatest possible satisfaction of the entire set of requirements. This is perhaps the most obvious characteristic that distinguishes satisficing from optimizing.

2. *Number of Alternatives Generated.* A decision maker using a satisficing strategy sequentially tests each alternative that comes to his attention; if the first one happens to be minimally satisfactory, he terminates his search. Since he makes little effort to canvass the full range of possible courses of action by searching his memory or by seeking suggestions from advisers, the decision maker is likely to generate *relatively few alternatives.* If he uses an optimizing strategy, on the other hand, the decision maker makes a thorough search and attempts to generate as *many* good alternatives as he can.

3. *Ordering and Retesting of Alternatives.* When using a satisficing strategy, the decision maker typically tests the alternatives only once and in a haphazard order, as one after another happens to come to his attention, until he finds one that meets his minimum requirements. When using an optimizing strategy, however, he selects the best alternatives and reexamines them repeatedly, ordering them in pairs or in some other way so as to make comparative judgments.

4. *Type of Testing Model Used.* When testing to see if an alternative meets a given requirement, the satisficing decision maker typically limits his inquiry to seeing whether it falls above or below a *minimal cutoff point.* If there is more than one requirement, he treats each cutoff point in the same way, as equally important. In contrast to this simple, unweighted threshold model, the model used in the optimizing strategy is typically a weighted additive model, which requires the decision maker to arrive at an evaluation that takes account of the *magnitudes* of all the pros and cons with due regard for the relative importance of each objective. This gives him the opportunity to consider possible "trade-offs" from gaining very high values on some important requirements in exchange for tolerating relatively low values on less important ones.

Elimination by Aspects

Instead of a single decision rule in a satisficing or quasi-satisficing strategy, a set of decision rules, involving perhaps up to half a dozen considerations, is sometimes used. Still, the decision maker does not engage in anything like the amount of cognitive work that would be required if he were to evaluate and weigh the alternatives using an optimizing strategy. One such multiple-rule variant, designated as the *"elimination-by-aspects" approach*, has been described by Tversky (1972). It consists essentially of a combination of simple decision rules, which can be applied to select rapidly from a number of salient alternatives one that meets a set of minimal requirements. Tversky illustrates this type of quasi-satisficing strategy by citing a television commercial screened in San Francisco. An announcer says:

> There are more than two dozen companies in the San Francisco area which offer training in computer programming. [*He puts some two dozen eggs and one walnut on the table to represent the alternatives.*] Let us examine the facts. How many of these schools have on-line computer facilities for training? [*He removes several eggs.*] How many of these schools have placement services that would help you find a job? [*He removes some more eggs.*] How many of these schools are approved for veterans' benefits? [*This continues until the walnut alone remains. The announcer cracks the nutshell, revealing the name of the advertised company.*] This is all you need to know, in a nutshell.

When the elimination-by-aspects approach is used, decision making becomes essentially a sequential narrowing-down process, similar to the logic employed in the popular game Twenty Questions. Starting ordinarily with the most valued requirement, all salient alternatives that do not contain the selected aspect are eliminated, and the process continues for each requirement in turn until a single expedient remains. For example, in contemplating the purchase of a new car, the first aspect selected might be a $4,500 price limit; all cars more expensive than $4,500 are then excluded from further consideration. A second aspect might be high mileage per gallon; at this stage, all cars are eliminated that do not have this feature. Yet another aspect, say power steering, is examined for the remaining alter-

natives, and all cars not meeting this criterion are crossed off the "mental list." The process continues until all cars but one are eliminated.

Of course, the decision maker may run out of aspects before he arrives at a single remaining expedient; he will then have to introduce another decision rule in order to narrow his choice. Or he may run out of alternatives before he exhausts his list of minimal requirements. From a normative standpoint, however, a much more serious flaw of this complex form of satisficing lies in its failure to ensure that the alternatives retained are, in fact, superior to those eliminated. For example, in the alternative arrived at in the television commercial, the use of placement services as a criterion for elimination might lead to the rejection of programs whose overall quality far exceeds that of the advertised one despite the fact that they do not offer that particular service. Similarly, in the choice of a car, the use of power steering as a criterion for elimination could lead to rejection of vehicles otherwise far superior to the vehicle purchased. Part of the problem is that minor criteria may creep in early in the sequence or may survive to determine the final choice. Perhaps this drawback could be corrected in a way that would transform the elimination-by-aspects approach into a quasi-optimizing strategy by introducing procedures that reflect the decision maker's judgments about the differential weights to be assigned to various aspects. Even without any such refinement, however, this approach appears to be one of the most sophisticated and psychologically realistic of the quasi-satisficing strategies and might result in fewer miscalculations than the simpler variants that rely exclusively on a single decision rule (Abelson, 1976).

Some social science theorists would describe reliance on a single decision rule as less "rational" than the elimination-by-aspects approach, and all variants of satisficing as less "rational" than optimizing. But terms like *less rational, nonrational,* and *irrational* carry invidious connotations ("stupid," "crazy") that often do not correspond at all to the evaluations that would be made by objective observers. Indeed it could be argued that in certain circumstances it is not rational to waste time and effort in maximizing; even when the relevant information is available, a very simple form of satisficing sometimes may be the most sensible orientation, especially for many minor issues. For example, consumer research organizations have recommended that when purchasing aspirin at a registered pharmacy, one should follow the simple rule of selecting whichever brand is cheapest (because all brands must meet rigorous U.S. government specifications and, despite advertising claims to the contrary, there are no significant differences among them). As Miller and Starr (1967, p. 51) point out, "It is always questionable whether the optimum procedure is to search for *the* optimum value." Accordingly, we avoid characterizing the satisficing strategy or any other decision-making strategy in terms of "rationality" or "irrationality." We do not intend to bypass the important issue of determining the conditions under which one or another decision-making procedure will have unfavorable consequences for the decision maker; but we shall attempt to relate specific types of conditions to specific types of unfavorable consequences without using overinclusive, misleading labels like *irrational*.

Incrementalism and Muddling Through

Organizational theorists recognize that despite its shortcomings, a satisficing strategy can result in slow progress toward an optimal course of action. Miller and Starr (1967), for example, speak about *incremental improvements* that sometimes come about as a result of a succession of satisficing policy choices, each small change presumably having been selected as "good enough" because it was seen as better than leaving the old policy unchanged. "Over time," Miller and Starr assert "both individuals and groups may be better off to move in incremental steps of reasonable size toward the perceived and bounded optimum than in giant strides based on long-range perceptions of where the ultimate optimal exists" (p. 51).

Charles E. Lindblom (1965) has given a detailed account of the incrementalist approach in an analysis of "the art of muddling through." When a problem arises requiring a change in policy, according to Lindblom, policy makers in government or large organizations generally consider a very narrow range of policy alternatives that differ to only a small degree from the existing policy. By sticking

close to this familiar path of policymaking, the incrementalist shows his preference for the sin of "omission" over the sin of "confusion" (Lindblom, 1965, p. 146).

Incremental decision making is geared to alleviating concrete shortcomings in a present policy—putting out fires—rather than selecting the superior course of action. Since no effort is made to specify major goals and to find the best means for attaining them, "ends are chosen that are appropriate to available or nearly available means" (Hirschman and Lindblom, 1962, p. 215). The incremental approach allows executives to simplify the search and appraisal stages of decision making by carrying out successive comparisons with respect to policy alternatives that differ only slightly from the existing policy. Slovic (1971) postulates, on the basis of his experiments on the cognitive limitations displayed in gambling situations, that decision makers find the incremental approach attractive because it enables them to avoid difficult cognitive tasks: "Examination of business decision making and governmental policy making suggests that, whenever possible, decision makers avoid uncertainty and the necessity of weighting and combining information or trading-off conflicting values."

Often decision makers have no real awareness of trying to arrive at a new policy; rather, there is a never-ending series of attacks on each new problem as it arises. As policy makers take one small step after another to gradually change the existing policy, the satisficing criterion itself may change, depending on what is going wrong with the existing policy. If there are strong objections to the policy on the part of other bureaucrats who have to implement it, the policy makers may find a satisficing solution that involves making a compromise in accord with the realities of bureaucratic politics. Incremental changes are often made primarily to keep other politically powerful groups in the hierarchy sufficiently satisfied so that they will stop complaining and will not obstruct the new trend (Halperin, 1974).

Probably the same type of incremental change, based on a simple satisficing strategy, is adopted whenever a person is ignorant of the fundamental issues at stake or when he wishes to avoid investing a great deal of time and energy in wrestling with a problem that appears, at the time, insoluble. Important life decisions are sometimes incremental in nature, the end product of a series of small decisions that progressively commit the person to one particular course of action.

Many individuals do not make a deliberate occupational choice but in haphazard, trial-and-error fashion leave their job whenever something that seems somewhat better comes along. Ginzberg et al. (1951) suggest that incremental steps may determine the career choices made by a sizable number of people even in skilled occupations. A man or woman starts off getting a certain type of job training and then finds it more and more difficult to switch to another type of career. The person anticipates social disapproval for "wasting" his training, which tends to increase with each increment of training or advancement. And, of course, he is also deterred from changing by his own sense of prior investment of time, effort, and money in the direction he has already moved.

Matza (1964) indicates that the careers of lawbreakers are often arrived at in the same stepwise, drifting fashion, without any single stage at which the offenders decide they are going to pursue a life of crime. Rather, they start with minor offenses, get into more and more trouble with the police, and proceed slowly to enlarge their repertoire of criminal acts until they reach the point where they are regularly committing serious crimes. Each successive crime in the series appears to be not very much worse than the preceding one, and in this stepwise fashion the person proceeds to move from minor delinquency to major crime.

A similar stepwise process has been reported for the decision to marry. Waller (1938, p. 259) noted that during the early decades of the twentieth century the process of mating unfolded gradually, in a series of steps whereby the person became increasingly committed in his own eyes and in those of others to the decision to marry. Each step involved the use of a few simple criteria, with no effort to weigh alternatives.

These observational reports about incremental decision making on such vital personal choices as marriage and career, although not sufficiently detailed to enable us to draw definitive conclusions about decision-making processes, suggest that the succession of small decisions may be often based on a satisficing or quasi-satisficing strategy, just as in the case of the incremental policy-making decisions described by administrative scientists.

MIXED SCANNING

Etzioni (1968) has outlined a conglomerate strategy called mixed scanning, which he sees as a synthesis of the stringent rationalism of optimizing and the "muddling," slipshod approach of extreme incrementalism, displayed by bureaucrats who use consensus as their only satisficing criterion. The mixed-scanning strategy has two main components: (1) some of the features of the optimizing strategy combined with essential features of the elimination-by-aspects approach are used for fundamental policy decisions that set basic directions; and (2) an incremental process (based on simple forms of satisficing) is followed for the minor or "bit" decisions that ensue after the basic policy direction is set, resulting in gradual revisions and sometimes preparing the way for a new fundamental decision. Etzioni argues that this mixture of substrategies fits the needs of democratic governments and organizations. In noncrisis periods, it is easier to obtain a consensus on "increments similar to the existing policies than to gain support for a new policy" (p. 294). But in times of serious trouble, a crisis stimulates intensive search for a better policy and serves "to build consensus for major changes of direction which are overdue (e.g., governmental guidance of economic stability, the welfare state, desegregation)" (p. 294).

Etzioni uses the term *scanning* to refer to the search, collection, processing, evaluation, and weighing of information in the process of making a choice. The intensiveness of scanning can vary over a wide range, from very superficial to extremely intensive, depending on how much "coverage" the decision maker strives for when he surveys the relevant fields of information, how much detail he "takes in," and how completely he "explores alternative steps." Each time he faces a dilemma that requires choosing a new course of action, he has to make a deliberate prior judgment about how much of his resources of time, energy, and money he is willing to allocate to search and appraisal activities.

Etzioni's description of the mixed-scanning strategy includes a set of rules for allocating resources to scanning whenever a policy maker faces the type of crisis that leads him to realize that earlier policy lines ought to be reviewed and perhaps changed.

Put into a program-like language, the [mixed-scanning] strategy roughly reads:

a. *On strategic occasions* . . . (i) list all relevant alternatives that come to mind, that the staff raises, and that advisers advocate (including alternatives not usually considered feasible).

(ii) Examine briefly the alternatives under (i) . . . and reject those that reveal a "crippling objection." These include: (a) utilitarian objections to alternatives which require means that are not available, (b) normative objections to alternatives which violate the basic values of the decision-makers, and (c) political objections to alternatives which violate the basic values or interests of other actors whose support seems essential for making the decision and/or implementing it.

(iii) For all alternatives not rejected under (ii), repeat (ii) in greater though not in full detail. . . .

(iv) For those alternatives remaining after (iii), repeat (ii) in still fuller detail. . . . Continue until only one alternative is left. . . .

b. *Before implementation* [in order to prepare for subsequent "incrementing"] (i) when possible, fragment the implementation into several sequential steps. . . .

(ii) When possible, divide the commitment to implement into several serial steps. . . .

(iii) When possible, divide the commitment of assets into several serial steps and maintain a strategic reserve. . . .

(iv) Arrange implementation in such a way that, if possible, costly and less reversible decisions will appear later in the process than those which are more reversible and less costly.

(v) Provide a time schedule for the additional collection and processing of information. . . .

c. *Review while implementing.* (i) Scan on a semi-encompassing level after the first subset of increments is implemented. If they "work," continue to scan on a semi-encompassing level after longer intervals and in full, over-all review, still less frequently.

(ii) Scan more encompassingly whenever a series of increments, although each one seems a step in the right direction, results in deeper difficulties.

(iii) Be sure to scan at set intervals in full, over-all review even if everything seems all right. . . .

d. *Formulate a rule for the allocation of assets and time among the various levels of scanning.* . . . [pp. 286–88]

Although intended for policy makers, the same program, with minor modifications, could be applied to an individual's work-task decisions and to personal decisions involving career, marriage, health, or financial security. (Only a few slight changes in wording would be necessary—e.g., in step a (i), for personal decisions, *the staff* would be replaced by *family and friends*.)

The program for mixed scanning is presented by Etzioni primarily as a normative or prescriptive model, specifying what decision makers *should* do. The mixed-scanning strategy obviously has the virtue of adaptive flexibility at different stages of decision making, with a quasi-optimizing approach being used only while selecting the trunk of a new decision tree and a satisficing approach being used after the new fundamental policy has been chosen, as one moves out along the branches. Etzioni expects that decision makers will improve their effectiveness in attaining their actual goals if they follow his recommendations to differentiate "fundamental" from "bit" decisions and carry out the intensive scanning procedures he prescribes for the fundamental ones. It remains an open, empirical question whether any sizable population or sub-population of decision makers does, in fact, proceed along the lines specified in Etzioni's description of the mixed-scanning strategy.

THE DECISION MAKER'S REPERTOIRE

Implicit in Etzioni's account is the assumption that every decision maker has in his repertoire all the component substrategies and orientations we have described in the preceding sections. Adopting a given strategy at one stage of the decision-making sequence does not preclude use of another strategy at a later stage, particularly if the earlier one proves ineffective in resolving the conflict. For some people, the work of making a decision involves switching from low-cost, low-energy substrategies to more costly, effortful ones as they realize they are unable to settle the decisional conflict.

We expect that when different strategies or substrategies are used, different information-processing orientations in the decision maker's repertoire come to the fore. When he is trying to optimize, as we have seen, the decision maker consistently behaves like an intelligent realist, pursuing maximum satisfaction or utility with single-minded attention. He uses his mental capacities to a remarkable degree while searching for all viable alternatives and trying to understand all their possible consequences.

When operating as a "mixed scanner," the decision maker solves the problem of his limited capacity to process information by classifying decisions as either fundamental or minor. He conserves his time and energy by scanning intensively only those choices that are the most important or most troublesome, treating all other choices much more superficially.

When satisficing, on the other hand, the decision maker deals with fundamental decisions in the same way as minor ones; he relies on one or a few rock-bottom principles that enable him to reduce a complex decisional problem into a matter of judging what will do and what won't do, which requires much less time and effort for search and appraisal. When in response to a profound challenge the decision maker functions as an incrementalist muddler, he resorts to the simplest form of satisficing, making only slight adjustments in an obsolete policy after

doing little more than checking on the agreement of other interested parties. This crude form of satisficing is more likely than other strategies to lead to gross failures to meet the criteria for vigilant information processing. For vital decisions, the most damaging consequences are to be expected when the preliminary appraisal of the challenge is itself based on such a low level of vigilance that the person fails to realize the importance of the objectives and values at stake. But a muddling strategy might be adaptive in a stable environment, where few fundamental challenges to existing policies are encountered.

Irrespective of the strategy adopted—i.e., whether the decision maker strives to optimize, settles for satisficing, or tries to follow a mixed strategy—the likelihood of miscalculation and postdecisional regret increases as a function of the degree to which he fails to engage in vigilant information processing (as defined by the seven criteria) during the period preceding commitment. Hence, according to this assumption, when attempting to predict the consequences of a satisficing strategy—or any other strategy—one needs to inquire into the degree to which the decision maker meets the seven criteria.

If we make the additional assumption that practically all the various strategies and substrategies we have discussed are in the repertoire of every decision maker, we find ourselves confronting a new set of research questions that need to be answered in order to develop an adequate descriptive theory of decision making. The old question, which has been addressed by many social scientists, was "Which strategy is the one most decision makers use most of the time?" The answer is still being debated, because no consistent evidence has as yet emerged. But the analysis presented in this chapter inclines us to be dubious about ever finding a general answer that will hold across all types of major and minor decisions, and in all circumstances. After all, being extremely careful to meet the criteria for vigilant information processing would be almost as inappropriate for a trivial or routine decision among substitutable alternatives as superficial satisficing would be for a major decision. In *Up the Organization*, Robert Townsend, the former chairman of the board of the Avis Corporation, gives some conventional wisdom, well known to business executives who have managed to survive at the top, about how to approach different kinds of decisions:

> There are two kinds of decisions: those that are expensive to change and those that are not.
>
> A decision to build the Edsel or Mustang (or locate your new factory in Orlando or Yakima) shouldn't be made hastily; nor without plenty of inputs from operating people and specialists.
>
> But the common or garden-variety decision—like when to have the cafeteria open for lunch or what brand of pencil to buy—should be made fast. No point in taking three weeks to make a decision that can be made in three seconds—and corrected inexpensively later if wrong. The whole organization may be out of business while you oscillate between baby-blue or buffalo-brown coffee cups [Townsend, 1970, p. 45].

We suspect that in addition to using a simple satisficing approach to relatively unimportant decisions and an optimizing approach to the most important ones, many executives use some form of mixed strategy when dealing with decisions in the intermediate range that fall between the two extremes Townsend is talking about. The important point, however, is that people cannot be expected to use the same strategy for all types of decisions.

REFERENCES

Abelson, R. P. Script processing in attitude formation and decision making. In J. S. Carroll and J. W. Payne (Eds.), *Cognition and social behavior*. New York: Lawrence Erlbaum Associates, 1976.

Brim, O. G., D. C. Glass, D. E. Lavin, and N. Goodman. *Personality and decision processes*. Stanford; Calif.: Stanford University Press, 1962.

Cyert, R. M., and J. G. March. *A Behavioral theory of the firm*. Englewood Cliffs, N.J.: Prentice-Hall, 1963.

Engel, J. F., D. J. Kollat, and R. D. Blackwell. *Consumer behavior*. New York: Holt, Rinehart and Winston, 1968.

Etzioni, A. *The active society*. New York: Free Press, 1968.

George, A. The Chinese Communist intervention in the Korean War. In A. George and R. Smoke, *Deterrence in American foreign policy: Theory and practice*. New York: Columbia University Press, 1974.

Ginzberg, E., S. W. Ginsburg, S. Axelrad, and J. L. Herma. *Occupational choice*. New York: Columbia University Press, 1951.

Halperin, M. H. *Bureaucratic politics and foreign policy*. Washington, D.C.: Brookings Institution, 1974.

Hansen, F. *Consumer choice behavior*. New York: Free Press, 1972.

Hirschman, A. O., and C. E. Lindblom. Economic development, research and development, policy making: Some converging views. *Behavioral Sciences*, 1962, 7, 211–22.

Jervis, R. *Perception and misperception in international relations*. Princeton, N.J.: Princeton University Press, 1975.

Johnson, R. J. Conflict avoidance through acceptable decisions. *Human Relations*, 1974, 27, 71–82.

Katona, G. Rational behavior and economic behavior. *Psychological Review*, 1953, 60, 307–18.

Leites, N. *A study of Bolshevism*. New York: Free Press, 1953.

Lindblom, C. E. The science of muddling through. *Public Administration Review*, 1959, 19, 79–99.

Lindblom, C. E. *The intelligence of democracy*. New York: Free Press, 1965.

Matza, D. *Delinquency and drift*. New York: Wiley, 1964.

May, E. R. *Lessons of the past*. New York: Oxford University Press, 1973.

Miller, D. W., and M. K. Starr. *The structure of human decisions*. Englewood Cliffs, N.J.: Prentice-Hall, 1967.

Schwartz, S. Moral decision making and behavior. In J. Macauley and L. Berkowitz (Eds.), *Altruism and helping behavior*. New York: Academic Press, 1970.

Simmons, R. G., S. D. Klein, and K. Thornton. The family member's decision to be a kidney transplant donor. *Journal of Comparative Family Studies*, 1973, 4, 88–115.

Simon, H. A. *Administrative behavior: A study of decision-making processes in administrative organization*. 2nd ed., New York: Macmillan, 1957; 3rd ed., New York: Free Press, 1976.

Slovic, P. Limitations of the mind of man: Implications for decision making in the nuclear age. *Oregon Research Institute Bulletin*, 1971, 11, 41–49.

Steinbruner, J. D. *The cybernetic theory of decision*.

Princeton, N.J.: Princeton University Press, 1974.

Taylor, D. W. Decision making and problem solving. In J. March (Ed.), *Handbook of organizations*. Chicago: Rand McNally, 1965.

Townsend, R. *Up the organization: How to stop the corporation from stifling people and strangling profits*. New York: Knopf, 1970.

Tversky, A. Elimination by aspects: A theory of choice.

Psychological Review, 1972, 79, 281–99.

Vroom, V. H., and P. W. Yetton. *Leadership and decision making*. Pittsburgh: University of Pittsburgh Press, 1973.

Waller, W. W. *The family: A dynamic interpretation*. New York: Cordon Co., 1938.

Young, S. *Management: A systems analysis*. Glenview, Ill.: Scott, Foresman, 1966.

29   THE WISDOM OF SOLOMON
JOHN McCORMICK

In an approach to decision making not specifically covered by Irving Janis and Leon Mann, McCormick reports how researchers at the University of Chicago are investigating the ways people make decisions. These researchers are attempting to do two things. First, they are identifying the errors that people make in approaching and investigating problems. These errors may explain why decision makers often fail to use a reasonable strategy and instead only manage to "muddle through" their decisions. Second, McCormick describes the work researchers are doing in artificial intelligence programs that presumably would be better able to use information to make "correct" decisions. Fortunately for humans, these programs do not work all that well.

This is a story about how to make decisions, and you're about to make one: whether to keep reading. Let's analyze the factors that may go into your choice. *Curiosity:* you've probably noticed the intriguing [not reprinted here] drawings on these pages, and reading the story may explain what they mean. *Inertia:* you've already invested this much time in the piece, and you might as well give it a little more. *Reward:* learning some decisions skills might earn you that promotion to the Paris branch. But there are disadvantages, too. *Distractions:* ESPN is showing your beloved Pro Beach Volleyball. *Hopelessness:* no matter how well you hone your decision making, the boss may still think you're ditch-digger material.

And so we reach decisions, the building blocks of our lives. Some may be important, some inconsequential, but all of them are fascinating to the Center for Decision Research in Chicago. Nowhere else do so many scholars explore the incessant process of choice. The goal is to help business executives as well as business students improve their often rudimentary decision-making skills. Researchers labor to unravel the tangled directions of human thought, in part by analyzing heuristics, the imperfect mental shortcuts we all use in decision making. The exercise is more than academic: the center's autopsies of everyday decisions are now catching the blackened eye of corporate America, where big thinkers too often serve up such ill-conceived catastrophes as New Coke.

The decision center has survived for 10 years in hostile territory, the University of Chicago Graduate School of Business. Oil and water might be a likelier mix. Most of the Chicago school's theorists argue that economic man is supremely rational and calculating: in moments of decision he chooses what is genuinely best for him. Not so, the researchers at the decision center have sadly concluded. Most people, they contend, are woefully muddled information processors who often stumble along ill-chosen shortcuts to reach bad conclusions. If people really did act rationally, the decision center's researchers say, not one sap would join a Christmas Club at the bank.

The center's researchers have compiled a list of typical decision flaws so lengthy it would demoralize Solomon. A sampler of common mistakes:

POOR FRAMING

Decision makers often allow a decision to be "framed" by the language or context it's presented in, rather than exploring it from every perspective. To prove the point, the center's Paul J.H. Schoemaker splits his students into two groups. He tells the first that a hypothetical business maneuver offers an 80 percent chance of success, and most of the group tend to give the go-ahead. He tells the second group that the same maneuver carries a 20 percent risk of failure, and the students turn thumbs down. They have been given identical information but allowed themselves to be swayed by its form. Essentially the same mistake was made by the American automobile industry. For years U.S. car makers were slow to recognize inroads by the Japanese because the American companies viewed their market through just one frame: each measured its performance only against the other domestics.

AVAILABILITY BIAS

Many executives are suckers for the most readily available evidence, even if it contradicts the big picture. That's why, during the days just prior to

their salary reviews, mediocre employees subtly remind bosses of their few achievements. Salesmen often make a variation on this error. Instead of recommending the product that would best meet their customers' needs, they suggest the product they've most recently been trained to sell.

STRATEGIC ANCHORING

The mere mention of a dollar figure can "anchor" a financial discussion to a high or low range. Take a house being appraised by a real-estate agent. If the agent is asked, "Do you think this house is worth more than $150,000?" he is likely to come up with a figure not very far above that amount even if the real market value is $200,000. For the same reason, antique dealers, anticipating that customers will haggle, often overprice an object so that, even after giving ground, they still can turn a handsome profit.

ASSOCIATION BIAS

Executives often choose a course of action because they associate it with some past success. Never mind that a different solution would better suit the current problem, which is not really very similar to the old one if it's analyzed carefully. Past disasters can have the same unwarranted power of suggestion: a manager who once raised prices only to see sales plummet will probably be overly hesitant to order further markups when he should.

Many executives know little beyond cookbook decision making: they have read a bit and survived on intuition. Kepner-Tregoe, a Princeton-based firm that has given basic decision training to 2 million managers, says U.S. companies use good decision skills only 12 percent of the time. The Chicago approach, which draws on the work of California behavioral scientists Daniel Kahneman and Amos Tversky, burrows into the intellectual roots of choice to help executives improve their performance. "We've learned that our managers must actually mistrust their judgment," says Royal Dutch Shell executive Ron van Beaumont, noting that Schoemaker helped Shell calculate that geologists

''90 percent sure'' where to drill for oil were correct only half the time. T. Rowe Price investment managers and Kidder Peabody stock analysts have learned equally painful lessons—and become equally fervent fans.

Schoemaker says today's execs must improve their decision skills to keep pace with competitors. A tactic based on framing, he says, has taught Japanese companies to view complaining customers not as annoyances but as valued informants about their products. He shocks decision makers by exposing how they refuse to consider data challenging their pet solutions. The most seductive sin, overconfidence, ensnares bosses who are certain an impartial party would see things their way. Northwestern University's Max Bazerman, who uses Chicago-style axioms in his negotiations classes, says the Pennzoil-Texaco drama got out of hand solely because each side was overconfident the other would capitulate.

By breaking down the decision process, the professors hope to model human decision makers' rules of thumb so that they can be reduced to computer software. That would accelerate Artificial Intelligence, the evolution of computer systems that reason and create like the human brain. The goal is not to replace humans but to give them an important tool. ''Today we ask a computer to decide how many widgets we should build,'' says MIT researcher John Carroll. ''With AI we might ask it, 'Why are we in this business, anyhow?' ''

Scientist Rick Hayes-Roth of the Palo Alto firm Teknowledge says some 1,000 computers worldwide already make narrow business decisions. Today's systems typically manage 10,000 rules of thumb, a fraction of the 100,000 a chess master uses. But far more powerful systems will someday make strategic and even artistic judgments. First the software must learn to master nuance—a daunting task. Decision-center director Robin Hogarth cites an existing program that interpreted the headline WORLD SHAKEN—POPE SHOT to mean EARTHQUAKE IN ITALY—ONE DEAD.

Even short of AI, the Chicago center's work could alter the way American business makes decisions. In a forthcoming book titled ''Decision Traps,'' Schoemaker and Cornell University's J. Edward Russo envision executives who practice decision making on computers much as pilots train on flight simulators. The shrewdest bosses will become decision architects, framing problems and overseeing final judgments reached by human and electronic subordinates. But first, the new decision making will have to clear a fundamental hurdle. ''The most biased managers,'' says Kidder Peabody executive George Boyd, ''don't want to learn about their biases.''

30 COMMUNICATION NETWORKS IN ORGANIZATIONS
EVERETT ROGERS AND R. ARGAWALA-ROGERS

Network analysis bridges the gap between formal and informal communication by providing a technique for mapping perceived interaction in any circumstances for any purposes. Rogers and Argawala-Rogers make clear the important links between network research and organizational structure and emphasize the relational nature

Everett M. Rogers and Rekha Argawala-Rogers, ''Communications Networks in Organizations.'' Reprinted with permission of the Free Press, a division of McMillan, Inc., from *Communication in Organizations* by Everett M. Rogers and Rekha Argawala-Rogers. Copyright © 1978 by the Free Press.

of network data and analysis. They ground their discussion of networks in group dynamics and systems theory. The following selection provides detailed information about the history, research aims, analytic techniques, and conceptual problems of network studies. Other key issues to be mindful of when reading this selection are the perceptual nature of network data and the dynamic nature of communication relationships: How accurately do network data represent actual communication behavior, and how well can network analysis techniques capture the always changing boundaries, links, and content of interpersonal interaction?

The purpose of this chapter is to describe what is known about communication networks in organizations. A network is a grouping intermediate in size between the individual and the organization. It also is intermediate in the degree of structure that is present. Our work is relational in nature, and our data are generally sociometric. Our units of analysis are the communication relationships between individuals, rather than individuals themselves. After some preliminary discussion of communication networks, we review the results from two main types of network research: (1) laboratory experiments on artificial, small-group networks, and (2) sociometric surveys of communication flows in organizations, which are usually analyzed in order to identify cliques and such individual communication roles as liaisons and, more generally, in order to determine the degree of overlap between the formal and informal communication structures. We will find that the laboratory studies are of much less utility than the sociometric communication researches in studying organizational communication.

WHY ARE NETWORKS IMPORTANT?

Among a large number of individuals, where each person cannot talk easily and equally with every other person, communication networks soon develop. There is a natural tendency for these subsystems to form, so that the individuals within them interact more with each other than with individuals outside

of the subsystem. Needless to say, in a large organization composed of thousands of individuals, many, many networks exist. In fact, one way to think about communication in an organization is to see it as consisting of a great number of small communication networks, overlapping somewhat and interconnected so as to form a network of networks (Mears 1974). So our present discussion of networks is essential to an adequate understanding of communication in organizations. Network analysis is a type of microstudy that contributes to understanding the macro nature of organizational communication.

In most network analysis, the usual concern of communication research with the individual-level effects of a source-receiver communication event is replaced by a research approach in which no sharp distinction is (or can be) made between source and receiver. Communication flows occur among "transceivers" in the network, who are both transmitters and receivers (Pool 1973, p. 9). Communication, in this research conception, is truly a mutual interchange.

The term "network" is the communication analogue to the sociological concept of group; but "network" is distinct from "group" in that it refers to a number of individuals (or other units) who persistently interact with one another in accordance with established patterns. Networks can be measured sociometrically, but they are otherwise not visually obvious. Nevertheless, they are quite real. "The numerous case studies [of communication] show undoubtedly that sociometric patterns [that is, networks] are real" (Nehnevasja 1960, p. 751).[1]

[1] The best evidence for the validity of sociometric measures of communication flows comes from researches in which a multimeasurement approach is used. For example, a triangulation of measurements (perhaps including observation and tracer analysis along with sociometric questions) might be utilized in studying the same respondents in an organization. We agree with Webb and others (1966, p. 1): "No research method is without bias. Interviews and questionnaires must be supplemented by methods testing the same social science variables, but having different methodological weaknesses." Multi-measurement implies that "each method can be strengthened by appealing to the unique qualities of the other methods" (Sieber 1973). The general argument for a multi-measurement approach was posed by Campbell and Fiske (1959), and illustrated in the case of organization research by Pennings (1973).

A *network* consists of interconnected individuals who are linked by patterned communication flows. When we talk about networks, then, we imply a concern with the regularized informal groupings of individuals within a formal system. Each network is a small pocket of people who communicate a great deal with each other, or a multitude of such pockets that are linked by communication flows.

The basis of association that holds a network together may be a mutual concern with a common work task (in which case the group is often called a "work group"), a common liking for or attraction to each other, or a mutuality of interest in some topic. Whatever the basis for the patterned interaction, the existence of regularized flows of interpersonal communication lends predictability to informal communication.

Formal Structure and Communication Networks

In the previous chapter, we noted that one of the differences between formal and informal communication is the greater stability and predictability of formal communication, stability lent by the organizational structure. Now we see that certain of the informal communication behavior also has pattern and predictability, deriving not from the formal organization structure but rather from the regularized patterning of interpersonal communication flows. The fact that such networks exist leads us to speak of an "informal communication structure." We shall probe its nature in this chapter.

Still, communication networks are relatively much less structured than formal communication. Networks occur more or less spontaneously; they spring up out of the day-by-day communication behavior of individuals in an organization. Communication networks are constantly changing over time, and this is one main reason why they are not as predictive of human behavior as is the formal structure. So while the formal structure lends stability to communication relationships over time, the network flows energize the organization's daily activities.

One of the "true delights" of the organizational expert, says Professor Charles Perrow (1972, p. 42), is to find a wide discrepancy between the formal and the informal structure of an organization. The organization chart is simply a diagram of the expected or ideal communication relationships in an organization. What actually happens is usually quite different, as many organizational researches clearly show. And communication network analysis is one of the best available ways to find out the extent and nature of the difference.

We conclude that *while the formal communication system (like the organization chart) is to some extent forced on the members of an organization, the informal communication networks emerge spontaneously. Also, compared to the formal communication system in an organization, the informal communication networks are less structured, and hence less predictable.*

System Effects

In one of the first empirical studies of organizational behavior, the Hawthorne studies, cliques were found among the fourteen workers in the Bank Wiring Observation room. Of the two main cliques (there were also three isolates), one had a much higher rate of performance than the other; this was partly cause and partly effect, as the higher-producing workers tended to be drawn into membership in this clique (Homans 1950, pp. 54–72), and once they were in it, the clique's norms of high production tended to raise the workers' output even more. Similarly, workers in the low-producing clique were restrained by peer pressures from producing "too much." So if one wished to thoroughly understand why some workers produced more than others, the communication networks could not be ignored.

Networks provide an understanding of their members' behavior. The characteristics of an individual's friends (those with whom interaction is most frequent) are important in explaining certain aspects of the individual's behavior. This is true not only in organizations, but also in a wide variety of other contexts. *System effects* are the influences of others in a system on the behavior of an individual member of the system (Rogers with Shoemaker 1971, p. 29).[2] Certainly there are usually strong network effects on the behavior of the network's

---

[2]Other authors have referred to system effects as "compositional effects," "contextual effects," or "structural effects."

individual members in an organization.³ In fact,the norms and climate of the system exert their influence on the individual through his communication network relationships with others in the system.

Generally, we conclude that *the importance of networks in affecting behavior of individual members of an organization is suggested by system effects.*

"It's a Small World"

In addition to sociometric measurement of communication networks, some researchers use a technique perfected by Professor Stanley Milgram that is called the "small world" approach (Milgram 1967, 1969; Korte and Milgram 1970; Travers and Milgram 1969; White 1970). Who has not been asked by a stranger, "Do you know so-and-so?" only to discover mutual friends? We usually exclaim in surprise, 'My, what a small world!'"

Milgram asks his respondents to advance a message from a randomly selected starter to an assigned target person by sending it to any personal acquaintance the respondent thinks is more likely than himself to know the target person. Amazingly, Milgram (1969, p. 112) finds that an average of only about 5.5 intermediaries are needed to transmit a message from starters in Nebraska to targets in Massachusetts. Most of the dyadic transmissions are highly homophilous; for instance Milgram (1969, p. 114) finds that about 80 percent of the transfers are between sources and receivers of the same sex. Black starters are able to get a message through to a black target in somewhat fewer steps than a white target, and white starters are similarly found to be less distant from white targets than black targets.

Actually, Pool (1973, p. 17) argues, Milgram's small world findings are not so surprising when one examines the probabilities involved. Pool finds that the average individual has from 500 to 2,000 close acquaintances (this is the size of the individual's total "personal communication network"). If each individual averages about 1,000 persons, then one's friends' friends would number about 1,000,000 if there were not much overlap (there is, of course, due to interlocking personal networks). A list of friends

of friends of friends would number 1 billion, a staggering number. One can thus understand how a randomly selected starter in Nebraska, can reach a randomly assigned target person in Massachusetts in only 5.5 steps.

Pool (1973, p. 16) estimates that the longest possible chain in the United States would have about six intermediaries. What is the longest possible chain? Perhaps the "small world" linking two hermits on opposite coasts. but each presumably knows a storekeeper. Each storekeeper, in his or her list of acquaintances, has at least one individual who knows his or her congressperson. And there we are with another "small world"—with only a couple of more links, we could carry it to a peasant in India.

Small world studies have not yet been utilized very much in organizations,⁴ although they are a special type of tracer study that could tell us much about how messages flow in an organizational structure. One of the few such studies in an organization is Shotland's (1969, 1970) research among students, professors, and administrators at Michigan State University.

Many student activists in the 1960s claimed that deans and presidents were too socially distant from them, and hence that the only message from students that could "get through" was an act of violence. Shotland's research was designed to determine the social distance between students, faculty, and administrators at a megauniversity of about 50,000 individuals. He found that the average number of intermediaries between randomly selected starters and targets was about five, a figure approaching Milgram's for the entire United States. Students had the longest interpersonal communication channels, and administrators the shortest. The widest social distance at the university was, indeed, from students to administrators.

Personal Networks: Radial and Interlocking

The term "network" is actually used by communication scientists to refer to three different concepts:

1. *Total system network*—comprising the communication patterns among all of the individuals in a

³Although Shoemaker (1971) found only little system effects (from their school) on teacher's innovativeness among a sample of 585 teachers in 28 Thai high schools.
⁴Examples are the study of diffusion of a "planted" message in a boys' camp by Larsen and Hill (1958); and an investigation of the communication of planted messages among teachers in St. Louis high schools, by Wager (1962).

system, such as an organization. This network may consist of thousands of individuals if the organization is a large one. In the present book, we usually use "network" in this context.

2. *Clique*—defined as a subsystem whose elements interact with each other relatively more frequently than with other members of the communication system. Most cliques consist of from five to twenty-five members, with some much larger than this. Cliques are thus one of the main components of a communication network in an organization (along with isolates, liaisons, etc). We prefer to use the term "clique" for the type of subnetwork defined above, but some other authors also call this unit a "network," or a "group."

3. *Personal network*—defined as those interconnected individuals who are linked by patterned communication flows to any given individual (Laumann 1973, p. 7). For the purposes of our present analysis, we occasionally find it convenient to anchor a network on an individual, rather than on a clique or

the entire system (Mitchell 1969, p. 14). Each individual carries around with him a personal network of other individuals with whom he consistently interacts about a given topic. Thus each individual possesses his or her own small communication environment. This personal network partly explains the individual's behavior. In this book, we refer to this individualized type of communication network as a "personal" network, to distinguish it from our broader use of the term "network."

We illustrate a personal communication network in Figure 1. Obviously, if we want to understand the communication behavior of Individual #7, we should look first at the five other individuals in his personal communication network (shown in Figure 1 as connected by solid lines). We also may want to look further, at the larger network which includes the personal networks of the five others in #7's personal network, and at the degree to which these five individuals are interconnected with each other (shown as dotted lines in Figure 1).

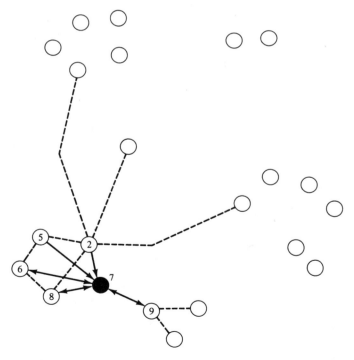

Figure 1   Personal Communication Network for Individual #7 in the ARC Company (shown by the solid lines)

The Strength of Weak Ties. The ingrown communication patterns in an interlocking personal network facilitate effective communication, but they also act as a barrier to prevent new ideas from entering the network. One's closest friends seldom know anything that one does not already know. Friends tend to tell other friends what they know more or less immediately. There is not much new information coming into an interlocking personal network; it needs some nonmutual communication flows to give it more openness. Otherwise, a pooling of ignorance may occur. For example, a study of the search for an abortionist by American women (conducted prior to 1973, when abortions were illegal) showed that most women went first to their best friends (Lee 1969). Unfortunately, these friends were members of interlocking personal networks with the respondent, so they were seldom able to provide any information about abortionists that the respondent did not already possess. One woman sought the name of an abortionist from several of her best friends, her mother, and a family doctor. All provided the name of the same abortionist (one, in fact, who was no longer performing abortions).

Human communication typically entails a balance between novelty and similarity. Communication research on personal networks has dealt with an issue that has come to be called "the strength of weak ties" (Liu and Duff 1972; Granovetter 1973; Rogers 1973). This research is summarized in the statement that *the information strength of dyadic communication relationships is inversely related to the degree of homophily (and the strength of the attraction) between the source and the receiver.* Or, in other words, a new idea is communicated to a larger number of individuals, and traverses a greater social distance, when passed through weak sociometric ties (in radial personal networks) rather than strong ones (in interlocking personal networks). There is little informational strength, then, in interlocking personal networks. "Weak ties" enable innovations to flow from clique to clique via liaisons and bridges.

Network analysis of the diffusion of a family planning method (the IUD or intrauterine device) in the Philippines demonstrated the strength of weak ties. The innovation spread most easily within interlocking cliques, among housewives of very similar social status (Liu and Duff 1972). But heterophilous flows were necessary to link these cliques; usually these "weak ties" connected two women who were not very close friends, and allowed the contraceptive idea to travel from a higher-status to a somewhat lower-status housewife. So at least occasional heterophilous dyadic communication in a network was a structural prerequisite for rapid diffusion of the innovation.

LABORATORY EXPERIMENTS ON SMALL GROUP NETWORKS

In this section we shall review and criticize the body of communication research obtained from laboratory experiments with small group networks, from the perspective of what useful knowledge such research provides about networks in organizations. These experiments entail creating small communication networks in the laboratory, with different types of miniaturized organizational structure, so that the effects of such varied structure can be determined as it affects communication behavior.

Laboratory small groups studies have attempted a unique contribution toward understanding communication behavior in organizations, but they lack the reality of an ongoing, "live" organization. They have focused on the nature of the task, motivation of members, group size, and emerging patterns of interaction.

Background of the Small Groups Studies

The studies we are concerned with are commonly known as "small group" research. About thirty years ago, most writings about small group behavior were only philosophical, intuitive, and theoretical. It was not until the mid-1940s that the small group became a focus of social scientific inquiry.

Laboratory experiments on small group communication sprang from three main origins:

1. the work of the social psychologist Kurt Lewin and his protegés: one of Lewin's researches (1958) dealt with the introduction of the idea of

eating "sweetbreads" (undesirable cuts of meat) to small groups of housewives in Iowa City;

2. the sociometric studies of Jacob Moreno and his students, who investigated the patterns of social relationships among the members of communities, classrooms, and other real-life groups (Moreno 1953; Moreno and Jennings 1960); and

3. the Hawthorne studies (Roethlisberger & Dixon, 1939), which indicated the importance of small work groups in the factory in determining workers' performance.

Communication network research with laboratory groups became a standard experimental approach in the 1950s and 1960s. What effect does the structure of the group have upon the efficiency of its communication behavior? What effect does an individual's position in the group structure have on his or her morale and job satisfaction? Three experiments, conducted by Bavelas (1950), Leavitt (1951), and Shaw (1954, 1964), are summarized herein, as they are perhaps most representative of laboratory research on small group networks.

Circle, Wheel, and Chain

Professor Alex Bavelas (1950) developed the technique of arranging small groups of individuals in cubicles, interconnected by means of slots in the cubicle walls through which the group members were asked to communicate by written messages. Various communication structures, such as the circle, wheel, and chain, were imposed upon the group members by closing certain of the cubicles' wall slots (Fig. 2). Each of the members was given certain information, which had to be shared in order to

complete the assigned task. Generally, all network members organized themselves into a pattern by which peripheral individuals sent messages to the central members, who solved the problem and communicated the solution back to the peripheral members. (All members had to know the solution in order for the assigned task to be scored as successfully completed.) The dependent variables were the amount of time required to achieve the correct solution, the number of messages exchanged, the number of errors committed, sociometric leadership nominations, and perceived satisfaction with the job on the part of the group members.

Bavelas concluded that (1) highly centralized communication networks like the "wheel" are superior for routine tasks, where errors are acceptable; while (2) a decentralized network like the "circle" is better suited for less routine tasks, where adaptation and innovative thinking are required. When only centralized communication (as in the "wheel") was allowed, the task was seldom completed successfully; performance improved when decentralized communication (the "circle") was allowed. However, a completely interlocking communication network (the "all-channel") was no more effective than the restricted communication network (the "wheel").

Professor Harold Leavitt (1951) examined the relationship between different communication networks and task performance by asking his subjects to identify the one correct symbol which had been given to them on a card depicting six different symbols. Information was exchanged until all five participants constituting a group knew the correct answer. Each small group of five subjects were given a total of fifteen consecutive trials in attempting this

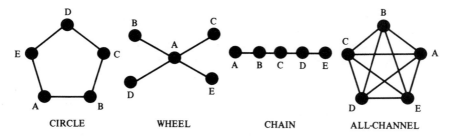

Figure 2   Some of the Five-Person Group Structures in Laboratory Experiments on Small Group Network Communication

task. Group members were allowed to transmit and receive messages according to a structure predetermined by the experimenters (and similar to Bavelas's).

In the "wheel," peripheral individuals funneled information to the center, where a decision was made and then disseminated to the other four individuals. The "circle," however, showed no consistent organizational pattern, as all available links were used at some point during a given trial.

Work performance was measured in terms of (1) the speed in arriving at a correct solution, and (2) the proportion of errors committed by the group. Leavitt (1951) found that the "wheel" was considerably faster than the "circle" in solving the assigned problems. However, the "circle" groups made more errors than those in the "wheel." Whereas the individual occupying position "A" in the "wheel" is alone able to recode the information and detect errors, all five individuals in the "circle" can recode and hence check a particular solution to the problem.

Building on Leavitt's work, Shaw (1954) studied the concept of independence—the degree of freedom with which an individual could function in a group. Independence was greater in decentralized networks like the circle or all-channel, regardless of the type of task, and was positively related to individual satisfaction. A second concept that Shaw elucidated was "saturation," rather similar to our concept of information overload, which was the information input and output requirements for the individual. It was highest for Individual "A" in the "wheel" network. Saturation (overload) was negatively related to efficiency in solving group tasks.

The small groups experiments led to the following conclusions.

1. *Network centralization (such as possessed by the "wheel") contributes to rapid performance (especially of simple tasks), but the error rate is high, presumably because two-way communication and feedback is discouraged.* The more interconnected a network is, the more likely it is to solve a problem requiring the pooling of information held by the network members.

2. *Low centralization or high independence (as in the "circle") is associated with member satisfaction.*

3. *The network structure served to elevate certain individuals into leadership positions.* For example, Leavitt (1951) did not designate a formal leader in a laboratory network, but Individual "A" in the "wheel" always emerged as the sociometric leader named by the participants. In the "circle," the participants were less likely to feel that a leader emerged during the experiment, and if they did select a leader, their choice was distributed among all the positions in the circle.

4. *Being in a key position in a network, however, also led to information overload for the leader, through whom all the messages had to pass.*

Criticisms of the Small Groups Studies

One communication scholar claims that since most work in organizations is done in small groups of five or six persons, a large organization can be conceptualized as merely a collection of small groups (Mears 1974). If one accepts this argument, perhaps the findings from laboratory experiments on communication networks might be useful in providing an understanding of the networks that are embedded in organizations. We have some serious doubts.

Findings from laboratory experiments on communication networks in small groups (like the wheel, circle, and chain) can be applied to organizational settings only with great caution. Student subjects in artificial, nonorganizational settings undoubtedly do not act in ways that help us understand the complexities of communication networks that are embedded in organizational structures. For this reason, Professor Howard Becker (1954) refers to the small groups research as "cage" studies, in a biting criticism of their unreality.

In retrospect, the paramount blunder committed by small groups researchers undoubtedly was the lack of a systems framework, as Starbuck (1965) points out. The individual-oriented psychological myopia of communication research in the 1950s and 1960s is well illustrated by these small groups researches.

Individuals were brought into experimental settings, as virtually total strangers, to perform tasks of a completely unreal nature. The experimental conditions did not reflect the real-life situations of large organizations. The integration of group networks within an organization through communication patterns was overlooked. So the lack of a systems approach was a serious oversight.

Perhaps the main contribution of the small groups studies was that they provided information about structural effects in communication networks. But the precise nature of the relationships among the variables involved still remained largely unclear. As Professor Donald Campbell (1969, p. 377) noted, experiments cannot prove theories, only probe them. And network analysis undoubtedly has benefited from the prior probing of conceptual issues in the small groups experiments.

NETWORK ANALYSIS

Network analysis is a method of research for identifying the communication structure in a system, in which sociometric data about communication flows or patterns are analyzed by utilizing interpersonal relationships as the units of analysis. Most past communication research, as well as organization behavior studies, has largely ignored the effects of structure on communication behavior. Network analysis is a tool that promises to capitalize on the unique ability of communication inquiry in ongoing organizations to reconstruct specific message flows in a system and to overlay the social structure of the organization on these flows. Communication inquiry in organizations makes manifest otherwise static structural variables; network analysis permits an understanding of the dynamics of organizational structure as it determines the flows of messages between units and across hierarchical positions. About the only example to date of communication research in which network analysis has been used to restore social structure to the communication process is that of several investigations of organizational communication centered in the Department of Communication at Michigan State University.

In the preceding section of this chapter, we reviewed the laboratory experiments on small group networks and expressed considerable reservations about the usefulness of this research in understanding the complex reality of communication in organizations. It was natural and logical for communication scholars to drop these laboratory experiments

(few such studies are being conducted today) and move from the artificial and controlled setting of the laboratory to the reality of actual organizations, where real-life communication networks abound. This shift in the research setting being investigated also entailed a change in experimental design from one in which the structure could be manipulated by the experimenter (as in the "circle," "wheel," and "chain") to survey sociometry, in which the structural arrangements of real-life networks and cliques could be determined by network analysis but usually could not be manipulated as an independent variable.

Background on Network Analysis in Organizations

Network analysis of organizational communication dates from a classic investigation of communication patterns among officials in the United States Office of Naval Research by researchers at the University of Michigan's Institute for Social Research in the early 1950s (Jacobson and Seashore 1951; Weiss and Jacobson 1955; Weiss 1956). This research caused little scholarly excitement at the time, and its impact went relatively unnoticed for almost two decades. But in retrospect, viewed from the vantage point of present-day approaches to research on organizational communication, the Jacobson–Seashore–Weiss research represents an important turning point in the study of communication in organizations.

In the early 1950s, the University of Michigan researchers were fully aware of the Hawthorne studies' earlier focus on "work groups" as communication subsystems within an organizational setting, and they were certainly alerted to look at informal communication patterns. But unlike all the Human Relationists of the day, who were largely ignoring communication networks, Jacobson, Seashore, and Weiss utilized survey sociometric techniques to gather data from naval personnel about their communication behavior. Each respondent in the organization studied was asked to indicate how frequently he talked with each other member of his organization. These sociometric data were then analyzed by using a modification of the matrix analysis procedures previously described by Forsyth and Katz (1946).

This technique arranged all of the organization's members down one side of a matrix (the "who," or "seeker," dimension), and all of the same individuals on the other side (the "whom," or "sought" dimension).[5]

For almost twenty years, no other communication researcher took up this type of network analysis, until Schwartz's (1968) study of 142 faculty members in the College of Education at Michigan State University. Soon thereafter, MacDonald (1970) used network analysis to investigate the cliques, liaisons, etc., among the 185 members of a federal agency located in the Pentagon. The studies by Schwartz and MacDonald were soon followed by several doctoral dissertations using network analysis in the Department of communication at Michigan State University. The invisible subcollege was forming.

Network Analysis Procedures

Network analysis of communication in organizations is usually carried out in order to determine the nature of interpersonal communication flows and how the formal and informal structures are related. This analysis is done by:

1. identifying cliques within the total system, and determining how these structural subgroupings affect communication behavior in the organization;
2. identifying certain specialized communication roles such as liaisons, bridges, and isolates (thus allowing communication research to proceed far beyond the relatively simpler issue of opinion leadership); and
3. measuring various structural indexes (like communication, integration[6] or connectedness, and system openness) for individuals, cliques, or entire systems.

We describe these procedures in detail later in this section.

Network analysis necessitated a new kind of sampling, as well as a shift to relational units of analysis. Instead of random samples of scattered individuals in a large population, network studies depended on gathering data from *all* of the eligible respondents in an organization or subsystem, or in a sample of organizations or subsystems (Table 1).[7] As a result, the ability to generalize the research results is traded off for a greater focus on understanding the effects of structure on communication flows. For if these effects were to be understood, intact structures (like organizations), or at least the relevant parts of them, had to be studied.

Several difficulties are involved in communication network analysis. For one thing, perhaps the dynamic process of communication relationships among the members of a system is so fleeting that networks cannot be accurately charted, and the plotting of sociometric communication relationships within a formal structure is but an evasive illusion. Imagine trying to capture, in quantified terms of "arrows" and numbers, the total human interaction that occurs in even a small organization in one day! Impossible, you say. True. Sociometric data actually reflect only the grossest of communication behavior, the main lines of communication that are most frequently and heavily used. The "weak ties" that occur in organizations, the lightly used flows, seldom are reported by respondents in organizational researches, and hence are rarely analyzed in network studies; Granovetter (1973) argues that this problem is especially serious because these "weak ties" are different in nature from the "strong ties" or regularized communication patterns that are usually reported by respondents and investigated in network analyses. For example, as we showed previously, weak ties are more likely to be informationally rich.

Communication networks are the "threads" that hold a system together; they are important but difficult to study, as they are so numerous. The threads can easily become a tangled ball to the investigator. One of the practical problems of communication

---

[5]Such a who-to-whom matrix is sometimes called a "communimatrix"; it is a method for graphically displaying relational data about communication patterns among the members of a system.
[6]*Communication integration* is the degree to which the units in a system are interconnected by interpersonal communication.
[7]A high rate of nonresponse can leave gaps in the data matrix, so network analysts typically try to achieve a nearly 100 percent response.

Table I COMPARISON OF MONADIC AND RELATIONAL ANALYSIS IN COMMUNICATION RESEARCH

Characteristic of the Research Approach	*Type of Communication Research Approach*	
	Monadic Analysis	*Relational Analysis*
1. Unit of analysis	The individual	The communication relationship between two (or more) individuals
2. Most frequent sample design	Random samples of scattered individuals in a large sample (in order to maximize the generalizability of the research results)	Complete census of all eligible respondents in a system (like an organization), or in a sample of such intact systems
3. Types of data utilized	Personal and social characteristics of individuals, and their communication behavior	Same as for monadic analysis, plus sociometric data about communication relationships
4. Main data analysis methods	Correlational analysis of cross-sectional survey data	Various types of network analysis of cross-sectional survey data
5. Main purpose of the research	To determine the independent variables (usually characteristics of individuals) related to a dependent variable (usually a communication effect)	To determine how structural variables affect communication flows in a system

network analysis is the immensity of the task. In a system of 100 members, each of the 100 individuals can talk to the 99 others, so that 9,900 communication relationships are possible. In a 200-member system, 39,800 communication dyads are possible, and in a system with 5,000 members, nearly 25 million, which exceeds the processing capacity of most modern computers (Lindsey 1974, pp. 1–3). One solution, of course, is to break the total communication system down into subsystems, or cliques; this technique makes the complexity of interpersonal communication more manageable.

A further problem is that there is not just a single set of communication networks. A given individual may have a different set of communication partners for each of a myriad of topics; each of these personal networks may be somewhat overlapping and can be superimposed on the others. For example Berlo and others (1971) found somewhat different communication networks for the members of a federal government agency when the sociometric questions dealt with work-related matters, with innovations, and with maintenance.

A common approach to network analysis of organizational communication consists of the following sequence of research steps:

1. Sociometric data about work-related (or other) interpersonal communication flows are gathered from each member in the organization, or from a subdivision or specific department of the organization. The sociometric data may be obtained via questionnaires or personal interviews, by observation, or by other means.

2. Cliques are identified among the members of

the system on the basis of which individuals communicate most with each other. Such identification may be accomplished by visually representing the patterns of communication in a sociogram and rearranging together those individuals who interact most with each other. Or a computer program can be utilized to identify cliques as is more often done when many individuals are involved.

3. These cliques are then superimposed on the formal organization chart to determine the degree to which the two correspond. Presumably the organization chart represents the formally expected patterns of communication, while the sociometric data constitute the day-to-day reality of actual communication flows.

4. This assessment of the adequacy of the formal organizational structure from a communication point of view may lead to recommended changes in the organization chart through reorganization, or to the reassignment of certain individuals in the organization. For example, the network analysis may show that the organization contains isolates who do not communicate with anyone else in their organization (or in their unit or department). Or it may show that the cliques are not adequately linked by liaisons or bridges, and these roles may need to be created.

COMMUNICATION STRUCTURAL VARIABLES

Almost all communication research to date uses the individual respondent as the unit of data analysis, and concentrates on determining the effects of communication. We have argued for the advantage of operationalizing communication *relationships* between two or more individuals, usually utilizing some types of sociometric measurement. Several types of relational analysis of communication behavior can then be utilized to probe the nature of the communication relationships at the level of: (1) the individual's personal communication network, (2)

the clique, and (3) the system. At each level, various indexes can be constructed to operationalize the type of communication structure that is present.

Personal Communication Networks

At the lowest level, an important structural characteristic is the degree to which a person is integrated with the individuals in his personal communication network. *Personal communication network integration* is defined as the degree to which communication links exist among the members of an individual's personal communication network. The greater the number of these links, the greater the degree of integration of a particular individual's communication network. As we showed previously (Fig. 2), an interlocking personal network has a high degree of integration, while a radial personal network has a low degree of integration. In the latter case, one's friends are not friends of each other; this type of unintegrated network is more open to its environment, and we expect that an individual who has this type of network will receive a particular message that is circulating in his or her system relatively earlier than one with an interlocking network. So more highly integrated personal networks are informationally weaker.

Liaisons in a network of agricultural extension specialists at a state university were found to have a higher degree of personal network integration than nonliaisons (Amend 1971, p. 46). The liaisons communicated about work-related matters with peers who were not linked with each other. Such a diversity in personal networks is exactly what we would expect to characterize liaisons, who are by definition in a marginal position between two or more cliques in their system. We also might expect opinion leaders in an organization to have less integrated (and informationally stronger) personal networks.

Personal network integration is greater for some topics of communication, like sensitive or taboo[8] issues, than for others.[9] Laumann (1973, p. 125) found that urban men in Detroit discussed such

---

[8]*Taboo* communication is that category of message transfer in which the messages are perceived as extremely private and personal in nature because they deal with prescribed behavior.

[9]Kincaid (1973) found that the degree of personal network integration among slum dwellers in Mexico City, measured in an approach similar to Laumann's, was related to the adoption of family planning methods.

issues as voting and what kind of a new car to buy with less integrated personal networks (that is, in more radial networks), but the same respondents communicated about more sensitive topics, like a serious medical problem, with more integrated (that is, interlocking, or closed) personal networks.

So the degree of integration in personal communication networks has been related to (1) special communication roles in a system, like liaisons, and (2) different topics of conversation.

Clique-Level Analysis

At the clique level of analysis, we can consider a variety of structural variables that can be measured: (1) clique connectedness, (2) clique dominance, (3) clique openness, and (4) clique integration into the larger system.

1. *Clique connectedness* is the degree to which the members of a clique are linked with each other by communication flows. The actual degree of connectedness among the individuals in a clique (measured by the number of interpersonal communication flows) can be compared to the total possible degree of connectedness that could potentially exist. Such an index of communication connectedness can be computed for each clique, and the clique then becomes the unit of analysis. This index allows us to investigate the relationship between the degree of connectedness in a clique and various other clique-level variables, like the relative speed of diffusion of a new idea in one clique as compared with others.

For example, Berlo and others (1972, p. 14) found that the degree of clique connectedness among twenty-seven cliques in a federal agency in the Pentagon ranged from 85 percent (this clique was centered in the agency director's office) down to 11 percent (for a clique in the planning office, where presumably the need for clique members to work in close connection was much less). As might be expected, larger-sized cliques had less connectedness; it is more difficult for everyone in a larger clique to communicate with everyone else. The highest degree of connectedness was for work groups of about seven to ten members. The planning office clique, with only 11 percent connectedness, had seventeen members. An implication for reorganization of this agency might be to formally divide this unit into two subgroups if a higher degree of connectedness were desired (Fig. 3).

2. *Clique dominance* is the degree to which the patterns of communication relationship among clique members deviate from equality. The "wheel" network shown in Figure 2 has a high degree of dominance, in that all communication flows must pass through one individual. Such centralization causes information overload and tends to limit openness. Berlo and others (1972) measured clique dominance in a federal government agency and found it to be highly related (negatively) to clique connectedness.

3. *Clique openness* is the degree to which the members of a clique exchange information with the clique's external environment. Where new ideas

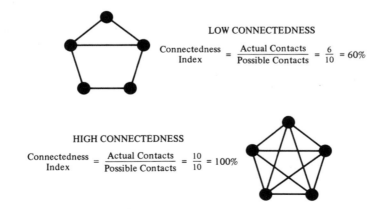

LOW CONNECTEDNESS

$$\text{Connectedness Index} = \frac{\text{Actual Contacts}}{\text{Possible Contacts}} = \frac{6}{10} = 60\%$$

HIGH CONNECTEDNESS

$$\text{Connectedness Index} = \frac{\text{Actual Contacts}}{\text{Possible Contacts}} = \frac{10}{10} = 100\%$$

Figure 3   An Illustration of Low and High Communication Connectedness in a Small System

must enter a clique from external sources, as is often the case, those cliques with greater openness are expected to be more innovative.

4. A final structural index at the clique level of analysis is *clique integration* into the larger network. This measure is analagous to the integration index for personal communication networks discussed previously, but here we are measuring the degree to which a single clique is linked with others in the system. Such integration rests on the number of liaisons and their location in the total communication network for the organization.

To date few researches have been conducted using clique openness or clique integration indexes.

System-Level Analysis

Once we have isolated, measured, and analyzed communication structural variables at the personal network and clique levels of analysis, we can also compute structural indices for entire systems, like organizations.

System differentiation is the degree to which a system contains distinct cliques. The greater the number of distinct cliques within a social system (at a given constant size),[10] the more that social system is differentiated. *The greater the differentiation in a system, (1) the slower the rate of diffusion of innovations in that system (as compared with others), and (2) the lower the system's productivity in accomplishing tasks that require collaboration by the total system.*

System connectedness is the degree to which the cliques in a system are linked to each other by communication flows. This index enables us to represent mathematically the relative degree of clique interlinkage within a particular social system.

Betty's (1974) investigation of forty-one family planning clinics in the Philippines illustrates use of the system connectedness index. His dependent variable was the productivity of each clinic, as measured by the number of adopters of family planning methods secured by the clinic staff each month. Independent variables, such as the degree to which its staff were dependent on each other for information, were communication indexes for each clinic.

The connectedness of the clinic staff members was tested to determine its importance in intervening between the independent variables and the dependent variables of clinic productivity.

Although Betty's empirical results did not provide much support for his theoretical design, his paradigm is provocative in terms of further investigation. Significantly, it utilizes the organization (in this case, the clinic) as the unit of analysis.

Another research using system connectedness was conducted by R. K. Allen (1970) in two innovative and two noninnovative high schools in Michigan. The innovative systems have a higher degree of connectedness among the teaching staff; the noninnovative schools had more isolates, and the cliques among teachers there were interlinked less closely by interpersonal communication patterns. Generally, we expect that the degree of connectedness in a communication network is positively related to the rate of diffusion of innovations.

System dominance is the degree to which the patterns of communication relationships among cliques in a social system deviate from equality. Thus it is a measure of the degree of centralization governing interclique communication. The greater the control by a single clique over the communication flows within the entire set of cliques, the higher the system dominance. A system with high dominance should be able to make decisions quickly, but its openness to the environment should be less and hence information should be less likely to penetrate the boundary of the system. R. K. Allen (1970) found only weak support for this proposition, however, in his investigation of both innovative and noninnovative high schools in Michigan.

System openness is the degree to which a system exchanges information with its environment. Systems with greater openness are likely to be more innovative.

The possibility of using various indexes to probe communication structure's relationships with organizational innovation and productivity has been appreciated only in recent years, and so much of our preceding discussion of communication structural variables has necessarily been hypothetical, rather than a synthesis of completed research. These com-

---

[10]We can remove the effects of the number of individuals in a system by making the measure relative to the size of the system.

munication structural variables can help point the way toward new types of network analysis communication research in organization.

REFERENCES

Richard K. Allen (1970), *A Comparison of Communication Behaviors in Innovative and Non-Innovative Secondary Schools*, Ph.D. Thesis, East Lansing, Mich., Michigan State University.

Thomas J. Allen and others (1971), "The International Technological Gatekeeper," *Technology Review*, 36–43, 73.

Edwin H. Amend (1971), *Liaison Communication Roles of Professionals in a Research Dissemination Organization*, Ph.D. Thesis, East Lansing, Mich., Michigan State University.

Alex Bavelas (1950), "Communication Patterns in Task-Oriented Groups," *Acoustical Society of America Journal*, 22: 727–30.

Howard Becker (1954), "Vitalizing Sociological Theory," *American Sociological Review*, 19: 383–84.

David K. Berlo and others (1971), *Relationships Between Supervisor-Subordinate Communication Practices and Employee Turnover, Attendance, and Performance Evaluations*, East Lansing Mich., Michigan State University, Department of Communication, Mimeo Report.

David K. Berlo and others (1972), *An Analysis of the Communication Structure of the Office of Civil Defense*, East Lansing, Mich., Michigan State University, Department of Communication, Mimeo Report.

Samuel Betty (1974), *Some Determinants of Communication Network Structure and Productivity: A Study of Clinic Staff Interaction in Two Philippine Family Planning Organizations*, Ph.D. Thesis, East Lansing, Mich., Michigan State University.

Donald T. Campbell (1969), "Prospective: Artifact and Control," in Robert Rosenthal and R. L. Rosnow, eds., *Artifacts in Behavioral Research*, New York, Academic Press.

Donald T. Campbell and D. W. Fiske (1959), "Convergent and Discriminant Validation by the Multitrait-Multimethod Matrix," *Psychological Bulletin, 56: 81–105.*

E. Forsyth and Leo Katz (1946), "A Matrix Approach to the Analysis of Sociometric Data," *Sociometry*, 9: 340–47.

Mark S. Granovetter (1973), "The Strength of Weak Ties," *American Journal of Sociology*, 78: 1360–80.

George C. Homans (1950), *The Human Group*, New York, Harcourt, Brace.

Eugene Jacobson and Stanley Seashore (1951), "Communication Patterns in Complex Organizations," *Journal of Social Issues*, 7: 28–40.

Elihu Katz (1957), "The Two-Step Flow of Communication: An Up-to-Date Report on an Hypothesis," *Public Opinion Quarterly*, 21:61–78.

D. Lawrence Kincaid (1973), *Communication Networks, Locus of Control, and Family Planning among Migrants to the Periphery of Mexico City*, Ph.D. Thesis, East Lansing, Mich., Michigan State University.

Charles Korte and Stanley Milgram (1970), "Acquaintance Networks between Radical Groups: Application of the Small World Method," *Journal of Personality and Social Psychology*, 15: 101–108.

Otto Larsen and Richard Hill (1958), "Social Structure and Interpersonal Communication," *American Journal of Sociology*, 63: 497–505.

Edward O. Laumann (1973), *Bonds of Pluralism: The Form and Substance of Urban Social Networks*, New York, Wiley-Interscience.

Harold J. Leavitt (1951), "Some Effects of Certain Communication Patterns on Group Performance," *Journal of Abnormal and Social Psychology*, 46: 38–50.

Nancy Howell Lee (1969), *The Search for an Abortionist*, University of Chicago Press.

Kurt Lewin (1958), "Group Decision and Social Change," in Theodore M. Newcomb and Eugene L. Hartley, eds., *Readings in Social Psychology*, New York, Holt.

George N. Lindsey (1974), *An Alternative Method for the Evaluation of Networks in Large Organizations*, M.A. Thesis, San Jose, Calif., San Jose State University.

William T. Liu and Robert W. Duff (1972), "The Strength of Weak Ties," *Public Opinion Quarterly*, 36: 361–66.

Donald MacDonald (1970), *Communication Roles and Communication Contents in a Bureaucratic Setting*, Ph.D. Thesis, East Lansing, Mich., Michigan State University.

Peter Mears (1974), "Structuring Communication in a Working Group," *Journal of Communication*, 24: 71–79.

Stanley Milgram (1967), "The Small World Problem," *Psychology Today*, 1: 61–67.

Stanley Milgram (1969), "Inter-disciplinary Thinking and the Small World Problem," in Muzafer Sherif and Carolyn W. Sherif, eds., *Interdisciplinary Relationships in the Social Sciences*, Chicago, Aldine.

J. Clyde Mitchell (1969), "The Concept and Use of Social Networks," in J. Clyde Mitchell, ed., *Social*

Networks in Urban Situations, Manchester, England, Manchester University Press.

Jacob L. Moreno (1953), *Who Shall Survive? Foundations of Sociometry, Group Psychotherapy, and Sociodrama*, Beacon, N.Y., Beacon House.

Jacob L. Moreno and Helen H. Jennings (1960), *The Sociometry Reader*, New York, Free Press.

Jiri Nehnevasja (1960), "Graphic Presentation," in Jacob L. Moreno and Helen H. Jennings, eds., *The Sociometry Reader*, New York, Free Press.

Johannes Pennings (1973), "Measures of Organizational Structure: A Methodological Note," *American Journal of Sociology*, 79: 686–704.

Charles Perrow (1972), *Complex Organizations: A Critical Essay*, Glenview, Ill., Scott, Foresman.

Ithiel De Sola Pool (1973), "Communication Systems," in Ithiel de Sola Pool and Wilbur Schramm, eds., *Handbook of Communication*, Chicago, Rand-McNally.

Fritz J. Roethlisberger and William J. Dickson (1939), *Management and the Worker*, Cambridge, Mass., Harvard University Press.

Everett M. Rogers (1973), *Communication Strategies for Family Planning*, New York, Free Press.

Everett M. Rogers with F. Floyd Shoemaker (1971), *Communication of Innovations: A Cross-Cultural Approach*, New York, Free Press.

M. E. Shaw (1954), "Some Effects of Unequal Distribution of Information Upon Group Performance in Various Communication Nets," *Journal of Abnormal and Social Psychology*, 49: 547–53.

M. E. Shaw (1964), "Communication Networks," in Leonard Berkowitz, ed., *Advances in Experimental Psychology*, New York, Academic Press.

F. Floyd Shoemaker (1971), *System Variables and Educational Innovativeness in Thai Government Secondary Schools*, Ph.D. Thesis, East Lansing, Mich., Michigan State University.

Robert L. Shotland (1969), *The Structure of Social Relationships at MSU: A Communication Study*, East Lansing, Mich., Michigan State University, Educational Development Program, Project Report 302.

Robert L. Shotland (1970), *The Communication Patterns and the Structure of Social Relationships at a Large University*, Ph.D. Thesis, East Lansing, Mich., Michigan State University.

Sam D. Sieber (1973), "The Integration of Fieldwork and Survey Methods," *American Journal of Sociology*, 78: 1335–59.

William H. Starbuck (1965), "Mathematics and Organizational Theory," in James G. March, ed., *Handbook of Organizations*, Chicago, Rand McNally.

Jefferey Travers and Stanley Milgram (1969), "An Experimental Study of the Small World Problem," *Sociometry*, 32: 425–43.

Victor Vroom (1964), *Work and Motivation*, New York, Wiley.

L. Wesley Wager (1962), "Channels of Interpersonal and Mass Communication in an Organizational Setting: Studying the Diffusion of Information about a Unique Organizational Change," *Sociological Inquiry*, 32: 88–107.

Eugene J. Webb and others (1966), *Unobtrusive Measures: Nonreactive Research in the Social Sciences*, Chicago, Rand McNally.

Robert S. Weiss (1956), *Processes of Organization*, Ann Arbor, Mich., University of Michigan, Institute for Social Research, Report.

Robert S. Weiss and Eugene Jacobson (1955), "A Method for the Analysis of the Structure of Complex Organizations," *American Sociological Review*, 20: 661–68.

Harrison C. White (1970), "Search Parameters for the Small World Problems," *Social Forces*, 49: 259–64.

31 NORMS AND VALUES IN A CONFLICT SITUATION
Bruce Kapferer

The following excerpt from a paper by Bruce Kapferer is probably the best example of the explanatory power of communication networks that has been published to date. Kapferer's use of the idea of a network—or *reticulum*, as he calls it—redeems network analysis from criticisms that it lacks theoretical import. He shows how network analysis can be used to yield a very detailed explanation of one significant instance of organizational communication: a dispute between an old and a young employee over "ratebusting," or increasing the speed of production.

The first half of Kapferer's original paper includes a detailed analysis of the dispute and its normative basis. Unfortunately, space limitations prevent publication of that material. In its place we offer the following synopsis of the background and normative bases of the communication events that took place:

The dispute occurs between two workers in the cell room of a zinc production plant. The plant is part of a mining operation in Broken Hill, Zambia, in the southern part of Africa. The work force is drawn from several different tribes. The zinc is produced by a process of electrolysis: Zinc from the mine is reduced to a solution, which is then separated into zinc and by-products by passing a current through two electrodes placed in solution baths. The deposited zinc is stripped from the electrodes by the *strippers*. The stripped zinc sheets are collected and taken to the weigh office by *scale attendants*, and from there they are taken to be melted down.

Other personnel support the main production. When the electrodes become so dirty that their efficiency declines, they are delivered to the *scrubbers*, who clean the electrodes or replace them if they are badly worn. Some zinc sheets are wet when stripped, and the *dryers* must see that they are dried before a fire; dryers also occasionally help with difficult stripping jobs. The *titrator* is responsible for maintaining the proper chemical balance in the electrolysis baths. All cell room employees are responsible to the *crew boss*. The locations of these workers are shown in Figure 1. Other important demographic characteristics are presented in Table 1.

Kapferer describes one particularly interesting dispute that occurred between workers in the cell room in late 1964:

> The normal clamour and hum of the Cell Room is suddenly broken by Abraham who shouts across to Donald at Stand IV, "*Buyantanshe* (Progress), slow down and wait for us." A hush now settles on the Unit. For a while Donald takes no notice and Abraham calls "*Buyantanshe*" once more. This evokes a reaction and Donald retorts that he is not to be called by his nickname as he already has a proper name. Abraham replies that he only knows Donald

by his nickname, "*Buyantanshe*." His blood up, Donald shouts, "We young men must be very careful about being bewitched." Abraham assents, "You are quite right; you will be bewitched if you don't respect your elders." Donald is now almost beside himself with rage, and goes straight to lodge a formal protest with the Shop Steward, Lotson, against what he considers to be Abraham's threat of witchcraft. This done he then goes down the stripping stands reporting the matter to the Strippers and those Scale Attendants working nearby. He is just passing Stand III when he hears, as do others close at hand, Soft's very audible comment to Joshua that Donald must be drunk or else they (the Unit 3 workers) should not be seeing such behaviour. Donald storms across to Soft, and the latter, in an attempt to pacify him and to persuade him to return to his stand, says, "I didn't mean *you* when I said that." Jackson, the Crew Boss, who has hitherto been amusedly observing the dispute from the sidelines, now steps in and orders Donald to return to work, which the latter does, muttering angrily all the way back to his stand, "I don't wish anyone to call me '*Buyantanshe*'; I have my own name, Donald."

Work now returns more or less to normal. Occasionally small clusters of workers collect to discuss or enquire about the dispute; but the event is once more brought fully to the attention of the Unit workers when Soft comes to seat himself near Lotson at break time. Lotson asks him why he has quarrelled with Donald at work. "It's my own business; Donald didn't hear me properly," mutters Soft. Others who are seated near Soft and Lotson now stop whatever they have been talking about and crane forward to listen. Damian and Jackson come from where they have been standing near Stand I and hover at the outskirts of the group surrounding Lotson and Soft. Soft now elaborates, "Donald has taken too much beer and this is what has caused him to behave like this. Surely we all call him by his nickname!" Donald, who has been listening nearby, and prior to this had been discussing his version of the dispute with two of his friends, Godfrey and Stephen, impatiently breaks in, "In my case please, I don't want anyone calling me *Buyantanshe* as I have my proper name, Donald. Drinking doesn't enter the case—the quarrel was caused by Abraham who insisted on calling me by my nickname and instead of answering properly to my protests, threatened to bewitch me." At this Lotson bursts out with a disbelieving laugh and asks Donald for the real reasons behind his outburst: "Was it because Soft called you a drunk? If so, this is not a real case." Soft now intervenes and states that Donald has reacted in such a way because the comment came from a young man. "Really," he declares, "there is no excuse for Donald's behaviour."

Abraham, who is seated near Stand I, calls across to Donald to join him where he is sitting. (He addresses the latter as "Donald.") Everybody seated with Donald urges him to go, and after much prompting he does so. Lotson, Abel and Soft joke together that now Donald need not fear being bewitched any longer. Immediately on Donald's arrival at Abraham's seating place, Abraham asks him to go and sharpen his stripping hook. After having completed this service Donald returns the hook to its owner and then joins a group of Scale Attendants and Titrators who are seated near the Weight Office.

For most workers in the Unit, including Abraham, the dispute seemed to be at an end. But that this was not so for Donald was demonstrated a few days later. Donald again accused Abraham of witchcraft and used his suspicions of Abraham's malevolence as a pretext for applying for a transfer from the Cell Room to another section of the mine. His application was successful and he was transferred to underground work.

Kapferer develops a normative explanation for this dispute. Explicit norms regarding the speed of work govern the production rate in the cell room. Both management and workers have an interest in ensuring that the work is not done too quickly. Strict enforcement of the rates particularly protects the older strippers, who cannot work as fast at the strenuous manual task as the younger strippers. This explains why the accusations of rate-busting would go from Abraham, an older man at a stand with the oldest average age, to Donald, a younger man at a stand with the youngest average age.

However, norms fail to explain why Donald was not defended against Abraham's threat of witchcraft. The threat of witchcraft is taken very seriously. In this culture at this time, witchcraft was considered to be harmful to others and something not to be used. Negative events that could not otherwise be explained were attributed to witchcraft. Older men were thought to be especially proficient at casting spells, and Abraham encouraged this idea in his response to Donald.

Kapferer wondered why the others decided not to side with Donald, instead accusing him of drunkenness. He felt that the normative analysis could answer neither this question, nor why the dispute occurred between Donald and Abraham rather than some other old/young pair of workers in the cell room. The following *reticulum analysis* of the networks of the cell room employees shows how the dispute could hardly have occurred otherwise.

The material on which this analysis is based is drawn from data collected in the Cell Room in the months I was there before the outbreak of the dispute. There is no significant difference between Donald and Abraham in terms of the number of individuals included within each of their reticulums. Donald is linked directly in regular interaction with eight other workers, whereas, Abraham is tied to nine (see Figure 2). There are four individuals in Abraham's reticulum who are not directly linked to Donald and likewise three individuals in Donald's direct set of ties who are not directly connected to Abraham. This means that within both men's spheres of direct relationships there are five individuals who are commonly tied to them by direct links. I will examine the extent to which these individuals are differentially tied, if at all, to the two men, and

thus assess the degree to which either Donald or Abraham could expect to exert the greater pull over them. Similarly, starting with Abraham, I will analyse their relationships to the men who are not common to both their reticulums.

Three of the four men to whom Abraham is linked but who are not tied to Donald, Maxwell, Damian and Andrew, are also multiplexly connected to Abraham. The exchange in Abraham's relationships with Maxwell and Damian exhibits well the closeness of the bond which Abraham has with them; for he talks regularly with them sharing a diverse range of opinion and information about work and town life in general. Abraham also frequently shares cigarettes with them and on those occasions when they or Abraham bring food to the work place to eat at break, the food is shared between them.

Adapted from B. Kapferer, "Norms and Values in a Conflict Situation." Reprinted with permission from J. C. Mitchell (ed.), *Social Networks in Urban Situations*, Manchester: University Press, pp. 181–240. Copyright 1968 by Institute for Social Research, University of Zambia.

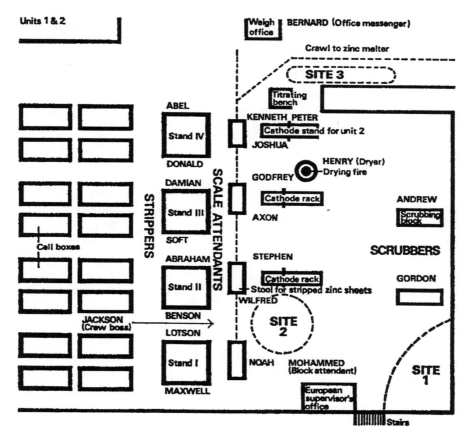

Figure 1   A Schematic Drawing of the Cell Room Showing in Detail the Work Area of Unit 3 and the Approximate Working Positions of Those Cell Room Employees Who are Engaged for Most or Part of Their Time in Unit 3.

This mutual exchange of conversation and goods of like kind between them reveals clearly the feeling of friendship which Abraham has for them and they for him. The closeness of the tie which Abraham has with the two men is most certainly influenced by the common position in which they find themselves in the Unit. Although, belonging to tribes with different cultural and linguistic backgrounds (see Table 1) all three are old men and as Strippers are subject to similar insecurities and pressures deriving from their old age and the competition of younger, more physically active men in the Unit. But Abraham's tie with Andrew must be viewed in a different light. Andrew converses with Abraham on similar topics as those discussed by the latter with Maxwell and Damian.

Abraham also has a personal service exchange content in his relationship with Andrew, but unlike his relationship with Maxwell and Damian the personal services involved in the relationship such as the fetching of drinking water and the giving of cigarettes flow from Andrew to Abraham, the latter to my knowledge never reciprocating in kind. In addition the two men regularly exchange jokes at one another's expense, their joking based on the institutionalized joking relationship which is recognized to exist in town between the members of the two tribal categories to which they belong. Although their age and their institutionalized joking behaviour might lead one to suspect the existence of a close emotional tie between them, as is evidenced in Abraham's

Table 1 OCCUPATION, TRIBE, AGE AND RELIGION OF UNIT 3 EMPLOYEES

Name	Religion	Age	Occupation	Tribe
Jackson	Roman Catholic	48	Crew Boss	Lamba
Bernard	Roman Catholic	56	Office Messenger	Bemba
Peter	African Reform Church	40	Titrator	Nsenga
Kenneth	Roman Catholic	39	Titrator	Chewa
Simon	Methodist	29	Titrator	Ila
Maxwell	Nil	66	Stripper	Kaonde
Lotson	Roman Catholic	37	Stripper	Bemba
Abraham	Nil	58	Stripper	Bemba
Benson	Roman Catholic	52	Stripper	Lozi
Soft	ex-Jehovah's Witness	33	Stripper	Lala
Damian	African Reform Church	57	Stripper	Chewa
Abel	Roman Catholic	44	Stripper	Bisa
Donald	Jehovah's Witness	36	Stripper	Bisa
Joshua	Roman Catholic	34	Scale Boy	Bisa
Godfrey	Roman Catholic	34	Scale Boy	Bisa
Stephen	Roman Catholic	50	Scale Boy	Bemba
Noah	Roman Catholic	26	Scale Boy	Swaka
Wilfrid	Jehovah's Witness	36	Scale Boy	Lala
Axon	Free Church	52	Scale Boy	Lozi
Mohammed	Muslim	55	Block Boy	Aushi
Andrew	Nil	52	Scrubber	Nsenga
Gordon	Roman Catholic	36	Scrubber	Chewa
Henry	Roman Catholic	31	Dryer	Lala

relationship with Maxwell and Damian, the nature of the exchanges in their tie reveals what I think is the most important characteristic of their relationship. Andrew is a Scrubber, an occupation which is regarded by other workers in the Room as being of low status, whereas Abraham occupies a high-status position as a Stripper. By performing small personal services for Abraham and manipulating a tribal joking relationship with him,[1] Andrew thus ties himself to a man who has status as well as some power and influence in the Unit, Andrew perhaps receiving in return Abraham's patronage.

The fourth person to whom Abraham is tied, but Donald is not, is Henry. There is only a conversational exchange within this relationship. Relative to Abraham's other links already discussed I regard it as weak, not only because the relationship is uniplex, but because in comparison with the other links, conversational exchanges are seldom made. But, nevertheless, as in Abraham's relationship with Andrew, Abraham is the dominant partner in the relationship. It is always Henry who initiates the conversation and I regard this as an attempt by him, as a low status and comparatively uninfluential man

[1]One factor which influences the presence or absence of joking is the membership of tribes which have an institutionalized joking relationship. However, it is not only the fact that two men stand in a tribal joking relationship to each other that is important but also the nature of other factors conditioning their relationship—for example, a tribal joking relationship can be manipulated as in Andrew's instance to establish a tie with a higher status person in a situation, or, alternatively, to alleviate tensions and strains produced by the work context. Not all people who stand in an institutionalized tribal joking relationship to each other joke.

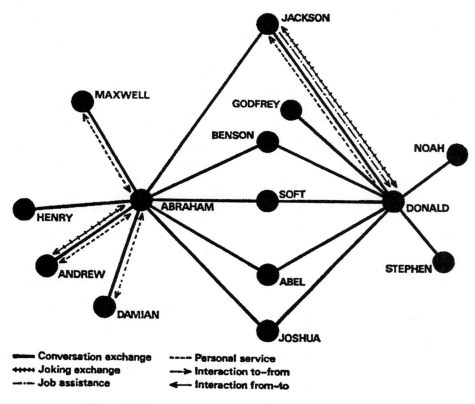

Figure 2 The Direct Relationships of Donald and Abraham

in the situation to establish an association with a much higher status and more powerful man in the Unit.

In contrast to Abraham, Donald is more "weakly" linked to the three persons to whom he is connected and with whom Abraham has no tie. All three of Donald's relationships to Stephen, Noah and Godfrey respectively are uniplex, conversation being the only content exchanged in them. Stephen, Noah and Godfrey are all Scale Attendants and come into contact with Donald in the course of their work activities but Donald regularly joins them at break when they seat themselves near the Weigh Office (see Figure 1). Although Donald is superior to them in terms of his occupational status, he does not show any dominance over them in his relationships with them, as for example, Abraham does in his relationships with Andrew and Henry. None of my information suggests that these individuals asso-

ciate with Donald out of a desire for his patronage; if anything it may well be the opposite as it is Donald who most frequently initiates the conversation with them.

Of the relationships discussed above connecting various individuals either to Abraham or Donald, Abraham's ties are multiplex whereas Donald's are uniplex. In terms of their social investment in their relationships with Abraham, coupled with their sharing of common interests arising out of their age and occupational position, it may be expected that Maxwell and Damian would be obligated to support Abraham. Abraham, in addition, could be expected to have some control, though admittedly limited, over the soliciting of support from Andrew and Henry. It could be surmised that a refusal to support him would be more disadvantageous to Andrew and Henry in the long run as it could result in the withdrawal of Abraham's patronage. At the very least, however, Abraham could expect support from Maxwell and Damian. But Donald could by no means be as confident, for as shown in the uniplexity of the content in his relationships with Stephen, Noah and Godfrey, they are not as heavily obligated to his support as for instance, Maxwell and Damian are to Abraham. It could be argued, however, that as young men and because of the sentiments arising out of their membership of the same tribe, Noah and Godfrey would be tempted to sympathize with Donald. But equally, Stephen, who was not observed in any interaction with Abraham, could, on this occasion, have supported the latter because they are of the same tribe and as older men in the Unit have many of the same interests. As events were to demonstrate, possibly for some of the reasons outlined, Abraham did receive support from the three persons to whom he is multiplexly linked, Maxwell, Damian and Andrew. Henry remained neutral. Stephen, Noah and Godfrey took very little action on Donald's behalf. Stephen and Noah made no move to support either party in the dispute, while Godfrey, far from aligning with Donald, commiserated with Soft over Donald's reaction to Soft's calling him a drunk.

One reason for examining Abraham and Donald's links to the individuals within their reticulums who are not jointly tied to both of them, was that these relationships involved persons who are least likely to be faced with a decision of making a choice between their support of one or the other of the main disputants in the case. As they are directly linked to only one of the two parties they do not have to make a choice between opposing loyalties and obligations which would arise if they were involved in social relationships with both Abraham and Donald. This is not so with the other individuals in their reticulums to whom they are both directly linked.

With the exception of Jackson, the Crew Boss, who has a multiplex relationship with Donald but not with Abraham, all the remaining direct ties which Donald and Abraham have jointly to the same individuals are uniplex. Donald could be regarded as

having a close tie with Jackson, for they exchange services with each other, as seen in Jackson's assistance of Donald at work and Donald's fetching of drinking water for Jackson. In addition Jackson and Donald joke with each other, though this is not part of a recognized institutional joking relationship, and they regularly engage each other in conversation. For these reasons Donald might have expected Jackson's support in the dispute. This did not happen, Jackson even appearing to align with Abraham through his action in sending Donald back to work when the latter was venting his anger against Soft. The obvious explanation for Jackson's behaviour is that he was acting according to the requirements of his job. But Soft also had stopped work and in fact had caused Donald's anger—Jackson could also have exercised his authority on Soft. An additional consideration which may further explain Jackson's action is the nature of his ties generally in the Unit. Jackson has many ties with other workers in the Cell Room similar to those he has with Donald. He uses these ties in an instrumental way, for by establishing close multiplex bonds with workers, he eases his task of supervision and the exercise of his authority.[2] If Jackson had supported Donald he might very well have jeopardized his ties with other persons in the situation, and so reduced the effectiveness with which he could perform his job.

This type of explanation, which depends on the nature of social ties to individuals other than the two main disputants, needs to be more clearly demonstrated, not only to explain Jackson's apparent opposition to Donald, but also the seeming desertion of Donald by Stephen, Noah and Godfrey. Furthermore some explanation may be given as to why the other workers to whom Abraham and Donald had ties of equal strength supported the former and not the latter, especially when on the surface it would appear that men like Soft, Abel, Godfrey and Joshua, who isolated themselves from Donald during the dispute, had more interests in common with Donald than they had with Abraham. All can be classed as younger men, and three of them, Abel, Godfrey and

---

[2]Moreover, because Jackson has multiplex relationships with a large number of the Unit 3 workers, he exposes himself to pressures from them. Thus he intervenes seemingly against Donald when the tide of opinion and support is obviously beginning to turn in Abraham's favour.

Joshua, are of the same tribe as Donald (see Table 1): a common bond which conceivably could have influenced their support of him.[3]

Although this examination of Abraham's direct links in relation to Donald's reveals the former's as stronger, at least in terms of the number of multiplex links which Abraham has compared with Donald, it does not provide sufficient explanation for the outcome of the dispute. Not enough evidence has yet been advanced which could adequately explain the apparent extent of Abraham's support and Donald's seeming isolation, let alone which could provide solutions of the earlier problems as to why Donald was accused of fast work and not Abel, or why trivial issues achieved prominence and not the more important ones of ratebusting and witchcraft. I have already suggested with reference to Jackson that some explanation could be given if the nature of ties to others apart from those to Abraham and Donald are examined. It will, therefore, be the purpose of the following analysis to examine the types of relationships which connect the individuals within the two reticulums to each other, and to other workers who were influential for the course of the dispute.

RETICULUM STRUCTURE AND THE COMPETITION FOR SUPPORT

Now that the character of Abraham and Donald's direct links has been described, and some assessment of the structural type of their reticulums and those of the other workers in the Unit has been reached, some solution to the problems preventing a satisfactory analysis of the process of the dispute should be achieved.

In Figure 3 I have drawn Abraham and Donald's direct links in the situation, the heavy lines indicating multiplex relationships and the light lines uniplex bonds. The figure is skeletal in that not all the ties between the many actors have been included, only those relationships which I consider important and illustrative of the general pattern of relationships with reference to Abraham and Donald being drawn. Beside each actor I have placed the structural type of his reticulum.

It is immediately clear from Figure 3, on information recorded prior to the dispute and on Abraham and Donald's relationships as well as those of other workers concerned, that Abraham's reticulum (and his indirect links to other people's reticulums) is much stronger than Donald's. Thus a pattern which was beginning to emerge in the discussion of Abraham's and Donald's direct relationships is now more distinct. Although, relative to the other workers in the Unit, Abraham is not the most strongly tied into the work situation set of relationships, he is more involved in them than Donald. Despite the fact that Donald and Abraham include almost the same number of individuals within their reticulums, of the measured reticulum structural characteristics, no factor appears to any marked extent within Donald's reticulum in comparison with other Unit employees. Abraham's ties in the situation cover individuals who are more closely interconnected with one another than those to whom Donald is tied, these interconnections tending to be multiplex in Abraham's reticulum, but uniplex, where they occur, in Donald's reticulum. Moreover, if the relationships of the persons to whom Abraham is directly connected by multiplex bonds are examined, it can be seen that they draw into their own reticulums, often by multiplex links, some of the individuals in Donald's reticulum who are not directly connected to Abraham, as well as other powerful men such as Lotson, the Shop Steward, who is directly connected to neither by any regularized interactional relationship. For example, through his multiplex tie with Damian, Abraham is able to draw Lotson into his web of influence. Likewise, Andrew, through his multiplex tie with Stephen, draws the latter into Abraham's set of relationships. Furthermore, of those individuals who are jointly linked

[3]It may be considered that Donald's being a Jehovah's Witness could have influenced the attitude of other workers to him. At the time of fieldwork there was considerable conflict between the United National Independence Party, to which the majority of the Cell Room workers belonged, and the members of the Jehovah's Witness sect, which does not permit the participation of its members in political activities. However, Jehovah's Witnesses do take an active part in trade union affairs. No evidence appeared before, during or after the dispute to indicate that Donald's membership of this sect had any bearing on the attitudes of his fellows. The issues which were raised referred specifically to the work context and did not involve the wider considerations of political party and religious sect affiliations.

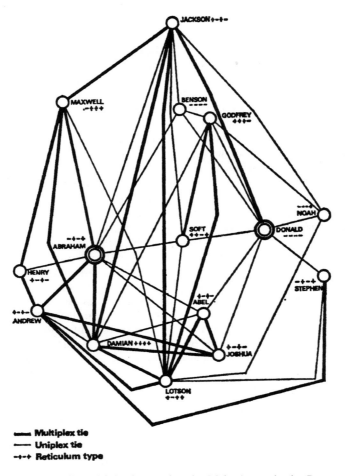

Figure 3 Direct and Indirect Links Connecting the Main Actors in the Buyantanshe Case

to Abraham and Donald, and who would seem to have their allegiance divided between the two parties as their ties are uniplex to both (with the exception of Jackson) all tend to be heavily committed in their relationships to individuals caught in Abraham's sphere of influence rather than in Donald's. Thus, in terms of the degree to which Abraham and Donald are differentially linked into the set of Unit 3 relationships, Abraham's reticulum and the relationships which spread out from it is more open to effective mobilization. Apart from the issues, norms and values which were involved in the situation it was predictable that Abraham should mobilize more support than Donald.

The structure of Abraham's and Donald's re-

ticulums, and of the other workers' reticulums, could also explain why the accusation of fast work should pass from Abraham to Donald and not involve other combinations of workers employed on the two stands. Abel was equally as guilty of rate-busting as Donald, but when their reticulum structure is compared Donald has by far the weaker set of ties. Abel's ties cover a wide span of relationships in the Unit, and, although the factors of density and multiplexity are not significant in his ties relative to other workers, he is strongly linked to some powerful men in the situation, in particular Lotson. By not reproaching Abel, Abraham was not embroiling himself with a man who could have had the potentiality of mobilizing effectively against him. His reprimand of Donald was likely, however, to have more certain success. Similarly, Benson could have met with some difficulties if it had been he who had initially reproached either Abel or Donald. He would have been in a much weaker position in relation to Abel but by operating his ties through Damian and Abraham, for example, he could have conceivably mobilized effectively against Donald. Later in the dispute he did voice his support for Abraham, but that he was not the initiator of the dispute could be explained by the fact that he and Donald had some social investment in each other, as is demonstrated by the regular conversation exchanged between them. If he had told Donald to slow down his work speed he could have seriously infringed this relationship. At any rate, he did this later in the dispute by siding with Abraham, but this was more brought about by the stronger pulls exerted on him by Abraham, especially through other links such as his multiplex ties with Damian to whom Abraham was also multiplexly linked. The process of events meant that he had more to lose by not aligning with Abraham than if he had remained neutral or supported Donald. The strength of his ties lay through his connections with such persons as Abraham and Damian rather than with Donald. Therefore, by reproaching Donald rather than Abel, Abraham was playing from a position of strength. Being, of the two men on Stand II, the more strongly linked man into the situation, Abraham was the better placed to warn Donald against his fast work.

This argument is strengthened when it is realized that the Unit employees are not ignorant of the character of other people's ties in the situation. For example, the small groups of individuals which regularly form at break and which vary little in composition from day to day, give an impression to the workers in the Room of others' main acquaintances at work. Thus Maxwell, Damian and Abraham regularly sit together at Site I (see Figure 1) at break; Lotson, Abel, Joshua, Soft and many other younger workers cluster at Site 2; while Donald and some of the Scale Attendants such as Noah and Stephen group together at Site 3 near the Weigh Office. It can be inferred therefore that Abraham, prior to the start of the dispute, knew roughly which people were involved in Donald's set of ties.

I have explained why Abraham should have re-ceived support in the dispute, and why it should be he rather than Benson, for instance, who should initiate the dispute. But no solution has been provided as to why some of the major issues involved in the dispute were not taken up and why there should even appear to be an interest in focusing on the seemingly more trivial issues. So that some reasonably satisfactory explanation for this can be presented it is necessary to examine more closely the process of mobilization in the dispute. The nature of Abraham's ties could be said to have had a cumulative effect which was to operate to Donald's disadvantage in the mobilization of support during the course of the dispute. Abraham was connected to individuals who in turn drew others to them, frequently by virtue of their multiplex links and so drew away from Donald any support he might possibly have hoped for. Donald's actions in fact facilitated part of this process as shown in his attack on Soft. Soft's position was difficult. His work position on Damian's stand placed him between two influential and committed men in the dispute, Damian and Abraham, and to have supported Donald could have infringed his work relationship with Damian. The difficulty of his work position could have contributed to his support of Abraham but, whatever the reason, his suggestion that Donald was drunk brought Donald's wrath down upon him. This reaction influenced Godfrey, with whom Soft is tied by a close bond, to commiserate with him, an action which aligned Godfrey with Soft, and therefore, by association, with Abraham.

This instance of Godfrey's support of Soft against Donald emphasizes an aspect of the various alliances which built up to support, seemingly, Abraham's position. Although the major issues raised in the dispute are important to an understanding of some individual behaviour (for instance, Damian and Maxwell's support of Abraham) they could cloud other factors which might also be important to understanding the support mobilized against Donald. It could be that for some of the individuals who were involved in this dispute that many of the issues raised were secondary to other considerations. Everyone did not enter the dispute at once, rather they were gradually drawn into it as other persons with whom they had close bonds, became involved. Their seeming alignment with

Abraham grew out of the discharge of their obligations to specific individuals to whom they were closely socially committed, as evidenced by the multiplexity of content in their relationships.

THE PROCESS OF MOBILIZATION

The above suggests that there are numerous ways by which people can be committed to a common alignment. Although I do not exhaust the possibilities, I discuss three kinds of mobilization which relate to this case. Firstly, people can be mobilized to the support of one or other of the parties in the dispute on the basis of issues, norms and values raised during the course of events. Secondly, they could be mobilized, like Soft, for instance, because of the formal position in which they are placed in the production system. Thirdly, mobilization in the support of a disputing party may arise out of the necessity for individuals to fulfil the obligations involved in the nature of their close relationships with others in the situation. It was the interplay of all these three factors which gave rise to Abraham's successful mobilization against Donald.

But, despite the importance for the consideration of the train of events in the dispute of the first two factors affecting the alignments, I consider the last factor to be the most important for understanding both the build-up of Abraham's support in the dispute and the reason why the issues involved were maintained at a trivial level. In the description of Abraham and Donald's direct links it was shown that Abraham had more multiplex direct links than Donald. This apart, however, Abraham as well as Donald in comparison with other workers in the Unit, had a limited span and multiplexity of direct links in their reticulums. This limitation to their reticulums meant that both men could not reach a significant amount of support through their own direct links but were dependent on indirect ties, and, in particular, those relationships which were multiplex, through individuals to whom they were directly connected in their reticulums. In fact it was the nature of these workers' ties which primarily was to determine the success or failure of Abraham's or Donald's respective mobilization. Because of this dependence on them by both Abraham and Donald,

these persons, to whom they were directly connected and who were the points through which they could gain access to other individuals, had control over those issues which were important, not Abraham or Donald. Earlier in the paper I made the point that the issues of ratebusting and witchcraft, if they had been seized upon, would most likely have divided the Unit into opposing factions, and that one explanation why they were not taken up was to prevent this. I regarded this explanation as not completely satisfactory as it did not lead to any understanding of why on other occasions when these issues again were involved in a dispute, they *were* taken up. The nature of the mobilization around the dispute I have been analysing and the degree of control which Abraham and Donald had over this mobilization may provide some solution to this problem.

For example, with regard to the successful man in the dispute, Abraham, some of the key men who contributed to the effectiveness of Abraham's mobilization were Damian, Andrew and Soft. In turn it was their links to powerful individuals like Lotson which led to the dispute's being settled very much in Abraham's favour. Here were people who had differing interests in the situation. Although Damian had reason to sympathize with Abraham's concern over Donald's ratebusting, if he had openly expressed support of Abraham on this issue he could have alienated other workers to whom he was connected but who had other interests in the situation. Thus he could have deprived Abraham of valuable access to other influential people in the work place and also have threatened the continuance of some of his own close ties which he had built up. To align himself effectively and also to influence the support of others to whom he was tied (and in fact make the discharge of their obligations to him easier), Damian had to appeal to a norm which was least likely to relate to a source of division within the Unit and which would not threaten the basis of his own relationships. Thus in his conversation with other workers who visited him at his work stand, and in his conversation with Maxwell and Lotson on the neighbouring stand, he remarked on Donald's lack of respect for an older man, keeping well clear of the potentially explosive issue of ratebusting. Likewise, Lotson's attitude had much to do with the outcome and alignments which were to be formed during the process of the dispute. Much of his power and influence in the Unit and Cell Room generally, as well as his ability to maintain this power and influence, stems from his ability to include relationships within his reticulum which tend to be multiplex and which cover a relatively large number of individuals who are densely interconnected. As with Damian's, Lotson's reticulum also includes many individuals who have divergent and in some cases opposed interests in the work situation. To have grasped at the issue of witchcraft or ratebusting could have seriously endangered the future of many of his relationships and thus have upset his position of power in the Room. It was not surprising therefore, that he should try to transfer the focus of the dispute to the relatively minor issues which emerged over Soft's *contretemps* with Donald, and insist that it was the former's statement that Donald was drunk which really lay at the root of the dispute. In so doing he tried to keep the grounds of the dispute trivial, thereby adopting a course of action which would result in the least damage to his own set of relationships and powerful position in the Unit.

I suggest then that because the effectiveness of the mobilization in relation to the dispute lay in the hands of key individuals like Damian and Lotson, and was not in the control of the major disputants themselves, that the issues of the dispute were kept at a trivial level. The importance of their successful attempt to play down the more divisive issues of ratebusting and witchcraft which were raised, was to preserve intact their relationships as much as possible. On other occasions when issues such as witchcraft and ratebusting have played a more dominant part throughout a dispute people like Damian and Lotson have had less control over the course of events. At these times the major disputants have themselves had a wide span of multiplex relationships and have managed to keep the issues over which the dispute was initiated, more in the forefront.

Some explanation has been given for the reason why Abraham should receive support in the dispute and not Donald, why it should be Abraham who accused Donald initially of ratebusting and why despite the seriousness of some of the charges, the issues surrounding the dispute were kept at a minor level. But what was the result of this mobilization? The obvious effect was that the dispute between Abraham and Donald was settled in Abraham's favour. It was Abraham who produced the opportunity whereby the dispute could be settled by calling Donald to join him where he was seated, at the same time offering a concession to one of Donald's objections by addressing him as 'Donald' and not '*Buyantanshe*'. Some of Donald's acquaintances in the Unit such as Abel, Soft, Joshua and Godfrey urged him to accede to Abraham's request. This Donald eventually did, and Abraham then asked him to carry out a personal service for him by sharpening his stripping chisel. In doing this service for Abraham, Donald publicly expressed an acknowledgement of Abraham's dominance in the situation and re-established an expectation accepted by most men in the Unit that a younger man should show respect and deference to an older man. Thus a norm which had been momentarily broken was now reaffirmed. Also Abraham, by requesting that Donald sharpen his stripping chisel established a relationship with Donald, based on his dominance within it, which had not existed prior to the dispute. By developing a relationship with Donald, initially through a personal service tie, the ground was prepared for an eventual more multiplex bond to be created between the two men. This meant that, in future, instead of working through other individuals in the situation to bring pressures on Donald and to control his behaviour at work, Abraham could now operate controls on Donald's behaviour to protect his own interests through a multiplex link. But another result of the mobilization in this dispute was to render unnecessary Abraham's attempt to build an effective direct tie with Donald.

In the eyes of the other Unit workers Abraham had emerged in a stronger position from the dispute than he had been in before it, whereas Donald had his isolation and the ineffectiveness of his current set of relationships in the Unit dramatically demonstrated to him. A few days later, Donald asked the European supervisor in the Unit to arrange his transfer to another section of the Mine Plant and a job underground, which was lower paid than his Cell Room task, was then found for him. Stephen and Noah, for example, remained neutral throughout the dispute and Godfrey supported Soft against Donald.

Others, such as Soft and Jackson, whom he considered to be his friends, did not support him either. Donald was particularly angered by Soft's support of Abraham. Although Soft was connected to Donald by a uniplex bond only, he was regarded by Donald as a close friend in the work place. Another person from whom Donald expected support was Jackson. He was the one person with whom Donald had a multiplex relationship. Both regularly talked about their experiences in the township after work, both men jested with each other, and Donald occasionally carried out some small personal services for Jackson while the latter occasionally assisted Donald with the stripping. As I have previously argued, this relationship can be seen as serving an instrumental purpose for Jackson, enabling him to perform his task of supervision more effectively. Additionally, in that Jackson has a number of similar instrumental links with other persons in the situation, he could have damaged these other ties by supporting Donald, thereby making his task of supervision all the more difficult. But his establishment of such a strong relationship with Donald might have led the latter to expect some support when he needed it. The only part Jackson played in fact was seemingly to intervene on Soft's behalf. It is significant that when Donald applied for transfer he gave as his pretext his suspicion that Jackson was assisting Abraham to bewitch him, Abraham having given Jackson a sweet to be taken to Donald. Thus not only did he recognize a break in his relationship with Jackson, but perceived Jackson as aligning in a hostile way against him.

The mobilization surrounding the dispute was not only immediately advantageous for Abraham, in that he was able to control Donald's behaviour, but also his success demonstrated to others in the work place the power and authority he could command. The dispute aligned with him people to whom he had no previous regularized interactional bond of a multiplex nature, and provided a basis for him by which such multiplex ties could be developed in the future. In the weeks after the dispute a tendency emerged for others to whom Abraham had been only uniplexly connected to develop multiplex relationships with him. This was particularly noticeable with Jackson and Soft. Moreover people with whom Abraham had had no regular interactional relation-

ship before the dispute, subsequently began to enter into more frequent contact with him. Lotson, for example, started to cultivate a regular conversational relationship with him. A result of Abraham's successful mobilization therefore, was to lead to a change in the nature of his direct relationships and to a certain extent, the ties of others in the situation.

As Abraham emerged in a stronger position from the dispute, Donald's position had been weakened. He chose to sever his ties in the Unit and transferred to another job. Thus the mobilization around the dispute which led to this action of Donald's also served to change the pattern of relationships within the Unit. Although he was not a significant member of the reticulums of those to whom he was directly tied, his opting out of the situation did alter the structure of these reticulums. The dispute and the various actions of the Unit workers redefined their relationships to one another and to the major disputants.

CONCLUSION

I have restricted the application of a network or reticulum approach to an analysis of the social process surrounding one dispute. The account of the dispute, following a short description of the industrial setting in which it took place, showed that the individuals involved in it, and the major disputants themselves, appealed to many norms and values in an attempt to define the normative basis in terms of which the conflict was to be resolved. This led me to make a brief description of the norms and values etc. which provided some understanding as to why certain types of accusation such as those of fast work and witchcraft could be expected. But although this description gave some broad impression of the structure of relationships and the general norms and values pertinent to the context, various aspects of the dispute could not be explained. For example, I was interested in such problems as why a particular worker should accuse one specific fellow worker of fast work when he could, just as legitimately, have accused another. The difficulties of explanation became more pronounced when I turned my attention to such problems as why the workers in the situation should select certain types of norms and not others in defining the, for them, important aspects of the dispute, and therefore the framing of their own reactions to it. This related directly to the question why, when the mobilization of support around the disputants was considered, this should result in the total isolation of one of the parties to the benefit of the other. The decision to support one or other of the disputants was by no means clear-cut in terms of the norms and values which appeared to be relevant, it being possible for a strong case to be made out for either one.

But the process of norm selection resulted in the more trivial aspects of a worker's behaviour being emphasized (to his disadvantage) and the comparatively more important norms, such as those relating to fast work and witchcraft, which largely occasioned the dispute, being pushed into the background. I suggested the possibility that witchcraft and fast work were potentially divisive issues, related to a separation of interests between older and younger workers: and if individuals' reactions to the dispute had been defined by the norms and values pertaining to fast work and witchcraft, then the workers could have divided into opposing factions on the basis of age. Although I do not disregard this possibility, this explanation was not completely satisfactory, as at other times of conflict the same workers, faced with similar alternatives, have not been loth to divide in this way. The need for further solution to these problems was necessitated by the realization that in the isolation of one disputant from the other workers (which was the result of this particular mobilization) many individuals aligned with, and by so doing appeared to reaffirm, norms, values and attitudes which protected more the interests of other workers than their own. In fact, by appearing to support an older against a younger man, many of the workers who had interests in common with the latter seemed to act against their interests.

I then suggested that the focusing upon general norms and values, although these are influential to the course of social action, tends to obscure the more specific norms and expectations which relate to the interaction between particular pairs of individuals. One of the most noticeable features of the conflict described was that those involved appealed to various norms and values in an attempt either to

rally support to their cause or to justify their own actions. Here my attention focused primarily on the mobilization of support, though rather than discuss the mobilizing potential of the general norms and values referred to by the participants, I turned to an examination of the mobilizing potential of the sets of interpersonal relationships, the efficacy of their manipulation and the exertion of pressures through them to other individuals for the winning of support in such a conflict.

In any situation individuals are differentially tied to others, and the extent of their obligation and commitment to these others varies. Thus the degree to which an individual will fulfil the norms and expectations governing his relationship with another will depend on the extent of his social investment in this other individual, and the returns on the investment should he act according to norms and expectations arising out of the relationship. It was at this juncture that a form of network or reticulum analysis was introduced as an additional approach to those already pursued in an attempt to explain some of the particular aspects of the process of the dispute. Therefore my first exercise in the application of a reticulum analysis was to examine the direct interactional relationships of each of the major disputants to the individuals in their reticulums, concentrating on such qualities of the relationships as exchange content, multiplexity or uniplexity, and directional flow of the exchange contents within them.

The analysis yielded some *index* as to the form of commitment which the actors in the situation had to the disputants, and the likelihood of the fulfilment of their obligations to them. Although a few of the alignments observed in the dispute fitted well with what could have been expected, many of the alignments, from the information presented up to then, could not have been anticipated. In particular this referred to those individuals who were jointly tied to the disputants and were involved in similar forms of exchanges with them. This led to a qualification of the earlier proposition which stated that the degree to which an individual is likely to fulfil the expectations specific to a relationship with another is dependent on the extent of his social investment in that other, and the returns on this investment should he choose to fulfil these expectations. But the nature of a social investment in a relationship with *one* other person, and the expected returns on this investment, which condition the likelihood of fulfilment of the norms and expectations in the relationship, also depends on the kinds of social investment and expected returns which an individual has to *other* persons in the situation. Therefore the alignment of an individual with one disputant cannot be seen in terms only of his relationship with this person, but has to be seen also in terms of his relationships with other individuals in the situation. Commitment to one disputant may not only involve the breaking of ties with another disputant but could also result in the severing of relationships with others. In addition to the loss or gain by supporting one disputant, actors appear to weigh the extent of the loss of their investment in other individuals which would be incurred by taking a specific line of action. A basic assumption then, is that persons will align themselves in a dispute in such a way as to incur the least loss to their investments in the total set of relationships in the situation. But the strategic placement of individuals for mobilization within the total set of relationships will differ, this strategic placement varying, of course, relative to the major disputants concerned. Through the application of various measures relating to span, density and multiplexity, some indices were produced to show the degree to which the workers were differentially tied into the situation and the extent of their social investment in each other. Thus some indication was gained of the pressures and forces which could be exerted through the relationships in the work context to influence and explain certain patterns of behaviour relating to a particular dispute.

The result of the analysis which used the concept of network or reticulum was to provide an explanation for why one specific worker should accuse another, and why the ensuing mobilization should end with the isolation of one disputant. Added to this was a solution to the problem why certain divisive issues should not receive prominence when more trivial issues defined the terms of the dispute. Individuals selected the issues (and the relative norms and values) which allowed them to discharge their obligations to others without incurring too great a loss in their social investments built up over a period of time. If the issues of the dispute had been defined in terms which showed the disputants as representing opposed interests which divided the Room (in this case fast work and witchcraft) the loss to others of their social investments could have been too great. Furthermore, the ability to define the dispute in terms of less divisive issues was greatly facilitated because defining the issues perceived as relevant largely lay outside the power of the disputants themselves; this definition was more controlled by others to whom the disputants were directly or indirectly linked. It was on these others also that the disputants depended for the effective mobilization of support. Possibly, as appears to be the pattern in other similar disputes, if the major disputing parties had had more control over the process of norm selection and mobilization in the dispute others may have been forced, at least momentarily, into opposing factions.

Although, through reference to the general structure and norms and values of the situation, many of the workers may have been seen in their alignments to have opposed their own interests, an examination of the interpersonal sets of relationships indicates the reverse. A reticulum or network approach, which concentrates on a close examination of such interpersonal relationships, accounts for the selection of issues and norms, and variations in the manipulation of these norms to serve particular interests in a specific context.

32   EPILOGUE: THE TWILIGHT OF HIERARCHY: SPECULATIONS ON THE GLOBAL INFORMATION SOCIETY

HARLAN CLEVELAND

The function of an epilogue is to round out and draw together the subject matter in a book, and give the reader something upon which to reflect. For this purpose we have chosen an article that considers the impact a large-scale shift to a new cultural age will have on our theories of organization and communication.

The theories discussed in this reader were developed largely to explain organizational communication phenomena of the industrial age. We might generalize by saying that industrial-age organizations are primarily concerned with control of tangible resources. Resources controlled by the organization are transformed or traded for gain; thus, much of the organization's efforts, including its communication, are directly or indirectly devoted to maintaining this control.

Now, many argue, society is in the midst of a change toward an information age. The chief resource in this new age—information—is most notable for its lack of controllability. This means that notions of organization developed in the industrial age may soon seem as archaic and strange as feudalism does today. More important for our readers, if communication has been an important part of organizations of the past, its natural role in the development and dissemination of information will make it absolutely critical in organizations of the future.

This concluding article, by Harlan Cleveland, scratches the surface of this subject by discussing the implications an information society has for a world based on scarce resources. Cleveland begins by explaining why information, unlike other resources, can only be shared, not owned or traded as are industrial-age resources. Among the consequences of this evolving kind of exchange are an inability to control who has access to what, a flattening of social hierarchies, and an increased need for cooperation.

When reading this article, think about the broader implications of this shift on our notions of organizing and communication, the perspectives we take on organizational communication, and the concepts we use and issues we consider important. How will these things have to be changed or adapted to accommodate the shift in emphasis from tangible resources toward information? How will it change the role of communication in organizations?

Harlan Cleveland, ''The Twilight of Hierarchy.'' Reprinted with permission from *Public Administration Review*, © 1985 by the American Society for Public Administration (ASPA), 1120 G Street NW, Suite 500, Washington, DC 20005. All rights reserved.

THE INFORMATIZATION OF SOCIETY

It is still shocking, 40 years later, to remember that the Manhattan Project, the huge secret organization which produced the atom bomb during World War II, did not employ on its staff a single person whose fulltime assignment was to think hard about the policy implications of the project if it should succeed. Thus no one was working on nuclear arms control—though I. I. Rabi says he and Robert Oppenheimer used to discuss it earnestly over lunch. We have been playing catch-up, not too successfully, ever since.

The Manhattan Project was not an exception; it was the rule. For 300 years until the 1970s, science and technology were quite generally regarded as having a life of their own, an "inner logic," an autonomous sense of direction. Their self-justifying ethic was change and "growth." But in the 1970s, society started to take charge—not of scientific discovery but of its technological fallout. The decision not to build the SST or deploy an ABM system even though we knew how to make them, the dramatic change in national environmental policy, and the souring of the nuclear power industry, bear witness.

The most prominent and pervasive consequence of the people's concern about the impacts and implications of new technologies is what the French call "l'informatization de la société." The made-up word, which we will Americanize to "informatization," will serve as well as any to describe what is happening to some of our key concepts and conceptions as information becomes the dominant resource in "post-industrial society." (The new word is certainly better than "post-industrial," which describes the future by saying it comes after the past.)

The revolutions that began with Charles Babbage's "analytical engine" (less than 150 years ago) and Guglielmo Marconi's wireless telegraphy (not yet a century old) started on quite different tracks. But a quarter of a century past, computers and telecommunications began to converge to produce a combined complexity, one interlocked industry that is transforming our personal lives, our national politics, and our international relations.

The industrial era was characterized by the influ-ence of humankind over things, including nature as well as the artifacts of man. The information era features a sudden increase in humanity's power to think and therefore to organize.

The "information society" does not replace, it overlaps, the growing and extracting and processing and manufacturing and recycling and distribution and consumption of tangible things. Agriculture and industry continue to progress by doing more with less through better knowledge, leaving plenty of room for a knowledge economy that, in statistics now widely accepted, accounts for more than half of our work force, our national product and our global reach.

A DOMINANT RESOURCE, A DIFFERENT RESOURCE

The size and scope of "the information society" are now familiar even in the popular literature. We can take it as read that information is the dominant resource in the United States, and coming to be so in other "advanced" or "developed" countries. To take only one cross-section of this startling shift, the actual production, extraction and growing of things now soaks up a good deal less than a quarter of our human resources. Of all the rest, which used to be lumped together as "services," more than two-thirds are information workers. By the end of the century, something like two-thirds of all work will be information work.

Table 1 shows one effort to describe the sweep of change—historical numbers and estimates pulled together from varied sources by G. Molitor of Public Policy Forecasting, Inc.

It is not only in the United States that the informatization of society has proceeded so far so fast. A study by the Organization for Economic Cooperation and Development (the club of richer nations, with headquarters in Paris) puts the average information labor force of several of its member countries at more than one-third of the total during the early- to mid-1970s, and rising: the information component of labor increased its share of the total by 2.8 percent for each five-year period since World War II.

Table I   UNITED STATES WORK FORCE DISTRIBUTION

	1880	*1920*	*1955*	*1975*	*2000 (est.)*
Agriculture and extractive	50%	28%	14%	4%	2%
Manufacturing, commerce, industry	36	53	37	29	22
Other services	12	10	20	17	10
Information, knowledge, education	2	9	29	50	66

Farming, which in some people's vocabularies is the most primitive of pursuits, is probably farther ahead than most industries in the embedding of information in physical processes. Says agricultural economist G. Edward Schuh: "All of the increase in agricultural output from the mid-1920s through the mid-1970s (a fifty-year period!) came about with no increase in the capital stock of physical resources. It was all due to new knowledge or information. That makes clear the extent to which knowledge is an output or resource."

If information (organized data, refined into knowledge and combined into wisdom) is now our "crucial resource," as Peter Drucker describes it, what does that portend for the future? Thinking about the inherent characteristics of information provides some clues to the vigorous rethinking that lies ahead for all of us.

1. *Information is expandable.* In 1972, the same year *The Limits to Growth* was published, John McHale came out with a book called *The Changing Information Environment* which argued that information expands as it is used. Whole industries have grown up to exploit this characteristic of information: scientific research, technology transfer, computer software (which already makes a contribution to the U.S. economy that is three times the contribution of computer hardware), and agencies for publishing, advertising, public relations, and government propaganda to spread the word (and thus to enhance the word's value).

The ultimate "limits to growth" of knowledge and wisdom are time (time available to human minds for reflecting, analyzing, and integrating the information that will be "brought to life" by being used) and the capacity of people—individually and in groups—to analyze and think integratively. There are obvious limits to the time each of us can devote

to the production and refinement of knowledge and wisdom. But the capacity of humanity to integrate its collective experience through relevant individual thinking is certainly expandable—not without limits, to be sure, but within limits we cannot now measure or imagine.

2. *Information is not resource-hungry.* Compared to the processes of the steel-and-automobile economy, the production and distribution of information are remarkably sparing in their requirements for energy and other physical and biological resources.

Investments, price policies and power relationships which assume that the more developed countries will gobble up disproportionate shares of "real" resources are overdue for wholesale revision.

3. *Information is substitutable.* It can and increasingly does replace capital, labor, and physical materials. Robotics and automation in factories and offices are displacing workers and thus requiring a transformation of the labor force. Any machine that can be accessed by computerized telecommunications doesn't have to be in your own inventory. And Dieter Altenpohl, an executive of Alusuisse, has calculations and charts to prove that, as he says, "The smarter the metal, the less it weighs."

4. *Information is transportable*—at close to the speed of light. As a result, remoteness is now more choice than geography. You can sit in Auckland, New Zealand, and play the New York stock markets in real time—if you don't mind keeping slightly peculiar hours. And the same is true, without the big gap in time-zones, of people in any rural hamlet in the United States. In the world of information-richness, you will be able to be remote if you want to, but you'll have to work at it.

5. *Information is diffusive.* It tends to leak—and

the more it leaks the more we have. It is not the inherent tendency of natural resources to leak. Jewels may be stolen; a lump or two of coal may fall off the coal car on its way from Montana; there is an occasional spillage of oil in the ocean. But the leakage of information is wholesale, pervasive, and continuous. In the era of the institutionalized leak, monopolizing information is very nearly a contradiction in terms; that can be done only in more and more specialized fields, for shorter and shorter periods of time.

6. *Information is shareable.* Shortly before his death, Colin Cherry wrote that information by nature cannot give rise to exchange transactions, only to sharing transactions. Thing are exchanged: if I give you a flower or sell you my automobile, you have it and I don't. But if I sell you an idea or give you a fact, we both have it. An information-rich environment is thus a sharing environment. That needn't mean an environment without standards, rules, conventions and ethical codes. It does mean the standards, rules, conventions and codes are going to be different from those created to manage the zero-sum bargains of market trading and traditional international relations.

THE EROSION OF HIERARCHIES

I am not a scholar of information/communication theory, but in my listening and reading as a practicing generalist I am struck with three seminal ideas as containing the most nourishment for our purpose, which is to think about how the new information environment is likely to modify our inherited assumptions about rule, power and authority.

One is that information (in its generic sense) is not like other resources, nor, as some would have it, merely another form of energy. It is not subject to the laws of thermodynamics, and efforts to explain the new information environment by using metaphors from physics will just get in our way.

A second idea I find nourishing is that the ultimate purpose of all knowledge is to organize things or people, arrange them in ways that make them different from the way they were before. This is true of rearranging the genes in a chromosome, and it is equally true of rearranging people's ideas to create a

movement. There is no such thing as useless knowledge, only people who haven't yet learned how to use it. This was the powerful message carried in a 1979 article in *Science* by Lewis Branscomb, chief scientist of IBM. He wrote that information is so far from being scarce that it is in "chronic surplus." There is still plenty for scientists to find out, but "the yawning chasm is between what is already known by some but not yet put to use by others."

A third insight, from the late British communications theorist Colin Cherry, is the distinction between the information ("message") itself and the service of delivering it. You may own the journal you hold in your hand, but you don't own its contents, the facts and ideas in the journal. Neither, now that I have written them down and you and I are sharing them, do I.

The historically sudden dominance of the information resource has, it seems to me, produced a kind of theory crisis, a sudden sense of having run out of basic assumptions. This is not only the product of information and communication technologies (and their fusion in the new systems that are sprouting daily in the deregulated environment created when the U.S. government by deciding to stop suing IBM and settle with AT&T said in effect that information and telecommunications were all really one industry—for which again the French have a name, *l'informatique*). Other dramatic extensions of scientific rationalism and engineering genius such as nuclear fission and gene-splicing—all with an indispensable assist from the new information technologies—have also made their contribution to the *bouleversement* of long-held social and political convictions.

But somewhere near the center of the confusion is the trouble we make for ourselves by carrying over into our thinking about information (which is to say symbols) concepts developed for the management of things—concepts such as property, depletion, depreciation, monopoly, "inevitable" unfairness, geopolitics, the class struggle, and top-down leadership.

The assumptions we have inherited are not producing satisfactory growth with acceptable equity either in the capitalistic West or in the socialist East. As Simon Nora and Alain Minc wrote in their landmark report to the President of France: "The liberal and Marxist approaches, contemporaries of the production-based society, are rendered questionable by its demise."

The most troublesome concepts are those which were created to deal with the main problems presented by the management of things—problems such as their scarcity, their bulk, their limited substitutability for each other, the expense and trouble in transporting them, the paucity of information about them (which made them comparatively easy to hide) and the fact that, being tangible, they could be hoarded. It was "in the nature of things" that the few had access to resources and the many did not.

Thus, the inherent characteristics of physical resources ("natural" and man-made) made possible the development of hierarchies of power based on control (of new weapons, of energy sources, of trade routes, of markets, and especially of knowledge), hierarchies of influence based on secrecy, hierarchies of class based on ownership, hierarchies of privilege based on early access to valuable resources, and hierarchies of politics based on geography.

Each of these five bases for discrimination and unfairness is crumbling today—because the old means of control are of dwindling efficacy, secrets are harder and harder to keep, and ownership, early arrival, and geography are of dwindling significance in getting access to the knowledge and wisdom which are the really valuable legal tender of our time.

Out of dozens of assumptions requiring a newly skeptical stare in the new knowledge environment, these five seem to me to bear most directly on leadership and management, because they are likely to affect most profoundly the ways in which, and the purposes for which, people will in future come together in organizations to make something different happen.

POWER AND PARTICIPATION

Knowledge is power, as Francis Bacon wrote in 1597. So the wider the spread of knowledge, the more power gets diffused. For the most part individuals and corporations and governments don't have a choice about this; it is the ineluctable consequence of creating—through education—societies with millions of knowledgeable people.

We see the results all around us, and around the world. More and more work gets done by horizontal process—or it doesn't get done. More and more decisions are made with wider and wider consultation—or they don't "stick." If the Census Bureau counted each year the number of committees per thousand population, we would have a rough quantitative measure of the bundle of changes called "the information society." A revolution in the technology of organization—the twilight of hierarchy—is already well under way.

Once information can be spread fast and wide—rapidly collected and analyzed, instantly communicated, readily understood by millions—the power monopolies that closely-held knowledge used to make possible were subject to accelerating erosion.

In the old days when only a few people were well educated and "in the know," leadership of the uninformed was likely to be organized in vertical structures of command and control. Leadership of the informed is different: it results in the necessary action only if exercised mainly by persuasion, bringing into consultation those who are going to have to do something to make the decision a decision. Where people are educated and are not treated this way, they either balk at the decisions made or have to be dragooned by organized misinformation backed by brute force. Recent examples of both results have been on display in Poland.

This is the rationale for Chester Barnard's durable theory of the executive function: that authority is delegated upward. As "director" of an organization, you have no power that is not granted to you by your "subordinates." Eliciting their continuous (and if possible cheerful) cooperation is your main job as director; without it, you cannot get the most routine tasks (for which others are holding you, not your staff, responsible) accomplished. Indeed, nowadays in many offices orders that used to be routinely accepted are now resisted or refused. In the modern American office, if you want a cup of coffee you don't take that co-worker, your secretary, off her (or his) own work to get it for you.

In an information-rich polity, the very definition of "control" changes. Very large numbers of people empowered by knowledge—coming together in parties, unions, factions, lobbies, interest-groups, neighborhoods, families, and hundreds of other structures—assert the right or feel the obligation to "make policy."

Decision making proceeds not by "recommendations up, orders down," but by development of a shared sense of direction among those who must form the parade if there is going to be a parade.

Collegial not command structures become the more natural basis for organization. Not "command and control," but conferring and "networking," become the mandatory modes for getting things done.

"Planning" cannot be done by a few leaders, or by even the brightest whiz-kids immured in a systems analysis unit or a planning staff. Real-life "planning" is the dynamic improvisation by the many on a general sense of direction—announced by the few, but only after genuine consultation with those who will have to improvise on it.

More participatory decision making implies a need for much information, widely spread, and much feedback, seriously attended—as in biological processes. Participation and public feedback become conditions precedent to decisions that stick.

That means more openness, less secrecy—not as an ideological preference but as a technological imperative. Secrecy goes out of fashion anyway, because secrets are so hard to keep.

Most of the history we learn in school is so narrowly focused on visible leaders that it may give us the wrong impression about leadership processes even in earlier times. We learn that Genghis Khan or Louis XIV or Ibn Saud or the emperor of Japan or George Washington said this and did that—as though he thought it up by himself, consulted with nobody and wrote it without the help of a ghostwriter. But even in ancient, "traditional" societies I suspect that effective leadership consisted in being closely in touch with where the relevant publics were ready to be told to go.

Consensus is a prominent feature of many cultures now dismissed as "primitive." The Polynesians in the Pacific Islands with their circular village councils and the American Indians around their campfires made (and in some degree still make)

decisions by fluid procedures which may induce more genuine participation than a "modern" meeting run by parliamentary procedure. In the agora of Athens and the Roman "Senate and public" (the SPQR), there seems to have been lively participation by those (well-born male citizens) qualified to take part.

The difference in the current sense is the sheer scale of the relevant publics. In "democratic" Athens slaves, women, tradesmen and other noncitizens didn't presume to play in the decision games. The notion that "all Men," let alone whole peoples, had inalienable rights came in only with the Enlightenment, a scant three centuries ago—and has been made effective, still in a minority of the world's nations, only in the 20th century. (In Switzerland, women still can't vote.)

Participatory fever is contagious. "Public policy" used to mean "what the government does." Now it includes corporate policies, collective bargaining agreements, the cost of health care, the recruitment of university presidents, lobbying practices, equal employment opportunity, environmental protection, tax shelters, waste disposal, private contributions to political candidates, the sex habits of employees, or just about any other "insider" activities that outsiders think are important enough to engage their time and attention.

The biggest issues so far have to do with the quality of public responsibility that shows forth in the actions of corporations, universities, hospitals, and the thousands of other structures in which executives make the decisions that serve people, cost them, anger or please them.

The rising tide of participation is reflected in dramatic organizational changes. Big corporations now usually have a vice president for keeping the corporation out of trouble with nosy outsiders, or even with their own stockholders and employees, who raise questions about what the company ought to produce, who it ought to employ, and how it ought to invest its money.

Should "my" company, or any American company, make and market nerve gas, even if the government does want to buy some? Should "my" company, or any American company, promote nuclear proliferation by selling to developing countries nuclear power plants that make plutonium, the fuel for nuclear weapons, as a byproduct of generating electricity? Shouldn't "my" company have more women, and blacks, and American Indians in its employ—and especially in its board and top management? Should a company whose stock I own invest my money in South Africa? Should "my" company, or any American company, pass the "social costs" of its profit-seeking—overcrowding, the paving of green space, radioactive risk, dirt, noise, toxic waste, acid rain, or whatever—to the general public? Should our community hospital perform abortions, splice genes, change people's sex, invest in expensive equipment that can help only a few affluent patients? Should our state university do secret work for the Defense Department? Should the CIA recruit our students for who-knows-what clandestine wars in other people's countries?

Such questions cannot be brushed aside without raising their decibel level. There are ways to deal with all of them: shifts of policy or consultative processes or diversionary moves or public explanations—in descending order or probable effectiveness. But the visibly responsible leaders increasingly have to build into their organizations, not as a public relations frill but as an essential ingredient in "bottom line" budgeting, staff members competent to help develop strategy on such issues as these. And the visible executive now has to be personally competent to defend the organization's public posture in public debate.

These "public responsibility" issues can make or break companies, products, and executive reputations. If you don't believe that, take a Nestle executive to lunch and ask him about marketing baby formula in the Third World.

DILEMMAS OF OPENNESS

The push for participation by all kinds of people, and the inherent leakiness of the information resource, combine to produce the modern executive's most puzzling dilemma. The dilemma must have been familiar to the first cave people who tried to bring other cave people together to get something done. But for us moderns, the scale of the perplexity is without precedent. The dilemma can be summarized in one question: How do you get everybody in on the act and still get some action?

The contemporary clamor to be in on the act is certainly impressive. In business, customers are feistier, more likely to complain; stockholders are more numerous and less passive; policy-holders are more inclined to follow through on their insurance claims; union members and other citizens give advice on what's wrong with the steel and automobile industries; employees assert the right to judge whether their employers should make fragmentation bombs; maritime unions decide whether shipments should go to the Soviet Union; advocacy agencies excluded from the United Way organize their own competing drive for community funds; ethnic groups keep a watchful eye on investments in South Africa and business with the Arabs. More and more parents have a world population policy; teachers organize to tell school systems what ought to be taught; students want tailor-made courses of study. Environmental groups, carefully avoiding questions about whom they represent, are articulate (and effective) beyond the wildest dreams of Gifford Pinchot and Teddy Roosevelt. New kinds and colors of people are breaking through the oligopoly of influence long controlled by businessmen and male lawyers from early-arriving ethnic groups. Even those deadly predictable circuses, our national political conventions, become increasingly interesting as minorities and women fill more delegate slots and live TV coverage enhances the risk that a delegate will be seen making a deal, picking his nose, adjusting her shoulder strap, or falling asleep—in millions of living rooms at once.

Openness, then, is the buzzword of modernization. In its firmament the deities are the public hearing, the news conference, the investigative reporter, "60 Minutes" and "20/20," Ted Koppel, Phil Donahue, and the *National Enquirer*. Its devils are also well-known: smoke-filled rooms, secret invasions, hidden or edited tapes, and expense-account luncheons at which The Establishment decides what to do next.

In consequence, compared with a generation ago, most public officials—and a rapidly growing number of "private" executives conscious of their ultimate public responsibility—are much more inclined to ask themselves, before acting, how their actions would look on the front page of the *Washington Post* or the *Wall Street Journal*, or on the evening telecast. Even former Vice President Agnew has conceded that taking cash from contractors in his government office might be wrong if judged by what he called post-Watergate moral standards. No one doubts that raising the risk of public exposure will improve the private behavior of executive leaders as they ask themselves. "How would I feel about this action if everyone were able to see me take it?" The moral of Watergate is clear enough: If the validity of your action depends on its secrecy, better decide to do something else.

But the yen for wider knowledge and broader participation has gone well beyond this sensitivity training for visible leaders and raised new questions about the "cost-benefit calculation" of more openness. A generation of experience suggests that it is high time we faced the next question: How much openness is enough?

Since this isn't a mystery story, I will reveal at the outset the conclusion of the next few paragraphs. Experience teaches that the procedures of openness are well designed to stop bad things from happening, and ill designed to get good things moving—unless the consensus for action has been built in private ahead of time.

A practical benefit of openness is simply that complex social systems work badly if they are too centralized. (In managing their agriculture the Soviets have put this proposition on public exhibit for more than half a century.) The opposite of centralization is of course *not* "decentralization," which is simply an effort to preserve hierarchical workways when your organization gets too large for grandpa to know everything. The opposite of centralization is what Charles Lindblom calls "mutual adjustment": in a generally understood environment of moral rules, norms, conventions, mores, very large numbers of people are adjusting their behavior by watching each other and modifying their behavior just enough to accommodate the differing purposes of others, but not so much that the mutual adjusters lose sight of where they themselves want to go.

What makes "mutual adjustment" work is the wide availability of relevant information, so each mutual adjuster can figure out what the others may do under varied conditions, and give forth useful signals about his/her own behavior. The market principle doesn't guarantee smoothly working systems, of course; perfect competition among buyers and sellers with full information is to be found only in textbooks for sophomores. Yet very large systems, many of them global in scale, based on massive information outputs and feedback systems, have been developed in this century. In recent years systems unimaginable before the marriage of computers and telecommunications (currency and commodity markets, world-wide airline and hotel reservation systems, global public health controls and weather forecasting systems come readily to mind) are accepted now as routine.

In other writings I have addressed the growing costs of openness. The very great benefits of openness and wide participation are flawed by oversimplification and confrontation, by apathy and nonparticipation, by muscle-binding legalisms, by too many meaningless public hearings, by an excess of voting and parliamentary process, by the nay-saying power of procedural objection, by the protection of mediocrity, by the inhibition of excellence in recruitment and the absence of candor in evaluation—and by one thing more. Mythology has it the other way around, but it seems clear now that wide consultation early in a policy process tends to discourage innovation and favor standpattism.

More openness in decision making is a radical litany, yet the multiplication of those consulted tends to water down radical reform. During the Vietnam war, I used to conduct seminars on this subject (among others) during the long hours spent with student leaders on the barricades. Why, I asked them, do you advocate openness with such passion when the reforms you want would be voted down if you put them to a big public meeting? They were regularly nonplussed by the question; evangelists, in David Riesman's phrase, often "mistake the righteousness of their cause for its marketability."

An action proposal, especially if it is new and unfamiliar, will seem threatening or at least postponable to most of the experts who haven't already been involved. It is no accident that so many memorable U.S. public policy initiatives (much of the New Deal and the Lend-Lease idea in the 1930s, the Marshall Plan and Harry Truman's Point Four in the 1940s, the Open Skies proposal in the 1950s, the

Peace Corps and Food for Peace and the War on Poverty in the 1960s, the Nixon Doctrine and the Carter human rights initiative in the 1970s) began as the products of leadership hunch and thinking-out-loud rhetoric, with most of the professional staff work and the needed consultations at home and abroad following after. In each case the executive leaders were sensing a trend the American people would buy if a credible salesman came forward to peddle it. But if all the relevant experts had been asked for their opinions before launching them, some or all of these great ideas might well have shriveled in the womb. Too many people, in Washington and abroad, would have said, "Let's study it some more."

Bold initiatives for change can thus be killed by premature exposure to the rough winds of public debate. Yet let us again remember that this cuts both ways: timely openness is also well designed to stop foolish change. Earlier and wider consultation would almost certainly have killed the ill-fated Bay of Pigs operation, drastically modified the Vietnam escalation, and illuminated the grotesquerie at Watergate for the foolish scheme everyone, including President Nixon, later judged it to have been.

Whatever the costs and benefits of openness in particular cases, it is clear enough that in every kind of hierarchy the winds of openness and participation by new kinds of people are whistling through the cracks, blowing in the windows and knocking down the doors. The result in each case cannot be so clearly judged in advance; it depends on how well those involved have analyzed and balanced the openness equation. Openness, like technology, is not properly an ideology. The answer to whether it helps or hurts basic human purposes is the same as the answer to most of the interesting questions in the study of society: It depends.

THE OBSOLESCENCE OF OWNERSHIP

The openness which the informatization of society brings in its train was bound to raise fundamental questions about the idea that knowledge "belongs" to a person or an organization—or a nation. The propensity of this "sharing resource" to leak is eroding the doctrine that knowledge can be owned, exchanged and monopolized the way "real" resources can.

That you or I can "own" a fact or an idea, that a message of any kind "belongs" to a person or a corporation or a government, is (for reasons already cited from Colin Cherry's work) rather a peculiar notion to begin with. The person from whom you got the message didn't lose it; any right you acquire by receiving it is at best shared with the sender, the carrier, and often a good many other nosy people who are privy to it. Even if you paid to get the message (if, for example, it was a piece of research you hired someone to do), or if someone paid to get it to you (a friend who sent you a cable, a company that sent you a commercial), it was the assembly or delivery service, not the information contained in the message, that was paid for. The researcher could not "own" the facts and ideas she or he strung together for your use, and neither can you even if you use them as your "own."

The new tide of information technologies makes the "ownership" of "intellectual property" more detached from reality with every new invention. Dynamic high-technology keeps developing better and faster techniques of piracy—xerography, videotape, the backyard dish for picking up signals from satellites. The knowledge explosion also produces new kinds of works (computer software), new means of delivery (microfiche, videocassettes, computerized videotext over a telephone line), and new ways to assemble great complexities of facts and ideas in more readily accessible form (computerized data bases, inventory controls, energy use data, on-line reservation systems for airlines and car rentals).

In this environment, laws written to protect books and phonograph records and broadcasts, the products of the past, are getting harder and harder to apply. Laws which address technologies not yet invented are hard to write.

The nervous breakdown of copyright protection is now an open scandal. It may be retarded in degree by technological fixes. Satellite broadcasters can scramble their signals to prevent pirating. Elaborate codes have been devised by the creators of some computer programs, though teenage computer hackers have been showing how inherently porous they are.

When I first acquired a home computer, I found the ethical dilemma right up front: in the instruction manual. On its cover sheet I was threatened with litigious mayhem if I copied any of the software. On the very first page of the manual I was told that before I did anything else I should make at least two copies of the floppy diskette provided with the manual.

Since then, the makers of software keep up their pitiful efforts to maintain a proprietary interest in their products, but the happy-go-lucky free distribution of copies of copyrighted diskettes has already become one of the friendly gestures that make the owners of personal computers feel like members of a new kind of guild. The leakiness of the information resource seems destined to overwhelm the backward-looking efforts to imprison it. The history of arms control, and the success of computer pirates, teach us that there is always a technological fix for a technological fix.

Is the doctrine that information is owned by its originator (or compiler) necessary to make sure that Americans remain intellectually creative? In most other countries creative work is overwhelmingly controlled by organizations and carried out by salaried people. In Japan, even the most inventive employee is likely to have a lifetime job and receive salary raises in lockstep with his age cohort, his morale sustained not by personal ownership of his ideas but by togetherness in an organizational family.

Most U.S. patents are held by organizations (corporations, universities, government agencies), not by the inventors. Many copyrights, perhaps most, are held by publishers and promoters, not by the authors and songwriters the Founding Fathers may have had in mind when they sewed information-as-property into the U.S. Constitution.

An author or songwriter who helps a publisher make money should certainly participate in the proceeds. But direct agreements about profit-sharing or joint venture arrangements (the movie industry is already full of relevant examples) seem a less fragile basis for such cooperation than the fraying fictions that the author owns the words in a book and that shared information is being "exchanged."

In U.S. universities and research institutes, creative work is already rewarded mostly by promo-tion, tenure and tolerant traditions about teaching loads and outside consulting. We generate a respectably innovative R&D effort in public-sector fields such as military technology, space exploration, weather forecasting, environmental protection and the control of infectious diseases without the scientists and inventors having to own the ideas they contribute to the process.

In the private sector, the leaders of industries on the high-tech frontier are already saying out loud that their protection from overseas copyists doesn't lie in trade secrets but in healthy R&D budgets.

The notion of information-as-property is built deep into our laws, our economy, and our political psyche—and into the expectations and tax returns and balance sheets of writers and artists and the companies, agencies and academies that pay them to be creative. But we had better continue to develop our own ways, compatible with our own traditions, of rewarding intellectual labor without depending on laws and prohibitions that are disintegrating fast—as the Volstead Act did in our earlier effort to enforce an unenforceable Prohibition.

In international politics the notion that knowledge is "owned" by sovereign states is in maximum disarray. Every newly miniaturized recording or micrographic device, and every new satellite launched for communication or photography or remote sensing, makes it more difficult to sustain the doctrine that national governments can own, or even control, their information resources.

In 1979 the U.S. government sent two delegations to two world meetings about the control of information. At a UNESCO conference in Paris, the delegates righteously advocated the "free flow" of information, meaning information furnished by U.S. news agencies, U.S. television producers, and U.S. movie studios. A few weeks later, at the UN Conference on Science and Technology for Development in Vienna, an equally righteous group of Americans came out against the free flow of information, meaning "information" as technology we were anxious to hoard.

Both principles are authentically American: the right to choose, and the right to own. In the international discourse, we will hardly be able to have it both ways. Yet there is no evidence that the two groups of delegates, and the government that instructed them both, perceived the irony or the contradiction.

The U.S. State Department, which instructed both delegations, seemed unusually disoriented by the new information environment when it ruled last year that Western European owners of IBM computers could not move them from, say, Birmingham to Manchester without first seeking U.S. permission. This assertion of extraterritoriality over equipment produced by a multinational company with headquarters in the United States was designed to prevent "strategic" equipment from flowing indirectly to communist countries. Regardless of the merits of the case, the edict is simply unenforceable. In the global information society, the long arms of "ownership" and "control" are shrinking fast.

If information is inherently hard to bottle up, policies based on a long-term information monopoly are likely to have a short half-life. For the 1980s and beyond, the principle is clear: if the validity of your action depends on its continuing secrecy, don't depend on it.

In our generation-long arms race with the Soviet Union, successive U.S. administrations have managed to persuade themselves that each new U.S. weapons system (its made-in-America technology a continuing mystery to our adversaries) would enable us to stay "ahead." In one of the most damaging of these actions, in the early 1970s, the U.S. decided to stuff multiple, independently-targetable, reentry vehicles (MIRVs) into single missiles. Despite elaborate secrecy on our part, the Soviets soon figured out how to do likewise. But since they (for other reasons) had built much bigger missiles boosted by more powerful rockets, they were able to stuff more MIRVs into their canisters than we could. Thus did we outsmart ourselves by taking an action which depended for its validity on technological secrecy, and created the famous "window of vulnerability" instead.

In the management of mutual deterrence the overclassification of information about what we could do, if we had to, may actually increase the danger of war by miscalculation. The core of the nuclear deterrent, that remarkably stable if unattractive substitute for peace, is the Soviet leaders' uncertainty about what the U.S. president would do in the event of Soviet moves against our allies or ourselves; combined with their certainty that we have the means to retaliate no matter what. Keeping our intentions credibly uncertain is easy: we cannot know what we would do "if," until we know what the "if" is. But keeping from our adversaries full knowledge of our capabilities merely adds another element of madness to the "mad momentum" of the nuclear arms race.

Our own government has for three decades engaged in half-hearted and demonstrably ineffective efforts to "own" strategic U.S. science and keep foreign nationals out of sensitive university research. In our mostly open society, it never worked very well. Americans have no corner on the market for brains; scientists talk quite freely across frontiers to each other; our European and Japanese allies never had much enthusiasm for controlling transborder information flows (because sales of equipment mean jobs for Europeans and Japanese); and Soviet technological espionage, like our own, has long been a thriving industry.

Keeping our R&D to ourselves is a policy that depends for its validity on secrecy. As informatization intensifies in the post-industrial world, strategic secrecy can be expected to work less and less well.

Similar government behavior used to work better for dictators and totalitarian bureaucracies in societies where keeping information from spreading is honored by doctrine and practiced *ad absurdum*. The last time I looked, Xerox machines still had to be licensed by the government in the Soviet Union: in Bulgaria, even typewriters are closely controlled. Ideas are harder to license: Russian youngsters readily learn about jeans and hard rock, and scientists on both sides of the porous Curtain seem to know how far along their peers are in unravelling (for example) the puzzlements of rocketry and space travel.

The good news is that information is leaky, that sharing is the natural mode of scientific discovery and technological innovation. The new information environment seems bound to undermine the knowledge monopolies which totalitarian governments convert into monopolies of power. In the horoscope of the USSR and the Soviet bloc, a future looms where nobody is in charge.

DOES ACCESS LEAD TO FAIRNESS?

The informatization of society may destabilize more than the Soviet bloc. It may help undermine the systems that keep two billion people in relative poverty, and more than a third of them in absolute poverty. In many ways the most exciting, and puzzling, question about the new knowledge environment is whether it will be good news or bad news for the global fairness revolution—and for that revolution's U.S. precinct, the upward mobility of women, minorities and the poor.

The most arresting trait of the information resource is that it is inherently more accessible than other resources—and that once accessed, it unlocks the other resources. What does that imply for access to the power and affluence that knowledge brings in its wake? Theoretically at least, compared to things-as-resource, information-as-resource should encourage:

- the spreading of benefits rather than the concentration of wealth (information can be more equitably shared than petroleum or gold or land or even water); and

- the maximization of choice rather than the suppression of diversity (the informed are harder to regiment than the uninformed).

In the industrial era, poverty was explained and justified by shortages of things; there just weren't enough minerals, food, fibers, and manufacturers to go around. Looked at this way, the shortages were merely aggravated by the tendency of the poor to have babies.

In the post-industrial era, the physical resources are joined at center stage by information, the resource that is harder for the rich and powerful to hoard. Each of the babies, poor or not, is born with a brain. The collective capacity of all the brains in each society to convert information into knowledge and wisdom is the measure of that society's potential.

But whether the informatization of the globe will actually mean a fairer shake for those who have been the victims of discrimination depends mostly on what they do. Most of the fairness achieved in world history has not been the consequence of charity, goodheartedness and *noblesse oblige* on the part of those in power. Always in history, it seems, fairness has been granted, legislated or seized when there was no alternative. And usually the reason there was no alternative was that the "downs" were determined (or at least perceived by the "ups" to be determined) to cast off their shackles and take the law into their own hands.

Societies flexible enough to adapt to the pressure from the "downs" (as the United States has been doing, not without conflict and coercion, on school integration, voter rights, sex discrimination and equal employment opportunity) manage to keep change comparatively peaceful.

Societies which try to maintain rigid hierarchies (and especially those which, like the Shah's Iran, at the same time encourage education for most of their people) get blown out of the water. In Iran it was the marriage of convenience between those who harbored two powerful resentments, about tradition (the mullahs who had been bypassed and downgraded by "modernization") and about fairness (the Iranian students at home and abroad), which brought the Shah down. Afterwards the tradition-defenders and the fairness advocates went after each other, and the fairness people lost.

In other countries the mix is different, but part of the stew of resentments is always the complaint we learn from infancy to make: "It isn't fair."

There will be less excuse in the future than in the past for depriving whole populations of the benefits of development. There will also be less excuse for the disadvantaged to blame their condition on the barons and bosses when the accessible knowledge to even the score is already floating out there in the noösphere.

The noösphere of knowledge that is power, this accessible resource, has many of the characteristics of a "commons." In considering the implications for fairness of information-as-a-resource, it is an intriguingly fresh thought, worth a moment of speculation.

In earlier times, sharing arrangements for a common resource were customary, for example in tribal ownership and nomadic practices. Vestiges of the idea survive in the Boston Commons, the National Park system, and in the way many major waterways, in Europe and North America, are managed.

For people in old England the commons, as Ivan Illich defines it, was "that part of the environment which lay beyond their own thresholds and outside of their possessions, to which, however, they had recognized claims of usage, [not to product commodities but to provide for the subsistence of their households]." The commons "was necessary for the community's survival, necessary for different groups in different ways, but . . . in a strictly economic sense, was not perceived as scarce."

The older commons, such as those for sheep and cattle, have disappeared through "enclosure." But the "commons" idea has now been revived in a big way, as the basis for worldwide cooperation in the environments that by common consent belong to no one or everyone (which seems to be about the same thing): the deep ocean and its seabed, Antarctica, outer space and celestial bodies, and the weather.

The Mediterranean Sea, the arena of bloody ancient feuds and lethal modern rivalries, has recently been formally recognized by all the coastal states (including the Arab states and Israel) as so precious a shared commons that reversing its degradation must be a matter for cooperation even among sworn enemies. The resulting international agreement, intermediated by the UN Environment Programme, is self-enforcing: violating its terms would be in a literal sense self-defeating.

For the management of an information commons, a sharing environment, these exotic precedents suddenly seem not so exotic.

Illich, in a Tokyo speech called "Silence as a Commons," argued that electronic devices (from the microphone to the computer) are a form of "enclosure," reserving to the few the privilege of breaking the silence otherwise available to the many.

I don't know about silence; I haven't much experience with it. But on the computer as a form of "enclosure," I demur. In its general impact the forced march of information technology, personal computers combined with global telecommunications, seems to me to be taking us away from the idea of enclosure. My hunch is that the fusion of computers and communications will further empower the many to participate in "making policy" in domains to which the few, with their moth-eaten monopolies of knowledge, will have to yield more and more access.

Neighborhood organizations are furnishing themselves with personal computers to deal more effectively with the banks and developers and government agencies that will otherwise make the neighborhoods' decisions for them. American Indian tribes might set up a computer teleconference to concert their political clout on fast-moving legislation. A single individual with a personal computer can even now get access to so much useful and timely information that she or he can, with a week's homework and without leaving home, intervene as an unusually knowledgeable citizen in almost any public policy issue on the national agenda.

To chart these potentials is not to fulfill them. The trends in information technology would make it possible to organize as a commons (with free though not necessarily costless access thereto) most of the world's useful knowledge. That is not to say it will happen. It just helps to remake the point that those who think "it isn't fair" will have plenty of opportunity to get access to almost any information that is being withheld from them to their disadvantage. But they will have to want to work at it, they will have to prepare their brains for the task. In the information society as in its predecessors, there is still no free lunch.

THE PASSING OF REMOTENESS

I have argued the mind-blowing implications of the informatization of society for four of the old hierarchies—based on control, secrecy, ownership, and structural unfairness. Let's look at what is happening to the fifth of the old hierarchies, those based on location.

The inherited idea is that the political importance of communities is based on their geography. Cities usually developed because they were seaports or on critical inland waterways, or (earlier) on important overland caravan routes and (later) on important railway lines. It made a difference whether you were in the city or in "the country"; if you lived in a rural area, you were remote. There was no choice about it, you were just remote.

The importance of countries was often based on the natural resources they had discovered, and developed, on "their" territory. The spices of the Orient, the rubber and tin of Southeast Asia, the coal and iron of Central Europe, the diamonds (and later uranium) of South Africa, the fruit of Central America, the petroleum reserves of Indonesia and Mexico and Venezuela and North Africa and the Persian (or Arabian) Gulf and the North Sea, the soil that produced those "waving fields of grain" in North America—these crucial resources left an indelible mark on the national sovereignties which happened to find them in their back yards.

Then there was the sense of place in military strategy, summed up in the once-popular word "geopolitics." This was the idea that a nation's power depended largely on its geography—how vulnerable its land mass, how defendable its frontiers, how rich its mineral deposits, how fertile its soil, how plentiful its waters, how extensive its coast line.

But communications satellites and fast computers are gradually erasing distance, eroding the idea that some places are world centers because they are near other places or obsolescent natural resources or old-fashioned means of transportation, while other areas are bound to be peripheral because they are remote from these centers.

Octavio Paz, a poet, caught onto what was happening well before most of the systems analysts and political pundits. "We Mexicans," he wrote in the 1970s, "have always lived on the periphery of history. Now the center or nucleus of world society has disintegrated, and everyone—including the European and the North American—is a peripheral being. We are living on the margin . . . because there is no longer any center. . . . World history has become everyone's task and our own labyrinth is the labyrinth of all mankind."

The passing of remoteness is one of the great unheralded macrotrends of our extraordinary time. Once you can plug in through television to UN votes or a bombing in Beirut or a Wimbledon final; once you can sit in Auckland, or Singapore, or Bahrain and play the New York stock markets in real time; once you can participate in rule, power and authority according to the relevance of your opinion rather than the mileage to the decision-making venue—then the power centers are wherever the brightest people are using the latest information in the most creative ways.

Distant farmsteads can, if they will, be connected to the central cortex of their commodity exchanges, their political authorities, their global markets. The fusion of rapid microprocessing and global telecommunications presents nearly all of us with a choice (and an obligation to choose) between relevance and remoteness. There will be costs and benefits to either choice—but the necessity to choose is new, and inescapable.

There is, of course, an alternative to geography as a principle of organization. The revised proposition was recently formulated by futurist Magda McHale: in the new knowledge environment, civilization will be built more around communities of people, and less around communities of place.

That this trend is well advanced can be seen in a quick review of what is happening to the great hierarchies which in this last couple of centuries have been dividing, and governing, the world.

The State is not withering away, as with their different motives Karl Marx and the advocates of world government would have desired. But power is leaking out of sovereign national governments in three directions at once.

The State is leaking at the top, as more international functions require the pooling of sovereignty in alliances, in a World Weather Watch, in geophysical research, in eradicating contagious diseases, in satellite communication, in facing up to global environmental risks.

The State is leaking sideways, as multinational corporations—"private," pseudoprivate, and "public"—conduct more and more of the world's commerce, and operate across political frontiers so much better than committees of sovereign states seem able to do.

The State is also leaking from the bottom, as minorities, single-issue constituencies, special-purpose communities and neighborhoods take control of their own destinies, legislating their own growth policies, their own population policies, their own environmental policies.

And what has Nation come to mean? Increasingly it means not a hierarchy of power but ethnicity—the Frenchness of Quebec, the tribal loyalties of the Ibo in Biafra, the separatism of the Scots, the rhetorical brotherhood of the Arabs, the world's many diasporas ranging from the Overseas Chinese to the Zionist, and non-Zionist, Jews outside Israel.

And Organized Religion? All of the great religious traditions have had to settle, so far in world history, for hegemony in one or another part of the world. But in a world of people-communities, not place-communities, the "parish" cannot be mostly geography-based. Now, even "established" religions are trying to break free from their national and regional parishes. The Roman Catholic Pope's ex-tensive travels and the terrorist outreach of Ayatollah Khomeini's Shi'ites form a grotesque correlation: both are breaking loose from historic geographic bounds to appeal to wider religious—and therefore political—constituencies.

The prospect of people rather than place as a basis for community has interesting implications for universities trying to serve a "local" clientele; for corporations that have bet heavily on regional organization; and for political systems that have bet heavily on geography-based constituencies. It implies that those institutions which exploit the electronic answers to remoteness may be "catching a wave" in the twilight of hierarchy.

INDEX